AF607842

My Struggle for Peace

The Diary of Moshe Sharett 1953-1956

My Struggle for Peace

The Diary of Moshe Sharett 1953-1956

Volume 1

October 1953 - December 1954

Edited by

Neil Caplan and Yaakov Sharett

Translation from the Hebrew

Yaakov Sharett and Neil Caplan

INDIANA UNIVERSITY PRESS

BLOOMINGTON AND INDIANAPOLIS

Publication of this English edition of
Moshe Sharett, *Yoman Ishi* (1978) was initiated by
The Moshe Sharett Heritage Society (MSHS)
30 Ben-Gurion Blvd., Tel Aviv, Israel 6458805

www.sharett.org.il

Cover and Graphic Design by Adi Chen

The MSHS and Indiana University Press gratefully acknowledge
the generous support of the
Israel Institute, Washington DC.

www.israelinstitute.org

Manufactured in the United States of America.

Cataloging information is available from the Library of Congress.

ISBN 978-0-253-04325-2 (cloth, 3-vol. set)
ISBN 978-0-253-03735-0 (cloth, vol. 1)
ISBN 978-0-253-03758-9 (cloth, vol. 2)
ISBN 978-0-253-03762-6 (cloth, vol. 3)
ISBN 978-0-253-03738-1 (ebook, vol. 1)
ISBN 978-0-253-03761-9 (ebook, vol. 2)
ISBN 978-0-253-03763-3 (ebook, vol. 3)

1 2 3 4 5 24 23 22 21 20 19

Table of contents

Volume 3: January 1, 1956 – December 9, 1956

List of persons cited by their first name and mini-glossary of terms

Abba	Abba (Aubrey) Eban
Abe	Avraham Harman
aliya	(Heb. lit., "ascent") Jewish immigration to Palestine (pre-1948) or Israel
the *Alliance*	*Alliance Israélite universelle*
Arthur	Arthur Lourie
Aubrey	Abba Eban
Barney	Dov Yosef (Bernard Joseph)
Beba	Beba Idelson
the Brother	Allen W. Dulles, CIA Director
Committee of Five	Mapai Cabinet Ministers Ben-Gurion, Sharett, Myerson, Eshkol and Aran.
Committee of Nine	Mapai Party leaders Ben-Gurion, Sharett, Myerson, Avigur, Kesse, Namir, Lavon, Bash and Govrin, set up in April, 1956.
CoS [of the IDF]	Moshe Dayan
the Dane	Vagn Bennike
DG [of the MFA]	Walter Eytan
Dodik	David Golomb (Sharett's nephew)
Dolik	David Horowitz
Ehud	Ehud Avriel
Eliahu	Eliahu Elath
Elias	Eliyahu Sasson
Eliashiv	Eliashiv Ben-Horin
Emile	Emile Najar
the Envoy	Robert (Bob) Anderson
Eppy	Ephraim Evron
erev	(Heb.) the eve of
Fati	Yehoshafat Harkabi
G.R., Gideon	Gideon Rafael
Giora	Giora Josephthal
Golda	Golda Myerson (Meir)
Haim	Haim Sharett (Moshe's son)
hasbara	(Heb. lit., "explanation") information services and public-relations
haver, haverim	(Heb.) friend, party member, colleague

haverenu	(Heb.) "our [Mapai] colleagues" in the Cabinet (see Committee of Five)
Isser	Isser Harel
J.P.	Jayaprakash Narayan
Joe	Yosef Tekoah
the Joint	the Joint American Distribution Committee (JDC)
Josh	Yehoshua Palmon
Kirya	(Heb.) Israel government compound/offices
Kol-Israel	Israel's national radio service
Kovi, Kobi	Yaakov Sharett (Moshe's son)
Leo	Leo Kohn
ma'abara, ma'abarot	(Heb.) immigrant transit camp(s)
Memi	Meir (de) Shalit
Nahum	Nahum Goldmann
Navot	Navot Sharett (Moshe's nephew)
Nehemiah	Nehemiah Argov
Reggie	Mordechai Kidron
Reuven	Reuven Shiloah
Ruhama	Ruhama Sapir, Sharett's secretary
Shabtai	Shabtai Rosenne
Shamai	Shamai Cahana
Shaul	Shaul Avigur
Shimon	Shimon Peres
Teddy	Teddy Kollek
Walter	Walter Eytan
Y.D.H., Yaacov	Yaacov Herzog
yishuv	(Heb. lit., "settlement") the Jewish community of pre-1948 Palestine
Yitzhak	Yitzhak Navon
Yosef	Yosef (Joe) Tekoah
Ziama	Zalman Aran
Zipporah	Zipporah Sharett (Moshe's wife)

List of Abbreviations

AFL	American Federation of Labor
AFME	American Friends of the Middle East
AFP	Agence France-Presse
AJC	American Jewish Committee
AMAN	*Agaf Modi'in* – IDF Military Intelligence Branch
AP	Associated Press
BBC	British Broadcasting Corporation
BG	Ben-Gurion / David Ben-Gurion
BGA	Ben-Gurion Archive, Sde Boker
CBS	Columbia Broadcasting System
CC	[Mapai Party] Central Committee
CIA	[US] Central Intelligence Agency
CIO	Council of Industrial Organizations
CoS	Chief of Staff
CPI	Communist Party of Israel
CZA	Central Zionist Archives, Jerusalem
Dept.	Department
DFPI	*Documents on the Foreign Policy of Israel*
DG	Director-General
DM	Deutschmark
DMZ	Demilitarized Zone
doc.	document
DP	Displaced Person
Ed.	Editor(s) – edited - edition
EDC	European Defense Community
EEC	European Economic Community
EIMAC	Egypt-Israel Mixed Armistice Commission
ETZEL	*Irgun Zvai Le'umi*
FADC	Foreign Affairs and Defense Committee
FBI	[US] Federal Bureau of Investigation
FDR	Franklin Delano Roosevelt
FM	Foreign Minister
FO	Foreign Office (UK)
FRUS	*Foreign Relations of the United States*
GA	[United Nations] General Assembly

GAA	General Armistice Agreement
GHQ	General Headquarters
GOE	Government of Egypt
GOI	Government of Israel
GS	General Staff
GZ	General Zionists
HMG	Her Majesty's Government (UK)
HQ	Headquarters
HUAC	US House of Representatives Un-American Activities Committee
IDF	Israel Defense Forces
IDFA	Israel Defense Forces Archives
IFR	*Israel's Foreign Relations*
IG	Israel Government
Ihud	*Ihud Hakvutzot Vehakibbutzim* – Union of Kvutzot and Kibbutzim
IJGAA	Israel-Jordan General Armistice Agreement
IJMAC	Israel-Jordan Mixed Armistice Commission
IL.	Israel Lira (pound)
ILGWU	International Ladies Garment Workers' Union
ILMAC	Israel-Lebanon Mixed Armistice Commission
ILO	International Labor Organization
IPU	Inter-Parliamentary Union
Irgun	*Irgun Zvai Le'umi* – also *ETZEL*
ISA	Israel State Archive
ISMAC	Israel-Syria Mixed Armistice Commission
JA, JAE	Jewish Agency (Executive)
JDC	American Joint Distribution Committee
JNF	Jewish National Fund
JTA	Jewish Telegraphic Agency
KGB	Komitet gosudarstvennoy bezopasnosti, the main security agency of the USSR (1954-1991)
LAC	Libraries and Archives of Canada, Ottawa
LEHI	*Lohamei Herut Israel*
m^3	cubic meter
MAC	Mixed Armistice Commission
ME	Middle East
MFA	Ministry of Foreign Affairs (Israel)
MK	Member of the Knesset
MP	Member of Parliament
NATO	North Atlantic Treaty Organization
NYT	*New York Times*
O.C.	Officer Commanding

PATWA	Professional and Technical Workers Association
PCC	Palestinian Conciliation Commission, UN
PEC	Palestine Electric Corporation
PEN	Poets, essayists, novelists – international association of writers
PICA	Palestine Jewish Colonization Association
PM	Prime Minister
PMO	Prime Minister's Office
POW	prisoner(s) of war
SC	[United Nations] Security Council
SCOR	Security Council Official Records
SEATO	South East Asia Treaty Organization
SG	Secretary-General
SOE	Special Operations Executive
TNA	The National Archives, London (Kew), UK (formerly Public Record Office / PRO)
UJA	United Jewish Appeal
UK	United Kingdom of Great Britain and Northern Ireland
UN	United Nations
UNA	United Nations Archive, New York
UNEF	United Nations Emergency Force
UN GA	United Nations General Assembly
UNRWA	United Nations Relief and Works Agency
UN SC	United Nations Security Council
UN SG	United Nations Secretary-General
UNTSO	United Nations Truce Supervisory Organization
UP, UPI	United Press, United Press International
US	United States / U.S.
USNA	United States National Archives
USNWR	*US News & World Report*
USSD	United States Department of State
WJC	World Jewish Congress
WW	World War
WZO	World Zionist Organization
ZO	Zionist Organization
ZOA	Zionist Organization of America

List of Illustrations

Editors' Introduction

Neil Caplan and Yaakov Sharett

The publication in 1978 of the 8-volume Hebrew edition of Moshe Sharett's *Personal Diary – Yoman Ishi, 1953-1957*[1] – was a remarkable achievement. The intimate revelations about the diarist's last years in government and his brutally frank comments about his colleagues and rivals – many of whom were still promoting their political careers -- surely contributed to the unusual popularity of the sometimes dense work running to some 2400 pages.

For decades the *Yoman Ishi* would continue to attract the attention of readers and researchers for a number of reasons. One was the diary's unusually high literary quality. Another reason was its insights into the personality – both strengths and weaknesses – of the junior member of the "troika" leadership of the Zionist movement. From the early 1930s, Moshe Sharett (then Shertok) had worked intimately with Chaim Weizmann and David Ben-Gurion. Yet another reason was the diary's testimony to the writer's unwavering commitment to sober statesmanship – which was incapable of halting the rising tension, jingoism and adventurism that accompanied Israel's road to the Sinai campaign of late 1956. As a personal account of the inner workings of Israel's political and military elites, the diary has maintained its political relevance and continues to resonate. In 2014 the long out-of-print Hebrew *Yoman Ishi* was posted in digitized format on the website of the Moshe Sharett Heritage Society.[2]

The genesis of this English-language edition began in the early 1990s with the production of a rough draft of a translation, which remained untouched until 1998, when Neil Caplan was introduced to Yaakov Sharett. Author of a multi-volume history of the Zionist-Arab and Arab-Israeli conflicts, Caplan was among many scholars from abroad who wondered why this important work had not appeared in English. He had already come to value the Hebrew edition of the *Yoman Ishi* among the primary sources consulted for his study of the "futile diplomacy" of the 1950s.[3]

1 Edited posthumously by the author's son, Yaakov Sharett, and published in Tel Aviv by Sifriyat Ma'ariv.

2 http://tinyurl.com/ms-yoman-ishi, or http://www.sharett.org.il/cgi-webaxy/sal/sal.pl?lang=he&ID=880900_sharett_new&act=show&dbid=books&dataid=30.

3 Neil Caplan, *Futile Diplomacy*, vol.3 - *The United Nations, the Great Powers, and Middle East Peacemaking, 1948-1954*, and *Futile Diplomacy*, vol.4 - *Operation Alpha and the Failure of Anglo-American Coercive Diplomacy in the Arab-Israeli Conflict, 1954-1956*, both volumes published in London: Frank Cass, 1997 – republished Routledge RLE, 2015.

When he learned of the stillborn translation project, Neil readily accepted Yaakov's invitation to work as his co-editor on the preparation of this English-language edition.

The editors' labors began with multiple passes over the preliminary translation, meticulously correcting its many errors, fine-tuning and standardizing historical and political terminology, and refining unclear English usage. A second series of passes involved further research aimed at clarifying allusions and references, augmenting the text with biographical notes, scholarly references and other annotations specially aimed at today's non-Israeli and English-speaking readers. The editors also determined which passages might be legitimately omitted as being of little relevance to today's English-speaking reader. These omissions are indicated in the pages below in brackets, thus [- - -]. Owing to considerations of space and interest, the editors decided to end the present English edition with the entry for December 9, 1956. Beyond this point the Hebrew diary continues sporadically until its final entry dated Thursday, November 28, 1957.[4]

This English edition is also an expansion of the original Hebrew diary; approximately 20-25% of the current edition is new material that was not available when *Yoman Ishi* first appeared. In the years since 1978, major archives in Israel and abroad have made available valuable diplomatic papers and reports that amplify Sharett's first-person diary accounts. This English edition interweaves excerpts from protocols of Cabinet meetings and closed-door meetings of Mapai Party committees at which Sharett lectured to his *haverim* (party comrades) on the delicate political issues of the day. This new material helps to compensate for gaps when Sharett did not supply detailed or polished daily write-ups.

Indeed, the original Hebrew *Yoman Ishi* was not the uniform product of Moshe Sharett's penmanship. Pressures of work and emotional strain caused him on a number of occasions to interrupt and then resume the writing up of his diary. In assembling the 1978 Hebrew diary, editor Yaakov Sharett often stitched together fragmentary materials to provide coherence and bridge many of the gaps between full entries. Similarly, the English edition of the diary presented here consists of several types of material, woven together but clearly demarcated by the editors:

1. "Pure" personal diary: pages written and polished by the meticulous author, composed mostly close to the events described and preserved in folders at his home. While Sharett did publish an account of his diplomatic mission to south-east Asia in late 1956 based on selected entries of his diary,[5] he never gave instructions regarding the future disposition of the full diary. It was left to his elder son Yaakov to decide on his own to publish it *in toto* following his death in 1965.

2. "Skeleton" diary: notes and lists kept by the diarist, usually on the same day of events described, preserved with the intention of one day writing them up as

4 *Yoman Ishi*, VII: 1911 to VIII: 2396.

5 *Mishut Be'asia* [*Roving Through Asia*], Tel Aviv: Davar, 1958 – in Hebrew.

full-fledged diary entries. Editors' interventions which "flesh out the skeleton" are indicated within [square brackets].

3. Supplementary primary material inserted by the editors, often reproduced here for the first time. These reports, letters and protocols are introduced by the editors' use of a special smaller font, with the texts slightly indented on both margins.

4. A further layer of supplementary material has been provided by the editors on a website offering the text of some 135 historical documents and background notes. These "WebDocs" are numbered in the footnotes, and readers may access them via the IUP websites: https://www.iupress.indiana.edu/9780253043252 or http://go.iu.edu/28TF. A list of these WebDocs is given on page 1884 of Volume 3.

The Editors wish readers to note that

- A list of first names of persons mentioned and a brief glossary of Hebrew terms used in the diary are given at the beginning of Volume 1.
- A list of abbreviations used is given at the beginning of Volume 1.
- Sharett often inserted foreign words in Arabic or Russian/Cyrillic script; for this edition these have been rendered into Latin script.
- Brief biographical notes are given on first mention; bold page reference in the index indicates a biographical footnote.
- Division of the diary into chapters was done by the editors.
- Breakdown into paragraphs has occasionally been altered by the editors.

Acknowledgements:

The editors are most appreciative of the assistance offered by hard-working staff members at the various archives they have visited and whose materials they have consulted (see "Sources"). We are especially grateful for the generous assistance provided by senior editors Yehoshua Freundlich, Yemima Rosenthal and Louise Fischer of the Israel State Archives [ISA]; the central importance of the *Documents on the Foreign Policy of Israel* [*DFPI*] series published by the ISA becomes evident in almost every entry of the diary that follows.

Moshe Sharett – The Man, the Statesman, and the Diary[1]

Yechiam Weitz[2]

Moshe Sharett (October 15, 1894 – July 7, 1965) was a prominent Zionist and Israeli leader who made major contributions to developing the diplomacy of the movement and the state. He served as Israel's first Foreign Minister [FM] (1948-1956) and its second Prime Minister [PM] (1954-1955). In his last years he was chairman of the Jewish Agency Executive [JAE] (1961-1965).

In the pre-state period of the British Mandate (1920-1948), Sharett directed a series of historic operations and projects, such as the *Homa Umigdal* ("Tower and Stockade") new settlements operation during the Palestine Arab rebellion (1936-1939), and the enlistment of thousands of Palestinian Jews into the British Army during World War II [WWII], culminating in the establishment of the Jewish Brigade which fought under the Zionist flag on the Italian front.[3] More significantly, he orchestrated the great Zionist effort at the United Nations General Assembly [UN GA] in 1947 which resulted in the historic resolution of November 29, 1947 to partition Palestine into two states, Jewish and Arab – without which the State of Israel would not have been established six months later. As Foreign Minister, Sharett oversaw armistice negotiations with Egypt, Jordan, Lebanon and Syria, and successfully steered Israel's candidacy for membership in the UN in 1949. He also led the negotiations between Israel and West Germany which brought about the Reparations Agreement which he signed in Luxemburg together with Chancellor and Foreign Minister Konrad Adenauer in September 1952.[4]

1 Segments of this Introduction are drawn from the author's article, "Moshe Sharett, his Diary and the Controversy over Moral Norms in Israel's First Decade," [in Hebrew] *Gesher* 139 (1999), 52-62.

2 Prof. Yechiam Weitz, The Eretz-Israel Studies Department, The University of Haifa.

3 On the Jewish Brigade, see below, page 78 n.26.

4 Yechiam Weitz, "Moshe Sharett and the German Reparations Agreement, 1949-1952," *Studies in Contemporary Jewry* XXI, ed. Eli Lederhendler (Oxford University Press, 2005), 213-31; Yaakov Sharett (ed.), *The Reparations Controversy: The Jewish State and German Money in the Shadow of the Holocaust, 1951-1952*, Berlin/Boston: Walter de Gruyter, for the Moshe Sharett Heritage Society, 2011.

A Zionist Statesman Molded by Palestine

Sharett was born Moshe Shertok[5] in the city of Kherson in southern Ukraine. His father Jacob Shertok (1860-1913), having joined the *BILU* organization,[6] emigrated to Ottoman Palestine in 1882. In 1886 he returned to Russia and married a young teacher, Fania Lev, in Odessa. They settled in neighboring Kherson where their five children were born, Moshe being the second. In 1906, following a further wave of pogroms which swept southern Russia, Jacob Shertok made his second *aliya*, but now as a head of a family. Moshe was then almost twelve.

Although born in Russia, with Russian as his mother tongue, Sharett was seen by many as Palestinian-born, for he grew up, was educated, and matured in Palestine. This was in sharp contrast to other leaders of the Mapai Party[7] such as Levi Eshkol, Golda Meir and Zalman Aran[8] who immigrated to Palestine as a result of a personal, psychological and ideological decision to leave the diaspora, to break with their families and to become Zionist pioneers tilling the land. Sharett did not experience such a personal revolution; he did not come to Palestine alone, but grew up in the bosom of a loving family whose patriarch had already made the decision to immigrate – or "make *aliya*" – there. Moshe's hands were never callused. He grew up in Palestine protected by pampering parents. One of the consequences of this difference between Sharett and his party peers – or *haverim* (lit. "friends" or "members") – was that he never had any intimate friends among them.

The Shertok family disembarked in Jaffa and soon settled in the Arab village of Ein Sinya, situated in the heart of the all-Arab Samarian hills between Ramallah and Nablus. After living for two years in this idyllic spot, far from any Jewish center, the Shertoks moved back to Jaffa and soon to Tel Aviv, where the family patriarch Jacob died in 1913, at 53 years of age. The death of his worshipped father was a heavy blow to young Moshe, a blow which he seems to have never overcome. For much of his life he felt an inner need to find a substitute father-figure, finding him first in the person of Berl Katznelson (1887-1944) and later in David Ben-Gurion[BG] (1886-1973). Following Katznelson's death in 1944 he wrote to his son Yaakov: "Ever since the death of my father thirty years ago, I was never devoured by such pangs of agony of orphanhood."[9]

---

5 Shertok Hebraized his Russian name early in 1949, not long after the establishment of the State of Israel.

6 On the *BILU* pioneers, see below, page 1258 n.81.

7 The Labor Party of Israel - a social-democratic workers' party which dominated the politics of the *yishuv* and Israel from 1933 to 1977.

8 Biographical details about Eshkol, Meir, Aran and other personalities mentioned in this Introduction are given at their first mention in the diary, below.

9 *Moshe Sharett: Rosh Hamemshala Hasheni: Mivhar Te'udot Mepirkei Hayyav* [Hebrew - *Moshe Sharett: The Second Prime Minister - Selected Documents*] eds. Yemima Rosenthal and Louise Fischer (Jerusalem: Israel State Archives, 2007), doc.71 – hereafter *Sharett: Mivhar Te'udot.*

Sharett's relations with David Ben-Gurion, his second father-figure, were complex and problematic in the extreme. Ben-Gurion, who emigrated to Palestine the same year as Sharett (1906), was eight years older, but Sharett viewed him as belonging to the previous generation. In July 1937, in a letter to BG when both of them were members of the JAE in Jerusalem, Sharett confessed:

> To me you are not only an older colleague and co-worker, not only the leader of the movement which is my very home. To me you are the man whose moral and personal authority I have absorbed when this movement was just born. [- - -] I shudder when I think what would have been my fate if not for your standing beside and in front of me.[10]

The ups and downs of Sharett's relations with BG – "whom he adored and hated, the man who was his friend and mentor, his colleague and executioner"[11] – were a decisive factor in Sharett's life, amply illustrated in the diary before us. Especially after April 1955 readers of this diary can share in the daily painful unraveling of relations between the two men. By late June 1956, although still smarting from the humiliation of his forced resignation, the introspective Sharett seemed at last to taste "the freedom [- - -] from the psychological shackles in which I have been bound for years and years due to my subordination to BG and which had forced me to take his position into account and fight him constantly, day after day."[12]

The Shertok family's sojourn in Ein Sinya, short as it was, had a deep and lasting influence on Moshe Sharett. When a group of foreign tourists met with him after having travelled through Samaria and reported that their guide had pointed out the village, saying "it was here that Moshe Shertok was born," Sharett replied: "True, it is there that I was born anew!"[13] A gifted linguist, he mastered Arabic there. Moreover, the experience significantly contributed to his special sensitivity to the "Palestinian Question." In a lecture to young Mapai activists in late June 1956, he declared:

> I cannot expect all of you here to have had the same experience I had when I lived surrounded by Arabs in an all-Arab village in order to become aware that Arabs are human beings, that they have brains, rational thinking, self-esteem and human emotions, and are capable of feelings of outrage just like us.[14]

Similarly, in October 1956, while visiting Malaya, Sharett explained to the Tunku (PM) Abdul Rahman Putra that he had spent part of his childhood in an Arab

10 Moshe Sharett, *Yoman Medini* [*Political Diary*] vol. II (1937) (Tel Aviv: Am Oved, 1971 – in Hebrew), 232-33.

11 Amnon Dankner, "Lonely at the Top," *Ha'aretz*, October 27, 1978.

12 Below, diary entry for June 23, 1956.

13 *Yoman Ishi* [*Personal Diary*]. 8 vols., ed. Yaakov Sharett (Tel Aviv: Sifriyat Ma'ariv, 1978 – in Hebrew), VII: 1966.

14 Minutes of the Meeting of the Mapai Ideological Circle, June 28, 1956, WebDoc #129, available at http://go.iu.edu/28TF.

village and that "that had not only enabled me to learn Arabic directly, but it also taught me to see the Arab firstly as a human being and only afterwards as an Arab, i.e., to see the human angle first and only afterwards the national angle."[15]

Sharett was a student in the first graduating class of the Herzliya Gymnasium in Tel Aviv. Historian Israel Kolatt pointed to the important implications of this fact, for as a result his general outlook was different from that of many of his party *haverim*.

> Unlike them he did not study in Vilnius or in Warsaw, in Poltava or Bobruisk. The revolutionary fermentation and ideological storms played no part in his mental development. The abstract and doctrinaire concepts of war, class struggles, social revolution, or the international solidarity of the proletariat were not sown into his thinking.

Sharett was not a prisoner of dogmas or "isms." He went through "a structured study program, inculcating systematic, clear and empirical thinking" and "saw the world through rational eyes more than through ideological ones."[16]

Members of a Missionary Elite

In the Herzliya Gymnasium Sharett befriended two classmates who became bosom friends, partners in Zionist activity and also members of his family. Like him, these two arrived in Palestine in their early teens. One was Dov Hoz, the father of aviation activity in the *yishuv* [Jewish community in pre-1948 Palestine], who married Sharett's elder sister Rivka. The other was Eliyahu Golomb, future leader of the *Hagana*[17] militia, who married Sharett's younger sister Ada.

Golomb, who died in 1945 at the age of fifty-two, was the leader of this "missionary" trio. The other two saw him as an elder brother in spite of his being older by only one year. In his obituary to Golomb, Sharett said: "Eliyahu towered above the two of us. Not only was he older – he was richer in experience. For us he was a moral and intellectual authority."[18] With Golomb's death Sharett lost not only a close friend and a brother-in-law, but also a person on whose loyalty he could always count and in whom he could always freely confide. The diary offers evidence of how painfully Sharett felt the absence of Golomb as someone who could have strongly supported him in his difficult, sometimes daily, battles with the party's and the country's leader, David Ben-Gurion. This was sharply evident several months after his dismissal from government. In a speech to a large gathering of kibbutz youth at Givat Haim in January 1957, BG found it appropriate to

15 Below, diary entry for October 14, 1956.

16 Israel Kolatt, "Moshe Sharett: A Local-born Zionist," in *Betfutzot Hagola* [in Hebrew] no. 75-76 (1975), 98.

17 On the *Hagana*, see below, diary entry for October 24, 1953.

18 Moshe Sharett, *Orot Shekavu* [*Lights Extinguished; pioneers' portraits* – in Hebrew] (Tel Aviv: Am Oved, 1969), 13-15.

retroactively justify Sharett's dismissal by remarking that the new FM, Golda Meir, although lacking the erudition and experience of her predecessor, had in short order succeeded in providing Israel with defensive arms – thanks to her ability "to act not necessarily according to rules of protocol and diplomatic etiquette, or to use bona fide channels. Golda's unorthodox efforts bore fruit." In other words, BG made it clear that the country's needed arms were provided mainly by France after Sharett's failure to attain them and only following his replacement by Meir. Sharett was enraged and deeply hurt by BG's accusations. First of all, it was he who had initially obtained the French PM Edgar Faure's promise to provide Israel with superior jet planes.[19] And secondly, he asserted that he had never opposed using "unorthodox" methods for the sake of arming Israel.[20]

But it was Sharett's sister, Ada, who reacted first and most sharply to BG's speech. In a letter to Ben-Gurion she accused the PM of slandering Sharett before the Israeli public. "I feel strongly," she wrote, "that if only two persons who are no longer with us had been alive today, this episode would not have happened and you would not have been able to do what you did to Moshe."[21] The two deceased persons to whom Ada Golomb was alluding were her late husband Eliyahu Golomb and Berl Katznelson.

Sharett's second intimate friend and brother-in-law, Dov Hoz, died tragically in a car accident in 1940 when only forty-six. To the end of his life Sharett lamented the loss of his only friends, both of whom known for their integrity and high standing within Mapai ranks. Frequently in his diary, usually during hours of tension and political loneliness, he would recall the old times when the three friends would meet together, discuss current problems and share agreed conclusions. Sharett was never able to find a substitute from among his Mapai *haverim* to replace them. In his will, Sharett left instructions to be buried in the old Tel Aviv Cemetery "beside the graves of Dov Hoz and Eliyahu Golomb,"[22] thereby renouncing his right to a special plot in the National Cemetery on Mount Herzl reserved for major Zionist and Israeli leaders.

It was from Golomb that the young Sharett imbibed a principle which guided him throughout his life, namely that one should devote one's energy to *serving* one's people, and to make this the overriding aim of one's life. The three brothers-in-law saw themselves as stalwart members of a "Limited Organization" of Herzliya Gymnasium's graduating class, led by Golomb, who vowed to serve the Jewish people under the inspiration and leadership of the older, pioneering generation.

---

19 See below, diary entries for October 25-26, 1955, April 3, 1956 and June 28, 1956.

20 On BG's Givat Haim speech and its fallout, see *Sharett: Mivhar Te'udot*, docs.153-154; Sharett, *Yoman Ishi* VII: 2008-18.

21 Quoted in Sharett, *Yoman Ishi* VII: 1947.

22 Sharett's last will was published in all the Israeli dailies on the morrow of his death in July 1965.

Sharett's fundamental loyalty to this principle was clearly a dominant characteristic of his very being, and was reflected in his adoption in 1949 of a Hebrew name deriving from the verb *lesharet*, meaning "to serve." Members of the "Limited Organization" were attracted by the dedication of the leaders of the two labor parties of the time (which would unite in 1930 to establish Mapai) and accepted their predominance. These youths, a product of local education under Palestine's skies, felt secure under the authority of these Second *Aliya* pioneers.[23]

Sharett's Road to Politics and Diplomacy

During WWI Sharett served as an officer in the Ottoman Army. In 1919 he and his friends Hoz and Golomb joined the *Ahdut Ha'avoda* socialist party upon its founding.[24] Being a member in a socialist party was a dream come true for Sharett. He firmly believed that he had found his social and political home. "The burning creative spirit of *Ahdut Ha'avoda*, its striving for great achievements, its dynamism and its political daring, its courage and free atmosphere of discussion captivated our hearts and intoxicated us," reminisced Sharett.[25]

In 1920 Sharett went off to England to study at the London School of Economics, from which he graduated in 1925. By aspiring to higher learning he again set himself apart from his party *haverim*. No other member of the Mapai leadership left Palestine in pursuit of higher learning. A remark attributed to Avraham Harzfeld, one of the fathers of Zionist settlement, likely represented the feelings of many of his contemporaries: "My university was Palestine's swamps."

By contrast, Sharett's political road was unique. His graduate studies, and the very fact of living abroad for five years and studying in the political, economic, and cultural capital of the world at the time, gave him first-hand experience of the daily workings of British democracy. He was able to experience the functioning of parliament, political parties and a variegated press – enriching his general erudition and widening his horizons and outlook. Unlike many of his more "provincial" colleagues, he was becoming a man of the world.

Sharett's first career was in journalism. Even before his return to Palestine in April 1925, he was asked by the soon-to-be editor of *Davar*, the labor movement's new daily, to serve as his assistant. Editor-in-Chief Berl Katznelson had become acquainted with the young Shertok in 1919, when the latter had assisted him in editing their new party's weekly and became one of its regular contributors. Sharett thus had no need to seek employment upon starting his life anew after returning to Palestine in 1925. He happily accepted his mentor's offer and became the front-page

23 Zionist immigrants who arrived in Palestine between 1904 and 1914. See below, page 1447 n.31.

24 The party would merge with the leftist *Hapo'el Hatza'ir* Party in 1930 to form Mapai.

25 Sharett, *Orot Shekavu*, 20.

editor of *Davar*, starting with its first issue. In 1929 he founded *Davar*'s weekly English supplement as an important outreach effort. Sharett was well satisfied with his choice of career, and might have stayed on at *Davar*, eventually becoming its Editor-in-Chief – until fate decreed otherwise.

In 1931, following the success of labor in the elections for the 17th Zionist Congress, the Mapai Party was awarded a seat on the JAE in Jerusalem, and as a result one of its leaders, the bright young intellectual Dr. Chaim Arlosoroff, was appointed head of the Agency's Political Department, the *de facto* "foreign affairs ministry" of the Zionist Organization [ZO]. Arlosoroff – well aware of Sharett's talents, including his mastery of English, Arabic, Turkish, Russian, and German, his acumen in writing and speech-making, and his wide knowledge of Palestinian and Middle Eastern affairs – offered him a job as his assistant. Sharett very much wanted to accept this new post which was both political and administrative; he was even prepared to abandon his journalistic career to begin working with this brilliant man, five years his junior, at the cost of damaging relations with his mentor, Katznelson.

Sharett's move from *Davar* to assume a political role in the Jewish Agency was – characteristically – not a result of personal initiative, ambition or maneuvering. The new post, which would abruptly change his whole life, was offered to him, just like his previous job as journalist and editor, in recognition of his proven abilities. Out of loyalty to the party, Sharett asked the Mapai Central Committee [CC] to decide whether he should stay on with Katznelson or join Arlosoroff. In the end Sharett was more than happy to accept the CC's majority decision in favor of him working with Arlosoroff.

But on June 16, 1933, Chaim Arlosoroff was gunned down on the beaches of Tel Aviv, an event whose reverberations have not subsided to this day.[26] Arlosoroff's death was a heavy personal blow for Sharett, who deeply adored him; he named his younger son, born only a few days after the murder, Haim. At a party gathering marking the twentieth anniversary of Arlosoroff's murder, Sharett said: "From his early youth he had shown his prodigious talents. Not only was he gifted with rare abilities, but had a soul emitting holy sparks of fire from its very depths."[27] Arlosoroff's death was a fateful watershed in Sharett's life, forcing him to assume responsibility for the Political Department of the JAE. Sharett, not yet 40 years old, now found himself at the center of Zionist politics, becoming in 1935 part of an informal leadership "troika" alongside ZO President, Dr Chaim Weizmann, and labor movement leader and *haver*, David Ben-Gurion. From 1933 until his dismissal by Ben-Gurion in mid-1956, Sharett would help steer the ship of Zionist and Israeli diplomacy.

---

26 The identity and motives of the killers have never been clearly established. See Shabtai Teveth, *The Murder of Arlosoroff*. Tel Aviv: Schocken, 1982 – in Hebrew.

27 Sharett, *Orot Shekavu*, 30.

It is important to recall that Sharett's rise to prominence derived not through backing from any particular group or powerful individual within Mapai, but rather from his personal "prestige" and his "ability to logically convince his listeners."[28] Unfortunately, his lack of factional support within the party would make it easier for PM Ben-Gurion to remove him in 1956. One could say regarding these two colleagues/rivals that, while Sharett was admired and highly respected by the *haverim*, Ben-Gurion was worshipped. In an open showdown between the two, Sharett would have no chance.

Sharett as Family Patriarch

Sharett always saw himself as a family patriarch – a dedicated and strict, but loving and beloved, father – not only vis-à-vis his immediate family (wife and three children) but also to his larger extended family. This last aspect was expressed especially in his loving care for his nephew Harai, whose unmarried mother Geula (the youngest of the five children of Jacob Shertok) died in childbirth, and towards his niece Tamar, the sole survivor of the 1940 car crash in which her father Dov, her mother Rivka, their elder daughter Tirza, as well as Sharett's brother Yehuda's wife Tzivia were killed. And after the death of his brother-in-law Eliyahu Golomb in 1945, he took special care of his sister Ada and her three children. When his younger brother Yehuda fell into a deep depression upon the death of his wife, it was Moshe who saved him from a serious mental crisis.

But Sharett behaved as a patriarch in an even wider sense – i.e., in his relations with the Foreign Ministry [MFA] which he had built up from among the pre-state Political Department personnel he had personally selected over the years. In late 1955, when he stepped down from the premiership (to be replaced by Ben-Gurion) and went back to his MFA office, he noted in his diary: "At the Foreign Ministry I was greeted with broad smiles by everyone. Although I had still been FM during the past twenty-one months, I was greeted like a long-lost son or an exiled father reunited with his family."[29] At his farewell reception in mid-June 1956 MFA employees were overcome with tears and emotion.[30] Upon replacing him as Foreign Minister, Golda Meir expressed astonishment at her predecessor's acquaintance with all the details of his staff, writing in her autobiography: "It was typical of Sharett that he knew everything down to the last detail about the ministry, including the name, family status, and personal problems of everyone who worked there. He even knew the names of their children."[31]

---

28 Avi Bareli, *Mapai in Israel's Early Independence: 1948-1953* (Jerusalem: Yad Ben-Zvi Press, 2007 – in Hebrew), 92-94.

29 Below, diary entry for November 4, 1955.

30 Below, diary entry for June 18, 1956.

31 Golda Meir, *My Life* (London: Futura Books, 1976), 242.

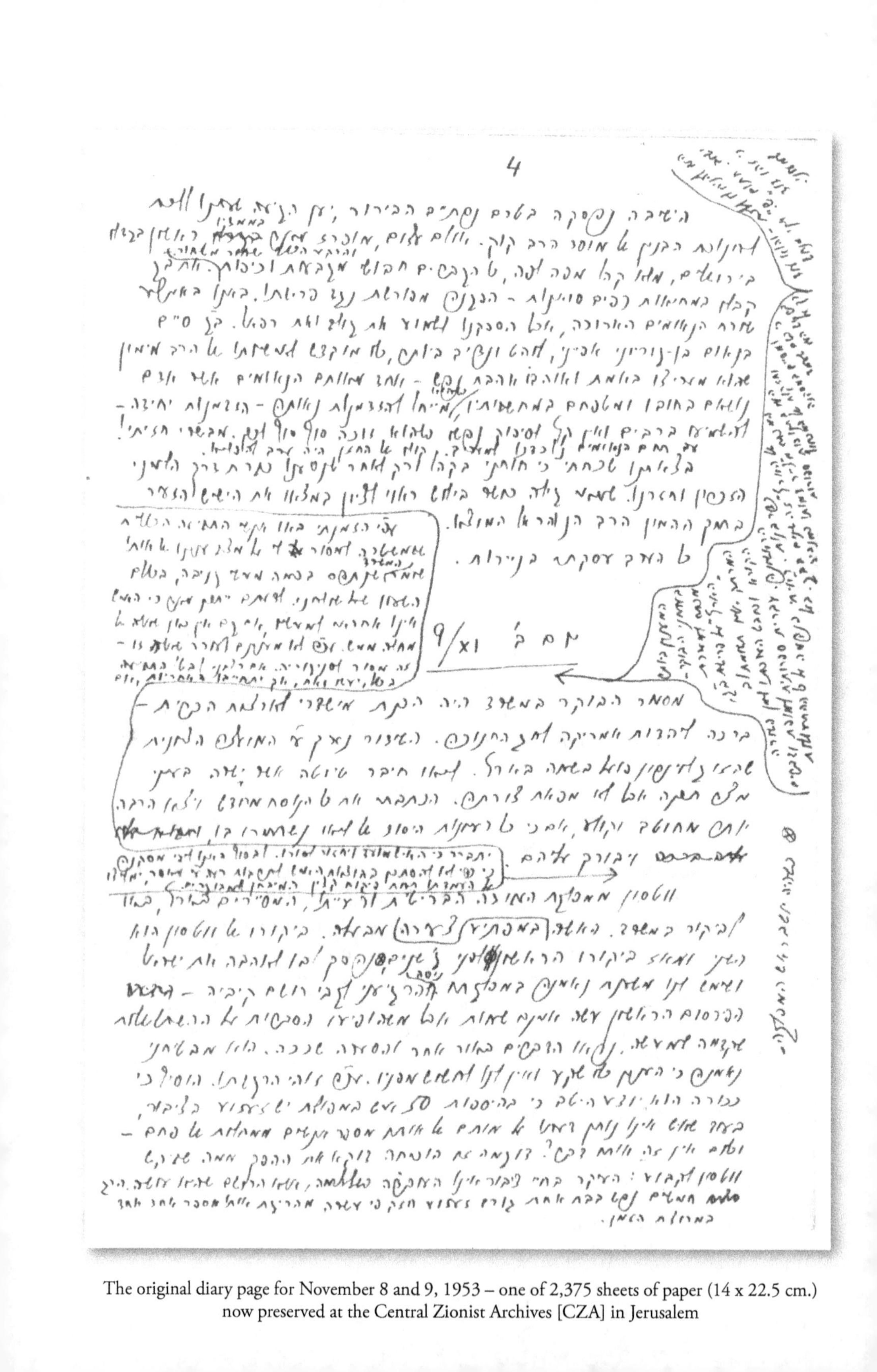

The original diary page for November 8 and 9, 1953 – one of 2,375 sheets of paper (14 x 22.5 cm.) now preserved at the Central Zionist Archives [CZA] in Jerusalem

Sharett and his Diary

Among Israel's prime ministers two are known to have kept a diary: Ben-Gurion and Sharett.[32] The main characteristics of Ben-Gurion's diary may be summed up as follows:

(A) Duration of writing. Ben-Gurion kept a diary for most of his long life (1886-1973). He wrote it day-by-day from age 14, until his last year. The importance of these diaries as a major source of information regarding the history of the *yishuv* and of Israel, as well as regarding Ben-Gurion the man himself, cannot be exaggerated.

(B) Character of writing. Ben-Gurion's diary is not one in which the diarist pours out his experiences, musings, and feelings. On such subjects there is very little in Ben-Gurion's diary. Apart from expressions of grief at the passing of close friends, it hardly touches upon any intimate issues. It is mainly a record of work and activity, a kind of daily agenda, "a handy archive helpful for recalling facts and keeping workdays in order."[33]

(C) The diarist's aim. There were two motivations behind Ben-Gurion's diary writing. The first was practical; to collect a lot of political and military information with the aim of bolstering his leadership. The second aim was to shape, for the historical record, his image in the eyes of future generations. Only a few portions of the voluminous diary have been edited for publication (e.g., for the fateful period 1947-1949),[34] while the complete diary is available for public consultation at the Ben-Gurion Archive at Sde Boker.[35]

Moshe Sharett's diary, which was published in eight volumes in Hebrew in 1978 as *Yoman Ishi*,[36] is by far different, as seen in its main characteristics:

(A) Duration of writing. Sharett wrote his diary over a short period, albeit the most important in his life. Following Ben-Gurion's decision to retire from government and settle on Kibbutz Sde Boker in 1953, many assumed that the mantle of primeministership would fall on Sharett's shoulders.[37] It was the

32 Shimon Peres, who served as prime minister in 1984-1986 and 1995-1996, kept a diary but it was not published or opened to the public.

33 Zaki Shalom, "Ben-Gurion's Diaries as Historical Source," *Cathedra* 56 (1990): 139 [in Hebrew].

34 David Ben-Gurion, *Yoman Hamilhama: Milhemet Ha'atzma'ut* [*War Diary: The War of Independence, 1947-1949*], 3 vols., ed. Gershon Rivlin and Elhanan Orren. Tel Aviv: Ministry of Defense Publishing, 1982 – in Hebrew.

35 The Ben-Gurion Research Institute for the Study of Israel and Zionism, online at http://in.bgu.ac.il/en/bgi/Pages/Archives.aspx. The original diary is preserved at the IDF Archive in Tel Hashomer, near Tel Aviv.

36 *Yoman Ishi* [*Personal Diary*]. 8 vols., ed. Yaakov Sharett. Tel Aviv: Sifriyat Ma'ariv, 1978 – in Hebrew.

37 Sharett officially became PM on January 26, 1954, and served till November 2, 1955 – a period of 21 months.

realization of the seriousness of the new personal and national responsibilities awaiting him that prompted Sharett to begin writing a diary, which opens with the following line: "I am starting to write a diary, prompted by a sudden urge to record for posterity something of the tumultuous stream of events which makes up my life."[38] The closing entry of the full Hebrew diary was composed on November 28, 1957[39] when Sharett, still bitter following his dismissal from government a year and a half earlier, at which point he abruptly abandoned his diary without explaining why – probably feeling that his life had become devoid of significant political content worthy of reporting. The diary thus spans a period of only four years and one month – an obvious difference in comparison to Ben-Gurion's lengthy diary.

(B) Context of writing and publication. About two months after he started writing his diary, he wrote to his elder son Yaakov, then a student in New York, that "the very existence of the diary is top secret."[40] Interestingly, only members of his immediate family, his close friend David Hacohen, and his brother-in-law Shaul Avigur (Zipporah Sharett's younger brother) were in the know. According to Yaakov, his father had not intended to publish his diary and had never instructed members of his family what should be done with it after his death.[41]

Close to the end of October 1965, a few months after Sharett's death, Yaakov Sharett published several passages of the diary in the Tel Aviv daily, *Ma'ariv*, where he was member of the editorial staff.[42] These excerpts appeared close to the end of a stormy general election campaign. Three days earlier, Ben-Gurion, then head of the small break-away Rafi Party ("Israel Workers' List"), had published in *Yediot Ahronot* an entire chapter from his book, *Devarim Kahavayatam* [Things as They Are] in which he stated that he had not been involved in the decision to mount the Israel Defense Forces' [IDF] retaliatory raid on the Jordanian village of Qibya.[43] While Ben-Gurion claimed that he had heard about the Qibya operation only afterwards, Sharett's diary painted a different picture: the decision to mount the operation had been taken at a meeting of three senior ministers – Ben-Gurion, Pinhas Lavon (then Acting Minister of Defense) and himself. The first two, who approved it, prevailed against Sharett, who had opposed it.[44]

Israel's newspapers had a field-day with Sharett's diary as published by *Ma'ariv*, and Ben-Gurion's role in the 1953 operations became an election issue.

38 Below, diary entry for October 9, 1953.

39 This English edition of the diary ends on December 9, 1956, with Sharett's return to Israel following his 82-day tour of Asia.

40 Yaakov Sharett, Preface, *Yoman Ishi* I: 7.

41 Ibid., I:8.

42 Yaakov Sharett, "Pages of Moshe Sharett's Diary," *Ma'ariv*, October 29, 1965.

43 *Devarim Kahavayatam* [Things As They Are]. Tel Aviv: Am Hasefer, 1965 – in Hebrew. On the Qibya operation, which killed more than 60 villagers, see below, diary entries for October 13-November 29, 1953.

44 See below, diary entries for October 16, 1953 and June 18, 1956.

At a campaign rally organized by opposition right-wing parties, *Herut* Movement leader and Knesset Member Menachem Begin stated:

> The diary of the late Sharett from that Qibya period is a frightening and shocking document. It makes it unequivocally clear that by claiming that he had heard about that operation only after it was mounted and by putting the sole responsibility for the action on Minister Lavon he said the very opposite of truth, demonstrating, in the words of Sharett, 'an elasticity of conscience.'[45]

Over the coming years Yaakov Sharett would publish additional excerpts of his father's diary, culminating in a series of 24 chapters in *Ma'ariv* in 1974 and, finally, the complete 8-volume set in 1978.

(C) The diarist's aim. During his time as Prime Minister (1954-1955) and then as Foreign Minister under Ben-Gurion (from November 1955), Sharett had numerous clashes and experienced many a frustration. And it appears that the main outlet for releasing his inner turmoil was by pouring out his heart and soul, and unpacking his various burdens, onto the pages of his diary.

He wrote freely about everything – without filtering or self-censorship. This obsessive psychological need turned his diary into a captivating historical document. A senior *Ha'aretz* journalist described Sharett's unbearable situation during those years: "He was suffering from an ulcer and from eczema in his feet. People under him were uncooperative, friends were abandoning him. The reins of power he had been holding were gradually slipping away."[46] In such circumstances the diary became his only refuge, the only place where he could allow himself to openly and fully write about whatever troubled and embittered him, revealing his true feelings toward friend and foe alike.

(D) Character of the writing. Perhaps the greatest contrast between Sharett's and Ben-Gurion's diaries is the degree of candor and personal disclosure of the former. Sharett devoted much attention to describing not just facts but also atmosphere, facial expressions and body language, even when reporting on Cabinet and party meetings. See, for example, how he describes Defense Minister Pinhas Lavon taking his leave of the Cabinet following his resignation in February 1955:

> I got up from my seat, went over to him and staunchly shook his hand. He left with his head held high. Thus ended such an important and tragic chapter in the life of this peculiar man, who by virtue of his intelligence and talent could have attained greatness if the distortions of his character had not led him astray. I have never felt with such intensity as I did at that moment the bitter truth that, in his failure and downfall, he was paying the price for the defects of his soul and his despicable actions.[47]

---

45 "Forty-thousand People at a Meeting Headed by GAHAL Leaders in Tel Aviv," *Herut*, October 31, 1965. Cf. below, diary entry for October 20, 1953.

46 Dankner, ibid.

47 Below, diary entry for February 20, 1955.

One can also feel Sharett's literary touch as he portrays awkward moments, such as when he took personal responsibility for meeting with Rega Oren, wife of Mordechai Oren, to inform her of the bad news that her husband had been given a harsh sentence following a show trial in Prague.[48] Perhaps most searing of all is Sharett's account of his final moments as a Cabinet minister:

> There was complete silence around the table. Not one of my colleagues raised his eyes to mine. [- - -] no one rose to shake my hand. It was as though they were suffering a kind of inner paralysis, as if their limbs had been shackled in the same way as their freedom of expression and action according to their consciences had been shackled earlier. They sat staring into space, oppressed in silence. I walked the length of the big conference room with measured steps and went outside. Only [Cabinet Secretary] Ze'ev [Sharef] jumped up from his place and ran after me, full of emotion, to see me out. It was a critical and harsh moment which ripped through my very soul. I felt so not because I had left the Cabinet table, the responsibility, or the position, but because of the absence of a friendly hand outstretched in human warmth, surmounting all the difficulty and breaking any stricture. It was a cruel lesson. I knew that they were most unhappy, but I also knew that they were faint of heart.[49]

Also in sharp contrast to Ben-Gurion, Sharett the diarist refers to quite a few cultural events, especially theater and concert performances, which he was not shy to critique, sometimes in picky detail and quite negatively. (Ben-Gurion's diary occasionally makes note of cultural events, but only superficially and from a political angle.) This difference underlines the wide gap in cultural sophistication of the two men. Sharett was by far better versed in the fields of literature, poetry, music, and translation.[50] His diary describes lively debates and conversations with noted journalists, intellectuals and academics, including Isaiah Berlin, Jacob Talmon, Margaret Mead, Gunnar Myrdal and Isaac Deutscher. In this sense, Sharett is closer to another Zionist leader widely admired for his cultural and intellectual prowess: Ze'ev Jabotinsky. Sharett's diary also includes detailed accounts relating to family matters, holiday celebrations, get-togethers and the like – topics which have no place in Ben-Gurion's diary.

Most important of all, however, the diary starkly exposes Sharett's mental state and spiritual anguish during and following his term in office. Descriptions of his moods are often gripping. On the day of the hanging in Cairo of two members of a ring of Israeli-directed Egyptian-Jewish saboteurs, he wrote:

48 Below, diary entry for November 2, 1953. Mordechai Oren, member of Kibbutz Mizra and one of the leaders of leftist party Mapam, was arrested in Prague while on visit there in December 1951 and accused of being an American spy. He was sentenced to 15 years in prison but was released in 1956.

49 Below, diary entry for June 18, 1956.

50 See, e.g., Moshe Sharett, *Mahberet Tirgumei Shira* [*A Booklet of Poetry Translated*]. Introduction by Aminadav Dickman. Tel Aviv: Moshe Sharett Heritage Society, 2003 – in Hebrew, Russian, German, French – originally published by Am Oved, 1965.

> I awoke under the heavy cloud of the execution of the death sentences in Cairo scheduled for this morning. I couldn't stop thinking and tormenting myself over the fate of the two Jewish lads in Cairo prison, who'd been delivered for nothing – for absolutely nothing! – into the hands of the hangman. What are they going through during these hours as they prepare in their solitude to meet bitter death, face-to-face?
>
> One after the other arrived the announcements confirming that the men had been executed, first Marzuk and then Azar. The nightmare which had dragged on for months has reached its end. All efforts and hopes have been dashed against the reality of the gallows. I continued to weigh every phrase and every word in the statement I had prepared for the Knesset, lest I say too much, lest I say too little.[51]

In the days and months following his forced resignation as FM, Sharett alluded again and again to the depression and distress in which he was submerged. Indeed, these feelings never left him, and he would never recover from the humiliating blow of his dismissal, inflicted by his erstwhile partner, David Ben-Gurion.[52]

Sharett's Diary: Assessments and Context

Reviewers from academia and commentators from all parts of the political spectrum were in agreement in welcoming the 8-volume *Yoman Ishi* as an important historical document – one that both shed much light on the period and gave unusual insight into the diarist's personality. Israel Kolatt wrote:

> The self-possessed and restrained man, who used to report on political situations in public meetings using general descriptions so as not to reveal too much, opens up to all an unprecedented exposure, unknown so far in the history of Israeli politicians, and even among that of non-Israeli ones.

Underscoring his assessment of the revelatory quality of the diary, Kolatt added:

> There is in Moshe Sharett's diary much of petty inner desire, no little frustration and even political evaluations tinged with grumbling. However, whoever accepts the diary as pure truth in view of the writer's integrity, must also accept the positive exemplary characteristics it reveals: the acumen of political thinking, the total devotion, the diligent working, the morality of his personal behavior, the high abilities of learning and expressing – all of which are evidenced in the diary.[53]

Writing in *Davar*, the daily in which Sharett had launched his career in public life, Danny Rubinstein echoed the above observations, heaping additional praises on the diary and its author:

---

51 Below, diary entry for January 31, 1955.

52 See: Yechiam Weitz, "Why Was Moshe Sharett Deposed? A Historical Question and a Historiographical Issue," *Israel Studies*, 20:3 (Fall 2015), 131–57; Neil Caplan, "Why Was Sharett Sacked?" *Middle East Journal* 70:2 (Spring 2016), 275-97; below, "Epilogue: The Premature End of a Political Career."

53 Israel Kolatt, "A Personal Diary and a National Reckoning," *Ma'ariv*, February 2, 1979.

> The candor and self-exposure of Moshe Sharett turned his diary into a unique document unlike diaries and reminiscences of other politicians and leaders, which are usually replete with much hypocrisy, pretensions and selectiveness aimed at enhancing their historic importance. Sharett's diary is by far different. This is an authentic document, absolving nothing. It was written secretly, at the time of the events portrayed, and without taking into account the "worthiness" of the diarist's historic stature. Now, for the first time in the annals of Israel's political life, we are presented with an intimate diary of a first-rate leader, detailing innermost thoughts, dreams and doubts, exposing human weaknesses and personal crises. [- - -] Sharett's obsessive devotion to his diary was limited to only four years – indeed fateful years in his political life – during which he succeeded in mobilizing an incredible spiritual and physical effort, producing about 2,400 printed pages, while at the same time fulfilling his onerous duties as foreign minister and prime minister. The result is a truthful, mesmerizing, and highly important document, and one of the most vital for understanding Israel's political life during its first and formative decade.[54]

Focusing on the unfiltered revelations retained in the published diary, Amnon Dankner noted that:

> There are many who would certainly have been happy had they managed to delete, throw away, and destroy certain passages in Sharett's diary. His acute observations, his sharp tongue, his doubting the integrity of and his lack of trust in many who surrounded him, strewn among the tens of thousands of the diary's lines, are indeed poisoned arrows which may hit many a person, alive as well as dead – statesmen and military figures, political leaders as well as party activists and journalists.[55]

How Will Sharett Be Remembered?

How was Sharett perceived on the day he passed away? A dominant typical observation in his obituaries was that Israel had lost a noble-minded man blessed with moral integrity and authority. In his last years he remained true to these qualities as he struggled heroically with his worsening lung cancer which confined him to a wheelchair. *Ma'ariv*'s editorial on the morrow of Sharett's death was titled "The Noble," and said: "The man Moshe Sharett shall forever be remembered as a well-rounded man of integrity, sincerity and warmth, a symbol of clear conscience and moral principles."[56] *Herut* daily, mouthpiece of the party which had consistently opposed Sharett's political line throughout his service as a minister in Israel's governments, noted that he was

> a formidable opponent, a man of impressive cultural standing which he inherited from his Zionist father and enhanced by academic study together with a noble personality bestowed on him by Providence. He was a man of letters, well versed in the Hebrew language and known for his fanatic devotion to its purity. He was a scholar, highly

54 Danny Rubinstein, "A Diary with No Embellishments," *Davar*, December 15, 1978.
55 Dankner, ibid.
56 *Ma'ariv*, July 8, 1965.

devoted to cultural attainments and as a result he was highly respected by his political opponents as well.[57]

It is my opinion, as an historian, that Sharett's most important quality was his consistent devotion to molding and maintaining a credible alternative to the stronger and dominant political and military line posited by Ben-Gurion's school of thought. A number of analysts have compared Sharett's and Ben-Gurion's worldviews and personalities,[58] and I wish to refer to this dichotomy in drawing these concluding remarks. The "activist" approach fostered by Ben-Gurion, Pinhas Lavon, Moshe Dayan, Ariel Sharon and others cultivated a machismo attitude and a hero-worship in the name of which excesses were at times committed by officers and officials who considered themselves above the law and outside moral norms. On a number of occasions Sharett courageously stood up against this attitude, although not always with successful outcomes.

Two examples illustrate this clash. In March 1955, four Israeli ex-paratroopers crossed the border into Jordan and cold-bloodedly executed three Bedouins, ostensibly in revenge for the murder of the sister of one of them. The IDF closed ranks to block inquiries, while others higher up (including Defense Minister Ben-Gurion himself) protected the perpetrators from facing the courts. Describing the contention between BG and himself over this issue, Sharett lamented:

> During the period of *havlaga* [self-restraint] in the thirties, we had managed to subdue the lust for vengeance and had enlightened the public to view acts of gratuitous vengeance as being totally unjustified. Yet today we justify this method of retaliation for pragmatic considerations without, Heaven forbid, lending credence to the principle of vengeance *per se*. Still, unintentionally, we have removed the moral and mental barriers against this primordial negative human passion. Thus have we allowed a paratroop unit to elevate an act of vengeance to the level of a moral principle.[59]

Several months earlier, when IDF jets intercepted a Syrian airliner flying outside of Israeli airspace – ostensibly to use its passengers as hostages to exchange for several Israelis imprisoned in Damascus – Sharett ordered its immediate release.[60] After reporting on this episode to the Knesset, he closed his speech by "posing a choice: was Israel to be a country of laws or of license, of reason and foresight or of anarchy and unbridled passions? I asked the Knesset to vote on these alternatives."[61] We can see these options as being as relevant today as they were over fifty years ago, when they were first presented.

Sharett's diary, written in perfect and rich Hebrew, opened with his personal

57 Editorial, *Herut*, July 8, 1965.
58 See the works of Michael Brecher, Avi Shlaim and Gabriel Sheffer cited below, Epilogue.
59 Below, diary entry for March 13, 1955.
60 Below, diary entries for December 19, 1954 – January 16, 1955.
61 Below, diary entry for January 17, 1955.

ascent to primeministership and ended with his political downfall. His was the lonely struggle of a man against a powerful defense establishment, headed by two charismatic leaders of the day, David Ben-Gurion and Moshe Dayan. This was indeed a historic and fateful confrontation – one between a moderate statesman who aimed at diplomatically lowering the flames of Arab hostility to Israel, and his opponents who sought a solution of the conflict primarily through military prowess, unconcerned about provocative actions that would fan those very flames. It was a struggle between a statesman who sought to avoid a second Arab-Israeli war at all costs, and those who were not averse to launching a preemptive war, or colluding in an Anglo-French attack on Israel's most powerful Arab neighbor.

The victory of the Ben-Gurion school over the Sharett approach was to be expected and was indeed inevitable. Sharett was clearly aware of this final outcome as it loomed ahead, and on several occasions he seriously contemplated resigning his ministerial posts. However, bound by his unflinching loyalty to the principle of serving his country, he fought on courageously until his rival found it necessary to rid himself of the nuisance and obstacle represented in the person of the moderate Foreign Minister, Moshe Sharett.

The diary which follows unfolds a spellbinding historical drama, one which was also a personal tragedy for the diarist. The war of 1956, which he opposed, erupted just over four months after his dismissal, while he was abroad attempting to expand Israel's relations with the new states of Asia. In a diary entry written near the historic ruins of Angkor Wat in Cambodia, he coldly noted that his own political career should be included on the list of "casualties" of that apparently successful war.[62]

The diary of the defeated statesman Sharett serves to remind us of the existence of a moderate political option which came to an end with his downfall in the eighth year of the young Jewish state. And for the English-reading public, the diary's publication in this current edition, four decades after its appearance in Hebrew, may help raise Moshe Sharett – a leader resolutely committed to peace – from oblivion.

62 Below, diary entry for December 2, 1956.

1953

Primeministership in the Offing

Friday, October 9

I am starting to write a diary, prompted by a sudden urge to record for posterity something of the tumultuous stream of events which makes up my life. This urge has arisen within me more than once, especially at times of toil and stress, but either my inner resources have failed me, or I have lacked the strength to respond to it, stifling the urge within me. I have told myself that I shall not be able both to live through these things and to set them down on paper. My strength is insufficient for this twofold pursuit. And so events and deeds have gone by, images have vanished, and voices have become mute. Some, surviving for some time, fade in memory, while most slip entirely into oblivion. I do not know why this evening in particular I should have found the vigour to begin writing, as they say in Russian, *s m'iesta v karier* [at one go]. I doubt if I shall persevere and make an established custom of it. Nevertheless, I will try.[1]

[- - -]

A long consultation at the Ministry of Foreign Affairs [MFA] in the *Kirya*[2] with Pinhas Lavon who is Acting Minister of Defense,[3] and the Army people, including the Chief of Staff [CoS] Lt.-General Mordechai Maklef,[4] Brigadier Moshe Dayan,[5] and Lt.-Colonel Aryeh Shalev.[6]

---

1 This was the first attempt at writing a diary found in Sharett's archives since 1940.

2 The term *Hakirya*, lit. "the town," refers to the Government compound (formerly the German Templars' colony of Sarona) in Tel Aviv, housing then MFA and Ministry of Defense Headquarters HQ), as well as liaison offices of other ministries based in Jerusalem.

3 Pinhas Lavon (1904-1976). Minister of Agriculture (1950-1951), Minister without Portfolio (August 1952-January 1954); Acting Minister of Defense (August-October 1953), Minister of Defense (January 1954-February 1955), Secretary-General (SG), *Histadrut* (General Federation of Labor in Israel) (1956-1961). In July 1953 Prime Minister (PM) David Ben-Gurion went on leave and asked Sharett to replace him as Acting PM and Lavon to replace him as Acting Minister of Defense. While serving as Acting Minister of Defense, Lavon was in constant contact with Ben-Gurion.

4 Mordechai Maklef (1920-1978). CoS Israel Defense Forces (IDF) (1952-1953); later Director-General (DG) of Dead Sea Works.

5 Moshe Dayan (1915-1981). At this time Chief of Operations at General Staff (GS); CoS of the IDF (1953-1958); later Minister of Agriculture, Minister of Defense, and Foreign Minister (FM).

6 Aryeh Shalev (1926-2011). GS officer, Intelligence Branch; Israel's representative on the Israel-Syria Mixed Armistice Commission (ISMAC).

We aired some ideas concerning the northern imbroglio.[7] Gideon Rafael[8] was with me. I suggested that I write another letter to Major-General Bennike,[9] which would offer us a way to gain another few days. Dayan was afraid the letter might do more harm than good; that it would hasten rather than postpone the stopping of the works. Shalev believed that a letter from Bennike, setting a deadline for the stoppage of work, might arrive on Monday, and then we would not be able to avoid staking out a final position: obedience or defiance. Meanwhile we were [still] working, even after Bennike's demand that we stop. Our pretext is that as long as Bennike has not set a deadline and we continue to deliberate with him, this does not constitute defiance of the United Nations [UN]. Once a deadline is set, however, the issue will have been decided. Nonetheless, it was concluded that we had best write to him and try to postpone the final verdict in this way. Our goal is to keep matters rolling for another week or ten days until the first link of the canal is finished. The question arose whether, once this work is completed, we would divert the Jordan into the canal. The IDF people held that we should do it because only thus would we demonstrate our proprietorship over the Jordan. My answer was that we had all along told Bennike and others (the US, and England) that we would not tamper with the Jordan for the time being, that we would not establish any new realities regarding water. How could we now justify the diversion of the river? Actually, I had already instructed Abba Eban[10] to tell Dulles[11] in a conversation held yesterday, that once we finish this part of the canal, we shall for the moment refrain from diverting the Jordan into it. No decision on this matter was reached during the consultation, for it was not yet time to decide. Let us see if we can finish the so-called "bend" [in the diversion canal], and then we'll decide in accordance with the circumstances on the day.

It was also decided to make use of the Electric Corporation in opposing Bennike's

---

7 In September, Israel's plans for a water diversion project at B'not Yaakov Bridge in the Israel-Syria Demilitarized Zone (DMZ) were challenged by General Vagn Bennike, rendering a decision in his capacity as Chairman of the ISMAC, responding to a Syrian complaint that the works violated articles of the Israel-Syria General Armistice Agreement (GAA). See Bennike to Sharett, September 23, 1953, *Documents on the Foreign Policy of Israel*, volume 8 (1953), ed. Yemima Rosenthal (Jerusalem: Israel State Archives, 1995), doc.381 – hereafter *DFPI* 8.

8 Gideon Rafael (1913-1999). Counsellor in charge of Middle East (ME) and UN Political Affairs, MFA; later Ambassador to Belgium and representative to the European Economic Community (EEC). From 1967 to 1972 served as DG, MFA. Close associate of Sharett since working together in the pre-state Jewish Agency (JA) Political Department.

9 Maj.-Gen. Vagn Bennike (1888-1970). CoS, UN Truce Supervision Organization (UNTSO), July 1953-September 1954.

10 Aubrey (Abba) Eban (1915-2002). Ambassador to the UN and to Washington (1950-1959); later Member of Knesset (MK), Minister without Portfolio, Minister of Education and Culture, Deputy PM, and FM. Close associate of Sharett since working together in the pre-state JA Political Department.

11 John Foster Dulles (1888-1959). US Secretary of State (1953-1959).

move. A letter will be written in the company's name proclaiming its rights to the Jordan waters, and threatening legal action – once again a deterrent and delaying tactic.

[- - -]

[Back home in the evening] I changed hastily. Zipporah[12] had gone to rest awhile, and I managed to wake her up with the noise I made. We drove to the home of the Argentine Consul, Pablo Mangel, to a dinner in honor of Vera and Jacob Tsur,[13] who are leaving on Sunday for Paris. Present were the French Ambassador, Pierre Gilbert,[14] and his Greek-Egyptian wife, several people from our Foreign Ministry, and others. The food was plentiful, and French and Spanish were spoken. I succeeded in amusing my Greek dinner companion three times! Later I explained to my other companion, the wife of our head of the Latin America Division, what constitutes the Levantine nature: a lack of any respect for values in themselves, from any universal – moral or cultural – viewpoint, but rather judging every issue only in terms of self-gratification. I joked with the French Ambassador over the differences between Israel and France regarding compliance with the UN. If Israel should defy Major-General Bennike by not stopping vital development operations, it transgresses; while if France boycotts the [UN] General Assembly [GA] debate on Morocco, it gets away with it. Gilbert succinctly explained: Everything depends on the US position, and the latter cannot renounce French aid – neither in Western Europe nor in North Africa. I went on to add that the fact that a third of the French nation are communists is also a great asset.

[- - -]

I went to bed at nearly one o'clock, and tossed and turned for a long time. I was gravely troubled. Should I accept the premiership when Ben-Gurion[15] [BG] retires,[16] or should I refuse, and ask that the burden be placed upon Pinhas Lavon?

---

12 Zipporah (Meirov) Sharett (1897-1973). Moshe Sharett's wife since 1922.

13 Jacob Tsur (1906-1990). Member of the Political Department of the JA, Jerusalem (1942-1944); Israel minister to Argentina, Uruguay, Paraguay, and Chile (1949-1953), Ambassador to France (1953-1959); later Chairman of the Jewish National Fund (JNF). Close associate of Sharett since working together in the pre-state JA Political Department.

14 Pierre-Eugène Gilbert (1907-1982). French Ambassador to Israel (1953-1959).

15 David Ben-Gurion (1886-1973). Born in Poland. Settled in Palestine in 1906. Founder and leader of the Mapai Party (1930). Head of the Jewish Agency Executive (JAE) (1935-1948). PM and Minister of Defense (1948-1953). Minister of Defense from February 1955. PM and Minister of Defense from November 1955 until June 1963. Left Mapai in 1965 to form the Rafi Party. Retired from political life in 1970.

16 Ben-Gurion had recently revealed to his close associates that he was weary of government responsibilities and anxious to rest and rejuvenate his energies by retiring and moving to Kibbutz Sde Boker in the Negev Desert of southern Israel. Mapai Party leaders were contemplating what changes would occur and who would replace him as PM. Two assumptions were current at the time: (a) that Moshe Sharett, as long-time associate and "number-two man", would succeed Ben-Gurion as PM, and (b) that this "retirement" idea was not final, and Ben-Gurion could be convinced to forego his decision.

Saturday, October 10

[- - -]

Last Monday, following a consultation of the Mapai Party ministers[17] concerning the conference [of wealthy diaspora Jewish leaders] in Jerusalem, BG notified us that, at a meeting of the party's Political Committee[18] scheduled for Wednesday, he is going to announce his retirement from the government "for two years." This was the first time his fellow ministers heard it from his lips, although some of us had known it for some time from his confidants Yitzhak[19] and Nehemiah.[20] He implored us not to argue with him. I said it must be clear to him that this decision meant general elections without delay. We immediately held a consultation without him in Lavon's room (the meeting was in the *Kirya* in Tel Aviv) and I proposed to ask him not to broach the subject with the Political Committee until we had a talk with him. Golda[21] and Lavon went to him with this proposal and the discussion was set for Saturday afternoon at his home in Jerusalem. Of the ministers, Lavon, Golda, Eshkol,[22] Yosef[23] and myself were invited, as well as Ziama[24] and Shaul.[25]

---

17 The Israeli Cabinet, in office since late December 1952, included the following Mapai Party members: Ben-Gurion (PM and Minister of Defense), Moshe Sharett (Foreign Affairs), Peretz Naftali (Agriculture), Levi Eshkol (Finance), Dov Yosef (Development), Benzion Dinur (Education and Culture), Golda Myerson (Labor), and Bechor-Shalom Sheetrit (Police).

18 The Political Committee, under the chairmanship of Meir Argov, comprised some 20 members and was the principal decision-making body of the Mapai Party on day-to-day issues. The next highest body was the Party Central Committee, with about 90 members, which met less frequently.

19 Yitzhak Navon (1921-2015). Sharett's Political Secretary (1951-1952). Ben-Gurion's Political Secretary (1952-1953, 1955-1963); Israel's fifth President (1978-1983).

20 Lt.-Colonel Nehemiah Argov (1914-1957). Military Secretary to the PM (1950-1953, 1955-1957); Aide-de-camp to the Minister of Defense (1948-1953, 1955-1957).

21 Golda Myerson (later Meir) (1898-1978). Israel Minister to Moscow (1948-1949), Minister of Labor (1949-1956); FM (1956-1966); PM (1969-1974).

22 Levi Eshkol (1895-1969). Director, JA Land Settlement Department (1948-1963); Mapai MK (1951-1969); Minister of Finance (1952-1963); later Minister of Defense and PM (1963-1969).

23 Dov Yosef (Bernard, "Barney" Joseph) (1899-1980). Minister of Development (1953-1955); Minister of Health (June-November 1955); Minister of Justice (1961-1966).

24 Zalman ("Ziama") Aran (1899-1970). Mapai MK (1949-1969); Minister without Portfolio (1954-1955); Minister of Transport (June-November 1955); Minister of Education and Culture (1955-1960).

25 Shaul Avigur (1899-1978). Moshe Sharett's borther-in-law. Deputy Minister of Defense; Special Affairs (1948-1950); since 1952, Head of *Nativ*, the autonomous *Mossad* organisation responsible for dealing with Jews in Soviet bloc countries with a view to bolstering their Jewish national feeling in hopes for their emigration to Israel. *Nativ*'s members operated in Soviet bloc countries under cover of being officials of Israeli embassies and legations. In Western countries they disseminated information regarding Soviet Jewry and lobbied for their right to emigrate to Israel.

[- - -]

The table was set for lunch when our old friend Hassan, the fisherman from Jaffa, and his son Mahmud showed up.[26] They always contrive their visits to fall on Saturdays knowing they will find us at home. Their boat was completely smashed several weeks ago during a storm that hit Jaffa port. They came to ask for a loan of IL600. to build a new boat. We arranged a loan of IL400 for them from Bank Hapoalim on my security. This time they came to plead for an additional IL150 without which the work could not be finished. There was no choice but to lend them the sum from our own funds. Meanwhile old Hassan went out to sea himself this morning, cast his net and drew up a large fish which he brought to us as a gift, as he is wont to do every week. I told them that once we move to Jerusalem[27] they would be relieved of the toil of satisfying our need for fish. They vehemently protested this aberrant thought, saying they would make their way to the Holy City, and that wherever we might be, they should surely get to us.

Just before leaving for Jerusalem Yosef telephoned and informed me that Ira Hirschmann,[28] whom I met a few days ago, had in the meantime seen Russell[29] and had something to tell me concerning the [water diversion] works in the north.

By 3:15 I was already at the King David [Hotel] where I received the envelope containing Eban's cable on his meeting with Dulles. Its contents surprised me with their ostensibly positive mood. Dulles went out of his way to assure us of the friendship of the US. He only pleaded that we not provoke the UN. The matter of the deferred grant-in-aid was not mentioned at all during the discussion.[30]

At any rate, this discussion in itself evidently doesn't add anything to the strain

26 Hassan Sabbag had been close to the Sharett family since the 1930s, when Sharett's brother-in-law, Dov Hoz, organized a group of Arab workers in the Jaffa port to be affiliated with the Hisatrdut labor federation.

27 The Sharetts' move from Tel Aviv to Jerusalem coincided with the transfer of the MFA to that city in July 1953. The MFA kept a liaison office in the *Kirya* in Tel Aviv. Sharett moved into the FM's official residence in Jerusalem in October 1953.

28 Ira Hirschmann (1901-1989). American business executive, financier and author, who was involved in rescue efforts during the Holocaust; later special inspector in Germany for the UN Relief and Rehabilitation Administration.

29 Francis Henry Russell (1904-1989). Chargé d'affaires, later Counselor, US Embassy Tel Aviv (1952-1955); Special Assistant to US Secretary of State (1955-1956).

30 The start of Israeli construction work on a water-diversion canal near the B'not Yaakov Bridge on September 2 led to serious strains in Israel's relations with both the UN and the US. Israelis would finally agree to suspend construction on the project, but only after the Eisenhower administration expressed its disapproval through temporarily deferring approval of a grant-in-aid Israel had been expecting. For details, Yaacov Bar-Siman-Tov, "The Limits of Economic Sanctions: The American-Israeli Case of 1953," *Journal of Contemporary History* 23 (1988), 425-43; Avraham Ben-Zvi, *The US and Israel: The Limits of the Special Relationship* (New York: Columbia University Press, 1993), ch.2.

of the conflict over the dredging of the Jordan [canal]. For the time being we are thus faced with a contradiction between words and actions.[31]

Accompanied by Joe Tekoah[32] [- - -] we went into a meeting with Rutenberg,[33] Levin[34] and George Bredlo [of the PEC London office]. Rutenberg agreed immediately to take action in regard to Bennike. We concluded that Tekoah would prepare a draft for them, and the letter would be sent tomorrow. Afterwards Rutenberg held me back for a short while and bitterly decried Dov Yosef's handling of the negotiations with the Electric Corporation delegation,[35] which had infuriated the visitors from London and made them consider a complete rupture.

I had a quick talk with Hirschmann. According to Russell, the American experts affiliated with the US Embassy were convinced that there was no practical need at this time for the work we are doing on the Jordan. It was being done [they felt] only with a political purpose, for sake of demonstration [of Israeli control of the river].

I arrived at BG's home tense in anticipation of the painful discussion. We – Golda, Eshkol, Lavon and I – confronted BG with our winning arguments, even if we didn't press him to the wall. But he did not waver. He can't go on. After twenty years of filling his post he has resolved to retire. He rejected the assumption that his retirement had to lead to a dissolution of the coalition and new elections. If anything had held him back until now, it was only his responsibility for security matters, but the special effort he has made these past few weeks to become acquainted with army affairs has set his mind at rest. It has been proven to him that there have been significant improvements and he will present the government with a three-year plan for additional substantial measures of improvements. He still has to do that and conduct the American [Jewish] conference [scheduled for Jerusalem], speak at the Weizmann[36] memorial ceremony, and dine with the scientists who will come for the occasion. All this should take up six weeks, and with that his term would end. In the next few days he would also notify our partners in the coalition

31 *Foreign Relations of the US 1952-1954*, vol. IX, eds. Paul Claussen, Joan M. Lee & Carl N. Raether (Washington: USGPO, 1986), doc.683 – hereafter *FRUS 1952-1954*; *DFPI* 8, doc.413.

32 Yosef ("Joe") Tekoah (1925-1991). Director, Armistice Affairs at the MFA (1954-1958); subsequently Deputy Permanent Representative at the UN and Ambassador to Moscow.

33 Avraham Rutenberg (1893-1982). Chairman, Palestine Electric Corporation (PEC).

34 Avraham Levin, Rutenberg's legal advisor.

35 The government of Israel was at that time negotiating for the purchase of the PEC. The enterprise had been established by Pinhas Rutenberg as a limited company with mixed Anglo-Zionist participation, registered in London in 1923.

36 Dr Chaim Weizmann (1874-1952). President of World Zionist Organization (WZO) (1920-1931, 1935-1946); President of the State of Israel (1948-1952).

government, the General Zionists Party,[37] of his intention to retire. It was not true that he was retiring in order "to write." He has been the victim of a libel that his object is to write a history of the War of Independence. There was only one reason: he can't go on. He'll go somewhere he can work at physical labor several hours a day, and be free to do what he pleases the rest of the time. The name Sde Boker wasn't expressly mentioned, but we all knew that is the intended spot.

Golda argued that his retirement expressly due to this rationale justified, in advance, the retirement of other *haverim*[38] for the same reason. I cautioned against the irresponsibility of such behavior which would abandon the country and the party to untold shocks. If that was his final verdict, he must hold on until the next general elections and cooperate in preparing the party for the change. If there is any justification for retirement, I added, it was only for the sake of a changing of the guard, and to make room at the top for younger *haverim*. But, if such is the case, then this same logic demands the retirement of other elderly *haverim* as well, and the planning of a more extensive changing of the guard. Eshkol tossed back in his face the conclusions to be drawn from his position in regard to security matters. If these matters had kept him from carrying out his plan until now, then the gravity of affairs on other fronts should require the postponement of his retirement henceforward. Lavon addressed the harshest remarks to BG. He ruthlessly analyzed the internal destruction of the party which BG's retirement could only exacerbate. He held up Churchill's example, older than BG by twelve years, suffering from several afflictions and illnesses, his contribution immortalized in the annals of his people, yet nevertheless feeling that he must not retire and working now with the last of his strength. If Churchill was forbidden to retire, all the more so BG. There was no comparison between Israel and England regarding their security and future.

I left the meeting before it ended since I was already late for a scheduled dinner at my home in Ramat Gan.

[- - -]

Meanwhile [on my way home], I started making plans for tomorrow with Joe. I must get in touch with Pinhas Sapir,[39] who visited the north today. At BG's home Eshkol told me that the news Sapir brought upon his return from the tour was that the work in the DMZ could be finished within twenty-two days. This greatly

---

37 The General Zionists (GZ) Party. A moderate right-wing party founded in 1922. Won 16% of the vote in the last general elections of June 1951. At present represented in the government by three ministers: Israel Rokach (Interior), Peretz Bernstein (Trade and Industry), Yosef Sapir (Transport).

38 Party colleagues (Hebrew: *haver* = member, friend).

39 Pinhas Sapir (1909-1975). DG, Ministry of Defense (1949-1951); DG, Ministry of Finance (1952-1957); Minister of Trade and Industry (1955-1965); Minister of Finance (1963-1968, 1969-1974).

differed from what Baruch Amir, the man from *Tahal,*[40] told me only last week, namely that it would take ten months! Sapir also supposedly has a new suggestion about a meeting of experts with Bennike. All this is quite astonishing, but it must be looked into without delay. I also asked Joe to find Amir "*min takht el ard*" [Arabic: from under the earth; i.e. from wherever he may be] and notify him that he must drive with me to Jerusalem tomorrow morning -- the only opportunity I will have to hear about the situation from him. It is urgent because I must send a letter to Bennike tomorrow as we decided at the consultation held on Friday.

[- - -]

Sunday, October 11

At 6:00 am the telephone woke me as prearranged last evening. Baruch Amir arrived at 7:30 and we set out immediately with Zipporah for Jerusalem. On the way Amir offered an explanation for the miraculous shrinkage of time from ten months to twenty-two days in the work [required] on the Jordan [canal diversion]. The work has been going on since September 2; night work meant three shifts a day – i.e., every day counts as three. The large number of machines makes it possible to cut up the dredging into sections, etc., etc. I also questioned him about what I had heard from Ira Hirschmann. The assumption that there is no practical need for the entire project at this juncture is groundless in Amir's opinion. It is, however, true that a diversion of the Jordan waters into the 450-meter-long section of the canal now being dredged, so that at the end of that same section the water should be returned to the natural channel, serves no practical end and would merely seem a provocative action.

Upon arriving at the Prime Minister's Office [PMO] at 9:15 I found Sapir waiting. He also offered proof that work in the DMZ might be shortened to three and something more weeks, and pleaded that we decide in the affirmative.

I told him about the disappointment of Rutenberg and his colleagues who had come from London at the course of the negotiations. Curiously, he defended a few of Dov Yosef's positions and took it upon himself to persuade Rutenberg that a compromise must be sought. [- - -]

During the Cabinet meeting[41] [- - -] I delivered a detailed report on Eban's talk with Dulles and reviewed the situation concerning the project in the north and attendant circumstances. Authorization was provided me for the proposals that we make use of the Electric Corporation, that I should address a new letter to Bennike to continue the debate and postpone the deadline, and that meanwhile we should start working at full speed and with added machinery in order to try our luck at finishing the work in the DMZ.

---

40 Israel water planning corporation founded in 1952, later creating the National Water Carrier.

41 The Israeli Cabinet met every Sunday for its regular weekly meeting.

Upon leaving the meeting [Pinhas] Rosen[42] asked to talk with me. In the morning he attended the swearing in of the judges in the President's[43] presence. At the end of the ceremony Michael Simon,[44] head of the Foreign Ministry Protocol Division, came up to both of them and repeated what he had heard from Paula[45]: that her husband is about to retire. He asked me with astonishment: Is it true? I told him to ask BG himself. I couldn't deny it and I didn't want to confirm it. At any rate, I said I'd give Simon "a good talking to." Paula may not know how to hold her tongue, but does that allow the Chief of Protocol to stoop to gossip? Between one thing and another it appears that the reins have been loosened. Paula has certainly revealed the secret to others as well – including BG's driver – while BG himself helped spread the word by ordering a wooden hut for his living quarters at Sde Boker. When I called Yitzhak Navon to warn him of the mischief, he told me that a reporter from the *Yediot Ahronot*[46] had just phoned him to ask if it was true.

From the meeting I drove to Golda's for the consultation with Lavon, Eshkol, Barney and Naftali.[47] Ziama [Aran] was present too. It was resolved that we must be merciless towards BG and announce that we would all resign. I said that at any rate I would write BG a letter in that vein in my name. It emerged that in the meeting on Saturday evening, after I had left, it had been settled with him that he would postpone any notice or discussion of the matter until the end of the timetable he had allotted himself, i.e., the beginning of November. But now that the word is out – what good is a postponement? Does it not seal the fate of the American conference, which instead of attending to plans for financial efforts will be entirely involved in guesswork and fancies about what has happened and will now happen in the highest echelons of power? It is as if we have invited all these good people in order to spread confusion among them!

It was concluded that a delegation of veteran *haverim* of the cooperative settlement movements be sent to BG to talk sense into him. Also Golda and Lavon will talk to him again, and try their hand one more time.

[- - -]

At 6:30 I came to the President and discussed with him the problem of the

42 Pinhas Rosen (Felix Rosenblueth) (1887-1978). Leader of the Progressive Party, later of Independent Liberal Party; Minister of Justice (1948-1951, 1952-1961).

43 Yitzhak Ben-Zvi (1884-1963). President of Israel (1952-1963). Settled in Palestine in 1907. Founder and leader of Mapai Party. Chairman and President of *Hava'ad Hale'umi* (National Council of the organized Jewish community of Palestine) (1931-1948).

44 Michael Simon (1901-1976). Born in Berlin. Settled in Palestine in 1924 and joined the JA Political Department during the 1930s. Head of the MFA Protocol Division (1948-1957). Later Israel Consul-General to Montreal, and Ambassador to Peru and to Austria.

45 Paula Ben-Gurion (1892-1968). Ben-Gurion's wife since 1917.

46 Popular evening newspaper.

47 Peretz Naftali (1888-1961). Economist. Born in Germany. Settled in Palestine in 1933. Minister of Agriculture (Mapai Party).

Italian minister, who remains in Rome and awaits our decision regarding the ceremony for presenting his credentials. He is willing to come to Jerusalem to visit me, but definitely not to present his credentials there to the President.[48]

Ben-Zvi is of a mind to be adamant, and it is to be feared that the matter will drag on, with the absence of an Italian Consul becoming the status quo.

The President, in his characteristic way, posed a few questions of great vision but no practical end, such as if there was any chance of us conquering the Sinai Peninsula, and how good it might be if the Egyptians initiated an attack which we could repulse and follow up with an invasion into the depths of that desert. He was very disappointed when I told him that the Egyptians show no inclination of making the work of conquest easier for us by a deliberate provocation on their part. [- - -]

Tomorrow at 8:00 am a meeting of the party's Cabinet ministers at BG's office upon his initiative. I wonder why and for what purpose.

Monday, October 12

Today was a day fraught with frenzy. At 8:00 am we convened at BG's. It turned out that the subject tabled for deliberation was once again the [water diversion] project in the north. It was Lavon who arranged for it. His behavior stands as a very strange token of friendship. We sat together reviewing the issue in the *Kirya* in Tel Aviv on Friday. We spoke about it on Saturday evening at BG's home in Jerusalem. On Sunday the greater part of the Cabinet meeting was devoted to it,[49] and now he convenes an intimate consultation of the *haverim* for the same purpose without breathing a word of it to me in advance. It is as if I had called a consultation concerning something to do with financial problems, and Eshkol had been summoned without anyone informing him beforehand that matters concerning his work and within his sphere of responsibility would be discussed. I wrote Lavon a note expressing my astonishment. He shrugged his shoulders and claimed that he had arranged the consultation through the services of Yitzhak Navon. A groundless excuse.

The question posed was what should we do if we are ordered to stop working

---

48 Most foreign countries were reluctant to accede to Israel's declaration of Jerusalem as its capital. Such recognition would have angered Muslim and Arab countries, and would have been contrary to the strict letter of UN Resolution 181 of November 29, 1947, whose (aborted) plan for partition declared Jerusalem to be "a corpus separatum under a special international regime ... administered by the UN."

49 During the Cabinet meeting Sharett, as Acting PM, discussed the political and technical problems involved in digging a 450-meter Jordan diversion canal running inside the DMZ as part of a longer one which would eventually reach the Kinneret (Sea of Galilee), thus creating a *fait accompli* in the face of Syrian, UN and US objections to Israel's changing the status quo in the DMZ as stipulated in the Armistice Agreement. It was concluded that a special effort would be made to complete the digging within 22 days.

on a given date: obey or defy? And what would then be our financial fate? Could we hold on without the American grant-in-aid or would we collapse? Eshkol said that we would be able to "hang in there" until the end of the budgetary year, but that afterwards we would founder. Lavon demanded that we not stop. Others supported him. Dov Yosef, of all people, demurred slightly. Everyone talked about the UN in the abstract – as if it were a factor apart from the Great Powers. Clearly, any conflict with the UN is undesirable, but if there is no other choice, the UN after all has no power to implement or impose, etc. I deplored the fallacy of speaking in the abstract. I also explained that from a procedural viewpoint my *haverim* had ignored the practical aspects. It was not the defiance offered to Bennike that stood at the crux of the impending debacle, but the non-compliance with a Security Council [SC] resolution. A conflict with the SC carries with it a much graver prospect. It might lead to a punitive campaign on the part of the Great Powers in the form of the suspension of credit and other benefits. It might also foster such a climate of relations with the American government as to be prejudicial to all American-Jewish financial efforts on our behalf. It would also strain our relations with that Jewish community. Therefore, even if we do not obey Bennike immediately and appeal to the SC, when the matter does come up for debate in the SC, it is inconceivable that we should appear to be working [on the Jordan water project]. We would forfeit by this half our chances of successfully winning our case. It would be better to announce in advance that, as soon as the SC debates the issue, we will stop. Thus we would also expedite the debate. On the other hand, if we should stop immediately and appeal, the debate might be postponed for who knows how long. If all else fails, and we find that our vital need of the Jordan waters justifies a headlong collision with the SC too, we shall always be able to resume working. But as long as we have a chance to obtain a SC decision in our favor regarding the project in itself – and such a chance does exist – we must not throw it away by a provocative transgression.

BG disagreed with me. As is his wont, he ignored the specific tactical considerations and focused on the crux of the matter – as if from that viewpoint there were any substantial differences. Without difficulty he proceeded to prove a new verity: that making continued work dependent upon Syrian agreement was tantamount to putting a lid over the entire Jordan water irrigation plan. This was an original and incisive idea which only incidentally lay at the basis of my letters to Bennike, all my talks with him, my talks with the Americans and the British and all my briefings to legations abroad. His conclusion was that we must appeal and not stop, and then see how things turn out in the SC. We might perhaps have to withdraw in view of future developments, but not in advance.

Regarding the matter at hand, BG rightly asserted that we must not take any irreversible action at the moment, since Bennike has not yet stipulated a date, and who knows if and when he will. When he does, we shall consult.

He posed a puzzler. For what reason or purpose had this consultation been convened? I certainly couldn't answer that. The consultation had been convened without anyone troubling to ask the person in charge if there was any need for it.

Upon leaving the meeting Yitzhak Navon placed a note written in Arabic in my hand, so that nobody else could read it: "BG is thinking of Eshkol as PM, Mordechai Maklef has resigned, and Brigadier Moshe Dayan is to be appointed CoS."

I drove to the office and wrote a personal letter to BG. I said there that I was not to be taken into consideration as his heir in case he should resign. I had already told my *haverim* yesterday that I had written such a letter, but in fact I did not get around to writing it. Now I regretted the delay. I feared BG might think that I had heard of his notion with regard to Eshkol, and had therefore written to him. Too bad.[50]

I read and dictated telegrams, and dealt with various matters. At 10:30 there was a sudden call from the PMO. Would I not come to the meeting with the Electric Corporation? I had had no intention of taking part in this meeting. This entire affair of the negotiations with the Electric Corporation is an unbearable nuisance for me. I thought I had done my share by chairing the start of the negotiations, and that now Eshkol and Yosef would be able to carry on without me. I replied that I would not be coming and that I have full confidence in Eshkol. But a minute later Pinhas Sapir phoned that the old man, Lord Herbert Samuel,[51] was offended by my absence. They had come all the way from London in response to my invitation, and they viewed my absence as a lack of consideration for the effort they have made. Having no choice, I assented and said I would come, but they should not wait for me and ought to start in the meantime. When I joined them, I found them discussing a new proposal by Yosef. Every shareholder would be free to sell his shares to the government at any time he chose, it being not dependent on the massive transfer of stock from the Corporation to the government. The Corporation officials asked for a recess to consult. We stepped out, and left them in the conference hall. Since our people too began consulting among themselves in the meanwhile, one of their number being Oscar Gass[52] whose presence I cannot bear, I made my exit and went to BG.

He was sitting alone in his room, and studying an old book which had evidently just been brought to him. The atmosphere about him was remarkably serene and he was in good humor. We had friendly and affable conversation, as if nothing had happened and all was going well. He told me about the changes in the GS. Maklef was resigning; he'll occupy himself with farming for a year, and

---

50 Letter not found.

51 Lord Herbert Samuel (1870-1963). First High Commissioner to Palestine; Liberal Member of Parliament (MP) and Cabinet Minister; Chairman, PEC.

52 Oscar Gass (1912-1990). Washington-based American-Jewish economic consultant. Worked for the Franklin D. Roosevelt (FDR) administration, the JA and from 1948 to 1955 for the State of Israel.

then he'll see. Moshe [Dayan] will replace him. Yitzhak Rabin[53] will return from his studies abroad and become Head of the Operations Branch [replacing Dayan]. Aharon Remez is designated for the Logistics Branch. I immediately said that Moshe Dayan was a soldier only in times of war, but in peacetime he was a man of political mind. He had no real interest in running the military establishment. This appointment means a "politicizing"[54] of the GS. The new CoS's far-reaching scheming talents will be the cause of multiple complications. BG conceded the truth of these worries. Moreover, he added that Dayan himself defined himself in this way and had therefore asked to be disqualified for the position. But, no matter; all will be well. I left his room with a heavily burdened heart.

We again entered the conference, and the PEC officials announced that they accepted Yosef's proposal. Now a price had to be set. It was decided that the experts should meet for that purpose this very evening.

I returned to the Foreign Ministry office and had time to hold the consultation scheduled and postponed several times in regard to the question of American military aid. The sum of all reports and impressions was that the State Department was resolved to supplying Syria and Iraq with arms, to supplying Egypt with arms too, after the signing of the Suez Canal Zone accord with Britain,[55] and to relegating us to the last place in line – and even then to offer us not arms but only military infrastructure items. Apparently the Pentagon shared this resolve, unlike in the period towards the end of President Truman's administration. The questions were: Shall we go on with the campaign of opposition to giving any arms to the Arabs? What were this campaign's chances of success? Should we submit a request of our own in the meantime? Should we accept infrastructure items if we are not given arms? I expressed my opinion in favor both of going on with the campaign, and of submitting a request. I cited weighty reasons for not accepting infrastructure if we are not given arms, but I refrained from taking irreversible action at this stage, and I asked to wire our Embassy in Washington asking how they view the situation before we make a final decision.

I drove to a luncheon held at the Tourism Club in honor of the departing Professor Carlsen, head of the UN team of experts, who was leaving for Bolivia. A proper meal was served, quite tasty. At the end of it I spoke and said that in the past our country had been a graveyard for the good name of experts. Now, on the other hand, we enhance their reputations. We cannot repay our debt of gratitude to such eminent men as Carlsen, who have put the best of their energy and experience into training us, except for the contribution we have made to sharpening their wits and improving their talents while wrestling with our problems. This gift is presented to them upon leaving, and it is our indirect contribution to the development of

53 Yitzhak Rabin (1922-1995). IDF CoS (1964-1968), PM (1974-1977, 1992-1995).

54 In Hebrew, *Midun*, a triple pun alluding to politicizing, bickering (*madon*), and Dayan's name.

55 Negotiations for an Anglo-Egyptian agreement governing the withdrawal of British troops from the Suez Canal zone would begin in April 1954.

the countries in which they will work in future.

From the luncheon I went back to the office. [- - -] I dropped into Leo Kohn's[56] office since I promised to help him finish editing the booklet about the Arab refugees he has been working on. I once again apologized and asked to postpone it for tomorrow. Meanwhile I told him that the BG crisis was threatening to explode any day.

[- - -]

Upon returning home a call came from the office to say that a letter from the UN had just arrived. I told them to bring it over immediately. I opened the envelope with some excitement and scanned its two pages quickly to see if it set a date. None! Thus the Army's apprehensions had been proven false. Bennike made an issue over an Arab plot of land. He claimed and proved that we did indeed do work there at the beginning, contrary to our statements (he's right in that – I was misled by *Tahal* in regard to this detail!). Finally he proposed a meeting tomorrow or Thursday. I breathed a sigh of relief.

Eshkol phoned to say that Moshe Tavor of *Davar*[57] won't lay off him in regard to BG's resignation. The editorial offices are seething, and tomorrow the story is going to burst out full-force onto the front pages. What is *Davar* supposed to do? A few moments later our Michael Elizur[58] phoned, and after that Tavor himself. I told him that all I could offer in the way of advice was to point to two facts: the PM would speak at the next Cabinet meeting on security matters, and on the 25th he would open the American [Jewish] conference. As regards the resignation I said I could not say anything. I decided to speed up the official announcement of the conference, which is late anyway, to serve as a palliative for the epidemic of rumors about the resignation. Having done that, I dealt with stacks of my papers until a late hour.

[- - -]

Close to midnight I began clarifying to Zipporah my thoughts about the premiership. I am in accord with my *haverim* in every action and effort to dissuade BG from resigning, but in my heart I am certain we must allow him to leave. It is clear that at the moment he has not the strength to carry the load, and it is best

56 Dr Leo (Yehuda Pinhas) Kohn (1894-1961). Political Adviser, MFA (1948-1961). Close associate of Sharett since working together in the pre-state JA Political Department.

57 The newspaper *Davar* was founded in 1925 as the organ of the *Histadrut* labor federation. With the establishment of Mapai Party (Sharett's party) in 1930 it became fully controlled by it and served as its mouthpiece. Sharett was the deputy editor of *Davar* from its establishment until 1933 when he became the right-hand man of Chaim Arlosoroff, Head of the JA's Political Department. Moshe Tavor (Fritz Tauber) (1905-1978). Born in Moravia. Settled in Palestine in 1939. *Davar*'s parliamentary correspondent (1950-1957); Spokesman, Israel's Reparations Mission; later, member of Israel's Embassy, Germany (1957-1966).

58 Michael Elizur (1921-2004). MFA Spokesman. Born in Germany. Settled in Palestine in 1933. Second Secretary, Israel Embassy, London (1949-1952). Press Officer, MFA (1954-1956). Political Secretary to FM (1956-1957). Later Israel Ambassador to Australia and to Austria.

to let him regain it. The well has dried up. Perhaps it shall flow again, perhaps not. But today there is not a drop left in it. With regard to his heir, my deepest and innermost conviction is that, from an objective viewpoint, the lot falls to me. There is no comparison between me and any other candidate as regards the ability to serve as a unifying factor – in the Cabinet, in the Knesset, in the party, among the people, both in Israel and abroad. It is not a matter for conjecture. It is an uncontested fact. It is the end result of many years of experience, the acquisition of a reputation, the consolidation of a status. All the same, it is not my business to present my own candidacy. On the contrary, if it should come to pass it should only be as a result of constraint exercised by my *haverim*, by no means otherwise. From a personal viewpoint, becoming PM is altogether undesirable. I have no intention of abandoning the MFA. The double load will be too much to bear, to the detriment of myself and both positions. Furthermore, for myself it would be best that they compare me to Eshkol or Lavon, if they should serve in this high capacity before me, rather than always to BG. In addition, if Lavon is in the Cabinet when I'm PM, there will be no curbing his impulses and the tendencies he's already exhibited as Acting Minister of Defense during BG's leave,[59] to go radically far in both internal and external affairs. It is a very bleak prospect of unceasing friction, conflict, and growing tension in personal relations as well as in affairs of state. On the other hand, if Lavon should become PM – on condition that the Ministry of Defense be given to another party member, say Namir[60] – it would apply an effective restraint to these tendencies, and the responsibility of office would demand caution and moderation. Another advantage of Lavon's premiership is that he would be that, and nothing else. This post thereby would only gain.

[- - -]

Tuesday, October 13

[- - -]

I consulted with the Director-General [DG],[61] Rafael, the Legal Advisor[62] and Tekoah about the position to take towards Bennike.

In his letter Bennike insists upon stoppage of the work as before, but this time

59 Ever since his appointment as Acting Minister of Defense in July 1953, and despite his past strong "dovish" principles, Lavon adopted a harsh activist approach vis-à-vis the neighboring Arab states, which led to frequent clashes with Sharett.

60 Mordechai Namir (1897-1975). SG, *Histadrut*. Minister of Labor (1956-1959).

61 Dr Walter Eytan (Ettinghausen) (1910-2001). DG, MFA (1949-1959). Formerly, a senior member of the JA's Political Department, Jerusalem.

62 Shabtai Rosenne (1917-2010). Born (Sefton W.D. Rowson) in London. Settled in Palestine in 1947 while working for the JA Political Department. Upon establishment of Israel, became Legal Adviser, MFA (1948-1967). Later Deputy and then Permanent Representative of Israel to the UN.

he bases his argument not on the need to obtain Syrian approval, but on the need to clear up unresolved problems. This is drawing closer to our position, but there is no sign of willingness to set a date for the resumption of work.

The letter's "direct hit" lies in exposing the fact that, contrary to our proclamations and the clear-cut remarks in my first letter to him, we did indeed work on Arab land at the start of the project in violation of the Armistice Agreement with Syria. Bennike uses this fact for added leverage in demanding that we stop. The relevant passage in his letter makes it clear that our assurances cannot be trusted, since it has been proven that we are not reliable in stating the bare facts.

The matter concerning this Arab plot of land on which we worked in building the dam and overturned some rocks is truly a scandal. How many times did I ask our men, and how many times did they swear to me that the project had nothing to do with any Arab land? But after Bennike told me at lunch at my home that it had been proven to him that our work began on an Arab plot of land, I once again questioned Amir from *Tahal*, and then he confessed it was true. There is no taming our people! I have been made a liar before the entire world.

To all appearances, the case of this plot is immaterial – nothing was taken away from it, and the piled rocks have been removed. Since then we have been working only on Jewish and state-owned land. The dredging of the canal itself has not touched on any Arab area. For what reason then the stoppage? Whatever we have done to that plot, Heaven forbid, cannot be undone. Now, though, the stoppage won't help anyone or change anything for the better. But in the morning papers the UN spokesman in Jerusalem was specifically quoted as saying that the stoppage of work has become a matter of honor for the UNTSO CoS, involving the very fate of his authority. The question is whether we can successfully persuade him to view a temporary stoppage as satisfaction for his grievances, and an honorable way out of the mess. Very doubtful.

Meanwhile one telegram after another arrived from Eban showing a growing nervousness. He is afraid that Syria will demand a meeting of the Security Council, and then we will be in an inferior position from the start, all the more so if we do not stop work beforehand. According to our information, Syria does indeed intend to submit a complaint to the SC, but it has not yet decided to demand a meeting. This is an exact duplicate of the course we took towards Egypt in the case of the freighter "Farnon" in the Suez Canal.[63]

At any rate, we decided to write Bennike a letter in which we would affirm that we had proposed a temporary stoppage and that this proposal still stands. This is to counter the impression made by the press, including the *New York Times (NYT)*, and press releases of the UN spokesman in Jerusalem, that I had only mentioned

63 A Greek flag carrying ship which sailed from Haifa Port with Israeli goods to Africa. It was detained by the Egyptians in Port Said for 12 days, then released and allowed to go south through the Suez Canal.

this matter orally in an offhand way, but had never officially proposed to stop.

Immediately after the consultation I dictated the letter and issued a précis for the press. Following this I arranged for a consultation with the Army for tomorrow afternoon.

[- - -]

At home in the afternoon I dictated a long letter to Eban. Aubrey's approach to the conflict in the north is marred by his thinking in the abstract. He only sees the external political aspects of the imbroglio, and not the basic facts of Israeli life -- psychological, territorial and economic – which are the essence of our policy and lie at the root of the problem. I explained the practical necessity of the northern project to the country's development as a whole, and what its indefinite postponement might mean.

Leo Kohn came. He was chafing for news about BG, vehemently opposed to Lavon's candidacy for PM, and deeply concerned over Dayan's appointment as CoS. I gave him permission to speak to BG about all these things. I only calmed him about Lavon. He is not proposing himself for the premiership, but it is I myself who am raising this possibility.

Lord Samuel telephoned me, and asked to see me to inform me of a breakdown of the negotiations and the departure of his colleagues for London tomorrow. I conferred on his behalf with Eshkol, Yosef and Sapir at the PMO, and heard about the current state of affairs. Afterwards there was a consultation concerning oil matters: Eshkol and Sapir came back, and with them Dolik[64] and Israel Kozlov.[65] The topic was Britain's refusal to sell us oil from Kuwait. The obvious became clear. There is nothing we can do, except perhaps to purchase some oil in the Soviet Union, in exchange for citrus. This is worthwhile anyway. We should also appeal to the British to lower somewhat the price of the oil we shall receive in place of the Kuwaiti oil.

At 6:00 pm I went to the King David and suffered through a bothersome conversation with Samuel and his colleagues. The imbroglio is at its peak, and woe unto me for having stepped into the thick of it against my will.

I returned to the PMO smack into the middle of the party's Political Committee [meeting]. I called Eshkol, Yosef, Naftali, Dolik and Sapir out into an adjoining room, and told them of the PEC officials' complaints. Without going into details here, it has been demonstrated to me without a doubt that despite the justice of some of our claims, the handling of this entire affair has been bungled by Dov Yosef. He has a special talent for honing antagonisms, overblowing problems,

64 David Horowitz (1899-1979). Born in Galicia. Settled in Palestine in 1920. Director of the JAE's Economic Department (1935-1948), and JA liaison officer with the United Nations Special Committee on Palestine (UNSCOP). DG, Ministry of Finance (1948-1952). From August 1954, a founder and Governor of the Bank of Israel.

65 Israel Kozlov (1921-2011). Born in Palestine. Fuel Advisor, Ministry of Finance. Later Director of Petroleum Division, Ministry of Development.

and provoking the other side through unnecessary contentiousness and the indiscriminate use of unsound arguments, several of which are totally objectionable. He's a great master at winning the battle and losing the war. One last attempt will be made this evening to come to a compromise with the Corporation.

In the course of a conversation with the *haverim* the telephone rang and I was informed that Eban wished to speak to me. Within a few moments his voice was heard. He wanted to know about the situation. I said I had a meeting with the Dane [Bennike] the day after tomorrow. He asked if there was reason to fear Bennike might submit the matter to the SC before then. I gave him a negative answer. He reported that the Syrians submitted a memorandum today but did not demand a meeting of the SC. I said that today I would affirm in writing our proposal to stop temporarily. The connection was very bad, and the conversation quite brief.

As I was leaving the conference hall where the Political Committee had convened, Lavon joined me and told me that a retaliation operation is about to be mounted in response to the recent incidents in the Jordan border area. These reached a climax with the killing of a woman and her two children in Yehud late the previous night.[66]

I came home to supper "dead beat."

Gideon Rafael showed up later in the evening. After making some apposite remarks about Aubrey's excessive anxiety in his telegrams ("he sees the American and the international processes, but he doesn't see the Israeli process"), Rafael then reopened the dispute which had erupted between himself and one of his colleagues, and tired me with it for a long while.

At 11:00 Sapir telephoned from the King David to inform me that all had ended well. A finalized agreement for the sale of the Corporation's stock to the Government had been worked out. I asked to say goodbye to Samuel. The amazing old man came to the telephone and expressed his complete satisfaction with the agreement. He gave me some excessive compliments. According to him I had intervened at the right moment, and helped to reach a solution. For myself, I think my only real contribution lay in restraining Dov Yosef.

Wednesday, October 14

[- - -]

Aryeh Aroch,[67] Director of the Foreign Ministry's Cultural Relations Division,

66 Kfar Yehud is a townlet near Lydda, opposite the airport. On the retaliatory raid on Qibya, see below and also "The 1953 Qibya Raid Revisited: Excerpts from Moshe Sharett's Diaries," introduced by Walid Khalidi and annotated by Neil Caplan, *Journal of Palestine Studies* 31:4 (Summer 2002), 77-99; Benny Morris, *Israel's Border Wars, 1949-1956: Arab Infiltration, Israeli Retaliation, and the Countdown to the Suez War* (Oxford University Press, 1993), ch.8.

67 Aryeh Aroch (1908-1974). First Secretary, Moscow Embassy (1953); Deputy Director of East European Division (1955-1956); later Ambassador to Brazil and to Sweden.

who has returned from his trip to Europe and America, came to give his report. He went out on a mission to generate publicity in the American press about the trials of Jews on the charge of "Zionism" in Romania, and to rouse the Jewish organizations to a public response. These initiatives were to coincide with the UN GA sessions thereby exploiting the Soviet Union's sensitivity in this season when she would like to show herself as striving for peace. He apparently succeeded in his first task, which had been dependent on non-Jewish journalists. Reports appeared in the New York press, some of which made an impact. By contrast, despite the help of Abe Harman[68] and Reuven Shiloah,[69] success did not shine on his second task, which had to do with rousing Jewish activists to action. The Americans wanted a more explosive issue than the one they were being given. Long prison terms aren't enough for them. If only there'd been at least one hanging! The British activists on their side do not dare take a line which should seemingly contravene the policy of their government which is now making overtures towards the Eastern Bloc. Anyway, what has been published has been published and that is good in itself, and who knows if the appeal against Bucharest's verdict, of which there was news today, does not already reflect some of the impact of this mission of censure.

Gideon came in. He knows that a retaliation is planned for the killing of the woman and children in Yehud. But only today there was a meeting of the Israel-Jordan Mixed Armistice Commission [IJMAC] at which a forceful denunciation of the act was adopted. Jordan's representative in the MAC also voted in favor of the resolution and said his government took it upon herself to do everything to prevent such atrocities in the future. Under these circumstances, is it wise to retaliate, even more so when we are already in conflict with the UN in the north and south? I have come to the conclusion that we now face the same sort of situation in which I once averted a retaliation, halting the chain of incidents of bloodshed for two weeks and more.[70] The Jordanians have been alarmed now and it will be incumbent upon them to act. If we do retaliate, we will only be giving the gangs of infiltrators new incentives and providing the Jordanian authorities

68 Abraham (Abe) Harman (1914-1992). Israel Consul-General to New York (1953-1955), Ambassador to the US (1959-1968) and later President of the Hebrew University.

69 Reuven Shiloah (1909-1959). Director (1951-1952) of the *Mossad* (*Hamossad Lemodi'in Uletafkidim Meyuhadim*, the Institute for Intelligence and Special Operations, Israel's external security agency); Adviser on Special Affairs, MFA; Minister, Israel Embassy, Washington (1953-1957). Close associate of Sharett since working together in the pre-state JA Political Department.

70 Sharett is probably alluding here to his role during the summer of 1953, and especially at the Cabinet meeting of May 31. For the build-up of tension and incidents along the Israel-Jordan frontier earlier in 1953 and Sharett's diplomatic efforts during those months, see: *DFPI* 8, docs. 40, 45-46, 50-51, 54, 59-62, 89-90, 97, 127; *FRUS 1952-1954*, docs. 550, 552-554, 556-557, 561-562, 566-569; Eyal Kafkafi, *Pinhas Lavon - Anti-Messiah: A Biography* (Tel Aviv: Am Oved, 1998), 162 [in Hebrew]; Morris, *Israel's Border Wars*, 224-25. On the evolution of Israel's retaliation policy, see Morris, *ibid.*, chs. 6-7.

with an excuse to sit back and do nothing. I telephoned Lavon and gave him my opinion. He said he'd consult with BG.

Teddy[71] returned from New York. When he entered the room it was as if a burnished ray of light had pierced the darkness. And it's not that the day was cloudy, but my spirit was gloomy from the press of troubles. "Prince Charming" came and dispelled the gloom. I found him pale and tired. He may have eaten well in the US, but didn't get much sleep. He told me about the preparations for the American conference [in Jerusalem] – the response was exhilarating. He expanded upon Aubrey's anxious telegrams in regard to our loss of international repute due to the conflict in the north, and the troubles awaiting us. I sent him along to BG and Lavon. It won't hurt them to hear things from a first-hand source who is acceptable at any rate to BG. I told him about the shock of the resignation and all it entailed, and also about the turnover in the GS.

Ze'ev[72] who came to take me back to the office, brought a new letter from the Dane [Bennike]. He had not been aware that we proposed to stop temporarily; he'd only learned of it from my last letter. But he no longer needed a stoppage to clarify unresolved issues, for all was clear. The main point was our admission that we had indeed worked on Arab land at the start. A memorandum was appended to the letter, with place-markers from the Book of Landholdings in regard to the four Arab plots which were amalgamated into one.

Two more telegrams came from Aubrey, in the same vein. It seems that Syria was about to demand a meeting of the SC.

At 4:00 pm a consultation about the works in the north with Walter, Gideon, Shabtai and Joe of my Ministry, and Lavon and Shalev from the Ministry of Defense and IDF. Wiener,[73] the engineer from *Tahal*, was also present.

It was ascertained that the matter of work on Arab land, which was by all means a scandal as far as our internal lack of policy coordination, was not as terrible externally as the Dane would like to make it appear. If they drove through, they used a fixed route which has since become a public thoroughfare. If they placed machines there, they were not necessarily on private land but on the strip between it and the Jordan stream, which is considered part of the river's bed. If rocks were piled up, they had been removed. However, Joe did relate that when he was there on the spot yesterday he found a new pile of rocks and ordered it removed. He also

71 Theodore ("Teddy") Kollek (1911-2007). Minister, Washington Embassy (1950-1952); DG, PMO (1952-1964); later Mayor of Jerusalem.

72 Ze'ev Shek (1920-1978). Born in Czechoslovakia. Settled in Palestine in 1946. Political Secretary [chef de bureau] to FM (1953-1956); later First Secretary at Israel Embassy, London; Israel Minister to Paris; Director, West European Division; Israel Ambassador to Austria and to Italy.

73 Aharon Wiener (1912-2007). Director, Department of Irrigation Projects, *Tahal*, and chief engineer, *Mekorot* Water Co.; chief planner of Israel's National Water Carrier project through the Negev.

related that the engineers at the site had been about to tear down a water-mill but he had been able to prevent them. That's just what we need!

Lavon suggested that I again hurry off a letter to Bennike about the matter this very evening and I accepted his advice.

As regards the matter itself, I suggested that since the Dane has announced that he has no need of a stoppage to clarify unresolved issues, yet does not retract his demand for a stoppage, then he intends it [as a way] to obtain an agreement with Syria and has reverted to his true colors – in the language of the fellaheen, "*reji'ana ila akl el-khara*" [Arabic: we are back at eating shit]. If such is the case, he will most probably submit a report to the SC in a day or two. He doesn't have the prerogative to demand a meeting, for in his official capacity he can only report to the UN SG. But it stands to reason the SG will convene the SC, perhaps Syria will jump the gun on the SG in demanding a meeting. Either way, we must not take the initiative. What do we do if the SC is convened? There is still time to consider.

Lavon, too, rejected our taking any initiative, but Gideon reasoned that we had best take the initiative, and he did not lack arguments to prove his point. Walter sided with me, saying it was worth our while to pretend that we are interested in having the matter out in the SC.

We went over the phrasing which Joe and Shabtai had prepared for the guarantees we need to give concerning use of land and water in the area we are working in. The text still requires a final revision.

In the middle of the consultation Shalev handed Lavon a letter from Bennike. This old fellow is a prolific writer! In it he says that General Glubb[74] has addressed a message to our CoS stating that he is willing to accept the help of an Israeli bloodhound to track down the murderers of the family from Yehud inside Jordanian territory. The message also states that Glubb has resolved to uproot this evil.

Shalev asked if under the circumstances there was "any change." Pinhas replied: "No change." I interrupted the meeting and called Pinhas out into the corridor. I asked him if they were indeed about to take action. He said yes. I said it was a serious mistake and explained my view. I also relied on precedents. After all, it has never been proven that retaliatory action helps in curbing terrorist infiltration in the final balance. Pinhas characteristically smiled. He didn't try to contradict my remarks in any way, but he remained unmoved. It seems that the Acting Minister of Defense feels obliged to provide satisfaction to his people. BG, he said, hadn't agreed with me – that means it's two against one. We went back into the room and I wrote him a note: "One day there's going to be a resignation over this." We did not return to the subject.

When the meeting ended I took paper in hand and wrote BG asking him to

74 Sir John Bagot Glubb (1897-1986). Also known as Glubb Pasha. British soldier, Arabist and author. Commander-in-chief, Transjordan's (later Jordan's) Arab Legion (1938-1956).

immediately take over the reins of government. Next Sunday I will no longer chair the Cabinet meeting as Acting PM. I reminded him that I had already explained the peculiarity of my position to him during Sukkot.[75] Since then the situation had become unbearable. Just think of it: the PM was traveling around the country, attending various functions, summoning a conference of diaspora leaders, and so on and so forth. And at the same time a deputy PM was performing all sorts of inconsequential tasks. His intention to resign and the excitement over it in the press also enjoin me from continuing to act in this role. I must leave this post, the quicker the better, so that it might not impinge upon another's candidacy or diminish my own. Finally, this decision in favor of retaliation was just too much. I was against it, but BG thought otherwise, and the decision has gone his way. There is no disputing his moral authority, but I am, after all, officially responsible at the moment, and why should I take the responsibility for an action to which I had objected as Acting PM, even though my opinion was not accepted? I entrusted the letter to Pinhas who returned to Tel Aviv, where BG today conferred with the GZ Cabinet ministers.[76]

[- - -]

I dictated a new letter to Bennike. I denounced his petty nitpicking concerning the proposal for a temporary stoppage, of which he ostensibly hadn't known, and also contradicted his claim about Arab land with signs and proofs. Among other things, I emphasized a new fact I had learned about from Wiener: not only had we not violated the individual rights of Arab ownership; on the contrary, in safeguarding them we had changed the course of the canal and lost height as regards the future waterfall.[77]

It was almost 9:00 when Baruch Amir suddenly appeared. I questioned him once again about that unfortunate plot of Arab land. He affirmed everything Wiener and Shalev had told me, but added something of his own. Yesterday, when he was at the site, he had seen – as Joe did – a new pile of rocks in a forbidden area. He yelled until he was hoarse. He made sure the pile was removed, but while he was yelling two UN men, camera in hand, took photos of the pile for posterity.

After he left silence prevailed at long last in the apartment and I sat at the table, first to write the day's diary and then – papers, papers, papers! Close to midnight Zipporah called from Tel Aviv and told me of her adventures. The mystery of BG's resignation is the talk of the town. I told her about my letter to him and soon was submerged again in the papers. I went to bed at 1:00 am.

75 The Jewish festival of Tabernacles, falling on October 4-12 in 1953.

76 Letter not found.

77 Letter not found, but see Sharett's earlier detailed letter to Bennike, September 24, 1953, *DFPI* 8, doc.387.

Qibya

Thursday, October 15

A nice morning, though a bit chilly. The clouds portend rain.

Arrived at the Foreign Ministry. Gideon told me about the events of the night. According to the first reports from the other side, over thirty houses were destroyed in one village alone – Qibya. There has never been a retaliation of such size or force.

I paced back and forth in my room at a loss what to do and utterly depressed by this feeling of impotence. Finally I decided to propose at the next Cabinet meeting that any decision regarding retaliatory action be subject to confirmation in advance by the Cabinet Committee on Foreign Affairs and Defense [FADC].

In this mood I prepared for my talk with Bennike. Gideon came to urge me to open with three searching questions for the UNTSO CoS to ascertain his position. I could not understand the reason for his request. I asked him to put the questions in writing. As soon as I saw the phrasing, I found this approach unacceptable. I preferred to ask Bennike simply if he had anything to say, and should he be obscure, later on during the conversation, he should be forced to give clear answers to our pertinent questions.

At 10:00 the retinue appeared: Bennike, Vigier,[1] and the legal (Danish) and military (American) advisers. For five minutes photographers bustled about us and filmed the meeting, filling the room with their lethal hardware. When they left we changed the seating arrangements and I came to the point.

From the start of the talk it was clear that there was no coming to any sort of understanding with the Dane. I suggested that he begin; lo and behold, he did. He reiterated the familiar litany: we had worked and were still working on Arab land. We were altering the character of the region from a military viewpoint. We had to stop until an agreement was achieved. I made a forceful reply, and a keen argument ensued. Tekoah and Rafael also took part for our side, and Bennike's military adviser, for the other. As the debate went on, it became clear that the Dane wasn't at all concerned about water or land, but about the strategic change we are ostensibly carrying out in the DMZ. He himself decreed that there was no recourse but to submit the question to the Security Council,

1 Henri Vigier. Political Adviser to the CoS, UNTSO.

and I agreed that only the SC was qualified to decide the matter of principle which he had broached. To all appearances I tore to shreds the fabric of his argument concerning military advantages to be had in the DMZ, but he and his legal adviser in his train remained adamant. My contentions and those of my colleagues once more showed that we had an excellent case, but who knows which way the wind may blow in the SC now. In short, he rejected three proposals of mine: (a) to stop work temporarily – a temporary stoppage, he replied, would not solve the problem; (b) to submit to him a draft of guarantees for individual rights concerning land and water – he showed no interest in it and explained that the guarantees had to satisfy Syria, which would not count on our goodwill as long as we were enemies; (c) to visit the project site together to clarify any misunderstandings in regard to the facts – at first he assented willingly, but then he reversed himself and said it would serve no practical purpose. Finally, I said to him, if that is how it is, then we will see you at the SC! The meeting ended with a feeling that we have reached a critical juncture.

The strain under which I had labored all these weeks since the beginning of September climbed another few notches all at once. I asked myself: who will wage this new campaign? Aubrey is torn in two between ambassadorships, Washington and the UN GA in New York. Would he have the strength to take charge of this new front upon himself? Furthermore, he doesn't have sufficient command of the facts at all. In addition, he has been infected by a defeatist spirit, and he fundamentally opposes the line we have taken. How can he do battle in such a frame of mind? But for me to go now to New York is like "parting the Red Sea." The many issues at stake in the Ministry, the continuing complications along our borders, and most important, the ominous resignation of BG.

[- - -]

After a quick lunch at home I napped for a few minutes and set out with Zipporah in her car to the PM's Garden at the *Kirya* in Tel Aviv for a reception in honor of Shinwell,[2] who came to visit the country at our invitation. The guests – Foreign Ministry, Ministry of Defense, other VIPs, and the staff of the British Embassy. The latter appeared at full strength, and surprised me with its size – no comparison with our embassy in London. The refreshments were of the finest, the Ministry of Defense having paid for it. The Foreign Ministry personnel, who ate and drank plentifully, burned with envy at the bounteous resources with which the Ministry of Defense has been blessed while our Ministry has to fight for every penny, especially funds for entertaining.

[- - -]

2 Emanuel Shinwell (1884-1986). Labour MP and Cabinet minister; after 1970, Baron Shinwell of Easington.

In the course of the reception, an officer of the IDF Command approached me and reported that the PM, who was now attending Army manoeuvers in the north, would like the Cabinet Ministers to fly to the north tomorrow morning and inspect the work on the Jordan which might be stopped shortly (It is interesting to note that this is the PM's assumption!) and have a glimpse of the end of the maneuvers. I said to Joe that it was my intention to visit the site of the works on Monday and inspect the whole business thoroughly. The visit suggested by the PM shall not suffice for this purpose and will only result in a loss of time and energy. However, I feel I should not turn aside the PM's request these days, especially after the shot I fired at him yesterday in my letter.

[- - -]

Back at home in Jerusalem, the evening broadcast already carried a fair summary of the press conference I convened in which I lectured in my capacity as MFA spokesman about our meeting with Bennike.

[- - -]

Horror gripped me upon hearing the Jordanian Radio Ramallah's description of the devastation in that village of Qibya.[3] Dozens of houses destroyed and dozens of people killed. I can just imagine the commotion in Arab capitals and those of the West tomorrow.

At 11:00 I telephoned the *Jerusalem Post* and as usual edited the report on the press conference over the phone. I found quite a few slips which I corrected.[4]

[- - -]

Friday, October 16

[- - -]

At 7:50 I arrived at Tel Aviv Sde Dov Airport. We flew above the Sharon and Western Samaria, crossed the Jezreel Valley and the Lower Galilee until we landed

---

3 Sharett was in the habit of listening directly to Arab radio broadcasts.

4 Sharett's frequent intervention with staffers became a legend at the English-language daily. As Meir Ronen recalled in 1992, Sharett "would often appear in the editorial offices of an evening, crying for 'the leader.' He was not referring to Ben-Gurion, but to the editorial. He would pore over the galley proof, not so much to check its political line, which was pretty much impeccable, but to *farbesser* [Yiddish: improve upon] the English. It was the Turkish-educated Sharett's conceit that his English was impeccable and much superior to that of the American-educated editors Agronsky and Ted Lurie." See M. Ronen, "The Agony and the Ecstasy," *Jerusalem Post* (anniversary supplement), May 6, 1992, p.74. Cf. Misha Louvish, "When The Medium Is The Message," *Jerusalem Post*, November 16, 1990, p.4. It should be noted that (ignored by Ronen) Sharett's "Turkish" English was further perfected during 1921-1925 while living in London and studying at the London School of Economics.

at the airfield in Mahanayim. The flight took 50 minutes. All the mountains seemed rather small while I was in the sky. When the Hermon appeared in the distance, I thought it was Mount Canaan at first. When we arrived at the real Mount Canaan it looked squashed. Mount Meron did stand tall, but it looked puny and flattened. Only the Hermon triumphed in its relative dignity and stature.

We set out by car to the Jordan canal, accompanied by the commanding officer of the Northern Command, General Assaf Simhoni. We drove alongside the canal and beheld the transformation of God's creations[5] by men digging like moles in the dirt with gigantic machines like tusks – steam shovels and bulldozers and all sorts of other titanic implements of destruction. It nevertheless became clear that although today was Friday – the target date for the completion of the first segment of 450 meters – it was even doubtful whether it would be completed by Sunday. However, the project has already gone far beyond this point and extends along a line two-thirds the length of the central DMZ. The work is in full swing and tension at its height. I can imagine what a thunderbolt the order to stop will be for all those laboring and directing the work, but undoubtedly we shall be forced to give it up in the next few days.

I closely examined the Arab plot of land on which, according to Bennike, work was being done and found it to be true. There had been a path there before, but we had widened it by transporting the machines and turned it into a regular thoroughfare. We had placed the machines not only in the strip between the water and the border of the Arab plot but inside the plot as well. It was also true that the police were using the abandoned Arab mill, that rocks had been piled in a corner of the plot near the mill. And that one tree had been felled. All these would count as petty trifles in a project of this kind under ordinary conditions. But in view of our Armistice Agreement with Syria and the Syrians' intrigues, each of these items has been blown up into a grave political problem. The fact that I was told nothing at all about this Arab land and its intended role in the course of the project, which was naturally known in advance to its directors, is of course a deplorable scandal, behavior lacking all discipline or responsibility. Somebody will have to pay for it.

At 12:35 I was back at home. I showered and changed and at 1:00 o'clock began receiving guests for lunch and serving them drinks. The meal was in honor of Shinwell. Mainly Party members had been invited. After the meal I organized the guests in a circle and tossed Shinwell a question about the peculiarities he had witnessed in our way of life in this country. Are they too complicated to comprehend? This resulted, in effect, in a discussion about the kibbutz, its mission and its future. It transpired that Shinwell had not at all understood the social nature of the kibbutz movement and had attempted to classify it as merely an economic unit.

---

5 Sharett used the Hebrew *sidrei bereshit*, i.e., nature formations from the first day of God's Creation.

The conversation grew interesting, and was interspersed with explanations about various complications in Britain's economic life. Finally, Shinwell said that though our life was hard and fraught with complications, we had nevertheless been blessed by Fate. [- - -]

As I left my home after the meal, two envelopes were brought to me – one from the American Embassy and one from the British. Russell informed me of the coming of Eric Johnston[6] as President Eisenhower's special emissary to the Middle East, to help in solving its problems. Evans[7] conveyed in the name of Her Majesty's Government (HMG) a scathing and most severe denunciation of the atrocious action in the village of Qibya.[8] Word has also arrived from the British Military Attachés announcing that they are ceasing their participation in [joint] manoeuvers because of this action.

At the office. A call from Aubrey. His voice was loud and clear, and his words well understood. He wanted to know what I would propose to the Cabinet. I said I had not yet made up my mind and would still mull it over tomorrow. He said it was best if we would stop immediately and ask for a meeting of the Security Council. Otherwise we would not create an atmosphere conducive to an arbitration of the issue. I expressed my doubts about our taking the initiative. He said that Syria had evidently decided to demand a meeting of the Council and we had best anticipate that, to avoid creating an impression that we are the offenders. The conversation ended with no decision taken. Afterwards I began summing up the situation to myself and listed several questions to which an answer from Washington would be desirable. It was I who placed a call now for Aubrey, and I had him on the line in a few moments. I posed my questions and asked for a detailed reply by wire. The gist of it: to establish why we ourselves should turn to the SC – why we should stop before an inquiry had been scheduled, and whether we should warn the Syrians that if they raised the matter we would attack them for not making peace and make known the negotiations which had taken place between us. This threat was Tekoah's idea.

I also talked to Reuven Shiloah who was eager to know the background to BG's resignation. I promised to write it up. I found that Reuven well understands my position in the complications of the last few days, especially in regard to Qibya. I told him the matter had been decided by BG and Lavon against me, and that I had not known about the nature or extent of the operation until afterwards. Indeed it should be stressed that when I opposed the retaliatory action I did not imagine there would be such bloodshed. I was thinking of a retaliatory action of the earlier variety which had become routine and even to that I objected. If I had had any reason to fear such a slaughter, I would have raised hell.

---

6 Eric A. Johnston (1896-1963). Special Representative of the US President to the ME; Chairman, Advisory Board for International Development.

7 Sir Francis E. Evans (1897-1983). British Ambassador to Israel (1952-1954).

8 Evans to Sharett, October 16, 1953, *DFPI* 8, doc.433.

Telephone conversations with Walter and Elizur regarding our portrayal in the press of the attack on Qibya. The IDF has carefully considered this question, was searching for a plausible public explanation, and wanted to know how we intended to explain it. During an IDF consultation with our people, Bendor[9] suggested maintaining that the Army had had no part in the operation; that border area residents, incensed at the recent murders and thirsting for vengeance, had risen as one and slaughtered their neighbors. This is a completely implausible story which would make us a laughing-stock. It is clear to any observer that the IDF had a hand in the matter. The Army itself rejected this tactic and came to the conclusion that the IDF's role could not be covered up. I told Walter and instructed Elizur that the Foreign Ministry spokesman should say nothing about the reprisal, except for stressing the murders which had preceded it. Best let the IDF spokesman wiggle out of the predicament as best he could. I do not see why the Foreign Ministry should assume any explicit responsibility for something that took place despite its objection.

Teddy and Ehud[10] came to supper. We talked about BG's resignation for a long time. They were both convinced that the matter was serious, and that the man could not be swayed from his intent. They were both depressed at the ensuing results. Both firmly acknowledged that only I was capable of inheriting the post. I threw back at them my reasons for not accepting the mantle. They did not accept them. Meanwhile we roamed the length and breadth of the whole expanse of personal, organizational and political problems in the Army's relations with the Foreign Ministry, the coordination of government activities in various spheres, the tangle in our relations with the USA, etc. I unburdened not a few of my troubles before them, but it gave me no relief. I most seriously pleaded with Ehud to re-enter the FM, and even offered him the role of Deputy DG, but he refused. He prefers to stand aside – and at a distance.

When the two left, I went to work on the papers.

Saturday, October 17

At 10:00 Walter, Gideon, Tekoah, Katriel[11] and Moshe Yuval[12] for a consultation.

---

9 Shmuel Bendor (1909-1991). Director, US Division, MFA; later Israel Minister to Romania; Director, West European Division and Deputy Director, *Hasbara* Division, MFA.

10 Ehud Avriel (1917-1980). Born in Vienna. Settled in Palestine in 1939. Israel Ambassador to Czechoslovakia (1948), Romania (1950); DG, PMO and Ministry of Finance (1950-1953); Mapai MK (1955-1957); later Director, International Organizations Division, MFA; Israel Ambassador to Ghana and to Italy.

11 Katriel Katz (1908-1988). Counsellor and Chargé d'affaires, Budapest. Later Israel Envoy to Hungary and to Poland; Cabinet Secretary; Consul-General to New York; Ambassador to Moscow (1965-1967); Chairman of Yad Vashem.

12 Moshe Yuval (1913-1982). Director, Research Division, MFA (1954-1957); later Ambassador to Australia and New Zealand.

Before we started Fati[13] dropped in on his way to a meeting at the GS, and asked to know the contents of the British letter and if we had received any more protests. I emphasized the letter's sting – its reliance on the Tripartite Declaration[14] and the Anglo-Jordanian Defense Treaty.[15]

I asked Fati how yesterday's deliberation had ended in regard to the phrasing of the IDF spokesman's announcement about Qibya: whether to admit that the Army had a hand in the matter, or to deny any connection. His answer was that it had been decided to make no response at all. The formula I had heard, claiming that the Army knew nothing, was not publicized. He told me about movements of Arab Legion units from across the Jordan River to the West Bank in two spearheads – from Irbid to the Nablus district, and from Amman to Jerusalem. I did not consider these movements to be preparations for an attack, but merely vigilance against aggression on our part. They could not have failed to be impressed by the assault on Qibya as part of a calculated plan to spark a war, or at least a willingness to accept war as a repercussion of the operation.

Fati reported that, according to Radio Ramallah, 56 bodies had already been removed from the piles of rubble.

After he left we entered into a long argument over what line to take now that it was certain we are on our way to the SC agenda. There were three possibilities concerning the project in the north: not to stop until the SC should issue an injunction; to stop immediately; to announce that we will stop as soon as the debate begins. We considered the arguments for and against each possibility, and tested my ideas in their presence. Walter was in favor of not stopping until there is an injunction. Katriel and Joe argued that it was best to stop immediately. Gideon and I supported the middle course, which I had already proposed at the consultation of our party's ministers at the beginning of the week.

Next, Gideon and Joe lectured me on the evolution of the Hula conflict two years ago: how it reached the SC, what happened in the debate there and what were its conclusions. The question remains whether we shall also submit a complaint to the SC. On this point I have not taken a stand. Meanwhile I invited Russell for a talk at 3:00 pm. The internal consultation took three hours, from 10:00 to 1:00. I dictated to Elizur over the phone a short reply for the Foreign Ministry spokesman in response to the United Press International [UPI] news agency report that the three Western foreign ministers in London had expressed their deep anxiety over

13 Maj.-Gen. Yehoshafat ("Fati") Harkabi (1921-1994). Deputy Head, Intelligence Branch, IDF (1953-1954), Director of Military Intelligence (1955-1959); Professor of International Relations, Hebrew University (1966-1994).

14 For the text of the Tripartite Declaration of May 25, 1950, see WebDoc #1.

15 In accordance with articles 2-4 of the Treaty of Alliance between the UK and the Hashemite Kingdom of Transjordan of March 15, 1948, Britain was obliged to come to the aid of Jordan if it were to be attacked.

Israel's attack on Jordanian villages. I expressed a wish that they should consider the only reason for the restive situation in the border area which is the murderous attacks on Israel by armed Jordanians infiltrators and the Jordanian government's inability to stem the tide. After Zipporah and I had our meal, I sat down to focus my thoughts in preparation for Russell. Then I slept my allotted time – 10 minutes.

A number of telegrams from Eliahu Elath[16] were brought to me. The most important dealt with his conversation with Selwyn Lloyd,[17] which included a demand that we pay compensation for the destruction and killings in Qibya and similar delicacies of the kind. Elath answered well enough, but to us he addresses most pertinent questions with regard to the logic of our action.[18]

At 3:00 Russell and Fried[19] appeared. With me was Gideon. Russell's face was gloomy. Qibya hung in the air. I began by expressing my satisfaction at Eric Johnston's coming, and I promised any and all assistance to help him carry out his mission of defusing the tension in the region. I reported on the results of our last conversation with Bennike and our preparations for the SC debate which would certainly focus on the matter of principle: does the regimen of the DMZ demand the physical immobilization of the area? From that I went on to events on the Jordanian border. I said I would not say a word in justification of the attack on Qibya, but I must warn against any detaching of this action from the chain of events. I announced our willingness for a high-level meeting to get the situation under control, and laid the blame for the restive situation on Jordan's impotence or lack of good will. From this point on I conducted an offensive against US policy as one of the elements in the encouragement of the Arabs and the isolation of Israel. I touched on Byroade's[20] conversation with Nahum[21] and attacked his misleading and harmful assertion that we aspire to war, and that all our actions in the north and in the south aim only to precipitate it.

Russell denied holding such an opinion but stated that our provocations of the UN are bound to arouse US ire, poison the atmosphere and set peace back. He once again raised the banner of loyalty to the UN – as in the previous talks. Gideon castigated him with their tolerance of Egypt, which ignores a Security Council

16 Eliahu (Epstein) Elath (1903-1990). Born in Russia. Settled in Palestine in 1924. Head of the ME Section of the JA Political Department (1934-1945), and Head of its Political Office in Washington (1945-1948). Israel Minister and first Ambassador to Washington (1948-1950). Israel Ambassador to London (1950-1959). Later Political Adviser, MFA.

17 J. Selwyn B. Lloyd (1904-1978). UK Minister of State for Foreign Affairs under Anthony Eden (1951-1954). Minister of Supply and of Defense (1954-1955). Secretary of State for Foreign Affairs (December 1955-July 1960).

18 The Elath-Lloyd conversation is reported in *DFPI* 8, doc.434.

19 Milton Fried. Attaché, American Embassy (until June 1954).

20 Henry A. Byroade (1913-1993). Assistant Secretary of State for Near Eastern Affairs, US State Department (1952-1955); US Ambassador to Egypt (March 1955-September 1956).

21 Dr Nahum Goldmann (1895-1982). President, Zionist Congress and WZO; Chairman of the American Section of the JAE; Chairman of the Conference on Jewish Material Claims against Germany.

injunction with regard to the freedom of Israeli passage through the Suez Canal,[22] as well as their forgiveness of Syngman Rhee, President of South Korea, who abused and mocked the UN for the entire world to see in his tactics undermining the ceasefire in Korea. I denounced this discrimination in light of three facts: a willingness to help Egypt while at the same time disregarding its violation of a SC resolution; denial of rumors regarding the deferral of the grant to Yugoslavia because of its preparations for aggression in Trieste; and the suspension of our grant and conveying this to Syria's knowledge. Bennike's position added to the US position concerning the northern matter is tantamount to a double victory for Syria over Israel – the sabotage of our development project and a denial of foreign aid.

Among other things, Russell inquired if we were going to stop work, given that matter has been submitted to the SC. I replied that the Cabinet would discuss the issue tomorrow. He also asked if we would disavow the attack on Qibya. I said I couldn't reply.

When they left I had a short farewell talk with Katriel Salmon,[23] who is returning to his post in London as our Military Attaché. Earlier in the day Fati spoke about a dinner that was held yesterday with Britain's Military Attachés. The attachés had, however, announced that in protest against the operation in Qibya they would no longer take part in IDF maneuvers, including the social functions held in connection with them. However, they did not boycott that dinner since it had nothing to with the maneuvers. Fati also mentioned that none of the Englishmen had alluded to Qibya, and the Israelis took their cue from them. But now Katriel tells me that Rosser, the chief Military Attaché, had talked to him in an agitated mood about the impression in England made by events. There they understand an eye for an eye, but definitely not fifty eyes for an eye; an outburst for an outburst, but not a planned military response for the rampage of a gang.

Katriel came up with an idea for a "diversion." The Qibya affair may overshadow everything if we do not succeed in riveting attention upon some dramatic turn. This is his scheme: we shall notify the British that we are about to exert our rights in the Suez Canal by sending a warship through it. They will then begin begging us to desist and we, out of regard for their worries, shall

22 The reference is to UN SC Resolution 95 of September 1, 1951, which considered the armistice regime to be "of a permanent character," and hence that neither party could "reasonably assert that it is actively a belligerent or requires to exercise the right of visit, search and seizure for any legitimate purpose of self-defence," and called upon Egypt to "terminate the restrictions on the passage of international commercial shipping and goods through the Suez Canal wherever bound and to cease all interference with such shipping beyond that essential to the safety of shipping in the Canal itself and to the observance of the international conventions in force." For the full text, see WebDoc #2.

23 Katriel P. Salmon (1914-1967). Military Attaché, London (1951-1954) and Washington (1954-1957); subsequently official at the Ministry of Finance; from October 1959, Minister to South Africa.

comply and win praise. I said the opposite was true. We would further infuriate them by once again exhibiting the mischievous spirit of adventure that burns unrestrainedly within us. Regarding the "sailing of ships through the Canal," I remarked that according to our plans we must first try to convey an oil freighter flying a non-Israeli flag from the Red Sea to Haifa, then a regular freighter flying the Israeli flag from Haifa to Mombassa. The thought of sending a warship was nothing but madness. Obviously the Egyptians would confiscate it and we would only make ourselves look ridiculous by protesting.

[- - -]

The call I had placed to Washington came through. Aubrey announced that the debate was set for Wednesday or Thursday. He dismissed his earlier thought of coming here for two days. He asked if I could come there. I said it would be very difficult. He again stressed its importance. "For the thing which I greatly feared is come upon me!"[24] I asked his opinion about submitting a complaint to the Security Council. He said certainly. Against whom? Against Bennike. And what about Syria? Yes, against Syria too.

At 6:45 I set out alone for Jerusalem. From Beit Dagon to Ramle I gave a lift to an Iraqi girl who told me she was a nurse at a nearby hospital and that she was the only breadwinner in her family of mother and younger brothers. I then asked her if she knew who I was. She said no, then stared at me and said: "I think something but I am not sure." She asked for my identity but I declined. From Ramle onwards I remained alone, brooding the whole way about BG. What will he do now? Will he understand that the Qibya affair is no trifling matter but the beginning of a new chapter in the course of our political affairs? He had ruled in favor of it – when he could have stayed his hand and allowed me, as Acting PM, to decide. How can he now withdraw and throw the responsibility for the results of his action upon others? Or maybe it really is best that he go, and for the first time an attempt be made to bring defense policy into full coordination with foreign policy considerations?

[- - -]

I arrived home at 8:30. Aubrey called to report that the three Great Powers were prosecuting us before the SC for our action at Qibya. We have certainly prepared ourselves a pretty pudding. Who's going to eat it now?

[- - -]

Sunday, October 18

This was an excruciating day, grating the nerves and exhausting the stores of energy.

---

24 *Job*, 3:25.

At 8:00 I left for the office. I readied myself for the detailed report I shall give this morning to the Cabinet meeting: the conflict over the Jordan [waters diversion]; my last conversation with the Dane; its repercussions in Washington; the serious crises caused by the Qibya operation.

Walter, Gideon and Joe came in and we reviewed the panorama, which had changed altogether since last evening. The three Western powers' decision to convene the SC to discuss the tension in the ME in light of the recent complications – i.e., those which can be ascribed to us – constitutes a serious turn which threatens us with severe damage. It is clear that we face one of our most perilous campaigns since the establishment of the state – perhaps the most serious since the War of Independence, at any rate much more serious than our struggles over the Hula drainage and the Suez Canal closure to our shipping. We must meet this new trial neither defensively nor apologetically, but in a spirit of rebuke and on the offensive. Gideon was quite right in posing the subject in this vein. It is clear that the dimensions of the debate will now expand. Accordingly we can now widen it even more and make an effort to shift the weight from complaints against us to our complaints against the Arab states.

The conclusion is that we should join the demand to convene the Council and submit our own proposal for the agenda, in which we may present our entire list of complaints against the Arab states for violations of the armistice, Egypt's blockade of the Canal, Jordan's violation of Article VIII of the Armistice Agreement which allows Israeli access to the Holy Places and Mount Scopus,[25] the infiltration incidents and murders in the border area near Jordan, Syria's sabotage

---

25 Article VIII of the Israel-Jordan Armistice Agreement defines a "Special Committee" which was to be "organized immediately following the coming into effect of this Agreement" and which was to "direct its attention to the formulation of agreed plans and arrangements for such matters as either Party may submit to it, which, in any case, shall include the following, on which agreement in principle already exists: free movement of traffic on vital roads, including the Bethlehem and Latrun-Jerusalem roads; resumption of the normal functioning of the cultural and humanitarian institutions on Mount Scopus and free access thereto; free access to the Holy Places and cultural institutions and use of the cemetery on the Mount of Olives; resumption of operation of the Latrun pumping station; provision of electricity for the Old City; and resumption of the railroad to Jerusalem."

Following the armistice, Jordan denied access to the Wailing Wall in Jerusalem's Old City to Israelis, and a small Israeli police contingent protected the Jewish "cultural and humanitarian" property (hospital, university) in East Jerusalem on Mount Scopus, which was declared a demilitarized enclave controlled by UNTSO inspectors. Many provisions of Article VIII were eroded at an early date or not implemented smoothly owing to complications and disputes. For details, see E.L.M. Burns, *Between Arab and Israeli* (New York: Ivan Obolensky, 1963), 146, 153, 157-58, 161; Nathan A. Pelcovits, *The Long Armistice: UN Peacekeeping and the Arab-Israeli Conflict, 1948-1960* (Boulder: Westview Press, 1993), 54-55, 197-201; E.H. Hutchison, *Violent Truce: A Military Observer Looks at the Arab-Israeli Conflict, 1951-1955* (New York: Devin-Adair, 1956), ch.3.

of development projects in the DMZ, also the Arab economic boycott[26] in general, and above all – the refusal of all the Arab states to comply with the SC decision requiring progress from armistice to peace.

I informed my colleagues of Aubrey's request that I come to New York and the conclusion I had come to at night that I must be cruel to him this time and stay at home. The Israeli Foreign Minister's hurried departure for the SC meeting would be evidence of anxiety and nervousness that would not add to our credibility. No Arab foreign minister will be flying to New York at this time. On the other hand, if the responsibility is assigned to Aubrey, he will doubtless recover his fighting spirit as he has in such situations in the past. I was only worried that the SC debate and the Assembly debate on the refugee question might coincide, for then Aubrey would be torn to shreds. But Gideon set my mind at rest, assuring me that if the SC debate should start, the debate on the refugee problem would undoubtedly be postponed; for the UN has a tradition that two of its institutions do not deal with the same subject at the same time.

Only yesterday I had thought it was a good idea to send Gideon to New York as reinforcement for Aubrey – not to make appearances with him but to provide information and ideas and in general to encourage and stimulate him. Before I could voice the thought I was told that it had already been aired at the DG's morning conference. I immediately authorized Gideon's departure.

At 9:00 I went into BG's office at the PMO. I found him all aglow as though everything were alright and smooth. At first I was surprised not to find any of the *haverim* with him. On Friday Lavon and I had agreed to a meeting of the Mapai members of the Cabinet with BG at this hour for a preliminary discussion before the Cabinet meeting. It turned out that the proposal had been rejected by BG, who did not think we would have time to look into anything properly in the space of a short hour. Once again I wondered why Lavon had not notified me that the preliminary discussion had been cancelled. However, to each his own manners and his own conceptions of friendship and courtesy. Anyway, I entered into conversation with BG. He asked me if I would deliver a "report" at the start of the meeting. I was surprised by this naive question. Certainly, I said, there was much to look at and more: a storm was raging around us and the nations of the world had focused their interest upon us. I had to report on the situation in the north, on the repercussions of the Qibya action, on the pending meeting of the SC, on what was happening on our US front – and not only report, but also read out a string of documents: Eban's telegrams, President Eisenhower's letter regarding

26 A campaign organized by the Arab League, begun in 1945 to boycott goods produced by the Jewish *yishuv* in Palestine, subsequently expanded to prohibit Arab companies and to discourage other companies from trading with Israel. The boycott was coordinated through a Central Office created in Damascus in 1951. The latter sought to punish "foreign companies and institutions acting in support of the economy of Israel" by blacklisting them. Examples of blacklisted companies and entertainers included Coca-Cola, Danny Kaye and Frank Sinatra.

the Johnston mission, the British note, the Elath telegrams, etc.

I saw an expression of displeasure on BG's face. He asked how long my survey would take. I said: "At least an hour." He said: "But I had planned to bring up security matters at this meeting." He was referring to the program of improvements in the organization of the Army over the next few years, to which he had devoted all his time these past weeks. I was again perturbed by the naivety and the lack of any sensitivity to what was transpiring in the world around us and to the urgent press of the events of the day. He became pacified, and said: "No matter, you talk for an hour and then I will take up two."

"No, indeed," I said. "After I talk for an hour the members of the Cabinet will want to pose questions and express opinions."

I saw that it was hard for BG to abandon his plans and reconcile himself to the reality which I had presented to him, so absorbed within himself was he and insensitive to external events. I was astounded by this phenomenon of impermeability toward external events in a man capable of exhibiting an electric sensitivity to every vibration and development and extracting from them conclusions in a flash.

I turned to speak to the heart of the matter. I said there were three problems before me, two external and one internal. The external were: do we stop work in the north prior to the debate at the SC, and how are we to portray the Qibya affair to the outside world? The internal was how should the authority to decide on retaliatory action be regulated henceforward, in light of the bitter experience of Qibya? In my opinion, it must be determined that only the Cabinet FADC is authorized to decide on retaliatory action, and not the Minister of Defense by himself. Here BG roused himself and requested that I not pose this last question at the Cabinet meeting. "It's best we first consult within our own circle of *haverim*." He suggested that we re-convene for this purpose at 8:00 in the evening. This was scheduled.

The Cabinet meeting opened in an atmosphere of unusual gravity and tension. Everyone was enveloped in a feeling that this was an hour of crisis and trial. My report lasted an hour and forty minutes. I spoke quietly, in an effort to suppress my inner turmoil, and not spoil the factual account with polemics. I strove to confront my colleagues with the gravity of the present imbroglio, and the harsh possibility of international complications in store for us if we do not wisely take steps to relieve the tension. I concluded with three proposals: to submit to the SC a severe indictment of the Arab states, especially Jordan; to stop work in the north pending the SC debate; to issue a statement in regard to Qibya expressing regret for what had happened while laying the blame squarely on Jordan.[27]

BG quickly discovered that his hopes for delivering the results of his inquiry into Army affairs at this meeting were an idle dream. A searching and prolonged

27 The full Cabinet protocol for this important meeting runs to 65 pages. For excerpts from Sharett's introductory speech, see WebDoc #3.

debate ensued. Except for Eshkol and Burg,[28] all members of the Cabinet spoke. Eshkol's silence spoke against him. He is in great distress over the suspension of the American grant, but his pride will not let him admit it and draw political conclusions from this critical predicament. The more the debate progressed, the more I suffered one disappointment after another. Not only most of my Party *haverim*, but Moshe Shapira[29] as well as all of the GZ were against my proposal to stop work. I quickly discovered that I was in for a resounding defeat on this front and desperately braced myself for a rebuttal. The radical position of the GZ surprised me. Immediately after the conclusion of my report, Rokach[30] asked for a recess – as if to rest awhile from the torment caused him by listening to my remarks. It turned out that his intention had been to allow the GZ to consult among themselves, the result of which was this display of hollow radicalism. When the meeting resumed, BG remarked that as long as he was chairman he would no longer agree to any recess for the purpose of party consultations. He went on to say that in the Cabinet each minister expresses his personal opinion and party positions must not be consolidated as such. I could imagine what had been the starting point of Rokach and his colleagues' consultation. Since BG was about to resign, and elections could be expected soon, the GZ could not lag behind Mapai with a tough foreign policy.

Moshe Shapira, who rejected the idea of a work stoppage with great ease, focused all his moral fervor on condemning the harshness of the Qibya operation. During the course of his remarks he asked me if I, as Foreign Minister, had known about this action in advance. I sent BG a note and asked his opinion. Could I abstain from replying? BG had earlier remarked that he had not been asked about the Qibya action, for he was on vacation, but if he had been asked he would have approved it. This was a rather peculiar articulation of the facts. He had definitely been asked [by Lavon], even if he seemingly was on vacation, and had not only expressed his opinion, but his opinion had tilted the decision against mine [by a majority of two to one]. Now that I asked him, he answered by asking me whether I had known about the operation in advance. This too was peculiar, for Pinhas Lavon had specifically told him that I was opposed to the action. I pointed out the facts by way of reply – all this in an exchange of notes. He wrote that Pinhas would soon be speaking. No doubt he would report my opposition himself.

But this was not the case. Lavon's chivalry did not extend to such heights. He focused on the fundamental political aspect of both our confrontation with the UN in the north and the explosive retaliatory action. It is interesting and most

28 Yosef S. Burg (1909-1999). Leader, *Hapo'el Hamizrahi* party; Minister of Health (until October 1953) and Minister of Posts (until 1958).

29 Haim Moshe Shapira (1902-1970). Born in Russia. Settled in Palestine in 1925. Leader, *Hapo'el Hamizrahi* Party; Minister of Immigration and Health (1948-1951); Minister of Religious Affairs (1951-1958).

30 Israel Rokach (1896-1959). Leader, GZ Party; Minister of the Interior (1952-1955).

enlightening to witness the metamorphosis taking place in the thinking and entire disposition of this intelligent and talented man, who also evidently possesses strong control over his inner brakes – to release or block them as necessary – now that he has tasted control over the mightiest machine in the country: the IDF. How much had his adaptation to the prevailing atmosphere within the officers' corps transported him beyond his previous political principles and the basic values to which he had always adhered. He spoke in favor of "stiff-neckedness," not worrying about transitory difficulties, not losing one's nerve, and so on and so forth.[31] Both Golda and [Dov] Yosef followed suit in the same vein.

The debate went on for hour after hour. BG sent me a note at one point saying he was already totally exhausted as a result of this one meeting. Fatigue spread among other ministers as well, and as the discussion continued some ministers left for the adjoining room to smoke or talk. When my turn came to reply everyone re-convened and rapt attention once again held sway. I spoke at length again, no longer to report the facts, but to get at the root of the problems at hand and clarify basic conceptions. I made a supreme effort to subdue my agitation, but it burst out. I warned against the glaring contradiction between our objective, concrete total dependency on the help and sympathy of the world, and our subjective mental isolation from the world, insulating ourselves in complete numbness toward the response of world public opinion to our actions and behavior. I condemned our narrow-mindedness in obstinately refusing to budge from a position taken along one section of the front while at the same time endangering all other sections and risking utter defeat. I brought up BG's attitude in the morning as an example, when he had not seen any need at all to devote this meeting to a review of our relations with the UN and Great Powers, as if nothing had happened and business was as usual. I rejected the strictly formal and cerebral approach to the problem of the work stoppage, and protested the lack of any practical sensibility and psychological understanding of the straits we had entered by defying the authority of the UN. I demanded the stoppage of work as the need of the hour, for without it we would not under any circumstances be able to create an atmosphere conducive to any consideration of our position prior to the Security Council debate. In any event, we had already expressed our willingness to stop temporarily to enable Bennike

31 Pinhas Lavon was one of the main leaders in Poland of the Zionist youth movement Gordonia and of the Zionist labor party, *Hapo'el Hatza'ir*, both of which were ideologically moderate and clearly anti-militaristic. He pursued these lines as a labor leader in Palestine, to which he immigrated in 1929. His transformation from espousing a moderate, non-aggressive political philosophy to one holding extremist views in the political and defense arena took place quite suddenly in mid-1953, when, as Minister without Portfolio, he supported David Ben-Gurion's proposals in the Cabinet for undertaking reprisal operations. This transformation became even more acute in early July 1953, when Lavon became acting Minister of Defense upon Ben-Gurion's taking leave for six months. There can be little doubt that Ben-Gurion nominated him Acting Defense Minister in view of his "activist" views.

to ascertain the facts. In accordance with the very same logic, why should we not stop to enable a SC inquiry? Why wait until we are put in the dock and forced to mend our ways by an order to stop work? And more and more. It is too long to go into. Finally I replied to Shapira's question by relating the story in its entirety and I denounced the Qibya affair which had presented us to the entire world as bloodthirsty bandits capable of large-scale slaughter, who did not care, evidently, if it led to an outbreak of war. I warned that the stain that was cast on us in the eyes of the world would not be washed away for many years.[32]

When a vote was taken, only two joined me in support of a work stoppage – Naftali and Rosen. Their company was small comfort to me this time. Most of the others voted against. Eshkol abstained. I interpreted this as a sign that he had not the courage to vote for the stoppage – not that his conscience would not allow him to vote against it. But who am I to read a man's thoughts?

It was decided that a statement concerning Qibya be issued, and BG was entrusted with its composition. I again demanded some expression of regret. BG strongly insisted on not admitting the Army's responsibility for the action. Border area inhabitants, whose patience in the face of unceasing murder had been exhausted, had taken the law into their own hands in retribution. All of the frontier settlements were, after all, rich in arms and many of the settlers were ex-soldiers. Is it any wonder they had arisen and done what they did? I said that no one in the world would believe us and that we were showing ourselves as prevaricators and deceivers. But I could not seriously demand a statement that the IDF had done the deed, for such a statement would in no way allow any self-condemnation and would have only shown our defiant support of this monstrous bloodshed.

We agreed to turn to the Security Council with a long list of complaints which would embody Israel's indictment of the Arab states. BG was opposed to the inclusion of Egypt's sins in the list, and I acceded. In the first place, why should we arouse Egypt's ire? We should better emphasize our special attitude toward her. Secondly, what could we complain about? About the embargo in the Canal? After all, they had let the "Farnon" sail through, and in regard to oil we could not prove that they had stopped any ship, for no attempt had been made to stop any ship with such cargo.

Following this it was decided, against my opinion – the vote was 6 to 5 – that we exclude from the list Syria's disruptions of the northern project, but separately notify the SC that we should welcome an investigation of the matter.

The meeting ended at 3:30. In other words it had lasted five and a half hours.[33]

A second meeting was scheduled for tomorrow morning to hear BG's survey of the IDF. At the end of the meeting BG showed me a letter with a proposal that Moshe Dayan fly to New York as well. He asked for my assent and I gave it

32 For extracts of Sharett's rebuttal, see WebDoc #3.

33 For a summary of the Cabinet debates, see *DFPI* 8, doc.444.

readily. No doubt he will be helpful there while our case is deliberated in the UN. Meanwhile, he would not be causing any damage here and may well gain some wisdom there, and when standing at the very front of our international struggle he might learn something of the harsh realities of our political position. (While still at the meeting, I had sent a message to the Ministry that Gideon was to fly out this evening.)

With Ze'ev Sharef[34] I revised the communiqué concerning the meeting. He didn't grasp the heart of the matter. He thought he had discharged his duty well enough with an inconsequential statement. I insisted on publicizing our decision to turn to the UN SC.

Tired and hungry, I drove back to the Foreign Ministry. I summoned the DG and Gideon, one after the other, and told them about my defeat and the decisions that had been adopted. I found Dayan on the premises arranging for his passport. Meanwhile Lavon had suggested that engineer Simcha Blass[35] of *Tahal* go as well. I agreed, and told myself I would have to send a telegram of condolence to Eban upon the arrival of this help-mate whose immense erudition and enthusiasm for the subject of water is awesome, but who is inordinately intolerable to his interlocutors and a crashing bore.

I dictated to Walter the draft of a briefing to all the overseas legations regarding the Qibya action. At long last, three days after the event, an official version has been formulated which can be wired to our people in foreign capitals.[36]

I dictated a telegram to Eban and Elath about the Cabinet decisions.[37]

Meanwhile Gideon and Joe prepared a skeleton draft of our letter to the SC. In accordance with the line taken by BG, I erased from it every passage relating to Egypt or Syria. As a result Jordan was placed squarely at the center of the document, laden with good and charitable deeds, while the Arab states altogether were hallowed with a special blessing for their boycott and rejection of peace. This text too was immediately wired to New York. Finally I dictated to Michael Elizur a brief for the local press and the foreign bureaus. I guessed what questions he might be asked and instructed him precisely how to answer each one.

My secretary Lilian, bless her heart, came up with a modest sandwich and a cup of tea. Everyone felt I was undergoing a most arduous day, and that I was agitated to the core by all that was happening to me. [- - -] I finally left the office and arrived home at 6:30, eating a meal that was both lunch and supper.

At home I dictated short responses to yesterday's telegrams from Eliahu Elath, and to new telegrams that had arrived from Eban. Recovery is evident in Aubrey's

---

34 Ze'ev Sharef (1906-1984). Cabinet Secretary (1948-1957); DG, PMO (1957-1959); later Director of State Revenues, Minister of Trade and Industry, Minister of Housing. Close associate of Sharett since working together in the pre-state JA Political Department.

35 Simcha Blass (1897-1982). Engineer and inventor; Director, *Tahal.*

36 *DFPI* 8, doc.446.

37 *DFPI* 8, doc.445.

latest telegrams and a resurgence of his fighting spirit. There is no one like him! [- - -]

At 8:00 I went by foot to the PMO. Coming in I found Gideon there, who had come to take leave of BG and be briefed by him. Earlier I had summoned Zvi Maimon, the Cabinet stenographer, for the purpose of reading out to Gideon from today's Cabinet minutes the remarks of Lavon and Golda as well as my concluding oration. Afterwards he said that the speech was "vibrant with pathos, and heroic."

The consultation which I initiated [on the question of the decision-making process concerning retaliation operations] included our *haverim* in the Cabinet. Argov[38] and MKs Ziama Aran and Mordechai Namir had also been invited. So much the better. I presented the problem. Though there did exist a major issue of principle which required a searching examination for its own sake – what rationale underlies our military retaliations, what are the do's and don't's, when action is to be taken and when not, etc. – this was not the time for such an examination. The Cabinet's procedural routine was right now of a more pressing nature. As things stand, authority rests with the Minister of Defense. If I am informed beforehand of a retaliatory raid, I may at times appeal against it. If the matter seems serious to me, I may demand that the Cabinet be convened. But this is not always possible, and in such a case my appeal remains ineffective. This means that concrete facts – in my view, malignant facts – are established in the field of foreign policy, for which and for the results of which I am held accountable, though I myself have opposed their creation at the outset. Therefore a change must be made. The Minister of Defense must be stripped of his authority as sole arbiter, and that authority must be entrusted to a committee. To avoid the complication of establishing a special committee, it may be best to place the authority with the Cabinet FADC, in which our party has a majority (4 of the 7).

BG objected to this proposal. He claimed it would ensure a lack of responsiveness and perhaps abandonment of military reprisals. He maintained that he himself had always been careful to inform me in advance, and he had agreed to a resolution of the matter by the Cabinet if I appealed against taking action. At times he himself had chosen to ask the Cabinet's opinion beforehand. Other *haverim* were also opposed to having the Committee put in charge of the matter. Finally it was agreed that when the subject is brought before the Cabinet, we must insist upon placing the authority for a decision with the PM, Minister of Defense and Foreign Minister. If the latter should appeal, the matter would be brought before the entire Cabinet.

In the midst of all this the issue of Qibya came up. Eshkol criticized the needless dimensions of the operation. Pinhas [Lavon] hinted that the raid had unexpectedly exceeded its original plan (it is not yet clear to me how this developed;

38 Meir Argov (1905-1963). Mapai MK (1949-1963); Chairman, Knesset FADC (1951-1963).

I have asked for the operation report and it remains to be seen if it will be given to me). Since other *haverim* expressed their opinions regarding the deed itself, I saw fit to state my opinion as well, and I told of my opposition which had not been heeded. Pinhas affirmed at this point that he had consulted BG. He mentioned Glubb's message, but did not reveal all its contents. I filled in the gaps. I intended to emphasize that at the time of the discution concerning the operation I was still Acting PM, but upon the rejection of my appeal I ceased to serve in this capacity – but I forgot [to mention that].[39]

Upon leaving the meeting Dov Yosef told me that, although he had not agreed with my views this morning, he had to admit that I had defended my position with great skill.

[- - -]

Writing up my diary tonight took me more than two hours. It is now already 2:30 am and my head aches. As I said to Zipporah over the telephone: "*nu-de byl deniok*!" [Russian: What a harrowing day!]

Monday, October 19

At the Foreign Ministry I consulted with the DG over the organization of a *hasbara*[40] campaign throughout the world in light of the nightmare of the Qibya raid, in order to counter-attack and shift the focus from defense and apology to attack and indictment.

An idea came to my mind, and I wired Elath to present the following version in his talks: The very fact that during the first two days we had been unable to clearly

39 Additional Information regarding the Qibya operation was given by Arye Dissenchik, chief editor of *Ma'ariv*, in his article "Who gave the Order and When - From My Memory Archive": "At the time, Yehezkel Sahar, Chief Inspector of the Israeli Police, told me: Several days before the Qibya retaliation, I came to the *Kirya* in Tel Aviv for a meeting with Acting Defense Minister Pinhas Lavon. When it ended, upon leaving his office, I bumped into Nehemiah Argov, military secretary of PM and Minister of Defense, Ben-Gurion. I asked him: Nehemiah, what's the matter, aren't they going to retaliate for the terror incidents of the last days on the Jordanian border? He retorted: Don't worry. They will get their due within a few days. And indeed, several days afterwards the Qibya operation was executed. As it happened, I was summoned again by Lavon to his office, and was told by him that the picture of the Qibya operation as reported to him by the Army was not balanced and clear. He suspected that the results of the operation were not in line with the original orders given by the CoS, and asked me to try and find out what really happened. On my way out, I entered Argov's room and asked him: Nehemiah, who gave the order to operate against Qibya? - I did, he said. - You? In what capacity? - Ben-Gurion approved it to me this morning, beforehand, he said." (*Ma'ariv*, February 25, 1977). For a detailed investigative study of the operation, see Shabtai Teveth, "Secrets of Qibya" [in Hebrew, in 3 parts], *Ha'aretz*, September 2, 9 and 16, 1994. See also Kafkafi, *Pinhas Lavon - Anti-Messiah*, 173-82.

40 *Hasbara* (Hebrew: explanation), i.e., information services and public relations activity abroad.

define what had happened in that village testifies better than a hundred witnesses that we had been taken by surprise, and needed time to properly investigate the matter. Had it truly been an officially planned operation, we would have prepared a version for disclosure in advance as well. Katriel Katz thought it was a brilliant argument.

On the other hand, I was depressed by Ze'ev Shek's report on Walter's morning conference. The "brilliant" idea had been expounded that if the official version held that the attackers at Qibya had been frontier settlers, then this disclosure must be accompanied by real action to convince everybody of its veracity. Shabtai Rosenne, the dear man, for example, suggested that we apply the Collective Punishment Law to the frontier settlements, or at least make a show of such action. Even Katriel argued that the police had to conduct some investigation in the area, if only for the sake of appearances. This detachment from the psychological and concrete reality of the matter troubled me.

I recalled that at the meeting of the *haverim* last evening I had intended to inform them that I ceased serving as Acting PM last Wednesday – on the evening prior to the Qibya operation, and because of it – but had forgotten to do so in the course of my remarks. I therefore dictated a short letter on this matter to those who took part in the meeting, except for BG and Pinhas Lavon, who knew of the matter.[41]

The Cabinet meeting was at 10:00 am. BG lectured at length on the IDF deployment to meet the danger of a "second round" of an Arab-Israeli war. He spoke for two and a half hours. The speech contained a keen analysis – more profound than any appraisal of military matters I had ever heard from his lips – concerning the problem of defending the state against a renewed Arab attack. He cited detailed, precise and worrying numbers regarding the Arab states' growing military strength, and pointed to three trends in their preparations for an attack against Israel: the improvement of training, sophistication of equipment, and unification of command. Continuing in these directions, the Arabs were due to reach their aspired target in 1956. He stressed our principal advantages – professional ability and morale – and outlined the central problem in furthering our military might, which lies in improving its quality, in all respects, to the greatest extent possible.[42]

While listening to BG's analysis I pondered anew that we must consider how to combat the danger with non-military measures: implementing solutions to the refugee problem by a daring and realistic proposal on our part to pay compensation; the improvement of relations with the Western powers; a constant,

41 Letter not found.

42 An English translation of BG's report, "Army and State," is provided in Amir Bar-Or, "The Army's Role in Strategic Planning: A Documentary Record," *Israel Studies* 1:2 (Fall 1996), 115-20.

determined, effort to reach an understanding with Egypt. Each of these courses of action may lead us into some dead-ends, but nevertheless we may not be excused from trying.

The meeting was adjourned before BG could finish his speech – due to the funeral of Supreme Court Justice Rabbi Simcha Assaf, who died last night. BG read out to us the draft of a statement he had composed for publication. It was a long document with many redundancies, but containing some pertinent phrases about Qibya, based on the version of the raid that we had adopted.

[- - -]

The funeral cost me my afternoon nap. Although I did lie down for a quarter of an hour, I didn't sleep at all. I find myself these days calculating hours and minutes of sleep the way inmates of the Soviet concentration camps tell of how they fell victim to thinking only about food. At 3:00 pm I drove to the office, reviewed piles of telegrams, and dictated replies. Aubrey is suddenly upset over why we have decided to turn to the SC with a request to table a new item on the agenda.

Was not the existing one, which lays before us a broad canvas upon which to range, sufficient to us? I answered him that we had thought it necessary to take an immediate and vigorous step to shift the center of gravity, as I had already explained. In any event, the Cabinet had decided to act in this manner and made its decision public. There was no further argument. I spoke with Walter about the need for additional ammunition for our legations in the information campaign. Meanwhile telegrams arrived from Berne, Brussels, Paris, Rio, Buenos Aires, and Rome – all testifying to nervousness and discomfort in all corners [concerning the Qibya affair]. We shall have to supply them with additional argumentation.

At 4:30 I was asked by BG to come to his office to go over the revised version of the Government statement. He informed me that he had decided to turn it into a radio broadcast which he himself would read. I wholeheartedly agreed with this. I found him with a shortened and better honed text, but not quite enough. I could not change the structure, nor replace some slack and badly constructed turns of phrases, which serve the purpose of emotional release more than that of clarity in the delineation of the political facts, but I did insert many linguistic corrections for the sake of clarification and precision. He accepted them all. I summoned Walter to the PMO to help Moish[43] translate the statement into English and went home.

[- - -]

43 Moshe ("Moish") Pearlman (1911-1986). IDF Spokesman (1948-1952); Director of *Kol-Israel* (1952-1956); Advisor on information (*hasbara*) in the PMO. Author of numerous books, including *Ben-Gurion Looks Back*, New York: Simon and Schuster, 1965 [Schocken, 1988].

I returned to my papers, but after a short while Walter and Moish appeared with the English version of the statement in hand. We worked hard, the three of us together, over its final draft. Once again I noticed the extent to which inaccuracy or muddled thinking, which in Hebrew cloak themselves under a mantle of elegant phrases and flowery speech, cause endless trouble to whoever must express those same ideas in contemporary English, which is crystal-clear and precise as a Swiss watch. We somehow managed to bring our labors to an end.

They had but left when Teddy Kollek and Yitzhak Navon arrived. Teddy came to report on the preparations for the Jerusalem conference [of wealthy diaspora Jewish leaders]. Again he argued that I must make a speech about Israel's foreign affairs. I rejected this proposal, having been informed that in the Conference's opening BG would speak at length on almost the very same subject. After some arguments back and forth we agreed it would be best if I responded to the general debate. There would surely be many who would call for a review and criticism of Israel's policy in these past few weeks.

Teddy drove Zipporah and me to President Ben-Zvi's home for supper. We were just the four of us. It is forty years now that I love Yitzhak from the depth of my heart,[44] and am delighted for both him and the state that he, and none other, is now the President of Israel. The truth is that I was the first to think of his candidacy long before the passing away of Dr Weizmann. Therefore let it not be held against me if at this moment I take the liberty of indulging in good-natured gossip. Upon entering the dining room, Rachel, Yitzhak's wife, was meticulously strict that Yitzhak should march ahead of us. Also, in presence of others she refers to him only as "the President" and not, God forbid, as Yitzhak. This regard for Presidential gracious manners completely disappeared when we sat at table. I found before me the knives on the left and the forks on the right. The young woman who served us – bare-armed, not in accordance with customary manners – took the trouble to accompany each serving with a rote "Please" and insisted on serving from the right until Zipporah could no longer restrain herself and corrected her.

44 Sharett (then known as Shertok) first met Ben-Zvi (then Shimshelevich) in 1913, when he came to Istanbul after graduating from the Herzliya Gymnasium in order to study Ottoman law at the capital's university. Ben-Zvi had come there from Palestine, together with David Ben-Gurion, for the same purpose a year earlier. In 1916 they cooperated in Palestine as activists in the *yishuv*'s "Ottomanization" campaign, calling upon Palestinian Jews who were citizens of European countries to take out Ottoman citizenship so that they would not be expelled as aliens by the Ottoman authorities. In 1919, Shertok joined the new labor party, *Ahdut Ha'avoda* ("Unity of Labor," precursor of Mapai), created through the merger of the *Po'alei-Zion* Party, of which Ben-Zvi was one of the major leaders, with the so-called non-partisan labor movement led by Berl Katznelson. From that time the two men met regularly as party activists and participants in its various organs. In the 1930s and 1940s, when Ben-Zvi was chairman of *Hava'ad Hale'umi* (National Council of the local *yishuv*) and Shertok headed the Political Department of the JA, the two cooperated almost daily.

When we had soup, conversation was difficult because the President slurped it from his spoon with a deafening noise. When the chicken was served, the President displayed a daring streak of creativity in the proper utilization of knife and fork while progressively the various implements at his disposal were all piled upon and around his plate in a colorful array, and scraps of meat began flying over in all directions. In my conversation with Rachel I referred to Ben-Zvi as "Yitzhak." After a few minutes she made sure to remind me of her preferred usage by once again referring to him as "the President."

After the meal Ben-Zvi began interrogating me about the conflict in the north, the Qibya raid, and the SC debate. I spoke at length, and made an effort to hold on to my self-restraint. Finally the conversation drifted to the matter of the [BG] resignation. Ben-Zvi and Rachel both think that BG must be allowed to do as he wished, but they were sure he would not resign but be given an extended vacation, so that the door should remain open for his return. Rachel, too, believed that BG's going to Sde Boker would stir up a wave of pioneering enthusiasm and galvanize the "From Town to Countryside" campaign.[45]

Ben-Zvi agreed with me that this unusual and unexpected act would add a new romantic facet to BG's persona, serve as an additional element in his hero worship, and even more forcefully attest to his uniqueness, one whose creative power defied the imagination. But it shall not have any impact whatsoever on the Israeli public.

We listened to the news broadcast at the President's residence. We heard only the tail end of BG's speech. His reading was listless, and he stumbled and misread the text several times – a sure sign of fatigue.[46]

Afterwards we heard for the first time the Reuters announcement from Washington that the grant to Israel had been postponed.

[- - -]

Tuesday, October 20

At the office I was informed that during the morning conference a discussion was held regarding the disclosure of the suspension of the grant. Until now we had kept silent, but now that it had been made public, we had to voice our criticism. It was decided – and correctly so – that there was no cause for a response from the Foreign Ministry spokesman, but the press had to be briefed. Already there was a first response to it in the *Jerusalem Post* in a fine article, an exemplary dispatch

45 A national campaign initiated and organized by the *Histadrut* in 1952 with the purpose of moving urban dwellers to settle on the land, either in new settlements or in existing ones that needed buttressing.

46 For the official English translation of the text of the broadcast justifying the Qibya operation, see *DFPI* 8, doc.449.

written by Gershon Agron.[47]

I prepared a new briefing for all our legations as to why they must reject any idea of punishing the frontier settlements which allegedly participated in the Qibya operation.[48]

I am investing much ardor in justifying an action to which I objected from the start and which infuriated me, rationally and emotionally, after the deed was done. The telegram was sent to all the capitals.

I sent a telegram to Aubrey congratulating him on the fighting spirit which is evident in his latest telegrams. I knew that once he was put to the test, he would recover his courage for the raging campaign.

Walter also sent a useful briefing to our legations explaining how to portray the debate in the SC, not as intended to establish blame for one incident or another, but for creating an opportunity for a basic solution of the problem, since the armistice regime has failed to normalize relations and guarantee stability.[49]

The Dutch Consul, who has returned from a two-month vacation in Europe, visited at 9:30. He displayed a remarkable understanding of and complete sympathy with our position on the question of the B'not Yaakov Bridge canal. I explained to him the strategic aspect in detail and the absurdity of Bennike's attitude. On the other hand, he condemned the Qibya operation mercilessly and said, albeit with friendship, that we could not be forgiven such a thing. He hinted that it resembled Deir Yasin.[50]

He recounted that he had traveled through Nablus a day or two before. When he was but a short distance from the town, the police advised him to by-pass it because of the turmoil and angry demonstrations against the authorities for their lack of a vigorous response to the massacre in Qibya. On his way back he was allowed to pass through the town and he found it desolate. All the shops were closed as a sign of protest, and a transportation strike was in progress. He was advised to remove his hat, so as not to be recognized as a foreigner and come to unwanted harm.

At 10:00, a meeting of the Knesset FADC. I lectured for an hour and a half on

47 Gershon Agron (Agronsky) (1894-1959). Born in Russia. Emigrated with his family to the US in 1899 and grew up in Philadelphia. Settled in Palestine in 1924 after working in the press office of the Zionist Commission and for the JTA. Founding editor, from 1932, of the *Palestine* (later *Jerusalem*) *Post*. Director of the Israel Government Information Services (1949-1951); Mayor of Jerusalem (1955-1959).

48 *DFPI* 8, doc.453.

49 *DFPI* 8, doc.450.

50 Reference to the April 9, 1948 attack on the Palestinian village of Deir Yasin in the Jerusalem corridor by a combined force of the *Irgun Zvai Le'umi* (*ETZEL; IRGUN*) and *Lohamei Herut Israel* (*LEHI*), also known as the "Stern Gang." Apart from the fighting, Jewish forces massacred at least 100 of the village's inhabitants, a number believed by scholars today to be correct but lower than the figure of 200-250 considered at the time and for many years to be the number of Palestinian-Arab victims, some of whom were said to have been mutilated as well. For details, see Benny Morris, *1948: A History of the First Arab-Israeli War* (New Haven / London: Yale University Press, 2008), 125-28.

the unfolding of the B'not Yaakov conflict, and explained about the link between the electric power canal and the water reservoir planned in the Beit Netofa Valley being part of the large national water carrier project. I clarified the considerations that had led us to downplay this link, and to portray the canal dredging as an independent project only meant to generate electric power. I pointed out the possibility of severe complications if the SC debate reveals that our plans collide with US plans for the regulation of water interests in the region.

Lavon reported on the Qibya affair. I was impressed – amazed, more properly – by the icy calm with which he repeated the version of the raid having been carried out by frontier vigilantes. Colonel Meir Amit[51] reported on movements of the Arab Legion, for the most part to stake defensive positions against all possible points of attack on our part. The up-to-date expertise of our military intelligence regarding developments around us in the field of military deployment could not help but make a great impression.

A debate began. Just as I had been distressed at the Cabinet meeting by the meagre support of only Rosen and Naftali for my position on the question of a work stoppage, here I was discomfited by my complete agreement with Yaakov Riftin – a most leftist MK of the Mapam Party[52] – in his repudiation of the Qibya raid specifically, and in his outlook regarding the retaliatory policy in general. But this same Riftin opposed the possibility of a work stoppage, and even censured the Cabinet for having proposed a temporary stoppage to Bennike. The continuation of the debate was postponed to another meeting which will take place in Tel Aviv on Friday.

[- - -]

At 4:00 I was back at the office and dictated the draft of a reply to [British Ambassador] Evans' note [of October 16],[53] after finding Walter's text flawed by a weakness in argument and verbosity. My text seemed exceedingly biting to Walter. He asked that it be withheld until tomorrow morning.

A telegram arrived from Aubrey in which he insisted on a fresh consideration of the decision not to stop work. I cannot see any chance of it as long as BG does not change his position, and of this there is no sign.

At 6:00 I joined the Cabinet meeting where BG resumed his report on security matters. This part of his survey was inlaid with most penetrating and enlightening remarks concerning the human factor in the Army – women's service, the relations between the sexes, and the problem of illiterate young women. At the present time

---

51 Col. Meir Amit (1921-2009). IDF Chief of Operations (1954-1958) and Deputy CoS (1956-1957). Later Head of Intelligence Branch (*AMAN*), GS, and Head of the *Mossad.*

52 Mapam (*Mifleget Hapo'alim Hame'uhedet,* the United Workers Party), a leftist, kibbutz-based party formed in 1948 by a merger of the *Hashomer Hatza'ir* party and the *Ahdut Ha'avoda* movement. The party won 15 seats in the 1951 elections. Yaakov Riftin (1907-1978), Mapam MK, served on the FADC.

53 See *DFPI* 8, doc.433; above, entry for October 16, 1953.

such women were not inducted by the Army; nearly a thousand are disqualified this way annually. But BG thinks that this regulation must be changed and the women ought to be enlisted, taught and educated by the Army, for it is their only chance of obtaining any sort of education and a smattering of culture. The Army must view it not only as an opportunity to do some good, but as a worthwhile investment in the education of the mothers who shall raise its future soldiers. This led to the educational program in the Army in general, the customary period of one month of study for each battalion, the grant of an opportunity to officers to complete at least their high school education, the transfer of focus of paramilitary activities for youth from among high-school pupils to youngsters who are outside the educational system, and more. The time and effort BG invested in studying army affairs and the discernment he displayed were admirable.

[- - -]

Upon arriving home, Elizur called to tell me that Dulles, at a press conference, had confirmed the suspension of the grant. Shamai Cahana,[54] my personal secretary, telephoned to say that the PM had called a consultation on this matter for tomorrow morning. I wondered what arguments we could raise in our defense.

Stayed up until after midnight writing the diary and reading papers. Among these I found a most heartening telegram from Reuven Shiloah. Ambassador Davis,[55] who is expediting his return to Tel Aviv contrary to his doctors' advice in the hope that he may help extricate us from our difficulties, advanced an astute and most "penetrating" thesis: the Qibya mishap took place only because of the PM's absence. Had he been on the watch, this disaster would not have taken place. I could not refrain from wiring Reuven that this theory is surprisingly close to the mark, and truly elates me.

I told Zipporah that I would resign outright if I were forced to stand before the microphone and address the people in the Land of Zion and the entire world with a fabricated description of an actual event. Alas, BG himself initiated this fabrication and its public broadcast,[56] and did so with confidence in the justice and inherent inner truth of the matter. Man's conscience is indeed a thing of wonder!

Wednesday, October 21

Scanning the morning papers I found that *Ha'aretz* – that shaky crutch – has already changed course and begun preaching a retreat from the dredging of the Jordan channel in the north.

---

54 Shamai Cahana (1924-2012). Sharett's personal secretary (1953-1956). MFA official and diplomat (1950-1989), later serving in Peru, Cuba, Romania and elsewhere.

55 Monnett B. Davis (1893-1953). US Ambassador to Israel (1951-1953).

56 Official English translation in *DFPI* 8, doc.449.

I came to the office at 8:30, and I found there a fresh approach to the statement we thought of issuing regarding the suspension of the American grant. Since Dulles himself announced it, the morning conference had come to the conclusion that it behooved the government to issue an official response. I did not approve this idea. Any response would sound like a request for charity. If we do protest, then it best be by our silence.

I wired Aubrey – as a sequel to my response last evening over his insistent demand that the decision be changed -- that Dulles' announcement serves as an additional impediment to it.

At 9:30 at the PMO, a consultation concerning the results of the suspension or cancellation of the grant. Gass and Bell[57] expressed their views with vast erudition - especially the former. Pinhas Sapir filled in after him. He spoke in plain terms, and it was he who clarified the situation. Our $50 million budgetary cut is as follows: $9 million from services and food; $13 from investment, namely development; $10 from loan payments (in other words, rolling over this amount into the future); $18 to be raised in cash, mainly through increased contributions from the fund-raising organizations. Golda and Joseph predicted that Jews would give more precisely because of the political crisis, saying "American Jews always give more in times of trouble."

I said to BG: "Depending on what caused the trouble."

He did not agree with me. Gass, who spoke after me, vigorously substantiated the hypothesis that a crisis in relations between Israel and the US government would not encourage American Jews to contribute.

I took from BG the draft of the reply to Evans with his corrections. I returned to the office and summoned Walter. I informed him of the fall of this new axe on the foreign currency budget, which will be damaging to our own budget. We both found ourselves immediately thinking of the Rangoon legation as the first victim.

I listened to Elizur's concern over the deferral of the grant. The confusion in the press reflects the confusion of the public. A briefing must be given – all the more so if we are not issuing a formal announcement. I suggested convening the political reporters at 6:00 in the evening, when I would address them.

I passed the revised draft of our reply to Evans on to the DG.[58]

[- - -]

On my way home to lunch I went over to BG and obtained his assent to the press briefing as I had conceived it, especially with regard to our own public: a warning that there would be cuts in consumption and development.

[- - -]

57 Bernard R. Bell (1913-1994). American-Jewish economist. Chief economist of the US Export-Import Bank and a consultant to the governments of Indonesia and Israel.

58 The final version is in *DFPI* 8, doc.461.

At 6:00 I received the reporters. There were about twenty of them. I explained that we were making no demands on the US. There was no contract between us concerning the grant, and there was no question of an obligation on her part. It is the United States' own business to decide whether to help Israel or not. We condemn the decision, its motivation and the way it has been exploited. All this was done to ingratiate themselves in Arab eyes. If we must protest, then we'd best do it in silence, so as not to appear to be begging for charity. I proposed some guidelines for criticism and condemnation: the injustice and folly of the attempt to stoop before the Arabs, especially when one sees the ineffectual results of British policy in that direction, and the stupidity of the assumption that, by means of economic pressure, a weak and needy country can easily be brought to its knees politically. Experience demonstrates that such countries find it possible to harness untold hidden resources of endurance. In such cases national pride triumphs over economic necessity. But the people must know what the attempt to defend their political independence and freedom of judgement entails. It was groundless to assume that the reparations payments from Germany[59] will serve as a replacement for the grant. We must address the diaspora, especially in America, to increase their aid. All the same, there was no escaping budgetary cuts, and the public must come to grips with shortages if it wants to cling to our national aims.

There were numerous questions. At 7:00 all dispersed, and only Moshe Keren[60]

---

59 On September 10, 1952 Moshe Sharett, representing Israel, and Konrad Adenauer, for the Federal Republic of Germany, signed a reparations (Hebrew: *shilumim*) agreement which was ratified and came into effect on March 21, 1953. Under its terms Germany undertook to pay an amount of DM3,450,000,000 ($845,000,000) in goods, in annual installments over a period of 14 years (between April 1, 1953 and March 31, 1966). Thirty percent was to pay for Israel's crude oil purchases in the United Kingdom. With the balance of 70%, Israel was to buy ferrous and nonferrous metals, steel, chemical, industrial, and agricultural products. Goods bought and imported under the agreement represented 12–14% of Israel's annual imports and thus made an important contribution to Israel's economy.

This was accomplished only after fierce public and painful controversy in Israel. The Knesset resolution approving direct negotiations with Germany was passed by a small majority after stormy street demonstrations staged by the *Herut* opposition and a heated three-day debate (January 7–9, 1952). For details, see *The Reparations Controversy: The Jewish State and German Money in the Shadow of the Holocaust, 1951-1952*, ed. Yaakov Sharett. Berlin/Boston: Walter de Gruyter, for the Moshe Sharett Heritage Society, 2011; Nahum Goldmann, *The Autobiography of Nahum Goldmann: Sixty Years of Jewish Life,* translated by Helen Sebba (New York: Holt, Rinehart and Winston, 1969), ch.22; Raphael Patai, *Nahum Goldmann: His Missions to the Gentiles* (University, AL: University of Alabama Press, 1987), ch.7; Nana Sagi, *German Reparations: A History of the Negotiations.* New York: St. Martin's Press; Jerusalem: Magnes Press, Hebrew University, 1986; Ronald Zweig, *German Reparations and the Jewish World: A History of Claims Conference.* Boulder & London: Westview Press, 1987.

60 Moshe Keren (1900-1955). Counsellor, London Embassy (to September 1953); journalist and member of the editorial board, *Ha'aretz.*

of *Ha'aretz* remained – the only one to have come especially from Tel Aviv. I chided him over the article in his newspaper. In its defense he maintained that, on the one hand, he sees a grand delusion concerning our ability to stand up to the entire world which is being cultivated by certain newspapers. On the other hand, there is a deep concern among many sober-minded people concerning the gravity of the imbroglio we got ourselves into. *Ha'aretz* considers itself obliged to prepare the public for the possibility of a retreat – the certainty of a retreat, actually, if the SC should order us to stop work in the north.

A long telegram from Aubrey stating that the source of the entire complication lay in the American water plan. The B'not Yaakov project had raised ire in Washington, not because of Arab land or water rights, not even because of God-only-knows what strategic advantages we would allegedly gain (in Bennike's opinion), but only because it conflicted with that plan. We had already entertained tentative thoughts and apprehensions in this regard. Now Aubrey comes along and express matters clearly and incisively.[61]

Shmuel Bendor spoke to me about the need to clarify the problem of international conventions in Israel involving German participation. Especially pressing is the matter of the Modern Music Society's Convention. I promised to look into the matter with BG, and accordingly decide whether to bring it before the Cabinet.

I drove home and took Zipporah to Dolik's house for a buffet dinner in honor of Leon Keyserling.[62]

[- - -]

Alex Lowenthal came up and chattered endlessly in my ear about the plan to transform the multitude of Israel Bonds[63] purchasers into a large grass-roots organization for aid to Israel, instead of the Zionist organizations which have lost their vigour and are beyond rejuvenation. Leon Keyserling himself asked that we meet in more intimate circumstances. He wishes to convey his thoughts on the political confrontation between us and the US government. At this party there were two men whom I did not acknowledge: Henry Montor[64] and Oscar Gass. Both of them treated me most shamefully on my last visit to the US, each in his own way, and in his own field. I was reminded of our emissaries abroad who, upon entering a reception hall, first look about to see where the Arab representatives are standing, so as not to bump into them while making their rounds.

---

61 *DFPI* 8, doc.460.

62 Leon H. Keyserling (1908-1987). US economist specializing in the fields of employment and production; frequently consulted by Israel government agencies.

63 Debt securities issued by the Government of Israel through the American Finance and Development Corporation for Israel, established in New York in 1950 with the aim of creating a second means for economic support to Israel, besides the United Jewish Appeal (UJA).

64 Henry Montor (1905-1982). Vice-Chairman, American Finance and Development Corporation for Israel (1951-1955); Vice-President, UJA.

Thursday, October 22

It was a long and heavy day, like it was way back during the Arab Revolt or the War of Independence – and without any foreboding at that.

When I came to the office at 9:00 in the morning, I was notified of a serious border incident. In the early morning a freight train had driven over a powerful mine near Eyal, north of Qalqilya – a trouble-prone spot. The train consisted of empty oil tank cars. Seven cars had been derailed and nobody had been hurt. A great disaster was miraculously avoided.

The morning papers carried a rich harvest from yesterday's press briefing: admonishment concerning the suspension of the grant, condemnation of US appeasement of the Arabs, a warning to the public about "belt-tightening." All the newspapers toed the line in presenting the case to the reader. Only *Ha'aretz*, in keeping with its charity towards the Foreign Ministry, made sure to note that the information came from the mouth of an "official spokesman." The newspaper's Jerusalem correspondent, Yaakov Rosenthal, later telephoned my office to assure me that he was not to blame. He had reported as agreed between us and could prove it by means of the teleprinter, but somebody in the editorial board had changed the wording.

Moshe Sharett speaks at *Keren Hayesod* meeting

I consulted with the DG as to how we might leak to the press our speculations regarding the role played by the US regional water plan in Bennike's opposition to the continuing of the B'not Yaakov project. Aubrey had wired that they were making an effort in this direction. The PM had suggested that the matter be disclosed by the Israeli newspapers as if it had been reported by their correspondents in the US. I accepted the DG's advice that it would be best to wire New York and entrust the version to the correspondents there, so that the story should make its way to the newspapers here through regular channels.

[- - -]

The writer Isaac Deutscher, author of the famous biographies of Trotsky and Stalin, and his wife came for a visit. They are both typical Jews, Polish refugees who found asylum in England before the war. Deutscher posed one question: Is there any prospect of peace with the Arabs, and is time enhancing this prospect, or the other way around, weakening it? I expressed my philosophy: peace shall come, albeit in good time, and we must forbear patiently ten, twenty or thirty years.[65]

[- - -]

At noon I drove to the PMO. With Nehemiah Argov I looked into proliferating rumors concerning Syrian and Iraqi army movements to reinforce Jordan, and the probable arrival already of the first detachments in the Old City of Jerusalem. The exclusive source for these rumors is Damascus Radio. The IDF knows nothing about it.

At 12:30 a meeting of the Cabinet FADC was held [with] Eshkol, Bernstein,[66] Golda, Joseph and Sapir.[67] Lavon and Shapira were absent. Bernstein said he feared a retaliation due to the railroad attack and asked that I speak to BG. I reported on developments since the Cabinet meeting: Eliahu Elath's interpretation of Selwyn Lloyd's declaration as a warning that the Anglo-Jordanian Defense Treaty would be implemented if there should be a recurrence of the Qibya action;[68] disclosure of the UNRWA[69]- US State Department regional water plan and the way it undermines

65 Isaac Deutscher (1907-1967). The noted Marxist scholar had a reputation for being anti-Zionist. He published his impressions of this visit to Israel in an article entitled "Israel's Spiritual Climate" (*The Reporter*, April-May 1954), reproduced in *The Non-Jewish Jew and Other Essays*, edited posthumously by his widow, Tamara (Oxford University Press, 1968), 91-117.

66 Peretz Bernstein (1890-1971). Born in Germany. Settled in Palestine in 1936. Leader, GZ Party. MK (1949-1965); Minister of Trade and Industry (1948-1949, 1952-1955). Editor-in-Chief, *Haboker*.

67 Yosef Sapir (1902-1972). Born in Palestine. Leader, GZ Party. MK (1949-1972). Minister of Transport (1952-1955).

68 See *DFPI* 8, doc.434.

69 United Nations Relief and Works Agency (UNRWA) for Palestine Refugees in the Near East, established by the UN in 1949.

our own project; Dulles' official confirmation of the deferral of the grant and the stirrings of protest in the US; the exemplary response of all circles of Jewish leadership to Eban's appeal, notwithstanding its devastating criticism of Israel's policy both in regard to the non-stoppage of work and, in particular, to the Qibya action (Silver[70] was especially harsh in regard to the second matter.) Golda suggested that we engage experts such as James B. Hays and G.L. Savage, American irrigation engineers of international stature, as advisors to our government to help us secure favorable press coverage of our irrigation plan.[71] I promised to wire Eban. Yosef Sapir remarked that it would be worthwhile to re-examine all stages of the project in the north that led us to this point as well as the strategy we had undertaken. This would enable us to see if we took the right course all along in light of what has since become evident (a typical Sapir proposal!). I expressed my unqualified willingness for such an examination, and promised to prepare the documents which would make it possible. I also proposed to bring the complete American water plan before the Committee as soon as we get it and after obtaining our experts' opinion of it.

After the meeting I went in to see BG who was already entirely absorbed in preparing his address for the opening of the Jerusalem Conference. He bitterly complained about the paucity of the material which had been prepared for him and for the Conference in general. I had been constantly apprehensive about it. Now "what I feared was upon me."[72] I told him about the concern expressed at the Cabinet Committee regarding any new retaliatory action at this time. He told me that he had given orders to exercise "restraint" over the railroad incident. (Ze'ev Sharef, who knew nothing of my conversation with BG on this matter, had given him an identical opinion. BG had retorted that no retaliatory action would be taken this time, adding: "Anyway, you are going to get rid of me soon.") [- - -]

At 3:00, Berl Locker[73] came to consult over the utilization of the Zionist federations at this time of crisis. I expressed my views on the situation. In each and every capital where we have a legation, it was staying in close contact with the local Zionist movement and other Jewish organizations. As far as Jewish influence on policy was concerned, the US held center stage. There our Ambassador was

---

70 Abba Hillel Silver (1893-1963). American Reform rabbi and Zionist leader, chairman of the pre-state American Zionist Emergency Council and of the American Section of the JA. Active in promoting Jewish statehood in Washington and at the UN until late 1947, clashing frequently with both Chaim Weizmann and David Ben-Gurion for their presumed lack of militancy.

71 The Hays-Savage Plan for sharing the waters of the Litani and the Jordan was commissioned by the ZO in 1948; its assumptions and recommendations followed those of Walter Clay Lowdermilk in 1944. For details, see: Stephen C. Lonergan and David B. Brooks, *Watershed: The Role of Fresh Water in the Israeli-Palestinian Conflict* (Ottawa: International Development Research Centre, 1994), 164-65.

72 *Job*, 3:25.

73 Berl Locker (1887-1972). Mapai leader. Chairman, Executive of WZO and JAE (1948-1956).

maintaining close and intensive contact with the Jewish leadership and was doing everything possible to bring its influence and pressure to bear on the government. The Zionist Council[74] was helping the Embassy stir up a protest campaign throughout the country. Similar contacts existed in England, and Eliahu Elath's initiative should be credited with the important manifestos of the Board of Deputies and the Anglo-Jewish Association against the Foreign Office. In other countries, Jewish communities had no influence over their respective governments. To the extent that Jews had connections to the press and the public at large, it was incumbent upon our legations to utilize them. Locker asked about Latin America. I said that in Argentina the Jews had no standing vis-à-vis the government or within political circles. It was impossible for them to help the Israeli Legation with influence over the government on matters concerning Israel. On the contrary. They were requesting the Legation's intervention to help in matters pertaining to the local Jewish community. In other countries – with the exception of Brazil and Mexico, where we also maintain Legations – there was a tradition of activating Jewish influence by means of contact people, who received suggestions and recommendations from the Foreign Ministry or from our delegation in New York.

I suggested to Locker that he dispatch an order to the Zionist federations that they stay in touch with Israel's legations for instructions. On my part, I promised to send a circular to our legations to avail themselves [of the federations] in assisting the Jewish communities and the Zionist movement.

I took this opportunity to voice my remarks concerning Yeshayahu Wolfsberg's[75] book on Chaim Weizmann, to be published by the Zionist Library. It was neither a biography nor a historical evaluation. It was a confession of love. Weizmann, who was a great man, was possessed of eminent virtues as well as grave flaws – all in keeping with the stature of his personality. Wolfsberg has told the man's story in a glowing light, eliminating every shadow, justifying every defect, praising every fault. All this may occasion no censure, since Wolfsberg himself confesses the shortcoming of love and expressed his preference of the subjective approach. That does not hold when it comes to the delineation of historical fact. No distortion of the truth is admissible here. No love can disguise the unseemly distortion of fact. Wolfsberg's version, according to which Weizmann was the central moving force and decisive factor at the historic campaign in the UN in 1947, is a figment of his own imagination. Except for obtaining Truman's decision in favor of including the area of Eilat in the territory of the Jewish state, Weizmann did not play any substantial role in that campaign.

---

74 The American Zionist Council (1949-1963), an umbrella lobby organization of American Jewish groups including the Zionist Organization of America (ZOA), Hadassah and other pro-Israel organizations.

75 Yeshayahu Wolfsberg (1893-1957). Born in Germany. Settled in Palestine in 1933. Rabbi, pediatrician, writer and publicist. Active in the *Hamizrahi* Party. In 1948 appointed Israel's Minister to Scandinavia. In 1956 Israel's Minister in Bern, Switzerland.

(Even this measure was due to an initiative on the part of Eliahu Elath.)[76]

This passage in Wolfsberg's work has to be rewritten or scrapped. I explained to Locker how difficult it was for me in particular to deal with this matter, but since I had been asked by the Board of the JA to go over the manuscript and express my opinion as an authority, I have no choice but to insist upon the truth.

At 4:00 I sat down to prepare my speech for the Zionist Conference [of American leaders] and worked at it until 6:00 in great mental anguish and nervous anxiety – my perennial lot prior to speaking before a large audience.

When Zipporah and I arrived at the Habima Theater to attend the Conference at exactly 8:30, we found the large hall with its wide balcony brimming with people. Many remained standing for lack of seats.

[- - -]

At 9:55 my turn came at last. I spoke for a full hour. The subject was the future relations between Israel and the diaspora. I myself had chosen this subject which preoccupies me more and more in recent years. Every one of my trips abroad adds more food for thought on it in my mind. I chose this subject over the humdrum proposal of the Conference organizers that I speak about "foreign policy," whatever that may mean. It was the second or third time I had tried to articulate my thinking on this matter in public, and I was still far from a having attained a formulation that satisfied me. I was still adding bricks to the pile, but had not yet begun to erect the building itself. At the start of my speech, I felt obliged to contradict the false idea which Yaakov Hazan[77] of Mapam had attempted to inculcate the audience prior to me. Every phrase in this part of my speech – citing the blessing of the US grants and being their recipient as a sovereign state – resembled a match thrown into a barrel of gunpowder, igniting a stormy outburst of cheers and applause. Every allusion to countries in which large numbers of Jews were cut off from their people and in which the wave of their Messianic fervor was stifled by the rule of oppression and isolation was like turning on a light switch. The main substance of my remarks was an analysis of the mutual responsibility between Israel and the diaspora, and presenting the task facing those who were engrossed in building the state in these terms: to implant within the consciousness of the people of Israel and its younger generation the sense of being an integral part of our nation scattered throughout the world. In the same measure that Israel needed to draw upon support and reinforcement from Jewish communities in the diaspora, Israel carried a commitment towards [maintaining] their stature and enriching their spiritual fiber.

I had all but collapsed in exhaustion, covered with sweat, when notes and

---

76 See Elath's detailed memoir of the period, *Hama'avak al Ham'dina: Washington 1945-1948*, 2 vols. Tel Aviv: Am Oved / Hasifriyya Hatziyyonit, 1979, 1982.

77 Yaakov Hazan (1899-1992). Born in Russia. Settled in Palestine in 1923. Leader of *Hakibbutz Ha'artzi* movement and Mapam. MK (1949-1973).

whisperings were thrust at me from all sides. I was wanted on the telephone. My wife, who was sitting behind me on the stage, wanted to speak to me immediately. I was being summoned by Jerusalem. Something urgent had come up.

I immediately left the hall with Zipporah. I learned that BG wanted me to come up to Jerusalem immediately. He was convening a Cabinet meeting at 8:00 tomorrow morning and insisted that I return to Jerusalem this very night. At first I thought there might have been another serious Arab raid, and that BG wanted to consult over a proper retaliation. His urgent summons had to do with Arab Legion movements in the vicinity of Jerusalem. I still did not understand why I had to come to Jerusalem that very night. Would BG be sitting and waiting for me? As it was, I would not be arriving before close to 1:00 am.

I tried to contact BG's home but there was no answer. I telephoned Ze'ev Sharef and he gave me clearer information. There was serious worry about an offensive operation on the part of the [Jordanian Arab] Legion this very night. This operation may block off the road to Jerusalem. In this state of affairs, BG would not like me to remain cut off from the capital. I must therefore hurry back to Jerusalem. I understood the logic of the demand, but did not regard its underlying assumption as logical. Could Jordan possibly take leave of its senses to the extent of mounting a hostile action – and against Jerusalem, of all places! – at this very hour when the SC was about to commence deliberations, when the Arab states had taken the line of condemning Israel as an aggressor, when Jordan was doing everything to set Britain at odds with us, and when it was clear that Britain would not fall in with such a provocation against us and the UN? I considered the anxiety which enveloped our men in Jerusalem to be lacking any realistic political basis, even if it did have, apparently, a realistic military basis. I also questioned the wisdom of the demand that I drive in the dead of night, specifically in view of the assumption that the capital might be blocked. That meant that in the course of the drive I might encounter Jordanian army units taking part in the hostile operation.

Zipporah immediately voiced a heated objection to this nocturnal drive. I overruled her. It is precisely at such an hour that the authority of command was necessary and had to be obeyed. There was a person who bore the crucial responsibility, and there was no other choice but to rely upon his judgment. I added that she had evidently never been a soldier. Whoever tastes but once military experience doesn't ever raise questions.

Ze'ev called again. He had called up BG, who said I must come immediately. During the night things would clear up and accordingly the Cabinet might be convened. Then Walter called. He was summoned to BG and upon being informed of the Legion movements got in touch with the British Ambassador and the British Chargé d'affaires and told them of situation. He assumed as I did that the Legion had no intention to strike.

We arrived in Jerusalem at 1:15, and I still found something to do. As was customary whenever the *Jerusalem Post* published a speech or announcement of mine which was of special importance, I telephoned the editorial offices and asked to be read the report on my speech at the Zionist Conference so that I could edit it. I did discover some awkward phrases and corrected them, also adding whole sentences. When I went to sleep at 2:00 in the morning, I asked the telephone exchange to wake me up at 7:00.

Friday, October 23

The heartless telephone rang punctually at 7:00, and I found it hard to raise my head from the pillow. And so without raising it I telephoned Ze'ev at home to ask if the meeting was still on. He said no, it wasn't, since the PM hadn't notified him at 6:00 in the morning to convene it, as they'd arranged last night. That means that the tension had eased.

I tried to go back to sleep but did not succeed and tossed in bed for another short hour, vainly seeking further sleep. I got up lazily, and went about my morning routine quite slowly. I arrived at the PMO at close to 9:30, and BG told me what had happened. During the afternoon, IDF observers had seen units of the Legion taking position and digging in around Mount Scopus, as if preparing for an attack to capture the mountain. At 5:00 an agent had notified the IDF that the attack would be mounted at night. Since we knew that night operations aren't the Arabs' forte, the IDF had proceeded under the assumption that the attack might take place early in the morning.[78]

It was clear to the PM and CoS that hostile action on the part of the Legion at this was time completely devoid of political acumen. Nevertheless, they could not rule out [the possibility of] Jordanian aggression only on the basis of suppositions stemming from political logic, when first-hand evidence bore witness to its feasibility. Therefore the PM had taken the liberty of troubling me at night. He had also asked Rokach to return to the capital immediately, as the senior member of his Knesset faction. He was sorry to have troubled me, but under the circumstances there was no other choice.

I came to the office and Walter rounded out the report. When BG had notified him of the information that had been received, he had asked him quite simply: Do you consider a Legion attack desirable or undesirable? BG resolutely said that it was altogether undesirable. In that case, said Walter, let us tell the English and Americans what we know, and prompt them to stand in the breach. BG had agreed and then Walter had driven to the office and telephoned Evans and Russell in Ramat Gan and Gilbert in Jaffa. They had gathered at Evans' and at 2:00 in

78 Cf. *DFPI* 8, doc.462.

the morning the latter telephoned Walter informing him that they had contacted Amman. In the meantime he hoped Israel would not take any *anticipatory* [italicized word in English in the original] action. Walter gave his word that there was no fear of that.

It was clear that the intention behind the Legion movements, which evidently did take place, was to take up defensive positions against the possibility of an attack on our part in light of the Qibya raid. The Jordanians had every reason to interpret that operation as an initial provocation for the purpose of inciting a war.

[- - -]

I dictated a detailed telegram to Elath in London regarding a verbal response to Selwyn Lloyd's allegations. This was a sequel to my written reply to Evans' letter.[79] It was based on it and brought it to further completion. I dictated a memorandum to be wired to our legations clarifying our position on UNRWA's – i.e., the State Department's – regional water plan, and how we should present it in talks with government officials, the diplomatic corps, and in our briefings to the press. I dictated a telegram to Eban about mobilizing experts' public support of our water plan, and the rejection of Gordon Clapp's proposal.[80]

As one of the main bulwarks of our position, I pointed out that in the UNRWA-Clapp – or State Department – plan there was an utter disregard of the existence of the Litani River.[81] They were taking half or most of the Jordan's water away from us for the purpose of irrigating areas in Jordan and even in Syria; in so doing, they were giving a kiss of death to the plan to exploit the Jordan's surplus water to irrigate the Negev, thereby precluding any large-scale agricultural

79 *DFPI* 8, docs.433 and 461. A week later, Eban and Lloyd continued discussion of these issues in New York. See Lloyd memo of conversation, October 28, 1953, The National Archives of the United Kingdom (TNA – formerly Public Record Office, PRO), London, FO961/14.

80 Also known informally as the "TVA plan", the "Unified" plan, and the "Main" plan, presented to UNRWA and to the American government in August 1953 in response to a 1952 request by UNRWA. See Miriam R. Lowi, *Water and Power: The Politics of a Scarce Resource in the Jordan River Basin* (Cambridge: Cambridge University Press, 1993), 83-88. In August 1949, Gordon Clapp (1907-1963) – head of the Tennessee Valley Authority (TVA) in the US – was appointed to the UN Economic Survey Mission, whose mandate was to recommend ways to promote a major economic development program that could help reintegrate the Palestinian refugees into the economic life of the ME and promote peace in the region. Faced with insurmountable political and emotional obstacles, Clapp and his colleagues submitted an Interim Report in November 1949, which recommended that the UN GA establish an agency and provide it with enough funds and authority to carry out both sustained relief efforts and also a public works program. The final Report was submitted on December 18, 1949.

81 The Litani River runs exclusively through Lebanese territory. The distance from its nearest point to Israel – where it changes its north-to-south course and starts flowing westward towards the Mediterranean Sea – is about 6 km.

development there. For this reason alone we shall fight against it; but were we to be offered the Litani's water as compensation for the Jordan's which was being taken away from us, it would be an entirely different matter. I also pointed out, to both Washington and the legations, the principal danger today: on the one hand, freezing our own efforts on the pretext that we must avoid undermining the regional plan by a *fait accompli*; on the other hand, the lack of any progress towards a regional settlement because of the Arabs' refusal to cooperate with us in such a settlement, and, furthermore, to trust us in view of their water sources and reservoirs placed within Israel's borders. The result is that American policy was once again pursuing a direction which may be defined as dissatisfaction guaranteed on all sides.

[- - -]

Precious Waters

Saturday, October 24

[- - -]

Milton Fried telephoned to say that the American Embassy had received information from Washington that necessitated an urgent interview. He apologized for speaking directly to me since he had not been able to find our staff. When could Russell see me? I made an appointment for 6:30.

I sat over the Clapp (UNRWA-State Department) regional water plan, and reviewed its main points to myself. The plan completely ignores international borders, and views the Jordan basin as a single hydrological unit. Its purpose is to facilitate maximal irrigation at minimal cost. For this reason it is almost entirely based on gravitation, and encompasses in the main those lands which can be irrigated in this manner. This principle limits the plan to the Jordan Valley between the Lake Kinneret[1] and the Dead Sea, on both sides of the river, and precludes diversion of the Jordan waters to the Negev. To sum up: an area of 234,000 acres will be watered, of which 104,000 are in Israel, 122,500 in Jordan, 7,500 in Syria. Regarding Israel the division is as follows: 17,750 in the the upper Hula Valley, 7,500 around Ayelet Hashahar, 28,250 in Lower Galilee, 5,500 in the Yavniel Plain, 22,750 in the eastern Jezreel Valley, and 22,250 acres in the area called "Western Ghor." The amount of water to be collected for irrigation totals 1,213 million cubic metres [m^3] per annum, of which 394 is for Israel, 774 for Jordan, 45 for Syria. The striking discrepancy between the size of areas and amount of water is due to the differences in the water allowance per acre in the north and south. The farther south one goes in the Jordan Valley, the more the land needs water due to both high temperature and salinity; the minimal allowance in the northern Hula Valley is 192.5 m^3 per acre per annum, and 465 in the southern Jordan Valley.

Lake Kinneret will serve as a central regulatory reservoir into which the surplus waters of the Jordan and the Yarmuk will be channeled. The water level of the Kinneret will rise by two meters. From the overall supply of water from the Jordan's three sources including the Hula springs, which comes to 640 million m^3 per annum, 300 million m^3 will be allotted for irrigation in Israel by means of a

1 Also known as the Sea of Galilee, or Lake Tiberias.

diversionary channel from the Hasbani reservoir. The remainder – 340 million m^3 – will continue to flow through the Jordan into the Kinneret, even though not all of it will be devoted to irrigation because of losses incurred due to evaporation from the Kinneret (this is one of the plan's weaknesses!). Nor will all the rest be lost to Israel, for some of it will irrigate our sections of the Jordan and Bet-She'an Valleys. Nevertheless, the net loss to Israel is manifest. In reckoning this loss, the drop in the Dead Sea's water level must be included: 85 meters over 200 years, until the inflow of water balances the evaporation from a lower and more limited surface area. This reduction of the Dead Sea will not change its shape in the north, where the shores are steep, but large portions of its shallow southern half will entirely dry up. At any rate, the change is bound to have a far-reaching effect on the Potassium Works. The picture invoked by the entire plan cries out for the Litani.

I wasted endless time trying to reach Pinhas Sapir and Aharon Wiener by telephone. I wished to find out whether they were studying the plan, and to ask Wiener about the flow of the Litani. My phone calls were to no avail.

My brother-in-law Shaul dropped by to enquire about BG's resignation, which was deeply troubling him. He asked me if I thought that BG was serious. I said yes, without a shadow of doubt. He asked if the *haverim* had begun to discuss the future. I said no, the subject was taboo, because we were still in the midst of campaigning against the resignation. He asked if I was aware of the details of the Qibya action, and why the women and children had not been evacuated from the buildings. I said no, I was not. I had asked the CoS, Mordechai Maklef, for the operational report. He had promised to send it to me, but had not done so. After a day or two I had had the opportunity of asking Nehemiah Argov if there were any of "my people" – that is, in the private secretariat – in the PMO. He became angry and protested: "We are all yours!" I told him: "'My people' means that when I ask for a report on something they deliver it immediately. Now I have asked for an operation report on Qibya and I have yet to be given it. Can you get it for me?" He said: "Of course! You'll get it immediately!" To this day I have not received it.[2]

I went out to accompany Shaul, and we strolled in front of the house because his car had not yet arrived. When I saw Russell and Fried getting out of their car, I returned inside with them.

Russell began with the subject of Eric Johnston's visit. The Arabs, we know,

2 In her biography of Pinhas Lavon, Eyal Kafkafi writes: "Following the PM's radio speech, Lieut.-Col. Rehavam Ze'evi was ordered by the GS to destroy all copies of the Qibya operation[al order], but he kept one copy which he sealed with red wax and labeled: 'This is the sole copy at the disposal of IDF. All other copies were destroyed by order of the Security Officer after the PM's speech.' It is possible that this was one of the reasons for Sharett's difficulty to receive the operational report he had requested." *Pinhas Lavon - Anti-Messiah*, 177.

have launched a smear campaign against him because of his supposed excessive sympathy for Israel. Under the circumstances, the State Department would like to avoid unnecessary complications, and therefore asks if we would agree to conduct our talks with him in Tel Aviv. I immediately said that on my part, and insofar as it concerns myself and those subordinate to me, I am quite willing not to mix issues. I would just venture to hope that the State Department too will go back on its wrong position in due course. He immediately promised to relay my remarks. I added that I could not speak for the PM. He's very sensitive about this issue. After all, he had not moved to Jerusalem as I had with the Foreign Ministry in July but has been residing in the capital these past years, and he has become used to receiving the most distinguished visitors from the US there, including the Secretary of State himself.[3]

I asked when Johnston was coming and found out that he was already in Amman, and could be expected any day. I said I would be occupied with the Jerusalem conference on Monday and Tuesday, but free from Wednesday on. I made a note to myself that we must prepare meticulously before meeting with Johnston about the water issue. We must re-examine and refresh our memory on the data concerning the Litani, and make a strong effort to place this new subject at the center of our discussions with the US.

I received a call from the office to say that urgent telegrams had arrived which required a telephone call to Washington tomorrow at the latest. An envelope had been sent to me which I must, upon arrival, immediately read its contents.

[- - -]

Towards evening our dinner guests began to arrive. They were Samuel Gottesman[4] from New York, a very rich man, an important donor who helped with the purchase of the Dead Sea scrolls, currently abstaining from investments in Israel; his daughter and son-in-law by the name of Ungerlaider, he is a newspaper editor in Atlantic City; an old man named William Saltzman and his wife, he is a dedicated, long-time Zionist, excelled in his efforts for the *Hagana*[5] during the years of crisis, invested heavily in Maiser's paper mill in Hadera, an important donor, visiting Israel for the fifth time, fluent in Hebrew; the conductor Leonard

3 John Foster Dulles had toured the ME in May 1953, visiting Israel on May 13 and 14.

4 Samuel David Gottesman (1884–1956). US merchant and financier; established the D. S. and R. H. Gottesman Foundation in 1941 to donate funds for higher education, local welfare, Jewish studies and other causes. Among the foundation's charitable contributions were four Dead Sea Scrolls, purchased for the State of Israel in 1955, and the donations of funds in 1961 for the construction of the Shrine of the Book in Jerusalem to house the Dead Sea Scrolls at the Israel Museum. See below, entries for February 13 and 24, 1955.

5 *Hagana* (lit. defense). A Jewish underground paramilitary organization founded in 1920 in Mandatory Palestine by the Zionist labor movement, subsequently answerable to the JAE. After May 1948 became the core of the IDF.

Bernstein[6] and his Chilean-born wife; the mayor of Tel Aviv, Chaim Levanon[7] and his wife; and Chaya Fischer.

I held forth during dinner. Both old and young were spell-bound by my stories and anecdotes of times gone by. The atmosphere became extremely amiable and warm. The conversation came round to the turbulence of today, when the subject of Qibya reared its head. I told them about Nathan Alterman's[8] weekly column in *Davar* which yesterday was devoted to the matter.

The guests, who came from so far away, considered the moral issue as if they were one of us. They had all been enthralled by their tours and what they'd seen. When I remarked that we needed settlers from America like the very breath of life, Gottesman's daughter, a woman with a frank and warm spark in her eyes, said to me: "Tell that to my husband!"

Our dear guests enjoyed sitting and talking so much that they did not leave – as though they had forgotten they were in someone else's home and were entirely unaware of the late hour. Finally Mrs Levanon got up to depart, and only then did the rest of the company take heed of the fact that they would not be sleeping in our home tonight. Even then they lingered for a long time in the hallway.

The moment they left I seized the envelope which had arrived during the meal. It contained one telegram after another from Aubrey – long, detailed and full of surprises.[9] The State Department has begun pulling back from its suspension of the grant. Byroade had hinted in conversation with Aubrey, and fully confessed in conversation with Proskauer,[10] that the State Department had committed a blunder and that Dulles was now interested in repairing the mistake, instructing Byroade to find an honorable way out of the situation. There was a proposal concerning our work on the Jordan diversion. We should immediately inform the State Department that if the SC turns to us and asks for a short stoppage of work during the time of the debate, we will comply; and once we have complied, the grant will be renewed. In effect this is a return to my proposal at the last Cabinet meeting, but it is far better that it emanate from an understanding with a shamefaced, repentant State Department than we should first hold out our hands to them.

Reading and digesting the telegrams took up the greater part of an hour. I came up against several incomprehensible points and telephoned Walter half a dozen times. Like myself he was still working into the night reading documents at his home. I consulted him about several obscure points. Much more material has

6 Leonard Bernstein (1918-1990). American Jewish composer, conductor and pianist.

7 Chaim Levanon (1899-1986). Mayor of Tel Aviv (1953-1959).

8 Nathan Alterman (1910-1970). Poet, playwright, translator; published a popular weekly political column in verse in *Davar*, entitled "The Seventh Column."

9 See *DFPI* 8, docs.468-69.

10 Justice Joseph M. Proskauer (1877-1971). Honorary President, American Jewish Committee (AJC).

been provided for my report to the Cabinet tomorrow.

Within the pile of documents I discovered Blass' initial summary of the Clapp plan. While reading it now I happily realized that I had previously succeeded in mastering the main points of this complex, technically-detailed plan on my own.

When I finished studying the telegrams, Zipporah brewed some strong hot tea and sat down opposite me to read the weekly crop of my diary. The quiet around us banished the fatigue and dissipated the anxiety that has lately accumulated within me. Perhaps these latest telegrams from New York were a first ray of light slipping through a narrow fissure in the gloom of overhanging clouds? Indeed, US Jewry hasn't lost its vigour. It has raised its voice of protest against the injustice to Israel, and it was able to force a man as tough and unyielding as Dulles to reconsider his actions and seek conciliation.

I took to bed at 2:00 am in order rise at 6:00.

Sunday, October 25

At 7:30 I was driven to Jerusalem. Before the Cabinet meeting I went into BG's office and asked him about his reaction to Aubrey's latest telegrams. As is his habit in such cases, when the time has come to retreat from a cherished position, there being no recourse but to make a compromise, he did not say a word to defend the former position. But I understood from the tenor of his remarks that he would come to terms with the compromise. He told me that he had finished preparing the outline for his opening speech at the American [Jewish] conference [in Jerusalem], and had found it too long. He is therefore engrossed now in shortening it. Between the Security Council confrontation and the Jerusalem conference matters, I squeezed in a short inquiry regarding the PEN[11] and Israel Modern Music Society Conventions at which Germans are invited to participate. I found him resolved to take an affirmative position, and ready to do battle with those who would keep the Germans out.

Moshe Shapira and Yosef Burg were late for the Cabinet meeting, and asked to postpone my review until their return. I took advantage of the opportunity and brought up the PEN and Music Society issue. There was a keen argument, in which Golda took the extreme view, and Rokach supported her. By a large majority it was decided to let both conventions be held in Israel, but to announce that we reserve the right to inquire into the past of every participant. BG was a tower of strength.

I spoke at length, first on the Clapp plan, and then about political developments in the US – the State Department's repentance over the suspension of the grant, Byroade's talks with Eban and Proskauer (avoiding any mention of the latter's name), the proposal for a combined solution to both the northern [B'not Yaakov]

11 International PEN ("poets, essayists, novelists"), a worldwide association of writers founded in London in 1921 to promote friendship and intellectual co-operation among writers everywhere.

project predicament and the crisis over the grant. There was general opposition to Moshe Dayan's proposal, which the delegation in New York had endorsed, to seek the immediate renewal of the American grant before the SC debate began, so that we could agree there to stop work temporarily. Lavon attacked this proposal, and others joined in. They were opposed to any manouvering concerning the grant. On the other hand, the large majority accepted Byroade's proposal that in response to a "courteous" appeal to us from the SC – free of condemnation for our not stopping work until now and not formulated as an order, perhaps not even a Council resolution, but rather a request from its Chairman – we would immediately announce that we were willing to stop work temporarily in order to create a relaxed atmosphere for the debate. Golda was opposed to this too, and suggested that we make no decision, but wait until the SC demands that we stop working, and only then according to the wording of its decision. This dear and worthy woman betrays a surprising lack of practical political instincts. The GZ leaned heavily towards a compromise solution. Only Serlin[12] remained obstinate. When I proposed to instruct Eban to make an effort to obtain a US promise to adopt a supportive position at the debate regarding to the project itself, making continued work conditional only upon the protection of individual rights of the Arab landowners, Serlin suggested that we state this position in advance as a condition of our willingness to stop work. Both Golda and Serlin remained solitary champions of their respective positions. Rokach, with ingenuous cunning, insisted on hearing the PM's position. BG ignored his bothersome questions, and proceeded to a vote without revealing his opinion. A large majority voted in favor of the proposed solution. The chairman did not vote. He was clearly in favor of the solution. Nevertheless he did not want to have a hand in the decision.

At the end of the debate, I pointed out that in principle we had not scored a victory over the State Department. They had held up the grant because we had refused to stop working. Now we are about to stop, and then the grant will be renewed. Nevertheless, we have profited in three ways which, although not decisive, are not unimportant. First, we have gained time and made progress working – even though this progress does not determine its future. Second, the appeal to us will be most restrained, bearing no condemnation, as if there were no indictment of our defiance of Bennike. Third, the State Department had come to us, not we to them, to search for a way out of the imbroglio. The Cabinet ministers were deeply impressed by the fact that when Proskauer (I withheld his name) asked Byroade if Eban had demanded any satisfaction for the insult of holding back the grant, he replied: "It isn't Eban who needs the payment of the grant, but the Secretary of State!"

With this decision there was finally some hope that we may extricate ourselves from the crisis in our relations with the US, but it is still anyone's guess how matters

12 Yosef Serlin (1906-1974). Leader, GZ Party; Minister of Health (1953-1955).

will turn out during the debate regarding the project itself. Will the SC be satisfied with the conditions imposed in the past for the draining of the Hula, or will it impose stricter terms? Above all, will the US decree a prohibition of the entire project so that it doesn't interfere with Clapp's "grand" plan?

[- - -]

Yitzhak Navon sent me the notes which BG prepared for his speech tonight at the American conference. I made a few comments on some of the details, but I was unable to propose fundamental corrections at this late hour. For the most part, the speech was a review of the past, in the best the Ben-Gurionesque tradition of beginning at the beginning, while the main goal of the conference was to direct its participants towards the future, its needs and prospects. The speech was faultily constructed as well; in fact, it lacked any structure.

[- - -]

BG began his speech at an extremely lofty level and in eloquent and expressive English. His opening phrases immediately riveted his audience, and elevated them to an exalted spiritual plane. It was truly a magnificent appearance of the "Old Man." Everyone present must have thought: here is the man who can give unique expression to the eternal values of Judaism and Israel. But immediately after the opening passage he got derailed. The thread running through the speech snapped, and he began meandering from one subject to another with no apparent connection or well-considered transition. His English also suffered lapses, and fell apart in its misuse of idiom, grammar, syntax and diction. His verbosity was also overwhelming – an hour and a half. At the end he again soared upwards, but the overall impression was one of fatigue and lack of a coherent vision, a hovering over reality and an escape from it by flights into other worlds.

I came home at 11:00 and sat down over my papers. Among them was a letter from Gideon Rafael in New York, in which Moshe Dayan [is reported to have] said there that I hadn't opposed Qibya and that the PM had expressed his satisfaction over the operation,[13] and that he himself was convinced that continued infiltration and consequent retaliations must lead to war and there was no escaping it.

Monday, October 26

I had thought that the morning session of the conference began at 10:00 and that I would have time to drop by in the office, but it turned out that it began at 9:00, so I drove directly to the King David.

Berl Locker delivered a welcoming speech. It is quite strange that he is not the least hesitant about coming forth with a dull speech which is nothing but a rehash

13 *DFPI* 8, doc.464.

of BG's speech of last night and at any rate contains not an iota of originality. Yet, nevertheless, he believes himself highly honored as the chairman of the JA's Board of Directors.

Following Locker, Lieutenant Colonel Mattityahu Peled[14] (is he a delight!) spoke on the security problems of the state and the organization of the IDF. It was a wonderful appearance, doing great justice not only to the IDF but to the pick of our youth as well. BG gave him a proper and most generous introduction – relating his entire life story, his having been groomed in the *Hagana* and the *Palmach*,[15] having been wounded during the War of Independence, having risen through the ranks in the IDF. (True to nature, BG could not restrain himself from straying from the subject and sailing far afield by describing in detail the last campaign in the Negev. When BG has a story dear to his heart, he cannot hold back from telling it whether his listener is interested or not. Actually, his main motive in talking is always his wish to express himself rather than a need to state or explain anything.) Matti spoke excellent English – simple, cultivated, precise and lucid – like the speech of an educated and refined English officer. His lecture was structured with great talent to focus on the heart of the matter, an abstention from cumbersome details, the clarification of fundamental concepts and the choice of the most apt expressions and definitions. With it all he displayed a winning modesty and a thoroughness worthy of respect. My amazement knew no bounds. I later told him what I thought of the speech, including a few words of criticism, and asked him to convey my remarks to his wife.

As for the content of the lecture, two implicit conclusions stood out: first, that the Army regarded the existing border with Jordan as utterly illogical, and it was convinced that it had to be replaced with a linear one; and second, that the Army was bent on a war to conquer the remainder of the western Palestine.

When the morning speeches ended, the debating session began. It was actually long on questions, and short on views. BG dealt with two subjects: "the socialist regime in Israel" and the Qibya affair.

Then came my turn. At first it had been assumed that the debate would go on until 12:30 and I would have an hour left. However, by 11:00, as there were no more questions or remarks, BG cut it short and I was given a broad canvas upon which to range. Last evening and this morning I had covered a page

14 Mattityahu Peled (1923-1995). Chief Instructor, Military College, IDF; Head of Training Department, Instruction Branch, IDF (November 1954-1956); later Major General, Head of Logistics Department, GS.

15 *Palmach* (Heb. abbreviation of *plugot mahatz*, strike force). Elite force of the *Hagana* established in May 1941. Its members were stationed in kibbutzim throughout the country where they trained for two weeks and worked two weeks alternately for their up-keep. *Palmach* forces played a major role in Israel's War of Independence and enjoyed an autonomous command structure. In November 1948 *Palmach* command was dismantled by Defense Minister David Ben-Gurion, who insisted that the Army could have only one unified command.

with notes. I began with an additional explanation concerning "socialism" and I elaborated upon workers' initiative and the *Histadrut*[16] holding companies. I described the development of Israel's society and economy, and the crucial role played in this process by the collective responsibility and initiative of the organized worker, whose production had been integrated and continues to be integrated within the framework of society and the economy at large. I explained that it was nothing other than the embracing implementation of the two principles hallowed in America – freedom of initiative, and equal opportunity. In the context of Israeli life, these principles mean freedom of initiative not only for the capitalist but for the worker as well; not only for the individual or company of stockholders, but for the workers' collective and a country-wide workers' organization. I refuted the allegations of excessive privilege and the fable concerning the compulsion upon investors to hand over 51 percent of all shares to the *Histadrut*. I said that this regime of mixed forms of ownership and production within a national framework was a characteristic element of the Israeli economy. The government's task was to ensure equal opportunity for all these forms, to coordinate and unite them.

When I came to the crucial part of my talk, I began with an explanation of the problem of achieving peace with the Arab states. Just as building and establishing the state was the labor of the entire life-span of a generation, so too was the project of peace. I described the tremendous shock in Arab consciousness caused by the sudden emergence of the State of Israel in the heart of this region, the factors which delay the surrounding countries' acceptance of the reality of the state's existence, the patience we must exercise on our part over a lengthy period of expectation of compromise and peace, and the conclusion which arose from all this: that the less we press for peace – the more we shall expedite its coming. I analyzed the situation created by the Armistice Agreements, and the contradiction between the static nature of these accords, on the one hand, and the needs of development and progress in Israel through the transformation of established geographical facts and the creation of new realities, on the other. This has led to inevitable clashes and conflicts – political and sometimes military – between us and the neighboring states, sometimes involving conflict with UN authorities, which the imperatives of state-building sometimes impel us to defy. Finally, I touched upon the contrast between us and the Arab states in our network of relations with the Western powers, and the threat to our standing posed by our neighbors' quantitative advantage in land, population, natural resources and

16 *Histadrut* (Hebrew, lit. "organization"). The General Federation of Labor in Israel, a powerful umbrella organization created in 1920 initially to protect and advance the interests of immigrant Jewish workers in Mandatory Palestine. More than a trades-union, it created and operated agricultural and industrial cooperatives, corporations and an extensive health-care, social-services and cultural network.

advantageous geographic position. I pointed to the assets upon which we could rely as a counterweight to these advantages: the full exploitation of our own potential from a military and geopolitical standpoint, the cultivation of our special political and spiritual values, the utilization of the support offered us on the part of Jewish communities in the diaspora throughout the free world, and the sympathy of the democratic, progressive world for our endeavor. I ended with a call for an active Jewish unity, and the grooming of the younger generation to carry the burden of this union onward, and deriving strength and purpose from it in the future.

I spoke for two whole hours, and when I realized it I was embarrassed and regretted my annoyance with BG, who had spoken for only an hour and a half last night. But I must admit that the audience was completely attentive. Before me I saw faces concentrated and eyes sparkling. I was interrupted several times by lively applause, not in response to flights of oratory but in response to the bare articulation of essentials. I myself was satisfied that there was a tight cohesion between its several parts. I had an inner confidence in the worthiness and logic of my remarks, and I felt the verve with which I was speaking was justified.

When I finished, I was bombarded with a generous shower of compliments and praise. A few Americans said that their whole trip would have been worthwhile if only for this one speech. The Canadians were also spellbound. The stream of praise did not stop all day. My first emotion upon finishing the speech was one of intense relief, but after only a short while, as is usual with me, more ideas which I hadn't developed and apt phrases which I failed to employ came to mind, to my great torment.

[- - -]

Haim[17] came to Jerusalem to see me. He looked most lovely in his short leather jacket and summer khaki trousers. I served him tea and cakes and we fixed a date for my lecture in Hamadiya. Then he opened his heart and told me of his dream to work among Jews in the East [the Soviet bloc]. He said he was aware of his lack of command of the languages, but was sure he would be able learn. He yearns for adventurous and risky undertakings. His trouble is being born too late to be able to serve in the Jewish Brigade or the *Palmach*, in the bringing in of "illegal" immigration to Palestine, or in the fighting of the War of Independence. But he must take part in activity among east European Jews. After all, it's a family undertaking. I myself and Shaul are partners in this sphere.[18]

I had dinner at the King David [Hotel] with Nahum Goldmann. He milked me for information on BG's resignation. In his opinion, if BG was serious, he should be allowed to go and maybe it's for the best. We exchanged ideas about

17 Haim Sharett (1933-). Sharett's youngest son, member of Kibbutz Hamadiya.

18 See note 25 page 6.

the Qibya affair, the solution to the SC predicament and the grant, and so on. According to Nahum, the latest rumor has it that BG had Golda in mind for PM. He let me know that BG's talk with the GZ, evidently about his retirement, would take place tomorrow.

We went down to the evening session. I listened to the debate that had begun at the afternoon session. There were many speakers and their remarks displayed great zeal and dedication. Deep satisfaction with the conference and its inspiration was also expressed. A recurring motif was criticism of the competition between the fund-raising organizations in the US and the squabbles among their leaders. Unity and central authority were demanded. The affirmative and realistic line was laid down by Joe Schwartz,[19] whose speech ended the evening session. He made an effort to prove that all this talk about strife and contention was wholly exaggerated, that what characterized Jewish life in the US today was decisive unity in devotion to Israel, that the two separate frameworks of financial endeavor – the UJA and Development Bonds – were the product of necessity as was the partnership between the Appeal, which is principally directed towards Israel, and the local welfare funds. He emphasized that we had to increase our efforts in both directions without wasting energy over an impossible merger.

Tuesday, October 27

[- - -]

I met with hydrological engineer Wiener to look into some questions concerning our water plans, both in themselves and as well as vis-à-vis the Clapp plan. This consultation had a twofold purpose: to prepare for my speech at the conference, and for my conversation with Eric Johnston tomorrow.

I heard the last half of Dov Joseph's speech. It was an impressive report on the mineral deposits discovered, the chances of exploiting them and the possibilities yet undetermined – oil above all. He sowed a spirit of great, perhaps exaggerated, optimism. He spoke warmly and persuasively. Jokes have begun to make the rounds that the Americans would soon be asking us for a grant for them for the purpose of building an infrastructure.

I had been wondering whether to speak about the B'not Yaakov crisis or to let it be, but in response to the requests of many, from both our own Israelis and among the delegates, I took up the subject. Only after I had begun did I realize the length and intricacy of the affair I had to discuss and explain: the substance of the Armistice Agreement with Syria, the Syrian invasion of the Mishmar Hayarden area

---

19 Joseph J. ("Joe") Schwartz (1899-1975). Chairman, European Committee of the American Jewish Joint Distribution Committee (JDC – also known as "the Joint"), (1950-1951); Executive Vice-Chairman, UJA (1951-1955); Vice-President, Israel Bonds Organization (1955-1970).

in 1948 which hadn't been repelled, UN mediator Ralph Bunche's[20] innovative idea of establishing a DMZ, the non-resolution of the question of sovereignty in the DMZ, the origin of Syria's demand for border corrections, the history of the Syria-Israel border that had been drawn by England and France after WWI, and the conflict which preceded it, the history of the conflict over the draining of the Hula lake, the favorable principles which had been fixed as a result, the restrictions imposed upon us with regard to individual rights of Arab landowners, the B'not Yaakov canal's importance as a power-generating project and as a link in the chain of the grand irrigation plan, the data in our hands at the start of the project, Syria's appeals and Bennike's pronouncements, and the situation as we come to the SC debate. My remarks were quite lengthy, lasting over an hour and a half. Many took notes.

At the afternoon session of the conference, Dolik Horowitz spoke on the stages of our progress towards economic independence. He made a big impression with his explanatory ability and erudition. Meanwhile, tension grew at the conference over the problem of the rival competing institutions – [United] Appeal and [Israel] Bonds – in the US. BG was supposedly trying to work out a compromise between the two groups.

I drove to BG's to obtain his assent that, if Johnston should want to meet with him, he would have to come to Jerusalem. In unaccustomed fashion BG himself began with the matter of his resignation. It was the first time he had ever brought up this subject in private conversation with me. He told me that the GZ had come to him this morning and expressed concern over the fate of the coalition in his absence. His *haverim*, they had said, did not firmly believe in the coalition and were hostile to their partners. BG tried to put them at ease, and assured them we were all united and that his *haverim* were no worse than himself. He rejected their demand for a deputy premiership: it would mean two governments and was a bad precedent in general. He also stated that there was no justification for giving them additional Cabinet posts, and that at any rate they must not provoke a crisis upon his retirement. He promised them that he would talk to each one of us concerning their complaints of non-cooperation. It was his impression that he had convinced them.

I told BG it did not seem at all likely to me that they had accepted the verdict. They would have to be the purest of saints to content themselves with lean pickings now, and not take advantage of the opportunity at hand. Undoubtedly, they viewed his retirement as a devastating blow to the position of our party in the government and in the country as a whole. It was therefore just improbable that they should not try to turn the situation to their advantage by posing new demands. Could they be expected to push things even so far as to break up the coalition and force

20 Dr Ralph J. Bunche (1904-1971). American academic and diplomat, seconded to the UN. Director of its Trusteeship Department (1947-1954), Under-Secretary for Special Political Affairs (1955-1957), and later Under-SG. His role as mediator resulting in the signing of the GAAs between Israel and Egypt, Jordan, Lebanon, and Syria in 1949 earned him the Nobel Peace Prize.

new elections? BG had no reply. It is interesting to what an extent this man with his penetrating mind can delude himself with wishful thinking when the matter concerns a burning desire in his heart. His strong desires overrule his logic.

At 6:15 we set out for Tel Aviv. I sank down in the seat hoping to nap. Suddenly Gideon stopped the car in mid-course and jumped out: there was DG's car stopped in the middle of the road in the dark, with Mordechai the driver tinkering under the hood trying to fix something. We collected Walter and continued. On the way, he asked me if I had seen the exchange of telegrams between Dayan in New York and CoS Major-General Mordechai Maklef here concerning the removal of a certain "plug" in the Jordan, and if I had any idea what it was all about. Some change was evidently in the making. Nothing had been said to us in the Foreign Ministry. We were once again about to face a *fait accompli*; but above all, the SC would be handed a surprise just as it sets out to debate the issue. I said that I had certainly seen the telegrams before I left, and I had resolved to look into the matter this very evening.

I told Walter of the Canadians' praise for Michael Comay.[21] He reported what Yosef Nevo,[22] our Consul in Montreal who was currently in Israel, had related about the daring and combative exploits of my friend Sam Bronfman[23] – Canada's mighty baron – who has stubbornly refused to visit Israel these many years despite all our invitations and appeals. A few years ago he had $100 million; today his fortune undoubtedly reaches a billion. He is the wealthiest man in the western hemisphere, perhaps in the whole world. He made his first fortune smuggling liquor to the US during the era of Prohibition, and has done well since in the manufacture of whiskey and other such elixirs. One of his new business ventures alone brings in $40 million a year. He hands out money right and left to a variety of institutions in order to strengthen his position in Canada and the US and to forestall any possible disaster. He donated $1.5 million to Columbia University and a million dollars to McGill University. He gives a lot of money to Canada's Liberal Party. The Catholic Church is another one of his beneficiaries. His greatest fear is that a law specifically drafted to target him might be passed, for example, taking from every capitalist of everything in excess of $500 million. In such a case he would lose hundreds of millions at one stroke, and would be the only victim of such a law. For this reason he makes such an effort to appease all influential circles with donations. With regard to his donations for the needs of Israel and Jewry at large, Nevo had calculated that in relation to Bronfman's wealth, his overall contribution

21 Michael S. Comay (1908-1987). Born in South Africa. Settled in Palestine in 1946. Israel Minister (1953-1954) and Ambassador (1954-1957) to Canada; later Deputy-DG, MFA, and Israel Permanent Representative to the UN.

22 Yosef Nevo (1919-2001). Born in the USA. Settled in Palestine in 1922. Israel Consul to Montreal (1952-1955).

23 Samuel (Sam) Bronfman (1891-1971). Canadian Jewish businessman and philanthropist. Acquired Seagram Distillery under which he created a financial empire.

was equivalent to a contribution of only $3.00 from Nevo himself. Despite all this, he labors under the delusion that those who seek his company must appreciate him as a human being, and not as a bag of gold. There is a story about a dinner to which he had been invited along with Chaim Weizmann, and when the host began hinting that the Weizmann Institute was an important institution worthy of support, he'd got up and left in a fury.

When I arrived home I began a search for Baruch Amir. Finally, with the help of Pinhas Sapir in Jerusalem, I located him in Mishmar Hayarden, overseeing the night shift dredging of the canal. He was called to the telephone from the field. I asked him about the "plug." He explained that it was a temporary primitive damming of the Jordan which was now being removed to allow the water to reach the permanent dam that had been built in the meantime. The water could be channeled through this dam into the canal at any time by flipping a switch. I asked him what for. He began claiming that it was absolutely necessary. I asked him who had made the decision and he answered that there was a Ministry of Defense directive. I immediately thought this must mean Lavon. I said that I could not approve the action. He said that the job of removal had already began. I replied that it must be stopped at any cost. He said he would like to pose a question. I said I was unwilling to hear any, for he had not looked for me but vice versa. After finding out about the whole thing by accident I am ordering him to stop, and if he would like to state his case, then he must come to Tel Aviv to see me tomorrow and report. He said: so be it.

I telephoned Walter and told him the whole story. In the meantime, Walter had heard news of the SC session. The Pakistani [delegate] had proposed a stoppage of work. The British delegate had objected to raising the question of a stoppage before an inquiry. After a short query the debate had been postponed till tomorrow. This had taken place at the morning session, while the Council was to hear Bennike's report on the border situation at the afternoon session.[24]

I had plunged into my papers when the phone rang. It was the CoS: could he come see me right away? "Of course!" I said. To myself I thought: Baruch must have given him warning. And so it was. CoS Mordechai Maklef appeared with the IDF Spokesman, Lieutenant-Colonel Nahman Karni,[25] and he began explaining the matter of the plug and the dam. First of all, he informed me that a week ago the Army had taken over the project. (I had not known this, and had been wondering all this time about the Army's invasion of *Tahal*'s domain). They had thought it necessary to remove the plug and allow the water to reach the dam so that it would be possible, at only the flip of a switch, to channel the

24 Lengthy extracts of Bennike's Report to the UN SC are reprinted in Hutchison, *Violent Truce*, 154-74.

25 Nahman Karni (1926-1977). IDF Spokesman (1953-1955). Later worked in military intelligence and served as Military Attaché to Israel's Mission at the UN.

water into the first 450 meters of canal should that be necessary. The water would thence return to the Jordan, and the first diversionary *fait accompli* will have been established. If the plug remained in place, we would be unable to put the dam into operation except by removing it – a 12-hour job. We could now destroy the plug under cover of darkness, even tonight. Should we miss the opportunity and the SC decide in favor of a work stoppage tomorrow, and if in future we should decide to continue work and divert the water, we would find it very difficult to do so. Furthermore, removal of the plug in violation of a SC decision may provoke the Syrians into opening fire. From every aspect, it was vital that this affair be concluded before the stoppage of work.

I was not satisfied with this analysis. I told Mordechai there were two problems here. The first was about procedure: how had it come about that they had launched such an operation without asking my opinion? Why had I only found out about it by accident? But about this I shall follow up on another level. The second question concerned the operation itself. I was not convinced that it was necessary to bring the water to the dam. I had never entertained the notion that we might divert the water in defiance of the SC and, if we did, then it was neither here nor there whether the water was held back by a plug or reached the dam and was held back there. But I had also understood from Baruch Amir that the removal of the plug was already under way, and now it was impossible to leave the situation as it is – the plug would have to be rebuilt. Could this be done in time? I questioned Mordechai about the potential results of the removal of the plug. I explained the sensitivity of this matter in the SC, and in view of the accusations weighing upon us. The last thing we needed on the eve of the debate was that UN Observers should submit a report condemning some new trick played by Israel which was once more an open conspiracy to establish a *fait accompli* while flouting the UN. So what will actually happen?

The CoS said that a previously unflooded sunken area would be inundated, that the famous "Arab plot of land" would not be flooded at all, and that, on the other hand, the flow would be renewed in the Jordan's two western streams, the farther of which had entirely dried up due to the sealing of the river wall with the plug, while the middle one's level had dropped drastically. I seized upon this fact, seeing in it a ray of hope. Would this mean, as far as the Jordan was concerned, a reversion to the status-quo-ante? Mordechai affirmed that it would be so. I said to myself that, if it would be possible to present this entire operation as such, then there would be reasonable justification for it. I went on questioning the CoS about the amounts of water in the three streams and discovered another possible justification for the operation. Since the Jordan had already begun to rise because of the first snows on the Hermon, we could claim that renewing the flow in the three streams was necessary to prevent the flooding of the sole eastern stream when the rains came, thus benefitting from an additional pretext to justify our work on the dam.

I again called up Baruch Amir. I attempted to ascertain the truth of the CoS's statements. He confirmed the matter concerning the three streams. He was not much impressed by the argument about flooding of the Jordan during the rainy season, but at the same time he added that some water would seep into the canal through the dam. I was alarmed by this bad news, perceiving the danger that we might be accused of diverting the Jordan's waters deliberately. A sudden suspicion flashed through my mind that our people might again be misleading me, and that their intent was to present both me and not only the UN with a *fait accompli* by channeling the water into the canal (the IDF's and *Tahal*'s ardent desire from the start!) and thereby demonstrate our control over the Jordan – even though this demonstration did not in any way further the completion of the project. Amir swore to me that there was no such intention, and that the seepage could be brought under control within a few hours.

My mind was not put to rest. Since hydrological problems had come up, I decided to call Wiener. Karni set out to find him in Tel Aviv, and Mordechai and I sat down to wait. I said to myself: why don't I dispel the tension that has in recent weeks set in between myself and this good officer and outstanding warrior, the liberator of Haifa in the 1948 war and one of the conquerors of the Galilee, with whom my personal relations date back to the time of the "Jewish Brigade"?[26]

I asked him why he had handed in his resignation. In reply, he opened up his heart and poured out his bitterness. It was a devastating condemnation of the PM, who had all but abandoned him to carry out the painful cuts in the officer corps which the PM himself had decreed; of Pinhas Lavon, who since assuming office as Acting Minister of Defense had not lent an ear to his advice, had not taken advantage of his experience, but had made decisions on his own, contrary to his opinion as CoS; of the Ministry of Defense DG, Shimon Peres,[27] who was constantly undermining him

26 In the closing years of WWII Maklef served as Major in the Brigade. The Jewish Brigade of the British Army was formed in September 1944 by the amalgamation of three Jewish Palestinian regiments and other Palestinian Jewish units established from local Jewish volunteers recruited into the British Army. These volunteers numbered close to 30,000 men and women. The Brigade, consisting of about 5000 soldiers, fought on the Italian front under the Zionist flag during the last months of the war. After the war its soldiers operated clandestinely among the Jewish survivors of the Holocaust who were concentrated in displaced persons camps in Germany and Austria. Brigade operatives were instrumental in transporting many of the survivors to ports in Italy and France, from which they were shipped by the *Hagana* as "illegal immigrants" to Palestine. The British, aware of this large-scale activity, disbanded the Brigade in June 1946. Sharett (Shertok), as head of the Political Department of the JA, had been instrumental in organizing the volunteer campaign as well as in negotiating with British military authorities for the creation of the Brigade.

27 Shimon Peres (1923-2016). DG, Ministry of Defense (1952-1959); later Deputy Minister of Defense, Minister of Posts and Transport, PM, FM and ninth President of Israel (2007-2014).

and attempting to appropriate several branches of activity to himself; and of Moshe Dayan, who was no officer at all, but performed unconventional actions on his own devices and subverted every proper framework of collegial action.

I was shocked by the picture he portrayed and sat wondering at the gloomy prospects for the Army with the imminent change of command, the third in the short history of the IDF. I had sought to dispel tension, and instead I became burdened with anxiety. Nevertheless, it was good I brought up the subject and heard Mordechai's version of the new crisis in the GS, because it's incumbent upon me to hear from him personally on these matters and, all in all, it's best I learn the inside story concerning the changes about to take place.

Wiener finally arrived. I explained the situation to him and pointed out the problems. He reassured me about the seepage. It would involve only a small amount of water that would hardly affect the flow in the streams. He confirmed the version concerning the preparation for the rainy season. On the other hand, he brought up another problem. The dam was still fresh since the concrete was poured only a few days ago. It was therefore doubtful whether it could stand up to the pressure of the water. As soon as I get one foot out of the mud, the other sinks into it.

I telephoned Amir in Mishmar Hayarden for the third time. He vehemently refuted Wiener's fears concerning the strength of the dam. He told me these fears were groundless. We once again discussed the seepage problem, and the time required to overcome it. In the course of the conversation – which was torture for both of us because the connection was impossible – the young man got excited, began calling me "Moshe" and imploring me in the name of all that I hold dear to allow the completion of the operation, for without it all the work done until now will have been for naught. I rejected this peremptory assumption, but I was impressed by his ardor. I also agreed that, to the extent that the entire canal is important to us as a *fait accompli*, the same holds true for bringing the water up to the dam and presenting, by silent demonstration, our control over the water.

This conversation gave me an opportunity to look into the state of the "Arab plot of land" properly with Amir. It turned out that my visit to the site had not been in vain in this regard. The plot had been fenced in. I asked if we were still driving through it. His stammering made it clear that we were still sinning there. I ordered, and Amir gave me his word of honor, that this would be stopped. I asked if we still had earth-moving machines there. He solemnly promised me that the last tractor would disappear from view. Both my strength and Amir's were exhausted by this conversation.

In the end, I ruled that the plug had to be completely removed. I gave detailed instructions as to how the operation should be explained to the outside world. They were not to wait until a UN Observer passed by, and leave it to him to report, but they should invite an Observer, show him what we have done and explain the intention behind it, and thereby influence the tenor of the report. For this purpose, Lieut.-Col. Aryeh Shalev must be sent to the site tomorrow morning. He will portray the removal of the plug as one part of our effort to revert to the status-quo-ante, another part of our effort concerning the Arab plot of land. The CoS promised that all this would be done. To be on the safe side, I put it down in writing for him.

They left at midnight. Only then did I sit down to compose a detailed telegram to our delegation in New York. I clarified how to portray the affair of the dam should word of it reach the SC and raise a flurry there. This whole commotion will one day seem unimportant and ridiculous, a storm in a teacup! But if an abandoned and dingy Arab water mill was accorded such serious attention and such a painstaking analysis by Bennike in an official document, with international publicity in its wake, then this complex affair most certainly will too. I read through some more of my papers, seeking relief in them from the tension, and went to bed at 1:00.

Wednesday, October 28

The distinguished guest from the US, the President's special envoy, Eric Johnston, was scheduled to arrive at 9:00. I was hardly dressed properly when the CoS came by. Had I heard the news on the radio? No. "Eban announced at the SC session that Israel was willing to stop work!" I was bewildered at this quickening pace of events, but assumed that Eban knew what he was doing. It turns out that at its afternoon session the Council had returned to the matter of the canal and hadn't heard Bennike's report. I told Maklef that as long as there was no telegram from Eban, I could not know if we had already committed ourselves to a stoppage, and that therefore work should continue. Most probably we would stop sometime during the day, and I would let him know the hour.

Eytan and Bendor came in a few minutes before 9:00. Punctually at 9:00 Johnston, Russell and Fried arrived. Johnston is the civilized American type, polished and refined, careful in his speech, sees the essentials quickly, the glitter of his intellect cold, no warmth in him. Though he is a captain of world business, he looks and talks like a professional diplomat, to external appearances at least.

We immediately plunged into the thick of the matter. His mission, he said, was to look into the attitudes of the countries involved regarding the idea of a regional water settlement in the Jordan Valley. Thus did he explicitly and in advance fix the purpose of his mission. The plan which had been publicized – he didn't call it the "Clapp Plan" but the "Main Plan" after its author Charles Main[28] – was not binding on the US government. Its only purpose was to draft a framework, and it was subject to

28 The "Main Plan", or Unified Plan, was created under the direction of the Tennessee Valley Authority (headed by Gordon Clapp) by Charles T. Main, Inc., of Boston. For a summary, see Lowi, *Water and Power*, 83-86, 207-08.

adjustment and correction. The intention was not necessarily to create direct contact between the countries. It would be best to establish an agreed central authority, under the aegis of the UN or the US, which would separately engage each country in the overall implementation of the plan. The initial objective was to determine how much water was sufficient for each country. I told him that only for Israel did making do with a small amount of water entail a problem, since Jordan would get by far more water than what it had today. He confirmed this, and justified the discrepancy with the need to resettle refugees. All the same, he pointed out that Syria too would be relinquishing the waters of the Yarmuk in favor of its needier neighbors. I said that the most effective way to induce the Arabs to cooperate was to prove to them in tangible terms that they were incurring losses and missing opportunities because of their intransigence. I saw that this remark, quite well-reasoned and far-reaching in its conclusions, was unacceptable to him, probably precisely because of its far-reaching implications. This way of thinking was evidently out-of-step with the spirit of the times, in which appeasement and accommodation prevail.

Walter Eytan asked what he had heard from the Arabs. He said that the question was not relevant. An arrogant answer indeed! He should have answered simply that he could not reply to the question.

I said that we had subjected the Main Plan to a preliminary examination and found it faulty on two principal aspects: the sources of water it encompassed, and the amount of area it was to irrigate. With regard to these two, the plan is wanting. I pointed out our need to irrigate the coastal plain and the Negev, and the crucial importance of including the Litani in the plan.

He answered straight and to the point. As regards the amount of land to be irrigated, we were free to irrigate whatever areas as we see fit within the framework of our allotted amount of water. About the Litani, they had considered it, and had come to the conclusion that it was not to be integrated within the plan at the present time.

I refused to accept the position about the Litani, and an argument ensued. I contended that 700 million m^3 of water flow through the Litani to the Mediterranean every year without benefit to God or man. In any event, the plan already encompassed Lebanon, for the Hasbani reservoir was to be formed in its territory. If Syria was expected to participate, how much more readily would Lebanon, more moderate by far than its neighbor, be enticed into participating? Syria would only benefit to a small extent, while Lebanon could gain an important source of power for its industry.

The reply was decisive. They had examined the issue carefully and had concluded that to try to include the Litani would be grasping for too much and miss the mark of obtaining the Arab states' cooperation. The plan consisted of the Jordan Valley and nothing else.

I dropped this question, and said that we would return to it. At both the start and end of the conversation, I emphasized that as long as there was no regional settlement, we considered ourselves free to implement our plans. I said that the plan we were currently executing in no way contradicted the Main Plan.

With that we took leave of each other. At first it was agreed that we would meet in the afternoon, but after consultation among ourselves we decided to postpone the second meeting until tomorrow. I invited Eshkol and Pinhas Sapir to take part, but they could not make it because of the heated negotiations going on in Jerusalem to reconcile the "Appeal" and "Bonds" people with each other. During the day it occurred to me that it was best for the coalition to have Peretz Bernstein's participation as well, and I invited him.

I asked Walter to report to the PM on the substance of the discussion, and to propose that we set the time for the stoppage of regular work at noon, and for the completion of the sealing of the dam at 6:00 pm. Walter went up to Jerusalem while I hurried to the *Kirya* for a meeting of the FADC. This was scheduled as a continuation of the previous meeting which had been twice postponed.

The meeting lasted more than three hours. I reported on developments over the past few days up to the opening deliberations of the SC, including Eban's statement concerning the work stoppage. I surmised that Eban had seen fit to speed up the delivery of his statement in order to win a more favorable SC resolution than had he had anticipated. An abstract of a telegram from Eban arrived in the middle of the meeting to confirm my speculation.

There was a lively debate. Eliezer Livneh[29] made a rare discovery and proposed a new and refurbished idea: an extensive peace offensive against the Arab states. The Qibya affair was the hinge of the argument, and Livneh forcefully disapproved of it. Ziama Aran termed it a stain that would not be quickly erased. Mapam and *Herut*[30] argued against the stoppage of work, and voted against it in the end. The majority approved the stoppage.

At the end of the debate, I spoke my mind about Qibya for the first time (at the previous meeting I hadn't touched this open and bleeding wound, and had allowed Lavon to find shelter behind the official version). I said that as a representative of the Cabinet I had nothing to add to that version. Personally I could state that the large-scale slaughter had caused a shift from quantity to quality concerning the moral nature of the act in the eyes of the rest of the world. I described the uproar everywhere, and the strong echo of outrage and condemnation we had received. I also pointed to the political significance and possible consequences of the raid.

---

29 Eliezer Livneh (1902-1975). Veteran Mapai MK, maverick and rebellious (expelled 1956); writer, publicist.

30 The *Herut* Party was established in 1948 by members of the *ETZEL (Irgun)* under the leadership of Menachem Begin, formerly the commander of the *ETZEL*. Towards the general elections to the second Knesset in 1951, it absorbed members of the pre-state Revisionist Party, who failed in the elections to the first Knesset.

It must appear that whoever carried it out was ready for war, and from there it was but a step towards the presumption that the instigator desired war and was deliberately provoking it. If that was the case, we had to take into account the certainty that any repetition of such an act on our part would involve military intervention by Britain on Jordan's side against us, and that such an intervention might also take the form of a blockade by sea. I did not relate that I knew, all too well, that these possibilities had been discussed in certain quarters.

A question came up regarding the holding of a political debate in the Knesset immediately upon its reconvening next week. I said that I would consider delivering a statement concerning the situation at the start of the session, and that in the meantime we should postpone the scheduling of the debate.

When the meeting ended, I stayed behind with Argov, Aran and Namir - at their request. The content of BG's conversation with the GZ, including his announcement to them that his resignation was final, has been disclosed in full by the press. Now his resignation has become a public and political fact. In this state of affairs, confusion in the party would be most unfortunate. It is necessary that we expedite our deliberations and reach full clarification within a few days. We decided that the Political Committee should convene on Monday, and the Party Central Committee[31] two or three days later. Somebody said that BG was willing to come to the Political Committee, but had announced that he would not attend the Central Committee meeting.

Even as they were speaking, Walter telephoned from Jerusalem to say that BG would like to put off the work stoppage for a few hours in order to avoid any loose ends. So be it. Meanwhile the telephone call I had placed to Rosh Pina came through. I asked Amir how much time he needed to get the dam under control. He said: "Until midnight." Thereupon I immediately set midnight as the deadline for the cessation of all work.

At home in the afternoon I met with Isser Harel.[32] He reported to me on a few current matters, including post facto authorizations of activities undertaken during my days of turmoil when I couldn't get away to consult with him and he had to meet deadlines. They had all been in order and I gave my authorization without hesitation.

I attended the first part of the Mapai Knesset caucus meeting, called in view

31 Central Committee (CC). The central and most important Mapai Party body, meeting almost every month, consisting of around 90 members.

32 Isser Harel (1912-2003). First head (1948-1952) of the *Shin-Bet* (*Sherut Bitahon*), Israel's internal security agency; Head of the *Mossad* (1952-1963). The *Shin-Bet,* founded in 1948, was built on the *Hagana*'s pre-state intelligence service (*SHAI - Sherut Yediot,* Information Service) for the purposes of gathering information about Arab anti-Jewish activity as well as preventing foreign espionage and internal and external sabotage. *Shin-Bet* was later changed to *Sherut Habitahon Haklali* (General Security Service), accronym: *Shabak*.

of the resumption of session following recess. When I saw I was the only Cabinet minister present, Golda and Lavon being absent, I left the meeting. These days I have become overly sensitive not to do anything or say anything which might seem to indicate that I consider myself a "candidate" for the PM's post.

When I returned home I learned that Michael Elizur was looking for me. What's the matter? More trouble. Representing the *New York Times*, Moshe Brilliant[33] had heard from someone that we did not intend to stop work entirely, and that the Jordan would burst the dam tomorrow and flow into the canal.

I had been alert to this danger, and I could not overcome my suspicion that our own people might be conspiring to present me too with the *fait accompli* of diverting the stream contrary to all my statements and solemn promises. Since Brilliant's source was military, I turned to the CoS. Half an hour passed until I reached him, and while waiting I became thoroughly agitated. Mordechai put my mind at rest. He promised that there was no such intention, and all measures were being taken to seal the dam.

My brother-in-law Shaul dropped by for a short while at my request. I simply wanted to unburden myself of accumulated worries, especially my anxiety over developments in army affairs with the appointment of Moshe Dayan as CoS. Shaul concurred with my analysis at the gloomy outlook, but he could offer no advice. Moreover, where I was concerned about the future, Shaul turned backwards and spoke about the impetuous step taken in the very appointment of Mordechai Maklef as CoS. In that position he had been ruthlessly put upon and virtually eliminated as a creative power in the Army. Had he remained Deputy CoS, he could have stayed at the same post for years and years, and gone on building and improving the Army with all his diligence and efficiency. In the areas of internal organization and economic management he was most capable, but he was no leader, and the CoS's mantle has never suited him. It only diverted him from what he did best and hastened his demise.

There were times when two or three of the brothers-in-law, and sometimes all four,[34] would meet together and would pick each other brains, arrive at some constructive solution to the problem at hand, and work towards its implementation. Now, there were two of us left, and all we can do is discuss the wretched situation between ourselves, and contemplate the hopeless deterioration with cruel clarity, helplessly. Thus did we take leave of each other. Both of us are closer to sixty than

33 Moshe Brilliant (1915-1995). Knesset correspondent, *Jerusalem Post*; Jerusalem correspondent, *New York Times*.

34 Moshe Sharett, Eliyahu Golomb (1893-1945) and Dov Hoz (1894-1940), all students of the first graduating class of the Herzliya Gymnasium of Tel Aviv in 1913, became bosom friends in their teens and brothers-in-law when Golomb and Hoz married Sharett's sisters Ada and Rivka in the early 1920s. Both Golomb and Hoz became prominent leaders of Mapai and occupied high posts in the *Hagana*. Avigur was a brother-in-law to Moshe Sharett only, being Zipporah Sharett's younger brother.

fifty. I still have the vigour to work, but Shaul is a bereaved father suffering from physical ailments and withdrawn into himself.[35]

At 9:00 I telephoned Rosh Pina and asked Gittelson, a *Tahal* employee, about the state of affairs. He promised me faithfully that the lights would go out at midnight and no machine would be left in the canal dredging area. On the other hand, he notified me that the sealing of the dam would not under any circumstances be finished by then. Water was still seeping through, though not in any disturbing quantity. This work was impossible to do in the dark, and there would be no choice other than to continue it tomorrow in daylight, unless we let the seepage continue.

I said that the dam must be sealed come what may and that, having no other choice, I would permit the continuation of work tomorrow. It took precedence over any other consideration. If a UN Observer should appear, it must be explained to him that it was an emergency job meant to maintain the status quo concerning the flow of the water rather than stopping it.

I composed a telegram to Eban regarding this minor complication. Baruch Amir showed up after 10:00. He confirmed the facts of the sealing of the dam. He broached three questions. First, was work on the canal outside the DMZ permitted to continue? I said: "Certainly." Second, was work on the preparation of agricultural ground for the *Nahal*[36] settlement in the DMZ at a distance from the canal area permitted? I assented. Third, there was a gully that cuts across the canal that has been dug, and if the gully floor traversing the canal was not set in concrete, rain waters might ruin the work that has been done. Was casting the concrete permitted? I answered immediately in the negative, but agreed to its being done after the space of a week or ten days.

I composed a telegram to New York regarding all these matters too. At 11:00 pm the renewal of the grant in Washington was announced on the radio.[37]

Thursday, October 29

At 9:00 Eshkol, Sapir, Wiener, Ra'anan Weitz,[38] Amir and Bendor came to my house for a preliminary consultation. After 20 minutes Bernstein also arrived. I gave a summary of yesterday's conversation with Johnston, and we discussed the outline of our argumentation for today and the relevant objections which Wiener was to table. We spent an hour and a half at it, right until the Americans appeared.

35 Avigur's 17-year-old son, Avraham ("Gur"), was killed in the War of Independence.

36 Acronym for *No'ar Haluzi Lohem* (Fighting Pioneering Youth), a regular IDF unit whose companies were established by members of youth movements that prepared their members for founding or joining existing kibbutzim after completion of their military service. *Nahal* military service combined agricultural and military training on a kibbutz or at a *Nahal* outpost. During the 20 years of its existence, *Nahal* founded 36 outposts, of which 22 became permanent settlements.

37 *FRUS 1952-1954*, doc.711.

38 Ra'anan Weitz (1913-1998). Deputy Director, Department of Rural Settlement.

They arrived, nine in number: Johnston, Russell and Fried; Bruce McDaniel[39] with his two aides; and three experts accompanying Johnston. There were eight of us. We sat down in the dining room, on either side of the long and narrow table, Johnston and myself seated opposite each other in the middle.

I made a brief opening statement. Johnston once again enunciated the main points of his mission. I invited Wiener to present the technical analysis. His speech was above and beyond praise: the explanation clear, the speech moderate in spirit, but precise and penetrating in its content, the English cultivated, though of stumbling pronunciation at times. In seemingly mild language, and with exemplary forbearance, he demolished some of the basic assumptions and principal conclusions of the Main Plan and demonstrated their lack of any engineering and economic sense. He also exposed some serious errors in the calculation of the amounts of water and irrigation allotments; and all this without laying himself open to the charge of ignoring the fundamentals of the international settlement, or rejecting the plan outright. A masterpiece!

Johnston was unsparing in his praise for the speech and declared it to have been quite convincing – which did not mean, of course, that he accepted its conclusions, which were of a political, and not a technical, nature. The reply offered by one of his experts was ludicrous. He didn't trouble to contradict any of Wiener's figures, and he did not touch upon his criticisms at all, but repeated the principles of the Main Plan by rote in sloppy language, like a melancholy mourner. It was clear that he hadn't been prepared for an analysis as penetrating as the one Wiener made and did not have enough time to gather his wits and offer a proper reply.

Ra'anan filled in Wiener's lecture with some agricultural observations and he too was a sharp marksman, making a deep impression with his command of agrarian facts and agricultural issues covered by the irrigation plan. Without a doubt our people's two speeches, delivered to the point, considerably raised the reputation of Israeli experts in American eyes.

The thrust of Wiener's and Weitz's contentions was that the southern Jordan Valley area could not absorb the full amount of water earmarked for it in the plan; that the surplus of water could much more efficiently serve irrigation projects in Israel; that proclaiming the Kinneret as the sole regulatory reservoir and abandoning the Beit Netofa Lake reservoir plan would involve the loss of a huge amount of water to the project as a whole; that the exploitation of water flow for the generating of power incorporated in the plan was smaller by far than the evident potential.

As regards the first contention, which was the heart of the matter, for it directly touched upon the possibilities of irrigating the Negev, Johnston had a ready reply: his mission was to "sell" the plan to Jordan. To make the sale, the merchandise stood

39 Bruce W. McDaniel, Director of the Technical Cooperation Administration ("Point Four") Mission in Israel.

in need of embellishment. If he didn't promise them a much greater amount of water than what Israel would be getting, the attempt would fail. In the final analysis we had a greater interest in the success of the plan than our neighbors, insofar as we felt the urgency of a solution to the refugee problem, and were also interested, over the long run, in the increase of the standard of living of the neighboring countries so that in future they might be able to buy our industrial produce.

When I said that we were determined to develop our agriculture to the utmost possible extent and settle as many people as possible upon the land, Johnston wrinkled his brow. It was clear these sentiments were not to his liking.

Eshkol took up the gauntlet and in brief, terse remarks he stated the overwhelming importance of agriculture within the project of national renewal that we had undertaken.

I again brought up the problem of the Litani. I said that Johnston had come to us as an emissary of the President, that he must listen to what we had to say and report back. I warned against the squandering of a historic opportunity to harness the Litani to the regional development plan. One option of the two must hold: either no effort can persuade the Arab states, in which case they would refuse to cooperate regardless of the Litani; or they may be persuaded, in which case the addition of the Litani would do nothing to lessen the chances of success.

Johnston promised to faithfully report these matters to the President and Secretary of State, but nevertheless stood his ground and again unrelentingly gave the Litani plan a kiss of death at this stage. It was evident that the Americans considered the problem of the addition of the Litani's waters as one that should be left for the Messiah to solve. The reason for their obstinacy remains obscure. I said that the Cabinet's ultimate position might depend on the inclusion or exclusion of the Litani.

At the end of the discussion I focused on a few points. I emphasized that we considered ourselves free to go on with our development and irrigation plans. I stated that the B'not Yaakov/Kinneret canal project did not contradict the Main Plan, but could serve as an addition to it. I also said that this plan could be viewed in its own right. If it is viewed as the first stage of a larger project (that is, in connection with the diversion of the Jordan to Beit Netofa), then it would be a matter for 1959 or 1960. Secondly, even then the amount of water diverted would not surpass what is allotted to us by the Main Plan. Finally, I pointed out that the matter of an intermediary agency to be established for implementing the plan had yet to be clarified, and we would have to consider the plan carefully from this aspect.

Johnston requested that we formulate our position within a month to six weeks so that we could arrive at practical conclusions on talks with him during his second visit, or with another Presidential emissary, if he should find it necessary to return to his business in the meantime and the President send someone else in his place.

When the meeting ended Johnston told me privately that he had a great desire to see BG, but the trouble was that Dulles specifically forbade him to see anyone in Jerusalem.

I rested a bit in the afternoon, and set out with Zippora at 3:30 for Rehovot, for the laying of the cornerstone of the Chaim Weizmann Memorial. The ceremonies marking the anniversary of the first President's death have been too extensively planned and are spread over almost a full week. The impulse dominating Meyer Weisgal[40] does not allow him to be content with little. He is not blessed by the wisdom embodied in the words of our Elders: "too much is too little." Since I would be going to the laying of the cornerstone, which would be intimate with limited participation, I had decided in advance to permit myself to be absent from the official memorial ceremony and inauguration of the Institute to be held on the morrow.

The guests from England gathered, the distinguished men of science who had come for the memorial event and the entire family. The President and his wife came. Of the Cabinet ministers there were only two: Rosen and myself; the rest were occupied with the Jerusalem conference. Many other guests were present. Weisgal conducted the ceremony with his inimitable use of pomp and circumstance. He scuttled about, shouted, uttered outlandish expressions, and deprived the ceremony of its solemnity. To add to the disgrace, he constantly spoke English. After the first part of the program, when the entire gathering went on to the grave, I left and set out for Jerusalem.

[- - -]

I briefed Elizur by telephone about the meeting with Johnston, and asked that our statement emphasize that we thoroughly object to the plan. It was important both for internal reasons – to prepare public opinion in Israel for the possibility of a renewed conflict with the US over this point, and for external reasons – so that the Americans won't be able to claim that we undermined the chances of the plan's acceptance by the Arabs by showing too favorable an attitude towards it.

At 8:30 I went to the King David [hotel] for the closing dinner of the Jerusalem conference. I found that the negotiations towards a reconciliation between the "Bonds"[41] people and the "Appeal"[42] people had borne no real fruit. Although a resolution had been adopted which was equally binding on both organizations, as long as the personal relationships don't change – and change they won't! – and as long as Henry Montor rules at the UJA – there is no chance of a substantial improvement in the atmosphere.

40 Meyer W. Weisgal (1894-1977). Aide to Chaim Weizmann; Chairman (1949-1966), President (1966-1970) and Chancellor (1976-1977) of the Weizmann Institute.

41 The State of Israel Bonds Organization.

42 The UJA.

Some time earlier Eshkol had tried to convince me to make peace with Montor, whose existence I have refused to acknowledge since he made light of me in the US last year. I said that if, upon his return to the US, he wrote me a personal letter of apology, I would read what he wrote, and respond accordingly. He must steel himself in advance for a very harsh letter on my part, because he behaved in a base manner, and he must be told what he has done. For once, he must learn his lesson, if there's any hope for him at all.

In the evening at the King David I told Eshkol that I doubted it was worth his while to trouble himself with this matter. I haven't badgered Montor and I find contact with him unnecessary either for me or for any general benefit. In any event, I have renounced fund-raising activities in the US and shall not return there in the near future. Regarding the personal relations between Montor and myself – once upon a time we enjoyed friendship and good-fellowship, but he murdered them and in such matters there is no resurrection.

At the beginning of the meal there was a pretty spectacle. Somebody arranged to take a photograph: BG in the middle, Eddie Warburg,[43] Joe Schwartz and Morris Bernstein[44] of UJA on one side, and Henry Montor, [Rabbi David] Wanefsky and Sam Rothberg[45] of the Bonds on the other. As if concord had been achieved and all was well. I gazed at Warburg's face and it looked shriveled and ossified. I told Nahum Goldmann who was sitting beside me that Eddie's face looked like the face of an Arab mayor during the Mandate posing to one side of the British High Commissioner with me on the other side.

True, this affair concerning relations between the UJA and the Bonds is a serious obstacle. But if we don't dwell on it, then the conference itself succeeded beyond expectations. In fact, not only wasn't the conference called upon to solve this problem, but it had been specifically dropped from the agenda. Moreover, avoiding it was expressly a condition for holding the conference. The UJA people had at first refused to convene with the Bonds people under one roof in Jerusalem and the idea of a conference was almost scrapped because of their position. Then I came and proposed to the *haverim* in Jerusalem, and to Aubrey who was here at the time, that we promise the UJA people that the problem concerning relations between the two organizations should not be discussed at all at the conference, and the question of coordinating their efforts would not be placed on the agenda. Furthermore, the conference would be organized so as not to seem at all like

43 Edward (Eddie) Mortimer Warburg (1908-1992). Jewish community leader and philanthropist; founder and trustee, Museum of Modern Art (New York); Chairman, JDC (1941-1966); Chairman, UJA (1950-1955).

44 Morris W. Bernstein (1912-1962). UJA leader.

45 Sam Rothberg (1910-2007). US businessman and Jewish community leader; a founder of the Israel Bonds Organization (chairman from 1955); member of UJA National Cabinet; chairman of Board of Governors of the Hebrew University and of the American Friends.

a gathering of the two organizations under one roof. For that purpose we would invite delegates from other countries, and also important personages unidentified with either organization from America. This course was adopted and by means of it Aubrey later obtained Warburg's, Schwartz's and their colleagues' agreement to come to the conference. In other words, failure to achieve coordination between the two organizations should not in any way be construed as a failure of the conference.

On the other hand, there is no doubt that in view of the goals set for the conference, its success was complete and unanimously recognized by its participants. A weighty report on the achievements and challenges was heard, the participants from abroad were provided with direction, encouragement and inspiration. The Cabinet ministers' appearances (nine speeches!) made a great impression, and gave cause for immense gratification. The delegates clearly felt that they were being taken seriously, and treated as if they shared in the responsibility. They were spoken to frankly, dangers and difficulties were not suppressed, and the problems were spelled out frankly before them. Each and every one felt that his trip had been worthwhile and important, that he was returning home with a precious cargo, that he had heard, learned and seen what he hadn't known before. It was said that their visit to the Jordan River work site had made an especially strong impression – the sight of the lads on the bulldozers transforming the primordial face of the earth, while Syrian soldiers stare at them taking aim with their machine guns from a distance of only a few hundred meters.

The meal was a long drawn-out affair and the speeches began at a late hour. The Chief Rabbi[46] spoke and was charitably brief this time. Rokach spoke, so that no faction should be missing. He read the speech from his notes. It was not a bad Zionist speech, devoid of any brilliance and unsullied by any new idea. After him Nahum Goldmann spoke at length. For the most part his speech was light and shallow, even slightly cheap. Nevertheless his listeners were delighted, perhaps because they'd tired of hearing serious things and wanted to make merry after the food and drink. At the end of his remarks, Nahum touched upon the problem concerning BG. Here he became serious and somewhat more uplifting. He spoke with deep and frank admiration for BG, the great Jew, and defined his work and value for the Zionist movement in a few pointed, substantial statements. But, in truth, he accepted his resignation as a fact, specifically saying that it made no difference should he leave the PM's post, and only expressed the wish that in future he would take part in such conventions as a private individual so that others could benefit from his advice and indeed from his presence, as the

46 Isaac Halevi Herzog (1888-1959). First Chief Rabbi of Ireland (1921-1936); Ashkenazi Chief Rabbi of Mandatory Palestine (1936-1948) and of Israel (1948-1959). Father of Chaim (Vivian) Herzog and Yaacov Herzog, and grandfather of Isaac Herzog.

moving force among his fellows. This closed the door on the last hope – perhaps entirely imaginary – that this conference might still sway BG from his intention. Things standing as they are, the important and honest words of praise rang like a requiem for the departed.

Golda had been scheduled to speak at first, but at the beginning of the evening she fell into a "funk" and refused. I wrote a note to encourage her and saw by her expression from afar that, if cajoled, she would relent. I told BG to try to implore her again, and so it was. But her speech was disappointing. The music of her speech is always wonderful, her voice comes from the heart, and goes to the heart, and her simple English, with no adornment of learning, flows naturally and relieves the listener of any intellectual effort. But it was a speech that might have been delivered three or five or ten years ago. Plain "Zionism," [hackneyed ideological clichés] with a huge helping of arrogance dressed up as modesty in such language as "we the sons of the *yishuv* and the builders of the country." It is interesting to note that neither BG nor Golda can overcome the tremendous mental shock of their immigration to Israel, prompted by their inner selves, alone in their surroundings, flaunting their parents' wishes, disregarding the scorn of their [diaspora] friends. And therefore they cannot forgive others the sin of not immigrating to Israel. This emotion emerges from almost every speech they deliver to visitors from abroad, each according to his and her own approach and level. At any rate, Golda's speech also lacked any new substantive ideas.

BG closed the conference with a few short and heartfelt words. Inadvertently he made the closing moments feel ordinary by announcing the next day's touring program. But the audience refused to accept the verdict. Someone in the hall began singing "*Hatikva*"[47] and all joined in with fervor.

I returned home on foot, and went through my papers for a while. I had meant to sit peacefully when the phone rang. Michael Elizur reported a new headache. The same Baruch Amir, whom I thought I had managed to tame, has again overstepped the limits. He held a press conference and put on a swaggering show. We may have stopped working, but we were resolved to go on and finish, and in fact even now, at a flip of a single button, we can divert the Jordan into the new channel we have dug. There was more in the same vein of bravado and idiotic provocation. I couldn't believe my ears. It turned out the military censor was already dealing with the subject, Lieut.-Col. Aryeh Shalev was on the case, and his proposal was to impose a complete blackout on news concerning work on the project. I made a series of telephone calls to Elizur in Jerusalem, to the military censor and to Amir himself in Tel Aviv, and finally gave my assent to the blackout. Meanwhile I harshly reprimanded Amir, and ordered him to keep silent and say nothing to the press without authorization from the Foreign Ministry. It turns out that Nehemiah Argov

47 "*Hatikva*" (Hebrew: The Hope), Israel's national anthem.

persuaded him to say something to one reporter, who reputedly "invited" others, and what came out of it all was a big mess that he himself regrets and has labored for an entire evening to resolve. I told him there was nothing to resolve. The whole story was to be suppressed. Finis.

Went to bed at 1:00.

Friday, October 30

[- - -]

At 10:00 there was a gathering of the members of the Writers' Union Committee. The debate on [holding] the PEN Club Convention in Jerusalem in 1955 was conducted on a high plane, and lasted over two hours. I opened and concluded the meeting. The arguments back and forth began in a tone of sharp dissent and ended in complete mutual understanding. My "summary" was that any recall of our invitation was not to be entertained, but we had to see to it that the Germans understood that they either refrain from coming or send a representative or representatives with a distinctly anti-Nazi background, preferably émigrés or concentration camp prisoners. Those opposed spoke with great feeling and analysed this historic reckoning in depth. I also made an effort "to place issues on an erudite level," as Nachman Syrkin[48] used to say, and to invest these people of letters with an outlook which is more commensurate with Israeli statehood than Jewish emotion. The latter, with all due respect, was fundamentally "*galuti*"[49] and nothing else.

[- - -]

Late in the evening I telephoned Baruch Amir to see what was doing. Work on sealing the dam was continuing. A serious rupture was discovered in the dam which is made of logs. It was sealed today. The seepage has decreased, and there was a chance it may cease entirely tomorrow. Amir asked what to do with the large number of machines. I said it was best to leave only a few in the digging area in the DMZ. It would be a pity to leave the rest idle, and therefore they should be returned to their previous places of employment.

Amir mentioned in passing the work being done on the preparation of the ground for the *Nahal* settlement group and the leveling of access roads. Only after I had hung up the receiver did it dawn upon me that Amir had snuck in something new here. We had not discussed access roads at all, and I made a note to myself to look into it. Our people are incorrigible!

---

48 Nachman Syrkin (1868-1924). Leader of the labor Zionist movement in Europe; emigrated to the US in 1908.

49 *Galuti*, belonging to, or characteristic of, the Exile of the Jews from the Holy Land. *Galut* in Hebrew and Yiddish is a disparaging term denoting the dispersion and exile of the Jewish people, especially highlighting their weakened condition and lack of self-confidence because they were not living in their own sovereign nation-state.

I spoke at length with Zippora about my situation and state of mind these days as I go from crisis to crisis, internally and externally, especially in view of BG's determination to retire and considered intention, evidently, to propose Levi Eshkol for the prime ministership.

Saturday, October 31

I slept for eight hours. Took a hot bath, the first of the season after a summer of showering, and lay down again.

Shabbat [the Hebrew for the Sabbath] was completely quiet. Peace and tranquility reigned. It was entirely devoted to the composition of my speech for the Weizmann Memorial assembly in Jerusalem. The labor of creation was most painful. For days I have been afflicted by the distress preceding this mental and intellectual effort. I was resolved to compose a very short speech, but of concentrated essence. I worked throughout the morning and finished a first draft only in the late afternoon.

[- - -]

After dinner I continued non-stop my work on the speech. Early in the evening we went to the Russell residence for a reception in honor of a dozen American mayors who are touring the Middle East. They were about to visit me in Jerusalem, but I was forced to cancel this plan because of my meeting with Johnston. The Russell residence was full of people, and by the prevailing atmosphere one might have concluded that we had no better friend in the world than the US government, and that this friendship has never glowed as warmly as it does these days.

We returned home and after a hurried meal drove to a concert at Ohel Shem Hall. The concert, conducted by Lenny [Leonard] Bernstein in memory of the conductor Sergei Kousevitzky, comprised works by Mahler, Ravel and Beethoven's Third. Lenny showed himself to be devilishly talented, both as a conductor and as a pianist (Ravel's concerto), but there was nothing in him of the grandeur and immensity which conducting Beethoven's symphonies demands. Instead of an erect poise and expansive, measured movements, with leonine leaps at the dramatic junctures, he exercised constant jerkiness and twitching of the limbs. Very *shtetl*-like - or am I reading my own sentiments into it?

We avoided the traditional gathering after the concert owing to supreme tiredness, but also because I did not want to be seen in public too much.

Sunday, November 1

I left Ramat Gan at 7:30 and got to the office in Jerusalem before 9:00. The road was jammed with traffic. I went over telegrams and reports until 10:00 in order to prepare my review of Security Council affairs and the talks with Johnston for the Cabinet meeting. But the first telegram I saw from the bundle which had accumulated over *Shabbat* was from Shlomo Kaddar[50] in Prague, disclosing the fate of Mordechai Oren[51] and Shimon Orenstein.[52] I was stunned upon reading it. Both have been sentenced: the former to 15 years in jail and the latter to life imprisonment.

I kept the Cabinet meeting close to two hours with my review. Afterwards Lavon began his report on the problems of the Arab minority in Israel. In general he spoke much sense. The debate was postponed to the next meeting.

Ze'ev Sharef told me that at Sde Boker BG intends to shut himself off entirely from visitors who come to bother him with affairs of state. He will come to Tel Aviv only once or twice a year: for the Independence Day military parade, and for the Party Convention, if there should be one. Now this problem too has been satisfactorily solved and everything is falling into place.

I ate lunch alone while reading the morning papers. I was horrified upon perusal of Lavon's speech at Kibbutz Afikim, which *Ha'aretz*, with its conscientious regard for Mapai Cabinet ministers, took pains to present at great length and with all possible prominence.[53] A blatant anti-American speech and destructive in its corruptive effect on Israeli public opinion. The renewal of the grant was neither here nor there. The US government was against us. This is the enemy today and that is the threat. The Clapp Plan had to be rejected out of hand in advance. Most of all, the armistice regime was nothing but a conspiracy to destroy Israel and could not be tolerated under any circumstances. What is the reader supposed to conclude from all this froth and fulmination? Clearly, the only way out of these straits is a "second round" at Israel's initiative. And upon whom shall we lean in this predicament?

---

50 Shlomo Kaddar (1913-1987). Chargé d'affaires and Minister, Czechoslovakia (1953-1957).

51 Mordechai Oren (1905-1985). Leader, Mapam Party. In November 1951, while visiting Prague, he was detained, tried and sentenced to 15 years for espionage by Czechoslovak authorities. He would be released in 1956.

52 Israeli businessman detained in November 1951, tried and sentenced to life for espionage by Czechoslovak authorities in Prague. He would be released in 1954.

53 Lavon's speech of Friday, October 30, at the convention of the *Ihud Hakvutzot Vehakibbutzim* organization (below, page 203 n.11), held in Kibbutz Afikim, was fully reported on the front page of *Ha'aretz* of November 1, under the headline: "Lavon: Israel Will Not Accept US Diktat." He was quoted as saying: "Israel will not give up its sovereign right to develop its area according to its ability and understanding, and will not succumb to political pressure exerted on her by the US in this connection." He also said: "The present challenge is a result of a fundamental development within American policy to the detriment of Israel, which we have sensed for a long time but tried to ignore. However it has now reached a crisis point. [- - -] The armistice regime under which we have been living now for 5 years is built upon the sinister intention of the Arab countries to wage a total war of annihilation against us as soon as they are capable of it, while meanwhile weakening us by boycott and constant blood-letting. [- - -] Such an armistice is totally insufferable, in terms of Israel's vital interests, or in terms of the interest of global and regional peace. [- - -] Israel wishes to maintain its friendship with the USA, but on condition that it is a true friendship, not a dictating one."

Upon world Jewry and nothing else! A convention such as the one we just had in Jerusalem – that will be our savior. And this at a time when in fact we are declaring war on the US government! I was stupefied by this strange phenomenon. How can a man so talented, intelligent and seemingly level-headed sell himself to the devil and with dizzying speed change track from responsible statesmanship to unbridled demagogy? Where is he headed and what shall be the fate of a Cabinet without BG's restraining authority, despite all his eccentricities and outbursts? What will happen when these wanton drives explode unhindered at any time?

At the Cabinet meeting in the morning, during Lavon's long report, there were moments when I almost fell asleep from exhaustion. But after having been upset by his speech I couldn't shut my eyes.

[The following handwritten note from Sharett to Lavon, undated but most probably written on this day or close to it, was found among Lavon's papers at the ISA:]

> I'm against yielding to Johnston beyond a certain point – I am constantly on guard – but if your line predominates, a line which to my mind is definitely negative and unproductive, then another foreign minister will have to implement it, the outcome being BG's return in order to become PM and FM – and me going to Sde Boker.
>
> Don't think these words are written in a bad mood. In view of the last meeting of the [Mapai] political committee, I realize clearly that I don't represent the party, and that the party is not behind me. I cannot function this way as FM in the party's name, nor can the party demand this of me.

When I lay down to rest after lunch I fought to still my raging heart and to stop my thoughts gnawing at me but to no avail. I got up and dressed. I went over my papers and sat down again to work on the Weizmann Memorial speech. I rewrote it all, added and integrated, went over it again and again, and polished every phrase.

David Hacohen[54] telephoned. He returned from America this morning. I told him he had done well to send me such a furious letter concerning Qibya.[55] I had shown his letter to BG and Lavon. I also said that I would dearly like to see him, being very lonely these days as I have not been for years.

In the evening we went to the memorial service at the JA. Upon arriving I was shocked at the sight of the empty hall. It turned out that the organizers in their wisdom had been overly fastidious in dispensing tickets. From the Foreign Ministry, for example, only the DG had been invited. The end result was that barely 120 people had gathered. While Berl Locker was speaking I glanced at the audience and failed to count ten people who could be expected to understand each and every word of my speech. Locker was chairman and delivered a speech himself. My speech and Nahum's were not enough, as far as he was concerned.

---

54 David Hacohen (1897-1984). Israel Minister to Burma (1953-1955). Mapai leader and MK. Close friend of Sharett since serving together in the Ottoman Army in WWI.

55 *DFPI* 8, doc.435.

I couldn't believe my ears. So tepid and shallow and cheap was his address. He told jokes about Weizmann and jokes by Weizmann, spicing his stories with Yiddish expressions and in general playing the comedian. I would never have expected such lack of taste. Into this cold and empty expanse, due to the absence of audience and the chairman's opening, I was forced to deliver my speech which was made of concentrated thought and concise expression, the labor of the best of my ability. Although the mood of the audience immediately changed and assumed a serious air of rapt attention, only few understood everything. The rest merely marveled at my Hebrew – a compliment more wounding to me than virulent criticism.

Nahum spoke in English. He had prepared to address a multitude of guests from England and the US. Although they hadn't arrived, the speech remained in English and under the circumstances came out incongruous and almost spurious. Again, the text related neither to the audience nor to the previous speeches. In itself Nahum's speech was rich in content. It dealt mainly with the ethical foundations of Weizmann's Zionist policy.

We returned home, myself downcast and depressed. The supreme effort I made, mentally and emotionally, had come to naught. Moreover, it is clear that the speech won't even be published by the press. My mood was bleak also due to Lavon's Afikim speech, which lays down a rabid and reprobate foreign policy, the prospect of additional crises on the external front, internal dissolution and, above all, my wretched solitude these days and in the days to come. I do not know when I shall rid myself of this melancholy.

Ben-Gurion Resigns

Monday, November 2

A lethal lead article appeared in *Ha'aretz* on Lavon's speech: "Arrogance is not Statesmanship." Probably by Walter Gross.[1] He's nicely gathered all of the sparks which flew from Lavon and stoked them into a big fire.

At the office there was another telegram from Kaddar. He views the sentences as opening the way to a pardon. The logic is simple: as long as they were only under detention, their release might have been interpre ted as an admission that they had become suspect and been arrested for nothing. To open the possibility to set them free, it was first necessary to convict them in court, following which a pardon may be legitimately granted without impinging upon the dignity of Czechoslovakia's judicial system. There is confirmation of this possibility in Kaddar's conversation with [Gertruda] Sekaninová, that charmless woman whom I once met in New York and who is now Acting Foreign Minister. When Kaddar asked if it was possible to appeal the sentences, she replied in the negative but of her own accord added that the wives' requests for pardon were on the President's desk now.

I consulted with Levavi[2] and Bentsur[3] on our response to the sentences. We decided to disclose the sentences publicly immediately after notifying the families. The disclosure should be a carefully-worded announcement by the Foreign Ministry Spokesman. The East European Division is already composing a draft. Rega Oren, Mordechai Oren's wife, who had already written me to ask for an interview, had been invited for tomorrow anyway. I now asked that the meeting be advanced to today. Bentsur will see Orenstein's wife.

[- - -]

A telegram arrived from Elath to say that he is meeting with British Foreign

1 Dr Shlomo Yaacov Gross (1908-2003). Journalist and political commentator, *Ha'aretz* (pen name: "Poless").

2 Arye Levavi (1912-2009). Born in Lithuania. Settled in Palestine in 1932. Director, East European Division, (1950-1952) and Deputy DG, MFA (1952-1954). Israel Consul to Belgrade (1954-1958); later Ambassador to Argentina, Deputy DG and DG, MFA. Close associate of Sharett since working together in the pre-state JA Political Department.

3 Shmuel Bentsur (1906-1973). Director, East European Division, MFA; later Deputy to DG, MFA.

Secretary Anthony Eden[4] today. I replied immediately that on his own accord he ought to be the first to bring up the Qibya affair. He should say that it has shocked the Israeli public and evoked profound regret for the innocent blood shed; but that it has, at the same time, united the public in the awareness that a one-sided string of murders can no longer be tolerated, and that continued turmoil may lead to unforeseeable consequences. I also requested that he confront Eden with the responsibility Britain would bear for further encouraging warlike sentiment in the Arab states should it proceed with its design not to support a SC resolution calling on both sides to make peace. According to our information, France is willing to vote in favor of such a resolution, the US is wavering, while England is determined to defeat it.

[- - -]

Returning to the office I went over the draft of our response to the Prague sentences. Since I found it unsatisfactory I dictated it anew and honed its angles to suit both journalistic and political considerations.

I again spoke to Rosh Pina. The sealing of the dam continues, as does the seepage. Some new breach has been discovered which will require several days' work. This affair is getting more and more complicated.

[- - -]

I received a letter from BG. Yesterday at the Cabinet meeting he had taken issue with me over delaying the disclosure of the Prague sentences. I contended it would not be humane to disclose them before notifying the wives of the condemned. He dismissed this, and said that it was possible to send them letters. There was no need to summon them at all. I refused to accept his opinion. I do not know why this so exasperated him as to take the trouble to send me a letter protesting the "deliberate suppression" of the "horrible news" from the public. I immediately answered him that I do not see anything remiss in my duty towards the public in holding back the disclosure for 24 hours in order to perform the simple human act of charity required in such cases.[5]

I gave Michael Elizur guidelines concerning the press in the spirit of our formal announcement – a vigorous protest against perverted justice, but no assault on Czechoslovakia, and in general to refrain from any slander. A few reliable journalists may be informed of the possibility of a pardon, but not a word in print.

Baruch Amir telephoned concerning the same matter again. A crack appeared in the rock beneath the dam, through which a lot of water is seeping. Mending the situation requires bringing in a special machine to inject cement into the crack underwater. It'll take several men five days to do the job. I authorized the action. He again inquired about casting the bottom of that selfsame gully in concrete.

4 Sir Anthony Eden (1897-1977). British Foreign Secretary (1951-1955); PM (1955-1957).
5 Letters not found.

I forbade it for the time being. I asked about the work on the preparation of the plot of land for the *Nahal* settlement. He said they were about to begin on the western edge and leave a space of at least 500 meters between the work area and the canal.

[- - -]

I composed a cable to our legations on how to present the Prague sentences in their talks [with diplomatic colleagues].[6]

At 4:15 I went to the Knesset which reopened today after the holiday recess. Sprinzak[7] was already in the middle of his speech on Weizmann when I entered. His reading was horribly unbecoming.

In the interval between the eulogy and the regular session, I called Yaakov Riftin to the Cabinet room upstairs and informed him of the sentences. He was stricken. I realized Mapam had had no idea of Oren's predicament. Even though I told him about the possibility of a pardon, in accordance with Kaddar's version, I saw that he had fallen into a bottomless despair over the trial itself, and the conviction for treason and espionage. He was filled with emotion when he thanked me for making him privy to the facts and asked my permission to share them with Yaakov Hazan. It was typical of him not to propose to tell Aaron Zisling[8]. I told him that Rega was due to visit me tonight. He asked me to tell her to come see him and Hazan at the Knesset afterwards.

In the cafeteria I ran into David Hacohen whom I had not seen since his return from the US. I took him aside. Our conversation was wonderful. There was nothing we could not go into: Qibya, BG's resignation, the problem concerning the prime ministership, and David's own mission to Burma,[9] Lavon's speech, Moshe Dayan's serving as CoS, Aubrey, Reuven Shiloah, and so on and so forth. He refused to believe it when he heard that BG had never once talked to me about his resignation and had not sought my opinion on the question of a successor to the post.

In the mist of our conversation [Meir] Argov interrupted us. He wished to talk to me. I said goodbye to David, and bid Argov enter. He asked whether I believed everything he told me was the truth. I said yes, in all honesty. Argov has many faults, but not that of dishonesty or dissembling. On the contrary, he sometimes errs in his haste to unburden his heart even if it is not exactly prudent. He said that continued malaise and confusion over the question of the prime ministership was destroying the party from within, while the rampage of the yellow press was

---

6 *DFPI* 8, doc.487.

7 Yosef Sprinzak (1885-1959). Founder and leader, Mapai; Speaker of the Knesset (1949-1959).

8 Aaron Zisling (1901-1964). Minister of Agriculture (1948-1949); MK, Mapam and *Ahdut Ha'avoda* (1949-1955).

9 Hacohen's mission to Burma and his subsequent diplomatic service there are recounted in his memoir, *Time To Tell: An Israeli Life, 1898-1984*. Ttransl. Menachem Dagut (New York: Cornwall Books / Herzl Publications, 1985), 212-18.

damaging it from without. He, as Party Secretary, was launching a vigorous effort to put an end to chaos and establish complete clarity within three days. I encouraged him with all my heart. He said that I no doubt knew that I was not BG's candidate for the prime ministership. I said I certainly did. He said that BG's candidate was not to his liking, and that he was sure he would not be accepted by the party. I said that my candidate was Pinhas Lavon, and this for three reasons. First, as PM he would cease to be Defense Minister (I would designate Mordechai Namir for that post) and should serve in only one capacity, which is a great advantage for the PM. Secondly, as PM he may be restrained by the responsibility, for otherwise he was swerving down the dubious path of extremism which has deranged his mind and was hurtling himself down the steep slope of demagogy. Thirdly, he was younger than BG by at least twenty years, while other [candidates] were younger than him by only 10 years or less.

Argov rejected Lavon's candidacy as totally unacceptable. He went on to say that of the three acceptable candidates, only one, that is myself, had the qualities of a PM. Eshkol's virtues were obvious, but he did not have these qualities. Golda was a wonderful personality, but lacked having her own opinion. He asked if there was any possibility I could divest myself of the foreign minister's portfolio. I said no. I described the state of the ministry. Despite all its weaknesses and the criticism lashed at it – may there be many others like it! The atmosphere inside it was unsullied, the mood congenial. It boasted several excellent people and good fellowship ruled within. All these assets were associated with me. I was the one who recruited most of the people and achieved a closeness with them. They were my friends and companions. They had become accustomed to working with me and accepting my guidance. If I should go, the bond, I am afraid, may be severed. He asked if Eban could be taken into consideration to replace me. I said I was afraid not yet. He was brilliant to external appearances, but he lacked roots in the country and was not enough of a heavyweight in the internal arena. His non-membership in the party will also pose a difficulty. For this reason I was not at all keen about the prime ministership, and proposed Lavon. He said it didn't solve the problem and was entirely out of the question.

I stepped into the Knesset for a few minutes while Dinur[10] was expounding on education matters. I stayed there until it came time to drive home and prepare myself for the difficult trial of the meeting with Rega Oren. I hadn't seen her since the 23rd Zionist Congress in 1951 when she gave me a cold shoulder and refused to respond to my greetings, and this after years of friendship, albeit a strange friendship. She now met me with a broad smile, but I could see her face had withered, had become narrow and pointed, all the blood drained from it. I immediately came to the heart of the matter. I laced the bitter news of the sentence with the hope of a pardon.

10 Benzion Dinur (1884-1973). Historian; Minister of Education and Culture (1951-1955).

She heard it without any outward sign, but I felt she was stifling something inside. She asked if it would be publicized. I said: "In the morning papers." She asked: "And on the radio?" I said: "To night at 8:30." She blurted out: "With the children by themselves!" She got up and turned her face to the wall. I inquired as to the ages of the children. She replied: "The girl is sixteen, the boy is six." I said I could postpone the broadcast till tomorrow morning. She thanked me for it. (In BG's opinion I must have been remiss in my public responsibility again.) She turned her face away from me again, and asked me to leave the room for a moment. I understood she needed to compose herself. When she left she said she would try to get to her kibbutz, Mizra, by tonight, to be with the children when the newspapers arrive.

I telephoned [my secretary] Shamai to notify *Kol-Israel*[11] not to broadcast the announcement of the verdict tonight, but only tomorrow morning. After only a few minutes had gone by, the news editor was on the telephone: Could it be possible? The announcement has already been relayed to the agencies, in a short while the news would start rebounding from all the world's stations while we ourselves should remain silent. I telephoned Riftin at the Knesset and, after ascertaining that Rega had already left for Mizra, telephoned *Kol-Israel* and allowed them to broadcast the news at 11:00 tonight.

I worked on my papers until the time came for the meeting of the Political Committee of the party. It convened at 9:00 and lasted till midnight. I counted some forty people. From the very first moment the atmosphere was heavy and the tension did not abate till the end. The opening was most peculiar. In BG's presence, his secretary Yitzhak Navon read out his letter to the President – the resignation and his reasons for it. The letter in itself is a well-crafted and elegantly-phrased document, but all the expressive skill and heated emotion is devoted to justify a step which has no rationale. As soon as the letter had been read, BG asked for the floor, and said he would like to propose his suggestions for arranging matters. He proposed Levi Eshkol as PM and Pinhas Lavon as Defense Minister. He added that he was willing to concern himself with arranging coalition affairs, and hinted that he would be willing to postpone his retirement until this work was completed, and in any event until a final resolution in the SC.

When he finished, he immediately wrote a note and handed it to me. I could imagine what our *haverim* were thinking – he's written Moshe a personal note to explain and justify his position. The note, however, was about his conversation with the Agudist Dr Yitzhak Levin[12] from New York, on the chances of the *Aguda [Agudat-Israel]*'s returning to the coalition....

So, at last, the die was cast regarding the prime-ministership as far as BG is concerned! This in itself didn't surprise me, but BG's haste to announce this upset

11 "The Voice of Israel" – the country's national radio service.

12 Rabbi Yitzhak Levin (1906-1996). Leader, *Agudat-Israel*, US.

my plans to speak immediately after him. I kept silent and let Shmuel Dayan[13] and one or two others pose their innocent questions and emotional protests at BG's resignation. Finally I took the floor, and said I had meant to speak, but BG's proposal had prevented me from doing so. I accepted his proposal without hesitation, but if I now said what I held in my heart, my *haverim* might misinterpret my words. They must certainly agree that to a certain extent the matter concerned also me. I was also afraid that in describing the gloomy prospects I saw I might be tempting fate. I had therefore decided not to speak.

The debate progressed lazily for a while until its heat slowly began to rise. Zalman Shazar[14] spoke most vigorously, [basing his arguments] on the basis of the very "touching document" – that is, BG's letter [of resignation] to Ben-Zvi. If the state of the country as described therein was true, then the retirement was a glaring sin. He disagreed explicitly with the choice of Eshkol, for whereas the Treasury was the consolidation of the means, the PM needed to symbolize the necessity.

Eshkol himself declared in a level-headed manner that his candidacy for the post of PM was out of the question. Akiva Govrin[15] rose to great heights on this occasion. He challenged BG with the fact that there was no precedent in the history of Israel whereby the greatest man of his generation, from Moses to our own times, should abandon his post at the nation's helm of his own will. Would BG himself now repudiate this tradition of responsibility?

I decided to speak. I had been thinking: "damned if I do, damned if I don't," but Dinur's quote of the Mosaic dictum "if he does not utter it, then he shall bear his iniquity," [Lev. 5:1] tipped the scales of my inner conflict. As a *haver* who has known BG these past 40 years – more than anyone else in this room – and who has been working with him these past 20 years,[16] I would be happy if I could say to him: "Do as you please, you've earned it."

I could not say it. I could not grant him any moral release. For, against his personal need to retire stood the public need not let him do it. I'm not of the opinion that the nation cannot exist without any one person. A replacement shall of necessity be found; apportionment of responsibility in a different way shall of necessity give rise to new blood. The question is what to do in the meantime. For other nations, the meantime may not be critical. With us it determines our fate.

---

13 Shmuel Dayan (1891-1968). Born in Russia. Settled in Palestine in 1908. Mapai leader and MK (1949-1959). Leader, National Organization of Cooperative Settlements (Moshavim). Father of Moshe Dayan.

14 Zalman Shazar (1889-1974). Born in Russia. Settled in Palestine in 1924. Founder and leader, Mapai. MK (1949-1956). Minister of Education and Culture (1949-1950). Third President of Israel (1963-1974).

15 Akiva Govrin (1902-1980). Born in Russia. Settled in Palestine in 1922. Mapai MK (1949-1969); later Minister without portfolio.

16 Sharett and Ben-Gurion joined the JAE in 1933, and Ben-Gurion became its Chairman in 1935.

BG's retirement was tantamount to the removal of a machine's central pivot. The machine would break down. The retirement connoted the departure of the group's central figure. It would fall apart. The retirement was equal to the elimination of moral authority. Inescapable strife would ensue, not only among all parties, but inside our own Party too. Internal dissension and personal animosities would be unleashed. Contradictory inclinations would be sharpened and differences of opinion would become more serious. BG was perhaps oblivious to these considerations, not from any lack of desire but because of emotional inability. We had no choice but to voice them, even if only for our own ears. Was it really not possible to make an effort to reconsider? By all means, let Pinhas Lavon serve as Defense Minister. It would lighten a heavy burden. There could be other palliatives. Eshkol would take on some of the PM's duties. I will too. We shall lighten his load as much as possible. Only let him not strike his name from the Cabinet, let him not abandon his cardinal responsibility within the party and the coalition, let him not cease to serve as the spokesman of the nation.

Haim Ben-Asher[17] spoke after me: "Let BG leave the helm, if he so wills, but only on condition that from now on he devotes himself to building the party and the nation." As if this was his intention!

At this point BG burst into the fray like a wounded animal, in a raging fury, as if having been hurt to the depths of his soul. Why is he not being believed? Had he come to deceive the *haverim*? What would be the gain of all our rebuke? He couldn't go on. Finis. He'd come to the end of his ability. This "fellow" cannot do the job anymore. Was it possible to force him? This glass on the table – was it possible to compel it to become a gun? And lies have been bandied about by his *haverim* in the party and in the country at large and even in the coalition. The entire horrific prospect was nothing but a vain conceit. The *haverim* may have said what they were feeling at the moment, but that was not the exact truth. Moshe had known him these past 40 years? He'd known Moshe too these past 40 years. Moshe did not accurately present himself here. The situation was not terrible at all. Matters would be arranged, and all the apprehension was for naught. And so on and so forth.

After this I was prepared to get up and propose accepting the verdict, but the matter of Eshkol's candidacy bothered me, [so I remained silent]. But this [proposal to accept BG's resignation] was made by Lavon. But the meeting refused to take the responsibility upon itself and decided to transfer the matter to the Party Central Committee; that if its appeal to BG should prove fruitless, it may enjoin the Political Committee to propose the necessary arrangements.

As we walked home, I told Shaul Avigur I now had a very interesting channel for learning about BG's thinking – the *Shin-Bet* reports about his talks with leaders

17 Haim Ben-Asher (1904-1998). Born in Russia. Settled in Palestine in 1924. Mapai MK; member of the FADC until 1955.

of *Hapo'el Hamizrahi*.[18] Eshkol isn't his only candidate for the prime ministership. The other candidate is ... Barney. When we got back home I sat down to correct the proofs of Leo Kohn's booklet on the Arab refugees. According to the telegrams, the UN GA debate on the refugees begins this week already. Leo was late anyway – as he always is – and I saw fit not to put off my final proofreading for even one day more. I worked quickly and finished the entire booklet. I lay down after 1:00 am, and for a long time found it hard to fall asleep.

Tuesday, November 3

In the morning papers there was an enigmatic report on the explosion of a water pipeline in the vicinity of the Old City of Jerusalem.

The first appointment at the office was with Dr Levin, that same *Aguda* leader from America. In New York I always spoke English with him. Here he had addressed the Jerusalem conference in clear, fluent Hebrew in a flawless Sephardi accent. I complimented him upon it, and we continued in Hebrew as if we'd never spoken anything else. He outdid himself in proclamations of allegiance and devotion to the State of Israel. He fervently desired to see the return of the *Aguda* to the coalition. He complained bitterly about the regimen within his party, whereby every possessor of a beard and sidelocks, be he a member of the *Aguda* or not, be he a learned Torah scholar or just a common ignoramus, takes the liberty of voicing an opinion and issuing an edict regarding party policy.

[- - -]

Dr Lowdermilk[19] dropped by to say goodbye before returning to the US. He's lately been working here as an expert on behalf of the UN Food and Agriculture Organization. He was very gentle in his criticism of the Ministry of Agriculture's deportment. He'd received no reply to all the reports he had submitted to the Minister of Agriculture [Peretz Naftali]. In fact, he had had no contact at all with the Minister of Agriculture and his DG. His only contact was with the Land Conservation Department (the managing director of which, Nathan Gil, came with him). He did not think we had learned enough from him. We were repeating serious mistakes in land cultivation practices meant to prevent erosion. In certain areas, erosion in Israel was greater than it was in the time of the Mandate and Arab agriculture. His honest advice to us is – fewer experts, but greater exploitation of their expertise, and more attention to their counsel.

---

18 At this time the *Shin-Bet* (see above page 83 n.32) still secretly gathered information about the various political parties other than Mapai.

19 Walter Clay Lowdermilk (1888-1974). American soil conservation expert who was very impressed with Zionist land reclamation work in Mandatory Palestine, and whose 1944 water development plans would later be of importance for the building of Israel's National Water Carrier.

I took this criticism very seriously, all the more so coming from a friend and an expert whose only wish is to see wrongs corrected. For a while now I have been ill at ease concerning our attitude towards experts in general and UN experts in particular. I had meant to raise the issue in the Cabinet a few times and it seems to me it should be postponed no longer.

I asked Lowdermilk if he had seen the Main Plan, and when he replied in the negative, I edified him with the main points of the plan, and the thrust of our objection to it and asked him to maintain his interest in the matter after he returns to the US.

At 11:00 I drove to the Knesset for a meeting of the Foreign Affairs and Defense Committee. First I addressed myself to what had transpired since the last meeting: the chain of events at the SC, and our talks with Johnston. My very first item gave me an opportunity to settle a score with Mapam. They had voted against the stoppage of work, whereas Vyshinsky[20] had expressly demanded a stoppage and had even pestered Eban in his desire to ascertain that the work would be stopped without delay. It seems there was a most unfortunate lack of coordination here, no doubt the fault of Vyshinsky, who had not made sure to contact Riftin in time to receive instructions.... There was a big round of laughter. After I had finished my report, the problem concerning the debate in the Knesset came up. I presented the Cabinet's position which was against a general debate as long as the question was being discussed in the SC. In any event, not within the next two weeks. I said that artillery fire from the rear to support the assault of an infantry platoon was of use if it hit the enemy, but not if it wiped out the attackers. Of course, *Herut* and Mapam demanded a general debate forthwith, but failed to achieve it. Indeed, Riftin was much less forceful than last time in demanding a debate. The reason was obvious. Mapam had no interest in bringing the matter of the Prague sentences to the debate in the Knesset. I reported to the Committee on these sentences too – in slightly greater detail than the published version.

[- - -]

In the middle of the meeting, I was called out into the corridor on an urgent matter. Lt.-Colonel Aryeh Shalev had come to suggest that we not continue sealing the dam by means of that machine on our own, for fear of getting into trouble with the UN. Let us first ask Bennike's deputy if it was acceptable with him. I agreed.

I returned to the office for a talk with Leo Kohn. All my corrections of the proofs of the booklet on the refugees are being put in today and the booklet will be published in the very near future. There is hope it may be ready in time for the debate in the UN GA.

[- - -]

---

20 Andrei Y. Vyshinsky (1883-1954). Soviet FM (1949-1953); Permanent Soviet Representative to the UN.

Moshe Sharett and Andrei Vyshinsky

In Leo's presence I thought out loud about the course of events surrounding BG's resignation, and the things that had been said at the meeting of Mapai's Political Committee last night. He was pleased with Eshkol's candidacy as the lesser evil – at least not Lavon.

On my way home, I bid Shamai to look into the explosion of the pipeline with the Army and BG.

At home, I sat down with gusto over my papers. An hour later Shamai telephoned to say he had news that had best be delivered in person. He came to report. The Army claims we had nothing to do with the matter. No order to do any such thing was given. There has been no word from our men on Mount Scopus either, and nobody could imagine that they might have done anything on their own without receiving proper order. Still, the people on the mountain had been asked to report and their answer was soon due. Meanwhile, UN Observers and Arab Legion officers set out with a tracker, and the tracks led very close to the fence of Mount Scopus, right up to the guardpost which our people man at night.

I said that under the circumstances it was clear we must disseminate our version saying that this was a calculated act of deception on the part of the Jordanians. They are constantly harassing Mount Scopus and inventing pretexts to justify large-scale action by them against us, at the least a thorough search of our people by UN officials. Bennike had already tried to carry this out at their instigation. I telephoned Michael Elizur and briefed him. All the same, Shamai said that he had heard from *Shin-Bet* sources that, according to another version, our people have nonetheless had a hand in the matter. Anything is possible with us!

Shamai also had more to report on the dam. The UN CoS's deputy [Henri Vigier] was opposed to any work on it. If there was any seepage – no matter, let it continue, just so long as there's no infringement of a SC directive. The prohibition can only be lifted by the authority that issued it. That is, if we wanted to obtain permission to work, we had to turn to the SC.

I asked Shamai to find the DG. Walter was found, and responding to my summons came at once. I told him about the complications concerning the dam and other problems pertaining to the work in the DMZ. I said that it had been quite a few days that I had been thinking that I should go and verify the situation for myself. I saw no possibility of doing so, and therefore had to ask him to go instead. Walter said he was willing, but suggested sending Zvi Avnon[21] instead since the latter was more knowledgeable than he was about technical matters. I agreed.

I told Walter about the state of affairs in the Cabinet. He tried to persuade me to accept the prime ministership if there should emerge a majority in my favor within the party. I contended that the combination of both posts would tear me apart. He tried to ease my mind. Everyone would help me; hadn't BG also occupied himself

21 Zvi Avnon (1902-1996). MFA since 1949; Israel First Ambassador to Denmark.

considerably with security and foreign affairs? The combination of PM and Foreign Minister was a common practice in the world, and had the most striking precedents.

Returned to my papers, and at 9:00 went with Zipporah to a memorial concert for Weizmann by the *Kol-Israel* Orchestra. The main part of the evening was Beethoven's "Emperor" piano concerto, played brilliantly by Nadia Etingon. It was a pity that no one could see her because of the strange arrangement of the members of the philharmonic. It is difficult to listen to piano music properly when one cannot follow the running fingers.

On the way home I said to Zipporah: Just think of the lack of wisdom and foresight in BG's haste to propose Eshkol as a candidate. First of all, if he is retiring, why should he try to impose his will upon the public? The public should be allowed to choose the successor it desired. Most importantly, what if this candidacy does not appeal to the party? That would have serious negative consequences. First, the exposure of a serious rift between BG and his Party, which is neither to his nor the party's greater credit. Second, the damage to Eshkol for no reason at all. Third, the grave weakening of a candidate preferred by the party. Was BG really so sure that his opinion would be accepted? If he was confident and erred, that in itself is a serious failure. And if he wasn't confident, why did he propose it?

Sat up for two hours writing my diary.

Wednesday, November 4

In the newspapers there were splashy headlines about Eshkol's "resignation," meaning to say his withdrawal from the candidacy for PM. This opening-up of our party "kitchen" for everybody to peep in and smell is indeed an endearing and exhilarating spectacle.

The day at the office began with a meeting about our consulate in Rangoon. [- - -] After the meeting, David Hacohen told me that quite a few *haverim* in the party could not imagine that all of BG's proposed arrangements, foremost among them Eshkol's candidacy for the prime ministership, were not the outcome of consultations between BG and myself. Even he finds it hard to believe that BG never once spoke to me about all these matters. I said that BG could not be taken to task. Having come to the conclusion that I am not the man, he could not have been expected to confide his innermost thoughts to me.

[- - -]

I had a very interesting conversation with Dave Ginsberg[22] and found that some of his views concerning the state of our affairs correspond to mine. He

22 C. David Ginsberg (1912-1990). American Jewish lawyer, a founder of Americans for Democratic Action, and active supporter of the Democratic Party. Served as legal counsel for the JA and later the Israel Embassy in Washington.

remarked on our hopes for foreign currency income which are floating in the air. He considers them overestimated. The US grant this year won't exceed 50 million, and it is good that the budget was based on this sum exclusively; but there will be a further reduction next year, even if not total liquidation as yet. Regarding income from Jewish sources, this year we may perhaps receive from the UJA and the State of Israel Bonds Organization as much as last year, but next year there will be another drop. The effort behind the Israel Bonds will yield at most $10 million and not 30, as Teddy is hoping. He wondered if our leading experts had taken an exact accounting of the extent to which we are dependent on this outside income to maintain our standard of living, and what its decrease or liquidation may mean in terms of our way of life.

In his opinion, the Treasury errs in its exaggerated preference for agriculture and irrigation. Both Eshkol and Sapir are too much *Mekorot* men at heart.[23] All the actual planning is directed towards agriculture. No serious thought is being given to industry.

On matters of foreign policy, Dave's analysis was realistic, but his conclusions unusual: the key to peace was in Egypt's hands, and for the time being Egypt was embroiled in negotiations with the British. An opportunity for progress should come with the end of these negotiations. Up to now, he had stated the obvious and what was already known. I said the only question was how the Suez settlement may influence Egyptian President General Mohammed Neguib.[24] In any case, it should be a glorious victory for him. But what course will he embark upon thereafter? Will he consider himself strong enough to compromise with Israel as a result of his victory? Or, rather, intoxicated by victory, will he prepare for war with us? Dave accepted my assessment, but argued that our aim should be to offer Neguib a settlement which he could present to his own people not as a compromise but as an additional victory.

What did that mean? Well, Dave suggested a new and innovative idea. We should propose to Neguib the establishment of an Egyptian-Israeli "corporation" for the joint exploitation of natural deposits in the Negev and other projects, with a concession to a certain stretch of territory in Israel, including the right to maintain an army there. I said: "Do you mean mutual exploitation of natural deposits, in both Israeli and Egyptian territory?" Not exactly. The main thing was to give Egypt the satisfaction of having obtained something it hadn't had before. The whole idea

23 The *Mekorot* company was established in 1937 jointly by the JA, the *Histadrut* and the JNF for the development of water resources for the *yishuv*. In 1956 the State of Israel joined its directorship and in 1959 it became the National Water Company of Israel.

24 General Mohammed Neguib (1901-1984). Decorated veteran of the 1948-1949 Palestine War, later joined with the "Free Officers" group which overthrew King Farouk's dynasty in the coup of July 1952; served as the titular head of the Revolutionary Command Council until his deposition in November 1954.

seems premature to me. Dave knew about Dolik Horowitz's plan that we propose a tunnel near Eilat to Egypt to renew the territorial link between Egypt and Jordan. Interestingly enough, BG himself told him about it while voicing agreement to the plan (it was the first I had heard of BG's willingness). But, in Dave's opinion, this trifling concession wasn't likely to make an impression on Egypt.

Hurried home, snatched some food, and within a quarter of an hour set out for Tel Aviv. I drove alone, and picked up three soldiers on the road, all of them dark-skinned. It seems to me that Gideon reached top speed this time. We left Smolenskin Street at 1:58 and at 3:01 the car pulled up at the gates of the *Histadrut* Executive Committee's new building. And this after stopping four times to pick up and drop off the soldiers, and turning off into a dirt track next to Mishmar David because of road repairs. And why the big hurry? Because the meeting – the fateful meeting! – of the Party Central Committee, which had at first been scheduled for this evening, had been moved up to 3:00 in the afternoon.

It was my first visit to this new building, nicknamed by the bourgeoisie "The Kremel."[25] I have heard much about its luxurious style, but what I now saw with my own eyes was beyond all anticipation – the marble columns, the bright walls, the width of the stairs, the modern elevator and, above all, the huge space of the meeting hall with its impressive furniture and wood paneling – all these cried of exaggeration, a boasting imitation of Americanism, a move following in the steps of the ZOA building [in Tel Aviv], an example of bad ways. How superior is the modest beauty of the Foreign Ministry's pavilions.

The Central Committee members were seated according to the hall's shape. In the old *Histadrut*'s Executive building we used to sit around an oval table, many of us crowded within the egg-shaped center and others filling up the hall's corners. Here we are seated in rows, each row seeing the backs of those sitting in front of it, instead of seeing their faces. The chairman is elevated and distant, the speakers move up to the podium and use the microphone instead of each speaking from his seat. Thus is an exaggerated amount of formality introduced into the whole business and the atmosphere of intimacy is gone. We shall certainly in time get used to this new regime, but meanwhile it's difficult to digest. The luxurious, almost arrogant, look of the hall with its huge windows overlooking Tel Aviv removes any sense of intimacy.

The meeting opened with the reading of a document, this time a letter from BG to the party secretary, a second version of his letter to the President, containing the same explanations. Most of the members of the Central Committee, and this time almost all members were present, that is, some one hundred and fifty, were

25 "Kremel," the Russian word for citadel or fortified complex, is translated into English as "Kremlin," denoting the seat of Soviet power in a walled area of Moscow. Israeli anti-socialists regarded the imposing building of the *Histadrut* labor federation headquarters in Tel Aviv as the Israeli equivalent of the Kremlin.

hearing it for the first time and were clearly dumbfounded. Until now they had evidently thought that despite all the official announcements there must be some explanation, and who knows what internal complications had brought the "Old Man" to take this surprising step. But as it turns out, no such thing. He simply could not bear the mental stress any more. The man is tired. That this should be the real reason and none other made people vacillate between astonishment and incredulity.

Shmuel Yavne'eli was first to speak. He spoke with great admiration, elevating BG to the highest rank of the unique leaders in their generation, but solemnly enjoining him not to retire. There was a glaring gap between the tremendous moral authority of the substance, and the weakness and ineptitude of the manner of its presentation (Yavne'eli mentioned that he was older than BG).

BG immediately rose to reply: again the same irrefutable reason, the fact cannot be argued away; such is the predicament he has reached, and no amount of words and persuasive effort could make him change his mind.

The debate which ensued was unprecedented in character and in the makeup of its participants. People spoke not from any simple need to express or distinguish themselves. They pressed up to the lectern with an inner sense of responsibility, as representatives of the multitude of rank and file of the party. Three women spoke, almost one after the other, and each made a greater and more moving impression than the last. The first of the three was Yehudit Ginzburg of Jerusalem, a natural speaker, whose flights of oratory rose this time to greater than ordinary heights. She spoke in the name of the multitudes of the House of Israel, the plain Jewish folk and the children of the streets. She related how a neighbor of hers, a shop-owner from *Agudat-Israel* circles, had burst into her home in the evening and admonished: "How can you let him go? He belongs to us all, but only you can influence him! It's up to you!"

The second was Lily Menachem, a Greek-born Sephardi. I believe it was the first time she had ever spoken at a meeting of the Central Committee. Her emotions filled her with choked tears. Her Hebrew was excellent, flawless, charming in simplicity. She too spoke in the name of the "neighborhoods," expressing the emotions of legions of simple Jews. Every word of hers came from deep in the heart, and pierced the listener's heart.

The third was Rivka Guber, the woman from Moshav Kfar Bilu, a soldier in WWII, who'd lost two dear sons in the War of Independence. She is not a member of the Central Committee, but requested permission to attend. When she sent the chairman a note to ask for the floor, it was passed on to me for counsel and I asked Golda's opinion. We both thought that we could not deny such a woman the right to speak her mind, even though it would rip out BG's heart [to face this tragic woman]. From the very start of her speech, it was clear that an extremely complex personality stood before us, highly refined in thought and expression, but well aware of her own merit and not given to curb it. The language was eminently literary, the sentences splendidly thought-out and polished. "There are soldiers who have not received their discharge; accordingly they cannot grant a discharge either." "From the depths of my bereavement I cry out: Recant!"

The string of speakers was broken, laced with intervals of silence and weighty anticipation between one speaker and the next. When the chairman prepared to wind the meeting up, a mutiny broke out. Argov sought the CC's agreement to an "appeal" to BG to withdraw his resignation. And if he should fail to respond – this would not constitute any breach of discipline. Then the CC could proceed to arrange matters and entrust the task to the Political Committee. The members refused to accept the verdict. It was inconceivable, they argued, that the CC should absorb the blow and adjust to the shock at a moment's notice. Some time must intervene. Let us not make any decision this evening, but gather together again in a few days' time.

My opinion was that any procrastination, expressing malaise and confusion, could only worsen the situation and deepen the crisis in public confidence. I did not voice it aloud. Golda came out in support of those who demanded a deferral. Finally a compromise was reached. It was decided to address an appeal to BG and reconvene on Sunday evening. All of BG's entreaties – that no dishonor be brought upon the CC by means of an appeal to which he could not respond – did not help one bit. The CC remained adamant and thus dispersed.

Zipporah attended only the first part of the meeting. She had to go to the dental clinic. I told her what transpired. We ate, and I remained alone. Zipporah drove into town once again to Shaul and Sarah [Avigur] in order to offer Sarah advice about her trip abroad with Shaul. Shaul is returning to the rescuing front. Perhaps it shall prove to be his own salvation as well.[26]

[- - -]

I returned to my diary and brought it up to date. Afterwards I sat over my papers. On arriving home this evening, I found a nine-word letter from my brother Yehuda: "A work of art – may you be blessed." The allusion was to my speech on Weizmann which Yehuda heard over the radio. I was pleased. Today I received a short letter of very generous praise for the same speech from the old writer Yaakov Fichman.[27]

Thursday, November 5

This morning the newspapers were full of BG's letter to Argov, which was read out to the CC yesterday.

---

26 Avigur had recently founded and become director of *Nativ* (see above, page 6 n.25, and also below, page 248 n.44). By saying "Shaul is returning to the rescuing front," Sharett is alluding to his previous rescue work as head of the pre-1948 *Mossad Le'aliya Bet* (the Institute for "Illegal" Immigration), smuggling Jewish Holocaust survivors from central Europe to Mediterranean ports in Italy and France, and from there aboard ships to Palestine.

27 Yaakov Fichman (1881-1958). Hebrew poet, critic and literary editor.

Set out for Jerusalem at 7:45. I drove alone. Zipporah is to come with the CoS in the afternoon. I gave soldiers rides in the car, picking them up on the road one after another and dropping them off. One couple – a soldier and a civilian girl – came in together and began chattering as soon as they entered. At first I tried to restrain myself, but failing it I finally said to the girl: "Excuse me, I would like to think." They immediately apologized and fell silent. This has happened to me a number of times. When they departed I said: "Don't be sorry, but this car is a private room and I'm accustomed to quiet inside it."

At the office I took care of this and that until it was time for the President's father's funeral. I drove to the cemetery with Eliyahu Dobkin.[28]

[- - -]

In the car, returning from the funeral, Dobkin spoke incessantly about the resignation, and the latest meetings of the Political Committee and the CC. Except for the disjointed remarks I had heard from David Hacohen, this was my first opportunity to plumb the feelings which were in the air among the *haverim* – to the extent that Dobkin can be considered to express them.

Well then, much criticism of BG's manner of speaking at the meetings, his style in his response to me at the Political Committee meeting and the spirit of his remarks at the CC meeting yesterday, the anger and harshness with no vestige of compassion or friendship. On the other hand, Dobkin was unsparing in his reproach of Rivka Guber: how dare she speak in the name of the dead and take BG to task in the name of those whom he had sent to their deaths. His harshest criticism of BG was because of his proposal of Eshkol for PM, both regarding the candidacy itself and the manner of its presentation. The real reason for this candidacy was apparent to him and other *haverim*: BG was determined to return after a spell of time, and it would be foolish on his part to vacate his place to someone it might prove difficult to remove after having achieved success. Eshkol himself has stated, according to Dobkin, in conversation with some *haverim*, that if he should accept BG's proposal it would be digging his own grave. Regarding the *haverim* at large, the decisive majority, almost all members, rejected it. Dobkin viewed Eshkol as the weakest candidate of all four being mentioned. Eshkol was a clear-cut "improvisationalist." Improvisation is a good quality in a settlement administrator, in a Finance Minister too – under our specific circumstances, but not by any means in whoever must take responsibility for overall policy, both internally and externally.

28 Eliyahu Dobkin (1898-1976). Mapai leader; Head of the JA's Youth and *Hehalutz* Department (1951-1968); Chairman of *Keren Hayesod* (1951-1962). The Youth and *Hehalutz* Department of the JA assisted diaspora youth groups in preparation for immigration and kibbutz life in Palestine, later Israel. The *Keren Hayesod* ("Foundation Fund"), created in 1920, was the main fund-raising arm for diaspora contributions to the upbuilding of the Jewish national home in Palestine, and later Israel; subsequently became the UJA and the United Israel Appeal.

Finally he turned to me and said: the *haverim* know how strained your situation is, but you must accept the verdict if they demand it; there is no doubt that they will.

As to the real reason for the resignation, Dobkin thinks, much like Leo Kohn, that it is not so much the result of tension accrued in the past as the lack of tension in the present. There was no war into which he could throw all his emotional resources, no decisive political battle in the offing. The country has sunk into day-to-day routine in which the emphasis is on the economic effort. This was not the type of situation in which a dynamic and fervent personality like BG could find his place and feel he was fulfilling his role.

[- - -]

I sent a telegram to the delegation in New York about the conclusions stemming from Avnon's consultations with *Tahal* about the dam yesterday: no repair work was to be done on the canal as long as the stoppage continued.

Leo's booklet on the refugees was finally published. It looks elegant enough and I sent him a note of congratulations upon the completion of this important task.[29]

Meanwhile, a small cloud "like a man's hand" [*I Kings*, 18:44] appeared in the morning newspapers. The US is intending to apply serious pressure for the solution of the refugee problem. It would exert influence on the Arab states to speed up resettlement, and on us for accepting back some of the refugees.

Eliezer Livneh came by at 4:00. He's going to America and requested a talk before he leaves. Rumor has it he has been letting out that BG is sending him to establish a Jewish committee on behalf of Israel to be headed by Abba Hillel Silver. This is not the first time that Livneh has gone to the US, ostensibly on a special mission for BG that is shrouded in mystery; that is, he's the one who hints at the mission and the one who shrouds it in mystery, while BG only succumbs to his pressure, which can drive a man mad, and lets him have his way in order not to be bothered. At any rate, I was very curious to know what was really on his mind this time.

A mountain out of a molehill. It is all baseless gossip. Surprisingly enough I enjoyed a pleasant easy-going conversation with the man. Though his intellectual arrogance exceeds all limits, the interesting thing is that this is no artificial or affected pose, but a natural trait contained in his very essence. He is sincerely convinced that all he need do is talk to a few centrally placed rabbis in the US or to people like Joseph Proskauer and maybe to some Zionists for added glory, in order to bring about a metamorphosis in the fiber of life of American Jewry and its relations with Israel. This would revolutionize the internal structure of the Zionist movement and the allocation of roles therein. He also assumes he is capable – by means of a few explanatory talks with AFL-CIO leaders and with one statesman or one or two journalists – of bringing about a change in the main thrust of US policy

29 The English-language booklet, "The Arab Refugees," was published in November 1953 by the Israel Office of Information, New York (45 pp.). No author's name was given.

in Europe. They should entirely abandon the plan to arm Germany and instead foster a strong tendency towards the complete neutralization of central Europe.

[- - -]

Walter read out over the phone the draft of a cable to Bennike, to be sent tomorrow over my signature, against Jordan's machinations against us – the Jordanians are accusing us of acts which have never taken place. The sending of this protest cable for the sake of balancing-out was Eban's idea. I found the draft excellent – Walter is a superb drafter – it was only that the end lacked sharpness and I added a sentence castigating Jordan's move to tilt the scales against us while the SC was meeting.[30] By the way, it has been ascertained meanwhile that we were not involved in the blowing up of the water pipe.

At 7:30 Zipporah and I drove to the King David for a dinner held by the PM and his wife in honor of the scientists who had come for the week of lectures held in memory of Chaim Weizmann. We found a large crowd. I made the acquaintance of Niels Bohr, the greatest physicist of his generation, and of chemist Linus Pauling. I also had a friendly encounter with Ernst Boris Chen, the inventor of penicillin, whose acquaintance I had made in Rome. We spoke in Russian.

It was a rather noisy dinner with a lot of commotion, but a convivial atmosphere reigned. There were some speeches, all of them to the point, except for Bohr's. His speech may or may not have been to the point, for it was impossible to understand one word of it. His diction was extremely cloudy.

[- - -]

Yitzhak Navon came to tell me about the PM's conversation with the GZ ministers. They had insisted upon the posts of Deputy PM, Finance Minister and Minister of Education. All of the PM's arguments and efforts of persuasion that they had no right to pose such demands upon his retirement were for naught. They remained adamant. If so, the PM said, there will be no choice other than to renew the small coalition – Mapai and the religious parties, including the *Aguda*. This is exactly what I had feared and had told BG when he thought the GZ had accepted his dictate. The PM's successor – whoever he may be – will inherit the disintegration of the coalition.

At 11:30 I sat down over my papers. I then brought my diary up to date, and lay down to sleep at 1:00.

Friday, November 6

There was nothing special at the office.

I answered a telegram from the Washington Embassy which conveyed a query by the State Department concerning Lavon's speech: what was the Cabinet's authorized

30 *DFPI* 8, doc.496.

position on the Main Plan? Was it in Lavon's speech, or in my statement to Johnston?

[- - -]

At home, lunch for 12 guests: four New York bankers visiting Israel as guests of the JA; Gottlieb Hammer,[31] JA director in the US, who is their guide; Isidor Lubin, a renowned American economist, member of President Roosevelt's staff and his wife; Teddy and Tamar Kollek, Dolik and Riva Horowitz, and Chaya Syrkin, President of "Pioneer Women" in the US.[32] After the meal, at Hammer's request, I conducted a discussion on the problem of peace with the neighboring states.

At 6:30 we set out to Haifa for a farewell party for David Hacohen who is about to depart for Rangoon.

[- - -]

I had a short talk with Yaakov Dori.[33] I found him full of recrimination regarding the ousting of Maklef before he completed even one year as the IDF CoS. He saw this move as destructive of both army and people.

[- - -]

We stayed there late after midnight. At the end of the party, which was entirely given to jest and frolic, Shulamit Klebanov, an old friend who had been won over by Mapam, spoke some weighty words of farewell. Among other things, she made favorable mention of the strong friendship in this circle among people of different socialist outlooks. Evidently encouraged by this remark, an ex-pupil of mine in the late 1920s, when I was quite active in the life of our party's youth movement, who had also embraced Mapam, came up to me and took the opportunity to take me to account. Why, she complained, had I said in one of my speeches that, even if I do have good friends in Mapam, I feel no ideological bond between us; on the contrary, in terms of political ideology there is a chasm between us – Marxists and pro-Soviet members of Mapam, and the social-democrats of Mapai. Could it be, she contended, that we have ceased to be one political movement, united at the roots? I told her that to my great regret what I had said was the solemn truth. A wall had sprung up between us, a wall called the Soviet Union; the cloud of revolutionary

31 Gottlieb Hammer (1913-1993). Executive Vice-Chairman, American Section of the JA; longtime supporter of the Weizmann Institute. Later Executive Chairman, United Israel Appeal.

32 Pioneer Women (since 1981, *Na'amat*): a women's organization founded in the US in 1925, part of the Labor Zionist movement. Its activities include fundraising for social services for Israeli women, youth and children. Aside from fundraising, it runs social services (e.g., a training school for nurses, children's homes, day-care centers, vocational and agricultural schools, and community centers) and promotes educational and cultural activities to encourage women to be active in Israeli and diaspora Jewish affairs.

33 Lieut.-General Yaakov Dori (1899-1973). CoS *Hagana* (1939-1945); first IDF CoS (1948-1949); President of Haifa Technion (1951-1965). Member of the Olshan-Dori Inquiry Commission; see below, entries for January 2, 1955 and following.

mythology in which it was clad was completely at odds with our true values. This wall divided us, and totally. If we could still get together on a friendly basis, it was only due to our shared past, which had nothing to do with our political life of the present. My children already had no common political ground with theirs, and as long as that mountain existed, the division between us would only widen more.

[- - -]

Saturday, November 7

[- - -]

From 3:00 in the afternoon until midnight I sat over the papers. A considerable pile had accumulated. The DG telephoned to report on two men who had been killed last night on their way to Sdom at the southern shore of the Dead Sea. This only a day after the killing of the railroad station guard in Hadera. The toll of blood was increasing again.

[- - -]

Sunday, November 8

Set out for Jerusalem at 7:15. [- - -] On the way, I peeked into *Ha'aretz* and – lo and behold – a good report maketh the bones fat! Eshkol having pulled back from the PM's post, Sharett's chances have improved! That is to say: "Next best."

At the office, I went over SC matters with Ze'ev Shek and the alleged signs of progress in immigration from Romania and Hungary. All this in preparation for my report to the Cabinet meeting.

[- - -]

My report was brief this time and the meeting went on to discuss the question concerning the Arab minority upon which Lavon had expounded at the last meeting. My proposal included: (a) a speedy resolution of the problem of the dispossessed through the allocation of land or payment of compensation; (b) a more humane attitude and a more authoritative handling of economic and administrative problems on the part of the military government; (c) official authorization of permanent residency for dispossessed Arabs who lack documents; (d) a more humane system for the approval of requests for family reunification in cases of deportations; (e) the appointment of a special committee to handle Muslim community affairs – holy places and religious courts; (f) the appointment of a new Arab Affairs Adviser to the PM, with clear-cut authority over inter-departmental coordination.

At the end of the meeting, BG announced that he would almost certainly not attend the next meeting. Evidently this was not yet his final retirement, he merely intended to spend some time in Tiberias. I wrote Ze'ev Sharef a note asking whether

BG understood that I could not serve as his deputy this time.

It turns out that the police think that the murder of the two near Sdom is of a criminal nature.

Ate lunch at home, slept half an hour and returned at 3:30 to the PMO for an extraordinary Cabinet meeting to discuss BG's proposals for the reorganization of the IDF along new lines. When I arrived the CoS informed me that the mystery surrounding the death of the two brothers had finally been unraveled. Neither infiltrators nor criminal elements had had a hand in the matter. A simple misfortune had befallen them. They had been hauling a waste container. One brother evidently fell into the container and either drowned or suffocated from the poisonous fumes. The other one also fell from the container as he tried to save his brother. He too may perhaps have become intoxicated and fainted. In falling he struck his head and died. A most peculiar incident. There were no signs of violence on the bodies, and no tracks in the vicinity of their vehicle.

All the same, word arrived of another incident. Three soldiers had been patrolling close to the Egyptian border near Nahal Oz. Two Egyptian soldiers set out towards them, crossed the border and engaged them in conversation. As they were talking, more Egyptian soldiers appeared, a few of them armed. Suddenly the Egyptians fell on one of the Jews and stole his rifle, hit him with the butt and stabbed him with the bayonet. The wounded soldier ran for his life. One of his companions was also wounded and then abducted. The remaining soldier escaped too. Now it is been announced that the Egyptians will return the body of the soldier they had captured. This is also a most peculiar story and bitter lesson.

[- - -]

The meeting ended before the end of our examination, since we had to go to the inauguration of the Rav Kook Foundation's new building. A gigantic auditorium, of extravagant dimensions, the largest in size in Jerusalem, overflowing with people, all the men wearing hats and skullcaps and the background generally as black as can be. BG was received with thunderous applause. It was surely a demonstration against his retirement. We came in the middle of a long string of speeches, but in time to hear some. BG concluded with a typical BG speech, very fervent and big-hearted, devoted in its entirety to the character of Rabbi Yehuda Leib Maimon[34] whom he truly admires and deeply loves. It was one of those speeches which a man carries inside him and nurtures in his thoughts, waiting for the right opportunity – the one and only opportunity! – to deliver it publicly and finding boundless satisfaction when such is finally granted to him. I know it only

34 Rabbi Yehuda Leib Fishman Maimon (1875-1962). Born in Besarabia. Settled in Palestine in 1913. Founder and leader of the world *Mizrahi* movement. Helped establish the Chief Rabbinate in Mandatory Palestine; established the Rav Kook Yeshiva in 1936; signatory to the Declaration of Independence; member of First Knesset; Minister of Religion (1949-1951).

too well! At the end of the session we were "taken prisoner" for the evening prayer. The voice of the cantor was strikingly sweet.

All evening I was occupied with my papers.

Monday, November 9

[- - -]

The highlight of the morning at the office was the preparation of my broadcast to the US: a Hannukah greeting to American Jewry. The broadcast is being conducted by the [American] Zionist Council, on behalf of which the Levinson couple is active in Israel. Leo composed a draft which I found acceptable in content but not in form. I dictated the entire text anew, and it came out much more polished and direct, even though all of Leo's basic ideas were retained, for which he is to be blessed.

[- - -]

Samuel Watson[35] of the British Labour Party and his wife came to visit at the office. The wife is surprisingly younger than her husband. It is Watson's second visit here. Since his first one three years ago, when he was chairman of the party, he has become a true friend of Israel and its staunch supporter within his party. He tried to allay my fears regarding Qibya. The initial disclosure had indeed been most damaging, but when reports concerning the chain of events leading up to the operation appeared, things were seen in a different light and the storm abated. He faithfully assures me that the entire matter has been forgotten, and we should have no fear of it. At any rate, that is how he feels. He added that, as a miner, he knew that when 50 men die in a cave-in disaster, the public is shocked. At the same time, nobody pays any attention to the death of the same number of men from coal-related diseases. Was this not the same thing? The example proved exactly the opposite of what Watson wished to demonstrate. The main thing in public life is not the fact in itself, but the impression it makes. The slaughter of fifty souls at a stroke produces a shock ten times more powerful than the killing of the same number, one by one, over a period of time.

[- - -]

Moshe Bartur[36] came in for a consultation. One of the subjects was the growing importance of Russian oil. The Arab boycott against us was worsening on all levels. Its last achievement was the cancellation of our ties with an Italian oil tanker. Russian oil is rich with salt, but we can desalinate it rather cheaply in [the]

35 Samuel Watson (1898-1967). Trades-union leader, National Union of Mineworkers; member, National Executive Committee, British Labour Party. Was made a CBE in 1946.

36 Moshe Bartur (1919-1985). Director, Economic Division, MFA; later Assistant DG, MFA; later Ambassador to UN Economic and Social Council and to Tokyo.

Haifa [refineries]. Bartur asked whether we should inform the Americans of our prospective deal with the Russians – bartering oranges for oil. I said certainly, and we should enumerate the reasons: the boycott, the stopping of sales of Kuwaiti oil and now the Italian setback. Bartur then reported on the development of our commercial ties with the Eastern European countries. He doubted whether we should try to do business with the Hungarians while linking it with emigration [of Hungarian Jews to Israel]. I said we would lose nothing by trying. We should make an attempt, by all means.

After lunch with Zipporah David Hacohen burst in like a tornado, bearing tidings of the "people's will." Throughout the party – among old-time members and in circles of Party activists in the local branches throughout the country – a surging demand to have me declared the sole candidate. He faithfully assured me that he had absolutely no hand in the matter, but the echoes have been reaching him from all directions. Ziama Aran had also affirmed to him that the situation within the movement was such; no other candidacy was to be considered at all if public opinion was what mattered. Ziama intended to warn Pinhas Lavon not to bring on another head-to-head collision between two candidates, as happened with the election to the Presidency in December 1952, when Ben-Zvi and Sprinzak contended at the meeting of the Central Committee and Sprinzak gained nothing from it.

After 4:00 I went over to the Knesset. Ben-Zion Yisraeli[37] came for a talk about the internal situation in the party following BG's retirement. An "overhaul" was necessary. Somebody – preferably one of the Cabinet ministers – must take it upon himself to coordinate the forces active in the party and direct them towards the main tasks. This first, and secondly – the leadership must work together as a team.

I told him he was perfectly right as regards the teamwork. Too bad it hasn't existed until now, but BG by the force of his personality and his immense authority did much to fill the void. Regrettably, however, he himself was never a team player, and seems never to have felt the need for it. At any rate, when he retires, if no team is consolidated, total ruin would ensue. If one is, it will be a replacement of sorts and perhaps even more than that. As regards a central figure within the party, that was the Secretary's duty. And concerning one of the Cabinet ministers who should devote a good part of his time to the affairs of the party and the movement, the natural candidate would be Golda. But this matter should not be brought up with her. I at any rate would not do so as long as there was a possibility she may be assigned the PM's post. In my opinion, this was a realistic possibility. The conclusion was that nothing should be done until the question of the Cabinet was settled. Since BG is ostensibly willing to postpone his retirement until the coalition

37 Ben-Zion Yisraeli (1887-1954). Born in Russia. Settled in Palestine in 1905. Leader, *Ihud Hakvutzot Vehakibbutzim* organization; founder of the date industry in Israel.

problem is resolved, while the GZ have evidently decided to be stubborn and are willing to bring on a coalition crisis, the prospect is bleak.

In the Knesset lobby I was approached by Haim Landau[38] of *Herut*. His story: two Syrian Jews who crossed the [Israeli-Syrian] border a few days ago told him that a third Syrian Jew was recently caught while trying to cross the border and was sentenced to death by hanging in Aleppo. What could be done? The story sounded doubtful in my ears and I told him to advise the two informants to come over to the Foreign Ministry for a full report. I entrusted the matter to Shamai.

Upon my return home to the piles of my papers, Ze'ev Shek telephoned to announce that King Ibn Saud had died.

[- - -]

After supper, I went with Zipporah to the President. The visit was for the purpose of condolences, and also to talk about the affairs of the day. Ben-Zvi posed the problem of our relations with Asia, and wished to be told anew why we have no diplomatic relations with India. He asked about our chances of relations with Persia[39] and whether it was really impossible to establish good relations with Pakistan and Indonesia? Many other such apt and most practical and reasonable subjects were raised.

[- - -]

Tuesday, November 10

The *Jerusalem Post*'s political reporter[40] knows for a fact that Eshkol is the only serious candidate for PM. He enumerates some of the man's basic qualities, all of them correct, which mark him for the post. He also views his candidacy as a sign of the times, for the economic front is the main one now.

Among the morning telegrams at the office there was Elath's report on Liberal leader Davies'[41] talk with Churchill.[42] The old man was furious over Qibya. Not since the murder of Lord Moyne, British Minister of State to the Middle East [in Cairo in 1944 by two Stern Gang operatives] had Israel aroused such outrage in him. Had Weizmann been alive, such a thing would never have happened. As a Zionist he has been hurt to the depths of his soul, etc. I'm afraid this reaction trumps Watson's.

[- - -]

Shmuel Bendor came to report on reverberations from the US Embassy

38 Haim Landau (1916-1981). Born in Poland. Settled in Palestine in 1935. Founding member and MK, *Herut* Party.

39 Known today as Iran.

40 Sraya Shapiro (1910-1999). Born in Russia. Political correspondent and columnist of the *Jerusalem Post*. Presumed to be mouthpiece of Shimon Peres, Defense Ministry DG.

41 Clement Davies (1884-1962). Welsh MP, leader of the British Liberal Party.

42 *DFPI* 8, doc.495.

on the whirlpool surrounding BG's retirement. The source is [S.Z.] Abramov,[43] Chairman of the Israel-US Friendship Association, who had heard it from Russell. They are anxiously watching developments regarding his successor. BG, as far as they are concerned, is the man behind the dynamic and aggressive policy which embroils Israel in conflicts with the US; Sharett represents the moderate course. Their main fear is that Lavon will succeed BG, with the result that the aggressive line will become even stronger. Lavon's speech has raised grave concern in their hearts. According to Russell, they have the full text and are analyzing it thoroughly. Moreover, Lavon is a member of a kibbutz and they are afraid that if he should become PM, he may seek to give Mapam a share of the power. The US government's attitude towards an Israeli government which includes Mapam will be completely different from its attitude towards the present government. In this conversation Russell returned to the subject of Qibya and made the following observations: if Israel had meant to scuttle Britain's standing in Jordan, it could not have chosen a more effective way; for the Qibya action had struck Britain with a lethal blow, and destroyed all trust in her. The attack on Qibya would have been logical if the goal had been to undermine the current regime in Amman. This regime is barely managing to survive anyway, and an atrocity like Qibya destroys its ability to serve as a shield against the total anarchy which could ensue in the wake of an outburst of Palestinian rage against the government in Amman. A third consequence which may arise is the renewal of political conflicts and the first victim would then be General Glubb. Russell is trying to use the Friendship Association's social gatherings to publicly promulgate the doctrine of US policy in the Middle East and hinted to Abramov that he would be pleased if Foreign Ministry officials were present at his talks.

[- - -]

Shamai gave me an interim report on the situation in Syria. The matter of the Syrian Jew sentenced to be hanged has not yet been clarified. He has asked the *Mossad* people to investigate it. But meanwhile he was given fresh information concerning the cruel treatment of Jews especially in my Aleppo and also, in smaller measure, in my Damascus.[44]

The last wave of harassment of Aleppo's Jews started last August; they were told to make ready for their deportation to an unknown place. It seems the situation

43 Shneur Zalman Abramov (1908-1997). MK, GZ.

44 From February to the end of March 1916, Sharett (then Shertok) worked as chief secretary to a Palestinian Jewish engineer who served as chief engineer in the headquarters of Jemal Pasha (commander of the Turkish southern front) in Damascus. In April, he was conscripted into the Ottoman Army in which he served as an officer until the end of the war. In his last year of service he was stationed in Aleppo. See: Moshe Sharett, *Shall We Ever Meet Again? Letters of an Ottoman Soldier, 1916-1918* - in Hebrew, Tel Aviv: Moshe Sharett Heritage Society, 1998.

worsened after the news about Qibya reached Syria, when the authorities in these two cities started to concentrate the Jews in certain quarters supposedly for the sake of their protection from the wrath of the masses. I said that in view of this perhaps we should inform Syria via UN channels, as well as proclaim it publicly, that we are ready to accept any Syrian Jew who wishes to settle in Israel, and that we hold Syria fully responsible for the life of any such Jew unless they let him come over to us in time. The question remains, of course, whether the remnant of the Syrian Jewish community really wishes to come over.

During lunch I received a telephone call from London. Joseph Segal, an old acquaintance from my student years in London back in the 1920s who swims in London's high society, told me that his friend, the Spanish Ambassador, had just returned from a visit to Spain, during which he saw Franco. Franco discussed Middle East affairs with him and suggested – no more, no less – that he would invite General Neguib of Egypt and myself over to Spain, so that we two could reach an agreement. I said the whole story sounds very whimsical, and advised him to bring the matter before our Ambassador Elath. He agreed reluctantly, since his relations with Elath are bad. It would be interesting to see if anything serious comes our of this strange adventure!

A report by our Research Division was brought to me concerning the great efforts of Bennike's deputy [Vigier], supported by his master who is now in New York, to convince the Jordanians to put a complaint before the Israel-Jordan MAC, accusing us of rupturing a water conduit and attacking the village of Budrus in the West Bank – two actions which never happened. In my telegram to Bennike I said that the fact no complaint was tabled by the Jordanians demonstrated that they were aware that initially they were caught in a lie. Now Bennike comes along and is pressing them to complain notwithstanding. I was astonished by this meanness of Bennike and wrote to our DG advising him to find out whether it is possible to have it publicized in Jordan with the aim of it spreading all over with a big noise.

With rapt attention I read Yaacov Herzog's[45] report on his conversation with the American Bishop, Thomas G. McMahon, Secretary of a Catholic-American relief organization in the Near East, and the permanent envoy of the US Catholic Church (in effect of the Vatican as well) to the Middle East. It's been a long time since such a revealing and eye-opening document has come to my notice. According to this report, there has been no change in the Vatican's position. Nay, it has even stiffened and hardened. The Vatican supports uncompromisingly three immovable fixed principles – the 1947 boundaries, the return of the refugees, and the internationalization of Jerusalem. It seemingly has no fear of appearing as a

45 Yaacov David Herzog (1921-1972). Born in Ireland. Settled in Palestine in 1937. Adviser on Jerusalem Affairs, Israel MFA; Acting Director and Director (from September 1954) of US Division, MFA; Adviser to PM on US Affairs, 1956; later Chargé d'affaires and Minister at Israel Embassy Washington; Ambassador to Canada; DG, PMO.

non-peace-seeking element both in the Middle East and throughout the world. It does not care if the Land of Israel reverts to the situation as envisaged by the 1947 UN partition resolution by means of a war, as long as it does. In the international sphere, it is clear that war cannot be avoided, sooner or later, and all the contrivances resorted to by Churchill – a genius, but now almost a has-been – to bring about a truce in East-West relations are nothing but idle nonsense. I had not imagined there could be such a concentration of evil passions. It's good to know all this, but a shiver ran down my spine as I read it.[46]

I did learn something positive from McMahon. The number of refugees in the camps has gone down considerably. He estimates the overall number of refugees at not more than 750,000. Of these, only 400,000 are still in the camps. The others have dispersed and are working, but only few of them can be said to have actually been absorbed in the countries of their stay. All the same, the refugees' resolve to return is as firm as it ever was.

[- - -]

I directed Shamai to convene a consultation of people in the appropriate intelligence bodies, together with a knowledgeable Syrian Jew, regarding the actual situation of the Jewish remnants in Damascus and Aleppo. Are they really caged-up birds who, if only there were an opening, would immediately flee for their lives? Or do they rather, in fact, cling to their bits of property and miserable livelihood, and would they only curse us if we furnished Shishakli[47] with a pretext to expel them, naked and empty-handed?

Nechama Jacobs[48] came to see me. Her financial situation is most difficult. She is in dire economic straits, and she must have her house back in Rehavia, which has served until now as the PM's residence in Jerusalem, so that she can sell it; otherwise the government must buy it immediately. I promised her I would look into the matter.

[- - -]

At 10:00 in the evening the party caucus began in the Knesset. I reported on the conflict over the Jordan [water diversion] project and the problem of

46 Herzog's report, dated November 17, 1953 (ISA 2468/13), discussed in Uri Bialer, *Cross on the Star of David: The Christian World in Israel's Foreign Policy, 1948-1967* (Bloomington: Indiana University Press, 2005), 28-29. McMahon, who also headed the Catholic Near East Welfare Association, promoted the Vatican's hardline attitude on the internationalization of Jerusalem. He visited Israel in 1948, 1949, 1951 and 1953. See also Sharett's reports of conversations in 1949, *Documents on the Foreign Policy of Israel*, volume 4 (May-December 1949), ed. Yemima Rosenthal (Jerusalem: Israel State Archives, 1986), docs. 179, 215; Bialer, *Cross on the Star of David*, 18-20.

47 General Adib Shishakli (1909-1964). President and PM of Syria (1953-1954).

48 Widow of Julius Jacobs, deputy chief secretary of the Mandate administration, who was killed in the bombing of the King David Hotel by the *Irgun* in 1946.

a regional water settlement. This and my replies to questions lasted two hours. The explanations were well understood and, it seems to me, highly appreciated. But in several of my remarks I showed impatience towards a few *haverim*. When I got home past midnight I was tortured by regret and couldn't calm down. I went to bed in painful spasms of contrition. Damn my temperament!

Wednesday, November 11

[- - -]

I summoned Bendor to a consultation on the problem of American military assistance. Jacob Zanzibar, the Jewish American contractor who is paving a road to Eilat and draining the Hula, is sure it is possible to obtain an allocation of funds from the US Military Assistance Fund to complete the road. This in itself would require an application to the State Department. Furthermore, we must demand our share of the American Military Assistance Fund's allocation of $30 million.

[- - -]

Leo has an idea for a new essay. It has to do with a vivid reportage of the infiltration issue and all its damaging aspects, providing a look at life in the borderlands through first-hand experience. The idea appealed to me, and I suggested to Leo that he arrange the matter with Moish Pearlman.

At 12:30 went over to Sprinzak in the Knesset at his request. He told me of an idea he had tried to sell to Watson: that the British Labour Party declare that, as far as it was concerned, the treaty with Egypt was conditional upon the making of peace between Egypt and Israel. This declaration would imply that the party is committed to acting in this way when it should come to power. Not a bad idea. It is commensurate with the tenor of our activities in London. I told Sprinzak that Nye [Aneurin] Bevan[49], who is about to visit Egypt as a guest of the government, intends to talk to Neguib in just this vein. (Nye is seeking a government invitation to visit Israel).

[- - -]

At the end of the conversation Sprinzak broached the subject: the resignation and what would follow! He wanted to hear from me the reasons for the retirement. I said that I too had my guess. It seems that BG wasn't simply tired of bearing the load, but was unable to sustain the mundane routine of governing when there are no daring projects in the offing which promise grand results: a breakthrough towards a new wave of immigration, peace with the Arabs, another war, and the like. The struggle with day-to-day difficulties is what has drained him of his strength. He was not retiring because of continued high tension, but from the lack of it.

49 Aneurin "Nye" Bevan (1897-1960). Welsh Labour Party politician, Secretary of State for Health (1945-1951), instrumental in creating Britain's National Health Service.

Sprinzak "proclaimed" that he viewed me as the sole candidate. I could not, heaven forbid, protest against this declaration of sympathy and support. But if he only knew how hard it was for me to rely upon him, of all people, in the bubbling ferment surrounding the problem of an heir! He himself bitterly derides Eshkol and Lavon, the last two pillars of the old *Hapo'el Hatza'ir*,[50] who had completely fallen under BG's influence in the sense of Isaiah's complaint: "I have nourished and brought up children, and they have rebelled against Me."[*Isaiah*: 1:2] I told him: "Maybe Golda will be PM after all?"

I went down to Tel Aviv, and arrived at 4:00 exactly at the *Histadrut* "palace" [for the meeting of the Central Committee]. Once again I was shocked by the extravagance of this building and blessed myself at the extreme modesty of our Foreign Ministry barracks. The *Histadrut* missed an opportunity here to demonstrate a model of economy and modesty; instead it chose to show off with the exact opposite. What an unforgivable moral failure.

At first I thought the meeting would be very short, for I had not imagined any debate would be possible following BG's final reply. But the Mapai Central Committee exercises a logic all its own, whose devious pathways are obscure. BG arrived late. Argov, the chairman, again read out a letter from him. This time it was addressed to the CC. In frank and friendly language he resolutely announced his decision to retire from the Cabinet. Argov had barely finished reading the text when hands were raised from all directions. One speaker after another deplored the resignation as a disaster, and called upon the CC not to accept it, but to convene a Party Convention, to raise a cry to the heavens, anything but accept the verdict. After some ten people had spoken, someone proposed that the debate be curtailed. Again there was an opportunity to stop the flood of words which only disgraced the party by exposing its impotence, but the majority voted against. Another ten or more people spoke until the outpouring dried up. Later on some *haverim* demanded in strong language and with great moral passion that BG be allowed to do as he wished. Nevertheless, the impression left by this meeting was depressing. Some well-meaning and faithful *haverim* were not aware of the bad mark they were giving the party. They were making the damage worse, and turning it into a calamity by predicting anarchy in the face of BG's abandonment of the reins of power. "I have followed in BG's steps for thirty years, I've never disputed him, the whole Party is united around him, how can we hold on without him? I cannot imagine how we will be able to continue. We are on the brink of an abyss. Total destruction stares us in the face. We must not yield. He has got to change his mind. We shall convene a Party Convention. We will turn to the mass of workers. We mustn't accept the resignation under any circumstances," and so on and so forth in this vein. What

50 *Hapo'el Hatza'ir* (The Young Worker). A non-Marxist socialist-Zionist group active in Palestine from 1905 until 1930, founded by A.D. Gordon and Yosef Sprinzak.

hysteria! I could not believe my ears.

Yet this was the substance of what was said. It was voiced by people who were gripped by fear and whose thinking was paralyzed. They could not look straight into the future, lest this weeping should be to no avail and BG, in spite of everything, retire. [- - -] There were those who demanded that BG be allowed to go. A few of the people from the kibbutz movement raised the departure for Sde Boker as a banner of a sublime moral step, which should rejuvenate the pioneer movement and serve as a living example to the many. [- - -] Golda was the only Cabinet minister to take part in the debate and defended BG's ultimate right to decide his future by himself.

Towards the end of the debate I also asked permission to speak after having overcome grave doubts. But, meanwhile, another proposal to curtail the debate was submitted and won a majority this time, and the chairman for his part could not find the flexibility to understand that it was permissible and perhaps imperative to exempt me from the rule.

I had intended to say that after having spent all my outrage over the resignation at the Political Committee discussion, I had not the emotional strength to repeat my remarks here and would therefore say nothing to the heart of the matter. I only wished to assure the *haverim,* with all due respect, that all of us here were of one mind and the only difference was between those who have already gone through all the venues of persuasion and rebuke and found that the sentence has been irrevocably passed, and those who in their naiveté still think it can be repealed through exhortation. They [the latter] must be invited to open their eyes and see the situation as it really is.

In the midst of the debate, Argov sent me the draft resolution which he'd composed for the CC to vote on. I corrected its style, crossed out superfluous words, and added some articulated expressions about BG's role in the leadership of the people and the party. Argov then read out the corrected text as the CC resolution. There were a few futile attempts on the part of some members to prevail upon the CC not to accept the resignation and to convene the Party Congress, but Argov's text was unanimously adopted, that is, without any opposition. The large majority voted in favor, while about twenty people remained obdurate and abstained.

The meeting lasted until 7:00 and it was immediately announced that, without recess, the Political Committee would convene at Party Center headquarters.

At the start of the meeting of the CC, I had hastily gone through the file Shamai gave me and found an important and urgent telegram from Aubrey about Qibya.[51] He isn't satisfied with a reiteration of the expression of regret which was included in the PM's broadcast, but is asking for permission to make some blunter and more far-reaching statements. These statements would in effect imply a disavowal of the Qibya action, and would be construed as a commitment not to resort to retaliatory action at all in future. In the same telegram Aubrey makes

51 *DFPI* 8, doc.500.

so bold as to note that the PM's announcement excelled in neither courage nor candor and that few accepted his explanations as the truth. He contends that a harsh condemnation of the Qibya action may be a serious impediment to our future international standing. The only way to soften the resolution that will be adopted is to expedite our efforts and be first to make a statement which would not only express regret over Qibya, but repudiate the action altogether.

I saw that we could not grant him the authority to make such a statement so long as the Cabinet's policy concerning retaliatory action in general remained in force. When BG arrived at the meeting, I sent him the telegram with a note attached. In it I asked him not to fly into a rage at Aubrey, who was in a dire situation. On the other hand, he ought to compose an acceptable statement, since it would be improper to approve the text of the statement which Aubrey proposed to deliver.

BG's reactions, written in the margins of the encoded telegram, came in a series of explosions. Regarding the assumption that a more vigorous repudiation on our part could soften the condemnation, BG wrote "Eban is a child if he thinks so"; "the Great Powers' political interests lie in humiliating us, and no repudiation on our part can help here." Regarding the criticism of his own statement – Eban must be notified that Bennike's version (that the attack was carried out by regular army troops) is a "fantastic lie."(!) On the other hand, regarding the text proposed by Eban, he had no objection to these things being said.[52]

To all appearances, I could have immediately telegraphed Eban authorization for the proposed statement. I had the PM's consent to it, written in his own hand on the telegram slip containing the wording of the statement. But in his consent, too, I saw a singularly strange conception of the principle of moral and political consistency such as was manifested in his definition of Bennike's statement as a "fantastic lie"! I called Lavon over to me and showed him the telegram and the remarks I'd exchanged with BG. He immediately realized that Eban's wording was entirely out of the question. He went over to BG and presented it to him (and, all the while, speakers belched fire, cried to heaven and poured out their bitterness!) and finally came back to me and said that BG simply hadn't read the statement thoroughly. We consulted over the wording to be used, and worked something out. I asked Lavon what meaning he, who was acquainted with the details of the matter, might ascribe to "fantastic lie," but he only shrugged his shoulders. Clearly enough, BG was simply infuriated by the expression of a lack of confidence in his

52 Ben-Gurion's marginal notes are given in the endnotes to *DFPI* 8, doc.500, as follows: "He is wrong in this case; he does not understand what motivates England and its allies to make this condemnation." "For Eban's information: Bennike's version is a fantastic fabrication." "He must add–that if the UN declares open season on Israeli blood by setting different criteria, it would be undermining the moral basis of the UN." "I have nothing against this statement–but he is totally wrong in his prognosis as to the reaction of England and its allies." For Sharett's response, see *DFPI,* loc. cit., and below, entry for November 16.

statement. He simply exploded in anger, as was usual with him.

I toiled long until I formulated a telegram to Eban with firm instructions not to employ the text he had proposed, but to say such and such. I also specifically added that he must by no means say anything that may be taken to mean the repudiation of any retaliatory policy in advance.[53] Be that as it may, this was the first time I included in an official statement words of my choice expressing disavowal of the Qibya action as it had in fact happened.

[- - -]

I didn't stay for the meeting of the Political Committee, for it had come time to return home for a dinner held in honor of Isaac Wolfson[54] and his wife from London. I was glad I could rely on such a respectable pretext not to attend the Political Committee. But for this, who knows how I should have explained my absence and who knows whether it would have been made possible. Before leaving, I arranged with BG that he should summon Teddy to him tomorrow in Tiberias and order him to fly to the US to continue his activity on behalf of the Israel Bonds and to prepare a gathering to follow up on the Jerusalem conference.

[- - -]

Our dinner had at first been deliberately scheduled for 8:30, the timetable being well forecast. However, when I got home at 8:00 I found the Wolfsons, the Weisgals and the Jacobsons from Rehovot already deep in conversation in the living room. They had arrived early at 7:30. I changed with no rush, planned the seating arrangements and placed the cards on the dinner table, shielded from all eyes by the curtain. Only then did I step out to the guests and received their apologies. Finally the others gathered too: Rena Behrman, Avis Shulman, Leo Istoric, Dina and Yehezkel Sahar,[55] and Hannah and Yitzhak Bavli.

The meal passed with much gaiety. Weisgal joked constantly and I too contributed my share of stories and humorous anecdotes. After the meal, Wolfson confided in me how greatly amazed he was by what he had seen in Israel. He showed acuteness of penetration and expression, and hit the target regarding my remarks about the preparatory talks for the Jerusalem convention. It was not a matter of winning a war this year, or of handling such and such number of immigrants the next, etc., but the herculean project of building the country, which was in question here. It would go on for many years. It demanded the long-term participation of all segments of the Jewish people. Well stated! He was especially full of praise for the progress in industry. He had seen great things such as he had not imagined. And

53 Cable not found.

54 Sir Isaac Wolfson (1897-1991). Scottish-Jewish businessman and philanthropist. Founding director, Great Universal Stores. From 1962, 1st Baronet, FRS.

55 Yehezkel Sahar (1907-1998). Born in Palestine. Inspector-General of Police (1948-1958); later Minister and Ambassador to Austria.

all this had been accomplished with an untrained work-force! Wonder of wonders! He'd also seen plants of the *Ta'as* military industry[56] and spoke admiringly about the level of production and its quality. He is a primitive Jew, uncouth and from a lower class, but he is blessed with a brilliant head for business, a sharp eye for production, and with all that a warm and Jewish heart and soul. Yesterday, after a thorough discussion with the leaders of the *Histadrut*-owned *Solel Boneh*[57] Corporation, he offered them credit of one million pounds sterling.

We had invited this wealthy tycoon to our home so that Hannah Bavli, who came too – she is honorary secretary of the Israel Philharmonic Orchestra – should obtain from him a promise of a substantial contribution towards funding the Philharmonic Orchestra's tour of Europe in the spring of 1955. Weisgal, who for years has successfully dealt in emptying gold from Wolfson's bag into the coffers of the Weizmann Institute, tried to undo her design and place obstacles in her path. But Hannah knows her way around, and in the end she caught Wolfson in the corner and got what she wanted.

[- - -]

56 *Ta'as,* the state-run consortium for the development and production of armaments.

57 Israel's major construction and civil engineering company, founded by the *Histadrut* in 1923.

Ben-Gurion Undermines My Candidacy

Thursday, November 12

In the morning I drove to Jerusalem by myself. The newspapers printed BG's last letter and the Central Committee resolution under a bold title. The headline in *Davar* was "Goldmann Offered Place in Cabinet." By whom? Ostensibly by his Progressive Party.[1] The source? Yosef Serlin reported it to the press. Why Serlin? Because Serlin had had a talk with Nahum about his future, the future of the coalition and the future of the GZ. It turns out that Nahum had told him he aspires to foment a revolution in Israel's foreign policy and with his bit of magic he would bring peace to the world. Serlin, on his part, had promised his personal support – not in the name of the party, heaven forbid! – for Nahum Goldmann's policy. An enigma: how could Serlin, who always objects to the "concessions" which I propose, support Nahum, who's willing to yield ten times more than I? No enigma at all. The answer is simple: in the war against Mapai, there are no holds barred.

Ze'ev Shek told of a handsome deed on the part of the UN's press officer. He had informed a reporter that, at a meeting held on account of the attack of an armed band in the north, the Israeli representative to the Israel-Lebanon Mixed Armistice Commission [ILMAC] had threatened that retaliations on our part would follow if Lebanon did not get the situation under control. Even if an IDF man did say such a thing during the course of the meeting, what business is it of the UN representative to disclose it for publication? Only the decisions of the MAC's meetings are published, and not details of their deliberations. But the IDF denies that these things were ever said at all by its representative. According to its own version, it was the chairman of the Commission who invented it all. I summoned Walter and asked him to personally handle the matter, to invite Bennike's deputy [Vigier] over and give him a good thrashing.

[- - -]

Leo came to tell me about the progress on his idea for a book on the subject of Arab infiltration into Israel across the borders. Moish Pearlman thought that

---

1 Progressive Party (1948-1961). Founded by Pinhas Rosen. Held 4 seats in the Knesset at this time and would shortly become part of a new coalition under Mapai.

first-rate talent should be enrolled for the project and suggested Quentin Reynolds.[2] I cabled Reuven Shiloah in Washington to see if they could get hold of Reynolds. [- - -]

Came home for lunch, and after a short break returned to the Foreign Ministry for a consultation on Brazil's proposal to mediate between us and the Vatican on the question of Jerusalem. The DG, Levavi, Leo, [Avraham] Darom[3] and Yaacov Herzog participated in the meeting. The sting of the proposal lies in the demilitarization of Jerusalem on both sides of the line. Some interesting and sober opinions were voiced in favor of demilitarization. Although the CoS rejected the idea, the two Jerusalem commanders, both present and future, consider it a blessing – provided, of course, it applied to the other side as well. The one catch, of course, is the danger of Arab terrorist gangs, on the one hand, and a Jewish underground, on the other. But at first sight it seems that these elements can be brought under control by special police forces which must be adapted and qualified for the job. It will also be possible to concentrate military forces with heavy weaponry on the very edge of the DMZ. This zone doesn't necessarily have to expand with the expansion of Jerusalem. That is, as the city grows, not all of its territory shall be demilitarized.

The principle of demilitarization – to ensure the Holy Places' immunity from any danger of war – was mentioned by Vatican Minister of State, Cardinal Tardini,[4] to the Brazilian Consul [José] Fabrino [de Oliveira Baião]. The chain of events seems to have been as follows: During my visit Rio de Janeiro in April 1953, I thoroughly explained our position on the question of Jerusalem to Minister of External Relations [Joao Neves de] Fontoura. The latter said, as if thinking out aloud, that the deputy Vatican Secretary of State was expected in Rio soon; perhaps it would be a good opportunity to sound out his opinion regarding the chances the Vatican might accept my proposal of supervision over the Holy Places as a solution. When I returned to Israel, I told Fabrino about this conversation. Fontoura was removed in the meantime, but Fabrino kept it in mind. When he visited Rome, he began talks on the question of Jerusalem in the Vatican, and the result was Tardini's proposal of demilitarization, Fabrino's report to Rio, and the new Foreign Minister's proposal to Israeli Consul David Shaltiel[5] that Brazil be mediator.

It was evident in advance that the Vatican would by no means be satisfied with mere supervision. It may be that the Vatican views demilitarization as

2 Quentin James Reynolds (1902-1965). Prolific American war correspondent, journalist and author; associate editor, *Collier's Weekly*.

3 Avraham Darom. Director, Latin America Division MFA until March 1954; subsequently Israel Diplomatic Representative in Greece.

4 Cardinal Domenico Tardini (1888-1961). Longtime aide to Pope Pius XII; Vatican Pro-Secretary of State for Extraordinary Ecclesiastical Affairs.

5 David Shaltiel (1903-1969). Military Attaché to France (1950-1952); later Israel Minister to Brazil, Venezuela, Mexico.

a first step towards internationalization. Even though, according to the Brazilian proposal, our agreement to demilitarization should occasion Vatican recognition of our sovereignty and the elimination of the entire conflict – which means UN recognition of Jerusalem as the capital of Israel. If this is the case, not only is demilitarization not prejudicial to sovereignty, but it is a means to its achievement. Walter stated this at the start of the consultation and we all agreed. I added that the historic compromise between Jerusalem as the capital of Israel and Jerusalem as holy city to Christianity must come at a bitter cost to us and that demilitarization is not too steep a price. True, the problem of security still remains, but a practical solution should not be impossible to find.

Nevertheless, I was of the view that it's still too early to enter into binding negotiations on this basis. Moreover, this could not be done without the consent of the Cabinet. It was best to wait and see how things fared in the UN Assembly, and whether its results might include a thaw in the icy US position over the transfer of the Foreign Ministry to Jerusalem. If there should be a thaw, then a compromise with the Vatican becomes less pressing, though compromising with the Vatican remains important in its own right. If there should be no change in the US position even after the UN GA concludes its sessions without advancing any new proposals on the question of Jerusalem, there will be added reason to try to compromise with the Vatican through the good offices of Brazil. For the time being, we must gain time with Brazil. Let us say nothing rejecting demilitarization, but let us not hurry to commit ourselves. We shall inform them that we are looking into the matter, and meanwhile propose to study the questions which I had already asked Shaltiel in my last telegram to pose to them. Did they think there is any chance of Jordanian consent? And how did they propose to solve the problem of security in the DMZ to protect it from falling victim to endless gang warfare?

[- - -]

I returned home and at 6:00 Harry Beilin,[6] our Consul in Los Angeles and an old assistant of mine from our days at the JA's Political Department, came to visit. I had thought he'd begin with: "Moshe, what's to be with me in the end? How long will you keep me and Judy in the US? And what shall be my lot when I return?" Not so! He began: "Moshe, give me a slogan I can proclaim upon my return to Los Angeles. What should I tell the Jews now?" I responded immediately with few short sentences portraying the issue of American Jewry's financial assistance as the task of a generation and not the pressing need of a single year, a task directed towards building a country and rehabilitating a nation rather than towards absorbing such and such a number of refugees – a task designed to ensure the economic growth and political acceptance of Israel as the homeland of the entire Jewish nation. He said

6 Harry Beilin (1906-1959). Joined the Political Department, JA Jerusalem in 1936; Israel Consul, Los Angeles.

that participants from the West Coast at the Jerusalem conference had expressed to him their gratification at having been addressed this time in this vein and not otherwise. Now they knew what they had to do.

[- - -]

Friday, November 13

[- - -]

Jacob Halevy[7] from England came for a meeting. He's taken up a new position – chairman of the board of directors of the World Jewish Congress (WJC) in England. They are shocked and outraged by the Qibya action. They'd had a board of directors' meeting devoted to this issue. They'd "heard" (from Nahum Goldmann!) that I'd been against it. He isn't asking and doesn't expect an answer. He understands my lips are sealed. He merely wishes to point it out. The act was a desecration of the name of Israel. It created an abyss between the state and the diaspora, destroyed the state's moral repute in their eyes, and so on and so forth. Do we in Israel know, do we understand, what this action has done to our political stature in the eyes of the diaspora and the nations of the world? With what shall the state draw Jewish youth to its pioneer undertaking? If it loses its moral authority, with what spiritual strength will it struggle against communist ideology? This Jacob Halevy, whom I've known since youth, who had been shortchanged at birth in the allocation of "gray matter" and who was always slightly inflated and generally dull as death, this time spoke words which penetrated my inner core and caused me great mental anguish. He said he would like to see BG. I encouraged him with all my heart to request an interview.

[- - -]

Upon the DG's suggestion I telephoned Israel Rokach, Minister of the Interior, and asked what has become of my appeal to do away with the fee paid by Christians for crossing the border in Jerusalem for the purpose of praying in churches of the Old City at Christmas. Suppose Jews were allowed to cross the border for praying at the Wailing Wall – would we then make them pay the fee for going abroad? He said he already made his opposition to this fee known to his people.

[- - -]

Saturday, November 14

[- - -]

In the cables which arrived at the Ministry there was proof of the strong impression made by our appeal in New York to the Jordanian kingdom to enter

7 Jacob Halevy (1899-1978). Member of the WJC's World Executive and chairman of its British section; GZ leader; chairman of the British Zionist Federation.

into negotiations with us to settle peacekeeping and security arrangements in the border areas. This step has dispelled the tension surrounding us to a certain extent and laid a burden of responsibility upon Jordan.

A telegram from Walter informed me of the final outcome of the nasty disclosure by that UN officer concerning the meeting of the ILMAC. The man responsible in Jerusalem has admitted that improper action was taken in disclosing *in camera* proceedings, but claimed that, regarding the substance of the disclosure, there had been no misrepresentation. Everything was based on the transcript of the meeting. A quick check revealed that the IDF representative had indeed said something like what had been reported in his name. The IDF's denial has thus been refuted, and the Army Spokesman was no longer claiming to Walter that the statement had not been made by our officer but by the chairman of the commission. Instead, he now contended that the remarks had been unfaithfully reported because they had been taken out of context. This is an entirely different claim. Walter had been satisfied with the declaration of the UN Chargé d'affaires in Jerusalem that there would be no further disclosures of things said at meetings and with that the matter ended. But, once again, we have been undermined by a patently imprecise – actually fallacious – statement by our own army.

Sunday, November 15

[- - -]

At the Cabinet meeting there was continued debate on the problem of the Arab minority. Serlin [GZ] accused the Mapai Party: our policy had failed along the whole front; we had to change the line drastically; and so on and so forth. Deep thoughts fraught with wisdom.

The highlight of the debate was the report by the Head of Military Government, Lt.-Colonel Shani.[8] As opposed to the flood of criticism and self-abasement which is all a display of abstract principle, he exposed the naked reality. In the past three years, some 20,000 infiltrators have settled in the country. This is in addition to the 30,000 who returned immediately after the country's establishment and the completion of the conquest of the Galilee and the Negev. Altogether there are 50,000 returned Arabs. That these 20,000 haven't been issued permanent documents is the only thing to have stopped the flow of infiltration with the purpose of settlement. The abolition of military government would mean the opening of the borderlands to an unchecked, growing flow of infiltration directed towards residency. Nonetheless, even under present conditions, some 18,000 Arabs in the Galilee have permanent travel permits, but only to the West and South and not to the North and East. This military government's control over Arab movements inside the country is of inestimable

8 Lt.-Colonel Yitshak Shani. Head, Military Government of the Arab sector in Israel.

importance from a security standpoint. True, the problem of the dispossessed can be eliminated by means of permanent resettlement, but the dispossessed firmly refuse to settle on the land of refugees who now reside outside the borders. Even when they lease land from the Abandoned Property Administration, on their own account they pay rent to the landowners in the camps, in addition to what they pay to the Overseer of Refugee Holdings in Israel. They are certain that one day everything will return to the *status quo ante* and they will then be held accountable for what they have done with their countrymen's property. Even when stone houses are built for them, they refuse to take possession of them if the houses have been built on abandoned property. The Arabs who do live on their own land have an advantage with regard to the prices of various produce, since their production costs are immeasurably lower than the Jews'. And they are also exempt from the expense of guard duty and the resultant waste of manpower, for the infiltrators do no damage to their property. Regarding educational services, they are also privileged: they benefit without contributing, or contribute much less than the Jews.

One of the interesting things related by Shani is the smuggling of women into the country from across the border. A girl is brought. Somebody marries her. She is hidden from the authorities until she conceives, and gives birth, only then is a request for permanent residency submitted, for by then she is somebody's wife and the mother of his child. There is another trick. When a woman dies, a woman from a refugee camps is smuggled in to take her place. Since there is no photo attached to the identity cards of women, she uses the identity card of the deceased and her problem is solved. This custom is responsible for the fact that in some Arab villages women have stopped dying!

It is to be expected that, following this report, the GZ will cease their demand to abolish the military government.

In the afternoon there was another Cabinet meeting to discuss army affairs.

In the evening newspapers there appeared an item on Golda's rising star as a candidate for the prime ministership.

Sat over this diary and my papers all evening.

Monday, November 16

The Jerusalem winter, cold and gray, engulfed us suddenly with no warning. Upon entering my office I was beseeched by my secretaries to return home immediately. My room was cold as a grave, and what's more, its walls were dripping from the rain; they had to roll back the carpet and make room for the puddles. I agreed and went back home together with Levavi and Bentsur for a consultation in view of the arrival of the group [of immigrants] from Hungary, to whom we must immediately return the worth of what they deposited with us in Budapest.

[- - -]

I dictated a brief for the debate with the US on the question of the Litani's inclusion in the regional water plan, based on a new idea. Our previous contention gives the impression that the Litani's waters are essential to Israel, and that the river's inclusion in the plan means benefit to Israel out of Lebanese generosity. In this case, the Americans would be justified in claiming that we were pressing too heavily upon the Arab world with this demand. So, in order to facilitate the implementation of the plan with the cooperation of the Arab states, we should withdraw it; certainly at this stage. We should portray the matter differently and contend that the Litani's water is needed not by us but by Jordan. We are willing to make do with the water we have – that is to say, if we are allowed to use it as we see fit. But if the plan proposes to require us to concede a substantial amount of water which is essential to us in Jordan's favor, we would reply: Take the water needed by Jordan from the Litani, whose flow goes to waste anyway. In other words, the water flowing to no use in one corner of the Arab world should be exploited to irrigate land in some other corner of the Arab world, and the matter has nothing to do with Israel except for our willingness to serve as a conduit for it.

I telephoned Wiener to notify him that I was sending him the draft of the brief for review, and conveyed to him the essence of the idea. He endorsed it enthusiastically, and said he would use it immediately to advise the American Technical Cooperation Administration in Israel in view of their imminent meeting with Senator [Arthur V.] Watkins [from Utah]. I asked Wiener when his memorandum on the Main Plan would be ready. He said it would be ready at the end of December.

Yosef Nevo, our Consul to Montreal, who is in the country now because of a death in the family, came to say hello. We discussed the eternal subject: how to entice Sam Bronfman into visiting Israel. Yosef puts great hope in the budding friendship between Bronfman and our Ambassador to Canada, Mike Comay. He confirmed everything I have heard about Mike and Joan's undisputed success among both Jews and gentiles.

A meeting was convened with the DG, Levavi and Aroch on Foreign Ministry activity in the area of Israel's relations with the diaspora. We have been dealing with the subject extensively in recent months. There was no consistency whatsoever among the various delegations regarding relations with Jewish communities in their respective posts. Vigilance was lacking, and the home base did not provide them enough encouragement and direction. Though an improvement has been registered upon Aroch's assumption of his post, the situation leaves much to be desired. There was progress in Argentina, relationships may perhaps be mended in South Africa and the Scandinavian countries, and we may be certain that Jacob Tsur was dealing with the problem in France. I said that upon Chaim Yahil's[9] return, we would

9 Chaim (Hoffman) Yahil (1905-1974). Deputy Head, Israel Purchasing Mission in Germany (1953-1954); Director, Information Division, MFA (1951-1956); later Ambassador to Scandinavia and DG, MFA. Subsequently served as head of the Israel Broadcasting Authority, and became a leader in the "Whole Land of Israel" movement.

build the Information Division upon two foundations: constant transmission of information to the delegations, and routine activity to strengthen cultural bonds with the diaspora and establish channels through which we could convey our guidance. This had best be done within the framework of the Information Division, and no special department for relations with the diaspora need be established. This step should be taken, first, in order to avoid a problem regarding relations with the JA, whose work this initiative was meant to replace; and, second, in order to avoid fanning jealousy within certain Jewish circles and also in certain governments lest the Foreign Ministry be considered to be invading fields where it did not belong and interfering in the internal affairs of Jewish communities abroad. We also concluded that we had best first try to establish an active center inside the Foreign Ministry, and not start prodding the delegations before we are ready to meet all their demands.

In my papers I came upon a report by Katriel Salmon, our Military Attaché in London, on the doings of General Brian Horrocks,[10] who had been commander of British forces in the Middle East, returned to Britain enthused with the IDF, and became a faithful supporter of Israel. Among other things, he has aroused Field-Marshal Montgomery's enthusiasm. The latter is prepared to visit Israel, if he should be officially invited, with a disposition towards placing Israel under the wing of the North Atlantic Treaty Organization (NATO).[11]

I dictated a memorandum opposed to Monty's invitation. We haven't yet decided to seek entry into the Atlantic Alliance, and even if our disposition should be such, we must first talk to those who formulate Alliance policy and not appear to cut corners by trying to forge links with Alliance headquarters. Such an attempt on our part can only offend their Governments' policy makers, and undermine the entire project.

After lunch at home, Reuven Barkat[12] came by for a consultation on the political plans of Sam Watson. His devotion and amity towards Israel remind me of the tradition of those steadfast gentile Zionists in England – Josiah Wedgwood, Orde Wingate, Wyndham Deedes and others.[13] His attitude had been strengthened during this visit. Upon his return to England he intended to

---

10 General Sir Brian Horrocks (1895-1985).

11 For a later report of talks with Horrocks, see *DFPI* 8, doc.607.

12 Reuven Barkat (1906-1972). Director, Political Department and Arab Affairs Department of the *Histadrut* (1949-1960); later Ambassador to Norway, General Secretary of Mapai and MK.

13 Baron Josiah Clement Wedgwood (1872–1943), Major-General Orde Charles Wingate (1903-1944), Colonel Sir Wyndham Deedes (1883-1956). For an appreciation of their contributions to promoting the Zionist cause, see Chaim Weizmann, *Trial and Error: The Autobiography of Chaim Weizmann* (London: Hamish Hamilton, 1949), 273-74, 489-92; Norman A. Rose, *The Gentile Zionists: A Study in Anglo-Zionist Diplomacy, 1929-1939* (London: Frank Cass, 1973), chap.4, 110-11, 126-32, 184-5.

promote the establishment of a bloc of supporters of Israel within the Labour Caucus in Parliament, and he would like our blessing for it. He intended to exclude Bevan's people from any foothold in this Israeli bastion. I telegraphed Elath to ask his opinion. On Thursday Watson and his wife will be coming to tea with us at Ramat Gan, and I must be ready to state our position.

At 4:00 I went to the Knesset. The debate on the Knesset Bill continued. I again noticed that Ziama Aran wasn't speaking to me.

I returned home for a talk with Eliezer Livneh. It was a very long discussion in which we touched upon all sorts of matters, including the relations between him and myself. [- - -] He admitted he'd been in the wrong in some cases and had come to realize that my reprimands were justified. We also entered into an analysis of BG's character. I refused to go as far as Livneh in seeing tactical wisdom as the principal key to an understanding of his actions. I rejected the assumption that BG calculates his steps with cold rationality and always contemplates the end result from the start. I ascribed his vacillations much more to emotional impulses over which logic usually has no control.

After he left, I accomplished a lot on my papers, writing draft after draft. Among other things, I wrote a memorandum to BG to clear the debt I owed him on account of his remarks in the margins of Eban's telegram on our tactics in the Security Council.[14]

[- - -]

Tuesday, November 17

First on the day's agenda at the office was a meeting with the committee of three: Meir Argov, Akiva Govrin and Mordechai Namir, whom the Central Committee has enjoined to sort out the candidacies for the prime ministership.

Argov opened the discussion. He took the trouble to prove quite frankly that I am the only candidate, even following the tangle that has arisen, because Levi Eshkol has withdrawn his name in no uncertain terms. Argov did not conceal the fact that my political philosophy was not approved by many *haverim* and that a majority decision would be required on controversial matters. Govrin filled in after him with a slightly different choice of wording. Evidently there is no escaping the appearance of two candidates before the Central Committee, but it is plain in advance what the decision will be.

The three of them related the discussion held with GZ. It took place last night at Golda's and lasted until midnight. They had unfurled their list of demands: the

14 Memorandum to Ben-Gurion not found. See above, entry for November 11, for Eban's telegram of November 10 with Ben-Gurion's marginal notes, and also below, entry for November 18.

three deputyships, annulment of the red flag and anthem,[15] the independence of their ministries from Finance Ministry control, etc. At the end of the discussion, Rokach had blurted: "But just don't appoint a 'Galitzianer' as Prime Minister!"[16]

To sum up the negotiations, Eshkol had proposed that the existing government would remain intact and that only those changes made necessary by BG's resignation would be enacted, that is to say a new PM, a new Defense Minister, and another member from Mapai in place of the departing BG. All coalition negotiations concerning changes would be postponed for two months, in order to show that BG's retirement hadn't undermined stability. The GZ promised to think this solution over, but it was highly doubtful whether they would accept it. Among other things, they contended that since two of Mapai's three Arabs have left our party caucus, the balance of power between Mapai and the GZ in the Knesset had changed and that Mapai did not deserve the same number of ministers in the coalition as originally allotted.

When my turn came to speak, I began by talking about myself and my problem and said that I would speak with all candor. Until now I hadn't had the opportunity to explain my situation since I hadn't spoken at all with the *haverim* and nobody had spoken with me during all these weeks. I frankly confessed that my candidacy to replace BG must seem to many, both in Israel and the diaspora, as most natural and self-evident. For twenty years I have been his right-hand man at the helm. We entered the JA together to fill the vacancy left by Chaim Arlosoroff's death.[17]

I joined the Executive of the JA when he became its Chairman, and both of us became representatives of our people. I was his second-in-command and his deputy externally and internally within the *yishuv* and the party. My name always appeared immediately after his on the election ballots. Our working hand-in-hand in the JA carried into government, and thus we had reached the present day.

Nevertheless – and even if all were well in our relations – I would find it very difficult to accept the prime ministership because of my being Foreign Minister. It was not my intention in any event to abandon this post and the combination of the two positions involved serious drawbacks. First, the burden would be too great to carry and, notwithstanding, the double roles could not be performed properly. Even assuming that I could attain 150% efficiency, the result would be that the positions of PM and Foreign Minister would each be performed at 75% of what was required.

15 Ceremonies in school assemblies of the workers' movement included raising of the red flag and ended by singing the Labor movement Hebrew anthem "*Tehezaknah*" and "the Internationale."

16 Jews originating in the southern Polish province of Galicia were reputed to be clever manipulators. Rokach was alluding to Pinhas Lavon.

17 Dr Chaim Arlosoroff (1899-1933) headed the JA's Political Department from 1931 until his assassination on a Tel Aviv beach in June 1933. A trial failed to convict two accused Revisionists, leaving the identity of the guilty parties unknown to this day. Sharett (then Shertok) had served as Arlosoroff's assistant.

Second, it was not at all salutary that the Foreign Minister should also be PM. The preceding situation, when the PM was also Defense Minister, was very unwholesome. Some of the clashes I'd had with BG stemmed from his being Defense Minister, but were aggravated because of his being PM as well. Some of the extreme positions he had taken emanated from his being Defense Minister. Under ordinary circumstances as PM he could rein in their extremism, but by virtue of his serving in both capacities he had availed himself of the PM's authority to strengthen and harden the Defense Minister's position. To a certain extent, the same holds true of the dual capacity in my case. It would be unhealthy for the government that the PM's position should be determined first and foremost by considerations of foreign policy, or be unduly influenced by them. The PM's duty is to evaluate every matter from all aspects – foreign policy, security, economic needs, financial possibilities, etc.

Third, this dual capacity entailed a weakness for the party from a coalition standpoint. The GZ would have greater reason to demand a deputy to the PM when the latter is laboring under the onus of a dual role. Were he to serve in the post of PM alone they would be silent.

But in the situation which has arisen, I had not at all reached a final position, whether to accept their verdict or come to terms with it. New impediments to my accepting the task had emerged. They dictated that I must step aside and withdraw my candidacy. They were two in number: The first impediment was BG's open opposition to my candidacy. It is impossible to overcome it. BG has made a most serious mistake, perhaps more serious than he did in his actual resignation. There can be no argument against him, raised by me or by anyone else, if he has reached the conclusion that Eshkol and not me should replace him. However, in this case it was incumbent upon him to ask himself whether his proposal would be accepted by the party. If so – well and good. But if not – it should have been clear to him that the disclosure of the fact that he, BG, had proposed a candidate who would not be confirmed by the party, must lead to foreboding results. And he could easily have ascertained the chances of the candidacy had he decided to support his choice after preliminary discussions with four or five *haverim* who would not have leaked out one word. Instead, he had chosen to propose Eshkol at a meeting of the Political Committee before forty people, and it immediately became known and travelled around the world in a flash.

The results may be harmful and irreparable. First, if the party did not choose Eshkol, then a disagreement between BG and the party on such a basic issue as the selection of a new PM would be exposed. This must necessarily weaken BG's authority which would do great and irreparable harm. At the same time, it would damage the party's reputation. Second, it would be a grave disservice to Eshkol, again for no reason. Eshkol was currently in the ascendant. His position as Finance Minister was being consolidated. He surprised many with his skill in grasping and being in control of affairs and with his creative imagination. In the eyes of people from abroad as well, Jews and non-Jews, government officials, bankers, experts, he had won new prominence. Now BG had come along and by coercion tried to promote him to an even higher level, while the party had come to demote him. For what reason did Eshkol deserve such a demotion? Third, if this was truly the situation, that I and none other was the party's candidate, then my standing in Israel and the entire world had now been demolished without batting an eyelash. Instead of appearing as sole and undisputed candidate, one whose appointment was the inevitable outcome from which there was no other recourse and which everybody approved in advance, I had become overnight one of three, four or five candidates whose stock alternately rises and falls with the fluctuations of the market. Instead of enjoying BG's active support, given with the full weight of his immense authority, I appear unqualified in his eyes. Surely, even if he had unqualifiedly supported me in advance and if everyone had approved of me, I would have needed all the luck in the world, and heaven's mercy too, in order not to fail in the hellishly excruciating task. Having taken the moral liberty to undermine and endanger the stability of the regime by his surprising retirement, it was BG's duty to do everything in his power and more to strengthen the stature of the man who was obliged or forced to replace him. He had done the exact opposite.

Here I told the *haverim* that when the resignation had been initially announced and it had became clear that the decision was irrevocable, we, the party members in the Cabinet, had been ready to make any possible and impossible effort to sway BG from his course. We had considered ourselves obliged to do everything to frustrate his intention. We were determined to take this course, even when it was clear to us that we would achieve nothing by it and move him not a hairbreadth from his decision. But at that stage we hadn't lost hope that we might succeed. And so, at one of our consultations I had said, and Golda too had said, that we must all resign. After we dispersed I thought it over and found that the resignation of us all was out of the question. What would happen if it didn't help? For we would not carry out our threat. The Israeli government must be maintained. But I felt myself to be in an especially delicate situation. I could not ignore the presumption that I was to be the candidate. This fact placed in my hands a strong weapon against BG. Furthermore, I felt a need to take a vigorous step which would remove from anyone's mind the unwholesome thought that I might be expecting the vacated post. I then informed BG in writing so that it would be known that I was out of the running.[18]

Afterwards, when Eshkol announced that he wouldn't accept the proposal, it was reported in the newspapers that "Eshkol Resigns." From what? He hadn't been appointed yet! It was also reported that following Eshkol's withdrawal Sharett's

18 Letter not found.

chances had increased. It had not been reported that since Sharett announced that he was out of the running as PM, BG had offered the post to Eshkol. This was an utter cheapening of my name which was known throughout the world, in Jewish circles and in the international arena. The foundation upon which I've stood until now has been completely destroyed.

But that's not all. There was a second impediment, no less severe. I knew that the *haverim* in the Cabinet were not wholly satisfied with my candidacy. Well did I feel it. And this at a time when I was being called upon, seemingly, to unite them around me. I certainly agreed with Argov, and had already said so myself, that the only substitute for BG's enormous personal weight was teamwork. If a team should emerge, it would be possible to overcome the trials and dangers. Even if there should be drawbacks, from a few aspects these may be offset by gains in a cooperative effort. First of all, this meant the coalescence of the group in the Cabinet into a single unit, which would serve as a unifying factor for the Central Committee and the entire Party. In BG's absence we shall certainly have to consult among ourselves and make collective decisions much more than with him present. He used to decide things and persuade later; no one else would take such liberties. There may be a blessing in such activation of the party, its institutions and small cells. All this held true if the group in the Cabinet comprised a single unit, but how can internal unity be achieved if the man meant to be the central pillar was not accepted by the *haverim*? If, at best, they accepted him for lack of an alternative, but not willingly and with full trust?

In this situation, when everything had been done to undermine my personal stature and when my closest *haverim* refused to accept my authority, how could I be required to accept such a great responsibility and enter the struggle against the disintegration of the coalition and extricate our country from the dire straits in which it lies? There was no moral justification for coming to me with such a demand.

Namir spoke after me. He openly admitted that there was no envying whoever should take it upon himself to be BG's heir in his own lifetime, without BG's full endorsement. Nevertheless he thought that I had no choice. If it's not me, everything would revert to chaos. The party would not accept Eshkol. He [Eshkol] had himself explained with exceedingly clear-cut arguments why. First, he was entirely out of the running, and second, I and no other could take on this post. Eshkol's analysis of my character was very convincing. If so, there were two possibilities. Either the committee would succeed in bringing one candidate before the CC, and that depended upon me alone; or, for lack of alternative, it would present two candidates for the CC to choose between them, and again there was no doubt what the decision would be. My withdrawal would not help any and would change nothing. If both Eshkol and I withdrew, the CC would decide not to accept our withdrawals and would proceed to make a choice between us.

Suddenly I said to the *haverim*: Why shouldn't Pinhas Lavon be PM? I had been watching with deep concern the changes he was going through, and the development of my relations with him. His talents were dangerous if they are not harnessed by responsibility. He was undergoing a process of radicalization on both internal and external affairs. They must lead to severe clashes with me if I should be PM, all the more so when he doesn't accept my moral authority. As PM he should have two other advantages: he would be PM and nothing else. We would find another *haver* to serve as Defense Minister. He was younger than BG by at least 20 years, while I am younger than BG by only 8 years. This original and daring proposal was received with great amazement.

Meanwhile the discussion went overtime and my secretary came in twice to remind me of my next appointment. At the end of the discussion, Namir told us about his meetings with Beryl Raptor[19] and Yitzhak Ben-Aharon.[20] Raptor was eager to bring Mapam into the government. For this purpose he had arranged a meeting for Namir with Ben-Aharon. The latter reported that he'd talked for three hours with Ya'ari,[21] and found him to have taken a 180-degree turn. If Ya'ari determined *Hashomer Hatza'ir's*[22] position, then all of Mapam was willing and ready to join. They well understood that joining the coalition meant joining together with the GZ. They were prepared for it. In foreign affairs they based themselves upon my letter of July 6 to Soviet Foreign Minister Vyacheslav Molotov,[23] and are content with the formula contained therein.[24] I said that Mapam's entering into government at this time would create the most difficult problems for us in our relations with the US, but with a certain effort we might perhaps succeed in explaining the matter. In conclusion, Argov said that he was resolved upon having a single candidacy.

The three left and in came Charles Jordan,[25] Passmann[26] and Avnon. Jordan came to discuss the problem of emigration of Israelis to Germany, which in his opinion has been growing to the point of assuming scandalous international proportions, to say nothing of its negative results in Germany. These emigrants

---

19 Beryl Raptor (1902-1989). Born in Russia. Settled in Palestine in 1920. Former Mapai member. Mapam MK (1949-1951).

20 Yitzhak Ben-Aharon (1906-2006). Israeli left-wing politician and *Ahdut Ha'avoda* MK. Born in Bukovina. Settled in Palestine in 1928. Member of Kibbutz Givat Haim from 1933. Mapai SG (1938–1939). After serving in the British Army during WWII he left Mapai to form the leftist *Ahdut Ha'avoda* faction. Minister of Communications and Transport (1956-1962).

21 Meir Ya'ari (1897-1987). Born in Galicia. Settled in Palestine in 1920. Mapam leader and MK.

22 A leftist political movement, consisting mainly of members of the Marxist *Hakibbutz Ha'artzi* organization, headed by Meir Ya'ari and Yaakov Hazan, which merged with *Ahdut Ha'avoda* party to form Mapam in 1948.

23 Vyacheslav M. Molotov (1890-1986). Soviet Deputy PM and FM (1953-1956).

24 *DFPI* 8, doc.288.

25 Charles Jordan (1908-1967). JDC Representative in Germany.

26 Shmuel Charles Passmann (1888-1971). Head of the JDC office in Israel.

number now above 2,000, 700 of whom had no formal status and were posing a serious problem needing social and economic support. Most of them came to Israel five or six years ago, established themselves in work and accommodation but claim Israel was a "concentration camp" as far as they are concerned, that it was impossible to live in Israel and that tens of thousands Israelis were willing to follow in their steps. Jordan demanded that this emigration from Israel be stopped. If it were, then it would be possible to overcome the problems of the present emigrants. Otherwise, things would become complicated beyond repair. I said we were already tackling the problem. A special ministerial committee was considering a change in our passport system with the aim of stemming this phenomenon of emigration.

[- - -]

At 6:00 Namir came by again. The entire committee was due to meet with BG during the course of carrying out its task, but he decided to speak with BG privately beforehand and try to prevail upon him to renounce Eshkol's candidacy and support me in order to prevent a dangerous split in the party and a grave weakening of the new regime. He asked for my assent. I tried to persuade him not to do it. Even if BG should defer to him, it would be nothing but lip-service. He would have had no change of heart and that would be obvious to the *haverim* and, therefore, the threat of a split would remain. Again I argued that I could not be forced to accept responsibility under the impossible conditions which have been created. He remained adamant that there was no other choice and that everything had to be done to save the situation by bringing BG to his senses.

He related that, although Eshkol had made weighty and resolute remarks to consolidate my candidacy and renounce his own, it was hard to escape the impression that this wasn't a total rejection. This fact was not the only one to consider. Lavon too expressed his complete objection to my candidacy. He was willing to support any other candidate, but not me. Apprehension would certainly affect some *haverim* if a PM were chosen whom BG didn't support, since this connoted BG's exemption from responsibility for the new government. He would be completely severed from it. All of these combined to create a bleak vista of severe schism within the Central Committee many of whose members would not flinch from an open conflict and were willing to wage a holy war against me, come what may.

I asked Namir if he had the impression that Golda would be willing to be PM. He said certainly: he knew for a fact that Golda was willing, but her close friends, including Zalman Shazar, disagreed with her. He asked me if I had spoken with Golda. I replied that there had been no exchange of words between us. Under the present conditions this could only come about at her initiative, which had not happened.

I asked for Ziama's opinion. He said that Ziama had been appalled by my proposal concerning Pinhas as PM. In his view this would be a real horror. Ziama was convinced that Lavon undergoes waves of mental eclipse. He went on to add that Argov's absolute support of my candidacy at our meeting this morning had come as a most pleasant surprise to him. Nevertheless, after the meeting Argov had immediately driven to Lavon. Could things be more complicated?

Namir asked if I had spoken with Ziama. I said no, Ziama had not spoken with me, neither for good nor ill – not a word all these days. True, I did not initiate a conversation with anyone. Namir then recounted a detail from his talk with Ben-Aharon. If Mapam's association in the government should not work out, they would be prepared for an interim settlement. This would oblige us to maintain contact and keep them informed of the state of affairs, and in the same measure would oblige them to restrain their opposition both in the *Histadrut* and the Knesset. He also expressed the hope that in this framework some of their ex-officers would be able to return to service in the IDF.

Finally I said to Namir that perhaps it was really best that Eshkol should be PM and handle the Finance Ministry as best he could. He would certainly survive until the elections. Then we shall see what happens. Meanwhile he and Lavon would compromise somehow, as opposed to the most acrid conflicts that may erupt between me and Lavon. I fear this consequence more than any other danger. It may destroy all internal unity among us in the absence of BG's palpable unifying authority. He did not accept my opinion.

I returned to my papers and drove to the Knesset at 9:00.

[- - -]

In the cafeteria downstairs I ran into Govrin. He sat me down and inquired quite seriously why I had remained silent and revealed nothing to the *haverim* if relations between me and BG had come to what they had. I burst out with laughter upon hearing such an assertion, and explained that my relations with BG were excellent, most amicable, so far as can be expected in this situation. The root for our falling-out lies in deep and obscure strata of the soul. All this is food for a psychoanalytic inquiry for which I have no desire, and see no benefit in occupying myself with it.

I returned home and wrote up my diary till midnight. Over the last cup of tea I outlined to Zipporah the conclusions stemming from the conversation I had had in the morning with the three, and the one I had in the evening with Namir. I said: if I do not withdraw my candidacy, then Eshkol's withdrawal is a fact. I would remain the sole candidate, my election would be assured, and the Central Committee would be saved from an internal split. But if I withdraw, then the CC would decide not to accept withdrawals. Then the result would be that Eshkol's withdrawal is not accepted, which means his candidacy is valid. In that case, two rival candidates would appear and a split would ensue. Having ascertained for myself and explained the situation to Zipporah, we both reached the conclusion that I must withdraw, and the CC should decide. Not withdrawing would mean imposing myself upon the CC, in which case the CC would select me in the absence of another candidate. This would mean the CC's confidence would not be put to the test. But if I should withdraw, and the CC nevertheless selects me, it would mean that the CC was compelling me to be PM. The party would then become responsible in a much more concrete way for my selection, while I, at the same time, would legitimately win the confidence of the CC by virtue of a clear and definite majority. The die was cast.

Wednesday, November 18

In the morning I continued to ponder my decision of yesterday. Am I acting properly towards the party when I deny it an honorable way out by posing a single candidate? Am I not giving preference to considerations of my personal dignity over the public good? I don't know whether it was due to the inclinations of my heart or to pure logic that I came to the conclusion that it was best for the party too to decide this issue by a test of confidence rather than recourse to the easy solution of endorsing a candidate who must in any case be embraced for the sole reason that there was no other.

I arrived at the office early for the purpose of collecting the material for the meeting of the Cabinet FADC, and to study it in time.

At 9:30 Zanzibar came accompanied by David Moushine.[27] Zanzibar is originally from Israel but he was raised and became an adult in the US. He is a most experienced contractor who undertakes large projects in the US and Latin America. In Israel he is overseeing two projects: the drainage of the Hula, and the construction of the road to Eilat. He came to outline his ideas. This is the essence: The late Eliezer Kaplan[28] had asked him to study three problems: (a) the possibility of utilizing peat in the Hula; (b) the value of mineral deposits in the Negev; (c) the construction of the southern port. Regarding the peat, he has come to the conclusion that the deposits of this substance are not viable as a source of fuel. Its combustibility is insignificant; the amount of ash left after burning is enormous. The transportation costs are high. On the other hand, he has found that it's a superb organic fertilizer for enriching the soil. Unlike an inorganic fertilizer which always leaves deposits of salts in the soil which eventually destroy fertility, it is like manure which increases flora growth. As for mineral deposits, they are by nature and quality low-cost substances that demand cheap transportation, for which reason he has rejected the plan for a port near Ashkelon and recommended a port in Eilat. Phosphates loaded in Eilat to be sent to India or Japan will compete successfully with Morocco's phosphates, since the latter will incur the extra costs

27 David Moushine (1916-2005). Engineer. Secretary, Scientific Council and Director, Technical Assistance Department, PMO

28 Eliezer Kaplan (1891-1952). Treasurer, JAE (1933-1948); Minister of Finance (1948-1952).

of transportation from Morocco to the Red Sea and the price of passage through the Suez Canal.

Here he digressed to express a sensible idea. We here in Israel were excited by our ability to manufacture new products, and we forget that the manufacture of the product is, in itself, of no value. We had to keep in mind that the main thing was its production at a competitive price in world markets. We had to develop an awareness of production costs, otherwise we would achieve nothing. As to reducing these costs, one of the most serious problems was the infrastructure of roads. We should think of several factors: the width of a road, its endurance under heavy loads, the gradient of its inclines and declines, the arcs of its turns. All these determined speeds, loads per vehicle, rates of utilization of equipment per unit of time. In short, transportation costs were an important constituent of production costs. He had calculated and found that by improving the efficiency of the country's network of roads it was possible to save $50 million a year. As a great contribution to such improvement, he had conceived the idea of the Eilat-Metula highway, built according to all the considerations which help the acceleration of passage and the price-reduction of transport. He had sounded out the Pentagon and found a complete willingness there to authorize an allocation for us for such a road from military aid funds. This was the final conclusion he was leading to. I thanked him for his fascinating information. Regarding the practical aspect of the matter, I said that we were already working on it. As a matter of fact, immediately after speaking with him I would be going to a consultation on the military aid problem. The question of the road to Eilat would constitute its kernel.

Indeed, as soon as he left I drove to the PMO for a consultation on the same subject. It had been scheduled beforehand. I had tried to convene this consultation two weeks ago, but diverse problems and chores had kept on postponing it until the date was set because of Eshkol's insistent prompting. Our Finance Minister, having sniffed an opportunity to snatch another few millions in addition to the regular grant and devote them to a development project, gave me no rest and asked for a "green light" from a political standpoint.

Lavon, Maklef and Yehoshafat Harkabi participated. Shmuel Bendor came with me. I posed for examination the question of our recourse to the US government to demand our share of the military aid to the Middle East ($30 million altogether) in the form of an allocation for the road to Eilat. We would not demand arms – first, because we would not get any; second, because the demand itself would serve to justify giving arms to the Arabs; and third, because the granting of arms would mean the dispatch of a committee which would poke about the innards of the IDF. If an affirmative answer concerning the road should be forthcoming – conditional upon the dispatch of an American delegation – we would welcome it. That delegation would be specially detailed to the road plan and would automatically be unable to stick its nose into our army's strength and the rest of our military secrets. The receipt of aid for building the road would not interfere with our campaign against the granting of arms to the Arabs. If the US government should proceed to grant allocations to the Arabs too for military infrastructure, we would not oppose it. It would be impossible to argue against the preparation of the region for defense against outside aggression. In other words, objecting to the arming of the Arab states so long as they refused to make peace with Israel did not apply here.

Lavon and the Army people demurred. From a political standpoint, we were liable to stumble over a pitfall and subvert the whole campaign against the granting of arms to the Arabs. A study group that comes ostensibly to examine the road plan would use it as a stepping stone for delving into other realms. Once we established working relations with them, we shall not be able to restrict them for fear of appearing to refuse to cooperate with the US on defense issues. On the other hand, by receiving part of the military aid, with our own hands we would legitimize the granting of aid to the Arabs. Moreover, had not I myself said that they were planning to give the Arabs arms, and to give us only military infrastructure? Another point: it may have been worthwhile considering if the sum spoken of was a large one. But everyone agreed that we would not obtain more than $6 million. We were not that poverty stricken yet. Furthermore, if a study group should come, how could we be sure that it would approve the route we desired? Simple military logic dictated that they would prefer a road in the Arava Valley, along the Jordanian border, and totally ignore our need for a road to cross the heart of our Negev, protected from both Egypt and Jordan. Regarding the practical aspect, the road we were currently constructing, though it's not wide enough and not all of it will be paved, does suffice for our military needs and the transport of mineral deposits to Eilat for a few years. The port of Eilat was still far from being built. It was highly doubtful whether we would obtain an allocation for it from the US, the reason being that the Pentagon would certainly prefer the development of Aqaba. Why, therefore, should we hasten to demand an allocation for the road leading to the port? Last of all, in addition to the $6 million, the road just as far as Be'er Sheva would cost another IL. 14 million. Where would this sum be found? Would the Finance Ministry indeed be willing to put it in the budget for next year?

In short, they buried the plan and rolled a heavy stone over its grave. I could not dismiss the weight of their contentions. I said that I would still consult with our Embassy in Washington, and we would discuss the matter again. I suggested that, meanwhile, the GS prepare proposals for both a request for arms and for infrastructure in case it transpired that the Arabs were getting something anyway and we were liable to miss an opportunity for ourselves.

I returned to the office and found Zipporah there. We dealt with the filling-in of invitations to the two dinner parties this week on Thursday and Saturday. I also dictated a few telegrams. It was bitter cold at the office. The heating had not been turned on, and there were cruel north winds and heavy rains outside. My room resembled a captain's cabin atop a ship. The winds attacked it from all sides, as if to topple it or send it flying. Driving home to lunch along Ruppin Street, the car seemed to be borne by the wind into one of the ravines, there to be crashed.

[- - -]

I sat all evening alone in the room, reading and writing, while outside the storm wailed, interspersed with lashes of rain. I telephoned Namir in Tel Aviv to ask what had come of our *haverim*'s meeting with the GZ. It seems that the pressure for a deputy PM had weakened, but they remained adamant about a deputy finance minister and a deputy education minister. Their position was that a new government had to be installed upon BG's departure, and that they had to discuss its platform and composition with us before entering it and carrying on.

I told Namir what I had resolved between me and myself: to withdraw my candidacy in the Central Committee in order to bring about a vote between two candidates which should serve as a test of confidence. If I should be chosen as sole candidate, I explained, that did not mean that the CC truly viewed me as deserving of the post. It could mean that the CC approved of me for lack of choice only because it was inconceivable that the party should waive its right to promote a PM from among its ranks.

Namir disagreed with me, of course, and asked that I not shackle myself to this line. Meanwhile he told me that in addition to the meeting of the party committee of five[29] with the GZ, the committee of three had met today with the party's four prospective ministers for the future Cabinet, three of them actually in office – Golda, Yosef and Lavon – and one due to be appointed, Ziama Aran. Three of these four – that is to say Golda, Yosef and Ziama – wholeheartedly supported his proposal to go to BG and demand that he give his support for my candidacy. This came as a surprise to him and accorded him much gratification. Lavon, of course, remained intransigent.

I said to Namir that I must nevertheless ask him to convey my position to BG. I viewed Eshkol's candidacy as standing. I did not like to clash with him, as it appeared, but I had no choice. If I withdrew, and the CC decided not to acknowledge my withdrawal, then his withdrawal lacked sanction too and the CC would have to choose between the two. This was best for both the party and the *haver* who would be selected.

Namir asked if there was any news. I said that the reverberations from

29 A powerful informal working committee of Mapai's senior ministers in Cabinet – known in Hebrew as *Va'adat Hahamisha* ("the committee of five") – consulted together and coordinated their interventions on important issues. Members of the committee were Ben-Gurion, Sharett, Eshkol, Aran and Myerson. Frequently referred to as "the five" or as *haverenu* ("our [party] colleagues") throughout the diary.

New York were worrying. There were signs that resolutions against us would be adopted regarding both Qibya and the B'not Yaakov canal. I said that I was still being deluged by an unending stream of very bitter reactions to the Qibya action. I added two reports which came in today. One was from Elath about his talk with [Sir William] Haley, the editor of *The Times*, a true friend who has been a bulwark towards the outside world for us during these days of chill. The other one was from Amir,[30] our Consul in The Hague, about his talk with Dutch Foreign Minister [Joseph] Luns. He too is a loyal friend. They were both severely critical.[31]

I wrote BG to remind him that at the last meeting of the CC I had shown him a telegram which had arrived from Ambassador Eban and he'd written some remarks in the margins.[32]

At the time, I'd been involved in formulating a directive to Eban regarding the way in which to express regret over the Qibya action, and was not free to reply to his remarks, it being all the more difficult to do so on the spot. Even though several days had since passed, I expressed my wish to expose my mind to him on one point he'd touched upon, lest my silence be taken for assent. Eban had contended that a clear-cut expression of regret over what had happened at Qibya, which would imply moral disapproval of the act, might soften the resolution of condemnation which the SC adopted against us. He had expressed the fear that a harsh and unqualified resolution of condemnation might brand Israel as an international outlaw, and that such a shameful verdict would be harmful to our future international relations. For this reason, he had thought it vital to make a vigorous effort to persuade the Council of the sincerity of our regret for the act. This, he hoped, would take the wind out of the sails of those eager for the condemnation. BG had written that Eban was wrong here, and that he didn't understand what underlay Britain's and its allies' espousal of this condemnation. If I had understood him right, he meant to say that Britain was resolved to bolster the Arabs come what may; and it especially desired to strengthen its position in Jordan which was seriously undermined by the Qibya raid. It was therefore unlikely that Britain would be influenced by this or that version of our declarations.

I disagreed with BG. In my opinion he had been quite right in his assumption that we were speaking of a political or diplomatic step which Britain – or the US – was about to take against us directly in order to publicize it later, or at least to inform Jordan of it. But this wasn't true of the adoption of a resolution by an international institution, formulated after open deliberations to which several other countries – apart from Britain and the US – were party. Our experience of UN

30 Rehavam Amir (1916-2013). Born in Lithuania. Settled in Palestine in 1935. Israel Minister to the Netherlands.

31 For Amir's report of his meeting with Luns see *DFPI* 8, doc.504.

32 See above, entry for November 11 for Eban's telegram of November 10 with Ben-Gurion's marginal notes.

institutions – in both the GA and the SC – showed that in most cases (certainly not all!) the US did succeed in turning the scales in its favor regarding the substance of the position it would like to impart to the international body. Regarding the form of any specific resolution, its wording and details, the picture was quite different. There the US felt obliged to consider public opinion which was formed during the course of the debate, and the sensitivities of the different delegations whose votes were needed to obtain the required majority.

In other words, a Great Power acting on its own does not wield the same measure of independence when it seeks to activate an international institution which, at least formally, practices equality among its members. In the case in question it was entirely possible – although certainly not guaranteed – that a more vigorous and explicit statement on our part, with the intention of weakening the brunt of those interested in a severe condemnation, may help those advocating moderation or willing to take the sting out of the condemnation by broadening the scope of the resolution to include the issue of peace. The candidates for applying such pressure on Britain are France, maybe one of the Latin American countries, and even the US itself, at least as it is represented in the SC in the person of Cabot Lodge.[33] I ended by stressing that, while there was no prior guarantee of softening the verdict, one could not rule out entirely such an outcome.

I drank my last cup of tea in the company of my thoughts. The storm in my heart merged with the tempest raging outside.

Thursday, November 19

The Jerusalem winter – frosty, cold and bleak – has descended upon us in a flash, without warning or preparation. I had my hair cut this morning. After this feat, when I came to the office, the secretaries urged me to return home and have the appointments transferred there. My room is as cold as a grave, its walls are leaky, and it has been necessary to roll up the carpet at the corners to make room for the puddles. I concurred with them and returned home.

[- - -]

Yaacov Herzog came to look into several matters. The [Israel] Bonds people in America were pressing the President to record a greeting for broadcast to the Chicago Convention. It would be held in honor of 3,000 years of Jerusalem and the sixth anniversary of the UN resolution on the establishment of the state. Harry Truman was due to attend. In their profound wisdom, the Bonds people were asking that the President make a far-reaching political statement. If there was no other choice, they were willing to settle for a few words of greeting. I said that this direct appeal to the President was a scandal. I had already reprimanded these people

33 Henry Cabot Lodge, Jr. (1902-1985). US Ambassador to the UN (1953-1960).

a few times for not channeling such requests through the Washington Embassy, but they refuse to learn their lesson. Regarding the actual issue, it scarcely seems worth our while to append a greeting from the President of Israel to an appearance by the ex-US President who is the adversary of the current President, Dwight Eisenhower, all the more so at this stage of unduly strained relations. In any event Eban had to be consulted. Hopefully he will reply in the negative.

Yaacov told me of a talk he'd had with one of the B'nai Brith[34] people who'd come to the Jerusalem convention. Yaacov learned from him that they spend two and a half million dollars a year to campaign against anti-Semitism. He had thought of utilizing that gigantic budget for the benefit of our network of information. His American companion foresaw the chance of an allocation of $100,000 for a Jerusalem campaign, which would be an information campaign designed to crack the US government's boycott of the Foreign Ministry since its relocation to Jerusalem. I cabled Shiloah to meet with the man as a preparatory stage before an appeal is made to the President of B'nai Brith.

Lord Nathan[35] from London came by. Nathan's mission this time is as a solicitor for the Electric Company following the negotiations conducted by Lord Samuel with the government. We talked, of course, about the resignation and Qibya. Regarding the first, he said that BG was making a mistake if he thought that after retiring for two years he would be able to return. He was bound to be forgotten and to lose his place in the public eye. No parallel could be drawn with Churchill. First of all, the latter didn't retire willingly but was forced to resign. And second, he didn't go into isolation. On the contrary, he stayed in Parliament. His speeches during this period of being cut off from any position of power were of historic value in educating the nation and eventually in shaping national policy.

Regarding Qibya, he proposed mitigation rather than vindication. He confessed that when he heard of the matter he had been unable to muster within himself the same bitter acrimony that had erupted around him. Now he believed that, as time goes by, the matter will be dropped from the public's interest and eventually will not weigh upon us as it did at first. I said that, to my mind, the Qibya action contained one element that will remain fixed and constant: the fact that we are capable of such killing has been deeply engraved upon the memory and will not be erased. This fact cannot be excised. Here too Nathan begged to alleviate matters. In the annals of every nation there were acts of horror; over time they ceased to shape outside attitudes towards it.

When Nathan left I found Yaacov Herzog waiting for a car in the next room. Since I had ten minutes' time, we entered into conversation about BG, of whom he's a close personal confidant. I found him sunk in concern for the propensity

34 Heb., "Children of the Covenant" – an international Jewish fraternal organization founded in 1843. Based in the US, affiliated with the WJC.

35 Lord Harry Louis Nathan (1889-1963). Solicitor frequently retained by the JA and other Zionist institutions.

shown by the "Old Man" to delve into the supernatural. He had shown him a pile of the 20 volumes of the new edition of the *Zohar* which he was taking with him to Sde Boker. Moreover, he announced solemnly and firmly that he had resolved to study the Kabbalah and plumb its depths.[36]

Yaacov knows a company of kabbalists whose knowledge of secret wisdom has driven them out of their minds, uprooted them entirely from the ground of reality, and sentenced them to hovering in higher spheres, oblivious to the mundane. He was full of concern for BG's intellectual development if he too should take this road from which no one returns. In his opinion, this was a most serious matter which had to be addressed, and against which we must take steps by staying in contact with BG in order to keep him grounded in real life.

I did not subscribe to this apprehension. I said that the study of the Kabbalah for BG was no different than any other intellectual endeavor per se, just like the study of Greek philosophy or of Indian occult philosophies. It had nothing to do with his inner spiritual life. Yaacov also said that, as far as he has been able to draw BG out, he was hoping to put together a book of his views on Judaism. He would dispute Ahad Ha'am's[37] premise that the essence of Judaism's philosophy of life was the pursuit of justice. He would try to prove that the element of mercy in Judaism was no less important. From this Yaacov passed on to the conjecture that perhaps the source of BG's decision to resign was this desire to express in writing his heart's hidden thoughts and to hand them to the next generation while he was still in full possession of his faculties. [- - -]

In the evening I had a conversation with my brother, Yehuda, who made some sparkling and penetrating remarks in comparing the personalities of Berl Katznelson[38] and BG. I was amazed at his keen observation of the mystery of the "Old Man"'s character. I was, of course, forced to reveal my own thoughts and to explain – or merely try to explain – the knotty thicket of our relations these many years, and what this great and bewildering man had done to himself, to the party, to the future government and to me by proposing Eshkol for the prime-ministership.

---

36 Kabbalah is the name applied to a whole range of Jewish mystical thought and activity, going beyond the study of the codes of Jewish law (Torah, Talmud) in a quest to understand God's essence itself. Traditionally, the rabbis of the Talmud regarded the mystical study of God as important, yet dangerous. The most famous work of Kabbalah, the *Zohar*, revealed to the Jewish world in the thirteenth century by Moses De Leon, is written in Aramaic, in the form of a commentary on the five books of the Torah.

37 "One of the People." Pen-name of Asher Zvi Ginsberg (1856–1927). Noted Jewish scholar and Zionist thinker. Born in Russia. Immigrated to England in 1908. Settled in Palestine in 1922.

38 Berl Katznelson (1887-1944). Born in Russia. Settled in Palestine in 1908. Central figure of the Second *Aliya* [i.e., second wave of Jewish immigration to Palestine, 1904-1914], a leader of the Zionist labor movement, educator and writer. Founder of *Ahdut Ha'avoda* Party in 1919 and Mapai Party in 1930. He maintained intimate contact with Sharett from 1919 onward. In 1925 he founded the *Histadrut* daily *Davar* and enlisted Sharett as his assistant, in which capacity he served until 1931.

We returned home at 2:00 am and I couldn't take a bath because the tub was full of washing which had not been hung outside to dry because of the rain.

Friday, November 20

The morning's newspapers were quite bleak. The draft resolution concerning Qibya and the situation along the borders submitted to the SC by the three Great Powers was made public. It is worse than anything we had expected. It contains an explicit condemnation of Israel. Such a condemnation was never leveled against the Arab states during the War of Independence when they mounted an invasion expressly to defeat a UN resolution. The passage concerning the infiltrations is quite harmless, and rather than berate Jordan and denounce its responsibility, it implies a justification of Jordan, saying that it has already implemented measures to stop infiltration and cannot but continue. Most poignant is the absence of a call for peace, and a demand to enter into negotiations.[39]

Our delegation has already issued a harsh reaction to this slanted verdict, and emphasized the falsification it contains. Concerning the conflict in the north, there has been another debate and no follow-up was scheduled. Could this be the unfortunate start of procrastination and delay? Does it not confirm the apprehension that the US intends to stop us until the fate of the regional [water-sharing] plan becomes clear?

Telephoned Walter and exchanged impressions with him. Telegrams from the delegation had not yet arrived or been deciphered.

[- - -]

Before dinner, I leafed through newspapers and discovered two articles in *Yediot Ahronot*. First, an extensive interview by the editor with BG in Tiberias on the state of the nation, its problems and goals. I didn't read it all, put it down thinking, "God knows what is inside." The second was a portrait of me, the eminent work of [political commentator] Yeshayahu Porat. Here I was instantly cut to the quick. I had talked to that journalist under the assumption – so I had understood from our press people and my secretaries – that the interview was not for publication, but a background briefing on the basis of which the writer would write whatever he would with no mention of my name. But this was not the case. Although it is not written as an interview, the story includes a few conversations with me and I am explicitly quoted as saying things which I had no intention of saying for publication. From a few statements explicitly attributed to me, the reader could learn that I was the source of some others not said in my name. I was especially galled by the end of the article. Porat accurately reported an idea

39 The draft resolution would be adopted on November 24 without amendment. See *DFPI* 8, doc.534; http://avalon.law.yale.edu/20th_century/mid009.asp.

I had expressed, that BG was a leader of the highest order, that leadership was a quality bestowed by fate, that a man cannot make himself a leader, that standing at the head of a nation was possible even without the quality of leadership, and that the vacancy created by BG's retirement must be filled by teamwork. But he had found it necessary to add, as if I had said: "This will be the case whether Eshkol or I shall be PM." This I had not said, and by putting these words in my mouth Porat was making me publicly declare my candidacy for the post of PM. Grinding my teeth, I cursed myself for yielding to the urgings of my associates to receive that Porat at all, after I had previously refused to see him as one associated with the vulgar *Yediot Ahronot*. But what's done is done. The printed word in the newspaper cannot be erased. Any attempt to repair the damage might only complicate things further.

Went over telegrams which had arrived in the meantime and discovered that the wording of the Great Powers' resolution was even harsher than might have been understood from the press. Telephoned the DG and proposed to immediately order our London and Paris Embassies to mount a vigorous last-minute campaign against the conversion of the draft into an official resolution which would afflict us until doomsday. I added that we would have to issue a declaration immediately after the adoption of the resolution. Our delegation to the UN had responded to the draft with a statement, but the government itself must respond to the final resolution. I made the calculation that the resolution would not be adopted before Monday. Nevertheless, I took it upon myself to compose a draft of a statement over *Shabbat*.

At dinner at the French Ambassador's residence there were twenty people around the table. They included the British Ambassador, the American Chargé d'affaires, the Belgian and Turkish Consuls, the French First Secretary and Military Attaché and their wives. The house had been refurbished with elegance and splendor – draperies and furniture newly arrived from Paris. There was plenty of food, and it was cooked and served with all the finesse of French cuisine and table etiquette. I compared their manners with ours, and was astounded by the gap. Silver instead of porcelain, three kinds of wine instead of one, four waiters instead of two serving girls. And for the quality of the cooking – we were simply a hundred years behind. If this were at least known to all the cries of waste in the Foreign Ministry!

After the meal I entered into conversation with British Ambassador Evans. I broached the issue of his coming to see me in Jerusalem, and asked how long they would remain obdurate. After my trying to bring him to Jerusalem had failed, I would not invite him again. If it was true that to visit the Foreign Ministry in Jerusalem was not entirely forbidden him, but that he must ask for an authorization in each case, then he must choose the opportunity to undertake a visit and receive authorization for it. He said that he well understood this. I said that my official residence in Ramat Gan would be shut down at the end of December. The General

Assembly [session] will end at approximately the same time. If they do not wish to deny themselves all contact with the Foreign Ministry, they had best make up their minds as to what line to take.

From this I turned to the draft resolution in the SC. I said that if such a resolution should be adopted, it would be a very serious matter as regards the UN's moral standing in Israel. The resolution would also cast a heavy pall over our relations with the Great Powers. We would have to respond harshly. Among other things we would contend that, despite our denial concerning the participation of regular forces in the attack on Qibya, and with complete disregard for our expression of regret over the action, they had found it possible to pass an unprecedented shameful, slanted verdict upon us. In that case we were free to point out that none of the three powers responsible for the wording of the resolution had abstained in certain cases in the past from recourse to indiscriminate mass killings, that such activities were going on at this very time. He was very hurt, and said that if what I had said had been done, then it was not under similar circumstances. I said: "Why are the circumstances not similar? The thing is always done either as a response to, or in the face of, an unruly situation which seemingly could not be controlled otherwise." He argued that the Qibya action was of a special nature, and that it had been necessary to deal with it specially apart from the rest. In reply, I spared no words to express my shock at the act itself, but I added that I could see no sense or show of responsibility in this compulsive picking on this specific action without keeping in view the developments preceding it, and the results which must stem from its one-sided condemnation. With this he ostensibly agreed. I added that, concerning the conflict with Syria, I presumed that the opportunity to add insult to injury will not be missed – that is to say, the insult of preventing the renewal of the [B'not Yaakov diversion] project to the injury of the one-sided condemnation. He argued that this assumption was totally unfounded.

When we returned home I took, at long last, a real bath.

Taking Over from Ben-Gurion

Saturday, November 21

Slept for ten hours last night – from 1:00 till 11:00. *Shabbat* began quietly but before half of it had scarcely past, the storm broke out. Early in the afternoon an urgent telegram came from New York. The *New York Times* received a report from its correspondent, Moshe Brilliant, about the interview with BG in *Yediot Ahronot*. It said no more and no less than that BG had called the new immigrants a pack of thieves and crooks, and had only taken comfort in the hope that we may be able to educate their children to lead virtuous lives. He also declared that he had despaired of the American Zionists, and that it was no wonder when Rabbi Abba Hillel Silver prefers to conduct weddings in Cleveland to settling in Israel. The *New York Times* had contacted Silver by telephone, asking if he had anything to say? Silver replied he had nothing to say, but immediately after the conversation, he contacted Emanuel Neumann[1] in New York and induced him to do what he could to prevent a scandal (all this was spelled out in the same telegram.) Neumann notified our people. Hazy[2] immediately went into action, and managed to delay the publication of the report for 24 hours. Our people – Hazy and Abe Harman were signatories to the telegram – viewed as devastating the publication of these comments at this time. While listening over the phone to the telegram being translated into Hebrew I thought to myself: take the Qibya action – it's no wonder that Jews could have performed such a monstrous act of bloodshed when their PM himself testifies to their being a band of murderers and plunderers! It's no wonder too that he is resigning. He was only doing it out of despair. Not only had he despaired of the new immigrants in Israel, but of the Jews of the diaspora as well, first and foremost the Jews of America. On the other hand, the response of these Jews was clear. In troubled times for Israel, they are enlisted to help. At one and the same time, the Prime Minister of Israel stands up and openly defames them in front of the entire American nation.

1 Emanuel Neumann (1893-1980). American Zionist leader; co-founder of *Keren Hayesod*; President, ZOA (1947-1949, 1956-1958); Head, Economic Department, JA (1951-1953); later chairman of the American Section of the WZO.

2 Harry Zvi (Hazy) Zinder (1909-1991). Press Officer, Israel delegation to the UN (1952-1953); Director, Government Press Bureau (1953-1956).

The telegram continued: Hazy had not told the *New York Times* that Brilliant had distorted BG's remarks – how could he have done so? – but had suggested that the newspaper which published them had distorted them. So he confronted the paper with this allegation. The *New York Times* then promised to wire Brilliant, and ask him whether the report was reliable. Now we must not let Brilliant off the hook until he gives a satisfactory reply. It is likewise highly desirable that BG himself should publicly refute the published report, and deliver a positive statement on the same issues. That was the gist of the telegram.

So here's another scandal for you. As always, it further complicates and aggravates the existing crisis. I was immediately reminded of BG's proclamation to Cyrus Sulzberger of the *New York Times*, on December 14, 1952, about Jerusalem: "In our view, the status of the city is as established as the future of Washington or London." It was made at the height of the campaign in the UN for direct peace negotiations. It struck us a mortal blow, perhaps being solely responsible for the setback we suffered in that campaign, after victory had all but been assured.[3]

I said to myself: even though it is clear that BG did say all the things reported in his name, they are but crumbs scattered throughout his extensive tracts on the tasks of facing this generation and the prospects of the state. Along comes this evil malcontent, Brilliant by name, and collects them one by one to be served in a dish of concentrated bitter poison to *New York Times* readers. As if the departing PM of Israel had said this, and only this. I have already taken notice of this vile character, and found him to be diligent not to miss a single opportunity for shaming the government and its officials, and to drag them into whatever mire exists by exploiting every slip of the tongue.

At the same time, I was furious as hell that once again I was called upon to be the rescuer, the fireman, the man on the white horse. Where would I find BG? He was in Tiberias. My turning to him with an implied criticism of what he did or did not say to that self-same Rosenblum,[4] editor of *Yediot Ahronot* and an inveterate enemy of our party and the government led by it, would raise his ire and upset the tenor of his rational response. And how was I to get in touch with Brilliant? In his great piety, he is an observant Jew who doesn't answer the telephone on *Shabbat*.

Suddenly my spirits lifted and I ordered that Teddy and Moish Pearlman be informed of the mess, and be told in my name that it was theirs to tackle. I reckoned that Teddy would turn to BG, while Moish would give Brilliant a good talking to.

---

3 On the UN GA debates of November and December 1952, see Walter Eytan, *The First Ten Years: A Diplomatic History of Israel* (New York: Simon & Schuster, 1958), 110-13; Neil Caplan, *Futile Diplomacy*, vol.3 - *The United Nations, the Great Powers, and Middle East Peacemaking, 1948-1954* (London: Frank Cass, 1997; Routledge, 2015), 213-20.

4 Dr Herzl Rosenblum (Vardi) (1903-1991). Former aide to Revisionist Party leader, Vladimir Ze'ev Jabotinsky. Signatory to Israel's Declaration of Independence. Editor (1949-1986) of *Yediot Ahronot*.

Still, I decided to talk with Teddy myself, but while looking up his number the telephone rang. [- - -] It was [Zionist activist] Joseph Segal, of all people, calling from London. "Well, what's up?" He was again at his Spanish adventure. Meanwhile, however, I learned from Elath that it was Segal who had taken the initiative in talking with the Spanish Ambassador to London, and it was he who had suggested that Franco mediate between us and the Egyptians. I challenged him on this point. He denied it, of course, saying that the idea was not his; it just popped out during his conversation with the Ambassador. I asked him how it was that he ventured into discussing such subjects without asking for permission first. He evaded my question and said that one could not disregard such a chance for peace. I replied: "And do you seriously think, that any of us, or of the Egyptians, would go over to Madrid?" (Elath had told me that this indeed was his plan). No, he said, not necessarily in Madrid. We could meet any place, say, in Rome, for instance. I said: "Do you really think that the other side would be impressed by Franco's invitation to the point of agreeing at once to meet us?" He was sure of it. To this I replied that he didn't know what he was talking about, and calmed him down by suggesting that he submit a report on the whole affair. What a meddler that guy is!

I spoke with Arthur Lourie[5] in New York. Had I received Abe's and Hazy's telegram? Yes, I had received it, Teddy and Moish were working on it while BG's in Tiberias. It was the holy *Shabbat* at Brilliant's. The whole country was awash with fierce rains. I saw that Arthur was impressed by my concise description. He repeated that they were waiting for Brilliant's reply. I said that I knew this, and that we would do what we could. Meanwhile I asked him when the SC would presumably adopt the resolution on Qibya. He said not before Thursday, but perhaps on Tuesday after all.

Then I telephoned Teddy. He had not yet read the telegram verbatim. He well understood the complication which had arisen. He had already contacted Moish, and was willing to talk to BG.

Immediately after this conversation, Moish spoke with me from Tel Aviv. He was also ready for action. He only said: "We are geniuses of the first order to needlessly complicate matters!" I told him too that the interview was on the whole of a positive nature, but it did contain the usual ingredients: the denunciation of American Zionists, the lashing out at Silver, the frank admission of our moral faults within. And then along comes this busybody to lick the morsels one by one.

Moish telephoned later. He had met with Brilliant and given him a good dressing-down. He had proved to him that he, Brilliant, had distorted BG's remarks by taking them out of context, and assembling them into a single paragraph. Brilliant

5 Arthur Lourie (1903-1978). Israel Consul-General, New York (1948-53); Assistant to the DG, MFA (1954-1956); Ambassador to Canada (1957-1959); Ambassador to UK (1960-1965); Deputy DG, MFA (1965-1972).

was willing to mend matters. BG was on his way to Jerusalem, and Teddy was waiting for him. The aim was to obtain some statement from BG which will be conveyed to Brilliant upon which the latter will be able to repudiate his first version and rewrite it.

[- - -]

Later, midway through dinner, Moish rang and Bendor answered the telephone. His report was that Brilliant had wired to delay publication and promised a new version. Tomorrow BG will issue a denial of what had been published, which he claims he had never said. There you have it![6]

Sunday, November 22

I left for Jerusalem at 7:30. A biting chill reigned at the office. All the girls were working in their overcoats and rubbing their hands. Avnon came to promise me that my own office would be heated by Tuesday, and the entire office by the end of the week.

As usual, I went over the material for the Cabinet meeting and drove to the PMO. In the corridor I bumped into Argov. He informed me with a grave and solemn expression that they had succeeded in persuading BG to support my candidacy. The news grated on my ear.

Upon entering the conference room, Barney came up to me. His expression was serious and excited. He had heard from some about the impression I had that the *haverim* in the Cabinet were dissatisfied with my candidacy. He wished to disabuse me of my error. Except for one, everybody supported me.

The meeting began with my review of the situation in the SC debate. The review and the ensuing discussion lasted the entire three hours and we did not get to any other item on the agenda. The first and main argument concerned the government statement in response to the resolution about to be adopted by the SC [regarding Israel's attack on Qibya].

To my great distress I clashed with BG at every point. He subscribed to an immediate statement in response to the three powers' draft resolution, while I favored a statement following the adoption of the resolution. My contention was that we had already responded to the draft in New York, and had nothing new to offer. He wanted to condemn England in particular, but I objected. All three powers were officially responsible for the wording, so why should the other two be given preferential treatment? By all means, let them all feel our anger for having been swayed by the British. He forcefully demanded that we condemn the Bennike report as a libelous document, while I viewed such a condemnation as damaging to us rather than to Bennike, all the more so when our own statement had not been

6 A search of the *New York Times* online archive for this period reveals no story containing extensive interview quotations from PM Ben-Gurion, suggesting that Sharett, Kollek and Pearlman managed to prevent publication of the article originally submitted by Brilliant.

a model of truth. BG demanded that we conclude the statement with a proclamation of our right to self-defense, while I said that this could only be detrimental. To expand my point: if this truly meant self-defense, then we were not saying anything new. Would anybody deny our right to defense? Something else might be read into it, a hidden hint that we would repeat the Qibya action if we thought it necessary. This would constitute an open provocation of the SC and an arrogant declaration. It was bound to lead the Council to adopt the present wording in order to teach us a harsh lesson, rather than to produce a willingness to soften it.

Regarding most of the points in contention, the decisive majority was on my side. But it suddenly emerged that BG had not meant a simple statement by the government spokesman, but a personal statement by himself to be delivered in the name of the government. When I saw that he had an emotional need to close this account before retiring, I could not oppose it, and thus the way was cleared for a not large majority in favor of his proposal.

BG immediately stepped out to the adjacent room to draft the wording, and asked me to conduct the meeting in his stead. I went on with a review of the situation concerning the Jordan River. A great debate developed here whether to accept Eban's proposal of a new line of argument which proposed relying on the possibility of situating the entire canal in territory outside the DMZ by drawing the canal from the Hula Lake and digging a tunnel. Most of the ministers were against this innovation. They viewed, perhaps rightly, its dangers as outweighing its benefits. At the end of the meeting BG summoned me to go over the draft he'd composed. It did not appeal to me at all. I made a few small changes in phrasing; to repair its defects was beyond my powers.

I shut my eyes for half an hour after lunch, worked through a pile of my papers, and at 4:00 pm returned to the office for the afternoon Cabinet meeting. It was at first planned to take up the question of Jerusalem, which has been on the agenda for weeks. But once again this hapless item proved unlucky, because BG presented the wording of his statement [on Qibya in the UN SC] for confirmation by the entire Cabinet. Many grappled with him, and succeeded in persuading him to accept a few corrections. In the end there emerged a statement marred by careless wording and superfluous repetitions, with a few forceful passages, but with others whose logic was weak. I returned to the task of editing it after the meeting, experiencing for the 101st time the sad lot befalling anyone called upon to be the editor of BG, or, for that matter, to be edited by him.[7]

7 Sharett is alluding here to his aggravation over BG's editing of the draft that he, Sharett, had prepared for Israel's Declaration of Independence in May 1948. See Moshe Gur-Ari, "Moshe Sharett and the Declaration of Independence," in *Shoher Shalom: Hebetim Umabatim al Moshe Sharett* [A Statesman Assessed: Views and Viewpoints about Moshe Sharett], eds. Yaakov and Rina Sharett (Tel Aviv: The Moshe Sharett Heritage Society, 2008 – in Hebrew), 117-24.

Meanwhile a new telegram from Eban arrived. The Israeli delegation to the UN – meaning Gideon Rafael with Abba's authorization – is proposing that we have recourse to the famous Article XII of the Armistice Agreement with Jordan.[8]

Accordingly, we should demand that the UN SG convene a conference of both sides to review the whole agreement again for the purpose of peace. It is clear that Jordan will refuse to meet, but then it will be accused of open defiance of the agreement if it does not submit to it. This, then, should enhance our repute, and deflate Jordan's, and give us a sharp weapon against them in public opinion. This stratagem of Abba's – or of Gideon's – is certainly on-target under the given circumstances. I was surprised at myself and at others in my office for not having thought of it ourselves.

I sought BG's opinion, and he assented to the proposal with enthusiasm. He too asked why we hadn't done it before. There is some justification for the delay. We had gone from the lesser to the greater. At first we had brandished a light weapon by proposing to meet with Jordan to settle affairs in the border areas. Jordan not having responded, and we ourselves having been clobbered by the three Great Powers' draft resolution, there was now the need for a cannon.

A propos, BG asked me what had happened to our complaint to the SC. I myself was stunned to realize I had forgotten all about it, and had not kept track of progress concerning this step we had taken. To complicate matters, I remembered that tomorrow there was a meeting of the Knesset FADC and that the *Herut* representative was bound to hound me about it. Lo and behold, I have got no clear reply to deliver! True, it was incumbent upon the delegation to report and they hadn't, but it was my fault and the office's that we had not kept up with it. The absence of Gideon, whom we had sent to New York as reinforcement, again proved to be detrimental. Moreover, Tekoah's and Rosenne's going abroad at the same time had not helped either. I immediately placed a telephone call to New York, but rather than rely upon miracles, I sent off a telegram, and asked about the fate of our complaint.

At home, Yaacov Herzog came by with the translation of BG's statement into English. I revised it thoroughly from top to bottom, in many places straying from the original in order to tighten the logic, blunt the sharp edges and improve the style. Yaacov told me, in strictest confidence, something he had found out. The IDF's Northern Command has given an order to destroy another six abandoned

8 *DFPI* 8, doc.523. Article XII(3) of the Israel-Jordan General Armistice Agreement (IJGAA) states that: "In the absence of mutual agreement..., either of the Parties may call upon the United Nations Secretary-General to convoke a conference of representatives of the two Parties for the purpose of reviewing, revising or suspending any of the provisions of this Agreement other than Articles I and II. Participation in such conference shall be obligatory upon the Parties." For a detailed discussion of Israel's appeal to the UN SG under this Article, see Caplan, *Futile Diplomacy* III: 225-56.

Arab villages within the next few days. Just what we need right now, when the Assembly is still in session and the SC debate hasn't ended! Could it be true that someone is trying to exploit the interim period to establish *faits accomplis* which would be hard to make after BG's departure? I wrote to Lavon and asked him the meaning of it.[9]

The radio shortwave exchange informed me that the lines to New York were not functioning. I phoned Walter and updated him with the news and then we drafted a cable to Aubrey, approving his suggestion concerning Article XII. Afterwards both us, each at his home, set about re-learning the IJGAA.

The rest of the evening was completely devoted to my papers in general, and the diary in particular.

Monday, November 23

Walter came by early because I had decided to receive my visitors at home this morning due to the chill at the office. We discussed preparations for coordinating and explaining our pending dramatic appeal to the UN SG in New York.

[- - -]

At 10:00 Emanuel Celler[10] and his secretary came, along with Simcha Pratt,[11] our Consul-designate in Chicago. He is now accompanying Celler on his tour. I had also summoned Daniel Lewin[12] to the meeting, because the main subject to be was Celler's visit to India. I briefly explained to Celler past developments and Nehru's domestic constraints. My advice was not to impinge upon the latter's sensitivity by pressing for diplomatic relations with Israel. But when reviewing India's web of relations with the countries of Asia, I suggested he slip in a question on the state of relations with Israel, and see what response it elicits.

Celler thinks he will also be visiting Egypt. I don't believe they will let him in. Be that as it may, I suggested that in talking to [Egyptian President Mohammed] Neguib he begin by relating the esteem shown him in India, Pakistan, and other countries, and mention Israel in passing. Then he could say three things: (a) the leaders of Israel viewed him with great respect; (b) Israel wished Egypt the complete fulfillment of its national aspirations, but at the same time was resolved to stand

9 Letter not found.

10 Emanuel Celler (1888-1981). Lawyer, long-serving member (Democrat, NY), US House of Representatives; liberal, supporter of Irish and Indian independence; Chairman, American *Magen David Adom*.

11 Simcha Pratt (1916-2003). Israel Consul (later Consul-General) to Chicago, subsequently in New York. Later Ambassador to Mexico and Australia; held various other MFA appointments.

12 Daniel Lewin (1907-1971). Director, Asia and Africa Division, MFA. Later Israel Consul to Rangoon, Ambassador to Burma and non-resident minister to the Philippines, Laos and Ceylon, Minister to Japan.

on guard and protect its rights and needs, mainly on two issues: the freedom of passage through the Suez Canal, and the preservation of a proper balance of armed forces; and (c) Israel did not see any basic conflict of interest between Egypt and itself serving as an obstacle to peace that could not be overcome. Here, too, he should mark the response before going on.

[- - -]

At 11:00 I drove to the Knesset FADC. I was to update the members' awareness of developments in the SC. This time my lecture contained a "whopper" – the dramatic step we were about to take in New York [by invoking Article XII against Jordan]. It turned out that members of the Knesset Committee had heard about this initiative before the Cabinet knew about it. The news provoked a long debate. The opposition voiced remarks not entirely devoid of logic. Are we really sure that this is our path to glory? Are we not relying too heavily on Jordan's refusal? Certainly if it does refuse, the stratagem will have given us the upper hand vis-à-vis public opinion. Also, our political stature, which was severely damaged by the Qibya action and the resolution concerning it, would have been somewhat rectified. But what would happen if Jordan should acquiesce? Just as we would come prepared with contentions and accusations, so would they. We were only demanding a "review" of the [Armistice] Agreement, but they may demand the emendation or cancellation of articles it contains. Then it would be our turn to oppose their proposals. How could we be sure that our opposition will win favor in public opinion? How could we be sure that Jordan won't turn the tables on us? If the conference should prove a failure – and fail it must, for a new agreement will not be attained – was there no danger that in the final analysis we shall be held accountable for the failure, and this after we ourselves had initiated the conference? Generally speaking, were we not speculating thoughtlessly with our chances of success? Were we not ignoring long-term considerations while being misled by the immediate tactical gains? Doubt was also expressed whether we should raise the banner of peace once again in our appeal to the UN SG after we had seemingly resolved to stop doing it, since it brought us no nearer to it and simply hardened the Arab position.

I listened carefully to these doubts. I did not, however, change my mind. Even though the step entails a certain risk, in the situation which has unfolded the time was ripe for taking it. Chances are that the potential profit outweighs the fear of loss. On the other hand, I was impressed by the argument against the declaration of peace as the object of the conference, and not necessarily for the reasons given.

At the end of the meeting the discussion focused on the question of a debate on these subjects in the Knesset. I announced that the government opposed any open debate while the SC was in session. I explained that any talk about Qibya at this stage could only be detrimental. Making allowances for Qibya would serve as a provocation and toughen the resolve of the authors of the draft resolution not to soften it. Condemnation of Qibya would achieve exactly the same end. In conclusion, our activity in the SC would work for us, while our debate in the Knesset would do the contrary.

During the first part of the debate, Yaakov Riftin noted the differences in the wording of Eban's speech in the SC as opposed to the PM's radio broadcast concerning the expression of regret over the shedding of innocent blood. Eban had expressed explicit regret over Qibya, while the PM had spoken in general and vaguely about all innocent bloodshed. Wouldn't a plain renunciation of Qibya have strengthened our position? In replying, I recalled that in his first broadcast, the PM had announced that the government regretted the shedding of blood in Qibya and in every other case. I added that the paragraph about Qibya in Eban's superb speech had been dictated from here, after consultation with the PM.[13]

There were two things which were on the tip of my tongue but I couldn't utter: (a) that I'd urged BG to say something explicit about Qibya in his second broadcast, but hadn't been heeded; (b) that on the other hand, BG had been willing to authorize Eban to repudiate Qibya in much blunter terms than I myself had allowed him.

The *Herut* representative kept on asking why Eban had condemned the Qibya action in his speech. He didn't stop pressing the issue even after I denied it. To put him in his place I took the speech out of my briefcase and read out the passage for all to hear. It contained a vigorous expression of regret, but no condemnation. On the contrary, it voiced certain justification of the outburst in view of the background. I read the passage in the English original and then Ziama Aran asked: "Do the members of the SC really understand such English?" I said: "The English of this passage was dictated from here as well."

When I came home for lunch, I read the editorial in *Ha'aretz*. It dealt with BG's interview with the editor of *Yediot Ahronot* in Tiberias. This was a new pinnacle of venomous spite and raging malice. The writer of the article found it timely to discredit the PM publicly for the *faux pas* he was caught in, and bask in his humiliation. He seemed to say to himself: While it is doubtful whether honorable and cultivated people read that evening yellow rag, certainly they all read *Ha'aretz*, or at any rate its editorial. Let us therefore serve them this delectable dish filled with all the pungent spices of [BG's] interview – with all the outlandish expressions, rash epitaphs, indecent attacks on others (living, like Silver, and dead, like Weizmann, who "... didn't teach his sons Hebrew"!) which were to be found there. When I finished reading the editorial, I felt like someone who had just finished building a dam to stop an imminent flood, only to find a gushing stream bursting through in another place, and who raises his hands in despair. The thought that it would have been better not to have brought on the first flood to begin with didn't help any.

While still at the Knesset I had placed a telephone call to New York since last

13 Eban's speech to the UN SC on November 12 is summarized in *DFPI* 8, doc.507.

night's efforts had come to naught. The call came through at 3:00. I spoke with Eban and Gideon one after the other. I gave them the core of the doubts which were raised in the Knesset FADC. Aubrey contended that if Jordan should acquiesce and a debate ensue, it would be in our interest to keep the initiative in our hands; and with proper handling we would defeat the other side. It was my opinion also in this matter that we must proceed as planned. I wanted them to be aware of the other side of the coin. Afterwards I explained my view concerning the question of peace. If we should again define peace as our aim, we would miss our mark. The entire world knows that the Arabs aren't prepared for peace and that any pressure on them to this end is in vain. Raising the demand for peace once again would impress people as an empty stratagem, not be taken seriously by anyone. On the other hand, it was best we focus this time on the full and faithful implementation of the Armistice Agreement. This would be the best answer to the draft resolution of the three [powers]: you accuse us of violating the agreement? We turn the tables and accuse Jordan of systematic violation. You extol the sanctity of the agreement? We do too, but in its entirety, according to its letter and spirit. I felt that my remarks had been understood.

Gideon himself said that they would replace the language about progress towards peace with wording favoring the full implementation of the GAA. At the beginning of the conversation, I asked Aubrey when he would be submitting the appeal to the UN SG. He said he was scheduled to confer with the SG in two hours, whereupon he would deliver it in writing.

At 4:00 I came to the Knesset. [- - -] In the cafeteria I walked up to the table at which Argov, Lavon and Aran were sitting. I heard another story from Lavon about the negotiations with the GZ. They had submitted a list of demands extending to 28 items! In the course of our conversation Lavon casually blurted out: "Now it is already clear who is going to be PM...." As if he was bowing to the inevitable an adding his Amen to it.

Namir wanted to tell me in detail about the talk the three of them had with BG. When they had gone to him in Tiberias, they thought they would have to do battle to persuade him to abandon Eshkol's candidacy and support my own. What if he should refuse to relent, and remain adamant? But it had not turned out that way at all. They began by saying they had come to consult on two issues: the changes in the Cabinet and the negotiations with the GZ. He replied: let us start with the first issue and declared: "So Moshe must be PM. Now it is clear."

Clear indeed! This "clear" doesn't even begin to give me solace. On the contrary, I feel its sting. It could now mean that since Eshkol has announced that he is completely out of the running, no one else is left except for Moshe. And indeed that's exactly what Namir went on to say: "BG said that it was clear from the start that there are only two candidates and now only one is left."

I couldn't contain myself and again explained to Namir what injustice BG had inflicted upon me by his impetuous and wicked proposal, contrary to all logic, and what a mortal wound he had dealt to our relations. These relations had not entirely healed from the devastating blow he had dealt them back in 1943, when I went from London to New York at Weizmann's call in order to save the Zionist cause. The State Department had set a snare for us by setting us up for negotiations with King Ibn Saud. Weizmann and Goldmann almost fell for it. BG had completely severed relations with Weizmann at the time. He had been hurt to the depths of his soul by Weizmann's treatment of him in America, and considered my willingness to come to Weizmann's assistance as a betrayal of him and a desertion to the enemy camp. Berl Katznelson and the party took my side and I left for America. BG could not forgive me for it. He was so obsessed with personal animosity that he didn't pay any attention to the real issue which had to be addressed then, and to my responsibility for its fate. Upon my return he met me like a stranger. He stopped calling me "Moshe" and began calling me "Shertok,"[14] announced that all confidence between us had expired, mounted a deadly interrogation and cross-examination of me at a meeting of the Party Political Committee – and hounded me, pure and simple, in more ways than one. One day my patience ran out, and I expressed my anger at him in the presence of some *haverim*. I asked why had he never explained to me in a comradely way why I should not have gone to America? Why had he only spoken to me in threats and commands? Why had he permitted himself to ignore my position and my responsibility, and so on. The day after that harrowing evening, he telephoned me at a very early hour. From his hoarse voice I understood that he had suffered a sleepless night, and I don't remember exactly what he said to me. It is not important. The main thing was that he called me "Moshe" once again. That was the point of the conversation.

Nonetheless there was no atonement for putting me on the rack. I compared my relations with him then to a precious crystal vase which has cracked. The vase continued to serve its function as before, but the crack also remained and was beyond repair. Now, once again, our relations had been injured and again they were beyond repair. I spoke on and on and got very excited. Now I'm not sure whether I did well to pour my heart out.

Namir spoke about BG's plans in Sde Boker. He'd felt a need to disclose them to his *haverim*. Again he spoke of "four hours of work on the farm." He didn't yet know where he would work, but he had resolved to fiddle around and poke here or there. Afterwards he'd do a lot of reading. He would also write. He would like to regularly write articles for *Davar* on public affairs. He also said he doesn't want excessive contact with people; they shouldn't appeal for his advice too frequently. He himself would not come to Tel Aviv except for Independence Day and the Party Congress. But he would attend the Central Committee session next Wednesday, and the Party

14 Moshe, born "Shertok", Hebraicized his name to "Sharett" in February 1949.

Conference next month, and would speak about the future activity of the party....

He was displeased at the attempts made by old party veterans like Ben-Zion Yisraeli and Abraham Haft[15] and a few other *haverim* of the kibbutz movement to extol his departure as a symbol and example for the renewal of the pioneering spirit. He did not believe that the step he was taking would spark a following among young or old. He didn't consider this step as a call for mass mobilization to make the Negev bloom. He'd been dealing with the Negev's problems for many years, but only after several visits and close-up inspections had the bitter truth become clear to him: extensive tracts of the Negev were parched desert where no settlement or cultivation could succeed. (How many times, when writing briefs and composing affidavits and speeches, had I argued to my wits' end with BG over this very question. I had contended that we must not let ourselves slip into exaggeration, for we would then be viewed as idle dreamers who could not be relied upon; that we had best keep our language realistic and talk only about the wide strip of the northern Negev as an area of agricultural settlement which needs water for irrigation. He, on the contrary, disagreed with me angrily and yelled that there was no such thing in the world as land which could not be cultivated. It was all a matter of means, and of technical capability, and that any distinction between the northern Negev and the southern Negev from an economic aspect was the invention and wishful thinking of experts.) Though there were possibilities of mineral deposits and areas of agricultural settlement too, this development project was not geared to the masses. He had heard that there had been talk of the idea of putting up a camp for 5,000 people. What would these thousands do if the camp would indeed be built? It was truly impossible to absorb such numbers today. Certainly there must be a rejuvenation of the party, in the course of which the pioneering spirit must be reinvigorated, but we must not slip into vain fancies.

And while he was thinking out loud in this vein, he suddenly emitted a question and confession of this kind: "Tell me, do you have any idea who the people of Sde Boker are? I don't know them at all. I know only one – Haggai Avriel – and actually I do not know him all too well either. I am completely unfamiliar with the rest of the boys. Perhaps you know what kind of people they are?" And this after he'd been resolved for months to go to Sde Boker in order to stay there for two years!

At the end of the discussion, when they had accosted him with the matter of the interview in *Yediot Ahronot* – precisely this newspaper out of all the others in the country! – he wondered in all innocence: "Did I have any idea he would publish our conversation in the newspaper? It didn't occur to me at all that he would do such a thing." When the others burst out laughing and scoffed at him: "For what purpose did that self-same Herzl Rosenblum come to you? Is he any

15 Abraham Haft (1892-1965). Born in Russia. Settled in Palestine in 1913. Leader, Mapai; founder, Kibbutz Degania Bet.

friend of yours? Why, he's a journalist and he came to you only in order to publish what you tell him." He didn't accept their opinion, and argued seriously: "But he didn't take any notes at all. How could I have known that he intended to write it all down later for publication?"

Beyond repair. Beyond repair! Such is the man and no amount of wheedling or persuasion can move him. Take him or leave him.

[- - -]

At 9:00 I drove to the PMO for a "fateful" meeting of the party's Political Committee. The conference room was full and the atmosphere most solemn. BG's absence was conspicuous. He was in Tiberias and it was known in advance that he would not be coming.

Argov opened and announced that the "three" had come to the conclusion that a single candidate must be proposed for the prime-ministership – Moshe Sharett. He mentioned that I had announced my inability to accept the post, but that they would nonetheless keep to their opinion. They had had a talk with BG who had announced his support for me. This was the proposal which they have brought for approval. They also proposed that Lavon and Aran join the Cabinet.

I immediately asked to speak and collided in the act with Aran, who seemingly tried to pre-empt me. Argov bid me to speak. I subdued my inner turmoil and spoke softly, but I could not conceal my tension. I repeated what I had explained in my talk with the "three." Why under normal circumstances I would have perceived the joint posts of PM and Foreign Minister as posing a great difficulty for me and inherently faulty. And why, in view of what has transpired, my stature had been completely undermined. And why the *haverim* had no moral right to demand of me that I assume this burden. I had the feeling that my remarks went to the hearts of my colleagues, many of whom were probably hearing for the first time any candid analysis of the situation which had arisen.

Ziama spoke immediately after me and took a middle road between not trampling on Eshkol's dignity as one of two candidates proposed, and stressing the fact that the party viewed me alone as worthy of the title. Golda, who had meanwhile signed up to speak, announced that she was satisfied enough with Ziama's remarks. This retreat on her part at that moment and with her special position did not demonstrate excessive generosity.

Argov put my candidacy to a vote. Everyone raised their hands, nobody was against, and nobody abstained. I felt as if something weighty and fateful, from which there was no escape, had suddenly fallen on me. The die was cast. With inordinate difficulty I rose from my chair and left for the secretaries' room. I telephoned Zipporah at home and told her.

On my way back to the conference room, I saw that Lavon had come after me. He approached me and shook my hand. He said: "Don't worry, everything'll be alright, just as long as the *goyim*[16] don't mess things up." I replied: "The main thing is that the Jews don't mess things up."

Aran also stepped out and I bumped into him in the corridor. I said to him: "Ziama, if it was destined to happen that BG should resign and I take his place, did it have to happen the way it did? Was there really no choice other than this ugly transfer? It is hellishly difficult as it is. Was it really necessary to add this insult to injury so cruelly?" He answered me: "But you know BG quite well. We all know him, and must accept him as he is."

David Hacohen stepped out, and told me that I should appreciate the devotion and effort of the three. He especially praised Akiva Govrin who had thoroughly examined the situation in the various centers of the party, probed the depths and found that the rank and file would not accept the selection of anyone else. David added that he himself hadn't dared to hope for such a wave of support for me in view of the great esteem in which the public holds BG. Nevertheless, the public had not given up its own opinion. It had viewed BG's proposal [of Eshkol] as completely inappropriate and had rebelled against it.

I returned to my seat. I received a note from Haim Ben-Asher, who referred to BG's first proposal as "an assault on public sensibility." I also received a note from Eliyahu Dobkin that "the unanimous vote was not a matter of chance. All those here present know that is the clear wish of the entire Party."

In my absence, the meeting had voted on the candidacy of Lavon as Defense Minister, and of Aran as Minister without Portfolio. The chairman went on to deliver a report on the negotiations with the GZ. After this discussion had concluded, when it was already after 1:00 am, to the perplexity of many I once again asked to speak. I said that I must beg the forgiveness of the *haverim* for taxing their patience at such a late hour. I had to return them to the first part of the meeting. A portentous vote regarding myself had transpired here. I accepted the verdict. I believed in the honesty of the vote held and appreciated that honesty. I assured Eshkol – he'd known me these 39 years and knew that I was speaking the truth – that if the circumstances had been different and if the vote had come out differently and the lot had fallen to him, I would have been willing to stand at his right wholeheartedly and amicably as a foreign minister by his PM, and to help him to the best of my ability. The only substitute for BG could be a united and loyal team. Initially I had had serious doubts about my ability to serve as the coordinator of a team, because I wasn't sure of the attitude of *haverim* in the Cabinet. This uncertainty had been somewhat dissipated, and it depended upon my *haverim* to eliminate it entirely. Regarding BG, even after everything which had transpired and the harsh remarks I had made here, my attitude towards him will only be one of the deepest esteem and loyal friendship.

16 Hebrew and Yiddish term for gentiles, people who are not Jews. Sometimes, but not necessarily, derogatory.

The meeting ended at 1:30. I sat down to help Govrin and Namir draft a reply to the GZ. When I went down the stairs, I found Argov delivering a summary of the meeting to the reporters crowded around him. I was spotted and immediately surrounded by the reporters of several dailies: "May we congratulate you, sir?" I said they had best commiserate with me.

I went home on foot and to my boundless joy found Zipporah awake and waiting for me. We made tea and settled down in the kitchen. I first wrote a cable to my son [Kovi][17] and daughter [Yael][18] in New York. They are entitled to be the first to know. Only then was I ready to tell her about the course of the meeting. We both felt ourselves standing on the threshold of a new chapter in our lives, ominous in view of its unknown dimensions and awesome in its responsibility. We went to sleep at 2:30.

Tuesday, November 24

In the newspapers there appeared prominent headlines on the Political Committee's decision. The *Jerusalem Post* went so far as to add to the announcement of my election that "there was no other candidate."

At the office I was greeted by smiling faces, and not only because of the news of my election, but because this morning the heating had finally been fixed and was working at full capacity. People telephoned from various rooms in the office to congratulate me. Meanwhile the string of appointments continued as if nothing had happened.

[- - -]

A consultation on the "Balkan Alliance."[19] The question came up at the initiative of the Army, which would like to join the Turkey-Greece-Yugoslavia "family." Our Military Attaché in Ankara has already blurted out some such remarks in his talks with the Turkish Defense Minister. Ambassador Maurice Fischer[20] has embraced the idea. But is there really any substance to it? The conclusion was negative concerning our chances of being accepted and the very sense of attempting to ascertain this possibility. On the other hand, I advocated sending out feelers to strengthen our relations with each one of the three, especially on the military level. I also accepted the Army's idea of checking into the possibility of exchanging Military Attachés with Yugoslavia.

A document arrived which contained the complete wording of Eban's letter to

17 Yaakov (Kovi) Sharett (1927-). Sharett's eldest son, who was studying at Columbia University, NY, during this period.

18 Yael Medini (1930-). Writer.

19 "Agreement of Friendship and Cooperation" signed by Greece, Turkey, and Yugoslavia on February 28, 1953 to act as a counterweight against Soviet expansion in the Balkan area. It provided for the eventual creation of a joint military staff for the three countries. At that time Turkey and Greece were already full-fledged members of NATO.

20 Maurice Fischer (1903-1965). Ambassador to France (1949-1952), Turkey (1953-1956); later Assistant Deputy and Deputy to DG, MFA.

the UN SG concerning our appeal in accordance with Article XII.[21] My directive not to present peace as the major aim had been disregarded. This raised my ire. In his further clarification at the press conference, Eban had also gone too far in acclaiming the step we had taken as a historic turning point and spoke about the aim of peace in hallowed terms. I sent him a telegram which was in effect a reprimand for disregarding an explicit directive, and asked for an explanation.[22] My opinion has been further hardened that we must explain our recourse to the application of Article XII as a means to fortify the Armistice Agreement and the full implementation of the Agreement, rather than to make progress towards peace. In the last analysis, the GAA does not involve any commitment to make a peace treaty, but it does contain an explicit commitment to honor the agreement itself, and we would do well to put our pressure on Jordan, and compel the powers to put their pressure on Jordan, as regards the limited rather than the greater aim.

[- - -]

The front page of *Ma'ariv* had two gems. Again, that most gratifying choice phrase: "following Eshkol's withdrawal, Mapai chooses Sharett." And, on top of it: "Sharett posed the condition that BG must propose him in the Central Committee, otherwise he would not accept the PM." I asked Michael Elizur to see to it that this fallacious version is not repeated in the morning newspapers. Regarding the first allegation, I could not restrain myself from writing to Carlebach,[23] saying: criticize ideas and censure deficiencies – to his heart's content! But, for God's sake – no distortions! On the other hand, on an inside page of *Ma'ariv* there were a few gracious and refined lines about me upon my exit from the Political Committee last night.

After working on my papers for two hours, I went to the President in the late afternoon. I found him bed-ridden due to a slight bout of bronchitis with fever. I told Ben-Zvi that I had felt an inner need to come to him today specifically. He thanked me and congratulated me. I did not stay long. [His wife] Rachel [Yanait-Ben-Zvi] also showered congratulations upon me and displayed signs of emotion.

After I returned home, Moshe Bartur showed up to ask permission for giving Argaman[24] in Moscow the "green light" to enter into negotiations with the Russians to ascertain the possibility of commercial trade on a larger scale. Argaman's telegram

---

21 *DFPI* 8, doc.531.

22 *DFPI* 8, doc.532.

23 Azriel Carlebach (1908-1956). Born in Germany. Settled in Palestine in 1937. Editor-in-chief, *Ma'ariv* (1948-1956). Sharett's letter to Carlebach (marked "personal & secret") is reproduced in *Moshe Sharett: Rosh Hamemshala Hasheni: Mivhar Te'udot Meperkei Hayyav* [Hebrew - *Moshe Sharett: The Second Prime Minister - Selected Documents*] eds. Yemima Rosenthal & Louise Fischer (Jerusalem: Israel State Archives, 2007), doc.126 – hereafter *Sharett: Mivhar Te'udot*.

24 Ze'ev Argaman (1903-1983). Settled in Palestine in 1922. Joined MFA in 1950. Commercial Attaché, Israel Embassy, Moscow; later, Israel Minister to Bucharest; Deputy Legal Adviser, MFA.

expressed an interest in the import of consumer goods from Israel – fabrics and the like. It is a most interesting possibility. I endorsed the idea wholeheartedly.

[- - -]

Wednesday, November 25

The newspapers reported on the adoption of the SC resolution concerning Qibya. Thus at least one of Aubrey's hopes regarding our recourse to Article XII has not been fulfilled. Our application to the SG did not force the Great Powers to postpone the adoption of the resolution and our dependence on the Trieste precedent didn't help any. The resolution was adopted by a majority of nine. Lebanon and Russia abstained.

In the *Jerusalem Post* there appeared an editorial about me as "Premier Designate." It was simply wonderful. I found myself overly praised, but in a knowing and candid fashion. The clarity of the style was superb. I immediately recognized the fingerprints. Walter Eytan must certainly have written it.

At 9:00 at the office, a meeting with the IDF people – Dayan, Shalev, Harkabi. Dayan had returned from New York only yesterday or the day before. When we got down to business, he began with a complaint against the Foreign Ministry. Why had we decided on such a crucial step as the application of Article XII without consulting with the GS? I said the time was right, and we had also thought that the delegation's decision to propose this approach was made while he was still in New York. I thought it below my dignity to tell him that I had obtained the assent of the Defense Minister – BG himself.

He went on to express his opinion. Bennike would return prepared for battle on all fronts: a search for weapons of Mount Scopus by mine detectors, a return of Arabs to cultivate their lands in the northern DMZ, confirmation of the decision on the return of the Arabs of Majdal [Ashkelon] and the Azazmeh bedouin tribe in the south adjacent to the Nitzana area. There was no recourse against it other than to attack first.[25] We should announce that we will obey no order concerning

25 According to Benny Morris, the majority of the inhabitants of the Arab town of Majdal/Ashkelon fled to the Gaza Strip during the 1948-1949 War. In 1950, after the town served as a magnet for infiltrators from the Gaza Strip bent on theft, smuggling, visiting relatives, or pushing further inland, the remainder of the town's Arab population, numbering some 2,000-2,500 people, were evicted to the Gaza Strip. A small number of inhabitants, who cooperated with Israel, were transferred to the town of Ramle. Many members of the large Azazmeh Bedouin tribe left Israeli territory temporarily during 1948, then infiltrated back. This tribe, residing in the DMZ of al-Auja, was regarded by the Israeli authorities as a perennial nuisance in view of its harassment of other bedouin tribes and occasionally sabotaging Israeli targets. Beginning in August 1950 the IDF launched a series of round-ups and expelled about 4,000 people into the Egyptian Sinai. Expulsions were continued under orders from Brigadier Dayan in September 1953, with operations conducted by Unit 101 commanded by Ariel Sharon. See Morris, *Israel's Border Wars*, 109, 139, 155; Moshe Dayan, *Story of My Life: An Autobiography* (New York: Warner Books, 1976), 191.

Mount Scopus as long as the Arabs don't comply with the conditions imposed upon them concerning Augusta Victoria area on Mount Scopus and the nearby Arab village of Isawiyya.[26] The same goes for the south: no return as long as Egypt doesn't comply with the decision pertaining to the Suez Canal.

Walter made some apt remarks on the need to first check into the possibility of settling with Bennike by all direct and indirect means before getting entangled in new conflicts with him. For myself, I didn't repudiate the wisdom of attacking first and posing our own demands, but I warned against viewing frontal collision as a solution. We would end up being condemned before the SC again, and we had to learn a lesson from the bitter experience we had just had. We must not make an international name for ourselves as a rebellious lot, because then we shall certainly be punished. Since Dayan had brought his proposals in writing too, I suggested that we meet again on Friday and meanwhile I would study them.

I remained lost in thought for a moment after this discussion. I reflected about this young man who bears the name of Moshe Dayan. I still remember him as a tanned-skinned little boy in Degania [where he was born in 1915]. He is blessed with an extraordinary mind, piercing and inventive, but a stubborn and devious nature and a most elastic honesty. Now he'll be CoS and I'll be PM and Pinhas Lavon will be between us. There's no harmony at all among the three. Who knows what complications and crises await us!

[- - -]

Left for Ramat Gan and had tea at home, which warmed my bones after a most chilly ride. Then I immediately set out for the *Histadrut* Executive Committee building for the meeting of the Central Committee. Zipporah stayed behind to change. She was going to come to the meeting in her own car. I warned her not to be late for they would certainly begin with none other but me.

I was ten minutes late. Already downstairs I sensed that I was one of the latecomers. I asked and was told that BG had already arrived. In the main entrance I ran into a battery of cameras and a storm troop of reporters, their notebooks open in their hands and their pencils drawn. I dismissed them with some insubstantial remarks and hurried upstairs. I sat opposite the entrance and kept my eyes on the lookout for Zipporah's arrival. A subdued solemnity surrounded me. Meir Argov opened with succinct remarks and the same old story: there had been two candidates, Eshkol had withdrawn, the committee proposed Moshe Sharett as the sole candidate (my face

26 Israel frequently complained of lack of Jordanian cooperation in implementing Article VIII of the Israel-Jordan GAA, which called for the operation of a Special Committee whose purpose would be, inter alia, to formulate agreed plans and arrangements for the free movement of traffic on vital roads; a resumption of the normal functioning of the cultural and humanitarian institutions on Mount Scopus (i.e., the Hebrew University and the Hadassah Hospital) and free access thereto; free access to the Holy Places and cultural institutions; and the use of the cemetery on the Mount of Olives.

becoming quite contorted). He emphasized the point that this was the first time the Central Committee was electing the candidate for PM. With BG no election was held at all, the matter had been so self-evident. He went on to speak about the candidacies of Lavon and Aran for the Cabinet, and invited BG to take the floor. The tension in the hall grew. My eyes were glued on the entrance, but no Zipporah.

BG was in one of his good moods, but not serious and warm-hearted, rather light and frivolous. Perhaps it was an unconscious device to quiet his conscience. Perhaps I'm wrong. Perhaps the joy of relief from responsibility ruled his heart and expelled from it any concern for or obligation towards the gravity of the moment. At any rate, he ascended the lectern, all smiles and good humor, and spoke in a relaxed vein and with no emotional effort. First he corrected Argov's error in saying that the official election would take place in the Knesset. The Knesset does not elect but merely confirms, then he took a note from his pocket, glanced at it and spoke as follows:

> *Haverim*, I don't think any one of the three candidates needs introduction – not to the party, and not to the people of Israel. The two *haverim*, Aran and Lavon, won't be insulted if I say that Moshe Sharett needs no introduction to the diaspora either. I want to express my confidence that these three *haverim* – and I understand that Moshe is to remain Foreign Minister as well – will carry out their duties with honor, ability and success, and in close cooperation with the rest of our *haverim* in the government, and along with all the other members of the government will boost the repute of the government and the state. May this day, upon which the new government is established, serve as a great juncture in the national progress of the State of Israel. I move that we adopt the proposal unanimously.

And that was all.

It was then that Chairman Argov got to his feet and declared: "If no other candidates are proposed, I put this proposal to the vote. It can be an open vote. If there are no other candidates, I put Moshe Sharett to the vote as candidate for PM and as Foreign Minister."

A thicket of hands.

Who's against?

Silence.

"Who abstains?" - "No abstentions!"

Voices: "Yes there are, over there!"

All eyes turned in the direction of a corner of the hall behind me. I didn't turn my head. Later I was told that sweet Shlomo Hillel,[27] MK, a kibbutz member and of Iraqi origin, abstained for some reason – I wonder why. Afterwards Lavon and Aran were voted in, but since the best of all teachers is experience, the chairman was careful not to ask about abstentions. In the middle of the vote the door opened

---

27 Shlomo Hillel (1923-). Born in Bagdad. Settled in Palestine in 1934. Organised Iraqi *aliya* to Israel 1950-1952. Mapai MK from 1952. Subsequently joined the MFA and held ambassadorial posts in Africa and at the UN. Later returned to the Knesset and served as Minister of Police, Interior Minister, and Speaker of the House.

and closed in a flash. Zipporah arrived and sat down in a distant corner.

At the end of the vote, Argov announced that he had something to say to the *haverim* elected. His speech was prepared. He first turned to me. He spoke frankly and honestly in his usual way, and this time with a deep expression of friendship as well. He could not keep from mentioning the days of the Jewish Brigade, seemingly responding to an emotional need of his own, as an ex-soldier in its ranks, rather than fulfilling a duty towards myself.[28] He ended by offering the other two *haverim* his best wishes.

I had expected that I would have to say a few things and tried to formulate some disjointed phrases in my mind. The chairman evidently thought otherwise, and after concluding his remarks said that he would now deliver a report on the negotiations with the GZ. But suddenly he changed his mind and turned to me. Perhaps someone whispered in his ear. Perhaps BG, who was sitting exactly opposite him, signaled him. At any rate, he stopped short and called my name. There was no choice and I ascended the lectern.

It seems to me that I managed to subdue my inner turmoil. I explained the twofold difficulty I'd had in accepting the post: the two tasks and the circumstances that led to this point. Unlike before the Political Committee, I did not elaborate. I also noted that I had spoken in detail in the Political Committee and that I wasn't obliged to or could not repeat what I had said. I explained that I accepted the verdict for lack of any choice for the party, something I was not doing for the first time in my life. It was no easy matter to accept the reins which BG had held for so long, and immediately after him. Since the protagonists had changed, the regime must change (here I saw that many were startled and evinced surprise). BG's immense personal power had to be replaced by teamwork. His immense authority had to be replaced with a cooperative effort based on mutual counsel and assistance. I called on my *haverim* in the government to act in this spirit, to respond to every summons, to tender advice and aid. I called for such a spirit within the party. I asked for initiative, help, advice, support, but I also demanded criticism. I said that I viewed what I have been assigned as something precious given to me for safe-keeping to be returned in due time. But it must be clear that it is my right as well as my colleagues' to handle this precious deposit as we see fit and in accordance with our freedom of judgement. I would be happy to receive advice and guidance, but their use was also subject to my and my colleagues' sense of responsibility. I was sure that BG felt the same. After the hard struggle we had all had with BG, having agreed to release him and taken it upon ourselves to handle affairs without him, we had to put an end to defeatist sentiment and proclaim to the party and the entire public our faith and confidence in both the future of the nation and our appointed stewardship.[29]

---

28 Sharett (then Shertok) was instrumental in winning the British Government's agreement to establish a Jewish Brigade in 1944. On the latter, see above, page 78 n.26.

29 Sharett's remarks are reproduced in *Sharett: Mivhar Te'udot*, doc.127.

They listened with rapt attention. After I sat down I received a few congratulatory notes. The chairman returned to the negotiations with the GZ. Meanwhile BG got up, blurted to the chairman that he had to go, stepped up to me briskly showing both his agitation and his mastery of it with a smile, shook my hand mightily and said: "I wish you well, Moshe." After a moment he added: "*Ma'alesh!*" [Arabic: no matter] He left me and on his way to the door shook hands with the two others. He'd driven all the way from Tiberias to attend the meeting for half an hour and to take part in the vote. Once it was over he went back there.

The chairman continued his report on the negotiations, following which comments were exchanged. When I saw that things were coming the end, I decided to leave. It was a precaution against being surrounded by dozens of *haverim* wishing to shake my hand. I beckoned to Zipporah to leave with me. Reporters and photographers again pounced on me, until we made it out into the dark and the mud and found our car. Later I heard that Lavon and Aran had also spoken.

From the Executive Committee building we drove to my sister Ada[30] and from there home. We were brimming with emotion and stunned. Even after being stewed in this for weeks upon weeks and knowing that the thing was certain for days upon days, the final decision nevertheless shook us to our depths and we were overwhelmed.

Later I called up Walter in Jerusalem. I related what happened and asked him if he was the culprit; he admitted it was he who wrote the article [in the *Jerusalem Post*], and I heaped on him my compliments.

Thursday, November 26

In the newspapers there appeared screaming headlines on the results of the meeting of the Central Committee.

In the morning, at my residence in Ramat Gan, Isser Harel came for a talk about current matters. In the midst of our discussion a letter arrived from the American Embassy. It pertained to our initiative on the application of Article XII of the Israel-Jordan GAA. If the conference should take place, they wished us success – as if doing so under protest. But, for God's sake, we mustn't grab for too much in order not to endanger the position of the Jordanian government, but content ourselves with the little which is within reason.[31]

[- - -]

I later composed a telegram to our UN delegation in New York concerning

30 Ada Golomb (1897-1970). Sharett's younger sister, widow of *Hagana* founder, Eliyahu Golomb.

31 US Embassy Aide-Memoire, November 26, 1953, *DFPI* 8, doc.540.

the American missive. Lavon telephoned to propose a consultation on our move towards Jordan, to which the GS has made an objection. I said that it was still too early for it; we would consult in due course.

[- - -]

People from the Legal and US Divisions of the Ministry were waiting for me in Jerusalem with a letter to be signed. It was the confirmation of the grant contract for this year, the third of its kind. In the past we, the US Ambassador and I, used to sign this exchange of letters, which served as the draft contract, while seated together at the same table in the *Kirya* in Tel Aviv in a solemn ceremony. This time [Chargé d'affaires Francis] Russell signed his letter at the American Embassy in Ramat Gan, while I signed in Jerusalem.

Spent the entire evening reading my papers and writing various things. The telegrams from Washington and New York sketched a most complicated picture of the possible outcomes of the SC debate on the Jordan [diversion] canal issue. Everything depended again on the US, while the US was teaming with intrigue and susceptible to pressures. There's still no telling which way it will decide.

Friday, November 27

At the office I had a conversation with the DG. He said some of the Ministry officials had deliberated on the question of holding talks with Jordan under the assumption that the latter would favorably respond. The general drift indicated a preference for Switzerland as the meeting place and a recommendation for sending a high-echelon delegation. I said that I was in favor of a delegation consisting of Walter Eytan at its head, and alongside him Gideon Rafael and an officer from the GS. I proposed that at this stage Walter consult with the GS people without me, since we would have to hold another, more official, consultation with ministerial participation – Lavon and myself.

At 10:00 a second talk with Dayan and his men on the line to be adopted towards Bennike upon his return, and on the whole range of questions on the agenda between ourselves and Jordan, Egypt and Syria. Last night I studied Dayan's memorandum carefully and formulated conclusions. These were accepted at the meeting along with Dayan's usual additions. His position had appreciably softened between our first talk and this one. This time he spoke much more to the point. The GS people again betrayed a strain of irritation at our having taken the initiative concerning Article XII without having consulted them. Dayan left me a memorandum from CoS Maklef on the same issue, which begins by noting that they had learnt about it from the newspapers.[32]

We had previously decided that Walter would continue to consult with the

32 *DFPI* 8, doc.541.

Army people without me regarding the preparations for the conference. I asked him to let them know that I had specifically sounded out the Defense Minister – meaning BG – before authorizing Eban to submit the application to the UN SG; that, not only had he concurred and expressed great enthusiasm for the proposal and urged me quite strongly to act upon it, he had even wondered why we hadn't done so till now. In other words, the Defense establishment had been in effect partner to both consultation and decision. If the Defense Minister had not seen fit to consult with the CoS, or even to inform him about all this, then he should be the address for their complaint, not the Foreign Minister. For my part, I found it uncomfortable to present the GS with this fact; however, in view of their resentments and protests, I felt that they must be confronted with the truth.

I dictated a detailed memorandum on the consultation with the Army people.

A telegram arrived from Aubrey which was an irritated response to my grievance at the insubordination shown in his wording of the application to the UN SG by mentioning the peace issue.[33] I was offended by the tone of his reply and decided to postpone my reaction for the time being.

We went for tea at Hannah Bavli's[34] and found there Isaac Stern[35] and his wife, a couple from Chicago, Hannah Rovina,[36] the Justice Minister [Pinhas Rosen] and his wife, and others. Yitzhak Bavli[37] took this opportunity to enlighten me about the decision of a group of American financiers who decided to reverse their decision to invest a large sum in the country in exchange for Israel Bonds. This came as a result of their having failed to reach a satisfactory agreement with the Finance Ministry on the conditions for their financial activity in Israel. Bavli viewed it as a disaster. There was a severe shortage of investment capital and credit for industry. The prospective sum was $10 million; even $3 million today could boost up our economy, check unemployment and give exports an uplift. I said I would propose to Eshkol that he send off a telegram to that group of people to postpone their final decision, and await his arrival in another week.

We drove back to Tel Aviv to the Party Conference meeting. There was only one item on the agenda: implementation of the Education Law aimed at unification of the various "streams," which meant, among other things, that no more shall the schools of the "worker's stream" fly the red flag or sing the *Histadrut* anthem. Education Minister [Benzion] Dinur lectured, and was followed by the chairman of the Knesset's Finance Committee. Both speakers

---

33 See *DFPI* 8, doc.532 (n.2).

34 Hannah Bavli (1901-1993). Violinist and socialite; wife of Yitzhak Bavli.

35 Isaac Stern (1920-2001). World-renowned Jewish-American (b. Ukraine) violinist; often traveled the globe as a "musical ambassador" and was a strong supporter of Israel.

36 Hannah Rovina (1892-1980). Actress and founding member of Habima Theatre.

37 Yitzhak Bavli (1898-1968). Dutch-born Israeli engineer; briefly in the foreign service as Minister to South Africa (1955-1959).

were examples of obtuseness vis-à-vis the interests of the audience. A few hundred *haverim* had assembled. The house was packed. Many educators were present, many young people came too. And these two men, excellent in themselves, were hopelessly long-winded, spoke in soporific cant, delved into minuscule details of organization and administration. They heaped such boredom upon the audience that, instead of raising attention to their subject matter, they elicited, as if intentionally, a general loathing of it.

Suddenly BG burst into this wasteland with all his might. The man whom fatigue of body and spirit had forced to retire from office was like a gushing flood in a parched desert. He spoke exclusively about the flag issue, devastated his opponents with the venomous acerbity of his tongue, crushed and trampled them and scattered insults right and left. He too was inordinately long-winded, endlessly repetitive, though varied in his language. Although he dealt with the same issues and ideas, he stirred the audience and, most importantly, filled their minds with basic concepts with mighty persuasive power.

Moshe Sharett and David Ben-Gurion at Mapai conference, November 1953

Saturday, November 28

We were late getting up and I vacillated between preparing my speech for the Knesset on Monday and going to the Party Conference. I decided in favor of the latter, partly because of my special responsibility now and certainly because of anxiety regarding the mood of the Conference. But mainly, to be sure, because unconsciously I tend to postpone the preparation of a speech to the last day.

[- - -]

In the afternoon, I again put off the preparation of my speech and poured over my diary. I was interrupted by Hassan and his son Mahmoud, the fishermen from Jaffa, who came to congratulate me on my promotion. Hassan is convinced that if my brothers-in-law had been alive, Dov Hoz would have been PM, Eliyahu Golomb[38] would have been Defense Minister, and I could have stayed Foreign Minister.

Russell came at 6:00, and I argued with him about the fate of the conference with Jordan. He tried to propose US mediation for settling the agenda before convening the conference – in fact, even before Jordan had given a reply whether they are willing to confer with us. I rejected this. I said that Jordan must first indicate whether they accepted the invitation. Even afterwards it was best to avoid mediation and determine the agenda in a direct meeting at the beginning of the conference. In any event, this conference was entirely dependent upon consent and we won't be able to order Jordan about. At the end he gave me his word that the US government was interested in bringing Jordan to the conference and ensure its success. Ambassador Davis was returning tomorrow, evidently not in the best of health.

[- - -]

On the eve of his departure for Rangoon, David Hacohen took me aside to ask what *Solel Boneh*, the *Histadrut* building corporation, should do to cover the $36,000 it had already invested in the construction of BG's cottage in Sde Boker, with more yet to come. Paula was demanding furniture, appliances and all sorts of amenities, and *Solel Boneh* was the contractor for all these. I said that I would consult with Eshkol. David added that Paula had poured out her misery to him. What would become of her and BG in that desert and under those primitive conditions? It seems that BG has only now become aware of where he is headed. In conversation with David he said: "I've made no commitment to stay in Sde Boker. If it doesn't work out, I shall leave." He evidently does not understand how such a departure would affect his standing in the party and his reputation.

38 Eliyahu Golomb (1893-1945). Born in Russia. Settled in Palestine in 1909. Served in the Jewish Legion of the British Army in WWI. Founder of the *Hagana* in 1920 and its leader till his death. Married Ada, Moshe Sharett' sister.

Sunday, November 29

[- - -]

At the Cabinet meeting I began with the coming political debate in the Knesset. I said that I wished to bring to the Cabinet's attention in advance what I was planning to say on one issue alone – Qibya. I wanted to dwell on three points: (a) it had been a deep shock for public opinion; (b) it had put certain friendly circles towards us in an agonizing position; (c) it had led to our complete isolation in the Security Council. A storm broke out immediately. Golda was furious. After such a resolution, we should go and rebuke ourselves? Had anybody decided to condemn us out of [genuine] moral outrage? Why, it was only because of political exigencies, etc. Rokach also argued against "self-flagellation." Serlin and [Dov] Joseph sided with him. BG announced: (a) – yes, (b) and (c) – no. I said that I had no choice but to side with the majority, but I had not changed my mind that my duty was to apprise the Knesset and the public of the true situation lest we become victims of a delusion. The fact that the three powers acted in their own interests does not remove one iota of the genuineness of public opinion's moral outrage. People in the Land of Zion should be well aware of this. It was the duty of the Foreign Minister, who stands on the lookout, to act in this manner; all the more so in a speech which will settle accounts with the SC resolution and its true motives. Thus did I pour out my dismay, but the conclusion remained in force. This session was most illuminating.

The main portion of the Cabinet meeting was devoted to the appointment of the new CoS. When BG announced Maklef's resignation and his own proposal to appoint Dayan in his place, a storm broke out. The GZ and Moshe Shapira led the attack. A deep distrust of Dayan was evident, as well as a candid appreciation of Mordechai. There was a general objection to the change itself since [Yigael] Yadin[39] had been replaced only a year ago. In particular, there was objection to Maklef's departure, and even more so to Dayan's appointment. BG, to be sure, was adamant and a strained tension ensued. Our *haverim* did not rush into battle. Lavon kept silent. I was forced to say something on BG's behalf, otherwise my silence might have been taken as support of the opposition, which was my true position. I wrote Golda a note on my attitude towards this change: "Moshe Dayan is neither an army man nor a man who bows to discipline. He is a daring independent fighter in wartime and a gifted adventure-prone statesman in peacetime. He has no idea and no interest in managing the military establishment." It was finally decided to pass the question on to the Cabinet's FADC. BG pressed for a speedy resolution

39 Yigael (Sukenik) Yadin (1917-1984). Soldier, politician, archaeologist. Born in Palestine. Joined the *Hagana* in 1932 and later became one of its leaders. Second CoS of the IDF (1949-1952). As an archaeologist was renowned for recovering the Dead Sea scrolls and for excavating the Masada fortress. Later founded the Democratic Movement for Change and served as Deputy PM.

so that the change-over of CoS would be complete before his departure.

[- - -]

Returned to the PMO. Moish Pearlman came to share with me his concern over the manner of publicizing the change of CoS. Could it be explicitly said that Motke [Maklef] was going because BG was going, that the one refused to stay on without the other? That would redeem the CoS's dignity. Otherwise it might seem that he'd been fired, or even do grave damage to Lavon. Meanwhile Moish elaborated upon the change itself, defining it as a *calamity* [English in orig.]. Dayan was completely incapable of managing an organization as complex as the IDF, of dealing with all the personnel, economic, technical and organizational problems which arise day in and day out, and of following them up diligently. [Pearlman] was very wary about the impact this will have on the Army. He couldn't believe it when I told him that the decision was made and there was no overturning it.

[- - -]

Arrived home after 10:00. We drank tea and at 10:45 I sat down, full of revived energy and a clear mind, to compose the speech I shall have to make tomorrow in the Knesset. I sat over it for four hours and lay down close to 3:00.

Monday, November 30

[- - -]

[At the MFA] I received a delegation consisting of Rabbi Morris Lazaron[40] with two reporters, one Protestant and one Catholic. The three of them are supporters of Dorothy Thompson and belong to the American Friends of the Middle East [AFME].[41] They've already toured the Arab states and Israel is their last stop. They sat for a whole hour and bombarded me with questions: the chances of peace and the refugee problem. The gentiles were much more amenable to persuasion than the Jew, who is a member of the American Council for Judaism – a rabid anti-Zionist and a typical Reform Rabbi of the previous generation, his tongue oozing milk and honey, his eyes fluttering as if he is about to break into tears, his voice trembling in feigned excitement. His last question wasn't a question but an apocalyptic vision: "What will happen if someday hundreds of thousands of refugees, men, women and children, get up and cross the border *en masse* with no weapons in their hands,

40 Rabbi Morris Samuel Lazaron (1888-1979). US Reform Rabbi; founder and vice-president of the anti-Zionist American Council for Judaism.

41 A pro-Arab group headed by Dorothy Thompson (1893-1961), well-known American journalist and author. During the 1940s, she was a close friend and supporter of Chaim Weizmann. After 1948 she abandoned her earlier pro-Zionist stance and joined the AFME, founded in 1951. On Thompson's changing attitudes to both Zionism and the AFME, see Peter Kurth, *American Cassandra: The Life of Dorothy Thompson* (Boston/Toronto/London: Little Brown & Co., 1990), 382-84, 422-30.

as if going to their deaths? Would Israel not open its gates to receive them, and even shelter them in camps? Would it not make a great impression throughout the entire world and boost Israel's repute to the heavens?" I said that it is undoubtedly possible to make a great impression on the world by means of suicide. One of the Christians immediately told me that he did not entertain any such possibility. The other one also disclaimed it following the conversation. This Lazaron had visited the country back in 1921. Upon leaving he begged me to believe that he wished us only well in this "experiment" of ours.

[- - -]

Tuesday, December 1

[- - -]

At 3:30 a crucial meeting of the Cabinet FADC to decide on the CoS. The opposition's lack of confidence in Dayan remains firm. I was obliged to report Maklef's hint that he felt he wasn't wanted by the new Defense Minister. Lavon squirmed, but again didn't utter a word. BG saw no choice other than to put the change up to a vote. Thus, and for the first time, the appointment of a CoS was confirmed not unanimously but by a majority.

At the beginning of this meeting there was a meaningful episode. Before we sat down at the table, BG said that something was still to be weighed upon, whereupon I humorously responded that surely in Sde Boker he would have enough time on his hands to look into that matter. "Who said I am going to Sde Boker?" – he retorted – "I have never announced this. Where did the newspapers take it from? On what is it all founded?" The whole group of ministers heard him and everybody laughed. "Certainly, certainly" – said Eshkol – "it is all groundless. We just put up the wooden house meant for you for nothing!" As far as I was concerned, BG was hinting that he might withdraw from his Shangri-la at any moment. [- - -]

Wednesday, December 2

[- - -]

At 12:00 I returned to the office in preparation for the first visit of the new Soviet Minister, Alexander Nikitich Abramov.[42] He is a most agreeable gentleman, a pleasant conversationalist, amiable, the exact opposite of his predecessor, the sour and small-minded [Pavel] Eershov,[43] and of that crook of a man, Mukhin, the Embassy Counselor. He is 48 years old, hailing from the heart of Russia,

42 Alexander Nikitich Abramov (1905-1973). Ambassador of the Soviet Union to Israel (1953-1958).

43 Pavel I. Eershov. Soviet Union First Minister, later Ambassador to Israel (1948-1953).

in the region between the Volga and Moscow. He immediately said that he was very impressed with our momentum in building the country. I replied that it was a twofold process – building the country and molding the newcomers into one people. From this I went on to explain about the renaissance of Hebrew and the teaching of it to the people. He suddenly asked: "And does not English interfere?" He must have thought that this was a quick feint on his part to disconcert me, following which he would proceed to demand satisfaction for the insult to Russian. But he'd dug his own pit – and fell right into it! I said that English was no hindrance at all, but necessary and beneficial: "It is a universal language and particularly the language of most of the Jewish people with whom we are free to maintain contact." I immediately noticed a twinkle in the eye of Counselor [Gennady] Fomin, who seems most clever. Encouraged by this hint of understanding, I went on to explain the reasons for our involvement with foreign languages: freedom of contact, possibilities of study, tourism, and above all – immigration of Jews from all corners of the globe. There had been a time when Russian was the principal language of the *yishuv*, for most of the immigrants then came from Russia. Again a flash of distinct understanding. As an example I brought up the fact that the President, PM and Foreign Minister are, all three of them, Russian-speaking, for they all emigrated here at the same time and from almost the same region. When I mentioned the PM, I said the "departing PM." Fomin immediately asked: Has it been decided? I answered: Decided, but still not signed. They laughed.

At the beginning of the conversation Abramov handed me his letter of accreditation and the text of the speech he would deliver on Friday before the President. I glanced through it and saw that its main point was the Soviet Government's wish to strengthen economic and cultural relations between Israel and the Soviet Union. I seized on this opportunity and said that I was impressed by the intention to strengthen cultural relations. He said: "Certainly, certainly, even though this is only a protocol visit, allow me to point out that we intend to publish here a newsletter about the Soviet Union's economic and cultural achievements." I said: "On the basis of reciprocity – by all means!" He said: "Reciprocity?" I said: "Certainly, reciprocity. Clearly, we are taking here about relations. But relations cannot exist unless they are two-sided." He said: "A Hebrew newsletter in Moscow?" I said: "We will discuss this matter in due time. The main thing is reciprocity in publishing as well as in disseminating."

Later I thought that it was good that I demanded reciprocity in disseminating, but how could we practice it, even if we were allowed to? Clearly, any Soviet citizen who would receive our newsletter would be considered a carrier of a microbe or a plague, and would curse the publisher.

[- - -]

A conversation [- - -] with Teddy. [- - -] He is thinking of resigning his post.

He is disappointed at the ineffectiveness of his contributions to restoring order into the chaos all around. Efforts toward planning the economy are frustrated by the traditional practice of improvising, a deeply ingrained distrust of foreign experts, narrow-minded conservatism, etc. At the same time he is seriously troubled by the evolving views of the IDF chiefs and the inability of the foreign affairs people to resist their power and domineering. All these are pushing him towards leaving.

I said he was talking like a political leader weighing whether or not to enter into a coalition, the principles of which were not to his liking. But he was not [a politician]. He was a civil servant, a subjugated slave of the state – what moral right does he have to retire? What disorder would be mended by his leaving? What satisfaction would he get by stepping aside? And how could he justify withdrawing now, at a time of the changing of the guard, when it is incumbent on all of us to lessen, as much as possible, the trauma of BG's retirement? Under my tough attack he gave in. For the time being he is prepared to stay put.

[- - -]

Thursday, December 3

[- - -]

Pinhas Rosen came at my behest. He started by asking whether it was true that BG was about to submit his resignation at the beginning of the week, and whether he fully understood that this meant the resignation of the entire Cabinet. [- - -] He told me that an acquaintance of his, a Mapam man and not one of their worst, had complained to him about the frightful waste incurred by the state because of BG's mania to settle in Sde Boker. According to him, the Army was moving a whole company to the same area exclusively for the sake of BG's security. Constructing the camp with all its facilities and arrangements will cost... $3.6 million! A gross exaggeration, to be sure, but it is bound to cost something.

Drove alone to Jerusalem. At the office I composed the President's speech to be delivered before the Soviet minister. I put in a clear sentence concerning the right of diaspora Jews to return to Zion.

Then I cabled our London Embassy directing them to protest against Eden's speech in Parliament, in which he justified in advance Jordan's refusal to agree to our call for a joint meeting according to Article XII.[44]

Friday, December 4

Walter told me this morning that he had dined last night with French Ambassador Gilbert at his residence in Jaffa. The latter told him that he had already almost

44 See *DFPI* 8, doc.559 (n.2). Following Sharett's instructions, Elath met with Roger Allen at the Foreign Office (FO) on December 4, 1953, *DFPI* 8, doc.560.

maneuvered the Quay d'Orsay into giving him liberty regarding a visit to Jerusalem, when along came the Qibya affair and set him back to square one. The diplomatic corps view the change of the CoS as Maklef paying the price for Qibya. How naive of them! Had Dayan been CoS at the time of Qibya and been replaced after that action, then there would have been some logic to their version.

[- - -]

Suturday, December 5

[- - -]

Sunday, December 6

[- - -]

The Cabinet meeting began with BG's announcement of his resignation. It was a strange feeling to witness the official accomplishment of a fact which has been known for some time but nevertheless lacked final sanction. BG announced that he would submit his resignation to the President tomorrow. For the present he asked the Cabinet to authorize a vacation for him in the interim period and to appoint me as Acting PM and Lavon as Acting Defense Minister. It was agreed, of course, without debate, and BG sought to start with the agenda. Yosef Sapir tried to launch into a speech but I hinted to him and to Serlin that it had best be postponed to the end of the meeting [which was devoted to the civil service demand for a salary raise and to the state purchase of the Palestine Electricity Company.]

[- - -]

At the end of the discussion, I asked to speak. My excitement surged but I managed to subdue it. I said that I was appropriating to myself the right of first speech because of the length of my acquaintance with BG and my work alongside him. I first met him in Constantinople 40 years ago, when we both studied law at the university there, and began working with him exactly 20 years ago. He is certainly aware of the meaning of his departure from this [Cabinet] table, the table which he played a crucial historic role in begetting and in determining the make-up of the people sitting around it. I extolled the spirit which he inculcated into Cabinet meetings and the standard he had set for its deliberations. I wished him health and long life; gratification with Israel's development; a quick return to shouldering [national] responsibility.

[- - -]

At 4:00 I returned to the PMO for the inaugural ceremony of the new CoS. All the Cabinet members and Army generals were present. This is the third such ceremony in which I have taken part: from Yaakov Dori to Yigael Yadin, from Yigael to Mordechai Maklef, and now from Mordechai to Moshe Dayan. BG read out the farewell missive, full of love and appreciation and containing a vivid, expressive description of the departing CoS's life story and service. Again, the same scenes recurred: the warm handshake and embrace, a speech by the former, a speech by the latter, the handing over of the flag, congratulations and handshakes from those assembled. I was throughout permeated with sadness and concern. It seemed to me that these feelings hovered over the entire room.

[- - -]

I was dead tired this evening and hardly overcame my headache. I went over the protocol of the Knesset debate on foreign affairs and scribbled down points for my response. Writing out my full reply was beyond my powers.

[- - -]

Monday, December 7

[- - -]

The new Italian Minister came for a first visit. This is the first time a Western representative has officially visited me at the Foreign Ministry in Jerusalem. The fact that he is a representative of such a distinctively Catholic country lends added importance to this act of breaking the ban on Jerusalem.

Dinner at the Hesse Restaurant on the occasion of BG's departure. Those present were BG and Paula, all the Ministers and Ze'ev Sharef. Dinur, Bernstein, Rokach, Serlin, Burg and Sheetrit[45] made speeches. BG spoke highly of the need to increase the [Jewish] birthrate.

At the opening of the Knesset at 4:00, I delivered the announcement of BG's resignation which had been submitted to the President this morning. Immediately after the announcement I began my speech in response to the political debate, which lasted an hour and a half. I thought the speech was well crafted, yet at the same time it was winding between problematic subjects. I made a few incisive remarks on the reaction of the Jewish public abroad to the Qibya action which must have angered many. My answers to the Left and to *Herut* were sharp and provocative and unleashed a shower of cat-calls. Upon stepping down from the lectern I wondered how the *haverim* had reacted to the speech.

[Here follow translated excerpts of Sharett's speech.]

> Let us not exaggerate the value of *hasbara*. *Hasbara* cannot function and convince [international public opinion] every time and in all cases. There are deep-rooted facts

45 Bechor-Shalom Sheetrit (1895-1967). Born in Tiberias, Palestine. Minister in charge of Minority Affairs in the Provisional Government of Israel (1948-1949). MK (Mapai from 1951) and Minister of Police.

whose impact no *hasbara* can erase. With the establishment of the State of Israel all displaced persons camps [of Holocaust survivors], which gave no rest to human conscience, were closed. But at the same time there arose Arab refugee camps, and no *hasbara* whatsoever, including myriad speeches and dozens of booklets, shall erase their factual existence. I would like to cite another case, a more recent one. The Qibya action. It is my duty to tell the Knesset – it is incumbent on the Foreign Ministry to function as a spotter of foreign occurrences and inform the people of what it sees there – that the Qibya action was anathema to the Jewish public [abroad]. It shook Jewish masses to the depth of their souls and depressed them to the utmost. It broke, on that day, their pride. [- - -] Perhaps the people who executed that action were right; perhaps there was no other choice. But we must be aware – each and everyone of us must be aware – that such [international shockwaves] were the result. Perhaps these [international] results are not decisive – if the action has improved our security situation, then perhaps this is more important; and, if so, we should put up with the negative reaction. However let us not ignore reality, let us be aware of concrete facts. [- - -]

A far-reaching change has occurred in our situation, from which some conclusions are clearly drawn. For dozens of years we were a political movement, not a political reality. We were a movement facing itself towards the future, we appealed to the world's conscience, we tabled before it a moral demand, we professed lofty principles: our historical right, our people's distress, our striving for freedom, the international justice which dictates the fulfilling of this striving. Now we have succeeded in becoming a political fact, a center of interests governed by us, a nucleus of might which is our own. The value of this change is immeasurable. However, we shall not be saved by force alone. We are still a spiritual movement, we are a movement of *aliya*[46] and the founding of new settlements, of the ingathering of exiles; we are still a nation in a process of being built and thus in need of help. But even we when we shall fully be a nation, when the day comes in which we would be able to say: we have reached the goal of fully being a nation and that is that, because we shall number millions – even if there will be peace between us and our neighbors – we shall still be here "a people that dwells alone", a single Jewish republic conspicuously in this whole area if not in the whole world, a single Jewish republic that would have to overcome its loneliness by maintaining a network of ties with the world at large.

But there is more to it. We have a past legacy and a mission for the future. We once had something to say to the world. We made a contribution to the treasures of its spiritual life and mores, and we feel and believe that we can still make a contribution. And hence our problem is how to fuse together the element of concrete might with the spiritual element, the element of the concrete reality with the element of striving, the moral striving. It is the task of our policy to fully utilize our being a concrete reality while at the same time preserving to the utmost our moral stature in the eyes of the whole world.[47]

When I went into the adjoining room, Lavon and Golda met me with resentful faces. Lavon assailed me as to why I had said things about Qibya which I was not authorized to say. Golda fumed in his wake. I confronted them with the Cabinet resolution which allowed me to report on the shock the act had evoked abroad. There was a short, acerbic and most annoying confrontation. I contended that our

46 Jewish immigration to Eretz-Israel, Palestine or Israel. Heb., lit. "ascent".

47 *Divrei Haknesset*, XV: 320.

public is blind, and its eyes must be opened. They stuck to their position, and we left with a residue of bitterness.

[- - -]

At 9:00 I went to the President. He told me about his conversation with BG this morning. He'd already invited delegates from all the parties for tomorrow to discuss the formation of the new Cabinet. I was puzzled as to why he had also invited *Herut*, Sneh[48] and the Israel Communist Party (CPI). Are they being considered for any sort of coalition? It's true that Weizmann observed this custom, but it is best not to go on with it. Ben-Zvi thought it best that he should invite everyone too, from wall to wall. For the small and extremist parties it is their only chance to see the President once in a blue moon. Why should he deny them this small amount of happiness? We concluded that I was to be officially invited for Wednesday morning.

Sat through the rest of the evening over my papers. After midnight the galleys of the *Jerusalem Post* report on my speech of reply were brought over to me. The job was so badly transcribed that I had to re-write it almost entirely.

Tuesday, December 8

In *Ha'aretz* an editorial: "Two Speeches" – a comparison between my speech of reply and BG's departure speech, both broadcast last night over *Kol-Israel,* not to the detriment of the first. *Ha'aretz* is biased, of course, but still there were several grains of truth in the article.[49]

[- - -]

[Azriel] Carlebach came for a talk at my request. He revealed to me that his newspaper [*Ma'ariv*]'s version that my candidacy fot PM was put forward only because Eshkol refused the post, which annoyed me greatly at the time, was leaked

---

48 Moshe Sneh (1909-1972). Head, National Staff of *Hagana* (1941-1946); since 1945 JAE member; Mapam MK since 1949; joined the CPI in 1954.

49 The editorial concluded with the following paragraph: "Nobody doubts the force of Mr Ben-Gurion's personality and his willpower; everyone will admit his historic achievements. However, many believe that the balance-sheet of his actions in recent years was not positive, and that present circumstances are asking for a different kind of leadership than what Mr Ben-Gurion is capable of giving to the country. There is no danger of Mr Sharett not being capable of vigorously guarding the stature of Israel among the nations. On the other hand, there are grounds for observing with some worry Mr Ben-Gurion's efforts in ignoring a few of the factors which Israel's foreign policy should have taken into account. Mr Ben-Gurion's pronouncements regarding the historical aspects of the phenomenon of Jewish statehood and the importance of personal and public mores are as true today as they will be in the distant future. However, no less important is that the Israeli public will learn from Mr Sharett's pronouncements the real measure of our abilities in the international arena."

by a member high up in my own Mapai Party. I took this opportunity to express my wishes as to how the formation of the new government should be portrayed. There is no justification for any negotiations, certainly not exploiting BG's departure for partisan gains. The emphasis should rather be put on the unconditional demand for the stability of the regime vis-à-vis the internal and external affairs of the state. Whoever upsets this stability will be guilty of speculating with his public responsibilities in this time of trial.

Since today marks the start of BG's "vacation" and my incumbency as Acting PM, I made it a point to visit the said office. I found BG still in his room. I took issue with him regarding the improper use of a certain verb (*leratzot*) he had used in his broadcast of last night. In his customary manner he refused to admit his mistake and stuck to his guns. He turned to Yehuda Gur's dictionary for vindication. Even when he found nothing of the sort there, he remained obdurate until I desisted. I went into the adjoining room, and was followed by him. He sat down. Now he too took issue with me over a word I had used in my speech of response in the Knesset. Why had I termed the Qibya action a "horror" (*zva'a*)? I said this had been my definition of Jewish public response abroad to the Qibya action. He contended that the Cabinet had expressed a negative attitude to the line I had proposed to take in my speech. I reminded him that he himself had concluded that I could speak about the shock which the Qibya action had engendered abroad. He began objecting to the very nature of the response abroad, and remonstrating against Eban and Elath. I said that the matter had nothing to do with our Ambassadors' response, but with the obvious phenomenon of outrage in Jewish public opinion, whether expressed or muted. In vain should we try to ignore and obscure it. He disagreed with me and I disagreed with him, and he left the room holding back his anger.

[- - -]

Walter came by for a moment. He said he had heard from journalists present at the Knesset many praises for my reply speech, together with a critical note that I had not dared to say what I should have said concerning Qibya. There you have it!

[- - -]

Drove from Jerusalem to the Tzrifin military base for a dinner in honor of both BG's departure and the change of CoS. Zipporah arrived from Tel Binyamin. There were more than forty people at the table, including BG and Lavon and senior army officers and Defense Ministry people with their wives. I again was impressed with the high quality of the human material our senior officers are made of. There were no speeches. Hanukkah candles were not lit. The national anthem was not sung. One sensed an unfulfilled expectation. Pressing dilemmas, hovering in the air, remained unanswered. Doubts were left in their place. The participants at the event dispersed with a pressing feeling of distress, unrelieved. [- - -]

Forming the Government

Wednesday, December 9

Today the President entrusted me with forming the government!

I got up a bit late and barely managed to get to the Presidential residence at the scheduled hour – 9:00. Photographers lay in ambush for me in Alharizi Lane. Reporters crowded around the entrance. I forced my way through all these obstacles and found the President, as usual unassuming in person and noble in bearing, fervent and solemn. He made some warm and candid remarks about me and my talents and my capabilities, and about his own longtime regard for me. He spoke about his meetings with the different parties yesterday. The Progressive Zionists had wholeheartedly supported me. Other parties had contented themselves with voicing no objection. I responded with few words. We got up, kissed as Russian do, and shook hands. Upon leaving, I spoke briefly to the reporters, and was once again a target for the cameras.

[- - -]

At the office an exhilarating surprise awaited me: a cable from my daughter Yael from New York: "I too was elected – Phi-Beta-Kappa." I couldn't believe my eyes – what a daughter! My heart kept singing all day long.

The latest telegrams from New York testify to a vigorous and determined struggle going on there to obtain an acceptable formula in the SC concerning the Jordan [diversion] project. The impression is that our chances have improved. The US is obviously favorably inclined; only England is opposed.

An article by Carlebach appeared in *Ma'ariv*. It adhered faithfully to the ideas I proposed to him yesterday. Inevitably, it contained the old Carlebachian malice and biting sting towards both Mapai and the GZ. This man cannot do without such adornment.

[- - -]

Thursday, December 10

[- - -]

At 9:00 at the PMO in the *Kirya*, BG organized a day-long symposium to look into the problems of the party. The invitations were personal. About thirty people attended. I heard that typical insults had been inflicted. Sprinzak and the members of the board of the JA had not been invited, for example. I did see Shazar, but Golda told me that he hadn't been invited either. She prevailed upon him to come on the pretext that there must have been some mistake.

Lavon, who according to BG was responsible for the initiative for this symposium, opened the discussion. He spoke candidly but with immoderate acerbity. He ruthlessly exposed defects: the spirit of volunteering in the party was all but extinct; the human fabric in the leadership has disintegrated; people were at each other's throats [expressing] virulent envy and hate, the source of all slander and libel was from within; people were hindering one other's success and taking joy in their failure. And on and on. On the whole, it expressed a bitter remonstration and a cry of distress. Halt! Where are we heading? What then is his remedy? Alas, his lips were sealed.

Ziama Aran was more concrete. He brought up several failures such as lack of contact between the party's leadership and rank and file, but he, too, had no basic answer except trying to promote the tackling of problems one by one.

I tried to help resolve things. I sought to pinpoint the root of the evil in the lack of all planning concerning the allocation of tasks, the proper apportionment of our forces, the lack of guidance by our leadership. Planning itself requires planning. I suggested the election of a planning committee of seven members, to be headed by Ziama, which should unhurriedly and systematically deal with our current problems. Public volunteering, too, needs planning and organizing. Without overall organization, the movement of volunteering to [to the British Army] in WWII could not have reached the dimensions it achieved. [- - -]

When I said that we must also send people to work among Jewish youth in the diaspora, BG opposed me immediately, arguing that work should be done mainly in Israel and all the rest was secondary. The discussion went on and on for hours, each pouring out his complaints. At one point I took my leave, having another commitment.

[- - -]

Friday, December 11

Today I effectively assumed my post as Acting PM from a ministerial aspect. I conferred with Teddy and his aide, Yitzhak Levi.[1] They spread before me a diagram showing the structure of the Ministry extending to all its departments.

[- - -]

Yochanan Böhm, secretary to the Advisory Office for Economic Planning, which is headed by Oscar Gass, came to initiate me into the thick of the personnel problems which have confounded this office and which Gass is a consummate artist

1 Yitzhak Levi (1907-1994). Deputy DG, PMO; later Head, information center, PMO.

at developing around him wherever he sets foot. The most malignant sore right now is in the relations between Gass and Pinhas Sapir, more properly in Sapir's attitude towards Gass. Eshkol has gone from aloof repudiation to a completely positive attitude, but in this matter Sapir hasn't adopted his master's approach. Relations with David Horowitz are also amiss.

I said that I certainly uphold the existence of such an office from a practical-national viewpoint. To be sure, the question remains as to whether Gass' aberrations can be endured for long. But because of what happened between us, it is patently undesirable that matters should come to a crisis when I am on the threshold of power or immediately after I officially assume the reins. I promised to look into things with Sapir as soon as he returns from abroad. Afterwards I shall delve with Teddy and Yochanan into the problem of guiding the office in its work and the channels of communication between it and the other ministries.

[- - -]

Saturday, December 12

[- - -]

My niece Tamar told me that among other things her husband [Moshe Gidron[2]], who is a communications officer with the Southern Command, is handling communication arrangements with Sde Boker. These arrangements include constant monitoring of Sde Boker from the center. Three people would take their turns daily to receive communications from there, should there be any. I was reminded of [Pinhas] Rosen's story.[3] The first thought which came to my mind was to find out what the arrangements at Sde Boker would cost, including security arrangements. But I quickly backed off. The gossip would surely spread immediately that I'm "amassing material." Squalid grievance will only flourish.

I asked myself whether BG knows what's going on around him and has any idea of the fortune being spent on him. Here he is, apparently returning to the bosom of nature, to a simple and even ascetic life. Such is the impression throughout the country and the world. Such is the subject of articles and poems. But it isn't so. As to the public purse, the exact opposite is true even if he himself certainly didn't mean it to be so. So what if he didn't mean it? Our duty always lies in foreseeing the outcome in advance. Man is only judged by the results of his actions! Well, did he give any thought to the results? I truly don't know. He perhaps has no idea and never entertained the need to take all this into consideration. But he may well be in the know and still treat such trifles of mundane life with lofty disdain. What

2 Moshe (Musik) Gidron (1925-2009). Husband of Tamar Hoz, Sharett's niece. Communications Officer in the Southern Command, IDF (1953-1956).

3 See above, entry for December 3, 1953.

weight do they carry on the scales of eternity?

[- - -]

At 10:00 pm, at Zipporah's prodding we went, together with my brother Yehuda,[4] to see the last showing of Charlie Chaplin's "Stage Lights." The whole country is going mad about this film, but the Sharett brothers came out disappointed. The acting is indeed superb, but the film is melodramatic and too long.

Sunday, December 13

[- - -]

Sat with Teddy and Yitzhak Navon to look into the problem of BG's settling in Sde Boker. Do the security arrangements really involve such heavy expenditures as the spreading gossip reports? They are both sure that these are wild exaggerations. Yitzhak, however, promised to carry out a meticulous inquiry.

Teddy told me that he'd begun talks with Dayan and his colleagues on the infiltration problem in an effort to explain once and for all the ruinous political consequences of our reprisals and also the need to consult over preventive measures. I told him that a Foreign Ministry research project had prepared a special paper on this question, pointing to a whole list of possible measures which the Army, adhering to its routine of reprisals, had disqualified as impractical. In my opinion, it was shunted aside without proper study of the problem.

While talking with Yitzhak about my fears concerning internal relations within our contingent in the Cabinet, I found out something I didn't know. According to him, not only had Golda at one stage thought that she deserved to inherit BG's place, but she'd explicitly said so to the committee of three. Her line of thought went like this: since two candidates had been proposed, Eshkol and I, and ostensibly there ensued a rivalry between them, it seemed to her that her candidacy was not only suitable but also a solution out of the quandary. If this is the case, it explains the despondency and tension that engulfed her. It was a result of a profound disappointment which she has suffered.

[- - -]

After not taking leave of Ben-Gurion all day Saturday I deliberated over whether to go see him. I finally let Zipporah visit Paula by herself. I wrote him a short letter which Yitzhak will take with him tomorrow. It runs as follows:

> David, I am very grieved at your parting and at the circumstances of the exchange of roles between us. I seek to bolster my faith that your instincts, which have proven themselves several times in the past, will not fail this time as well. I wish you health, fortitude of spirit and inner gratification upon this new chapter of your life.

---

4 Yehuda Sharett (1901-1979). Sharett's younger brother. Composer.

Monday, December 14

A red-letter day – BG left Tel Aviv for Sde Boker.

[- - -]

Conducted a thorough consultation with Walter, Shabtai Rosenne and Shmuel Bendor, examining the Western powers' draft resolution in the SC on the fate of the northern project. I dictated a detailed telegram to Aubrey in accordance with its conclusions.[5]

The most immediate and pressing point is whether there is any obstacle to the renewal of work there. We openly announced – and the SC confirmed – that we were stopping work temporarily only for the duration of the "urgent debate" in the SC. Now that the debate is over and the resolution doesn't contain any prohibition regarding the renewal of work, it seems we are free to renew it. But actually it was quite clear from the spirit of the resolution, and there were explicit indications in some passages as well, that it is incumbent upon us not to renew work except in concert with the UNTSO CoS. At any rate, after having gotten into trouble resulting from our first rejection, it is best that we explore now all avenues of renewed negotiation before we think of taking a direct step to renew work on our own, openly disdainful of the UN and its representative.

At 3:00 pm in the Knesset I outlined the draft resolution before the Cabinet FADC. I pointed out all the pitfalls and mines. It seemed to me that everyone agreed the resolution could have been much worse. It did not preclude a positive outcome, provided there was the will. Especially disturbing were the paragraphs introduced to link our project with the regional plan made in the USA.

I told Ze'ev Sharef what I had heard about Golda's craving for the prime ministership. He vigorously denied this. He knew that Lavon had tried to convince her to put herself up for the post, but she had rejected it out of hand.

[- - -]

At 6:00 I went to Golda's for a visit of conciliation and mending of fences. At the outset of our working in cooperation according to the new arrangement, there has already been a glitch. It was not exactly in accordance with the spirit of teamwork I had called for at the meeting of the party's Central Committee. When she found fault with my conclusions regarding the manner of integration of the demands of the administrative bureaucracy for higher pay within the framework of the salaries settlement with the State Workers' Union, she went into a sulk, and announced that she would no longer attend the Cabinet Committee on Civil Servants' Remuneration, of which she is not only a member, but the chair. She did not appear at the last

5 *DFPI* 8, doc.581. For the delegation's consultations and lobbying on this issue in New York, see the minutes of the meeting (8/52) of the Israel Delegation, December 10, 1953, ISA FM 130.03/1962/13; *DFPI* 8, doc.573.

meeting. I told her that I had come to ask her to return to the Committee, and to come to its meeting tomorrow. She consented, but under the condition that I would be the chair. It was an unreasonable demand. Not only was I not a member of the Committee, and could not carry such a heavy burden on my own, but I had never handled this issue and knew nothing about it. Be that as it may, I saw no point in being obstinate at this stage and paid one concession as the price of another.

She told me about the negotiations with Mapam [concerning their joining the coalition government]. They are still picking and poking into the platform on foreign policy which I had formulated [for my government]. Their representatives are posing all sorts of bright questions: Why don't we talk about the importance of Soviet aid as we talk about the importance of US aid? And on the other hand, why don't we demand the right of US Jews to emigrate as we demand the right of Soviet Jews to emigrate – and so on and so forth, with similar contentions demonstrating their sober and most realistic grasp of reality.

Sat over my papers all evening.

Tuesday, December 15

Upon arriving at the PMO at 8:30 am I discovered that Yitzhak Navon had brought me a letter from BG, written in pencil on a page torn from a duplicate notepad. It ran as follows:

Sde Boker, 14.12.53

Dear Moshe,

After managing (actually, the young men who came here with me managed) to get a bit settled, I wish to send you my first greetings from this place – to you and to all the *haverim*. (a) - to stabilize the Cabinet as fast as possible, (b) - to ensure "teamwork" in the Cabinet and the party. I feel quite the same as I felt on my first day in Israel, and I hope to be able to return to manual labor (if only for four hours a day) and to read the books I cherish, and maybe do something more as well. Time will tell. Warm regards to Zipporah and all the *haverim*.

Yours,
D. Ben-Gurion.

Yitzhak testified to the great regard with which my letter to BG was received. Navon has looked into the problem of expenses and found that it doesn't exist at all. True, the Army had enclosed the Sde Boker site with a fence, but this could and should have been done anyway within the framework of security measures now being implemented to defend isolated spots. The Army company at the site had been augmented and, once again, deliberations had long been conducted concerning this step and could have been carried out anyway, even without BG's having settled there. My mind was put to rest.

[- - -]

Wednesday, December 16

[- - -]

Gideon Rafael came for a long talk on our future policy in view of the lessons of Qibya and the SC. He came all charged up and was sure that in one smashing attack he could capture fortresses and topple towers. "The Cabinet must decide once and for all that the Army will not cross the border to operate on the other side under any circumstances." I rejected the wisdom of proposing such a wholesale and unrealistic principle to the government. I also rejected the practical possibility of tying our hands like that in advance of any eventuality.

Thursday, December 17

[- - -]

At the Foreign Ministry, I sat with the DG and Gideon Rafael on further steps towards the application of Article XII of the Jordanian Armistice Agreement, and on the preparation of a response to the SC resolution on the northern project.

[- - -]

Friday, December 18

[- - -]

At the end of the day, when I reached Ramat Gan, Zipporah told me that [Francis] Russell, the Chargé d'affaires of the US Embassy, had telephoned several times. I phoned him, and he said he would come immediately. When he arrived, he told me with a strained and somber face that Ambassador Monnett Davis was mortally ill. He had not recovered his good health at all in the US. The State Department doctor had objected to his returning to his post in Israel. His private doctor had allowed it. It seems he catered more to his emotional needs – his desire to return to work – than to his physical condition. He had arrived in Israel near death. At the beginning of the week there had been a change for the better, but today he suffered a severe relapse. The doctor anticipated that he might not last more than a few hours. Even if he should recover, it was hard to believe he will last more than three weeks. They had notified the State Department and decided to notify me, and they told the State Department that they were notifying me.

I was deeply moved by this description, and by the impending death of this dear, fanatically conscientious man, who out of concern for the fate of the matter entrusted to him – Israel's relations with the US which have deteriorated these last few months – had hastened his own demise. I thanked Russell for taking the trouble to inform me and asked him to stay in hourly contact with me.

[- - -]

Suturday, December 19

[- - -]

Sunday, December 20

Today our residence in Ramat Gan was closed for good. I left it for Jerusalem for the last time.

[- - -]

I took Gideon Rafael with me to the Cabinet meeting. [- - -] I reported in detail on the SC draft resolution – its lights and shadows and the dangers involved both for us and for the Council. Golda, she of all the participants, pointed out the positive elements of the resolution, while Lavon and Joseph were most pessimistic about it. Gideon answered questions and explained away misunderstandings, doing so, as is usual with him, in a cumbersome way, but thoroughly. There was no need to take any decision, for the Council had not yet voted on the issue, but the prevailing mood was not to hasten any confrontation, neither with the Council nor with Bennike.

[- - -]

On *Shabbat* I had heard over the radio, and today I read in the newspapers, about the killing of a Arab Legion army doctor on the Bethlehem-Hebron road. I asked Lavon whether I recognized the fingerprints of the IDF in this incident. He answered: "Yes."[6] Some *haverim* entered the room and our conversation was interrupted. When I came home, I wrote him with all due friendship that in no way could I accept this disregard of the arrangement decided upon concerning IDF raids on the other side of our borders, namely that nothing be done without my knowledge.[7]

[- - -]

Monday, December 21

Yitzhak Navon brought me news from Sde Boker. BG's mood was sky-high, and Paula's too. A truly idyllic life they were leading there! They were impressed with the quality of the kibbutz members around them. Physical work was giving him satisfaction, and everything was smooth and perfect. BG did some ploughing and worked in the sheep shed too. One is impressed with him there as with a man who had come to terms with himself, and found solace in this world. I could only bless this situation. Pray, let this continue for a long time!

Between 11:00 and 2:30 I participated in the meeting of the Knesset FADC.

6 On this incident, see Morris, *Israel's Border Wars*, 293.
7 Letter not found.

I reported in detail on the draft resolution of the three Western powers in the SC and its various aspects. A long debate ensued and it was decided to continue it tomorrow.

Teddy came by in the afternoon. We had a long talk. The most important problem on the state's agenda was Arab infiltration. He had read the Foreign Ministry memorandum on this subject, written by Yael Vered[8] of the Ministry's Research Division, and found himself in total agreement with it. He told me he had been continuing his discussions with Dayan, who was ready to admit before his IDF officers that Qibya's negative results clearly outweighed the positive ones. Ostensibly, Dayan seemed to be nearing the conclusion that different methods to stop infiltration should be tried. We discussed the subject of preventive measures to be taken against infiltration and I concluded that we should consult Ezra Danin[9] on this issue.

[- - -]

Tuesday, December 22

Stepped into the PMO for a moment, and then arrived at the Knesset at 9:00 for a resumed meeting of the FADC. The generous contribution of Soviet delegate Vyshinsky to the SC debate was published this morning. It expressed Bennike's line, naked and in extreme terms, to postpone any decision for an indefinite period of time, to make continuation of the Jordan canal project conditional upon Syrian consent, and a complete freeze until then. Gideon Rafael came to the meeting and passed me a note: "Vyshinsky's intervention on Syria's behalf may save the situation for us."

I replied that here too logic is a double-edged sword. A Western rush to win friendship with the Arabs may begin with competition with the Soviet Union; then we should find Vyshinsky's support of Syria was to our disadvantage. It was both pathetic and maliciously pleasurable to watch Mapam's [Yaakov] Riftin's intellectual contortions. He tried to put the blame of Vyshinsky's hostile stand on our votes against the Soviet Union in the UN. According to that logic, had we regularly voted as Riftin wished, we would have raised US ire against us, and then the SC resolution would have fallen against us from the start. Riftin also tried to sweeten Vyshinsky's demand for direct Syrian-Israeli negotiations. Hadn't we ourselves always proclaimed our willingness for negotiations with Syria as a neighboring state on all questions of neighborly relations, including water issues? When I reminded him that we had never made our development projects dependent on the results of such negotiations – and this is exactly what Vyshinsky is trying to impose on us – his face reddened.

Towards the end of the debate, it was ascertained that all of the coalition

8 Yael Vered (1922-). Arabist. Chief Assistant, Research Division, MFA; later acting DG, West European and Middle East Divisions.

9 Ezra Danin (1903-1984). Born in Palestine. Adviser on Middle Eastern affairs, MFA. Before 1948 was a senior *Hagana* intelligence (*SHAI*) officer and a leading member of the Arab section of the JA Political Department.

parties rejected the notion of a renewed conflict with the SC, and were willing to wait three months until the results of the renewed struggle with the UNTSO CoS became clear. Neither did the opposition parties, for their part, advocate immediate rebellious action concerning the necessity of trying to reach a compromise with Bennike. In case the attempt failed, in their view we should proceed with our work. According to *Herut*'s Landau, after 3-4 weeks; according to Mapam's Ben-Aharon, after 6-8 weeks. The main point was that renewal of work would take place before the end of the three months.

Gideon Rafael made some pertinent remarks on the Arab position, and their assumption that we would be tempted to defy Bennike. He did not rest content with explaining the situation. He went on to lecture the members of the Committee that we must not give the SC cause for hostility towards us. With this he exceeded the proper bounds of a foreign service official, and what is more, he did not contribute anything new or vital. As though this wasn't enough, he took it upon himself to promise that there were good prospects of achieving the renewal of work with the authorization of Bennike. In advance, then, in case of failure, he offered the critics an opening to contend that the Foreign Ministry had deluded itself and others with vain hopes, and had neglected efforts it should have undertaken to counter a possible disaster.

In summing up I satisfied myself by noting three facts: (a) that none of the Committee members had proposed to renew work immediately (in saying this I intently fixed my eyes on Landau, but he didn't say a word); (b) that all agreed that we first had to explore the possibility of a settlement with the CoS [Bennike]; (c) that it was not yet clear which way the decision might fall in the SC, the situation having been clouded by the Arab-Pakistani counter-attack with Soviet artillery support, and therefore it was not yet time to decide on our tactics.

[- - -]

The wife and brother of Shimon Orenstein, who has been sentenced to life imprisonment in Prague, came to complain about the discrimination against him in the press as opposed to the treatment accorded to Mapam leader, Mordechai Oren, to the detriment of the former. I said that we had brought this to the notice of the press more than once, and that on our part we had taken all of our steps on behalf of the two imprisoned Israelis without any discrimination. I added that the President's appeal in support of the two wives' application for pardon would be made within the next few days.

[- - -]

Wednesday, December 23

In the morning newspapers there appeared a description of complete disintegration in the SC. It was as though Western unity was falling apart at the seams. Britain and France had given way under Arab pressure. The US was ostensibly standing firm. It was as though the coalition of seven had never existed. The US tried to put off the entire matter until January – in the hope, no doubt, of a more amenable composition of the Council – and failed. For the time being the vote has been postponed till next week.[10] Bennike was returning.

Gideon Rafael came to the PMO for authorization to send Eban instructions to make an effort to talk to Bennike about the negotiating procedures to be employed with him for the purpose of renewing work, and also to drive in a wedge against a search of Mount Scopus. This serious nuisance never drops off the agenda.

[- - -]

From 5:00 until almost 8:00, in Tel Aviv, I chaired the annual meeting of the board of Am Oved, the *Histadrut* publishing house. It was a strange leap into another world, but greatly refreshing and illuminating. Representatives of *Ihud Hakvutzot Vehakibbutzim*[11] complained about the absence of socialist literature in the Am Oved publishing program. They demanded satisfaction for the absence of writings of old liberal socialists leaders like Otto Bauer and Karl Kautsky. [- - -] They argued that "the young must be given answers to their questions." A rather sophisticated member of the Am Oved editorial board retorted that these books were hopelessly outdated, that those who championed them now were relying on their own youthful memories and would be grievously disappointed were they to read them to-day. Concerning contemporary writings, he continued, the blatant fact was that the literature of the present was no longer a literature of answers, but of questions.

[- - -]

Thursday, December 24

My first appointment was with Isser Harel. We examined some problems concerning matters entrusted to his care.

After him came Ezra Danin, my adviser on Arab affairs. He absolutely rejected military reprisals as a method, and advocated a system of preventive measures and surveillance both to establish defense measures and to strike at the sources of this evil. This would require the establishment of an apparatus and a network of contacts that was non-existent at present. Months would pass before we should get results,

10 On the previous day's deliberations in the UN SC and the ongoing complications of re-drafting the tripartite resolution on the Israeli-Syrian dispute over the B'not Yaakov water diversion project so as to rally at least seven votes, see *Ha'aretz*, December 23, 1953; *FRUS 1952-1954*, docs. 755-58; *DFPI* 8, docs. 594, 597, 601-03, 606, 611.

11 *Ihud Hakvutzot Vehakibbutzim* (The Union of Kvutzot and Kibbutzim) was established in 1951 by the merger of the pro-Mapai Hakvutzot Union (established in 1929) with non-Marxist kibbutzim which seceded from the leftist-Marxist United Kibbutz organization.

but the sooner we began the better. He was ready and willing to provide counsel, assistance and enterprise. However, there was no chance of success if the Army itself did not perform the job, and wholeheartedly too. The question was whether the GS was prepared for it.

Telegrams were received from New York about the unholy mess in the SC. One of the obscure points was the US role in the disavowal of the earlier draft. The US Ambassador to the UN, Henry Cabot Lodge, and the State Department people were claiming that they had no hand in the matter, and that only their allies succumbed to panic. The latter, however, were swearing that the US delegation was of one mind with them regarding to the need for concessions to obtain a majority of seven in the Council. Most disturbing of all was Aubrey's telegram about being on the verge of exhaustion and his wish to depart immediately for vacation in Florida. I sent him a telegram expressing appreciation for the superhuman effort he had made these past weeks, and added a prayer that he might manage to hang on until the end of the campaign.

[- - -]

At 8:00 pm I arrived at the JA building for the opening of the Zionist Executive meeting. It was opened by Sprinzak. Then I pronounced short greetings which were followed by Berl Locker's long report – a most dull and uninspiring speech. In contrast, Nahum Goldmann who followed him spoke brilliantly, showering sharp insights. His main thesis – one which I have been advancing since 1948 – was that the strong influence of Israel's actions over the stature of the entire Jewish people in the eyes of the world's nations has placed a heavy responsibility on our shoulders.

Friday, December 25

[- - -]

Saturday, December 26

[- - -]

The first half of *Shabbat* passed quietly. At 3:00 Walter telephoned from Tel Aviv to inform me that Ambassador Davis had died half an hour earlier. All my plans were upset. I immediately composed a short eulogy in English. I telephoned Walter and read it aloud to him. After a short while he called me back with a revised version. I then telephoned Michael Elizur and dictated to him the text to relay to the news agencies. He then called back with a Hebrew translation for my editing. At 6:40 I set out for Ramat Gan. In one hour we arrived at the Russell home where I saw the son of the deceased.

[- - -]

Sunday, December 27

Opened the Cabinet meeting with a eulogy of Davis. I noted that, even though he had come to us from afar and his appointment had been accidental without any background of involvement or sense of mission, he had quickly become imbued with a recognition of the special responsibility for the execution of his duty, and had totally identified with two tasks – enhancing friendship between the US and Israel, and peace between Israel and the Arabs. I then reviewed the disintegration and confusion gripping the SC. The meeting dealt mostly with mundane matters. Several heavy issues, such as our policy concerning the Arab minority and the problem of developing Jerusalem, are being postponed week after week in expectation of the formal formation of the new government and because of fear lest airing them would awaken sleeping dogs, contributing nothing towards their solution.

Two issues, however, raised havoc. The first – the payment for our citrus export to West Germany. When I asked a few months ago for approval of the Israeli Citrus Center's idea to sell citrus products to West Germany, all government ministers voted for it except one who opposed it. It was only Dov Joseph who insisted on the extreme principle of no commerce whatsoever with Germany even if this meant losing a most important foreign market. But then it was assumed that we would receive hard currency for our exports. Now it turned out that the Germans were asking our approval for their paying a certain percentage in Deutschmarks (DM), and it might be that this would mean our purchasing German products, i.e., accepting German imports to Israel outside the limits of the Reparations Agreement. Golda revolted against this door opening and Joseph doubled his opposition as well. Eshkol claimed that with these DM we would be able to purchase Danish or Dutch products. The opposing ministers seemed to agree to this suggestion, but were adamant against any direct purchasing. The matter was put aside for further deliberations, but meanwhile Golda raised objections to the purchasing of foodstuffs with money received from the reparations, and this not because these moneys should be invested only in infrastructure and not in food, but because these foodstuffs were manufactured by Germans. The claim that morally there is no difference between food produced in Israel by using agricultural machinery manufactured by German hands, and food produced in Germany, was not accepted and this matter, too, was related to the committee of economic ministers.

In the afternoon, a consultation in my office on the lines of our argument for a conference with Jordan in accordance with Article XII. I was skeptical about the wisdom of this consultation as long as it was not clear whether the conference would take place at all, for Jordan has yet to give an answer. Nevertheless I saw no harm in a preliminary exchange of ideas within the Foreign Ministry, but objected to a second stage of further debate with the Army's participation. In the congenial atmosphere of the Foreign Ministry, an examination of concepts is always beneficial, even if not directed towards any operational end. But what gain is there in getting into a dispute with the IDF before we know there is any practical purpose to it?

[- - -]

Monday, December 28

[- - -]

From 9:00 till 11:00 took part in a meeting of the Committee for Coordination between the government and the JA, devoted to the problem of "*yerida*" [emigration from Israel]. Locker, Josephthal[12] and Raphael[13] represented the JA; Golda, Rokach, [Moshe] Shapira and I represented the government. The JA's principal demand centered on more rigorous standards for issuing exit permits. Avnon, who came with me, and I put the emphasis on issuing passports. Even though the question had been resolved in Cabinet, Rokach and Shapira saw fit at this gathering to challenge the Cabinet decision. Rokach returned to his old demand: there should be a law against issuing a passport to anyone residing in the country less than two years. I was again obliged to prove that (1) the Minister of Interior [already] had all the administrative authority to refuse to issue a passport, and (2) the two-year restriction would not help any, because most of the emigrants had been in the country longer than that and it was only because of their long sojourn that they had managed to save money for the expense of a trip. We also talked about the need for the renewal of strict administration of the repayment of debts to the JA before receipt of a passport, and about the return of the housing they received. There are emigrants who sell the housing they received from the JA to finance their travel and settlement abroad. Avnon stressed the need for vigorous police action against fraudulent agencies which promise visas to Canada and other countries and thus tempt many who end up stranded in Germany. As always, Josephthal raised the discussion to a higher level when he assailed the shallowness of Shapira's ostensibly liberal attitude, which upholds the right of people to leave the country and to go wherever they like. He said that, just as doctors and welfare workers have the right – actually the duty – to ignore the foolish wishes of people in their care and to prescribe to them instead a cure or a change of lifestyle that is for their own good as dictated by their expertise and experience, so too has the state the right – and the duty – not to give in to the wanderlust harbored in the hearts of people or to surrender to their whims, but to save them and their sons after them – against their will, if need be – from the curse of eternal gipsy-like wandering in which, in

12 Giora Josephthal (1912-1962). Born in Germany. Settled in Palestine in 1938. Co-leader of Israel's Delegation to the Reparations Negotiations with Germany; Treasurer, JA; SG, Mapai (1956-1959); later Minister of Labor and Minister of Development and Housing.

13 Yitzhak Raphael (1914-1999). Born in Galicia. Settled in Palestine in 1935. Head of JA Immigration Department (1948-1953); *Hapo'el Hamizrahi* MK.

their impatience, they seek relief from the travails of absorption in their only home in the world. This was Zionism made of iron – nay, of steel! It is not for nothing that I deeply love this great German Jew. I wish there were many more like him!

[- - -]

Went to Tel Aviv with Nahum Goldmann who is also going to attend the JNF gathering at the Habima Theater. On our way we discussed several subjects. He was furious at BG's letter to the Zionist Executive in which he again denied the right of the Zionist movement to exist as long as it does not press its members to immigrate to Israel.

When I arrived at Habima with Goldmann, the hall, including the balcony and stage, were overflowing. I marveled that the public is capable of flocking to a gathering like this which is being held purely in the name of "Zionism." The chairman, as usual, spoke at length. He placed no trust in the speakers following him, and exhausted the subject from all aspects. The second-to-last speaker was Nahum. With wondrous ease he absolved himself of any duty to stick to the subject of the evening and embarked upon entirely different issues. He served the audience a popular version of his speech at the Zionist Executive Forum on the response of US Jewry to events in Israel. From there he leapt to BG's letter and shot polemical arrows at it. The whole speech was anomalous within the framework of the evening, while its conclusion was a downright prank.

I wondered: Should I respond? It would be unworthy of me to clash with my co-speaker on the dais, even when the latter has not shown me the consideration I deserved. Regarding the matter itself, if I should demand satisfaction for BG's affront and without reservation, I would be twisting the truth. I was not at all in agreement with that letter. But if I should make reservations while defending him, it would not benefit me at all.

I stood up and said: "Much as it may appear strange and surprising, I will devote my remarks this time to the subject of the JNF, all the more for its being the subject of this gathering." A roar of laughter and applause drowned my words. Indeed, I think this was the first time in my life that I made a concise speech regarding the main historic essence of the JNF, both as a principle and an undertaking, all in a quarter of an hour.

[- - -]

Tuesday, December 29

The first event of the day was the memorial service for Ambassador Davis at St. Peter's Anglican Church in Jaffa. I brought with me from Jerusalem full-dress special attire for this ceremony, including a top hat. Our protocol officer telephoned to say that I must arrive at the church at 9:25, the last arrival before the entrance of

Mrs Davis and her entourage. I arrived punctually, but the French Ambassador, who is the head of the diplomatic corps, contrived to be late and arrived after the widow.

God's worship took an hour. An organ played and a choir of men and women from the US Embassy staff – the women monstrous in their ugliness – sang hymns. The ceremony was conducted by an English priest who delivered a most cultivated and dignified oration. There was a large crowd. The coffin was carried out by American Marines while the assembled mourners formed two lines on either side. An IDF paratroop unit stood as an honor guard and presented arms.

After he service I stayed on in Tel Aviv while Zipporah drove to Lod Airport to accompany the widow. Mrs Davis and many other members of the diplomatic corps were late. The reason was the TWA pilot's refusal to postpone his departure without special reimbursement which the Embassy refused to pay. The coffin flew with the cargo. The Embassy's inquiry as to whether a special plane would be sent to convey the Ambassador's body had received no reply. The gentiles' attitude towards death is both sensible and practical.

[- - -]

Wednesday, December 30

Spent all day in bed with low temperature. A doctor was summoned. His verdict: mild influenza.

[- - -]

Went through a mountain of papers. After a pause of two months I took a book into my hands and started reading *Interview with India* by John Muehl.[14]

Thursday, December 31

[- - -]

Shaul and Isser came from Tel Aviv to report on a new development in Poland. Suddenly a prospect for the emigration of 15,000 Jews to Israel has been opened in exchange of a big payment per head, paid in the guise of Polish goods. This would entail the immediate despatch of a special mission to Poland. Several questions arise: should we enter at all into such negotiations? (I immediately answered in the affirmative). Would it be possible to lower the price per head? Who is to finance the transaction – the JA, "the Joint" [JDC] or both? Perhaps "the Joint" would consult the State Department; what would the response be, and is there a way to bring about a positive response? Finally I added an iconoclastic question: are we certain that 15,000 Jews residing in today's Poland would pack and come? The answer was a clear yes.

[- - -]

14 John Frederick Muehl, *Interview with India.* New York, J. Day Co, 1950.

1954

A Talk With a Labour Leader

Friday, January 1

Dr George Russell Strauss,[1] a Labour Party member of the British parliament, came for a talk. He is a Jew who has only just recently begun to draw nearer to our concerns and is visiting Israel for the first time. He is intimate with Emanuel Shinwell. He is afraid that this friend of his may burn the roast through his overly strenuous opposition to an agreement with Egypt,[2] which could compromise his seriousness in the eyes of the government and thus curtail his ability to help us. He tried to sound me out on the use of the Gaza Strip as a substitute base for British bases in the Suez Canal area. I told him that if the British government would address a proposal to us we would consider it. I explained that one of the negative considerations would then be our fear lest a British foothold in the Strip should lead to pressure for bases in the Negev as well, and a pincer movement from the Strip on one side and Trans-Jordan on the other.

I asked: "What would be the legal basis for Great Britain's entry into the Strip? Doesn't Egypt have sovereign rule over it?" And more: "If the Strip should pass into Great Britain's possession, what will become of Egypt's commitments towards us under the Armistice Agreement?" His answer was surprising. He and his like-minded colleagues assume that Egypt will quit the Strip altogether, whereupon Israel would assume sovereignty over it and allow the British to establish a base there, while the establishment of the base would solve the problem of employment for the refugees.

[- - -]

At 4:00 Eshkol came. We went over a long list of items: the problem of Oscar Gass' advisory staff, the affairs of the state-run (German) reparations agency, the future of the Electric Company, and more. My mutual understanding with Eshkol is of the very best, and Teddy was right when he said to me a few days ago that if

---

1 George Russell Strauss (1901-1993). Later Baron Strauss. Long-serving British Labour Party politician and MP for 46 years.

2 Negotiations for an Anglo-Egyptian agreement governing the withdrawal of British troops from the Suez Canal zone would begin in April 1954, and would result in the initialing of an agreement on July 27, 1954. The agreement, signed on October 19 of that year, provided for the final departure of British troops by June 18, 1956.

there is anyone among my *haverim* in the Cabinet who is willing to work with me in good faith, that person is Eshkol.

Saturday, January 2

[- - -]

We went to a party in honor of Moshe Dayan's becoming CoS. Moshe told about an Italian boat carrying meat from Ethiopia to Eilat, chartered by an Israeli meat firm. None of our people are aboard her, and there is no direct wireless contact with her. According to intercepted Egyptian reports, upon approaching the Strait of Tiran, she was ordered to stop and one cannon-shot was fired at her. She stopped, but disappeared in the dark and he doesn't know whether that means she's retraced her steps or slipped into the Gulf of Eilat. The IDF sent planes to look for her. They did not find the ship because of her small size, and because the Egyptian shore batteries opened fire on them. The order had been given to return fire from now on, not with bombs but with guns. Moshe Dayan tried to raise a fuss about the situation that will arise when this route for importing meat from East Africa is blocked. I couldn't understand his excitement, and said that following the revision of the Blockade Law and the expropriation of cargoes of food and fabric at the Canal, it is clear that Egypt is aiming at a complete tightening of the blockade and that a major battle is awaiting us in the Security Council.

I told Moshe about David Hacohen's enthusiastic letter written after his talk with the Burmese Commander-in-Chief and about the interesting prospects in the making concerning extensive military cooperation between us and Burma.[3] Our Rangoon Legation has already become the pet of the Burmese Army, which has supplied it with a building and is now renovating it, to the amazement of everybody in the diplomatic corps there.

Sunday, January 3

[- - -]

The main issue at the Cabinet meeting was the long-standing problem of Jerusalem. Dov Yosef reported on the economic strengthening of the city and proposed a series of ways and means. A general debate ensued concerning the dismal and unruly municipal authority of Israel's Capital. The Interior Minister suggested a law to man 25 percent of the municipality with people designated by the Government. I said the Government was to blame for abandoning Jerusalem – the eternal capital of Jewry, a holy city to multitudes all over the world, a city on the very front of Jordan – to the free game of power between local, parochial parties

3 *DFPI* 8, docs.604, 616.

when it should have taken the reins of the city into its hands to protect it from shame in the face of the nation and the world at large. I suggested that a special law be enacted for the municipality, but not by coopting into the municipality designated members, who may find themselves in the minority, but rather by ensuring the Government's decisions, either by appointing the mayor by the Government, or in another way. The dilemma is how to reconcile the Government's decision-making monopoly with a regime which will ensure certain rights to the city's inhabitants and be conducive to the fulfillment of their obligations.

[- - -]

Attended dinner at Golda's with David Morse,[4] Director-General of the International Labor Organization [ILO]. I had not known that he was Jewish, as are his wife, his secretary and his secretary's wife. He is a handsome fellow and evidently a man of feeling, but not very forceful. I found him filled with impressions from his visit to Egypt. He had seen Neguib and the rest of the junta, including Fawzi.[5] He had been impressed by Neguib's integrity. He had little new to report on what especially interests us, and confirmed our assumptions. As long as the Egyptian dispute with Great Britain was unresolved, there would be no change in the position towards us. It was doubtful, however, whether a solution of the Suez Canal problem would inspire moderation in relations with Israel. He's afraid that the enmity will remain.

Monday, January 4

My analysis of the situation concerning the setting up of my coalition government, which I gave yesterday to Moshe Keren of *Ha'aretz*, appeared in the paper this morning, attributed to "Mapai circles." The editor's conscientiousness did not allow him to present the plain facts as presented by me, but slanted them according to his own views. Nevertheless, Keren has done an exemplary journalistic job.

At 9:00 am at the PMO I received Nahum Goldmann and Arieh Tartakower[6] as representatives of the WJC. The purpose of the meeting was the establishment of a research unit in Europe to gather information about Jews residing in Arab countries from Jews traveling to and from them.

Nahum later told me about his visit to Sde Boker on Saturday. BG is all aglow, but Paula decried the place and bewailed her fate. It seems she is miserable and BG's efforts to quiet her are having little effect.

---

4 David A. Morse (1907-1990). American lawyer and bureaucrat. DG of the ILO, 1948-1970.

5 Mahmoud Fawzi (1900-1981). Egyptian diplomat and politician; Consul, Jerusalem (1941-1944); FM (1952-1961); later PM, Vice-President.

6 Arieh Tartakower (1897-1982). Born in Galicia. Settled in Palestine in 1946. Sociologist and demographer. Member of the WJC Executive and the Zionist Executive.

[- - -]

A meeting at the Foreign Ministry, with wide participation, to deliberate on the subjects first and foremost on our agenda: the Anglo-Egyptian talks concerning the future of the Suez Canal Zone, the Egyptian anti-Israeli blockade at the Canal, American military aid to Arab states, and the problem of a conference with Jordan in accordance with Article XII of the Israel-Jordan Armistice Agreement.[7]

Tuesday, January 5

[- - -]

Gideon Rafael sat with me for an hour or more for consultations about items on his agenda. First and foremost: Jordan's answer to the UN Secretary General's invitation to confer with us in accordance with Article XII.[8] The newspapers are making a big noise about this answer, in which Jordan has ostensibly rejected the invitation; that is, it has violated the Armistice Agreement which obliges it to attend. But this morning the full and exact wording of the reply was disclosed. It contained no rejection, but an attempt at evasion. It seems that Jordan realizes the seriousness of its situation if it refuses to confer, and it is equivocating while employing delaying tactics. In my opinion, we must emphasize this in our reply, and open the gates wide for Jordanian repentance.[9]

Ze'ev Haklai,[10] the JA's emissary in Morocco, reported on the problems of Moroccan Jewry. The picture is one of disharmony among the three main Jewish organizations who are working there – the JA, "the Joint" and the *Alliance [Alliance israélite universelle]* – and of unhealthy fragmentation of the Agency's activity which is lacking in focus and central authority. He spoke highly of the *Alliance's* work there, even though it is not geared toward promoting emigration to Israel. His criticism was aimed mainly at "the Joint," which aims at deepening the Moroccan Jews' roots there instead of being a lever for moving Jews to Israel. Had the resources invested by "the Joint" in Morocco been devoted to the absorption of immigrants in Israel, the emigration from Israel back to Morocco would have been halted and a new wave of immigration would have started. I said that, since "Joint"

---

7 For follow-ups to the last three items mentioned, see *Documents on the Foreign Policy of Israel*, volume 9 (1954), ed. Naomi Barzilay (Jerusalem: Israel State Archives, 2004), docs. 5-7 – hereafter *DFPI* 9.

8 See above, page 163 n.8.

9 The official reply of Jordan's FM was addressed to the UN SG on January 3, 1954; text in UN Document S/3180 of February 19, 1954, pp.7-8.

10 Ze'ev Haklai (1910-1964). Born in Russia. Settled in Palestine in 1926. Mapai and *Hagana* activist. Served in the Jewish Brigade in WWII, then became active in organizing Holocaust survivors' "illegal" immigration to Palestine. Early in 1952 became head of the Moroccan section of the JA's Immigration Department, travelling frequently inside Morocco.

leaders Leavitt and Beckelman[11] will soon visit Israel, I would discuss with them the problem of coordinating work there. But first I would consult with the JA people for the purpose of building a united front.

[- - -]

Wednesday, January 6

[- - -]

Thursday, January 7

[- - -]

A consultation on oil problems was convened at my home with Eshkol, Pinhas Sapir and others. The problem was whether to enter into contractual obligations with the Russians, and how this would affect our relations with the British suppliers and their government. After an examination, I summed up by saying that the Russian oil was of inestimable importance to us as the basis for not being totally dependent on the other side, but we had to be careful not to become dependent only on it, exclusively, for we were sticking our necks into a much more dangerous noose. Russian oil held out a second advantage: it released us from the pressure of the Arab embargo. The third advantage pertained to the millions of dollars in annual savings. This was our strongest justification vis-à-vis the West. We shall remind the British of their surrender to the Arab embargo at the Suez Canal and in Kuwait, and of their refusal to help us with credit in our hour of need.

[- - -]

Haim Cohn,[12] the Attorney-General, came at my invitation to look into the matter of registering abandoned land holdings in the DMZ near Tel Katzir, south-east of the Kinneret, in the name of the State Development Authority. This ought to drive in a wedge against any attempt by the UN people to return these lands to the Arabs of that area.[13]

11 Moses (Moe) A. Leavitt (1894–1965). Active with the JDC since 1929. Worked together with Joe Schwartz during WWII to coordinate relief for Holocaust survivors after 1945. Also took part in channeling JDC efforts to immigration to Israel and the start of social service for the elderly (Malben) there. Moses W. Beckelman (1906–1955). Served as Overseas Operations DG of JDC.

12 Haim Cohn (1911-2002). Born in Germany. Settled in Palestine in 1930. Jurist. State Attorney, Ministry of Justice (1948-1949); DG, Ministry of Justice (1949-1950); Attorney-General (1950-1960); later Supreme Court Justice.

13 On the Development Authority, see Michael R. Fischbach, *Records of Dispossession: Palestinian Refugee Property and the Arab-Israeli Conflict* (New York: Columbia University Press, 2003), 53-58.

Arieh Eshel,[14] our Consul in Vienna, came to say good-bye upon his return to his post. We discussed the problem of the dispute with the Austrian Government over the return of Jewish property for which inheritors have not been found – a dismal affair in which all Jewish organizations have become entangled. Nahum Goldmann's personal charm was to no avail in trying to convince the Austrians of the justice and the logic of the Jewish claim. Arieh is of the opinion that, if the matter is resolved, we should then elevate our Consulate in Vienna to a Legation, a move necessary also in view of Vienna serving increasingly as a base for our connections in Eastern Europe.

[- - -]

Friday, January 8

[- - -]

It took me quite a while to solve the problem of finding an appropriate escort for Nye Bevan and his wife, Jennie Lee[15] during their travels around the country as guests of the state. Both are tough guests, and come "charged" from their travels in Arab countries. Nye is by nature aggressive, biting, haughty and very difficult to deal with.

[- - -]

Saturday, January 9

[- - -]

Met with Nahum Goldmann. He disclosed to me his plans for a merger of the Progressive Zionists with the GZ so that he himself should stand at the head of the united party when he settles in Israel. Yosef Sapir and Yosef Serlin told him that if the Progressives joined the GZ, their united camp would undergo a change for the better and he would be put at its head. I retorted that the GZ were a mish-mash of self-interest seekers lacking cohesion and a tradition of public responsibility whether in the Zionist movement or in the echelons of the state. The Progressives were rooted in the Zionist movement, and only in the course of time did they become class-oriented to a degree. But GZ grew up in a social atmosphere of each running after personal gain, and they can hardly camouflage their naked selfishness and internal conflicts. Just take a look at their inability to run their ministries cleanly and

14 Arieh Eshel (1912-1968). Born in Germany. Settled in Palestine in 1934. Member of Kibbutz Givat Brenner. MFA official from 1949. Israel Consul in Vienna (1950-1955). Director, East European Division, MFA (1956-1957). Served as Sharett's political secretary; later Ambassador to Canada.

15 Jennie Lee (1904-1988). Scottish socialist politician; later Baroness. Labour Party MP, 1929-1931 and 1945-1970. Her decidedly leftist views sometimes clashed with those of her husband, Nye Bevan.

with no corruption, and to man important government posts with people of stature. Those among them who agree to serve the state volunteer for only a year or two, throughout which they mostly tend to their private business and think only of their return home. Nahum argued that the Progressives would contribute the necessary constructive elements to the new united party. I said that, objectively, it may well be that the Progressives had no chance of alone becoming a real political force, and thus it seemed perhaps good for them to unite with the GZ. But, knowing him as I do, and the various personalities within the GZ, I could not imagine him functioning as their leader and them accepting his moral authority.

After he left me I mused. It was clear what my friend Nahum was aiming at. He coveted the Foreign Ministry. The whole unification plan revolved around the axis of this personal ambition. His soul loathes the meagre nourishment of heading the Jewish Agency, and perhaps his desire to settle in Israel for the last quarter of his active life is candid. However it's below his dignity to become a "head to the foxes."[16] These Progressives are indeed nice and decent people, but their quality does not offset their lack of quantity, and their allegiance to him is not tantamount to the respect and stature that only a large party can bestow. The fact that this big party would be composed of second-raters does not repel him at all – he is not sensitive to that degree. He is not aware of the basic facts of Israeli society, and he certainly believes in being successful in charming them with his rhetoric into reigning them. Obviously, he views himself as the future leading representative of the "Consolidated Zionists" in the Israeli Cabinet.

It is clear that his aim is the Foreign Ministry. In this respect, it's an act of providence for him that I am now Prime Minister. We are truly good friends, and I am sure he has no wish or intent to clash with me head-on. There are those who whisper otherwise in my ear, but I choose to believe in Nahum's pure intentions towards me. He does stick his pins into me in speeches and press releases, but I don't presume he's willing to enter into open conflict or, more correctly, an open rivalry. All this holds true as long as I'm Foreign Minister and nothing more. If he should aspire to this post, he would ostensibly be conspiring to usurp my position. But it's another matter entirely since I'm both PM as well as Foreign Minister. It would then seem logical and right that I share the load with such a distinguished and multi-talented colleague as himself. This entire calculation is keen and incisive and typical of Nahum, but its realization is highly doubtful. The GZ political outlook which abides by the acumen of "the man in the street" doesn't at all tally with Nahum's thinking on the issue of peace with the Arabs and foreign relations generally. On the other hand, it's hard to see Mapai not only renouncing this jewel in its crown called the Foreign Ministry, but entrusting it into the hands of a "free agent" like Nahum, who has a frivolous trait to his personality and lacks roots in Israel. Altogether, it is hard to see Nahum in the role of a leader if only from one

16 Cf. *Pirkei Avot* 4:15: "Better be a tail to the lions than a head to the foxes."

aspect: the requisite ability of a leader to win the confidence of the masses with the sobriety and comprehensiveness of his judgement. He is a splendid envoy who demands both a close watching and restraint. He lacks an independent character. He boasts the sheen of silver, but none of the hardness of steel.

I spent my afternoon sitting over my papers while dipping my eyes into the vastness of the Mediterranean Sea and the splendor of the sunset.

[- - -]

Sunday, January 10

[- - -]

Monday, January 11

[- - -]

Had a meeting with all our people involved in our water plans and planning on the Main (or Johnston) Plan. Blass revived an interesting idea. It is best we endorse the Jordanian Yarmuk project in order to fortify our own right to the B'not Yaakov canal project, while explaining that the regional plan could not be implemented right now anyway, both because its details have yet to be worked out and because of the Arab states' refusal to cooperate. Therefore, the two separate water projects, each executed within the framework of its own country, could serve as a first stage towards the larger plan without raising complicated international problems. We would thus be supporting the regional plan in principle, proposing a constructive and practical attitude towards it, from the simple to the complex, and at the same time guaranteeing progress in our own development planning. We concluded that this would be our contention during Johnston's next visit, and that meanwhile the *Tahal* people would prepare a critical analysis of the Main Plan and also entrust American water expert Joseph Cotton,[17] who is currently in Israel, with the preparation of our own regional plan, which would include the utilization of the Litani.

Gideon Rafael lingered in the room after the meeting, and began voicing penitent thoughts about our initiative in the matter of Article XII. Perhaps it was not at all worth our while that the conference with Jordan should take place? If the Great Powers forced Jordan to agree to come, it would certainly be at the price of renouncing any real progress. Then it would transpire that we ourselves would have made a mockery of the conference. Wouldn't it be best to content ourselves with the momentary gain of our constructive initiative as opposed to Jordan's negative

---

17 On Cotton's water plan submitted to the Israeli Cabinet, see below, entry for May 30, 1954; Michael Brecher, *Decisions in Israel's Foreign Policy* (New Haven: Yale University Press, 1975), 197-98, 203-04.

obstinacy, without pressing and demanding to convene the conference?[18] I did not support this retreat which could portray our initial demand as dishonest, as caring only about the tactical effect and not the substance of the matter. We concluded that we had to continue to press the UN SG to convene the conference.

In the afternoon went again to the PMO. I consulted with Giora Josephthal in preparation for my discussion with "the Joint" [JDC] people. Giora rejected the contentions of our man in North Africa regarding the nature of "the Joint's" work there. The JDC didn't support families at all and was not involved in direct individual welfare. Its entire budget was spent on education and health, and not through contact with individuals, but through the support of institutions: kindergartens, youth clubs, clinics, and one trade school. To demand that it spend less in Morocco and more in Israel was to disregard the hard facts. "The Joint" was already expending 62 percent of its budget in Israel. It has to camouflage this fact in its propaganda and cannot be pressed to spend no money in the centers of Jewish poverty in the diaspora. Today it devoted only 12 percent of its budget to the countries in the East – Persia and North Africa. Giora agreed that the problem was the three-way coordination between the JA, "the Joint" and the *Alliance* with a view to preparing Jewry for large-scale immigration to Israel, even if at a slow pace; and that the most pressing need was to unify and streamline the JA's activities.

Moe Leavitt and Beckelman came over, both enthusiastic about what they had seen around the country. They accepted in principle the idea of meeting once in a while with the *Alliance* and JA people in Paris, with the Israeli Ambassador's participation, for the purpose of exchanging opinions and coordinating activity. In private Moe discussed with me the Polish plan for bringing out Jews in exchange for payment. He is willing to start looking into the subject, but is very much afraid lest this serve as a precedent for other East-European countries; if this happens, it would be hopeless, since all the Jewish money in the world would not suffice to finance such an enormous operation of "redeeming our prisoners."[19]

[- - -]

Tuesday, January 12

[- - -]

I came home early to see whether the house was ready for our first dinner party. It was in honor of Aneurin Bevan and his wife Jennie Lee. Nye and Jennie came at six for a talk. All during their stay in Israel, I had heard worrisome reports

18 Rafael elaborated his views in messages to Kidron, Shiloah and Eban in the US. See *DFPI* 9, docs. 12, 21.

19 Sharett uses the Hebrew phrase *pidyon shvuyim*, echoing the traditional and Talmudic injunction encouraging individuals and the community to do everything possible to achieve the ransoming of Jewish captives.

about their position. They were demanding the return of the refugees. They were impressed with Neguib. They didn't grasp what was happening in Israel. They did not understand the Zionist cause, and the uniqueness of the State of Israel. Given all of these concerns, my fears were happily not realized.

Nye himself brought up the refugee issue, and declared that he had told the Jordanians that they could hope for a return in vain. If they were to return, they would remain refugees here too. They would find no deliverance. It was best to start settling the refugees in Jordan. From this he passed on to the Yarmuk Plan. He poured fire and brimstone on the American plan. Even if the plan had been different, Jordan was not prepared today for any regional plan which required Israeli participation. This was a fact, and had to be accepted. The question was whether it was possible to make progress under these conditions of separate national – rather than cooperative, regional – planning. It seemed that it was. We should go on with the B'not Yaakov project, and Jordan should be permitted to execute the Yarmuk project for the irrigation of the eastern Jordan Valley. This would immediately provide employment for tens of thousands, and serve as the basis for the settlement of many. I told him that his line of thinking was much in accordance with ours, but that we nevertheless had to examine the Yarmuk plan with regard to its infringement of our irrigation rights in the Israeli Jordan Valley.

The bulk of the talk revolved around Egypt. Neguib was honest but not forceful. Nasser[20] was more powerful as concerns holding the reins. (All this was well-known.) The entire group at the top had no idea of how to go about social reform and economic rehabilitation. For the time being, they were completely involved in the conflict with Great Britain over the status of the Suez Canal, the Canal Zone, and Sudanese affairs. Neguib said that if a settlement on the canal region was reached, it would be possible to deal with the problem of a settlement with Israel. However, there was no knowing whether he had said it candidly or was just trying to please.

The fact remains that Mulki[21] has said the same in Amman. Thus, it may be the truth. Regarding the conditions we had tried to link to the evacuation of the canal region by the British – guarantees of security and freedom of passage through the canal – they simply could not be attained, since the Anglo-Egyptian treaty expires in 1956 and Neguib won't pay anything now for something he's going to obtain anyway, free of charge, within a short while. Regarding the conflict itself, of the two problems – the uniforms of the British staff who were to remain and emergency activation of the base – the first would certainly be solved, and only the second posed a serious obstacle. The Egyptians were insisting that the base must be activated whenever any Arab state was attacked, while the British Foreign Office was demanding the addition of Turkey, or

20 Gamal Abd al-Nasser (1918-1970). Leading member of the "Free Officers" corps which overthrew the monarchy in Egypt in July 1952 and established a republic. Prime Minister (1954-1964) and President (1956-1970).

21 Fawzi al-Mulki (1910-1962). Jordanian politician and diplomat. PM (1953-1954).

that this be decided by the General Assembly. Nye expounded more on the attitude towards Israel. The Egyptians were sure that the embargo was crippling us. They also thought that the success of the embargo might propel us to war. All the same, they declared that they did not want a war with Israel. But was this not a contradiction? Yes, he answered me, they were truly irrational. A very lame answer indeed.[22]

[- - -]

Wednesday, January 13

[- - -]

Had a short and sharp argument with Lavon concerning the tone of our relations with the UN Observers. This matter must be brought to a final decision in principle and settled once and for all after the government is formed.

[- - -]

Thursday, January 14

[- - -]

Friday, January 15

[- - -]

Summoned Moshe Keren of *Ha'aretz* with the purpose of explaining to him the situation concerning the coalition build-up for Sunday's paper.

Came home thoroughly depressed. On the verge of the sixth week of my appointment and in spite of the huge effort made by my Party colleagues in pursuit of an agreement with the GZ, I am as far away from presenting my coalition Cabinet as I was on the first day.

Saturday, January 16

[- - -]

Went out with Zipporah on a pleasant *Shabbat* walk. Our destination was the King David Hotel to return Rose Halprin's[23] visit, and to discuss with her matters

22 A Jewish Telegraphic Agency (JTA) report, datelined Jerusalem January 6, bore the headline: "Egypt Will Not Attack Israel, Premier Assures British Deputy" and quoted Neguib's remarks as recalled by Bevan. A later JTA report, datelined London January 21 and which appeared in the *Daily Herald* on January 22, 1954, bore the headline: "Bevan Urges Arabs to Abandon their Boycott of Israel."

23 Rose Halprin (Luria) (1896-1978). American Zionist activist. National President of Hadassah, 1932-1934 and 1947-1952. Resided in Jerusalem, 1934-1939. Member and sometimes Chair, American Section of the JAE.

weighing heavily on her heart. She spoke about a significant intensification of Arab propaganda in the US, and the agitation of pro-Arab members of the Dorothy Thompson followers (American Friends of the Middle East) who are supported by the American Council for Judaism. At a time like this especially, there must be a fundamental change in the organization of our *hasbara* activity.

The FBI has an eye on our financial activities, and the Arabs and their friends are inciting the authorities against us. There is no doubt that the authorities already have proof that money collected by the UJA on the basis of income-tax deductions, being ostensibly wholly earmarked for charitable purposes, is being spent in part on political activity which cannot be construed as charity by any means. If things should come to an investigation, our prospects are bleak. It was therefore decided to differentiate between political information activity and educational activities and the like and, accordingly, to separate the American Zionist Council into two bodies. There then looms the problem of a source of funding for that part of the Council which will deal with political activity. To all appearances, this will be a purely American effort, borne on the shoulders of US citizens. But if they are unable to make use of money from the UJA – and they won't be able to mount separate fund-raising – from what source will they derive their means? The question remained open. Rose told us about the worrying phenomena of hostile public reaction to our *hasbara* activity. Among other things, she mentioned a wave of antagonism that followed Eban's latest appearances on television.

[- - -]

Sunday, January 17

[- - -]

In the evening, a call from *Davar*. Tavor reported that the Progressives had decided to join a narrow coalition government. The die is cast, then! A narrow coalition has become a reality after having been only an empty slogan for so long. I immediately started calculating: [various calculations and combinations omitted here, until a final idea] making it possible to save the state 4 ministers, reducing the number of ministers from 16 to 12, and avoiding the trouble involved in the addition of 3 ministers to ours. I asked Sharef to prepare me a list of 12 ministers and he produced it immediately: 1) PM and FM - Sharett; 2) Finance and Development - Eshkol; 3) Justice - Rosen; 4) Interior and Religious Affairs - Shapira; 5) Health and Welfare - Burg; 6) Defense - Lavon; 7) Labor - Golda Myerson; 8) Agriculture - Naftali; 9) Police - Sheetrit; 10) Education - Dinur; 11) Trade and Industry - Dov Yosef; 12) Communication and Post - Aran(!).[24]

---

24 Despite this early speculation about a smaller Cabinet, the Cabinet announced on January 26 (see below, entry for that date) would consist of 16 ministers.

A very impressive list. All this arrangement is only a result of a lack of choice, since logic dictates a wide coalition despite its ills, in order to prevent the GZ from making havoc and hell in the opposition. But it's good that they are now feeling the whip of the narrow coalition over them and realize that time is running out for them. I went to sleep feeling relieved.

Monday, January 18

[- - -]

Lunch at home in honor of the lovely Kenneth Younger[25] – Golda, Walter, Shabtai, Gershon Agron, Moish Pearlman, and others. I asked the guest to come over for a short political conversation.

[- - -]

At 6:30 a talk with Younger on the Anglo-Egyptian negotiations and the guarantees we must demand for our security.

[- - -]

Tuesday, January 19

[- - -]

Wednesday, January 20

In the morning at the PMO a talk with Baruch Yekutieli[26] regarding the fate of the Azazmeh. A rather complicated issue, which, in Baruch's opinion, could be solved by patience and an empathetic approach, while the Army prefers the easy way of the hard line, completely ignoring Jewish and Arab, as well as international, public opinion.

[- - -]

25 Kenneth Gilmour Younger (1908-1976). British Labour politician and barrister. Minister of State at the FO and deputy to Foreign Secretary Ernest Bevin (1950). Opposition spokesman during the early 1950s. Later Director of the Royal Institute of International Affairs (Chatham House).

26 Baruch Yekutieli (1926-1989). Born in Palestine. Adviser on Arab Affairs at PMO. Later member of the Bank Leumi executive and vice president of the bank.

Coalition Labor Pains

Thursday, January 21

[- - -]

Friday, January 22

Set out for Jerusalem at 11:00.

Walter came by to help me brief for my conversation with José Fabrino. I had invited the Brazilian Consul to lunch to give him an opportunity to report on his talks at the Vatican. Some plan for the demilitarization of Jerusalem is in the works, and the Brazilian government wants to serve as mediator. The problem is how not to commit ourselves to anything, and not say "no" to anything in advance either. I have no idea whether anything will come of all this.[1]

Fabrino is about to retire from the diplomatic service and intends to go into business. He is joining a large industrial concern which manufactures a synthetic substitute for wood. I told him to prevail upon his partners to open a branch in Israel. He said: "But you nationalize industrial concerns."

I asked: "Where did you get such information?"

He replied: "Your government demands that 50 percent of the stock should belong to the *Histadrut*."

I thoroughly admonished and shamed him, he who has resided in the country these past three years, for believing such nonsense and for his willingness to spread it abroad. He was quite embarrassed and apologized. In the meantime, I could see the extent to which this lie has taken root and become widespread.

[- - -]

Saturday, January 23

Spent all morning over Foreign Ministry papers. In the middle of it, the cipher department telephoned to inform me of the substance of a cable received from Eban assessing the results of the vote in the Security Council. Vyshinsky has vetoed the draft resolution of the three powers – US, Britain and France – and the prolonged

---

1 On the Brazilian proposal, see *FRUS 1952-1954*, doc.769; *DFPI* 9, doc.68.

and exhausting debate has come to naught.[2]

This was the first Russian veto in the SC on a matter pertaining to us, clearly against us and in favor of an Arab state. My first reaction was one of dejection. It is bad on two counts. The Soviet Union is defining itself anew as an element which supports the Arab front against us, and the US will have to draw negative conclusions with regard to us and step up its efforts to compete with the Soviets for the friendship of the Arab countries.[3]

Only in the wake of a telephone conversation with Walter in Tel Aviv did I begin to see the other side of the coin. First, the draft proposal of the three had been subjected to serious pejorative changes – this in order to appease the Arabs and forestall the threat of a Soviet veto. Nothing had come of this effort, but in the meantime the formulation had drastically worsened as far as we are concerned, to the extent that it would be better for it not to be adopted at all. Secondly, since the debate began following a Syrian complaint against us, its termination in a draw can be taken as a rejection of the complaint. True, the Soviet Union had no intention of extricating us from trouble, even less of handing Syria a defeat. Also, the fact that these are the practical results of the veto does not at all mitigate the grave nature of its malignant intentions. Nevertheless, we must promote these results abroad for the purposes of propaganda, to create a positive atmosphere and imprint these results firmly on our domestic public opinion.

Despite all this, I was not sure whether the "draw" had really put an end to the debate, and I put in a call to Abba in Washington. The call came through in the afternoon, during which time Gideon Rafael came by. Abba confirmed that it was over. The Americans were certain that any resolution which did not make continued work dependent on Syrian approval was bound to encounter a Soviet veto, while they themselves will not support any resolution that does so.

The question arises whether we shall now resume our work. Resumption strictly on our own accord may lead to two results: (a) renewed debate in the SC and a resolution demanding that we cease until we confer with the UNTSO CoS; (b) a military operation on the part of Syria, to which we shall respond, and then again an urgent debate in the SC and a cease-fire as well as a cease-work resolution for the sake of peace. I therefore came to the conclusion that the Cabinet's official resolution at its meeting tomorrow must be that we view ourselves free of the obligation we took upon ourselves to cease work "for the duration of the urgent debate," and no more – that is, without saying a thing about the resumption of work itself. I telephoned Pinhas Lavon in Tel Aviv with this proposal and found him pleased with the results

2 *DFPI* 9, doc.32.

3 For background, along with the text of Andrei Vyshinsky's speech and extracts of the debates, see *From Encroachment to Involvement: A Documentary Study of Soviet Policy in the Middle East, 1945-1973*. Ed. Yaacov Ro'i (New York / Toronto: John Wiley & Sons, 1974), 115-24. Cf. *FRUS 1952-1954*, doc.770.

of the veto. We are well rid of this nuisance!

[- - -]

Sunday, January 24

In the newspapers there appeared a confirmation of the coalition agreement by the GZ, although by a much smaller majority than that reached in Mapai. This means that (a) we have a government; (b) I have no escape or refuge from being PM; (c) I shall present the Cabinet to the Knesset tomorrow. Nothing stands any longer in the way between me and my fated destiny.

At 9:00 am I went to the President and solemnly, albeit quite simply, announced that the task [of forming a new government] was accomplished. Ben-Zvi was moved, and we kissed.

Prior to the Cabinet meeting I consulted with Gideon Rafael over the wording of the [SC] resolution and our tactics [for responding]. At the Cabinet meeting I spoke for an hour about the course of events in the SC – the changes made in the draft resolution, the Arab pressure, the threat of a veto, the surprising exercise of the veto, the implications of the resulting situation, the conclusions as they concern us. I also reported on the results of the debate in the Knesset FADC, at which even the members of the opposition had not demanded an immediate resumption of work [on the B'not Yaakov canal diversion project].[4] At the end of the meeting, I remarked that this was the last meeting of the outgoing Cabinet, and [- - -] announced that tomorrow morning a meeting of the incoming Cabinet would be held.

[- - -]

It occurred to me that, as early as this week, immediately after the swearing-in of the Cabinet, it would be a fine idea to hold a large stately reception at home: the President, Cabinet members, the secretariat of the Knesset, ministry directors-general, the CoS. I calculated that the swearing-in would most likely take place on Tuesday and scheduled the reception for Wednesday afternoon. The secretaries immediately sent out an order for printed invitation cards – "Prime Minister and Mrs Sharett." When the proofs were brought to me I couldn't believe my eyes and took one home to show Zipporah.

At 7:00 pm a meeting at my home with the four Mapai Ministers-designate, and the three *haverim* who conducted the negotiations for building the coalition. I summoned them for the purpose of discussing my Prime Minister's address to the Knesset. I presented the main points and a few of those present added several important points. Eshkol seized the opportunity and raised the problem of current government finances, which is extremely serious, especially because of the budgetary

4 For the Cabinet decisions regarding the UN SC vote on Israel's dredging work at the B'not Yaakov bridge, see *DFPI* 9, doc.34.

additions to security items. The discussion of this topic was not completed, and if not for Eshkol's insistence and his dire situation it would not have started at all. [- - -]

Around 11:00 pm I sat down to compose my Knesset speech and here hit a snag: I had already written down the "skeleton"[5] of this speech during the sleepless night I had about ten days ago at the Dan Hotel in Tel Aviv. I was sure it was lying around in my portfolio of private papers. But, lo and behold – it was not there! Feeling cold sweat all over my body, I was stricken: had that draft got lost? I was acutely aware that it contained some pointed remarks, including some lines chiseled out from hard rock about Ben-Gurion the man and his deeds, beautified with all sorts of embellishments like a work of art, and which I would never be able to recreate! I was devastated! I started to meticulously scrutinize the heap of my office files which had been accumulating on my desk. In the tenth file I found it and a shout of joy came out of my mouth. I immediately ran into the kitchen and asked Zipporah to dance the *hora* with me.

Only then did I go back to work and wrote till 2:00 am. I thought I did a good job – a not-too-long speech, well thought-out in content and well-shaped in form.

Monday, January 25

At 9:00 am a meeting of the incoming Cabinet. I reported on the arrangements at the Knesset and read out my speech. I could see that it was well received by one and all. [- - -] As I was about to bring the meeting to a close, Golda asked to speak. She began with her need to say something which would certainly express the feelings of all present – to congratulate "our colleague Moshe Sharett, who will be Prime Minister within a few hours. Around this table are colleagues who have gone quite a long way with him. When BG decided to resign, the nation in Zion and the nation in the diaspora accepted Sharett's assumption of his place as natural and self-evident." She wished me the strength to bear this new task, just as I have born difficult and weighty tasks all my life. It seemed to her that the patience and perspicacity that I had exhibited these past weeks were only a small indication of the powers within me to "do battle." She said, on behalf of all, that I should find in them not only colleagues in government, but faithful aides who would share the hard labor I had taken upon myself. She concluded: "I would like to express my personal satisfaction at Moshe's having achieved what he deserves." I thanked her.

I retired to my room and went over the [Knesset] speech once more. I again tarried over the passage devoted to BG. I wasn't content with one phrase where I described him as "staunch of faith and broad of vision." I summoned Yitzhak Navon

5 Sharett habitually jotted down the main points (the "skeleton") of daily occurrences in a pocket diary, and later expanded these points into this full diary format.

and told him that a third definition was missing here – firmness of character, in which the secret of executive ability resides. After weighing the problem Yitzhak proposed the term "resolute" and I inserted it.

[- - -]

At 4:00 pm precisely I went with Zipporah to the Knesset. Outside a crowd milled about, having a few minutes before cheered the President, who had preceded me. Inside the House was overflowing. I had just time to tell Moshe Rosetti,[6] the Knesset Secretary, to warn the Speaker not to call me acting PM or Foreign Minister, but "Knesset member Sharett." And behold the wonder – [Speaker] Sprinzak was careful in his language and did not get confused this time. I read out the speech with composure and in clear, measured diction. There were no interruptions. I spoke for 17 minutes. The debate began forthwith, and with it a headlong descent down the slope of barren polemics.[7]

I sat down to listen to the detractors, my own speech still reverberating within me. All my sensitivity was focused on the things I had said about BG. And suddenly a void in the passage shot into view. I had devoted one sentence to his leadership in the years prior to the establishment of the state, then one sentence to his victory in the War of Independence, and finally one sentence to his accomplishments as the first Prime Minister. I hadn't noted his historic role as the architect of the state. Only too well do I know the sting felt in not finding what I consider most essential in somebody's words about me. I immediately composed an additional phrase and gave it to Shamai to insert into the version released to the press. But my speech had been recorded for *Kol-Israel* during delivery. Was it feasible to splice something into the recording? Shamai thought it was. I sent him to call Hanoch Givton.[8] The answer was affirmative. Immediately at the end of the session, I drove to *Kol-Israel*. Hanoch suggested that I re-record the entire speech – to prevent any defects in the hearing of it. This I did. Thus was history counterfeited!

Then back to the Knesset, where the debate continued.

[- - -]

And with the close of the Knesset session at 10:00 pm we yielded to Eshkol's crushing pressure and gathered at the PMO for a consultation on the budget. It meant an open battle between Eshkol and Lavon until after midnight.

6 Moshe (Maurice) Rosetti (1903-1992). Born in England. Settled in Israel in 1948. Zionist activist and Parliamentary lobbyist for the JA. Served as Knesset Secretary until 1968.

7 *Divrei Haknesset*, XV: 717-18. See below, entry for January 26, for extracts of Sharett's rebuttals to several critics.

8 Hanoch Givton (1917-1976). Born in Poland. Settled in Palestine in 1935. *Hagana* activist and organizer of underground broadcasting while working for the Palestine Broadcasting Service after 1945. *Hagana* liaison with foreign press corps in Jerusalem during 1948. Head of the News Department of the Israel Broadcasting Service (*Kol-Israel*) from 1950, and later its DG.

Tuesday, January 26

The morning papers, and the evening ones even more so, congratulated me on my speech, emphasizing its novelties – my peaceful approach to the opposition and my appeal to the diaspora and the Zionist movement for a constructive relationship. [- - -]

News from Cairo: in a meeting between Bennike and Vigier with Neguib, Vigier said that in his opinion Israel was free now to resume working on the Jordan [diversion] project in the north. Syria approached the member states of the Arab League and asked whether they would come to help her if she intervened militarily.[9] [- - -]

Came to the Knesset at 4:00 pm for the continuation of the debate. The speakers of the various parties were done by the evening recess, and only the Cabinet ministers remained.

[Following are extracts from Sharett's reply to the Knesset debate of the preceding two days:]

> MK [Yaakov] Hazan [of Mapam] has accused Mapai, on behalf of which I am serving in the new Cabinet in the capacity imposed on me by the President, that we have forsaken the united front of the labor movement. I have been a member of Mapai from its very inception, and before that a member of the party which cooperated in the establishment of Mapai, which makes altogether more than 30 years, and I fail to remember when, during this period, there existed a united political front in the labor movement, except for a very brief time.[10]
>
> Was there any unity in the period when *Hashomer Hatza'ir* fought stubbornly for a bi-national state in Palestine? Did it exist during World War II, in the fight against Hitler, when it maintained that the *yishuv*'s men would volunteer into the British Army on condition that they serve only in the defense of Palestine and not on other fronts? Or when Hazan poured scorn on the political aims of the Zionist movement as laid down in the Biltmore Program[11] and fought against the idea of the immediate establishment of a Jewish State?
>
> And when did you help in the adsorption of immigrants? Was it when you voted in the Knesset against accepting the American loan for developing the country's agricultural and industrial potential? Or perhaps when you vehemently and ferociously fought against the German reparations? The other day we heard with satisfaction your admission of your

9 Resolution of the Arab League Council, January 1, 1954, reproduced in *The Arab States and the Arab League: A Documentary Record*, ed. Muhammad Khalil (Beirut: Khayats, 1962), doc.94.

10 During the War of Independence (1948-1949).

11 An emergency Zionist conference convened at Ben-Gurion's initiative at the Biltmore Hotel in New York in May 1942. Its resolutions called for immediate mass immigration and for the postwar creation of a Jewish "commonwealth" (i.e., state) in an undivided Palestine. The Biltmore Program constituted the first overt and full Zionist demand for Jewish statehood in the whole of Palestine. For the text, see http://naip-documents.blogspot.ca/2010/08/document-s6.html.

mistake regarding the Reparations Agreement,[12] but this came only after the reparations proved to be an essential foundation of the country's economy, after all your bleak prophecies regarding the futility of the Reparations Agreement proved completely wrong.

[- - -]

My honorable friend MK Rabbi Levin[13] has vehemently claimed here that the National Service Law, inasmuch as it pertains to the conscription of women into the IDF, is contrary to the laws of the Torah. I have already asked you once to point out the concrete Torah law according to which women's military service is not allowed, but to no avail. I am not opposing the right of rabbis to explain the laws of the Torah, but why do they keep secret the relevant law pertaining to this issue? Tell us where it is: is it written down in the Torah, in the Talmud, in the *Shulkhan Arukh*? Where exactly? On which page – on the top, bottom, or in the middle? Why is it secret? Is the Jewish faith a pageant of secrets and mysteries?

[- - -]

At 10:30 the Knesset proceeded to a vote, and the motion of confidence was adopted by a majority of 75 to 23. [- - -] Immediately after the vote, the swearing-in ceremony began. The ministers were called to the podium in alphabetical order, but the PM was summoned first.[14]

Descending from the podium after taking the oath, I felt that I was not the same man who had ascended it a few minutes before. Whispered congratulations accompanied me on my way to my place at the Cabinet table. I raised my eyes to Zipporah in the center of the gallery, and then I sent a cable to my daughter Yael in New York.

The Speaker briefly wished the new government well, and the session was closed. Knesset members immediately surrounded the Cabinet table on all sides. I found myself at the center of a tight circle. The State of Israel once again proved to be a country in which men kiss men – in Russian and Arab fashion – rather than women, as in the US. One of the first to kiss me, and with great warmth, was Pinhas Lavon, while many others followed suit. I myself only sought out my old teacher, Chaim Boger, of the GZ, who began to cry from deep emotion.[15]

There was no end to the handshakes. Those proffering them including opposition members from *Herut* and Mapam. While still sitting at the table

---

12 See above, page 52 n.59.

13 Yitzhak-Meir Levin (1893-1971). Born in Poland. Settled in Palestine in 1940. MK for the *Agudat-Israel* Party.

14 The 16 members of the new Cabinet were: M. Sharett (PM and FM), Z. Aran (Minister without portfolio with special responsibility for *hasbara*), L. Eshkol (Finance), Y. Burg (Posts), P. Bernstein (Trade and Industry), B.-Z. Dinur (Education and Culture), D. Yosef (Development), P. Lavon (Defense), G. Myerson (Labor), P. Naftali (Agriculture), Y. Sapir (Transportation), I. Rokach (Interior), P. Rosen (Justice), Y. Serlin (Health), B. Sheetrit (Police), M. Shapira (Welfare and Religion).

15 Chaim Boger (Bograshov) (1876-1963). Director of, and a teacher at, the Herzliya "Gymnasium" of Tel Aviv, where the then-Shertok was the brightest student of the first graduating class in 1913.

I received a most heartfelt note of congratulations from Yitzhak Ben-Aharon.

Close to midnight all the ministers – including myself and Zipporah – drove to the President's residence, and I officially presented my colleagues to him. There was plenty of picture-taking. Finally the President rose and offered words of congratulation, imparting to the gathering his unpretentious nobility of spirit.

I answered with an impromptu speech which came out smoothly. Then drinks were served and in came "the Lady President," as Ben-Zvi's wife [Rachel] calls herself, and the PM's wife. Then and there I pronounced the opening of the first meeting of the new Cabinet in the presence of the President (the ladies went out).

At home, to clinch it all, I sat down to compose answers to questions by Knesset members, which are to be given tomorrow morning. At a late hour we sat in the kitchen drinking tea, and wondered at our destiny. What had we come to, what would become of us, and how would we bear it all? We concluded together that we had no other choice, come what may.

Moshe Sharett presents his government before Israel's President Yitzhak Ben-Zvi, January 1954. From left to right sitting: Golda Myerson, Yitzhak Ben-Zvi, Moshe Sharett, Peretz Bernstein. Standing: Levi Eshkol, Pinhas Lavon, Benzion Dinur, Yosef Sapir, Yosef Serlin, Dov Yosef, Peretz Naftali, Bechor-Shalom Sheetrit, Moshe Shapira, Yosef Burg.

Wednesday, January 27

Went through a shattered night. Had difficulty falling asleep, and when I did, my sleep was interrupted. Woke up again and again, going in and out of sleep. Finally I rose at a very early hour and tried to find solace for my raging soul in some office work. I translated for publication in the press the report on the last session of the SC which we had received from New York, where Vyshinsky's pro-Arab explanations were underlined. Our press had failed to select the necessary raisins from this fine report by itself, so I felt a need to serve the public with this matter in a clear and effective formulation.

I drove to the Foreign Ministry and was showered with congratulations. Walter excused himself for not kissing me – Anglo-Saxons are hopeless.

[- - -]

Barney and Eshkol came to see me for a consultation on settling matters with the Electric Company. Yosef has come to the conclusion that we had best propose to Avraham Rutenberg that he stay on as DG for at least another year. This will ease the changeover vis-à-vis the public and the company's employees. This was agreed upon. If Rutenberg agrees, we will propose that Maklef join the senior management with a view to his being appointed Deputy DG in due course, and perhaps inheriting Rutenberg's place.

Drove home in time for the large reception. The invitation list had grown to include representatives of the parties in the Knesset, committee chairmen, members of the Supreme Court, all the senior workers at the Foreign Ministry, various notables and representatives of various organizations, etc. Altogether there were some 200 men and women.

The flow of people began at 4:30 until all the rooms on the first floor were filled. Over 150 people came. The President arrived after returning from his visit to Sde Boker. The atmosphere was warm and the spirit convivial. I was extremely exhausted by this affair, during which I stood on my feet from beginning to end. I slumped into exhaustion afterwards.

Zipporah and I again discussed the change in our lives and what was in store for us. I said that for the time being success had smiled upon us. The beginning had gone well. First, in the very formation of a government. Second, my speech presenting the government won hearts with its tenor and original style in comparison to other such speeches (Roy Elston[16] wrote: "The best thing of its kind the Knesset has yet heard." *Ma'ariv* lauded the contents of the speech and

16 Roy Elston (1901-1974). British writer and journalist, worked in the BBC, was sent to Palestine in 1941 to direct the British military radio station broadcasting to occupied Eastern Europe. After the war he worked in the British Mandate information office. He gradually became a staunch pro-Zionist, resigned from his governmental post and became a columnist for *The Palestine Post*, later *The Jerusalem Post*, under the pen name of David Courtney.

its polish. Shimon Samet of *Ha'aretz* wrote that while riding the bus in Tel Aviv during the broadcast of the speech, he heard my voice coming from every house. Evidently a large number of people listened and numerous responses reached me afterwards). Third, my rebuttal speech had elevated the Knesset from the depths to which the debate had fallen. Fourth, the reception in our home.

All these are only trifles which decide nothing for the time being. Will I find the strength needed for the post? I must gird myself as never before. But I have finally attained independence. Now, what I have inside me shall be tested. Until now I was smothered and chained by my subordination to the authority of others greater and older than myself.[17] My lot was always decreed: adaptation and submission. Now, I will be able to conduct matters in accordance with my own mind and put my stamp on the course of events. It is an enormous responsibility, but a grand opportunity as well.

Thursday, January 28

I yielded to Eshkol's appeals and entreaties and, in response to a flowery congratulatory wire from Montor (congratulatory wires and letters from Israel and from all parts of the diaspora continue to arrive in a constant flow), I sent him a telegram inviting him to Israel. I did not allude to his letter in which he had offered to come for the purpose of settling our relations, but rather designated the consultation over future Israel Bonds Organization plans as the purpose of his visit.

Over the Foreign Ministry DG's signature, a letter was sent to Bennike, who returned from Cairo yesterday, proposing talks to clarify land and water issues.[18] The letter had just gone out when there came a telephone message from Bennike, who wished to pay me a congratulatory visit. I invited him for tomorrow afternoon.

I instructed our Washington Embassy to inform the State Department that we intended to establish regular relations with China. The Chinese had approached us on this matter in Helsinki. Their Consul in Rangoon has told David Hacohen that his government was interested in establishing commercial links with us, and wished to know which industrial products they would be able to buy from us.[19]

[- - -]

17 Weizmann and Ben-Gurion.

18 *DFPI* 9, doc.46.

19 *DFPI* 9, doc.48. For background, see Michael Brecher, *Israel, the Korean War and China: Images, Decisions and Consequences* (Jerusalem: Hebrew University [Jerusalem Studies on Asia], 1974), 55-56; Brecher, *Decisions in Israel's Foreign Policy*, 135-36; Jacob Abadi, *Israel's Quest for Recognition and Acceptance in Asia: Garrison State Diplomacy* (London: Frank Cass, 2004), ch.3.

Friday, January 29

At 8:45 am we set out for Sde Boker. Arrived at 11:45 and found Paula busy by the cabin. BG was in the sheep-pen. The cabin is quite comfortable, with a wide vestibule, a sort of multi-purpose living room runs along the entire front, with doors from it to BG's study, beside it a tiny bedroom, a bathroom, etc., and a more spacious bedroom for Paula. The pantry is full of goodies. It seems as though the entire country and the whole world has been sending gifts: fruit and wine and plenty of sundry canned food. We went to see BG at work, and found him on his way to meet us. Although he had already finished his chores, Zipporah insisted on seeing the sheep-pen, and he went back to show it to us. Zipporah later contended that he had displayed no empathy towards his work and spoke about the kids and lambs he was handling as though they were mechanical objects rather than living creatures. We returned to the cabin, and Paula served him something to revive his spirits – sweet potato pancakes and coffee and compote – and all this just before lunch. Afterwards we went to the kibbutz dining hall for lunch. The meal was well-prepared but quite minimal. We returned to the cabin and then I began conversation about this and that, with no central theme. Zipporah had the impression that BG did not behave spontaneously, as though he were under some distress.

One remark may or may not have been an indication of his frame of mind, and perhaps a clue to the future. When I touched upon foreign affairs, he said: "I see signs that the Arabs are preparing for war." When I remarked that exactly the very same signs could be indicative of the Arabs' apprehension that we were set on war, for which reason they must prepare, he did not agree and stuck to his astrological prediction. He added that the Arabs knew that time was working in their favor, and were therefore set on a second round forthwith.

I again disagreed and said that his analysis was illogical. Those in whose favor time is working did not precipitate matters but, on the contrary, would seek to gain time. He did not admit that he had been caught in a contradiction. All in all, it seemed to me that he may quickly tire of the entire project of Sde Boker. I also got the impression that he was enjoying the publicity in the world press and was happy about visiting guests, especially from abroad. Altogether I spent an hour and a quarter in his company. We set out to go back north at 1:00.

It was *Erev Shabbat*[20] by the time we arrived home. After a short while, Bennike, Vigier and an American officer came by. Gideon was with me. The three congratulated me solemnly on my "promotion." I served them drinks. I wished to hear about their visit to Cairo, but could not obtain anything from them. Bennike was willing to tell me about the antiquities he had seen in the Cairo Museum but I showed no interest in them. Thus no conversation was generated, and before long they left.

20 Friday night, the eve of *Shabbat*.

Gideon told me that a reply from Bennike to our letter of yesterday had arrived in the morning. In his opinion, the Security Council debate has not come to an end yet. It was therefore too early to clarify matters here.

[- - -]

Saturday, January 30

[- - -]

Sunday, January 31

At 9:00 am at the PMO I conferred with Ze'ev Sharef on the Cabinet's code of procedure which required renewed confirmation. Chief among the problems was smoking at Cabinet meetings. It was prohibited during the previous regime, due to the request of the late dear Finance Minister Eliezer Kaplan, but strictly enforced after his death too. The result was that those ministers incapable of suppressing their smoking urge would go out to the adjoining room, carry on loudly there, some jamming the entrance craning their necks to listen to the course of the debate – a most undignified sight! It is clear that with this state of affairs it is best to allow smoking in order to maintain the meeting's decorum.

[- - -]

I had planned to report to this morning's Cabinet meeting on the visit of Professor Franz Böhm[21], head of the West German delegation to the reparations negotiations – the first formal visit to Israel by an important German figure. But after I learnt that our people had not yet consulted the police and the *Shin-Bet* on the security aspect of the visit, I deferred my announcement till next week.

The Cabinet meeting was devoted entirely to the budget. Eshkol painted the picture, and the first round of debate began. The vista is extremely gloomy regardless of how the decision goes. If public needs are to be met, the budget will balloon, and our income will be stretched to the limit, with the prospect of the public losing confidence in the Finance Ministry's ability to master such financial resources. This result, in turn, will have a destructive effect on the Israeli pound. On the other hand, if we cut down on meeting public needs and constrain the budget within a more limited framework, we will be faced immediately with one disaster after another, an IDF crisis with the resignation of Lavon, a jump in unemployment with the threat of Golda's resignation, and the failure of compulsory education with the danger of Dinur's departure. The point is that a leap in the percentage of current expenses for services at the cost of the development budget means sacrificing the

21 Franz Böhm (1895-1977). German economist, politician, and lawyer. Involved in anti-Nazi activity during WWII. Christian Democratic Union member of the Bundestag (1953-1965).

future on the altar of the past and abolishing all hope of balancing the economy. A bright and lovely choice!

[- - -]

When I returned to the PMO in the afternoon, I first conferred with Eshkol on matters pertaining to Barclays Bank and the blocked accounts of absentee Arabs. We have released a million pounds sterling but we have no intention of continuing on this course at this time. However, Barclays was taken to court in Nablus and lost the suit. Now, in effect, it has to honor every deposit, and demands therefore that we deal fairly and release its money, against which it is ready to lend us the sum. Eshkol contends that if we manage to extract from Barclays a loan double the sum of the deposits, it would be worth our while, for at some time we shall have to pay them anyway.[22]

At home in the evening, a consultation with some of our Mapai ministers with the participation of the CoS. It was convened at Lavon's initiative. Moshe Dayan presented one plan after another for "direct action." The first concerned what should be done to break the blockade of the Gulf of Eilat. A ship flying the Israeli flag would be sent. If the Egyptians fire on it, then we would air-bomb the Egyptian position, or capture Ras el-Naqb,[23] or break through south of the Gaza Strip to the Mediterranean shore. There was general outrage. I asked Moshe: "Do you realize that this means war with Egypt?" He said: "Certainly." I said: "And then they will be able to bomb Eilat or even Tel Aviv." He replied: "No, they won't do that." Whence the certainty? It's an enigma. Everyone rejected these mad plans, and Lavon was quick to retreat.

The second plan was an operation against the Syrians' interference with our fishing on the Kinneret and their establishing of *faits accomplis* for their own fishing there. This remains a subject for further examination.

The third plan dealt with the contingency if the present turbulence in Syria leads to its invasion by Iraq, and the realization thereof of the "Fertile Crescent" plan.[24] In this case, he said, we should pre-empt this by occupying certain areas.

---

22 The unblocking of Arab accounts was to become, in the words of one observer, "the one bright spot" in the work of the Palestine Conciliation Commission (PCC), resulting in the unfreezing of some £4,000,000 in Barclays Bank accounts by 1957. See David P. Forsythe, *United Nations Peacemaking: The Conciliation Commission for Palestine* (Baltimore: Johns Hopkins University Press, 1972), 114. Cf. UN Conciliation Commission for Palestine, *Thirteenth Progress Report*, January 4, 1954, UN Document A/2629; *DFPI* 9, docs. 18, 41.

23 A mountainous point to the west of Eilat near the Egyptian-Israeli border.

24 During 1954 and 1955, Iraqi politicians Fadhil Jamali and Nuri Sa'id revived their earlier advocacy of the creation of an Iraqi-centered union of Fertile Crescent states. The idea was not at all popular in Syria, and would become totally eclipsed with the rise of Nasser's Egypt-based plans for pan-Arab unity. See also below, entry and note for October 4, 1954; Bruce Maddy-Weitzman, *The Crystallization of the Arab State System, 1945-1954*, Syracuse: Syracuse University Press, 1993. Nuri's 1943 proposal and Jamali's January 1954 project are reproduced in *The Arab States and the Arab League*, 9-12 and 47-49.

I said that it was definitely too early to make conclusive decisions on something that's entirely "iffy." I further demanded with explicit clarity that nothing at all be done without a political decision, which should be taken on the basis of the circumstances created at a future time rather than basing it on views and assumptions gleaned for the time being from the imagination.

The most illuminating conclusion from this discussion was that such is the direction of the new CoS's thinking. Most disturbing.

[- - -]

Monday, February 1

[- - -]

This morning I did not go to the PMO, but drove directly to the Foreign Ministry. We had a meeting there on the problem of the blocked accounts of the absentee Arabs. We decided to let the Finance Ministry try its luck with Barclays Bank.[25]

Later I told the DG and Gideon about last night's meeting. I portrayed it as a conversation among myself, Lavon and Dayan. Gideon contended that there was not the slightest chance that Iraq would invade Syria, and that any planning against such a contingency was nothing but wishful thinking on the part of the imaginative CoS.

At 10:00 am drove to the PMO. Received the French Ambassador who had come to congratulate me on my new appointment. Pierre Gilbert conducts himself with admirable chivalry. Without asking permission from Paris, he defies the diplomatic corps' ban on Jerusalem[26] and pays me a visit – albeit at the PMO and in my capacity as PM, which is his cover! – in the Capital in broad daylight. Gilbert stayed for an hour or so. He enjoys talking, but his talk is always interesting, though not everything he says is well-founded.

---

25 Cf. above, page 235 n.22.

26 Three United Nations resolutions in 1947, 1948 and 1949 called for the territorial internationalization of Jerusalem whose territory was divided *de facto* between Israel and Jordan along the cease-fire lines produced by the 1948 fighting. In defiant rejection of Resolution 303 adopted by the GA in December 1949, the Government of Israel began taking steps to make Western Jerusalem its capital by locating a growing number of its offices and official functions (the PMO, the Knesset, swearing-in ceremonies of its Presidents, the Supreme Court) there. The opening of the MFA in Jerusalem in July 1953 represented Israel's boldest challenge to those who still viewed the UN's resolutions as insisting on the internationalization of the disputed city. At first the US, the UK and other states announced that they would not conduct any official business with Israel in Jerusalem, but by 1955 the ban was relaxed. For details see: Sharett to Dulles, July 27, 1953, *DFPI* 8, doc.314; Brecher, *Decisions*, ch.1; http://israelsdocuments.blogspot.ca/2015/07/13-july-1953-facts-israeli-foreign.html.

[- - -]

Gideon came by to report on the unrest among the Israeli Druze due to President Shishakli's persecution of their brethren in Syria, which has been agitating the Jebel Druze.[27] There are rumors about the imprisonment of their leader Sultan el-Atrash, and of the bombing of villages. Our Druze are furious. On the one hand they rejected Dayan's proposal that the IDF enlist and equip saboteurs among them. On the other, they are ready to give their blessing to an IDF invasion of Syria to capture and liberate the Jebel Druze enclave, but are unwilling to take any risks themselves. They have organized rallies and demonstrations in their villages. A delegation of their elders and notables would like to meet with the PM. Their representatives in the Knesset are willing to speak from the podium if I approve of it. We concluded that there was no harm in it and that, if they should appear, I would respond. Meanwhile it became clear that we do not know exactly what is happening on the "Mountain," and in Syria generally. At this time of trial, we have discovered a serious flaw in our intelligence.

I called in Ziama Aran for a talk. I told him about my visit to Sde Boker, and my impression that BG may tire of the whole "adventure." He expressed the fear that maybe he already has.

[- - -]

The two Druze Knesset members came to see me. They appealed to precedents in which the Knesset had intervened on behalf of Jews disenfranchised of their rights in other countries. The Druze of Israel, too, have persecuted brethren in Syria, and they were appealing to the Israeli government and to the Knesset for succor. What needs to be done? "*Hakumat Isra'il Akhbar!*" (the Government of Israel knows better). I promised them all my sympathy and an appeal to the Great Powers.

[- - -]

In the evening I returned to the Knesset. With the opening of the session, the Druze MK Sheikh Jaber Mu'adi was given the floor. He protested strongly against atrocities perpetrated on the Druze and called for help. He poured abuse on Shishakli's head, and declared that the Druze in Israel would not stand idly by. This was a blunt and groundless assertion which also needlessly endangers the Druze of the Jebel. After the Hebrew translation of the speech was read, I took the floor and spoke briefly and with all due caution. I limited myself to an expression of sympathy for the freedom-loving Druze nation, which had succeeded in retaining its religious and national identity, and for the members of the Druze community in Israel, to whom the state owed a great deal for their loyalty and aid in time of need. After all, it was they, and not we, whose kin were hostages in the hands of

27 A mountainous area in southern Syria, populated predominantly by Druze.

the tyrant of Damascus. Why should we surrender them to him as a fifth column of "the Zionists"?

[- - -]

Tuesday, February 2

Rose at 6:30 to work on my papers. Also prepared myself for the Knesset Foreign Affairs and Defense Committee.

At the Foreign Ministry for a short consultation regarding our problems with Egypt – the British evacuation of the Canal Zone and the blockade of our passage through the Canal.

The FADC, which convened to discuss Egyptian affairs, got absorbed in the Druze matter. In the course of the discussions, I rather incisively reviewed the question of our relations with minorities in the Middle East. Why were we obliged to support them, and why did this support have to be circumscribed? Both because we shall eventually have to make peace with the majority rather than with them, and because they, being minorities, cannot be trusted, for "variable adaptability" is their stock-in-trade, a traditional means of defense.

In the afternoon I received a delegation of Druze community leaders at the PMO. Some ten of them came and sat around me in a semi-circle – priests, Knesset members and heads of villages. Some flowery speeches were delivered, both impromptu and prepared. I replied with a well-considered statement.

Gave Moshe Keren of *Ha'aretz* a good dressing-down for the fine division of labor instituted by this newspaper. The lead article preached moderation with regard to the Jordan River diversion affair and demanded that the public be realistically informed rather than misled. The first page, on the other hand, incited the public against the government for offering concessions and virtually fumed with a lack of comprehension as to why we had not resumed work. Keren said the fault was with the paper's Tiberias reporter and with the *Tahal* people who were inciting him, but admitted that there was a serious lack of coordination inside *Ha'aretz*. He gave me his word that there wasn't any ill intention here – no Satanic intriguing.

[- - -]

Wednesday, February 3

Gave instructions to appeal to the three powers about the Druze matter. Hopefully they can provide us with news which may calm the agitated community in Israel. If the situation is truly as it is touted to be, they ought use their influence to restrain Shishakli.[28]

---

28 See *DFPI* 9, docs. 53, 82.

[- - -]

Thursday, February 4

[- - -]

Mordechai (Reggie) Kidron,[29] our Deputy Permanent Representative to the UN, who arrived in Israel a few days ago because of his father's death and was now about to return to New York, came to visit me. He told of the growing eminence of Abe Harman, our Consul-General in New York, especially within the Jewish community, of his distinction as an orator, and the splendid character of this unique man and his wife, Zena. He is resolved to return to Israel this coming summer. With whom can I replace him? He gave me a detailed report on Aubrey. His nervous tension due to the strain of work and the burden of responsibility was steadily growing.

[- - -]

Friday, February 5

[- - -]

Saturday, February 6

Sat all morning with Eshkol and Henry Montor, whom Eshkol had persuaded me to invite to Israel for the purpose of renewing my relations with him. I employed simple and courteous language, though without any friendly bonhomie. I told him that I had complete faith in him and that he would receive my full assistance in his capacity as director of the Israel Bonds Organization. On his part, there was an expression of satisfaction, relief and gratification, but not one word of regret or apology.[30] We reviewed the renewed issue of Israel Bonds, the problem of coordination with the UJA, and the possibility of operations in countries other than the US. Finally he brought up the question of my coming to the US in May for the opening of the new campaign. Both Eshkol and I deemed it to be neither possible nor appropriate.

After supper went over to Moshe Zmora,[31] to listen to the playing of his

---

29 Mordechai (Reggie) Kidron (1915-1997). Born in South Africa. Settled in Palestine in 1933. Joined MFA in 1948 and headed its International Organizations Division (1951-1953); Deputy Permanent Representative to the UN (1953-1958); later Israel Ambassador to Thailand and to Sweden.

30 Montor had clashed with Sharett (the exact reason is not known) during the latter's 1952 visit to the USA for a UJA fund-raising campaign, leaving Sharett deeply insulted. See also below, entry for February 11.

31 Moshe Zmora (1888-1961). Born in Germany. Settled in Palestine in 1922. Lawyer and legal scholar; headed the Organization of Jewish Advocates in Mandatory Palestine. Taught law at the Hebrew University. Upon establishment of the state, was appointed Chief Justice of the Supreme Court (1948-1954).

daughter Michal and her husband Gideon Roehr, the violinist. Their performance was excellent and I enjoyed myself immensely.

Later I went with Walter to the tenth anniversary of the PATWA [Professional and Technical Workers Association], at the birth of which in England I was present and whose first steps I had planned. I was surprised at the full house, not having realized that this organization had brought so many men and women to the country, mainly from England. I made a speech, of course both in Hebrew and English, which was recorded for purposes of *hasbara* abroad.

Sunday, February 7

Rose at 6:00 to work on the papers I had not gone through on Saturday. [- - -]

Lavon entered my office in the PMO to inform me of new regulations about to be issued, allowing travel in the areas of Military Government in the Galilee. This is good news for the Arabs and will be attributed to the new government. I told him to announce this change at the Cabinet meeting. [- - -]

At the Cabinet meeting I raised for discussion the rebellion in the Knesset, including some coalition members, against the amendment of the Law of Return.[32] This would allow the withholding of entry permits to Israel to those with a criminal past so as to prevent the country from turning into a haven for criminals. Those of refined sensibility have contended that there may be no tampering with the Law of Return, that there is room enough in the state even for Jewish malefactors, etc. It was decided to insist upon the amendment.

Lavon came in after the meeting to consult with me on the recruitment of Druze by the Army. I was gratified to hear that he is actually in favor of the recruitment of Arabs and considers it possible to organize them in Arab units integrated within larger Jewish units. I suggested that we submit this proposal to the Cabinet when it should come time to summarize the bases of our policy towards the Arab minority. Once the regular recruitment of minority group members by the IDF is implemented, it will be possible to make a subtle differentiation between the Druze and the Arabs, to the relative preference of the former.

[- - -]

The second Cabinet meeting, which was devoted to the budget, began at 4:00 and went on till 7:15. There was a harsh and depressing battle both between Mapai and the GZ, and between Eshkol and all the ministers. I was highly displeased with myself. As the new Prime Minister, it was my duty to raise the banner of budgetary cuts, and wage war valiantly against the dizzying growth of the budget, which can only culminate in our ruin. As Foreign Minister, I did not have the fortitude to

32 Israeli legislation, passed on July 5, 1950, which gives Jews the right to freely immigrate to Israel and gain Israeli citizenship upon settlement.

compromise with the severe damage [of cutbacks] to the foreign service, which threatens to break its spirit, clip its wings, forestall any new conquests and constrain any free momentum in our network of information in the world at large and among Jewish communities in the diaspora. And again, as Prime Minister responsible for his own ministry, I demanded a budgetary increase for the purpose of funding propaganda and information efforts in Israel, which Aran is designated to oversee.

Eventually I found a way out of these pangs of conscience which I believe makes objective sense. At any rate, the proposal was acceptable to several colleagues. I said that we and the ministries were not ready now for any ruthless shrinkage. We had no choice now other than to adopt a large budget, come what may. But immediately with the start of the coming budgetary year, we had to seriously consider how to shape next year's budget within the framework of our ability, and then, in due time, we would be able to prepare the ministries and the public for the constraints to be imposed upon us. Lavon also fought desperately and announced that he would leave the Ministry of Defense if he wasn't assured of the necessary minimum. From the meeting I sent messages to the Foreign Ministry regarding the proceedings, and received cries of despair in response. It's clear to me that my people have no idea of the dire straits in which the overall nation's finances lie. The meeting came to an end without any final conclusions. It was decided to hold another meeting for final deliberation and decision before the week is up. The GZ announced that they had to confer internally prior to the next meeting.

Came home at 7:30, hastily changed and placed name cards on the dining table which was set for 15 people. The dinner was in honor of Lou Boyar,[33] leader of the Israel Bonds Organization in Los Angeles, and his wife. Among the guests were Bob and Zip Szold, Montor, Eshkol and the Serlins.

[- - -]

Monday, February 8

[- - -]

A meeting with Golda and Moshe Shapira on *Shabbat* work permits, in fulfillment of that item in the coalition agreement with the religious parties. We authorized three permits with Shapira's grumbling consent and left two for further examination. We were again confronted, and this time most crucially and in the face of incisive technical and economic facts, with the absolute contradiction between the *galuti* nature nature of *Shabbat* as observed by Orthodox Jewry and the critical needs of Israeli sovereignty and requisite demands of modern technology.

33 Louis ("Lou") H. Boyar (1898-1976). American urban planner and developer. Zionist activist, communal philanthropist and leader of the Israel Bond Organization. Supporter and Governor of the Hebrew University of Jerusalem.

[- - -]

A consultation with Walter, Gideon, Arthur Lourie and Arieh Eshel on our relations with the military in the domain of the Armistice Agreements, pending the meeting with Lavon and the CoS tomorrow. I am embarking on a decisive campaign of radical reform, and the institution of a new policy which would make a clear-cut division between the military and political authorities. These had become completely obscured during BG's tenure.

[- - -]

Arrived at home at 2:10 and ate while listening to *Kol-Israel's* news in Arabic.

[- - -]

A quarter of an hour with Boris Smolar[34]of New York's Jewish Telegraphic Agency (JTA), who is now touring the country. In a conversation not to be published he extricated from my mouth words on my attitude towards BG's opinions concerning the future of the Zionist Organization (ZO). He also emerged with my approval of his appraisal that Nahum Goldmann's boastings about his ability to conclude peace with the Arabs were nothing but nonsense.

At 4:00 with Montor, Eshkol and Dobkin concerning Israel Bonds in countries outside the USA. Montor suggested that I come to the USA in May for the opening of the new campaign. His plan was not to my liking. It would be a pale edition of BG's visit. I can't leave the country so close to assuming my new duties. And my visit would inevitably cause tension in our relations with the American administration, which is obviously not at all interested in receiving Israel's PM as a guest but would be, in such circumstances, unable to ignore me.

Gideon came by and we discussed the Jordan diversion channel in the north and Article XII. What should be our response to Jordan's refusal, for the second time, to confer? Gideon proposed a statement to the press. I said that I would subscribe to an official complaint to the Security Council over the violation of the Armistice Agreement. Had I seen any chance of a thaw in the "cold war" the Arabs are waging against us, I would have been willing to forgive Jordan its refusal, anything to avoid fanning the flames of hatred again. But the "cold war" is in full force, with no sign of any truce. The other side is seizing any available weapon against us, and we must therefore strike at them without mercy.

As regards the diversion channel, it was clear from the UN SG's wires to Bennike that our people in New York were deluding themselves if they thought there was still any chance of resuming work – if not with Bennike's consent, then without any protest on his part. Clearly, in view of the cables at our disposal, the SG opposes any resumption of the work, and he was warning Bennike not to

34 Boris Smolar (1897-1986). New York-based journalist; editor-in-chief of the Jewish Telegraphic Agency (1924-1968).

gloss lightly over this matter. Against this background, the question is whether it is worth our while to enter into talks with Bennike on land and water rights, or perhaps best to leave him alone. Should we begin talks, the public may get the impression that the road is being prepared for the resumption of work, and we should be found to have misled it with false hopes. I said that it is best that we discuss it; we would lose nothing. In any event, we would not be able to resume work, even if we wished to, before the month of April. If we don't make contact with the UNTSO CoS in the meantime, it will seem as though we have accepted the freeze, whereas if talks do begin, it will seem as though we have begun a maneuver to pursue implementation of the project. We have time until April to decide what steps to take later. Also, we shall always be able to explain to the public the rationale for the tactic.

[- - -]

Tuesday, February 9

[- - -] Started waking up earlier, my going to sleep late not withstanding. This morning I began working before shaving.

[- - -]

Received Raphael Bash[35] of the party secretariat at the PMO. He beseeched me to participate from time to time in its meetings. I knew right from the beginning that my being elected to the prime-ministership would entail my active involvement and responsibility in Party affairs.

[- - -]

Dealt with matters pertaining to the Arabs of Israel. Baruch Yekutieli brought up a packet-full of vexing troubles that demanded urgent handling, foremost among them those of the Israeli Arabs whose lands had been taken from them and were eligible for compensation in land or in money. I hope that all these matters will start to be handled once the appointment of the new Adviser for Arab Affairs becomes official. The candidate is Ziama Divon[36] whom I am willing to remove from our Paris Embassy for this purpose. I wired Reuven Shiloah to ask his opinion and am waiting impatiently for an answer. In the meantime, Lavon's removal of travel restrictions has become known among the Arabs in Galilee and this was

35 Raphael Bash (1913-2000). Born in Latvia. Settled in Palestine in 1938. Mapai activist and MK. Party Secretary (1954-1956).

36 Shmuel Zalman ("Ziama") Divon (1917-2003). Born in Russia. Settled in Palestine in 1935. Headed the Arabic Department of *Hagana's SHAI.* Joined the MFA in 1949. First Secretary, Israel Embassy in Paris (1952-1954), during which time he maintained contact with a member of the Egyptian Embassy there who served as a conduit to Gamal Abd al-Nasser. Adviser on Arab affairs, PMO (1954-1956). Later Israel Ambassador to Ethiopia, to Brazil and to Turkey.

immediately credited to the "Sharett government."

Came to the Foreign Ministry and spent three hours there for the first time in several days. I enjoyed the excellent tea, the likes of which is offered only at the Foreign Ministry – a result of my needling all these years and the attentive and hearty assistance of [secretaries] Beba [Yanai], Lilian [Alizi] and Poriah [Avnon]. The atmosphere here is altogether different from that at the PMO – warm and familial, as well as resourceful and efficient.

[- - -]

Napped for a quarter of an hour and at 3:00 I was at the PMO. [- - -] A meeting of the Cabinet Committee on Foreign Affairs. I lectured on developments in the areas of the Jordan diversion; the Canal blockade; the Canal Zone evacuation. On the last subject there was an important discussion, which led to clarification of the problem and the emergence of conclusions. Lavon wanted to raise the issue of our action regarding the Syrian fishing in the Kinneret, but time was lacking.

[- - -]

In the evening, from 8:00 to 11:30, a most difficult and strained meeting at the PMO. The main issue addressed was the coordination between the Foreign Ministry and the Army. A clash between Eytan, Rafael and me on one side, Lavon and Dayan on the other. I began by defining the problem. The IDF people heard for the first time a clear-cut statement of the Foreign Ministry's sole authority in policy-making. They must have said to themselves: gone are the good old days, gone, never to return! "Oh, where is the 'old man', now?" An acrimonious argument ensued. Lavon tried his hand with arguments of a debating contest, but I brought him back to plain facts. What went completely sour, in addition to the internal contradiction as regards the main direction of our policy – whether towards war or holding our ground, towards the exhaustion of all possibilities of political action or the shorter recourse to the use of force – was the Army's utter distrust of Gideon as chief liaison for the Foreign Ministry. In this respect, the situation is bound to improve greatly with the return of Yosef Tekoah. Nothing was settled. However, my colleagues felt that what I had said would be beneficial and leave its mark upon future relations and conduct.

At the end of the meeting, Aryeh Shalev told me of two strange and worrying incidents: two soldiers, one in the north, one in our Mount Scopus enclave, deserted to the enemy. The one in the north was wounded by the Syrians. The IDF reported that he was insane, in order to discredit whatever he discloses. There is much worry as to what the second will disclose to the Jordanians about military arrangements in the enclave.

Came home after spending more than eight hours non-stop in meetings. Wrote my diary till I felt my eyes closing and my mind became numb. These days I am walking about as if with two heavy coins hanging down from my eyelids.

Wednesday, February 10

An extraordinary Cabinet meeting was held from 8:00 in the morning until 12:30, wholly devoted to the budget. There was a tortuous and stubborn struggle between Eshkol, aided by Golda and Lavon, and the GZ. Their chief whip was Yosef Sapir. The leader of the campaign, first to raise his hand and quick to send exhortative notes, was Serlin. The GZ position was a mixture of demagogy and conservatism, all wrapped in a mantle of concern for the state's economy, for preventing inflation, for stabilizing the currency and other exalted principles. But this position was a firm fact. The atmosphere within GZ ranks in the Knesset and around the country is even worse. The right-wing press is venomous and subversive. The coalition is like a concrete casting that hasn't set. One fatal blow could break it into smithereens. It was therefore necessary to somehow seek a compromise, or at least soften the differences. At a certain point, there was a retreat on their part. Lavon proposed an amended version to Sapir's proposal of budgetary cuts – or the prevention of any increases. Serlin then suggested that we choose a committee to study the possibility of finding common ground between the two proposals. I wrote Eshkol a note that this could point the way to a solution, but he insisted on bringing the budget to a final vote today. Strictly speaking, from a national viewpoint he was quite right, for according to parliamentary schedule we are long past the deadline. Still, there was a logic of prudence above and beyond the logic of justice (for instance, had I insisted at some crucial stages of the coalition negotiations on concluding "today," I would have brought things to a crisis and failure rather than agreement.) A vote was held on Serlin's proposal and I ostentatiously voted with the GZ, whom Rosen also joined. My *haverim* and the *Hapo'el Hamizrahi* ministers voted against. This proposal having been rejected, the GZ returned to their radical proposals and the budget in its entirety was adopted with the votes of Mapai and *Hapo'el Hamizrahi* against the GZ and Rosen. As chairman I wasn't obliged to vote and didn't. The meeting left a heavy residue and explosive sparks were buzzing in the air. I told the *haverim* when it ended that the coalition was on the verge of falling apart.

Went to the MFA for a few minutes. The question concerning a conference with Jordan has become quite complex. There are serious doubts whether it's worthwhile to press for convening the conference. The Army is entirely opposed and the Foreign Ministry people are also skeptical. Abba, on the other hand, thinks in terms of diplomatic logic and ignores realistic considerations. He was planning to see the Secretary-General tomorrow. I wired him to postpone the meeting till Monday to give us time for serious consultation here, either in the Cabinet or in a ministers' committee, or at least between me and Lavon. I collected all the papers on the subject in order to send a detailed cable to New York.[37]

[- - -]

37 *DFPI* 9, doc.64.

All evening long I fell prey to qualms and pangs of conscience. Had we – the Mapai ministers – employed the right tactic against the GZ? Had I failed in the last meeting in my capacity as chairman? This crisis, erupting immediately after the formation of the government, will come as a set-back which no one anticipated. Besides its deleterious effect on the state, it will be attributed with all its gravity to me personally.

Thursday, February 11

The budget crisis is the talk of the day in the morning newspapers. It turns out that I wasn't accurate on one positive point. *Hapo'el Hamizrahi* didn't vote with Mapai but abstained in the final votes on the budget. During the first ballot, they did vote with my *haverim* to reject the GZ proposals. But when it came to the decisive votes, they washed their hands of the matter. *Haboker*[38] serves up a delectable meal for the pleasure of its readers, making much of the fact that this budget was adopted with the exclusive votes of Mapai alone against the GZ and the Progressive Zionists, with the abstention of the religious parties. The disclosure of the course of the debate in the Cabinet, down to the details of the vote, has become common fare for some newspapers. Admonitions against this practice of leaking the substance of Cabinet meetings have ceased to make an impression. Serlin especially shines in this sphere of "public relations."

[- - -]

The DG of the MFA came in with some news. He had dined at Gilbert's and heard much from him. The French Ambassador had proposed to the Quai d'Orsay to allow him to regularly visit the Foreign Minister at the PMO and the DG at the Foreign Ministry. He hopes that he will at least be permitted the former, and he will be grateful for that alone. His example will no doubt influence others.

He [conveyed Gilbert's report] about the Israelis who had been removed from a plane in Baghdad and imprisoned there. All our appeals to the US and Britain in this matter won't help us, for American and British influence in Baghdad is as good as nothing. They have adopted an attitude of abject appeasement. By this means they have reduced the efficacy of their intervention to nil. The only way is retaliation. The plan is a pinnacle of recklessness, but the inclination of this Ambassador is interesting. He is now devoted diligently to studying Hebrew, and has just now discovered the beauty of the Bible.

Discussed with Walter the course I am pursuing as regards diplomats' visits to Jerusalem, and my meetings with them in Tel Aviv or Ramat Gan. The American Chargé d'affaires [Francis Russell] sent me a written note of congratulations and invited me to dine at his home in Ramat Gan. It was explained to him that he has

---

38 Rightist daily, mouthpiece of the GZ Party. Editor-in-Chief: Peretz Bernstein.

fallen into an overblown pretentiousness if he imagines that the PM will come to dine with him without his having first paid me a courtesy call. He then sent a telegram to the State Department for permission to pay such a call, and received a negative reply. No matter. Let him cool his heels. The Belgian Consul, Eugène Dubois, requested – through his wife, who visited Zipporah at home – to arrange a visit with me at home for him too. It was explained to him that he was free to invite himself for a visit to the PM or Foreign Minister at their office. It was certainly his right to request an interview. But he cannot initiate a visit to the PM's home, and must leave that initiative to the PM, should the latter so desire. Dubois then artfully invited me to dine at his place. Emile Najar[39] explained to him that if he did not first visit my office in Jerusalem, I would not be able to accept any invitation from him. On the other hand, I was visited and congratulated at the PMO in Jerusalem by the French Ambassador, the Soviet Consul and the Swedish Chargé d'affaires. The Italian, Swiss and Turkish are to be prevailed upon to come too. I shall then invite them to come dine at my home in Jerusalem, and afterwards be willing to accept their invitations to Tel Aviv or Ramat Gan or Herzliya. I shall honor those who honor me.

Montor came to say goodbye before leaving. This time he surprised me. As soon as he sat down, he began with our personal relations. He said that something untoward had come between us a year and a half ago. He knew that I was hurt to the depths of my soul, that I viewed that as malice on his part. There would be no point in explaining that he had not meant it. The main thing was that such was my feeling. He expressed his profound regret. He asked what he must do to make it clear that he was extending to me his unqualified apology. A decent attitude on my part towards him would not satisfy him, nor would my proffered help. He sought my warm and personal friendship as in days of yore. What must he do to bring our relations back to what they were?

I replied that he already had, by virtue of what he had said. There was no need of anything else to express his remorse. He had done well to have said what he said. It had been his moral obligation to do so. Now the injury was no more, and the rupture healed. He was very moved, and thanked me no end. We went on to discuss current matters. When he got up to go I said to him: "Henry, you insulted me most deeply." He said: "Please, forgive me." He fell upon me and kissed me. The Bible would have added in such a case: "And he lifted up his voice and wept."[40]

Drove to the PMO and conferred with Eshkol and Aran on the simmering budget crisis. At this point Eshkol was willing to concede to the GZ the resumption of subsidies in order to appease them, as well as to promise them that the Knesset

39 Emile (Amiel) Najar (1912-1980). Director, West European Division, MFA. Later Israel Ambassador to Belgium.

40 *Genesis*, 29:11.

Finance Committee will be given a full opportunity to examine every item on the budget with a view to savings without the whip of parliamentary discipline being held over the coalition parties. We concluded that tomorrow in Tel Aviv, after the meeting of the economic ministers on the income budget, the two of us would meet with the GZ and attempt to resolve the crisis.

Napped for three quarters of an hour in the afternoon – quite a feat – went through a pile of papers and set out for Tel Aviv at 7:00. It was a wintry moonlit night. The passenger seat beside the driver, always available for hitchhiking soldiers, was for the first time occupied by a permanent escort, a Security Service man. I did eliminate the military police jeep and additional Security Service car, but agreed to the demand that at least one bodyguard always accompany me in the car.

[- - -]

Friday, February 12

In the morning, in my apartment at Hayarkon 184, I started to rack my brain for ideas for my evening speech at the journalists' "open press conference" in Tel Aviv.[41]

Shaul came at 9:30 and we sat together for quite a bit. He is setting out to Zurich for a long sojourn. We discussed the Polish mater,[42] which Shaul views as not serious. We decided to begin preparing a weekly Russian broadcast within the framework of "The Voice of Zion to the Diaspora" broadcasts, although our Minister to Moscow, Shmuel Eliashiv,[43] tells us that the Yiddish broadcast [directed towards Soviet Jews] is regularly jammed. Shaul told me they [i.e., the *Nativ* organization] are preparing a Yiddish booklet about the State of Israel and a pictorial Jewish calendar for the Soviet Union.[44]

[- - -]

Returned to squeezing out ideas [for the evening's "open press conference"] and once I started to write them down I realized that a pattern was emerging.

Yitzhak Navon telephoned from the "front" where the economic ministers were deliberating over the budget. Pinhas Sapir telephoned after him. Both had the same news: the tension had dissipated. At 3:30 Eshkol and I met with Rokach, Bernstein

---

41 In these sessions, organized by the Journalists Association and open to the general public, VIP's were questioned by a panel of journalists.

42 The possibility of paying money for immigration permits.

43 Dr Shmuel Eliashiv (1899-1955). Born in Russia. Settled in Palestine in 1934. Member *Histadrut* Executive (1937-1945). Upon establishment of the state joined the MFA. Director, East European Division (1949-1951); Israel Minister (1951-1954), then Ambassador (1954-1955) to Moscow.

44 *Nativ* people in Israel prepared such items, as well as prayer books, prayer shawls, *teffilin*, Israeli stamps and coins, a Russian periodical) unavailable in the Soviet Union and considered anti-Soviet. They were distributed clandestinely among Soviet Jews by members of the Israel Embassy in Moscow, who were all in fact *Nativ* operatives.

and [Yosef] Sapir to iron out difficulties. There was an open exchange and mutual, though muted, accusations. At the end there were indications of reaching common ground. We made no final decisions but parted with the feeling that the crisis was past.

Went back to writing up my speech and at long last gathered momentum and filled page after page, writing up the speech almost in its entirety. In the evening we drove to the Mugrabi Cinema Hall, but stopped some distance before we reached it, and walked the rest of the way by foot, the way good American Jews do on the High Holidays. My speech lasted more than the right time – an hour and a quarter instead of the 50 minutes as I had planned, because I couldn't suppress my impulses and interwove long impromptu additions between the written lines. Nevertheless, the house, which was full, was mesmerized and the listening was steady all the way through.

When Zipporah and I came back to our apartment after having visited my sister Ada it was 1:00 am. By now I felt deeply relieved after shedding off the burden of the speech as if I had crossed a high summit, and also deep satisfaction with the speech's contents and its impact. I said to Zipporah that I was satisfied with the speech itself as well as with my composure, since both what I said and the way I lectured reflected the change which had taken place in my position. Formerly, when it was not I who carried the highest responsibility, I did not feel myself obliged nor free to say a few of the things which I said tonight on our foreign policy as well as on internal politics. The pressure and awareness of authority were at work here.

Pipedreams in Lebanon

Saturday, February 13

[- - -]

Back in Jerusalem I called [personal secretary] Shamai. He opened by congratulating me on the speech, which was very effectively broadcast over *Kol-Israel.*

After supper we went to visit Dolik who is still laid up in bed, his whole body in a cast. I found him full of bleak foreboding due to the budget. Immediately after the new economic policy went into effect, the difference between the dollar's official exchange rate and the black market one narrowed to only 10-15 percent. Now the black market rate has jumped to IL.2.95 as opposed to IL.1.80. Unimaginable consequences may ensue. He rejects the GZ opposition to the reduction of subsidies for fear of a rise in prices, as well as Mapai's opposition to budget cuts for fear of a cutback in services and a drop in the standard of living. He very much endorses my proposal to appoint a committee authorized to prepare the Financial Year 1955-1956 budget with a view to substantial reductions and setting finances on a healthy footing. But he also advocates a vigorous effort now to make immediate cuts.[1]

I told him about the emotional straits I was in. The premiership compelled me to restrain the expansive impulse generally and prescribe thrift to all, while my job as Foreign Minister obliged me to look after the utmost efficiency of the state's foreign service, which demanded additional resources. I said that my inner voice was telling me to reject the demand of my colleagues in the Foreign Ministry and serve as an example in cutting its budget of my own accord. He said that I would be doing a great thing and win enormous respect if I should serve as such an example. I replied that it would then demand devoting two full days to examine every item of expenditure with a fine-tooth comb. I added that even if a contraction were possible, it would cost the state serious damage in the efficiency of the [foreign] service and perhaps the loss of positions and support of public opinion.

I was quite annoyed by his wife Riva, who time and again intervened in our conversation, like the constant pestering of a buzzing fly, pronouncing definite opinions on financial and economic subjects on which she is a total ignoramus, but

1 During this period, Horowitz was involved in plans for establishing the Bank of Israel, which would be founded in August with Horowitz as its first Governor.

only absorbing and emitting things she had heard once from Dolik – and all this in his presence, when the visitor could have heard everything directly from his mouth.

Back at home, when I sat down at long last to do my paper work, the telephone rang. The *Jerusalem Post* asked for my help in editing my Tel Aviv speech, which I did on the spot. Then I called *Davar* after having given up waiting for their call. I found their report of the opening and first part of my speech a disaster and couldn't control myself, pouring buckets of wrath on the head of the poor reporter. Why hadn't they taken a stenogram? On whom were they relying? And this after I had given them my notes! How poorly did they utilize them! Why didn't they chase after me? Instead of me being furious with them for unnecessarily pestering me, here I was furious with them for not bothering me! How could I now dictate for them my speech anew over the phone? If this is how they operated, then let them publish whatever they could concoct – I was fed up and could not help them. In the end my anger rose to such a height that I felt I had to stop the conversation, but then I continued venting my diatribe into the ears of Zipporah. She tried to get *Davar*'s editor-in-chief, but he could not be found.

Moshe Shapira [Minister of Welfare and Religion] telephoned earlier in the evening. For several days we have been informed of demonstrations held by ultra-orthodox fanatics from Brooklyn in front of the New York Consulate against the National Service Law, because it applied to women as well, desecrating the name of Israel. Abe Harman had requested the intervention of Chief Rabbi Herzog, and our religious colleagues have also received from him telegrams for this purpose. Shapira appealed to the Rabbi and the latter asserted quite rightly that he had not yet received a reply to his own letter to me. This was true. Because of all the troubles raging around me, that letter still remained unanswered. I promised to repair this fault tonight. I asked Zipporah to go through the pile of files (there is always one at hand) to find the letter. And indeed she did. I then sat down to compose a proper letter, which encompassed the entire breadth of this complicated issue. When I finished this labor it was 2:00 am.

Sunday, February 14

[- - -]

At the PMO I poured out my vexed spirits into the ears of Ze'ev Sharef. The matter of the budget had caught me unawares. If not for the cursed crisis engendered by the GZ – for nothing, in the long run, seeing that none of their suits were fulfilled – I would have delved into this issue in time, that is to say many weeks before the crucial stage, and set myself a proper course. Under the given circumstances, I let myself be dragged after the deliberations instead of guiding them. Furthermore, I was caught in a vice between PM's responsibility and the Foreign Ministry's needs. Should I now propose a cut in the Ministry's budget? And what if, as a result of the contraction, the work should suffer and we should lose positions and election campaigns? Foreign affairs are at such a highly sensitive juncture. Every venture that we initiate advances us, but every such venture needs to be financed.

Eshkol came in and announced that, after going over the figures on Saturday, he had come to the conclusion that there was no escaping the cancellation of all increases, in addition to a 4% cut. He doesn't favor an additional cut of up to 7%, as I had proposed, unless Lavon concedes a million. I gathered my courage and, in order to provide him with a bargaining lever to make it easier for him with the others, said that I had renounced the IL.300,000 increase he wanted to allot me in exchange for the 4% cut.

Moshe Shapira showed me a letter that Rabbi Herzog had sent, even without waiting for my reply, to the rabbis in New York, protesting against the demonstrations and the vilification of our name, and demanding a stop to all public action against the National Service Law.

The Cabinet meeting heard Eshkol's report on Friday's deliberations and went on to concentrate on trifling matters. The tension between Mapai and the GZ has slackened but is by no means eliminated. There was therefore no point in posing other highly controversial questions for discussion to exacerbate the tension. The only important subject discussed was the abolition of the death penalty. Most of the Cabinet members supported my proposal to leave it to the courts to decide whether to sentence murderers to death or life imprisonment. [Pinhas] Rosen, Naftali and Serlin advocated the complete abolition of the death penalty.[2]

After the meeting, I conferred with Eshkol and Lavon. The former put strong pressure on the latter to forgo a million, on the basis of which he could demand additional cuts from other ministries. Lavon wouldn't budge.

[- - -]

Ziama told me about his visit to Sde Boker. He found BG worried about the state of affairs at the highest echelons of leadership at the Defense Ministry.[3] It had to do with a disposition towards irregular activities and playing with fire which even the CoS viewed as too extreme and was attempting to restrain. BG was evidently following Army affairs closely (that is, from a distance).[4] He was willing to take part

2 For a revealing account of earlier Cabinet discussions of this sensitive question, see Gidi Weitz, "Ben-Gurion in 1951: Only the Death Penalty Would Deter Jews from Gratuitous Killing of Arabs," *Ha'aretz*, April 1, 2016, http://www.haaretz.com/israel-news/.premium-1.712125.

3 CoS Dayan and Defense Minister Lavon did not get along well, and their relations would soon deteriorate, prompting Dayan to offer his resignation. See Dayan, *Story of My Life*, 220-21; Shabtai Teveth, *Ben-Gurion's Spy: The Story of the Political Scandal That Shaped Modern Israel* (New York: Columbia University Press, 1996), 150.

4 Dayan and the Defense Ministry's DG, Shimon Peres, were in the habit of paying regular visits to Ben-Gurion in Sde Boker, and reported to him on the evolving situation within the Army, the Defense Ministry, as well as on political matters.

in the party's political deliberations if held in Be'er Sheva or Sde Boker.

I conferred with the DG and Gideon Rafael on the three main problems occupying us at this time on the foreign front: (a) Suez passage: went over the draft resolution that we were submitting to the Security Council and decided on its final formulation; (b) the conference in accordance with Article XII: went over the draft of the letter to the SG which Eban proposed and edited it;[5] (c) the Jordan [diversion] channel imbroglio: we clarified the course we should pursue with Bennike, pending the possibility of a resumption of talks. This last was a most wearying affair. Bennike had received instructions from the SG to be careful not to say anything that might be construed as confirmation of our assumption that only individual rights[6] were on the agenda, and that once they were assured we would then be free to resume work.

Zipporah and I heard some impressions from our niece, Ruth Hillel-Avigur, of her trip to Sde Boker. She and her parents toured the Negev this Saturday. Haggai Avriel of Sde Boker, younger brother of Ehud, told them exactly what I had feared. The kibbutz members consider themselves held captive by BG, the entire place lies under his shadow, their own sense of importance is gone, and all this for only a fleeting moment. Now the place is bustling and everyone comes to visit, but when the spirit moves BG to leave, it will be forgotten by all and remain isolated and remote and of no interest to anybody.

Sat over my papers till 1:00 am.

[- - -]

Monday, February 15

[- - -]

Had a short and sharp argument with Lavon on the plan for a Kinneret military operation.[7] It is interesting to note how sharp and skeptical he is as regards any diplomatic initiative – always willing to foresee the worst and to view every step taken in the foreign affairs front as damaging and dangerous – while every military adventure seems to him necessary, auspicious and far from being harmful. When I said to him that opening artillery fire on Syrian positions east of the Kinneret could lead to a counter-bombardment of Tiberias, he rejected it out of hand, arguing that Syria would certainly act cautiously. I could only wonder at the emotional roots of this peculiar confidence.

Afterwards there was a meeting of the Cabinet FADC with the participation of the CoS. Lavon submitted to the meeting the plan for "Operation Kinneret."

5 Eban to Rafael, February 13, 1954, ISA FM 130.16/2948/6.
6 Of local Arab landowners inside the DMZ.
7 In response to Syrian fishing in the lake.

It received a cold and most skeptical reaction. The GZ immediately announced that it was a matter for the entire Cabinet rather than the Committee only. Rosen and Shapira posed serious questions. Ziama and I refrained from taking a position for the time being. I pointed out the need to look into the legal aspect of the matter by means of an authoritative opinion. The matter itself was inextricably complicated. The Syrians have taken control of the northeastern sector of the Kinneret. Their boats fished in those waters, while our boats were being fired upon. We had no way of returning fire, for the adjacent shore was in their hands, whereas we can be defended from the far shore only by artillery fire. Opening any such fire would mean, to be sure, armed hostilities which would raise echoes throughout the world, condemning us again as the aggressors. On the other hand, not breaking through to the eastern shore would mean accepting as a fact Syrian control over a shore and waters that are not theirs. Appeals to the UN Observers had gained nothing. In response to our complaint, the head of the [Israeli-Syrian] MAC replied that we had best not approach the shore and try to reach a compromise. But an appeal to the SC may well make matters only worse. On matters pertaining to the Hula and the Jordan channel, the SC has upheld the proprietary rights of Arab landowners in these areas. And in truth they were merciful toward us, for the Russians had demanded that before work on the diversion was resumed, an Israeli-Syrian agreement had to be reached. According to this line of thinking,[8] a majority of the SC might confirm Syrian fishing rights in the Kinneret, disregarding a plain stipulation of the Armistice Agreement forbidding civilian movements beyond the cease-fire line. Once again, the Armistice Agreement was like a noose around our necks; worse – a serious breach of the border's wall at a spot of crucial importance.[9]

From the meeting I went straight to the Knesset. I submitted the amendment to the Independence Day Law for a first reading. This year it falls on *Shabbat*. The amendment prescribes advancing the holiday to the Thursday before rather than postponing it to the Sunday after, as was prescribed under the previous amendment. This would enable the Army to make all due preparations for the parade without violating *Shabbat*. What complications and upsets are caused by the observance

8 Recognizing traditional fishing rights of Syrian citizens respected in Mandatory Palestine.

9 At one point in the Cabinet FADC discussions, PM Sharett asked CoS Dayan: "Do you think that the Syrians would be prepared to end this matter peacefully if their rights in the days of the British Mandate were acknowledged? Do you see this as something possible, not as a part of a general settlement but as an ad hoc arrangement? Is such a thing favorable to us? Is it possible at all? Is it worthwhile on our part to tell them: 'Let us assess what were your fishing rights in the Kinneret, establish this as a continuation of the status quo ante, and then, clearly, we would fish too and no fishing would be interfered with?' Do you see this eventuality as beneficial and possible?" CoS Dayan replied in the negative, claiming it would amount to a one-way concession.

of the Jewish Sabbath! Yizhar Harari[10] of the Progressives found it necessary to uphold the dignity of the historic date and demanded that the proposed law be returned to the Cabinet. The religious party members – Yitzhak Raphael (*Hapo'el Hamizrahi*), Mordechai Nurock[11] (*Hamizrahi*), Shlomo Lorincz (*Agudat-Israel*) – were quick to defend an amendment meant to ensure *Shabbat* observance, lauded the government and the person of the PM, and poured fire and brimstone on Yizhar – deservedly. With quixotic valor, he alone voted against the passage of the amendment to committee.

[- - -]

At 8:00 pm I returned to the Knesset to attend the meeting of the committee elected at the last meeting of our [party's] Central Committee for the renewal of the party secretariat. [Listening to the various suggested nominations,] I warned against continuation of a conventional approach, showing us as being completely cut off from the new reality. I demanded the cooption of at least one member of the Eastern [i.e., North African and ME] communities. I denounced the fact that out of the ten committee members present only one was born in the country, seven out of the other nine were Russian-born and the other two were Polish-born. There was not one of German origin, nor one from Western Europe or the Anglo-Saxon countries, to say nothing of the multitudes of Middle-Eastern Jews who are members of our party. I argued bitterly and censured this old-age conservatism. In the end a committee – myself, Namir, Raphael Bash – was elected to formalize a general proposal. I have no choice but to involve myself deeply – among all other things – in the party's affairs. Where will the time come from?

It was quite a day – for God's sake, what a day! Back at home I sat for two more hours on my papers and diary and at long last plunged into a hot bath.

Tuesday, February 16

[- - -]

At 11:00 there was a meeting of the FADC regarding the evacuation of the Suez Canal Zone by the British Army. I reported on the course of developments and posed the problem. I made no revelations. One of the speakers later said, and rightly so, that we hold no trump cards in this matter. It is clear that we have no interest in the evacuation. It is also clear that we cannot say so outright, because such a statement would disgrace us in Egyptian eyes for an entire generation, would avail us nothing,

10 Yizhar Harari (1908-1978). Born in Palestine. Jurist. Member of the Supreme Command, served as chief justice, of the *Hagana*. MK, a leader of the Progressive Party. Later joined Mapai. Member of consecutive Israeli delegations to the UN.

11 Rabbi Mordechai Nurock (1884-1962). Born in Latvia, leader of Latvian Jewry. Settled in Palestine in 1947. MK, first for *Hamizrahi*, later for the National Religious Party.

and would provoke the ire of most of the British public. On the other hand, it is clear that we can help in postponing the evacuation and must do so. It is also clear that in the final analysis, if an agreement between Great Britain and Egypt is reached, we shall not be compensated by it. Above all, it is evident that such an agreement means a complete restructuring of relations between the Arab world and the West to our detriment, at least in the short term. Such a development demands serious counsel on our part. However, for the time being we are at a loss. True, one conclusion does suggest itself, and that is to seek closer relations specifically with Great Britain on the basis of some mutual benefit. But I was careful here and refrained from hinting as much before the Committee. The *Herut* representative demanded that we openly oppose the evacuation. The Mapam representative demanded that we openly support the evacuation. It was easy for me to condemn the idiocy and harm of both these extremes. The meeting lasted until 2:00.

Gideon came in the afternoon and reported on his "conversation" with Bennike. There was of course no conversation, in spite of the fact that the meeting was requested by the Dane. In fact, Gideon tried to elicit information from the man and he only stuttered and murmured, or just remained silent. The only thing he said was that he was now awaiting the arrival of the experts. To Gideon's question whether he would be ready to meet with me if I invited him, he answered in the positive. I retorted that I have no reason to invite him over, for if he came only to keep silent I would be humiliated by demonstrating that we were courting him while he was avoiding us. It would be best if we take it that the aim of yesterday's meeting was to inform us about the arrival of the experts. We shall meet with them and make a serious effort at bringing them over to our side. We shall see then what they report, and then decide on our future moves. We have no choice but to get through this phase of clearing up the technical matters with the experts.

[- - -]

Went down to the Knesset chamber for the debate on the abolition of the death penalty. It lasted two-and-a-half hours and was conducted on a very high level. It also created an atmosphere of mental and emotional strife. A brilliant and incisive speech was heard, even if not entirely logical and well considered, from Baruch Azaniah[12] in favor of the proposal supported by most of the ministers. Yizhar Harari delivered not a bad speech, also against abolition. There was a comprehensive and first-rate speech by Yaakov Shimshon Shapira[13] in favor of complete abolition. There was a thoroughgoing speech by [Pinhas] Rosen in the same direction. Finally,

12 Baruch Azaniah (Osnia) (1905-1994). Born in Russia. Settled in Palestine in 1933. Leader of Mapai and the *Ihud Hakvutsot Vehakibbutzim*. MK (1951-1969).

13 Yaakov Shimshon Shapira (1902-1993). Born in Russia. Settled in Palestine in 1924. Jurist. After establishment of the state, became DG of the Ministry of Justice and first legal advisor to Government. Mapai MK. Later Minister of Justice.

in keeping with the Knesset's incomprehensible custom, we were obliged to hear an endless string of party announcements, as though these weren't the continuation of the debate at all! In the vote, all the leftist and religious parties were united in opposition to the death penalty. Mapai, the GZ, the Progressive Zionists and *Herut* were divided. The result: 61:33 in favor of abolishing the death penalty.

At home we received for dinner Judge Joseph Proskauer. The Judge and his wife (they are touring around the world on a cruise and staying in Israel for two days), Samuel Kramer, the Jewish-American Arabist and educator, and his wife, Shlomo Ginossar,[14] and Justice Cheshin[15] and their wives, Arthur and Jeanette Lourie, Gershon Agron and Hermona Simon.[16] Old man Joe has aged even more. In his talk there was nothing new and nothing of interest – except for a few incisive and painful remarks he made about the impression left by Qibya and the praise he accorded Aubrey's performance [at the UN] during that bitter trial.

Wednesday, February 17

[- - -]

Thursday, February 18

[- - -]

12 noon at the Foreign Ministry: a consultation on the problem of Syrian fishing on the Kinneret. The DG, Rafael and others condemned with no little skill and acumen the sheer absurdity of the GS's proposal to bombard the Syrian shore with artillery fire.[17]

[- - -]

Friday, February 19

[- - -]

Saturday, February 20

Worked through the whole day except for open house at tea time in the company of our guests, and then continued till 1:00 am. The result was a huge pile of papers.

14 Shlomo (Ginsberg) Ginossar (1889-1968). Born in Russia, son of Ahad Ha'am. Settled in Palestine in 1922. Among the founders of the Hebrew University. Israel's first Minister to Italy (1949-1951).

15 Shneor Zalman Cheshin (1903-1959). Born in Palestine. Lawyer. District Court Judge (1937-1944). Member of Israel Supreme Court (1948-1959).

16 Wife of Michael Simon, Director of the MFA's Protocol Division.

17 For details, see *DFPI* 9, doc.75, 80.

During the day, Gideon telephoned to report that [UN SG Dag] Hammarskjöld[18] had finally summoned Jordan and ourselves to a conference in Jerusalem. Gideon praised the guess I had made as to the meaning of Hammarskjöld's tactic, which has now been substantiated in the most explicit way. From Abba's wired reports on his talks with the SG, I deduced that he is using a smart ploy as an easy way out of the complication towards both sides – towards Israel by convening the conference at all, towards Jordan by imposing a stalemate at its very start. The latter will be achieved by means of a deadlock over the agenda. Along comes Hammarskjöld's letter to us stipulating in advance that, if the two sides disagreed on the matter of the agenda, it would in that event be understood that the conference could not proceed.[19]

Sunday, February 21

[- - -]

I cabled my best wishes to Lorna Wingate, widow of General Orde Wingate, on her marriage to one John Smith, an estate owner near Edinburgh.[20]

[- - -]

At the second Cabinet meeting there ensued a big debate on the question of the activities undertaken by Christian missions. Should a law be passed against those who preach conversion by offering material benefit? Most of the Cabinet members spoke strongly against such a law. It would certainly create a negative impression in the world. This would be followed by the straining of relations with the Vatican and the Catholic Church. Lavon launched the opposition and I concluded it.

Conferred with Moshe Shapira on his travel plans to the US to explain [to the orthodox community] the matter of the National Service Law and to counteract the accusations of [American Ultra-orthodox] denigrators of the State of Israel. They are exploiting the waves of bitterness and distrust aroused in the Orthodox community.

[- - -]

In the evening I summoned Murik,[21] *Davar*'s political correspondent in Jerusalem, and instructed him to denounce the stratagem hidden in the UN SG's letter to us, in which he asks us to convene the meeting with the Jordanians only

---

18 Dag Hammarskjöld (1905-1961). Secretary-General of the United Nations from April 1953 until his death in a plane crash while on a peace mission in the Congo.

19 For the February 18 correspondence exchanged between Hammarskjöld, the Foreign Minister of Jordan, and Israel's Permanent Representative at the UN, see UN Document S/3180, February 19, 1954. Cf. *DFPI* 9, docs.73-74; Caplan, *Futile Diplomacy* III: 240-42.

20 See above, page 138 n.13.

21 Meir ("Murik") Bareli (1922-2004). Born in Lithuania. Settled in Palestine in 1926. Journalist and writer. Activist, younger echelon of Mapai leadership.

for the sake of lip service, but in practice to cause its failure by creating an insoluble controversy over the meeting's agenda.

Monday, February 22

Early in the morning a meeting of the Committee on *Shabbat* Work Approvals – myself, Moshe Shapira and Aran. In most cases we decided to give approval, overriding the opinion of Shapira, who wriggled helplessly under the pressure of the dictates of modern technology.

Today I carried out the first part of my plan to conduct visits to each ministry, to review its work and become acquainted with its key officials. I spent an hour and a half in the Ministry of Justice. Pinhas Rosen gathered the heads of departments in his office. He and Attorney-General Haim Cohn and DG Yosef Kukya explained the substance of the Ministry's work and its division into departments. They also presented problems and needs. I asked many questions and encouraged the department heads to reply and explain. I learned a great deal and left much the richer. The Ministry's top echelon made a serious and professional impression.

At the Foreign Ministry Gideon came in to suggest that we invite Abba to Israel to represent us at the Article XII conference [with the Jordanians], should it be convened. I said that I did not relish the idea. First, because it would be an admission of the meagerness of our forces; as though there were nobody suited to represent us in the entire world except for Ambassador Eban. Not only was he our representative in Washington and at the UN, but he was also obliged to journey to Jerusalem to represent us here at an international conference. Second, because it would not be seemly vis-à-vis Abba himself – as though we were trying to pin the burden of the conference on him, and enjoining him to extricate us out of trouble after getting us into it. I decided that the DG would be chief representative and Gideon his deputy. To be sure, a high-ranking staff officer must also be enlisted.

Asked Yaacov Herzog to go to his father, Chief Rabbi Herzog, to obtain another statement from him on the National Service Law [pertaining to women]. In his telegram to the US, which was very effective, he protested against the demonstrations. What is now needed is an expression of satisfaction at the way the government is handling the implementation of the law.

Later at 3:00 pm there was a meeting of the Cabinet FADC. I reviewed the state of affairs regarding the Article XII conference, the Security Council debate on Suez passage and Eilat, and the Jordan [diversion] channel problem. I obtained authorization from the Committee to send a ship under a foreign flag from Haifa to Eilat with a regular cargo, and for pursuing the purchase of a ship that would receive its Israeli flag at an East African port and sail from there to Eilat. These two acts will test the Egyptians during the course of the SC debate.

At 4:00 I went to the Knesset, and listened to Eshkol's speech presenting the budget, a speech full of content but devoid of all brilliance. It was a realistic analysis and a vivid description of the situation, but it lacked a sense of balance and suffered certain shallowness in wording. The liveliest and most sparkling part was about agriculture. I whispered to Ziama, "Agriculture was and is the poetry of Eshkol's life." Indeed, he spoke with fervor about the new wave of settlement, rising productivity and production levels, discoveries of new sources of water, and irrigation plans. I said to Ziama, "Let's see what he says about industry." At that moment Eshkol concluded the passage on agriculture and said: "As regards industry, ..." I cocked my ear. On the subject of industry, Israel's Finance Minister uttered exactly two sentences, and then went on to another subject.

[- - -]

Tuesday, February 23

Worked all morning at the Foreign Ministry.

Yesterday Walter told me the following tale. Mira Avrech of *Yediot Ahronot*, a journalist who makes gossip her profession, told him that she knew absolutely everything about the fishing imbroglio in the Kinneret, and the problem of using artillery against the Syrians. Walter was amazed at what he heard. After applying a great deal of pressure he managed to extract from her how she had found out. [Interior Minister Israel] Rokach had revealed the matter from top to bottom at a party held for him at the Ramat Gan municipality, and one of his listeners had enlightened her. After this, how can one trust one's colleagues on the Cabinet FADC, where he is required not to reveal matters which are not even brought before the entire Cabinet due to their high degree of secrecy? I wrote Rokach a short note, polite though quite to the point. I confronted him with the facts of which I had been informed and warned him henceforward.

In *Haboker* I saw the disclosure of a question posed by Yosef Serlin to Dov Yosef during the last Cabinet meeting. This was no longer an indiscretion or a slip of the tongue, or plain contempt for secret political information from a lack of education, but plain and simple villainy. I wrote Serlin, but what is the use? What's the use! These people are beyond any hope.

[- - -]

Wednesday, February 24

[- - -]

Pinhas Sapir came in at my invitation for a thorough discussion of the government budget. Are our straits as dire as they are purported to be? Were the cuts in the Foreign Ministry budget to which I agreed for lack of another choice really necessary? He described the situation to me in abundant detail. His principal conclusion was that we are on the verge of a great disaster. He contended that Lavon has exaggerated the figures already pared from the defense budget. He went on to prove that substantial sums from this budget can still be saved. As to the Foreign Ministry, I once again discovered that we haven't succeeded in erasing the impression of excessive comfort in the service, as regards both the number of people and their terms of employment. In any event, this discussion with Sapir was meant to prepare me for a serious meeting with the senior staff of the Foreign Ministry. We must examine our internal situation strictly and tighten our belts to the utmost. We should also embark on an internal campaign aimed at the Finance Ministry, the Knesset's Finance Committee and key figures in the press towards changing perceptions of the Foreign Ministry and forging an awareness of it as a service of special importance and equal to the IDF in terms of national security.

[- - -]

From 11:00 until 12:30 I had an uninterrupted chain of meetings at the Knesset. [- - -] Among them was Yaakov Riftin, who was very concerned over the political path Lavon was treading as Defense Minister. He and his colleagues in the leadership of Mapam had profound differences with me, but they had faith that I would not be given to militaristic recklessness.[22] That by itself was not enough to create a political partnership between us; however, as citizens of the state, they were reassured to a certain degree. Lavon was a different story altogether. As an example, he [Riftin] quoted one expression that [Lavon] recently uttered in a speech to new cadets at their graduation ceremony: "Let us look forward to a renewed assault." Although there was one newspaper that innocently interpreted this statement as referring to a Second Round initiated by the Arabs, those blessed with sophisticated antennas well understood that it meant an assault on our part, and there was more of the same.

[- - -]

From the Knesset I went to the Foreign Ministry. Walter expressed his concern over the deterioration of relations between Gideon and the IDF people. They have no faith in him whatsoever. It is enough that he is the initiator of a proposal for the military to reject and strenuously oppose it. After this encouraging start, I went

22 Until his resignation in February 1955, Lavon's adventurist tendencies, intemperate statements, and devious behavior would continue to create friction and distrust within the military establishment and among his Cabinet colleagues, not to mention considerable embarrassment among Mapai leaders. Those closest to him were also aware of his mental instability and alcoholism. For details, see: Dayan, *Story of My Life*, 219-21; Teveth, *Ben-Gurion's Spy*, 66-67, 136-37, 150; Morris, *Israel's Border Wars*, 229, 293-94; Kafkafi, *Pinhas Lavon - Anti-Messiah*, 242.

into consultation with Walter and Gideon pending our afternoon meeting with the IDF on the agenda for the conference with Jordan in accordance with Article XII.

At 4:00 in the afternoon the consultation with the IDF was held. Lavon, Dayan, Fati and Lt.-Colonel Shalev. With me from the Ministry were Walter, Gideon, Arthur Lourie and Arye Levavi. The meeting was interspersed with sparks of tension. Opposition to Gideon's proposals was palpable at every stage of the discussion. Nonetheless, in the end, I guided the consultation towards some concerted conclusions.[23]

At 9:00 pm, after several hours of work at home, we went to the Edison [Hall] to see [Hebrew version of Shaw's] "Pygmalion". I have long wavered about going – what a shame to give up an evening's work – but Zipporah beseeched me and, what's more, I had promised the Cameri Theater director that I would attend, so I consented to the "sacrifice." All in all I did not regret it. First of all, it's a flaw in my erudition to have no idea of Pygmalion and what it's all about – I had never read it, nor attended a performance in England, and have not even seen the movie. Second, the acting was superb. The actress Hanna Meron surpassed all my expectations. They say she flew over to London for two days just to see how the part of that flower girl was being played on the English stage.

Thursday, February 25

A short while after arriving at the PMO this morning, the Foreign Ministry called to inform me that General Mohammed Neguib had been deposed and Gamal Abd al-Nasser had proclaimed himself Prime Minister. News of Neguib's declining prominence had accumulated over the past weeks, making clear that Gamal was holding the reins of power with a firm hand. Nevertheless the changeover came as a complete surprise. How are the mighty fallen! [24]

At 12:15 I set out with Zipporah to Rehovot for a lunch at Mrs [Vera] Weizmann's in honor of Prince George of Denmark and his wife. The princely wife is a cousin of the Queen Mother of England. The royal couple made a most pleasant impression. The Prince asked me about Bennike. I painted his person with no undue adornment. Lavon and his wife were present too. In the middle of the meal I was called to the telephone. Gideon announced that a revolt against Adib Shishakli had broken out in Syria. One of the commanders in the north had seized control of Aleppo and proclaimed from its broadcasting station that Shishkali had to leave within 24 hours, otherwise the rebellious provinces in the north and east would be torn from Syria. This threat most probably connoted joining with Iraq. In general, there were indications that the revolt was being organized from Baghdad. I came back with the news and everyone became excited. "Awake, O North wind,

---

23 Summary of the consultation is in *DFPI* 9, doc.86.

24 *II Samuel*, 1:27.

and come, thou South"![25] This time, though, in reverse order.

After the meal, Pinhas Lavon took me aside and began to cajole me. This was a providential time to take action; this is the time to move and seize the Syrian border positions beyond the DMZ. Syria was falling apart. The country with which we struck an Armistice Agreement no longer existed. At any rate, its government was falling and there was no other. Furthermore, Iraq had in effect entered Syria. This was a historic opportunity that we should not let pass.

I recoiled at this impetuous idea and saw ourselves on the verge of a potentially disastrous adventure. I wondered whether Lavon was indeed proposing to act immediately and was shocked to realize this was so. I said that if Iraq entered Syria militarily, that would constitute a revolutionary transformation which would demand and even justify far-reaching conclusions. However, for the time being it was no more than a threat. It was by no means a fact. It was not even clear that Shishakli would actually be removed. He might perhaps hold his ground. We had to wait and see how things developed before making any decision.

Lavon repeated that time was precious, and that we had to act. Who knew if we would be offered another such opportunity? I again replied that, under the circumstances, I could not give my consent to any action of the kind he was suggesting. In the end I said that, since we would be at BG's in Sde Boker together on Saturday for deliberations about Party affairs, let us consult with BG then about whether anything was to be done and what. I saw that he was very dissatisfied with the delay, but he agreed for lack of any other sensible choice. Nevertheless, I was indeed alarmed by this certainty that we were facing armed Iraqi intervention in Syria, and that events were about to take place that would demand an active course on our part.

When we returned home toin Tel Aviv, I gave up my rest and composed an announcement for the MFA Spokesman which I dictated over the telephone to Gideon in Jerusalem. It contained a phrase on the Iraqi intervention and the conclusions stemming from it for us, since Iraq was a country with which we have no armistice agreement, etc. I stipulated that this phrase should not be included unless Iraq's interference was confirmed by another authoritative source. We must not be the first to propagate this version, for by doing so we would draw suspicion towards us and, in so doing, kill it by our own hand. Gideon said that indeed there was no confirmation of it.

[- - -]

Sat over my papers all evening. I telephoned Jerusalem several times inquiring for news of Syria. The last report said that Shishakli was sending an army unit to the north. That means he didn't capitulate and events had not yet been decided.

---

25 *Song of Solomon*, 4:16.

I agreed to withhold the announcement.

[- - -]

Friday, February 26

Shishakli's gone! Done and finished. Headlines in the press speak about his surrender and flight from Damascus. No one really knows where.

Isser [came by] with a bundle-full [of intelligence], as usual.

[- - -]

Tomorrow, Saturday, had been originally designated for an "outing" to Sde Boker. This is how it came about. BG was approached and asked to help to prepare the party conference by participating in the meeting of the 21-member committee chosen for the purpose. He agreed on two conditions: the 21 would convene in Be'er Sheva, and their meeting would be preceded by a limited consultation at Sde Boker with myself, Aran, Lavon, Namir, Ami Assaf[26] and Aryeh Bahir.[27] This discussion was scheduled for Saturday. I was quite annoyed at the prospect of these six people compelled to make this long trip at the expense of giving up their day of rest. Especially me, who is working under such heavy burden, but I kept quiet. With events in the north [Syria] coinciding with those in the south [Egypt], Lavon turned to BG and suggested that he come to Tel Aviv. It was a great relief. The meeting was scheduled for 10:00, but Lavon suggested that the two of us and Dayan meet with BG half an hour earlier to discuss the situation.

Saturday, February 27

At 9:00 am Israel Kasztner[28] came by. He has been testifying lately in a libel case held on the initiative of the Attorney-General, Haim Cohn, defending himself against one Malkiel Gruenwald, who has accused him of cooperating with the Nazis in Hungary while trying to save Jews from extermination; his lawyer is

26 Ami Assaf (1903-1963). Born in Palestine. Leader of the moshavim organization. Member of Mapai CC; MK 1949-1963 and member of the FADC. Later, Deputy Minister of Education and Culture.

27 Aryeh Bahir (1906-1970). Born in Russia. Settled in Palestine in 1924. A leader of the kibbutz movement. Mapai MK (1949-1951, 1955-1959). In 1965 left Mapai with BG to form his splinter party, Rafi.

28 Israel (Rudolph, Rezso) Kasztner (1906-1957). Jewish-Hungarian journalist and lawyer. A leader of the Budapest Aid and Rescue Committee for Jewish refugees. Among other things, Kasztner negotiated with Adolf Eichmann to allow more than 1,600 Jews to leave for Switzerland on what became known as the "Kastzner train" in exchange for money, gold and diamonds. Moved to Israel after the war, becoming a spokesman for the Ministry of Trade and Industry in 1952.

the notorious Shmuel Tamir.[29] The problem is how to widen the general basis of Kasztner's testimony in order to prove his innocence clearly. I suggested involving Ehud Avriel in this matter.[30]

At 9:30, after a two-minute walk from our flat on Hayarkon Street, I reached BG's home. He himself hadn't arrived yet. His plane was late. I spent half an hour in the company of Paula and their daughter Renana. He finally arrived, wearing winter khaki, exuding health and vigor but quite aged in appearance. We went upstairs, Lavon and Dayan with us. The chill of the lifeless library enveloped us; neither did the ensuing discussion warm the heart. Lavon and Dayan described what had happened in Syria as an undisputed Iraqi ploy. In spite of this, Lavon opted for a meeker course and, instead of the seizure of hills in Syrian territory, merely proposed that in the meantime the IDF enter the DMZ. BG's approval of the proposal came like lightning. I began asking questions to clarify what would happen if we did so. Would we open fire? No, we wouldn't. What would happen if the Syrians opened fire? Lavon tried to count on them not to, since Damascus was now immersed in other worries. I said that it was reckless to assume that the Syrians would idly watch us enter forbidden territory to which they lay claim almost as much as we do. At this point BG said that of course we would return fire. And what would happen if the Syrians on their part entered various sections of the DMZ? Then we would shoot at them. Would this mean war, then? A shrugging of shoulders instead of an answer. Dayan, for his part, developed this line of thought

29 Shmuel Tamir (1923-1987). Jurist. Served in the *Irgun* and was exiled to Kenya in 1947-1948. Founding member and MK of the *Herut* Party. Made a name as advocate in several famous anti-establishment trials.

30 Kasztner was testifying in criminal case 124/53 – State of Israel v. Malkiel ben Menachem Gruenwald – which opened in Jerusalem District court on January 1, 1954. In August 1952, Kasztner had been publicly accused of having been a Nazi collaborator during his service as head of the Rescue Committee in Budapest. The trial immediately took on a sharp partisan-political hue because Kasztner was a Mapai Party member and government official, while Gruenwald was a Hungarian-born *Hamizrahi* political activist and his lawyer, Shmuel Tamir, was a Revisionist activist who made special efforts to litigate against members of the Mapai Party.

The trial lasted 18 months, during which time Sharett's Mapai Party was vigorously attacked under the general accusation of having uncaringly abandoned European Jewry to their fate under the Nazis. The verdict, handed down on June 22, 1955, acquitted Gruenwald and publicly chastized Kasztner (see below, entry for June 22, 1955). The judgment was appealed in a case which opened in January 1957; Kasztner was murdered two months later by two former *LEHI* assailants. See, e.g., Yechiam Weitz, *The Man who was Murdered Twice: The Life, Trial and Death of Israel Kasztner*, transl. Chaya Naor, Jerusalem: Yad Vashem, 2011; Tom Segev, *The Seventh Million: The Israelis and the Holocaust* (New York: Hill & Wang, 1993), part V; Yechiam Weitz, "Mapai and the 'Kastner Trial'," in *Israel: The First Decade of Independence*, eds. S. Ilan Troen and Noah Lucas (Albany: State University of New York Press, 1995), 195-210; Ben Hecht, *Perfidy*, [New York: Julian Messner, 1961] republished Jerusalem & Hewlett NY: Gefen, 1999.

in arguing that we would not be able to enter all three DMZ sections because there were some, such as El Hama, which would become death-traps for us. Also, in other sections, too, if battle erupted, we would be forced to advance into Syrian territory to seize strongholds and hold ground.

I announced that I was against the whole plan, which was bound to end in ignoble failure. It would be a provocation of the Security Council. We might perhaps invoke the real threat of a tripartite resolution against us.[31] We would eventually be forced to retreat in disgrace. The three contended that our entry was justified in view of the unruly situation in Syria. We were doing nothing but protecting our own border regions, all the more so since we have always declared the DMZs to be Israeli territory and this was the time to make it a *fait accompli*. BG added that we should accompany our entry there with an explanation, and suggested saying that we are doing so "for the time being," in order to leave us an avenue of retreat if there is no other choice. He, at least, took into account the possibility of SC intervention against us. But wasn't it clear to him that such intervention was inevitable?

I felt stifled, battling alone against the three of them. I sought refuge. I said: "In any event, no decision can be made in regard to this question except with Cabinet approval. Let's raise the matter at the meeting tomorrow morning." Gloom settled upon Pinhas' face. He understood that this would put an end to it. He looked to BG. I turned to BG and said: "Would you have decided such a question when you were PM without bringing it before the Cabinet?" He mumbled something which I was at liberty to take as consent.

I must add that at the start of the conversation, when Lavon was reviewing the situation and possible courses of action, he noted as one of the feasible plans a thrust from the Negev to the seashore south of the Gaza Strip in order to cut it off from Egypt. BG rejected any thought of provoking Egypt and suggested we concentrate this time on action against Syria.

BG opened another front. Now was the time to arouse Lebanon – i.e., its Maronite Christians – to declare a Christian state. I said that it was an idle dream. The Maronites were divided into different communities. Those advocating Christian separatism were the weakest, and wouldn't dare do a thing. A Christian Lebanon would mean the concession of Tyre and its surroundings, of Tripoli and the Lebanon Valley. No power could return Lebanon to its pre-WWI dimensions, all the more so since it would then forfeit its economic viability.

BG's response was furious. He began arguing the historic justice of a limited Christian Lebanon. If it should become fact, the Christian powers wouldn't dare to oppose it. I argued that there is no force on earth that can bring about such a fact and that, if we start fomenting and encouraging it, we will become entangled in an

31 Reference is to a condemnation in the UN SC jointly drafted and sponsored by the US, France and Britain, as happened in October-November 1953 following Israel's raid on Qibya.

adventure which can only bring ignominy upon us. At this point there burst forth a torrent of rebuke against [my] lack of daring and narrow-mindedness. Emissaries must be sent and money thrown in. I said there was no money. The reasoned reply was that this was nonsense. The money must be found, if not from the Finance Ministry then from the JA(!). For such an objective it was legitimate to gamble a hundred thousand dollars, half a million, a million – anything so long as the job gets done. Afterwards a major reorganization of the Middle East would follow, and a new era would begin.[32] I tired of battling against the whirlwind. I was rescued from my predicament by the *haverim* who arrived for the party consultation.

[- - -]

After the consultation, when the *haverim* got up to go, I pulled BG over to a corner and said: "Take note that, for the time being, in the *coups* that have taken place, both in Egypt and in Syria, not one shot has been fired nor one drop of blood shed. If we enter the DMZ, the shooting will start and we will have been found to be the ones who started it. We will ostensibly justify our entry as a safety measure to ensure peace and security. But the result will be that we will have provoked an international armed conflict. Headlines the world over will portray Israel as an aggressor always willing to play with the fire of war."

I thought that I had made a powerful statement that was irrefutable – but not so! BG betrayed no emotional inclination to be impressed by the vista I had painted. "Will we be the aggressors? No, it will be the Syrians who shall open fire! Why, they and not we would be to blame!" I contended that we would appear to be the instigators and hence will have to pay the price. He wouldn't accept this, but repeated the same litany. I let him go, utterly dejected. I said to myself: At long last I'm PM and not he. This time I shall impose my will in the framework of my official capacity.

---

32 On February 27, Ben-Gurion wrote to Sharett to elaborate on his arguments in favor of supporting Maronite elements with a view to creating a "friendly" Christian Lebanese state on Israel's northern frontier. This provoked a lengthy reply, reproduced below, entry for March 18, 1954.

Critics of Israel's penchant for interfering in the internal politics of neighboring states welcomed publication of these letters when they appeared in the 1978 Hebrew edition of Sharett's diary – and cited this historical evidence increasingly following Israel's 1982 invasion of Lebanon. See Livia Rokach, "Israeli State Terrorism: An Analysis of the Sharett Diaries," *Journal of Palestine Studies* 9:3 (Spring 1980), 3-28; Livia Rokach, *Israel's Sacred Terrorism: A Study Based on Moshe Sharett's Personal Diary and other Documents*. Foreword by Noam Chomsky (Belmont: Arab-American University Graduates Press, 3rd edition, 1986), chs.4-5.

In late 1956, while preparing to join with the French and British in launching the Sinai Campaign, Ben-Gurion would again return to his idea of a comprehensive plan for "reshaping" the Middle East. See "Ben-Gurion's Diary: The Suez-Sinai Campaign," translated and annotated by S. Ilan Troen, in *The Suez-Sinai Crisis, 1956: Retrospective and Reappraisal*. Eds. Selwyn Ilan Troen and Moshe Shemesh (London: Frank Cass, 1990), 306.

I walked back to my flat with Ziama Aran, who wanted to talk about his difficulties as a minister. On the way I told him about the debate, starting with the exchange with Lavon at Vera Weizmann's on Thursday and ending with my last private conversation with BG. He was aghast and severely critical, especially of Lavon. He contended, as though from personal experience, that the latter had periods of demented judgement and posed a serious danger as Defense Minister.[33]

[- - -]

Sat over my papers all afternoon and intermittently reflected about the problem of an invasion of the DMZs. As usual with me, after being pounced upon with some unusual proposal, only some time after the initial shock does my mind clear and my real responses, considered and reasoned, begin to take shape. I came to the clear-cut conclusion that this proposal is sheer folly and madness, and that I shall bury it with due rites at the Cabinet meeting tomorrow. I telephoned Lavon and informed him that the more I think about his idea, the less I am favorably impressed by it.

Set out for Jerusalem at close to 6:00. We had just left the city when my driver asked whether I would like to hear the news. I said certainly. He switched on the 6:15 news broadcast. I heard some more about the continuing turmoil in Syria between north and south. Finally the newswoman announced: "Here is a report that has just arrived from the news desk. In Cairo, the Revolutionary Council has decided to return General Neguib to the presidency of the country." Just yesterday, they reviled and scourged him like a beaten corpse, and bragged that in their great mercy they had not shot him with the bullet he deserved. Now they reinstate him as their leader, albeit, most certainly, with the powers of an Israeli president. At any rate they must have realized that without him it would not work. What a demonstration of seriousness, consistency and perseverance!

Back home, I asked Walter and Gideon to come by and told them about the idea of entering the DMZs. I explained my reasons against, and they added more of their own.[34]

Sunday, February 28

According to the morning papers, things in Syria have begun to stabilize with the capitulation of the south to the north and the placing of pan-Syrian authority in the hands of the elderly president, Hashim al-Atassi.[35] The age of this President, who had once been the mutassarif[36] of Acre in the days of Ottoman rule in Palestine,

33 Lavon was known to have a drinking problem.

34 See also Sharett to Eban and Shiloah, February 27, 1954, *DFPI* 9, doc.94.

35 Hashim al-Atassi (1875-1960). Syrian nationalist, statesman and President (1936-1939, 1949-1951, 1954-1955).

36 Ottoman governor.

is a symbol of the vitality and freshness of the new regime now being established upon the ruins of Shishakli's tyranny.[37]

Lavon came into my room before the Cabinet meeting with drawn face. I said: "You no doubt accuse me of having missed our chance." He said: "Yes." I replied: "We have been spared a great misfortune. How can you fail to understand that a clash with Syria would have been an attack on the UN? Why, the DMZs are under UN authority even by our own admission! This and more. If Iraq, indeed, has organized the northern revolt, then she played her cards very skillfully. Iraq is remaining behind the scenes, giving no one an opportunity to lay the blame on her. But if we had invaded the DMZs, we would have brought the Iraqi army into Syria by our own hand. We would also have quickly united the forces fighting among themselves over Shishakli's inheritance and breathed new life into the Arab League, to which the pro-Hashemite coup in Syria may well have given a fatal blow. These would have been the "positive" results of the adventure. The negative result would have been ignominious retreat and our standing in the DMZs would have been further undermined after a failed attempt to seize control."

The entire Cabinet meeting was devoted to an inquiry into the course of events in Syria and Egypt. I began with a detailed clarification that took a whole hour. The debate lasted two hours. No proposal of action was heard, but the subject of the debate was whether we had missed an opportunity or not. Lavon argued that we had missed a rare opportunity to strengthen our position. I said that we had missed an opportunity to get into trouble. Lavon explained that specifically because prospects were gloomy, and the US was about to betray us and enter into an alliance with the Arab world which will in any event be aimed against Israel, it was incumbent upon us to make a show of strength before it was too late, and demonstrate to the US that it was a life-or-death matter for us, so it wouldn't dare [proceed in that direction].

My reply was that this calculation was too complicated for the simple minds of the gentiles in Washington. Had we invaded the DMZs, they would not have seen it as a demonstration against their plans to integrate the Arab world in their defense planning, all the more when these plans are completely legitimate in the eyes of American public opinion. Rather, they would have viewed the action as indicative of our scheme to exploit a time of tumult in the Middle East for conquest and expansion, and as an out-and-out confirmation of the suspicions and accusations held against us by a wide circle. I added that, without our intervention, the upheavals would remain in the nature of internal developments in each of the two countries [Syria and Egypt] It is only our stepping out of bounds that would precipitate an international conflict, which will arouse international concern and resentment. Our disregard of the possibility of the application of the [1950]

37 See *DFPI* 9, doc.93.

Tripartite Declaration[38] was also quite astounding, and testified to a frightening superficiality in the assessment of the risks awaiting us if we are not careful.

I was supported in the argument by all my colleagues except for Serlin, who also contended that this was an auspicious time to take action, but he was in favor of a southern operation against the Gaza Strip rather than against the northern DMZs. In my reply I tore into this reckless man, who would exploit even as grave a situation as this for a despicable gamble.

[- - -]

A report in *Ma'ariv* has it that because of events in the neighboring countries, BG came to Tel Aviv for secret consultations with Lavon and the CoS. I immediately felt there would be an uproar over this.[39]

Monday, March 1

Matters have apparently calmed down in Syria, although a new government hasn't yet been formed. The morning newspapers repeat the story of BG's having secretly met with the CoS and the Defense Minister. My name wasn't mentioned.[40]

[- - -]

At the Foreign Ministry, a consultation was held on conclusions regarding the military alliance about to be signed by Turkey and Pakistan, following the US decision to grant the latter military aid. Pakistan's PM has declared that his government won't forget its duty towards the Muslims of Palestine and North Africa. Turkey immediately disavowed this declaration and also notified us that the disavowal refers to us. Nevertheless, Turkey supports Iraq's joining. Herein lie our differences and collision with her. Clearly, we cannot set out on a full-scale campaign against the arming of Pakistan. US Jewry will certainly not join us in this battle. But we must aim all our arrows at the arming of Iraq. Here we can make headway. All the same, we must strengthen our relations with Turkey at all levels – commerce, culture and military contacts. The Defense Ministry's decision to eliminate the military attaché post in Ankara at this specific time is a serious error and we must insist upon maintaining it.

[- - -]

38 For the text of the Tripartite Declaration, see WebDoc #1.

39 This is one of many indications that, owing to political and Party balance-of-power considerations, Sharett could not ignore BG's overwhelming authority, even with BG ostensibly in retirement, especially on matters of national security importance. Thus, against his will, Sharett had to accommodate himself to BG's various interventions. Sharett and others were well aware that not only was BG watching him closely and constantly following events, but also that the "Old Man" was almost certainly weighing a comeback.

40 Cf. above, entry for February 27.

Tuesday, March 2

[- - -]

At the Foreign Ministry I received two Orthodox rabbis from the US. They are emissaries from the Rabbinical Council who have come to look into matters pertaining to the National Service Law, in particular, and the position of religion in the country in general. Two well-built, muscular, clean-shaven young men, speaking excellent Hebrew, and with all that Americans in every respect, especially the one who is President of the Council, Theodore Adams[41] by name, who is a native-born American. They told me wonders about the revival of tradition in the lives of American Jewry, the allure of religion with the awakening of national consciousness, the rise in stature of the Orthodox synagogue, the reinforcement of the most pious with the influx of refugees from the remainder of Eastern Europe, the creation of an Ultra-Orthodox center in Brooklyn's Williamsburg, the growth of *yeshivot* in various cities all over the continent and much more. It was merely a courtesy visit and there is a meeting planned with them at the end of their tour, when we shall go into matters in-depth.

[- - -]

Wednesday, March 3

Meeting of the Knesset Foreign Affairs and Defense Committee at 11:00. I spoke at length on the course of developments in Syria and Egypt leading to the current crisis. Here, too, the whole debate turned on whether an opportunity had been missed or not. The castigators were the *Herut* people, of course, though they did not say clearly say what should have been done. Yaakov Riftin praised our restraint and refusal to follow the advice of adventurers. A *Herut* man brought up the question of the consultation with BG. This has spread throughout the press, and has given rise to a wave of stinging interpretations which are neither to BG's credit nor my own.

[- - -]

The [Knesset] debate over the Foreign Ministry budget was resumed in the afternoon. Menachem Begin[42] delivered a stupendous speech, wholly devoted to

---

41 Theodore L. Adams (1915-1984). Born in Bangor, Maine. Orthodox Rabbi. President, Rabbinical Council of America (1952-1954), later President of the Synagogue Council of America.

42 Menachem Begin (1913-1992). Born in Russia (today's Belarus). Settled in Poland and became an active member of the Revisionist Party. Upon the Nazi occupation of Poland in 1939, succeeded in escaping to Soviet Russia. Arrived in Palestine in 1942 as a soldier of the National Polish Army, organized in Soviet Russia. Since 1943 Commander of the *Irgun* (above, page 48 n.50) and since 1948 leader of the *Herut* Party. Later, Israel PM (1977-1983).

censure of our foreign policy – a thorough balance sheet, so to speak, of my sinful deeds ever since the establishment of the state. He visited upon me the iniquity of Israel's vote in the UN [in November 1949] in favor of Libyan independence as well as my declaration in Washington that US friendship with Israel did not automatically compel her to be hostile towards the Arabs, and so on and so forth.[43]

Despite its bombastic nature, the speech was restrained. It was devoid of the Begin-esque unruliness to which the Knesset has become accustomed. It seems that, upon coming back from his trip abroad, he has decided to try a new tenor of speech in the Knesset, more restrained and civilized. The debate ended, but owing to lack of time my answer was postponed until next Monday. So much the better, because I will have enough time to prepare well and phrase my answer meticulously.

[- - -]

Thursday, March 4

[- - -]

Conferred with Gideon Rafael on our agenda with [UNTSO CoS] Bennike: a response to his injurious report,[44] preparations for the technical consultations over the Jordan channel project, handling of the David Horowitz committee's report on the compensation for abandoned Arab land-holdings, and more.

[- - -]

The entire evening at my Hayarkon Street apartment was devoted to my papers. It was punctuated with two visits. Moshe Keren of *Ha'aretz* came to ask the meaning of the consultation with BG. He had thought to write about the subject and warn against the constitutional impropriety of this trespassing on the part of a "has-been." When I explained to him the chain of events leading up to it, he calmed down and agreed to hold back his censure. The other visitor was Fati Harkabi whom I invited for a talk in an attempt to untangle the new complications surrounding Gideon Rafael's relations with the GS. What I heard from Fati was not encouraging. All the same, Fati tried to persuade me to invite the CoS himself from time to time for a personal talk. It was a rather tricky piece of advice. It raises

43 In late June and early July 1952, Sharett visited the US. During this visit he met with President Truman and also addressed the Philadelphia Conference on International Affairs on the subject of "Israel and the Middle East."

44 On February 24 Bennike had submitted a report to the UN SC on the situation regarding Israel's Armistice Agreements with Jordan, Egypt, Lebanon and Syria, including resolutions that had been brought to votes in the various MACs. Copy in ISA FM 130.02/2425/11. The Report's conclusions were critical enough to merit being reproduced in full as an appendix to Cmdr. E. H. Hutchison's anti-Israel book, *Violent Truce*, 175-93.

the question of trust within a framework of very complicated circumstances.[45]

Friday, March 5

Spent all morning at my Tel Aviv apartment. Eppy,[46] came by to tell me all about affairs behind the scenes at the Defense Ministry. He sees no benefit in Fati's advice to my holding personal meetings with Dayan. Relations between Lavon and Dayan are not all that good either. What purpose does God seek when he complicates and entangles relations among his own creations, yet commanding them to work together in concord and goodwill?

[- - -]

Later in the day I went with Zipporah to Jerusalem. Once home I telephoned Walter and unburdened myself about matters concerning the IDF and Gideon Rafael's relations with it. We both agreed that, with Joe Tekoah's return and assumption of responsibility for armistice affairs, there is bound to be a great relaxation of the daily tension vis-à-vis the military which will result in avoiding complications. All that the result of the IDF people's high regard for Joe.

[- - -]

Saturday, March 6

[- - -]

Went through Friday's newspapers and, lo and behold – a bombshell of a story following that consultation with BG: a far-reaching plan was tabled by BG to the Cabinet; in the course of the Cabinet deliberations opinions diverged and only two people, both of Mapai, supported it while all the others demurred and defeated it. I decided to publish a denial and explanation. I summoned *Davar*'s political correspondent and dictated my version to him.[47]

Sunday, March 7

[- - -]

In the afternoon I received Dr [Karl Taylor] Compton and his wife for an

---

45 For some indications of the complicated relations between Rafael, Dayan, Lavon, Sharett and members of the MFA, see: Gideon Rafael, *Destination Peace: Three Decades of Israeli Foreign Policy, A Personal Memoir* (New York: Stein and Day, 1981), 30-33; Dayan, *Story of My Life*, 219-21.

46 Ephraim ("Eppy") Evron (1920-1995). Born in Palestine. Joined MFA in 1949 and for a short time was Sharett's secretary. In 1951 was BG's secretary and in 1954 became Lavon's secretary. Later Israel Ambassador to Sweden, to Canada and to Washington.

47 Sharett's denial appeared in *Davar*, March 7, 1954, under the headline: "The Truth about the Meeting with BG in Tel Aviv."

interview. Compton is the President of MIT, the high technology school in Boston, which is considered the best of its kind in the world. He and his wife are guests of the Haifa Technion. Both are representatives of the best American type, highly intelligent and modest, and both are offspring of families of clergymen, well-versed in the Old Testament. The wife has especially showed signs of a spiritual upbringing.

All through the evening I worked on my reply speech for the Knesset tomorrow. While initially I meant to make do with preparing an outline, in fact I wrote up the speech almost in its entirety. [- - -] Later I went back and sat long after midnight writing up my speech, which cost me, as usual, some painful thinking and pangs of labor over finding the right expressions.

Monday, March 8

In the morning at the FM I translated the political part of my speech into English and Arthur edited it.

Until the very opening of the Knesset I worked on polishing my speech, as well as its English translation. I spoke for about an hour. People listened intently. The speech's weakness was its partition into two disconnected parts: the first on the Foreign Ministry budget and the second on foreign policy. There was no way out of this complexity and it had a bad effect on the flow of the speech. Still, the second part of the speech, which was the main one, came out tight and raised tension in the hall. I was under the impression that I had hit my target. The main thrust of the speech was to demolish the false claim of our "missing opportunities" [for territorial gains] in light of the coups and troubles in our neighboring countries.[48]

At night a late telephone call from the Chief Rabbi's Office. Rabbi Herzog wished to see me urgently. I said that the hour was already late, and set an interview with him at my home for tomorrow. A few minutes later the Rabbi himself called me: the Defense Ministry had issued a regulation to conscript *yeshiva* students against all previous custom and assurance. The uproar reaches to the heavens. A new scandal would break out abroad. I must stand in the breach. I said I knew nothing about the matter, and would look into it tomorrow and notify him.

Tuesday, March 9

[- - -]

The press was full of my speech.

The big news is the return of Neguib to the seat of the Presidency. It seems Nasser was mistaken in his speedy ousting.

48 For extracts of the speech, see WebDoc #5.

At the PMO I received a Hadassah[49] delegation – more than thirty women, filling up the room, all eager to hear the words of the living god.[50] I let myself go and the women were "deeply impressed, moved, thrilled," [in English] etc.

[- - -]

Arthur Lourie and Kozlov were summoned for a discussion of our oil purchasing policy. Kozlov was of the opinion, supported by Elath, that we had worn out the patience of the British too much because of our growing oil purchases from Russia. We had to take seriously the hinted threats about British oil companies leaving Israel. They were in any case being pressured by the Arab embargo against us, and if we went too far in this matter that might tilt the scales. If these companies left Israel, it could lead to extremely harmful results the world over – deterring investors, cutting-off commercial relations, serious economic isolation.

In the afternoon at the Knesset. No Cabinet meeting was held due to a misunderstanding in arranging it. Into the void thus created burst Cabinet member Moshe Shapira, shocked and infuriated by the new bomb tossed by Lavon – the conscription of *yeshiva* students. Last night some heads of *yeshivot* came to confer with him and stayed until three in the morning. Their agitation surpassed all proportions, as if the world collapsed over their heads. Had Lavon consulted with me before issuing the regulation? Why hadn't he consulted with him? Being colleagues in the government, one's actions most surely harms the other.

Why indeed?

The *Aguda* people also wished to see me but I made myself scarce.

Back at home I sat with the head of *Kol-Israel*'s Arabic Service over the translation of my Knesset speech into Arabic for its broadcast.

Ehud came for a consultation over the Kasztner case. It seems the Public Prosecutor [Haim Cohn] had not taken seriously enough this bombshell and had appointed for the prosecution a second-rate fellow, who is totally ignorant of the political and public ramifications of the subject and is constantly put down by Tamir, the hooligan lawyer. Haim Cohn must be told to add somebody clever and agile beside him.

[- - -]

At 10:30 went back to the Knesset for the meeting of our party members to discuss the law of religious judges. The Public Prosecutor, who is not a member of our party, was invited to attend as a lecturer and did a good job. The ensuing debate was lively and important. I made pertinent contributions to it, picturing, among other things, the background of the religious front which has been established in

49 The Women's Zionist Organization of America, founded by Henrietta Szold in 1912. Its mission is to "connect Jewish women and empower them to effect change through advocacy, advancing health and well-being, and support of Israel."

50 *Jeremiah,* 23:36.

the USA and the battle waged there not between us and the religious Jews, but between Zionists and Zionist-haters among American religious Jewry.

At 1:00 pm I went home, taking with me the Public Prosecutor. In the car I discussed with him the problem of the Kasztner case. He told me he had already appointed an adviser to the prosecutor.

Wednesday, March 10

Raucous publicity abounds in the press regarding a new coalition crisis due to Lavon's attempt to conscript *yeshiva* students. Just exactly what we – and I especially – need at this time.

[- - -]

At the MFA I listened to a detailed report by Daniel Lewin about his trip to Asia – India, Burma, Siam [now Thailand], Japan. David Hacohen is an excellent Minister, active and full of initiative, beloved by all around him. Diplomatic relations with Thailand are secured. Ties with India are far away as ever.

[- - -]

Thursday, March 11

American rabbis Theodore Adams and Bernard Segal[51] came for a topical discussion after having toured the country and scrutinized things from all sides. They were pleased with the Army's religious arrangements, amazed by the achievements of education in the national-religious school sector. They wonder why all these haven't been properly publicized among Orthodox Jewry in the US. All the same, they are very apprehensive as to the results of the National Service Law and begged that it be postponed.

A consultation with the DG and Gideon Rafael over final instructions to New York on the course to be taken in the SC on the matter of freedom of Israeli navigation in the Suez Canal and the Gulf of Aqaba. I determined our options as: (a) specify Suez and Eilat in the formulation of the proposal; (b) specify neither the one nor the other, but advocate a general formula of freedom of navigation or non-interference with shipping regardless of destination; (c) specify Suez and not mention Eilat at all. It stands to reason it is better not to mention Eilat than to mention it, and thereby have it governed by the Egypt-Israel Mixed Armistice Commission (EIMAC) framework, where certainly the whole matter would be buried for good. In this we are at odds with Eban, who contends that the lesser

51 Bernard Segal (1907-1984). Conservative rabbi and administrator. Executive Director and Executive Vice-President of the United Synagogue of America organization (1953-1976).

evil is to mention the matter of Eilat in the resolution, even if this means handling the subject over to the MAC. Once again, the difference between Abba and us is that he views the problem from a legalistic-formulistic standpoint, while we anticipate the whole course of developments in advance and are certain that surrendering the matter to Bennike means putting a lid on it. It shall be a loss mourned for generations.

Cabled to our London Embassy a detailed letter to James de Rothschild,[52] inviting him to Israel as a state guest for the re-interment ceremony of his father.[53]

I received for an interview a Danish journalist who is now touring the Middle East. In answering her clever questions I described to her the harmful approach of Bennike, resulting not from negative intentions but from his rigid character, narrow outlook and total lack of experience in political and international affairs.

[- - -]

---

52 James Armand de Rothschild (1878–1957). British Liberal MP (1929-1945), Zionist and philanthropist. Born in Paris, son of Baron Edmond de Rothschild. Served on General Allenby's staff in the Middle East during WWI and was seconded to the Zionist Commission (1918) as liaison officer. Became close with Moshe (then-)Shertok during the latter's years (1920-1923) studying in London. After 1924, directed the Palestine Jewish Colonization Association (PICA). Benefactor of the Hebrew University, archaeological excavations, and posthumously helped finance the construction of a new Knesset building in Jerusalem.

53 Baron Edmond James de Rothschild (1845-1934). Born in Paris. Philanthropist, art collector, and one of the earliest patrons of Jewish settlement in Palestine. Known as "*hanadiv hayadu'a*" (the Well-Known Benefactor), his generous subsidies helped to rescue several key early settlements from economic collapse.

Terror at Ma'aleh Akrabim

Friday, March 12

[- - -]

Wiener and Amir of *Tahal* came over to report about preparations being made for Eric Johnston's second visit.

[- - -]

Saturday, March 13

[- - -]

Sunday, March 14

[- - -]

At the Cabinet meeting, the matter of [army service for] *yeshiva* students was reviewed. A committee was chosen to handle the matter. In the afternoon I met at home with the two emissaries of the Rabbinical Council of America. This was the concluding discussion, and it lasted from four until almost seven. They again began with declarations of boundless trust accorded me by Jewish Orthodox circles abroad. Afterwards they wished to hear my opinion on two issues: first, about the conscription of *yeshiva* students, i.e., their non-conscription; secondly, about the National Service Law, i.e., the postponement of its implementation. This could help them quell the furor in America and put an end to the conflict that threatens to utterly upset relations between Orthodox Jewry and the state. I told them there was no intention of drafting *yeshiva* students whose studies are bona fide. However, we would certainly not tolerate *yeshivot* serving as citadels of refuge for draft-dodgers.

As regards the National Service Law, I refused to commit myself to its postponement. I merely reaffirmed all the restrictions and exemptions we would make during the process of implementation in order to avoid any impositions upon certain young women to change their way of life. This didn't satisfy them. Once again they asked for some additional exemption concessions beyond those already granted in the regulations to give them a weapon against the ultra-orthodox hate-mongers. I couldn't think of anything else to give them and referred them to Golda. But they had already spent three and a half hours with her, to no avail. So the matter remained in a stalemate.

Alongside the major issues a long conversation ensued about the position of religion in Israel. They again expressed their deep appreciation of some arrangements and customs – keeping kosher dietary laws in Army installations, observance of *Shabbat* there and in the country in general, the level of education in the national-religious school sector, and more of the same. As in my previous meeting with them they contended that our information services were lacking in efficiency, for Orthodox Jewry in America had no idea about all these accomplishments. I confronted them with the far-reaching concessions made by the majority of the population in the country to religious demands for the sake of national unity, the provocations and frustrations this gives rise to throughout the country, the accumulated bitterness against this mental coercion, and the suffering and injustice caused in many cases by the rigid enforcement of outdated religious principles. I emphasized my conviction that religion as a spiritual entity and the rabbinate as an establishment were facing bankruptcy if they did not choose wisely to soften prohibitions which modern society could not tolerate. I also made a special effort to explain that the conscription of women and the National Service Law did not actually harm religious dictates. They did not constitute a religious problem at all; they only involved problems concerning family and social life. I went on to say that a country which was a besieged fortress surrounded by enemies, and also a melting pot by virtue of its absorption of mass immigration, demanded a regime of duties imposed upon everyone the likes of which exist in no other state. In view of the traditional equality between men and women, it was unthinkable that these duties should apply only to men. The conscription of women and the spectacle of both sexes in uniform was a direct sequel to integrated schools, youth movements composed of boys and girls, agricultural settlements where men and women shared efforts on the basis of complete equality, and even everyday life where they mixed without any barriers – all these with hardly any difference between religious and non-religious circles.

They said they had learnt a lot from me, that issues had been presented to them in a new light. They prayed that they succeed in explaining things with the same clarity. Still, they again asked for additional concessions in regard to national service. There was no putting an end to this request. When they left I was utterly and completely exhausted, to the marrow in my bones.

[- - -]

Some time later Shamai called. Lavon was requesting that I send Tekoah to attend the ISMAC which was convening tomorrow for the first time after a long intermission to discuss the exchange-of-fire incident which took place between us and the Syrians on the Kinneret a few days ago. This invitation is a good omen in view of internal relations between the GS and the Foreign Ministry. It must be seen as the result of the bitter argument between these two bodies, in which I soundly assailed the defense people for the lack of cooperation on their part.

Monday, March 15

As a result of my talk yesterday with the American rabbis, it has become clear to me that the *yeshiva* students affair is still creating an uproar, and the disclosure of the news concerning the Cabinet committee chosen to handle the matter may only add fuel to the fire. If a Cabinet committee is pursuing the matter, that means there is a serious plot to change the status quo and deny *yeshiva* students their right of exemption from the Army. In America they are left alone regardless of how long they remain in their *yeshivot*. They are treated there the same as monks who are called upon to serve only when they leave the monastery. As long as they stay there, they are exempt for life. Here in Israel the regime [is being accused of] treating them shabbily and conspiring to stop their Torah learning, thereby undermining an age-old Jewish tradition. I also understood from that conversation that Chief Rabbi Herzog is still awaiting a letter from me. If I send him a letter today affirming that we have no intention of conscripting *yeshiva* students, regardless of the length of their studies, and that we were merely consulting on how to prevent a travesty of this privilege and the transformation of the *yeshivot* into cities of refuge for draft-dodgers – then the uproar would calm down. I telephoned Lavon and said that I was about to write and pledge myself in this vein. He agreed that it had to be done, and I immediately sent the letter.

I spoke with Golda and sent Yaacov Herzog to convince her to overcome her impatience and to receive the two rabbis again. They have additional proposals on how to dissipate the tension over the National Service Law in Israel and America and it is worthwhile to examine whether it is possible to accommodate them. On these religious matters, I advocate unlimited patience in searching for compromise and persuading religious people who haven't been unbalanced by fanaticism and are enemies of Jewish sovereignty that those at the head of the state are sensitive to the responses of Orthodox Jewry and seek to find common ground with it, even if they do not satisfy its wishes on everything. [- - -]

Dr David Bergmann,[1] came in for a talk on atomic research in Israel. We have discovered uranium in our phosphates, and this discovery has served as an impetus for the discovery of uranium in the phosphates of France and the US as well. (I received this statement with reservations, for David Bergmann is very thrilled with himself and may be exaggerating the global importance of our discoveries). We have also invented a new process for the production of heavy water from ordinary water. The conventional process, electrolysis, is too expensive to be of

1 Ernest David Bergmann (1903-1975). Professor of organic chemistry. Born in Germany. Settled in Palestine in 1933. Scientific advisor to Ben-Gurion. Headed the research and development division of the Defense Ministry (1950-1966). Founder of the Scientific Branch of the IDF. Played a major part in building Israel's nuclear capacity and served as first Chairman of its Atomic Energy Commission (1952-1966).

use to us and all the electricity in the country would not suffice for it. Possessing uranium and heavy water, it should be within our ability to build a nuclear reactor and produce atomic power. However, this is a very expensive business and beyond the reach of our resources. (Here I learned something important, that the amount of power generated is not dependent on the size of the reactor.) In the meantime we are concentrating on the production of uranium and on improving the process for the production of heavy water. We shall be able to sell the uranium. Its official price is $200,000 a ton, but on the European black market it's $3 million. The production of one ton will cost us $30-40,000. The production of one ton requires the processing of 10,000 tons of phosphates. The facility for it already exists, but production experiments need be continued. Eight months' work and a IL.400,000 investment will bring us to the stage of production for sale. Phosphate from which the uranium has been extracted loses nothing of its properties for regular use. The only problem then is the allocation of the required sums.[2]

[- - -]

In the afternoon, at the Foreign Ministry, a visit by Professor Franz Böhm and his wife. When I said something reservedly about Israel being an accumulator of Jewish feeling and the resultant high tension of the public which unavoidably exists with regard to Germany, Mrs Böhm started weeping.

[- - -]

Tuesday, March 16

Today, the eleventh of *Adar-B* [of the Hebrew calendar], has been established from this year onwards as Reserve Officers Day. There are gatherings all over the country and the ministers have been asked to appear. To my lot fell a large affair of the Northern Command in Kiryat Haim. Some 1,200 people are expected to gather there. We left Jerusalem at 8:00 am and arrived there at 11:00. I directed my remarks for internal consumption and I explained the need for balancing our policy between the two poles of relying on our own strength, on the one hand, and taking account of international sensibilities, on the other.

After the gathering, a mass luncheon was served at the Northern Command's medical corps base. Seated next to Colonel Moshe Tzadok,[3] I questioned him

2 For a skeptical assessment of Bergmann's optimism, see Avner Cohen, *Israel and the Bomb* (New York: Columbia University Press, 1998), 32.

3 Moshe Lehrer Tzadok (1913-1964). Born in Poland. Settled in Palestine in 1933. Among chief commanders of the *Hagana*. During the War of Independence headed the Manpower Directorate of the IDF. Commander of the Southern Command (1951-1953); Commander of Northern Command (1954-1956). Sharett knew well all the *Hagana* commanders since being chairman of the *yishuv*'s Defense Committee – the civilian body overseeing the *Hagana* in the early 1940s.

on two subjects: the senior officers' course he recently attended in England, and Yigael Yadin. Tzadok, who is entirely a product of the *Hagana*, returned deeply impressed by British military doctrine, even more by their culture and manners. With us, he said, when somebody suggests a solution to a problem, critical barbs are immediately shot at him from all sides and everyone competes in finding faults and offering smarter proposals. Among the British, on the other hand, once somebody has proposed a plan, everyone immediately rushes to support and help him, unhesitatingly accepting his fundamental approach and only seeking to amend the details. He had asked them: "Is it really so clear that this is the only way to solve the problem? Might there not be a completely different and better alternative?" They told him: "We are preparing ourselves for combat tasks. In combat there is no time to compete and ascertain which method is better than the others. The main thing is to rush into action immediately while exploiting the order given fully and effectively in a spirit of complete unity and mutual assistance." He was also impressed by the way the people of Great Britain know how to utilize their time highly efficiently without tiring to exhaustion. He found that the secret lies in the quality of organization and the brevity of speech.

As to Yadin, Tzadok's feeling was that he was already a bit "restless." Indeed, he still had another year of study in Britain before him, after which he is supposed to teach archeology for about a year at the Hebrew University of Jerusalem. But he's already showing impatience regarding his future, since he's full of expectation about reaching heights in Israeli politics. At the same time, he wasn't sure of the Israeli public's attitude towards his aspirations and this tended to make him uneasy. Tzadok himself valued him highly.

[- - -]

On our way back we listened to *Kol-Israel* at 6:15 and heard a passage from my remarks at Kiryat Haim in which I slightly missed the mark in the wording. I was appalled. Up till now I've taken part in many officers' gatherings and my remarks have never been publicized. I had thought that I could speak freely this time too, with my remarks meant solely for internal consumption. But I was wrong. Now what's done is done, I must try to correct the press.

I was in a hurry to come to Jerusalem and immediately telephoned *Kol-Israel*. I told them that in a short while I would dictate to them an authorized summary of my speech. I composed and dictated and delivered the wording to *Davar* as well, and asked them to forward it to *Ha'aretz* too. For some reason I forgot the *Jerusalem Post*. I later dictated a long letter to Ben-Gurion on the issue of Christian Lebanon; it was a sequel to the debate that erupted between us on that Saturday in Tel Aviv.[4]

4 See below, entry for March 18.

Wednesday, March 17

This morning I was deeply unhappy. There was one passage in my speech to the officers in Kiryat Haim which definitely hadn't been meant for publication. Even for internal consumption it hadn't been properly articulated. I said that in terms of our technical ability there was nothing to stop us from opening the way to Eilat by force, and finishing the B'not Yaakov canal as well. But we had refrained from doing so until now because of our assessment of the international complications which such direct action might cause and the ruinous results it might entail for our overall position. And now this "malignant" passage has been published both in *Ha'aretz* and the *Jerusalem Post*. The "house-broken" *Davar* disclosed only what I sent over, but *Ha'aretz* apparently rejected the official version and published what it got from its reporter. I immediately realized that I would not be easily let off the hook for this slip.

In the press there appeared Lavon and Dayan's speeches at yesterday's gatherings – bombastic political declarations.[5]

I wired Abba to make every effort to strike the passage from the New Zealand

---

5 In his speech, Lavon declared: "We are told that the Arab states would promise not to use the arms they are supplied with by the Great Powers against Israel. With due respect to the Big Three [i.e., US, UK and France] – and we would like to promote their friendship with us – how are they going to guarantee this? What is the value of this guarantee? The policy of the Great Powers, objectively, is directed against us. It is disturbing the equilibrium in the Middle East and endangers Israel's security. It increases the danger to peace in the area, and we must draw from this policy, if it is not reformed and mended, all the necessary conclusions pertaining to our present and future security. ...There is a lot of talk about peace, but the fact is that the UN is oblivious to our territorial rights and to our rights of maritime passage, and this policy is only sowing the seeds of war. Tension along the border is increasing. The Arab states feel they can do whatever they like. The Israeli public feels that our appeals to the UN are being dealt with not on the basis of justice. On this background, our most decisive dictum becomes more significant than ever: Be prepared."

Ha'aretz of March 16 reported Dayan's remarks on the fifth anniversary of the incorporation of the city of Eilat: "The guns installed by the Egyptians in the Gulf of Tiran will not turn the open sea into a closed lake for us. It is not the shores of Egypt, Jordan and Saudi Arabia which are beheld from there, but those of Ethiopia, Africa, India and China – the free commerce and sea passage to them. The decision of Egypt's government to blockade the sea passage for us and the guns installed at the entrance of the straits shall not change the role of Eilat. The 12 km. of Eilat's seashore do not designate the end point of Israel's southern border. This seashore is Israel's gateway to the big sea, to the Red Sea, and from it to the ocean.

"The Government of Egypt once decided to strangle Israel and the Egyptian Army earmarked soldiers and guns for this purpose. When General Naguib came to power a year and a half ago, he quickly resumed this aggressive stance. Now the Egyptian government declares itself to be in a state of war with Israel and is allowed to blockade by guns the free passage of ships going to Eilat. An Egyptian regime that builds its policy on the economic strangulation of Israel and which aims at disconnecting the Negev from Israel is bound to fall."

resolution placing us at the mercy of the EIMAC on the question of passage to Eilat. [- - -]

A telephone call from Yitzhak Navon. He was informed by the GS that a civilian passenger bus returning from Eilat was shot at in an ambush near Ma'aleh Akrabim [Scorpions' Pass] in the eastern Negev, close to the Arava Valley. There are dead and wounded.

At 5:30 I was back at the Knesset for [an emergency] meeting of the Cabinet FADC [on the Ma'aleh Akrabim incident]. More news arrived meanwhile on the disaster at Ma'aleh Akrabim. The CoS, who attended the meeting, reported. About ten were killed; the driver died in the first burst of fire. By a miracle, the vehicle didn't plummet down the steep slope. A spray of bullets poured from all directions. Then a few men entered the bus and killed and slaughtered left and right. Two young women and an IDF sergeant survived, and a badly wounded boy too.

Israel Rokach suggested that one of the ministers should go to Be'er Sheva. I took it upon myself to go tomorrow morning. It was proposed that an announcement be delivered in the Knesset immediately, but before Lavon went down to do so the session was interrupted.

[- - -]

I wrote to BG with regard to Iraq's responsibility for events in Syria. I noted that since writing to him on this matter, I had received a GS "Special Intelligence Report" from the second of this month in which I read: "It seems the Iraqis did not play a part in organizing the coup... The Iraqi consulate in Damascus had no information on what was transpiring, and this is decisive evidence that it did not have a finger in the pie." In the meantime I also reviewed a Special Survey of the Foreign Ministry's Research Division on "Iraq's part in the fifth coup in Syria." It contained the most complete summary I have seen to date of evidence proving both that Iraq had a hand in organizing the coup, and that it did not. In the final analysis the question remained equivocal. At any rate it seems that Iraq's direct participation in initiating and implementing the coup has by no means been proven.

As for the conclusions, I proposed to draw from the non-corroboration of assumptions we had made about to Iraq's role upon receiving the first news of the coup, it seems I had not been precise in defining them and thus had caused a misunderstanding. I had by no means meant that "disciplinary" action should be taken towards our intelligence people, who ostensibly erred in their assessment of the source or nature of events. Such an attitude is alien to me. I had meant conclusions of a completely different nature, as well as caution dictated by this experience to us, who are at the helm, in drawing conclusions from our assumptions in similar cases in the future in respect to actions we deem necessary to take. In the present case, the suggestions and proposals for action were based on assumptions which at least in part were not substantiated and may have been disproved by facts ascertained a day or two later.[6]

Thursday, March 18

We drove to Be'er Sheva at 8:00, arrived at 9:50, and found officers of the IDF Southern Command waiting for us [- - -]. All faces were bloodless gray after a sleepless night. The corpses have already been sent north. The surviving sergeant, a Tangier-born fellow, educated in France, was brought before me to tell his story. For about two months now he has been on guard in busses running between Be'er Sheva and Eilat. During this period he had never had any inkling of danger. When his bus was attacked he was not able to use his rifle. All he could do was see to his own survival. Blood spilled on him from all sides and the attackers thought he was dead. The attackers he saw were Bedouins. I said: "Life has been given to you as a gift again," to which he answered: "For the third time, sir!"

Then I talked with the girl who survived. She is originally from Holland, now working in Eilat. She was lucky to come out with not even a scratch. The attackers moved her body about to ascertain that she was dead. She lay still. Two of the attackers she saw wore khaki trousers. We then drove to the local hospital, and saw the wounded female soldier. A bullet tore her flesh quite badly, but did not penetrate her body. She is serving in Eilat, and was going north on vacation. Saw five (!) attackers, all in Bedouin dress. Lastly we were brought to the bus which became a death trap for its passengers. A horrible sight. The sides were bullet-ridden, the windows shattered, the floor covered with congealed blood.

Meanwhile tracking dogs had been brought to the scene of the atrocity, and serious tracking work was in progress along the most rugged terrain with UN Observers participating. According to reports which have started to arrive, two paths of tracks were discovered: one leading to the scene from the east and one leading away from it westward.

[- - -]

At 2:30 we came back to Jerusalem. I dined and immediately went to the Foreign Ministry where I summoned the high echelon of the office for consultation. All of us were of the opinion that a retaliation to such a bloodshed would only blur its terrible impact and place us on the same par with the other side's murderers. It would be much better to use the deed at Ma'aleh Akrabim as lever for a political attack on the powers, demanding that they put unprecedented pressure on Jordan.[7]

---

6 Letter not found.

7 For British and American diplomatic reactions to the Ma'aleh Akrabim massacre, see: Evans to FO, March 18, 1954, TNA FO371/111098 VR1091/12; *FRUS 1952-1954*, docs.776, 778; *DFPI* 9, docs.114, 118.

At 7:00 I went to Tel Aviv, where I composed a text for CBS television for tomorrow morning and then completed editing my letter to BG on Lebanon.[8]

March 18, 1954

Mr David Ben-Gurion
Sde Boker.

I must apologize to you for the nth time for delaying my answer to your letter regarding Lebanon. While I indeed voiced on the spot my negative response to the idea you broached in our conversation at your home in Tel Aviv, I said to myself that the matter should be investigated and I ordered our Research Division to compose a background review regarding past endeavors to grant Lebanon the character of a Christian commonwealth, as well as present chances of any movement – if such a movement should materialize – to achieve this aim.

To my dismay our research people were rather slow; it seems they take their task too seriously. But meanwhile time was running by fast and even though I am extremely busy – there is no end to troubles and complications in which I am immersed, and certainly not only in matters of foreign policy – I am now going to make an effort to explain to you my views in some detail. I shall do so by relying on knowledge I had gathered long ago, which I am not certain is exactly pertinent today – this I will probably ascertain upon reading the background survey. In any case, because of lack of time I could not verify data or consult anybody, and so I am writing from memory only.

First of all, I must set out a basic assumption I have held from way back, which is that if there is sometimes some reason and point for outside interference in the internal affairs of another country in order to support a political movement inside it aiming toward some target, it should only be when that movement shows some independent activity which there is a chance to enhance, and maybe to bring to success, by outside encouragement and help. There is no rhyme nor reason trying to create from the outside a movement that does not exist at all inside. It is possible to strengthen the stamina of a living body; it is impossible to inject life into a dead body.

Well, as far as I know, in Lebanon today there exists no movement aiming at transforming the country into a Christian state governed by the Maronite community. This has been my clear impression for several years now. It may well be that such a slogan was put forward in Lebanon once, and it may well be that there were people and circles which professed it; but even then this did not grow into a serious movement and did not become the subject of organized, systematic activity. Over time even these voices completely calmed down. The slogan disappeared from the public arena and was not heard anymore – a complete paralysis of thought and freezing of action were evident. Whoever comes today to arouse from the outside the aspiration for a Christian Lebanon as a practical policy option would only be shouting into the wind.

This is not surprising. The transformation of Lebanon into a Christian state is

8 In his letter of February 27, Ben-Gurion had written, inter alia: "Perhaps [- - -] now is the opportune moment to bring about the establishment of a Christian state in our neighborhood. Without our initiative and our vigorous aid this will not be done. And it seems to me that this is the central task [underlined by BG] – or at least one [underlined by BG] of the central tasks – of our foreign policy. And this means that the resources, time, and energy ought to be invested, and action be taken in all avenues which could bring about a fundamental change in Lebanon." For the full text, see WebDoc #6.

unfeasible today if it is to be achieved by an [outside] effort initiated towards this end. When I say "an initiated effort" I must qualify myself, since I don't exclude the possibility of this goal being accomplished in the wake of those shock waves that sweep the Middle East, re-arrange regimes, throw existing entities into a melting pot, and create new ones. But in the present Lebanon, with its present territorial and demographic dimensions and its international relations, no serious initiative aiming in this direction is imaginable.

The Christians do not constitute the majority in Lebanon. Nor are they a unified block, politically speaking or community-wise. The Orthodox minority in Lebanon tends to identify with their brethren in Syria. Not only would it not be ready to raise this flag and go to war for a Christian Lebanon, that is for a Lebanon smaller than it is today and detached from the Arab League. On the contrary, there is reason to assume it would not be flabbergasted by the idea of unification with Syria, as this would contribute to strengthening their own community and the Orthodox community throughout the Levant. And this for two demographic considerations: there are more Orthodox Christians in Syria than in Lebanon, and the Orthodox in Syria and Lebanon together are more numerous than the Maronites.

As to the Maronites, the great majority among them has for years now supported those pragmatic political leaders of their community who have long since abandoned the dream of reviving a Christian Lebanon, and have put all their cards on a Christian-Muslim coalition in that country. These leaders have developed the consciousness that there is no chance for an isolated Maronite Lebanon [to exist] and that the historical perspective of their community lies in a partnership with the Muslims in power, and in Lebanon's membership in the League, hoping and believing that these factors can guarantee that the Lebanese Muslims will abandon their longing for unification of Lebanon with Syria and will nurse among them the urge for Lebanese independence.

Therefore, accordingly, the great majority of the Maronite community who have been pursuing this policy is liable to see in any attempt to raise the flag of territorial shrinking and Maronite independence a dangerous attempt at subverting the status of their community, its security and even its very existence. Such an initiative would seem disastrous to them because it could tear apart the pattern of Christian-Muslim collaboration in the present Lebanon which was created through the great efforts and sacrifices of an entire generation. It would mean throwing the Lebanese Muslims into the Syrian embrace and, finally, would fatally bring about the historical disaster of the annexation of Lebanon to Syria and the annihilation of the former's personality through its dilution in a large Muslim state.

You may object that these arguments are irrelevant as the plan is based on tearing away from Lebanon the provinces of Tyre, the Beka'a and Tripoli, whose populations constitute a Muslim majority. But who can predict that these provinces will actually give up their ties to Lebanon, and their political and economic connection to Beirut? Who can assure us that the Arab League will be ready to give up the status that Lebanon's membership confers to it on account of Lebanon's location in the middle of the eastern shore of the Mediterranean? After it lost its positions at the northern corner of this seashore due to the incorporation of [the disputed province of] Hatay [including Alexandretta] into Turkey, and its southern part due to the establishment of Israel – who will vouch that the bloody war that will inevitably explode as a result of such an attempt will be limited to Lebanon, and not drag Syria into the battlefield immediately? Who can be sure that the Western powers will look on as observers and will delay intervening until a *fait accompli* is created, so that they could say "Amen" on the occasion of the "reconstruction" of Christian

Lebanon? Who can guarantee that the Maronite leadership itself will not become aware of all the above considerations to begin with, and will therefore completely back out of the dangerous adventure?

In addition to the serious political considerations which coalesce here to negate the idea, there are also decisive economic factors which are working against it. We are not discussing the issue in 1920/21, immediately after the declaration of "Grand Liban" by [the French High-Commissioner General Henri] Gouraud, but 30 years later. Mount Lebanon has meanwhile integrated into one organic unit with the coastal plain of Tyre and Sidon, the Valley of Baalbeck and the city of Tripoli; the various regions are commercially and economically connected and interdependent. Mount Lebanon was not a self-sufficient unit even before World War I. I remember that Arthur Ruppin in his book *Syria: An Economic Survey* [1918] pointed out that on the eve of World War I Lebanon was receiving contributions and monies from foundations and individuals in America, all in all, about twenty million gold francs, while contributions to the Jewish community in Palestine from world Jewry amounted then to just ten million gold francs. There is no doubt that the annexation of the three regions plus the city of Beirut to the Lebanese state has rendered possible the creation of a balanced economy. A return to the past would not just mean a surgical operation but also a disintegration which Lebanon would not be able to survive.

Again, it is one thing if such a change is a result of a sudden internal wave, but another thing altogether if the idea is to bring this about intentionally as a fruit of a pre-meditated plan. I cannot imagine, even from this viewpoint alone, that any serious organization would collaborate with this plan that would in my opinion threaten Lebanon with economic suicide.

Having said this, not only would I not have objected to actively supporting any fermentation inside the Maronite community towards independence and isolation, even if this had no chance of achieving its aim, but I would have certainly supported this [movement]. [- - -] I would have considered positive the very existence of such agitation and the destabilization it could bring about, the trouble it could cause to the Arab League, the diversion of attention from the Arab-Israeli complications that it could cause, and the very kindling of a fire made up of impulses toward Christian independence so that it would not be extinguished. But what can I do when such agitation is nonexistent, as I already noted above? In the present condition, I am afraid that any attempt on our part to arouse the issue would be considered as a display of light-mindedness and superficiality, or worse – as an adventurous speculation upon the well-being and existence of others and a readiness to sacrifice their basic good for the benefit of a temporary tactical advantage for Israel.

Moreover, if this plan is not kept a secret but becomes known – a danger which cannot be underestimated in the Middle Eastern circumstances – the damage which we shall suffer in the context of our relations with the Arab states and the Western powers alike would be immeasurable. This damage would not be compensated even by the eventual success of the operation itself.

Finally, let me note that the last coup d'état in Syria was not the first of its kind, and one can assume it will not be the last. This is another in a long chain of cataclysms and changes, all testifying to a malignant weakness in the state-building of all the Arab regimes. If there was any chance at all for political separatism of the Maronites, then the crises which have erupted in Syria in rapid succession would have already produced and enhanced this movement. It is doubtful if such a trend would evolve from now on. Anyway, I do not see the last coup d'état as a basis justifying our taking an interventionist course and direct action in Lebanon, throwing out large sums of money which we don't have, and at the same time risking all the dangerous mishaps enumerated above.

I am sorry if I burdened you by the long survey. However I wanted to present you with my way of seeing the problem in its fullest analysis possible.

M.S.[9]

Later I was informed that a preposterous editorial would be published in tomorrow's *Yediot Ahronot* against Bennike under the headline *poshol von* [Russian: "Out You Go!"]. I told Moish Pearlman to demand from Herzl Rosenblum, in my name, that he drop the article. Later Moish called and said the article had been deleted.

Friday, March 19

At the Foreign Ministry in the *Kirya* I recorded my statement on Ma'aleh Akrabim after I had learned by rote the text I had composed yesterday. The recording is to be flown to the USA today, and will probably be broadcast on Monday.[10]

[- - -]

A meeting of the Knesset FADC at the Defense Ministry, devoted entirely to Ma'aleh Akrabim. Riftin preached suppressing of [the] desire [to relatiate], while Ben-Aharon demanded we invade Jordan "in order to catch the murderers."

At 5:00 I received Bennike and his entourage at the PMO. Rafael, Tekoah and Shalev were with me. When the UN people came, Bennike, while still on his feet, expressed their sorrow at the loss of life. When we sat down I poured on the Dane's head a livid denunciation of Jordan's crimes. I demanded that he immediately go to Amman and announce that no self-respecting regime could accept the continuation of such a state of affairs. The whip-lashing lasted an hour. At home I composed a communiqué on the conversation, in Hebrew and English.[11]

Saturday, March 20

[- - -]

Sunday, March 21

The morning papers carried the full text of the communiqué I had composed on my conversation with Bennike. My own feeling is that the very forceful wording of our stand gave some vent to the tension reverberating among the people.[12] According

---

9 *Sharett: Mivhar Te'udot*, doc.128.

10 The written text of Sharett's address is in CZA file A245/35/III.

11 See *DFPI* 9, doc.115.

12 Also appearing in the day's press was an article in *Davar* by David Ben-Gurion, entitled "The United Nations and our Security." See below, entry for March 26, 1954.

to the latest news, trackers had followed the murderers' footsteps to within 10 km. of the Jordanian frontier and then stopped because of the rocky terrain. But from that point onwards there is only one narrow ravine that leads into Jordan. The IDF sent Arabs to reconnoiter the Jordanian village of el-Saffi, opposite Sdom. They returned and reported that villagers had seen a band of 8-10 crossing the border westward; they also extracted three names from the villagers.[13]

The Cabinet meeting was wholly devoted to a report on the Ma'aleh Akrabim incident and a consultation on a course of action. Lavon himself proposed to refrain from retaliation for the time being and first explore all the possibilities of political action. There was much arguing. It was finally decided to turn to the powers with a demand that they take the initiative in convening the Security Council as they had over Qibya.[14]

It was also decided that if the IJMAC rules – via an abstention by its chairman [Cmdr E.H. Hutchison[15] of the US] – that Jordan cannot be held responsible for lack of decisive proof, we shall announce our withdrawal from it. There was an unanimous agreement in support of this drastic measure. It seemed necessary both in order to advise the powers of the gravity of the situation, and to satisfy the public.But differences were immediately apparent as regards the stages to be followed. Lavon advocated withdrawing, period. My opinion was that this step would merely be demonstrative, and we would have to immediately afterwards consult on means for an honorable return. The argument didn't go any further because the time was not yet ripe in practical terms. (The situation reminded me of the disagreement between Ben-Gurion and myself on the question of closing the JA's conscription offices to the British Army during the Second World War. BG saw it then as an irrevocable step, while I moved mountains to obtain some honorable compensation which would enable the reopening of the offices.)[16]

---

13 The 32-page report of the investigation by UN Military Observers Ely, Norgaard, DeBarr, Ringler, Pinon, and Svedlund (No.X486), carried out on March 17-21, 1954, is available in the UNA, file S-0163-0008-05.

14 See *DFPI* 9, doc.117.

15 Cmdr Elmo H. Hutchison (1910?-1964). US Naval Reserve officer seconded to UNTSO (November 1951 – October 1954); chairman of IJMAC from summer 1953.

16 The JAE's decision to reopen conscription offices (following their closure in protest against a British police raid) was reached owing to the persistence and energetic lobbying of Sharett (then Shertok), effectively overruling Ben-Gurion who remained adamant in his (minority) view that the offices remain shut. In retrospect, Sharett and others considered this operational decision a wise one which led, within 18 months, to the creation of the Jewish Brigade (which was formed out of the three existing battalions of Palestinian Jews) and sent to Europe to participate in the liberation of Italy. See, e.g., Sharett's letter of September 7, 1946 in *Ma'asar Im Niyar Ve'iparon [Imprisoned with Paper and Pencil: The Letters of Moshe and Zipporah Sharett during the period of his detention by the British at Latrun, June-November 1946]*, eds. Rina and Yaakov Sharett. Tel Aviv: The Moshe Sharett Heritage Society, 2000), 236-37 – in Hebrew.

At the end of the debate, I said that I would undoubtedly have to issue a statement on the situation in the Knesset this week.

After the meeting, Ziama came in to report on what he'd heard from BG when he visited him in Sde Boker on Saturday. It had to do with his reasons for his withdrawal from party activity. It was as I had feared; I am to blame. My sins are twofold. First, the speech I delivered at the Kiryat Haim gathering[17] and the political orientation implied in it. Secondly, when the press made a to-do over his participation in the consultation with the Defense Minister and the CoS following the coups in Syria and Egypt, why had I not immediately announced that I was the one who had asked for his participation in the consultation?[18] Why had I let him appear as though meddling in state matters without any authority? It seems that the malignant contrariness in our mentalities, which has gone on for years, continues to breed crises even in this period of his withdrawal from responsibility. Both in the pre-state JAE days and afterwards in the government, BG could never last long in a stable condition, but seemingly had an inner need to foment a crisis from time to time and submit his resignation. Now that he has completely resigned from the government, this need is still active within him. Now he is withdrawing from party activity and I am the scapegoat. Just the same, why should the party be punished? It is clear that I must write him a letter and explain what I can. It won't be easy to write, nor pleasant to read.

[- - -]

Monday, March 22

[- - -]

Conferred with Gideon on the probable results of the MAC discussion on Ma'aleh Akrabim. It is almost certain that the results will reach a stalemate and that we shall then withdraw from the MAC. The Americans have already drafted a statement comparing Ma'aleh Akrabim and Qibya – the former the action of a gang, and the latter of a regular army.

At home in the afternoon, I began to compose a letter to BG. I made an effort to overcome my emotions but the bitterness and insult found their expression. Nevertheless, I gathered my patience to describe to him the course of developments, and to explain both the business of the speech in Haifa [i.e., its suburb of Kiryat Haim] and the matter of the consultation in Tel Aviv. I sat over the draft of my letter until 2:30. I was not brief.[19]

[- - -]

17 See above, entries for March 16 and 17.
18 See above, entries for February 26 and 27.
19 For the text of the letter, see below, entry for March 24, 1954.

Tuesday, March 23

[- - -]

From 11:00 till 2:00 a meeting of the Knesset FADC. I delivered an extensive report following Ma'aleh Akrabim concerning our decision to exhaust the political response. I also announced that tomorrow I would deliver a statement in the Knesset and would not object to a debate.

[- - -]

Upon leaving the meeting I ran into Tekoah and Shalev. The battle in the MAC has ended at last. Chairman Hutchison ruled that he did not have enough data on which to pronounce a decision, so the matter of responsibility for Ma'aleh Akrabim remained moot. In his summary he even said that the testimony of the survivors did not prove sufficiently that all of the murderers were Arabs...[20] Our people acted in accordance with previous instructions, and announced their withdrawal from the commission. I consulted with Lavon over the wording of the statement we shall publicize. I instructed Gideon and Tekoah to prepare a draft.[21]

Sat with MK Esther Vilenska of the CPI. Told her that their application for entrance to Israel of three Soviet women, invited to a conference of "The Democratic Women's Organization"[22] was granted. I used this occasion to ask her how she, an apparently good-hearted Jewish girl, found it possible to become a believer in the foolish doctrine of Communism? She then and there started to give me a lecture, in a most serious tone, on Marxism-Leninism. I stopped her immediately, saying that this was the problem, not the solution. She failed to understand and looked at me pityingly.

Came home and lay down feeling helpless, devoid of any shred of energy. Such situations have become frequent of late. But within a few minutes Gideon came by, draft in hand. Accordingly, I composed a totally new announcement in both languages, one after the other.

At 9:00 pm I sat over the speech I had to give tomorrow in the Knesset. The task was easier than I had assumed. At 1:30 am the speech was completed and by 2:00 I was in bed. It took me a long time to fall asleep. The ideas I put forward in the speech were constantly trickling through my head and I was bothered by different wordings from which to choose – again walking a narrow path between giving vent to the public's emotions and leading it astray by bombastic expressions; between strong language and provocative exaggeration.

---

20 Ellipsis in orig. See Hutchison, *Violent Truce*,194-95. The complete 85-page transcript of the 177th IJMAC meeting is available in the United Nations Archive (UNA) file S-0163-0008-05.

21 *DFPI* 9, doc.120.

22 A Communist front.

Wednesday, March 24

Early in the morning I sent my speech to the office for typing and when I came there I toiled all morning on polishing and translating it into English.

[- - -]

After eating at home I edited the English version of the speech, and by 3:00 I was at the Knesset. With the opening of the session I rose to speak and the debate began immediately.[23] Begin delivered a speech bombastic in form but not in content. He again enumerated a long list of my sins from years of yore and in effect recommended waging a new war, though he was careful to avoid saying so explicitly. Of our *haverim*, Herzl Berger[24] and Eliezer Livneh distinguished themselves, especially the latter. Yona Kesse,[25] on the other hand, became entangled in a completely unnecessary attack on the Soviet Union.

The surprise came with the speech of Minister Peretz Bernstein. Only yesterday and this morning we had both participated in meetings in which I had said that I would make a speech indicating its main substance and he had not said a word about making a speech too. Then suddenly he ascends the podium! Rokach sensed my amazement and sent me a note saying that Bernstein was speaking not as a minister, but as his party's representative. A most illuminating explanation! But not only was his appearance itself irregular, but even more so one slip of his tongue. Suddenly I heard him proclaim that this time the government had decided to abstain from retaliation. I could not believe my ears. What point is there in offering this relief to the other side? More important, how foolish to admit by implication that, whenever there is a retaliatory action, it is the result of a government decision. I sent a very angry note to Rokach and Yosef Sapir. The latter nodded a sign of agreement with my outrage. Secretaries worked afterwards to erase these remarks from the Knesset protocol, and cajole reporters not to publicize them. Bernstein came up to me shamefaced and apologized. What can happen in our midst!

At night I copied out my letter to Ben-Gurion.

Jerusalem, March [24], 1954

Shalom, Ben-Gurion -

Last week Ziama relayed to me the notification he had received from you in writing that you considered yourself compelled to withdraw from participating in the preparation of the next Party Council.

Yesterday Ziama told me what you said to him in Sde Boker on Saturday – that generally speaking you refuse to do anything which may imply that you share

23 For Sharett's speech, see WebDoc #7.

24 Herzl Berger (1904-1962). Journalist. Born in Russia. Settled in Palestine in 1934. Joined Mapai and became political commentator in *Davar*. MK (1951-1962).

25 Yona Kesse (1907-1985). Mapai leader and SG (1938-1940, 1953-1956); MK (1949-1965).

responsibility in the present government. From this stems your inability to be a member of the committee of twenty-one and in general take part in activity on behalf of the party except for that which is purely educational. For this decision of yours you gave, as far as I understood from Ziama, two reasons. First, the speech I gave at the Reserve Officers' gathering in Kiryat Haim and the political orientation implied therein; secondly, the fact that, when the press began to criticize your participation in the reported consultation, I did not issue a statement that I was the one who had convened it.

What this means is that I am responsible for creating a situation which does not allow your participation in Party activity. I consider myself excused from having to say even one word as to the severity of this conclusion as regards myself.

I have no illusions about the chances of this letter having an influence over you – this letter or any other letter on my part. But in writing I am first of all fulfilling an obligation to myself, as well as to our relations as I have regarded them until now.

I may perhaps weary you with things that neither add nor detract in your view. But I feel compelled to review the course of developments as regards your two accusations.

I shall start with the speech. I don't actually know what you are upset about – the content of the speech or its disclosure. If it is the content, my way of thinking concerning certain questions of our defense policy which are closely associated with foreign policy has been well known to you for a long time already. The disagreement between us on these questions has been evident for many a year. I therefore find it difficult to believe that my remarks this time came to you as a surprise which required your drawing any new conclusions. But if it is the disclosure of which you are critical, here there is the tale to tell you.

This was not the first speech I have given at the invitation of the IDF before an audience of officers, whether professional or in active service or on reserve duty. I have spoken many times before such an audience in various centers throughout the country. Never have reporters been invited to these gatherings, or my remarks publicized. Neither have I ever considered these appearances of mine as meant to give me an opportunity to make proclamations – be they forceful or moderate – to the outside world. I rather viewed them solely as information for internal consumption. Until now I have not heard of any mishap – political-external or educational-internal – which resulted from my speaking before the Army.

This time too, when I responded to the invitation, I had only internal consumption in mind. Although the audience was larger than usual, it was chosen and select. The setting was military. Nobody told me the press was present, neither did I see a press desk. My remarks were directed internally, especially towards the reserve officers, as citizens and as military personnel. Only on my way back to Jerusalem did I discover that my remarks might be publicized. Therefore upon returning home, I hastened to compose a report for publication and had it delivered to *Kol-Israel* and *Davar*. I also requested *Davar* to relay it to *Ha'aretz*, as is customary among the different papers. Due to the press of a variety of concerns that evening, after I'd been away from Jerusalem all day, I forgot about the existence of the *Jerusalem Post*.

Now, indeed, a passage I regrettably made found its way into that speech. I did not succeed in articulating it properly and in any event it wasn't meant for disclosure by any means. But next morning I realized that there had been a journalist present at the gathering who'd taken down my remarks. My version appeared in *Davar*, but not in *Ha'aretz*, which published its reporter's version. *The Jerusalem Post* did the same. In both these newspapers the wretched passage appeared, and in a more "crude" and damaging form than it had coming from my lips. I was quite frustrated. There are those who know how I felt that morning, and how I berated myself. But what had been done could not be undone. I only made certain that no news agency should relay that passage abroad. In the end I had no choice but to assuage myself somehow, to add this incident to series of mishaps from which none among us is immune and learn a lesson from this experience for the future.

But now you come along and draw from this failure of mine – certainly not the first and I cannot be sure it will remain the last – far-reaching, absolute and ostensibly final conclusions. I am utterly perplexed. And again, if you object to the content of the idea I expressed, there is nothing essentially new there and I am always willing to argue about it. But if it is the disclosure which has drawn ire, let me tell you simply – and with great sorrow – and asking all forgiveness for the comparison – that you do not judge and treat others as others judge and treat you. Is it only over my slips of tongue that I have had opportunity to become frustrated?

And now for your second reason. Here too events took their course. On the Thursday before that Saturday on which we met at your home in Tel Aviv, I had lunch at Vera Weizmann's in Rehovot. Pinhas Lavon was there too. The first news of the revolt in Syria arrived in the middle of the meal. Pinhas immediately began to persuade me that this was an opportune time to capture the first line of positions in Syrian territory (this was his proposal immediately upon hearing the news; two days later he proposed to settle for less, and only enter the DMZs). I was against it. He beseeched me. I said: "We shall be meeting on Saturday in Sde Boker. Let us consult with BG."

The next day, Friday, at the meeting of the party secretariat, Pinhas informed me that he had sent you a message that we would be unable to come to Sde Boker because of the situation in the neighboring countries, and that you had best come to Tel Aviv – and that he had signed my name to the message too. This was a great relief to me, for which I was glad. All the same, it seemed strange that he had not asked me before signing my name, but I did not make an issue of it, for in substance I concurred with the step he had taken.

That same afternoon I was informed by telephone in Lavon's name that I was requested to come to your home the next day half an hour before the time scheduled for all the other *haverim*. I understood that this was to be the intended consultation. A short while after I came you arrived, followed by Lavon and Dayan. (In the beginning I had not even thought of inviting Moshe to Sde Boker, neither did I think that he would come to the consultation at your home. But once he was there – having been invited by Pinhas – I again put up no objection, and surely not in his presence.)

The next day, word of Lavon's and Dayan's consultation with you "leaked" to the afternoon newspapers. My name wasn't mentioned. The disclosure was entirely discomfiting. But I was doubtful whether it should be responded to. How many times have you refrained from responding to irregularities reported about you or the government in the press? How many times have you expressed to me and to other *haverim* your disdain for leaks and reporting of a certain kind, and behaved with utter indifference towards them?

But the report gathered momentum and tongues started wagging. Yet I hesitated to interfere for fear that any correction or denial would only cause more trouble. Were there not a few times when you were given to such hesitation? Indeed, is it not only natural and correct? Does it necessarily testify to any malfeasance or baseness? I must confess the truth: that it had not entered my mind to proclaim publicly that I had convened the consultation – perhaps because of the course of developments which I have described above and which became blurred in my memory, or because I was afraid that the publication of an announcement on my part would only emphasize the importance of the matter, while it seemed to me that it was best to make little of it. Had somebody turned to me during those days with a suggestion that I publicize an explanation, I am sure I would have done so immediately. But nobody proposed such a thing – not one of all the people with whom I rub shoulders from morning till night. You too, who thought – as I now understand – that it was my duty to do so, did not take the trouble, as a friend, to suggest this step to me. Why? I am asking myself, not you, and I do not expect an answer. There are many questions with which I continually worry myself, although only others can answer them.

And so I continued to hesitate until the celebrated *Yediot Ahronot* came along and added the last straw: a blunt report on some political-military plan that you ostensibly submitted to the government and which only two Mapai ministers supported while the majority rejected it outright. This disclosure unsettled me, and I gave *Davar* a suitable account which among other things refuted the fiction about the "plan" and explained that the discussion was of minor importance and devoted exclusively to relaying news on what was happening in the neighboring countries. In passing, it was emphasized that I also participated in the discussion.

Now it turns out that my failure to publicize a denial or explanation – whether at an earlier stage or in full – was a grave sin in your eyes, so grave that without ascertaining the facts with me or voicing your outrage to me and giving me an opportunity to explain what had happened, you decided to draw conclusions, not only in the sphere of your personal relations with me but at the expense of the party.

The matter is so grave that I am obliged to say things to you that under different circumstances I would have chosen to hold inside. Everyone knows that, upon first consideration, you did not favor my candidacy for the prime-ministership, as you yourself said to dozens of *haverim*. It was your absolute right, even your duty, since you thought so. But the movement did not accept your opinion. The movement forced me to accept the post. In the end, you too accepted (so it seemed to me) the movement 's verdict. But now, as a result of your displeasure over my handling of affairs in one case or another, you have decided to deny your party your assistance and counsel – and this in a pre-election year, and when we face the calamitous unemployment of tens of thousands! Have you truly given yourself a reckoning of the threat this step holds? My sins are apparently too great to bear – but how is the party to blame, that you should find it impossible to partake in the deliberations for its future? Malignant and destructive results, stemming necessarily from your detachment from the party, will be visited upon its internal situation, which is now deeply undermined due to the confluence of several factors. Is this not clear to you?

Decide what you may, but make your decision with open eyes – in an effort to foresee the future, and without any illusions.

Yours,
Moshe

Teddy and Yitzhak are driving to Sde Boker early tomorrow morning and taking it with them.

Thursday, March 25

[- - -]

At the FM a consultation with Gideon and the DG on steps to be taken following the Ma'aleh Akrabim incident and our withdrawal from the IJMAC. We shall demand that the powers bring the matter before the Security Council as they did following Qibya. Although I at first advocated a direct appeal on our part, I acceded to the proposal of some colleagues in the Cabinet, especially Lavon, who urged that we adopt this way. And indeed an appeal made solely by us, without a subscriber, would have been received by the public as a sign of our isolation. It would further depress public morale which had reached a low ebb as a result of an absence of retaliatory response to the massacre.

I dictated detailed telegrams to Elath and Eban on the line they must take in explaining our position.[26]

I set out for Tel Aviv in the afternoon. Here I read some dire news in the press and in my papers. The US press was amenable to Jordan's version regarding Ma'aleh Akrabim that the deed was done by Israelis. That same press had vociferously publicized the fallacious version of Lt.-Colonel Shalev's alleged threats to Hutchison. The UN SG had said something about Israel's obligation to allow the return of 100,000 refugees.[27] I telephoned Jerusalem that we had to respond to the reported threats immediately. A short while later I was notified that they had applied to UN headquarters and demanded a denial, which they got. At least that!

Afterwards there was another telephone call from Jerusalem: Gideon reported that the UN SG has washed his hands of convening the conference in accordance with Article XII after Jordan's third and final refusal to attend.[28] This decision by the SG contradicts his previous declarations that he would set a date and convene the parties, come what may. I said that we had to respond in the press. After a while Michael Elizur telephoned with the draft of the communiqué which had been composed in Jerusalem and focused wholly on Jordan. I added a last paragraph directing attention to the UN as bearing its own responsibility in this situation.

---

26 See *DFPI* 9, docs.123-26, 135.

27 Sharett's assessment appears to be based on faulty information. While the Washington Embassy's press review of March 26, 1954 does refer to criticism in the *Baltimore Sun* of Col. Shalev's alleged threats about the demise of Cmdr. Hutchison and the MAC, it notes that both the *Philadelphia Enquirer* and the *New York Herald Tribune* ridiculed and dismissed Hutchison's endorsement of Jordan's allegation that the attack may have been perpetrated by disaffected Israelis. See "Initial US Press Comments on Negev Outrage," Report yhl/4080 by Harry Levin, ISA FM 130.02/2440/2i. Later press reports also criticized Hutchison's abstention from condemning Jordan. Report yhl/4099, April 2, 1954, loc.cit.

28 The official announcement and correspondence are in UN Document S/3180/Add.1, March 24, 1954, esp. 4-6.

Teddy came by upon his return from Sde Boker. He had delivered the letter and collected the response. The issue of the consultation and my failure to issue a public statement has been settled. BG accepts that there has been a misunderstanding in this matter. But not so the speech. It was not a question of what was said for internal consumption and what was publicized; the main thing was the course of policy expressed in the speech. It was one for which he could not take responsibility, since he viewed it as potentially disastrous. When we worked together there had been a "coalition" of sorts between the two of us. Sometimes the decision went his way and sometimes mine, but in any case one of us would concede. He had supposed that this "coalition" would also continue after his resignation. But this was not the case. He realized that he'd been mistaken. He had no complaints, but he could not be a partner to it and therefore... he would not be able to participate in routine party activity except, perhaps, for educational work. But his overall inclination was to abandon this too and eventually withdraw into himself entirely. He sent his greetings, and said that he'd write me an answer.

I said: "I shall await his answer."

[- - -]

Friday, March 26

An article by BG appeared [on March 21] in *Davar*: "Our security and the UN." Its title was made known well in advance and caused some consternation. Who knows what this roar of the lion in the wilderness may bring us? I read it and found that it had been written with great restraint but was in effect quite simplistic. BG proves by irrefutable dictums laced with pure logic and factual analysis that we must not rely on the protection of the UN but on our own strength alone. Wise words with which nobody takes issue. But from this point on disagreement arises. Because we can only hope in vain that the UN will protect us from Arab aggression, can we therefore mount a military initiative against the Arabs without taking into consideration the existence of the UN? This is the question and none other. The article, though, says nothing about it.[29]

[- - -]

Surprising news arrived of an attempt made by the British government to mediate between Jordan and us. It reports London's turning to Amman with an invitation to a conference with Israel in London, under British chairmanship, for the purpose of arranging matters.[30] I saw distinct signs of yearning for the round-table conferences in Chamberlain's era when Britain reigned over both Arabs

29 For a summary of Ben-Gurion's *Davar* article of March 21, see WebDoc #8.

30 On the British attempt to convene Israeli-Jordanian meetings in London, see *DFPI* 9, doc.129; Caplan, *Futile Diplomacy* III: 243-44.

and Jews in Palestine.[31]

[- - -]

Saturday, March 27

[- - -]

Lavon telephoned about another murder last night. Two guards at the village of Kisalon in the Jerusalem corridor were shot at. One was killed, the other wounded. Both their rifles were stolen. I was asked to authorize a "limited" retaliation with the explanation that restraint over this act too would mean our utter loss of control over the situation. I authorized it.

[- - -]

At home at 9:00 I conferred with Walter and Gideon. It seems that Jordan has rejected England's proposal [of good offices in London]. I deduced this from Eden telling Elath that his associates had suggested the idea of mediation to him, but he had decided it was best to heed our request and convene the SC.

Contrary to this, Eban wired that there was no chance of convening the SC. The US was vehemently against it, fearing a Soviet veto. Eban argued that we have to return to the IJMAC. That's how insensitive he is to public sentiment in Israel.[32]

Sunday, March 28

[- - -]

Sorted piles of coded telegrams at the PMO in preparation of my report to the Cabinet meeting. My report took an hour and a half and the debate lasted as long. In the end there was a confirmation of my proposals not to return to the IJMAC, not to turn to the SC at this stage, not to take any position for the time being on the possibility of British mediation. On the other hand, to take affirmative action by stepping up pressure on the powers to convene the SC themselves, to demand that they base this on the massacre at Ma'aleh Akrabim and Jordan's impropriety as regards Article XII, to issue a new statement about this impropriety and the UN SG's evading the implementation of this article.[33]

As to the method of publicizing the announcement, I first thought of setting

31 For the 1939 St. James round-table conference involving Zionist, British and Arab delegations, see Moshe Sharett, *Yoman Medini* (*Political Diary*), vol. IV (1939)(Tel Aviv: Am Oved, 1974 – in Hebrew), 9-180; Neil Caplan, *Futile Diplomacy*, vol.2, *Arab-Zionist Negotiations and the End of the Mandate* (London: Frank Cass, 1986; Routledge 2015), ch.4 and docs. 26-27.

32 See Eban to Rafael, March 27, 1954, ISA FM 130.16/2948/6.

33 See *DFPI* 9, docs.130, 132.

up a question to me in the Knesset to which I would answer, but the ministers were against this, arguing that by using this subterfuge I would weaken the force of the announcement. I did not agree with this attitude toward the institution of questions in the Knesset, which I highly value and wish to elevate in our political arena. But I gave way to my colleagues and announced that I would hold a press conference tomorrow.

As regards the nature of the response to Jordan's impropriety over Article XII, there was a disagreement between Lavon and myself. He favored a strong statement charging Jordan with the blame for the unilateral cancellation of the Armistice Agreement through its violation of Article XII. I contended that we must not throw the slogan of annulling the Armistice Agreement at Jordan, even as an accusation. I proposed a more calculated formula. Golda supported me.

Even before the meeting, Lavon had informed me that the retaliation for the Kisalon murder had not been executed last night and was postponed to this evening. I warned him against its being done in dimensions which would be seen be seen as a response to Akrabim. If so, we would be found belying our statements that we were not set on direct action at this stage, but were seeking peaceful satisfaction via our appeal to the UN and the powers. He solemnly promised that he had given strict orders against any over-reaction, so that the operation would bear the distinct character of a local and limited response. I questioned him about the details of the plan and he told them to me.

At the Cabinet meeting Ziama, on the one hand, and Yosef Sapir, on the other, demanded a response to the Kisalon attack. They contended that the public could not bear additional proofs that our lives are at anyone's mercy without confidence of the Army's ability to respond.

Moshe Shapira is leaving for the US the day after tomorrow for a serious effort to strengthen the spirit of Zionism and loyalty to Israel among Orthodox Jewry. He had been solemnly promised at the last Cabinet meeting that this Sunday we would conclude the debate on the Rabbinical Judges Appointment Law. Since the Cabinet meeting, which lasted three hours, was entirely devoted to foreign policy, I decided that we would reconvene this afternoon.

[- - -]

The second Cabinet meeting began at 3:30. It lasted until 7:00 and was wholly devoted to the Rabbinical Judges Law. There was a tenacious conflict, but we came to conclusions by majority decisions on the two basic questions: the wording of the declaration of allegiance of the Rabbinical Judges, and the composition of the appointments committee. On both issues the secular ministers made concessions to the religious ones. But since the latter were by no means satisfied in all their demands, they didn't vote in favor of the decisions and let themselves be "coerced." Ziama Aran left the meeting fuming and frothing, utterly irate with the religious ministers. I told him that his fury was to no avail. Such was the make-up of the state and its people, and one must exercise boundless patience.

Zipporah went to a dinner party at our friends the Krongolds without me. I had been wedged among people and talked endlessly all day. I had an emotional need to be alone and rest. I dined by myself; my mind settled down. I then composed a telegram to Abba Eban and Eliahu Elath:

> You must make an effort, which is constantly demanded and especially necessary now, to sense from afar what the nation's soul is experiencing. There is a mood of dejection throughout the country over the lack of retaliation to Akrabim, which is interpreted as impotence and an inability to protect civilian lives. *Herut* is trying to exploit the spirit of despair by advocating fanatic madness, but that is not what is worrying. Throughout the party there is confusion and lack of confidence in the rightness of my policies. Among the officer corps there is pent-up unrest and, I fear, a growing lack of loyalty and no shortage of whisperings [against me]. Moshe Keren in *Ha'aretz* writes highly of me, but this affects only a small, insignificant circle. Herzl Berger in *Davar* is helpful too, but the masses are nourished by the *Ma'ariv* and *Yediot* tabloids. Intelligent people understand that the present regime's approach is one of restraint and rational deliberation, and a balanced policy between the threat of force and the enlisting of international support. Alas, the UN's repute is at a low ebb, the US is disqualified as being hostile, and London is suspected of conspiracies. There are many who cannot see any way out, and derision [of the government] is spreading. In this situation, it is vital that our effort to curb dangerous [military] outbursts be accompanied by strong and demonstrative measures of political pressure. Considerations of foreign policy also demand pressure on the powers for vigorous intervention aimed at the other side to prevent further trouble. Therefore the internal benefits of our withdrawal from the IJMAC outweigh any external damage to us, all the more so since the final balance-sheet on the external front regarding this step hasn't been rendered yet. Again, in this situation, our routine appeal to the SC, instead of pressure on the powers, would mean added humiliation and dejection. Therefore a supreme effort is necessary to activate the powers without despairing in advance, and while doing so we should make our leaving the IJMAC a spur for our benefit instead of letting them use it as ammunition against us. Meanwhile, the Kisalon murder, which demonstrates that our border settlements are defenseless, sows added dejection and threatens to break the spirit of the settlers, demands a local response [i.e., military reprisal] which I have authorized. I face a very complicated front. The considerations are manifold and require precise balancing, internally as well.[34]

BG's letter arrived in the morning [see below]. He admitted that his assumption concerning the continuation of the "coalition" between us even after his retirement had been naive and unrealistic. But if I'm going my own way – and it is clear to him that most of the ministers support me – he had no choice but to desist from any role in political activity, including that of the party. The letter testifies to an intractable emotional tangle, profound turmoil and depression. There are distinct

34 *DFPI* 9, doc.133; *Sharett: Mivhar Te'udot*, doc.129.

signs of agitation in the handwriting. The analysis is altogether unsound. For had BG really assumed a priori that a "coalition" between us would exist even after his retirement? Why then had he objected to my candidacy and preferred Eshkol? And if he had objected and gave in against his will, it means he had no illusions as regards the independence of my course. There's no question but that the idea of the ongoing "coalition" arose in his head only after the fact.

Sde Boker, 26.3.1954

Moshe – Greetings and Shalom,

Concerning the matter of the meeting in Tel Aviv, I accept your comments and I have put the matter entirely out of my mind.

I cannot dismiss the political matter in so few words, though I shall not attempt to exhaust it at all. I shall say what I consider fundamental and practical at this time (incidentally: Ziama did not take a stenogram of the conversation, and could not have reported my remarks with accuracy, but the different nuance doesn't matter).

Our joint work in the political arena already in the days of the Jewish Agency was a sort of coalition, because we had different approaches. This "coalition" endured within the framework of the state as well. I consciously upheld it – aware of the distance and the difference in approach and aware of the need and <u>benefit</u> of this "coalition." I reconciled myself to some things which were mistaken in my eyes, prevented some mistakes when I could, and tried to correct (what seemed a "correction" in my eyes) whenever it was possible. I saw political matters (and still do) as not the single thing, or the main thing, at any given time, and the natural cooperation in all other matters seemed "proper" and required in my eyes this "coalition" on political matters.

I had thought that this coalition would continue even after my departure from the Cabinet. And it has become clear to me that this was childish naiveté on my part. I should have realized beforehand that upon my departure from the Cabinet, this "coalition" was nullified. Almost all of the Cabinet members have the same approach as you, and it is natural that a clearly defined line should be implemented and declared (even though the line declared doesn't necessarily have to be the line implemented), which is the line that you represent. I accept this as a fact.

One thing was clear upon my decision to leave the Cabinet, and it is clear to me now as well: not to dispute the Cabinet's actions or inaction, not to argue with it, and to express no opinion about its actions. Although I am not in the "coalition," I am not willing to be in the opposition (a) because of the reason that has pushed me into the "coalition," (b) because of additional reasons of a personal nature that are no business of the public.

This prohibits any political activity on my part. I cannot say *Amen* to something in which I do not believe. I cannot dispute it and argue with it, even behind closed doors, because with us everything reaches *Ma'ariv* or another newspaper. And even if it did not, I would not wish to burden the Cabinet, least of all the Prime Minister, whoever he might be, certainly not a friend with whom I have cooperated for twenty years in the political arena.

I have an inclination to withdraw not only from political matters but from public affairs in general. But I do not know whether I shall be able to decide such a thing before the elections to the Third Knesset. If we were already past the elections, I would not hesitate in this matter – and the reason is not social or political, but internal and personal. I am not sure that I shall be able to do it this year. But I cannot conceive of any political activity on my part.

It is not a matter of this speech or that expression. I do not have to hear your speeches in order to know your opinion and your approach, just as you do not have to listen to my speeches in order to know my differing approach.

I wish to devote my activity – to the extent that and as long as I shall yet be active – to the educational affairs of our movement. If it is of no help to the party, neither does it harm it. I am not capable of anything more.

Before my departure you said that from now on team-work would be required. This is my advice as well. Weekly meetings of our *haverim* in the Cabinet, for discussion and counsel and personal criticism exercised together, and perhaps a more urgent consultation of 4-5 *haverim* (although I doubt whether there is time for it).

I do not know whether I have clarified my position. But this is how things stand as far as I am concerned.

D.B.G.

Monday, March 29

Upon arriving at the PMO, Yitzhak Navon informed me that at 7:30 Radio Ramallah had broadcast an extremely excited report about an attack of a mighty Israeli force on the village of Nahhalin in the vicinity of Bethlehem. There were some ten dead, many wounded; an attempt to blow up houses, including the mosque, had failed. I told Yitzhak to telephone the Defense Ministry immediately and ask them for information.

In the meantime I let Yitzhak read BG's letter. I pointed out the intrinsic unsoundness of the argument. He asked how I interpreted the term "coalition" in the context of the letter. I said that BG thus wishes to explain his assumption that even in his absence I would not act according to my way, but according to the compromise reached after the clash of our opinions had we continued to work together.

Yitzhak disagreed. BG simply meant to say that in his view it was incumbent upon me to consult with him on every important issue, stay in constant contact with him, exploit every opportunity to learn his opinion and act accordingly. In any event, I said that I would certainly write to him with the intention of bringing him back to party activity; that its cessation was completely unreasonable in light of the explanation given. The reason for the cessation is rooted in an emotional complex and it serves only an outlet for release from anguish.

The reply from [the Defense Ministry in] Tel Aviv arrived. It was true. But the force had been small. No houses had been blown up and, God forbid, no damage done to the mosque. I asked how the matter would be publicized by an Israeli source so that the truth be told. They said they had no idea: perhaps the Foreign Ministry could see to it?

I spent most of the first half of the day at the MFA and dealt with composing two main statements for the afternoon's press conference: the first, on my initiative, concerning Article XII, with which I shall open the conference, and the second, as an answer to a pre-arranged question, on Bedell Smith's[35] announcement concerning his justification for supplying the Arabs with arms. Gideon and Joe were of great assistance with the wording, and Arthur and the DG helped with the English version. It was a collective effort and the result was fine indeed. As always, when the warp is well written, the woof is not difficult to add.

[- - -]

In the afternoon a crowd of press correspondents from Israel and abroad gathered in my room, some sixty men and women. I conducted the press conference by alternating between two languages. I began by reading my statement in which I questioned the change made in the Secretary-General's course of behavior and warned Jordan that abrogation of the Armistice Agreement would raise the threat of serious consequences, first of all to itself.[36]

This unleashed a torrent of questions on the Nahhalin action. I said that I did not yet have any first-hand information, but initial impressions make it clear that this was a retaliation for the Kisalon murder. It was also clear from previous incidents that the Arabs always greatly exaggerate their estimate of the size of the Israeli force which conducts a retaliation. I wished to make it well understood that the Nahhalin incident should not be seen as an answer to Ma'aleh Akrabim. There were many more questions of all sorts, some of them quite annoying, but I succeeded in restraining myself and avoided responding tersely. I said to myself beforehand that my status as PM obliged me and I passed the test.[37]

I returned home some time after 4:00, and sat over my papers. At 5:00 I received a large party for tea – the renowned Bennike with the two experts on water who have come to examine issues concerning the Jordan channel. They were the American [J.W.] Dixon and the Dutchman [W.F.] Eysvoogel. They were accompanied by our experts Blass and Wiener, as well as Arthur, Gideon, Tekoah, Shalev, Arieh Eilan,[38] and last but not least the fox-like [Henri] Vigier [Bennike's deputy]. Dixon made a great impression. He's the epitome of the American expert, erudite and practical, pursues a straight path and sees nothing but the project at hand, its possibilities

---

35 General Walter Bedell Smith (1895-1961). Former Head of the Joint CoS, US Ambassador to Moscow (during the period that Golda Myerson was there). Director of the Central Intelligence Agency (CIA) (1950-1953). Under-Secretary of State for Foreign Affairs (February 1953 - October 1954). A friend of Israel and a personal friend of Ben-Gurion. Code-named "*hayadid*" (the friend) in Israeli documents.

36 The text of Sharett's statement is in ISA FM 130.16/2948/6. On this day, Eban conveyed a different version of Israel's official response (*DFPI* 9, doc.137). See below, entry for March 31.

37 See also *DFPI* 9, doc.134.

38 Arieh Eilan (1916-1995). Born in Russia. Settled in Palestine just before the establishment of the state in 1948 and joined JA Political Department. After working in the PMO (1951-1953), became MFA Liaison Officer with the IDF and the UNTSO (1953-1956). Later held several posts, including service on Israel's Permanent Mission to the UN and as Israel Ambassador to Kenya.

and benefits. The Dutchman also made a serious impression. They are evidently convinced of the possibility of ensuring a satisfactory supply of water to the B'tekha Valley[39] even after the diversion of the Jordan into the [B'not Yaakov] canal. They will meet in New York in April to compose a report in which they will list the measures we must take and the guarantees we must give. If this holds true, then we have safely overcome this stage of patient discussion with the experts.[40]

The trouble is that Bennike doesn't believe that the only thing needing proof is our ability to meet Syrian demands for water for irrigation. He still clings to the doctrine of military advantage which would ostensibly accrue to us from the execution of the Jordan diversion project. He contends that as long as the Security Council hasn't ruled otherwise, his opinion on this matter is unshakable. That forebodes a future of trouble for us.

[- - -]

At one point in the evening our son Haim telephoned from Kibbutz Hamadiya. He praised me for the Nahhalin retaliation, saying "well done" and adding that "everyone was satisfied." Undoubtedly, he was expressing in this way the general feeling in the country, which breathed a sigh of relief and felt a return of self-respect.

[- - -]

Tuesday, March 30

The morning newspapers are full of my statements and replies at the press conference yesterday. But the astonishing news is about the Soviet veto in the SC, which blocked the adoption of New Zealand's resolution concerning freedom of navigation in the Suez Canal.[41]

This is a great blow to the SC. It almost completely paralyzes it as regards any intervention in security matters between the Arabs and ourselves, except perhaps for those cases in which we are the accused. In those cases the West and the Soviet Union can vote together with the Arabs against us. This second veto proves beyond a shadow of doubt that the Soviet Union has made a decision of principle to support the Arabs against Israel in every way. The first question is not the future of

39 A fertile plain extending northeast from the Sea of Galilee, within Palestine's territory, in Syrian possession until its capture by Israel in 1967.

40 The Dixon-Eysvoogel report was submitted on April 3, 1954. See: ISA FM 130.03/1962/9; UNA S-0370-0027-06. The report's conclusions are reproduced in Aryeh Shalev, *Shituf Pe'ula B'Imut: Mishtar Shvitat Hanesheq Yisrael-Suriya, 1949-1955* (Tel Aviv: Ministry of Defense Publishing House, 1989), 398-99 [appendix 18].

41 For background on the veto and the text of the defeated resolution, see Editorial Note, *DFPI* 9, doc.139; Yaacov Ro'i, *Soviet Decision-Making in Practice: The USSR and Israel, 1947-1954* (New Brunswick, NJ / London: Transaction Books, 1980), 488-90; Ro'i, *From Encroachment to Involvement*, doc.34; Israel UN Delegation meeting, March 30, 1954, ISA FM 130.03/1962/14.

navigation in Suez and the Gulf of Aqaba – there is still time to consider it – but the fate of our demand that the powers convene the SC for a debate on the situation on the Jordanian border. If the US has been hesitating to accede to this demand till now, after this veto it will be even more so.

[- - -]

Last night I composed a telegram to Eban and Elath[42] that, although the Nahhalin matter [has] complicated things, they must know that the action has relaxed tension in Israel, annulled anguish, and lifted morale.

At the MFA I composed a restrained and measured statement for the Foreign Ministry Spokesman on the consequences of the Russian use of the veto on the problem of freedom of navigation. Consulted with Eytan and Rafael on the conclusions we must draw from the veto. Gideon suggested that we abandon our initiative to convene the SC and only exercise pressure on the powers to prevail upon the SG to convene the conference according to Article XII. I opposed this hasty suggestion. I contended that, specifically because the paralysis of the SC may perhaps offer an opening for freedom of action on our part regarding passage to Eilat and the Jordan channel, we had to demonstrate that we were exhausting all possibilities of activating the SC despite all our disappointments. Furthermore, we need to demonstrate that we would be the last to abandon the final line of defense in the war over its authority.

Walter supported my view, and in a highly original manner. Since the Soviet Union had substantiated its veto with the explanation that direct negotiations between the parties should be sought rather than force SC decisions upon them, it should be taken at its word. We must therefore convince the powers to convene the SC and bring before it one of the proposals for Jordan to meet with Israel – whether by means of directing the SG to convene a conference according to Article XII, or by means of accepting Eden's proposal concerning the appointment of a SC committee with Jordan and Israel participating. In accordance with this I composed a briefing for Eban and Elath of first thoughts on the veto and after,[43] and called a meeting of the Cabinet FADC for this afternoon.

[- - -]

Meanwhile a bunch of cables arrived. Eban is in total despair about the SC in view of the veto and recommends giving up any thought of resorting to it. Abe Harman, on the contrary, wonders why we ourselves aren't applying to the Council!

After a luncheon at which we entertained several guests I managed to rest for exactly a quarter of an hour, and at 4:30 reported to the Knesset for the meeting of the Cabinet FADC. I spoke about the significance and implications of the

42 Reproduced above, page 301.
43 *DFPI* 9, doc.140.

Soviet veto. Rokach again exasperated me with his naiveté, whether authentic or a stupid pretense of it. "What made the Russians decide on a veto?" and "Are they really against us?" and "If so – why?" and "Why don't we look into the matter 'in depth'?" and "What prevents us from finding out?" etc. The argument was waged principally between Ziama and myself, on the one hand, and Lavon, on the other, Rosen and Bernstein supporting us, the former in full force and the latter weakly. Lavon supported Eban this time, i.e., to wash our hands of any initiative towards the SC. Ziama supported me: to make another, perhaps last, attempt, but not to hasten to break the thread. In the end I concluded that we had to demand that the powers decide forthwith and not dally, so that we should know where we stand. At the end of the meeting, Lavon took me aside and asked for authorization for a daring, albeit non-aggressive, operation – sending a boat on a patrol from Eilat through the Red Sea to the straits at the outlet of the Gulf in order to reconnoiter Egyptian positions there. The boat would set sail under the guise of a fishing boat. I authorized it.[44]

[- - -]

Wednesday, March 31

According to the morning press there was another mishap. Eban's letter to Hammarskjöld[45] which doesn't accord at all with my statement at the press conference the day before yesterday, was published. I had aimed a sharp barb at Jordan and a slightly less blunt one, though explicit and blatant, at the SG. I had also hinted that we had asked for an explanation from him about his desertion of the front. But Abba has acted otherwise. All his arrows were aimed only at Jordan, while he heaped only praise and thanks on the SG for his efforts and patience.

---

44 Here follow extracts of the FADC minutes covering Sharett's remarks:

"This is the second time that the Soviet Union has exercised its veto over a matter pertaining to the Middle East, in favor of the Arabs and against us. Now the question is what are we to do. If this is the general Soviet line, it means the end of the Security Council as an institution in which we can find some protection from Arab machinations against us. Moreover, if the Soviet veto on Middle East affairs is constant, why should the Western powers accommodate themselves to Soviet dictatorship in the SC? In view of this, they would stop using this institution as an arena for their initiatives. This would mean that the SC has ceased to play a positive role for us; it can play only a negative one.

"My view, together with my colleagues at the MFA, is that we should be the last ones to leave the trenches of the SC, and this because we may find ourselves taking direct action on the Jordan and Gulf of Eilat fronts. In the Suez we cannot take the law into our own hands. Not so in Eilat. If we are to act in the Gulf of Eilat, it is better to first put it on record that we appealed to the SC in this matter. I suggest that, in view of the fact that we have already appealed to the Western powers to bring the problem of our relations with Jordan to the SC, we should now ask them to expedite their deliberations on this matter and inform us of their decision."

45 *DFPI* 9, doc.137.

My spirits were already dampened at breakfast.

Telephoned Walter from the PMO to find out how this had happened. Abba had been briefed on what he was to write; had another course been instructed to him? And if he had been properly briefed, why did he pay it no heed? Now he has no recourse other than to write a second letter. This lack of coordination between our UN delegation in New York and ourselves threatens to turn into a festering sore. [- - -] I later re-drafted a telegram to Abba composed by Walter about the letter to Hammarskjöld.[46]

[- - -]

At 3:30, Weltman[47] came to discuss the course of the Kasztner trial.[48] The Public Prosecutor evidently hasn't got a clue about the political and public character of the trial and of its sensational repercussions. The prosecutor, Amnon Tal, is a total failure. If Joel Brand, who was involved in the Nazi "trucks-for-blood" affair in Hungary,[49] is called as a witness, he will certainly complicate things, since in the period after the failure of his mission he went berserk and accused the leaders of the JA of responsibility in the slaughter of Hungarian Jewry. And now all this would be

46 Eytan to Eban, March 31, 1954, ISA FM 130.16/2948/6. Eban justified his position in his reply to Eytan, April 1, 1954, loc.cit.

47 Weltman (Tuval), Meir (1905-1981). Born in Yugoslavia. Lawyer. During WWII worked in Istanbul for the Rescue Committee of Yugoslavian Jews. Later, Israel Minister to Budapest.

48 Although it was Malkiel Gruenwald who was on trial, accused of slandering Rudolph Kasztner, from an early stage the trial became erroneously referred to as "the Kasztner trial."

49 Joel Brand (1906-1964) was a member of the Budapest Jewish relief committee set up during WWII under the leadership of Otto Komoly and Rudolf Kasztner. As a member of this committee, Brand met Adolf Eichmann, upon whose orders he left for neutral Turkey on May 17, 1944, to present the JA with a German proposition to enable Hungarian Jews to leave Hungary - but not to Palestine – in exchange for the supply of 10,000 trucks and other equipment to be supplied by the Allied powers. Despite the extreme unlikelihood of the transaction appealing to the Allies, Brand was allowed to travel to Palestine in order to meet with a more senior representative of the JAE. When he reached Aleppo, he was arrested by the British, who suspected him of being a Nazi agent; Sharett came there to meet him in the presence of a British intelligence officer, after which Brand was taken to Cairo for interrogation. Upon his release on October 7, 1944, he returned to Jerusalem and remained in Palestine.

Brand told his story in his book *A Mission for those Sentenced to Death*, published in Israel in 1957 with an illuminating epilogue by Sharett in which he surveyed the unsuccessful efforts to save Hungarian Jewry from slaughter by the Nazis, while commenting on Brand's political naiveté. See below, entries for February 15 and August 24, 1956. The English edition of Brand's book, *Desperate Mission: Joel Brand's Story as told by Alex Weissberg*, translated from the German by Constantine FitzGibbon and Andrew Foster-Melliar (New York: Criterion Books, 1958), does not include Sharett's epilogue.

On Brand's activities, see also: Ehud Avriel, *Open the Gates! The Dramatic Personal Story of "Illegal" Immigration to Israel* (New York: Atheneum, 1975), ch.14; Yehuda Bauer, *Jews for Sale?: Nazi-Jewish Negotiations, 1933-1945*. New Haven: Yale University Press, 1994; Ronald Florence, *Emissary of the Doomed: Bargaining for Lives in the Holocaust*. New York: Viking, 2010.

incriminating material for Shmuel Tamir to use. [Weltman's] only advice was that Haim Cohn must take the prosecution into his own hands after the recess.

[- - -]

At 6:00 met with Dolik. He described to me Pinhas Sapir's new idea for both solving the unemployment crisis and curbing the spiraling inflation. Instead of continuing to subsidize prices and demand a "refund" from those of means, it would be better to abolish the subsidies and compensate those of limited means. This would save the Finance Ministry some IL.50 million, which would be devoted to the development budget in order to create jobs for the unemployed. [- - -] In the end, he warned me about attempts being made to undermine me because of my policy of restraint and consideration of international opinion. He supported me whole-heartedly and viewed the opposite line,[50] which seeks its prop in Sde Boker, as perilous. He remarked: "He who established the state can also destroy it."

At dinner, Zipporah told me most excitedly about her visit to the Kastel Ma'abarah with her friend Zelda Yiron, who is doing social work there. Poverty and want, and Orthodox education, and children bursting with health from the mountain air, eyes sparkling with wonderful lively and alert intelligence, a slow but continuing move from tin shacks to permanent housing. Great work by the Health Ministry and Hadassah in the treatment of trachoma and infant care.

The radio announced that Great Britain has officially turned to the US and France for the purpose of convening the SC for a debate on relations between Israel and Jordan. It seems that the Soviet veto will not deter British Foreign Secretary Eden. Or is he perhaps relying on Vyshinsky not to defeat a resolution which would also condemn Israel – and perhaps mainly Israel – for withdrawing from the IJMAC and for the retaliation at Nahhalin? But the US is still opposed to convening the SC.[51]

Haim called from Tel Aviv. He had participated there in the founding of a party circle of young *haverim*. Their leaders have visited BG in Sde Boker and found him deeply immersed in philosophical-religious-moral thinking. The impression was of him being totally cut off from Party life. At the end Haim said everybody in the country was satisfied with the well-considered line – the clear and strong pronouncements of the PM in the Knesset and in the press, and the last retaliation which was executed without the killing of women and children.

Teddy came by upon his return from Tel Aviv. There's a report that Jordan has turned to Iraq for military aid in view of the danger of an Israeli attack, both infantry and air force. I said: "We have returned to square one: are we set on war or on preventing it?" According to Teddy, the IDF senior echelon was itching for war,

50 Emanating from the Army and the Ministry of Defense.

51 On the continuing manoeuvers around convening the UN SC over the issue of friction along the Israel-Jordan frontier, see *DFPI* 9, docs.144-46.

full of anxiety at the growing military strength of the Arabs. It was blinded as regards economic complexities and the pitfalls of international relations. I wondered out loud to what extent Egypt's military strength might have grown this year, when all of its army's fervor is directed towards fighting for power and is consumed by internal dissension. According to Teddy, some 500 officers, the cream of Egypt's military, have taken off their uniforms and gone into administration and political life.

[- - -]

Thursday, April 1

[- - -]

An Italian journalist visiting Israel at our invitation conducted a proper interview with me employing a written questionnaire. When I replied to a question of his concerning the situation in Egypt that "the 'fleshpot of Egypt' still boiling and bubbling and who knows what is cooking inside," it turned out that he had no idea what the metaphor meant and I had to explain to him the source of the idiom[52]. I forgot that Catholic children are none too familiar with the Old Testament.

[- - -]

At 8:00 pm we went to the Soviet Consul's for dinner. To their great fortune, the Soviets had succeeded in renting a magnificent building in the heights of Ramat Gan, meant once for a hotel, and had furnished it with a mixture of cumbersome and tasteless Russian furniture and pieces of Israeli furniture, coated with ugly show-off bright silk and velvet. There were magnificent rugs on the floors and the walls were covered by landscape paintings, all done by Soviet artists of the young generation, fully loyal to the realistic and simplistic Zhdanovist school with not a sign of innovative spirit.[53] The dinner served was superb, high in quantity and quality above any which I have ever seen or tasted anywhere in our country. There were five goblets to each of us, besides a glass, all filled up in the course of the feast. However, after the okra and the pickled mushrooms and the traditional Russian borsht with cream and the meatballs and the stuffed dumplings, there came a sudden drop when we were served with canned fruit compote, a disastrous demonstration of lack of culture. One could easily imagine to what a climax a French chef might have brought us with a dessert to this feast!

I had decided beforehand not to touch upon the matter of the Soviet veto on

52 "And the children of Israel said unto them, 'Oh that we had died by the hand of the Lord in the land of Egypt, when we sat by the fleshpots and we ate bread to the full!'..." (*Exodus*, 16:3).

53 The Soviet leader Andrei Zhdanov (1896-1948) was a "cultural commissar" who oversaw all aspects of cultural production in the Soviet Union and implemented a harsh policy of censorship and exile against any deviators from the Marxist-Communist line.

this occasion,[54] but to save the subject for a special upbraiding which I mean to give Ambassador Abramov next week, when I invite him to Jerusalem specifically for that purpose. But he himself brought up current affairs and began to muse about the lack of peace and lay the blame on Great Britain and the US. I contradicted this trite and banal assessment and said that the blame lies with everyone who is capable of furthering peace and does the exact opposite. I noted that this applies to the Soviet Union just as it does to the US. He made no reply to this, but began to question me about the conditions for peace. I said that there was no question of conditions – Israel as it is – and that it was only a matter of goodwill. He said: "Nevertheless, there is the refugee problem, and the Arabs contend that at least some of them must be returned."

I asked: "Where and when have refugees ever been returned? Has Russia perhaps done so? Has Czechoslovakia?" He remained silent. I went on to ask: "Who has ever offered to pay for abandoned lands like us? Again, perhaps Russia, perhaps Czechoslovakia?" He again remained silent. I sufficed with this.

I emerged sullen and angry from this evening and bored to the core. An insincere group of people – every word calculated, malicious and obtuse, devoid of any spirit – hiding behind the mask of sweet courtesy. And, to top it all off, every bit of conversation betrayed an astonishing and blatant lack of culture.

In the middle of the meal I was called to the telephone. I was sure that something untoward had happened and was ready for news of a new Arab terrorist attack. I guessed wrong. Lavon was on the other end of the line. The boat he had talked to me about has already managed to run aground near the Saudi Arabian shore. We are in wireless contact with the men by means of a reconnaissance airplane. Tomorrow another boat will set out for the scene of the trouble and an attempt will be made to land aircraft in order to rescue the stranded. The Saudi Arabian shore is desolate, but there is fear of the arrival of Egyptians who may take our men prisoner.

Friday, April 2

[- - -]

Eppy telephoned to announce that all the men on the boat that was stranded in the Gulf of Aqaba have been returned to Eilat in small airplanes. The boat itself was blown up.

In the afternoon returned to Jerusalem. Cold has returned to the city with heavy clouds and rain and we had to heat our apartment. At 6:15 I heard over the radio that on the occasion of the Book Fair this evening there will be

54 I.e., the veto cast on March 29, which in effect prevented the SC from criticizing Egypt for its restrictions on Israeli shipping through the Suez Canal. See above, page 305 n.41; *DFPI* 9, doc.150.

a literary soirée at the Tel-Or Hall featuring Shenhar,[55] Shamir[56] and Shalev.[57] The spirit came upon me[58] and I said to Zipporah: "'Let us go and hear the words of the living God'[59] and get acquainted with faces unseen before." (I have never met Shamir or Shalev.) Zipporah was enthusiastic, and drove there on the spur of the moment, but arrived too early. So we went over to our in-laws and convinced them to come with us. When we returned the hall was almost full, mostly with youth. Shenhar read out two short stories from the days of the siege of Jerusalem during the War of Independence, both full of charm and sincerity. At the end of the second story, in which a young boy from Galilee, who came to defend Jerusalem, is suddenly shot, his voice faltered and he almost wept – so deep was his emotion, living the tragedy anew, most probably since he was an eye-witness to the incident. Shalev recited poems about Jerusalem that were wonderful from a literary point if view, but harmful and poisonous politically as far the young listeners were concerned – an extremely chauvinistic content, harking back, evidently, to mandatory days, if not to the Ottomans, since they centered on the tombs of Abshalom and the prophet Zechariah, and the road to Bethlehem[60] and how he could not look into the eyes of his son because he could not visit his grandfather's tomb on the Mount of Olives – as if he was incapable of strengthening his son's pride in being a citizen of an independent Israel. At the end Nathan Agmon[61] was summoned to the podium and showered the hall with a torrent of empty verbosity to the point of nausea.

Saturday, April 3

[- - -]

The Public Prosecutor, Haim Cohn, came for a consultation over the proceedings of the Kasztner case. Joel Brand has already appeared as a witness for the prosecution. It is not impossible that Tamir will request my testimony. The court will reconvene in three weeks, so there is enough time to prepare.

[- - -]

All day long I haphazardly read material about Baron Edmond de Rothschild but have not reached the stage of writing up my speech about him which I am to deliver

55 Yitzhak Shenhar (Shenberg) (1902-1957). Born in Russia. Settled in Palestine in 1921. Poet, writer and translator.

56 Moshe Shamir (1921-2004). Born in Palestine. Writer, publicist and playwright.

57 Yitzhak Shalev (1918-1992). Born in Palestine. Poet, writer and essayist.

58 Reference to *I Samuel*, 16:13: "and the Spirit of the LORD came upon David."

59 *Jeremiah*, 23:36.

60 All on the Jordanian side of the city.

61 Nathan Agmon (Bisrtritzky) (1896-1980). Born in Russia. Settled in Palestine in 1920. Writer and playwright.

in the Knesset. Composing this speech has put me under stress for the last few days.

Sunday, April 4

Lavon came in this morning to tell me something about what has followed up. Last week, Bennike seized an opportunity to show his "wisdom" and "talent" wisdom and acumen again. The EIMAC had ruled that Egypt must return an Israeli sergeant they abducted some time ago. The Egyptians wished to appeal; the chairman said that he had to ask the CoS whether an appeal was possible in this case. According to the Armistice Agreement, appeals are allowed only on matters of principle. But, having been asked, Bennike ruled that it was always done. Accordingly, it was not incumbent upon the Egyptians to return the abducted person in the meantime. Also, since appeal is a prerogative rather than an obligation, they can drag out the matter without end. The special armistice committee which handles appeals has not convened for the past three years or so. Some dozen items have accumulated on its agenda, to remain untouched until doomsday. Meanwhile, the IDF decided that an Egyptian soldier must be abducted for the purposes of an exchange. The attempt was made, and it encountered armed resistance. An Egyptian sergeant was indeed abducted, but another three were killed, among them an officer. One of our own men was slightly wounded. So now we have a new Israeli aggression on the agenda.

At the Cabinet meeting I reported on the course of events as regards our appeal to the Security Council.[62]

[- - -]

The last item was the problem of the municipal elections in Nazareth. Our people there have become quite panicky lately in view of local developments. The Muslims have disintegrated. The power of Bishop George Hakim[63] is on the ascendence, and the same goes for the Communists there. Our party activists, as well as the officers of the Military Government, are demanding a postponement of the elections, which means a scandal here and negative reverberations abroad, and also the stoking of the fires of hatred in Nazareth and the widening of the gap between the state and the majority of the local population. On the other hand, holding the elections on time runs the risk of surrendering the city into the hands of Israel's enemies, underlining its Christian character and making it a center of enmity and disorderliness. The question

---

62 Despite evidence of British and American reluctance to antagonize Jordan or other Arab regimes and of increasing Soviet support for the Arab states at the UN, Israel was still hoping to have the three Western powers introduce a condemnation of the Ma'aleh Akrabim massacre in the SC and put pressure on Jordan. See Cabinet protocols for April 4, 1954, ISA; *DFPI* 9, doc.146; Ludlow-Eliav conversation, April 6, 1954, US National Archives (USNA) 684A.85/4-654.

63 George Selim Hakim (1908-2001). Melkite Greek Patriarch of Antioch; Bishop of Akka; head of the Greek Orthodox Church in Israel.

is which is the lesser of the two evils. Lavon said he was decidedly for a postponement, then left the meeting for dinner at the President's. Golda and Ziama were of the same opinion. The GZ were against. Eshkol proposed that we hold the elections on time but on condition that the municipal committee elected would function only until the date of the nation-wide elections to the municipalities. The majority of ministers voted for this solution. I abstained.

In the middle of the meeting, an envelope was handed to me which brought back old memories from the days of the British Mandate. The envelope was from the British Embassy in Tel Aviv, inside it a letter from Ambassador Evans to me, containing a personal communication from British PM Winston Churchill, which ran as follows:

> As a friend of Israel and the Zionist cause I feel bound to express to Your Excellency my concern at the recent serious incidents and the growing tension between Israel and her neighbors.
>
> We shall do what we can to influence the Arab States, but we look to you to make counsels of statesmanship and patience prevail on the Israeli side.
>
> A renewal of war between Israel and the Arabs would be a calamity. If the United Kingdom in virtue of its Treaty obligations, become involved in that war, it would be a sad ending to the hopes and achievements of the last few decades in Palestine.
>
> I am determined for my part to do everything I can to avoid a disaster and it is for that reason that I ask you now to do everything in your power to urge on your people moderation and restraint.[64]

At the end of the meeting, I read a translation of the letter out loud to my colleagues. They were astounded. Both Sapir and Ziama immediately insisted upon reading the original. They both said that such words had never been uttered to us before. Ziama saw the letter as a threat to destroy the State of Israel. I did not hold with this interpretation. The "sad ending to the hopes and achievements" which Churchill mentioned was the end of the entire historical chapter of contact and cooperation between Britain and us, not the end of the physical existence of the state. Nevertheless, it is a harsh document, and will demand a carefully thought-out reply.

Pinhas [Lavon] came home after dinner to inquire about the outcome of the Nazareth debate. When he learned about it he was flabbergasted and demanded we take steps to annul it [i.e., the scheduled election]. I said it was an impossible idea. He then sounded me out on the possibility of stirring up strife in the city, so that in view of potential rioting we could postpone the elections. I told him to banish such ideas from his head.

[- - -]

64 Churchill to Sharett, April 2, 1954, TNA, FO371/111069 VR1072/35, and quoted in *DFPI* 9, doc.152.

To Ben-Gurion, With Heavy Heart

Monday, April 5

In the morning I peeked in at the PMO for just a moment, and immediately drove to the Foreign Ministry. I composed a first draft of the reply to Churchill's telegram, and held a consultation on the briefing of Elath pending his talk with Eden tomorrow.

In the afternoon we held a prolonged meeting of the Cabinet Foreign Affairs and Defense Committee on the instructions to Elath. Apparently all agreed that, in view of the slant of the military and political center of gravity towards the Arab-Muslim pole in the Middle East with the signing of the Pakistan-Turkey alliance,[1] with the chance of Iraq joining it and the possibility of an Anglo-Egyptian agreement on the evacuation of the Suez Canal Zone, it was worth our while to again try to discuss cooperation on matters of regional security with Great Britain. Actually, most of my colleagues lodged such far-reaching reservations as regards the hints I wished to put in Elath's mouth – and I did not suggest anything more than hints – that in effect this idea was shelved. I myself proposed nothing other than reminding Eden of the exchange between HMG and ourselves following the visit of [General Brian] Robertson.[2] I wished to confront him with the fact that, following negotiations between the IDF people and the British military delegation that visited Israel, to this day they still owed us an answer. All the same, it was my opinion that, in view of the Anglo-Egyptian negotiations concerning the evacuation, it is worth our while at this time to stress the matter of facilities and warehouses which was then discussed. This would allow us to see whether Eden would be tempted to seize upon these remarks to broaden the discussion towards the possibility of an alternative to the Canal Zone. This could create the

1 On April 2, Turkey and Pakistan signed a treaty of "friendship and cooperation for security" which would later be expanded to include Iran, Iraq and the UK in what became known, after February 24, 1955, as the "Baghdad Pact" (later CENTO). Although not a signatory, the US was a strong backer of this alliance which it saw as a bulwark to "contain" the Soviet Union and to prevent the spread of Soviet influence in the ME.

2 Brian H. Robertson (1896-1974). Commander-in-Chief, British ME Land Forces. Visited Israel in February 1951 and held high-level talks with Defense Minister Ben-Gurion and IDF CoS Yigael Yadin. See *Documents on the Foreign Policy of Israel,* volume 6 (1951), ed. Yemima Rosenthal (Jerusalem: Israel State Archives, 1991), docs.68-69, 71-72, 77, 138, 259, 508.

background for renewed negotiations in which we could ascertain whether such an alternative can be implemented in a manner acceptable to us. I referred not to bases, but to installations which should be built with Britain's help and handed over to our possession to fulfill their desired purpose when the time comes. This proposal received sharp objections and I was forced to abandon it.[3]

The reply to Churchill's communication was also examined.[- - -][4]

Finally, I raised the question of our direct action aimed at achieving free passage through the Straits of Tiran to Eilat after the SC debate had proved fruitless because of the Russian veto. We were about to sail a ship under the Greek flag from Haifa to Eilat. If the Egyptians stopped it we could only protest, for it is under a foreign flag. The Defense Ministry is preparing two operations connected with vessels under the Israeli flag: a tiny ship sailing out from Eilat, and a larger one from one of the East African ports sailing to Eilat.[5]

Here I learned for the first time of the IDF's ideas concerning retaliations against the Egyptians in case they take action against us in either of these cases. In the first case, seizing some Egyptian ship in the Mediterranean; in the second case, sinking an Egyptian ship anchored near the Straits by means of a mine attached below the water-line. The first retaliatory plan puzzled me, since only a short while ago Lavon poured coals upon Rafael's head for even thinking of such a possibility. At that time, Lavon contended that in such a case we should have the worst of it, since the Egyptians would be able to harm us to a much larger extent than we could harm them. In regard to the second retaliatory plan, it seemed plausible to me at first sight. However, the questions remained as to how the IDF went about planning such audacious and perilous operations without any prior decision in principle by the government, and what would have happened had I not raised the issue in time. I had no desire to conduct an argument with Lavon within the framework of the Committee and said that there was still time to discuss these plans. My purpose was to scrutinize the matter within a more limited circle first.

[- - -]

All evening long, till after 1:00 am, I labored over two replies: a telegram to Churchill and a letter to BG [- - -]:[6]

Jerusalem, April 4, 1954

Ben-Gurion, Shalom,

With heavy heart I come to write you this time too. Perhaps not all of the bleak

3 See also *DFPI* 9, doc.156. For reports of the April 6 Elath-Eden interview, see *DFPI* 9, doc.157; Eden to Evans, April 6, 1954, TNA FO371/111070 VR1072/38. Lavon's reaction to reports of this interview is described below, entry for April 13.

4 See *DFPI* 9, doc.152.

5 See also *DFPI* 9, doc.160.

6 The final text of Sharett's reply to Churchill is reproduced below, entry for April 8.

premonitions which I foresaw when you first notified us of your decision to retire have come true. For instance, one "prophecy" of mine, concerning the disintegration of the coalition and advancing the elections, have been proven wrong in the meantime. On the other hand, a crisis which I had not envisioned at all is threatening the party, namely your withdrawal from all party activity.

To the extent that I thought in advance about your position and role in party life and activity after you ceased being PM, I consoled myself that when the cruel burden of official responsibility and the exhausting daily gnawing of rule and government had been removed from your shoulders, you would be better able to devote time and thought and initiative to party matters. This would serve as some compensation for your abandonment of the helm and a weighty addition to the public leadership of our party. I am horrified at the thought that apparently this was but a vain consolation and the contrary is destined to be the truth.

I have not yet reconciled myself to this decree and I am resolved to challenge it. This I shall do both as a party member and as a *haver* of yours.

Your remarks on the "coalition" between us in the JAE and the government are correct and apt. You will certainly agree that in this "coalition" – except for rare cases which I considered of utmost importance and concerning which I could not by any means renounce my position without bringing them to an authorized resolution, whether national or within the party – in most cases your view predominated over mine. This state of affairs was natural and justified, and even though it caused me much torment on frequent occasions, I did not object to it.

Even now, when I stand at the head of the government and ostensibly at the head of the party, I am still far from deciding things according to my view in every matter and in every case. It is my way to consult frequently and to take far-reaching consideration of the opinions of the *haverim*. At any rate, I consult with other *haverim* on matters which I could settle by myself more than anybody consults with me on matters which, it seems to me, one is obliged to. In the short period which has elapsed since you resigned, things have been done without my knowledge and against my views over which I made no protest. I have also authorized steps to be taken out of consideration for the views of others, steps which I would not have authorized had I been the "sole judge."

But that does not mean that I am willing to disregard the special responsibility which I bear by virtue of my position to the extent of subordinating my views to those of others on issues which are decisive and bear crucial consequence. In such cases, I consider myself not only permitted but obliged to decide according to my way, unless a contrary decision is made by an authorized institution, whether governmental or in the party, whose rulings I would obey. And if a decision against me is made, the question may arise whether I can be asked to continue bearing the responsibility. For the time being no such question has arisen.

As to the differences in our views, your assumption that the "coalition" between us would continue even after your withdrawal from the government raises a complex question. I do not know how you envisioned the realization of such a "coalition," whether by a system of frequent meetings for consultation in addition to the exchange of letters and communications by urgent messengers, or by means of my attuning myself to your view in every case in order to accept it as is, or in order to draw the line of a decision midway between my decided opinion and your conjectured view.

I will not linger over the question of the practicality of each of these two methods. Actually, I have already hinted that the government, upon your departure from it, has not chosen one unanimous, clear-cut position as regards certain problems. My lot throughout these days has consisted of quite sharp disagreements and I do not think that your line is unrepresented at these debates. Furthermore, if you would regularly attend the Party Secretariat and its Political Committee meetings, I have no doubt that the mere fact of your participation would induce us to raise important questions for examination and resolution by these institutions. I also have no doubt that your view would carry great and sometimes decisive weight in the results of these discussions.

On the other hand, it is incumbent upon me to say that it was not only clear to myself beforehand that the changing of the guard in the prime-ministership might bring about a change of policy direction on certain matters, or at least in certain instances, but I said so very explicitly and in public and prior to its taking place.

At the meeting of the Party Central Committee on November 25, 1953, at which my candidacy for the prime-ministership was confirmed, among other things I said the following (according to the stenogram):

> May it not be taken as arrogance, but merely as an expression of responsibility, if I say that it is my duty to view this trust is given to me and my *haverim* in the Cabinet as we see fit and with utter freedom of judgement. The use of this trust can only be dependent upon our sense of responsibility and our judgement – under the guidance of the party and the people. It may not be easy to say these things, but it is easier for me to say them because I know that in this I am expressing Ben-Gurion's conviction. I shall be gratified if I am accorded the possibility of [his] counsel and guidance. But the very *use* of such counsel and guidance is to be decided by me and my *haverim*, for it is we who are responsible [before the people], since it is on our shoulders that this task has been placed. And I say all this for the benefit of the *haverim* gathered here and for the entire membership of our party. They must understand that this task can be approached in this way only and none other.

I shall give you an example to illustrate the tenor of my thoughts and feelings. I have heard that after the Ma'aleh Akrabim incident you expressed an opinion that we should occupy some territory in Jordan. In my view, such a step would have immediately set us at war with Jordan, with Britain fighting on their side against us and the Soviet Union raising hell and condemning us before the entire world, in effect branding us as an aggressor. In this situation, the state would have been faced with a serious debacle and perhaps ruin. Perhaps I was right; perhaps I wasn't. But let us assume that I had subordinated my view to yours in this case, on the one hand, and that at the same time my assumption was proved right, on the other. What would history have said later? It would not have said that Sharett did what he did because such was BG's opinion and he is therefore absolved of responsibility. It would have said that Sharett's government made a fatal mistake and that it was responsible for the debacle or ruin. In such situations, when the man standing at the helm does not act in accordance with his incisive views and the strong voice of his conscience, while bearing moral and political responsibility for what is done, a concrete contradiction is created. This cannot be demanded of me.

I owed you this explanation because you raised the question – even though you ostensibly annulled it yourself.

But I do not see any connection, relation or linkage between your analysis of the "coalition" issue and the conclusion you have reached about your activity in the party. I view this decision of yours as not only boding severe damage to the party – and therefore blatantly wrong – but as entirely spurious from a logical point of view, and therefore as an inexplicable injustice.

Why, if the government's line on questions of foreign or security policy is mistaken in your view, are you bereft of the ability to contribute your share to strengthening the party internally and reinforcing it in the face of future public challenges? Justifiably, and with all your moral authority, you are claiming your right [to function] as a simple citizen and rank-and-file party member. What would be the fate of the party if every *haver* considered himself free to withhold his assistance and cooperation from it whenever the party adopted a course he did not advocate in some important, even crucial, field of activity?

Just because the government's position on certain questions is mistaken and detrimental in your view, would you not want the party to make a vigorous and efficient effort, so far as is possible, to win a majority in the coming elections? Would you not wish it such success whole-heartedly? Would you take a position of indifference and unconcern for the result of the elections and the party's fate in them? No one could conceive of such an attitude on your part. But if this is not your attitude – nor shall it ever be – how can you exercise this right to stand aloof and not do what you are capable of in order to express this attitude with generous, thoughtful counsel and concrete action?

Again I shall give you an example. We sat in your home in Tel Aviv on that Saturday morning and consulted on a difficult political question. Our views conflicted. You were in favor of the IDF entering the Syrian DMZs, and I opposed it. You advocated an effort to transform Lebanon into a Christian republic, and I objected to it. So there was no "coalition" between us this time. But immediately after this strained discussion we went into a meeting, together with other *haverim*, to discuss the convening of the party Council and preparation for the elections. Did the political dissension and the strain that pervaded it in any way exert influence on the atmosphere, course and results of the second consultation? You proposed some basic guidelines, and I wholeheartedly and openly subscribed to them. I proposed some organizational measures in the same vein and you supported my proposals. In what way did the political argument interfere with our mutual concern for the party?

You write to me that you have no wish to "burden the government, least of all the Prime Minister." It's not for me to decide to what extent you refrain from burdening the Prime Minister by your non-cooperation with the party. But I am permitted to complain and protest against the severe burden you do not refrain from placing on the party because the Prime Minister, in your view, is following an erroneous path.

I beseech you to re-examine the matter. Look at it from another angle – the party's angle. This party does not deserve to be forsaken by you. Even a sinful government does not deserve it. Israel has no other government. And if this government is different than what it was or might have been, its members are not to blame. And at any rate, Israel does not have another party to bear the burden of the state as this party does. And you have no way of helping the state other than by means of this one and only party. Or would you truly deny the state your help, even if "they that lead cause [it] to err"?[7]

Yours,
Moshe[8]

---

7 *Isaiah*, 3:12.
8 *Sharett: Mivhar Te'udot*, doc.130.

Tuesday, April 6

[On this date, Sharett composed a lengthy and eloquent diary entry (not translated here) about the state funeral, in which he participated, for the remains of Baron Edmond de Rothschild at his estate in Zichron Yaakov, and the speech he crafted for delivering at the Knesset on the occasion on the next day.
On the same date, the CoS Moshe Dayan made the following revealing comments during a conversation with Anthony Moore, First Secretary at the British Embassy in Tel Aviv. After criticizing Britain's erroneous assessment of Arab "mentality," Dayan spoke of the widespread feeling that "there was no forum to which Israel could bring her legitimate complaints. This was a most serious situation, which exacerbated the frustration so widely felt in Israel. There was no doubt that public opinion generally accepted Mr Ben-Gurion's thesis that, important though foreign opinion was, Israel should rely primarily on her own efforts.... There was very deep conviction in the country that there was a point beyond which Mr Sharett's policy of appealing here and complaining there could not be pursued."][9]

Wednesday, April 7

[- - -]

Went back to the PMO and worked with Arthur on a new draft of the reply to Churchill.[10]

[- - -]

A meeting of the *haverim* in the Cabinet was scheduled for this evening. I had an argument with Lavon concerning his attendance. He informed me that due to his tour of the Gaza Strip frontier where the situation has been deteriorating recently, he could not come. (He came back to Tel Aviv at 7:00 and could of course get to Jerusalem by 8:30. However it's one thing to respond to an urgent meeting in days past,[11] and another nowadays.) I ascribed special importance to this meeting because a meeting of the party's Political Committee was scheduled for tomorrow, at which I planned to pose for examination the searing question whether we are set on war or peace. I did not want to plunge into this maelstrom without first consulting with the *haverim* in the Cabinet. Golda and Eshkol and Dinur and Naftali showed up, whereas Lavon and Ziama did not.

[- - -]

Well did this enrage me.[12] We nevertheless sat and clarified some issues.

---

9 Moore to Falla, April 6, 1954, TNA FO371/111070 VR1072/46.

10 See below, entry for April 8.

11 I.e., when Ben-Gurion convened such meetings.

12 This was not the first or last time that Lavon's non-attendance angered Sharett. In August 1953, Sharett had written to Lavon: "Your refusal to attend the consultation of our members of the government [*haverenu*] is highly astounding and creates a very serious problem. If the intention is to push me into resigning from my function as acting prime minister, there is nothing easier… Is that what you are after?" Lavon was then acting Defense Minister. Quoted in Ben-Gurion, *Devarim Kahavayatam*, 23.

I announced that I would not limit myself to delivering a report on the situation at the Political Committee, but would go into the essence of our overall policy on the security front. After the ministers had departed, Ze'ev Sharef began to prevail on me not to present the problem of war and peace to the Political Committee. Word of it would leak out and result in great harm, both internally and externally.

Meanwhile, anger and pique at Lavon and Aran's absence from the consultation seeped into my innards and I finally decided to heed Sharef's entreaty, which was seconded by Yitzhak Navon, and to postpone the meeting of the Political Committee, though not for their reasons. After some consideration, I saw no point in convening the committee without its being preceded by an in-depth internal consultation among the five members who constitute the central core of the party in the government [i.e., Sharett, Lavon, Eshkol, Myerson and Aran]. I directed Navon to see to the publication of a notice in the newspaper tomorrow morning that the meeting has been postponed.

[- - -]

Thursday, April 8

Golda came early to the PMO to discuss "personal" matters. She suggested that "the five"[13] sit down to discuss retaliations policy with Lavon.

[- - -]

A serious discussion concerning progress in the Kasztner case from this point onward, with Haim Cohn, Ehud, Teddy and Amos.[14] I ordered Haim Cohn to take the prosecution into his own hands. I have deliberated and decided that I should not take the stand as a witness. I decided instead to call a press conference after the case is over and there to spread the whole truth about Joel Brand's story. When the case reopens, Ehud will be the main witness.

At the Foreign Ministry, I edited the final draft of the reply to Churchill and it was telegraphed to Elath for transmission. The missive became quite lengthy, but it was impossible to shorten it without sacrificing major fundamentals of content. It is not often that an opportunity opens to address the old man in such a direct manner.

> Personal and Confidential London, April 13, 1954
> My dear Prime Minister,
>
> I have been asked by Mr Sharett to transmit to you the following personal and confidential message:
>
> The anxiety which prompted your personal message and the reaffirmation of your life-long friendship for the Zionist cause, and now for Israel, are very deeply appreciated.

13 See above, page 150 n.29.

14 Amos Manor (1918-2007). Born in Hungary. Settled in Israel in 1948. Head of the *Shin-Bet* (1953-1963).

The effect of events along the Jordan border has been cumulative over the years. Since the conclusion of the Armistice, hundreds of Israelis have been killed and heavy losses of property sustained. Israel is most gravely concerned at this mounting toll. In every instance it has been action from Jordan which has initiated a fresh and tragic cycle of violence, in the end resulting also in the loss of Arab lives.

Israel does not want war, and will for her part do nothing to provoke it. Yet no-one will understand better than you, how difficult it is for a virile community to look on passively while its members in exposed localities or at isolated spots on its highways, sometimes deep within its territory, are murdered at random.

After the revolting outrage at Ma'aleh Akrabim (Scorpions' Pass) on 17 March, the people of Israel were profoundly stirred. But restraint was the watchword. The very enormity of the event forbade retaliation, and hopes were pinned on the international reaction.

But the UN investigation of the case bogged down; action by the Great Powers was slow in coming; the Kisalon murder and a new wave of Jordanian provocations followed quickly, and patience broke under the strain.

In the face of the Jordan Government's constant default in keeping the border under effective control, the conviction inevitably spreads that the only way to persuade that Government of its duty is by showing that it runs greater risks in condoning or encouraging murderous raids into Israel than by taking stern action against them.

The root of the problem is that the Arab States are promoting a virulent propaganda of incitement and hostility against Israel, are continuing to serve as bases of armed attack against her, and instead of advancing towards peace, are doing everything - by boycott and blockade, by violent words and scarcely less violent deeds - to aggravate the situation.

It is in this context that the Anglo-Jordan Treaty must, we believe, be viewed. As Mr Eden emphasized only a few days ago, the Treaty is subject to the duty of the parties to seek a peaceful settlement of their disputes. The Treaty further expressly obliged Jordan not to adopt in regard to other countries an attitude which might create difficulties for the United Kingdom.

In these circumstances, it is hard to reconcile Jordan's reliance upon the Treaty with its flat refusals, in repudiation of a clear injunction of the Armistice Agreement, to attend the conference with Israel convened by the UN SC to review the operation of the Armistice. And it is inconceivable to us that the United Kingdom should leave the Jordan Government under the illusion that it can find in the Anglo-Jordan Treaty a shield for the organization within its territory of terror and outrage against Israel citizens. Just because the eventualities to which you yourself refer are so grave - and we were painfully surprised to see that you considered them at all possible - a supreme effort must be made to remove the prime cause of the evil.

The Treaty indubitably gives Britain powerful influence in Amman. We are hard put to it to explain to our public why that influence has so far been inadequate to prevail upon the Jordan Government to abandon its present attitude, and put an end to the armed incursions.

You may rest assured that it will be the earnest endeavor of my colleagues and myself to curb passions and make sane counsels prevail. But we all believe that if the present grievous deterioration is to be stemmed and reversed, it must be by a new and determined move towards real peace. It is to this that the efforts of all concerned must be directed.

Through the clouds of the present local storms we see far-reaching vistas of beneficent co-operation between Britain and Israel in culture and trade, in the advancement and defence of democracy, and in all creative achievement. It would be appalling if these prospects were checked by the precipitation of a tragic crisis. Let us do everything in our power to avert a catastrophe, and to bring about the realization of the lofty vision which I know is ever present to your mind.

Believe me to be, my dear Prime Minister,
Yours very sincerely,[15]

Walter came by and told me of several mishaps, one of which I already knew about. Several days ago, at a meeting Walter had with Russell, the latter told him that he had found in the Government of Israel a man who well understands America's need to arm the Arabs, that all our protestations against this policy would be to no avail and that indeed Israel must not interfere with this activity since these arms are needed for the protection of the region. This most clever person, blessed with great foresight and a courageous tongue, is Teddy Kollek. I then immediately asked Teddy if all this is really true, and it turned out that it was a mixture of truth and falsehood. Teddy had indeed said that, in view of what he had heard in Washington, the Americans had decided to arm the Arabs despite our objections. But he had not justified this verdict; on the contrary, he had explained to Russell the stupidity and injustice permeating this American policy. Before I managed to castigate him, Teddy hastened to admit his mistake. There is no curing this most enchanting of men and no teaching will ever change him. He is oblivious to the differentiation between what is meant for internal consumption, and what is appropriate to be said for outside use.

Now I learn from the DG that Teddy had said more than that. He admitted saying that "not only would protests be in vain, but it is his opinion that there is no sense continuing protesting." I received a bitter and well justified cable from Aubrey: what was the point of all his efforts, which have been so far fruitful, if a man so high up in the hierarchy of our government releases the USA of any commitment to take them into account? He added that what Teddy did was tantamount to one person filling up his bath and another coming in and pulling the plug. And when people at the Foreign Ministry here criticized him, he gave them a cute answer: "But you know that I disagree with the Foreign Ministry on this issue!"

Another issue is Reuven Shiloah's proposal to Russell that he and Hart[16] come to my house for tea. Hart is in charge of Israeli affairs at the State Department, and is currently visiting Israel. He will not come to visit me at my office in accordance with the stupid US embargo of [i.e., against officials visiting] the Foreign Ministry

15 Sharett to Churchill, transmitted by Elath to Churchill, April 13, 1954, *DFPI* 9, doc.170. Original in TNA FO371/111070 VR1072/57/I, also in VR1072/68, with the following handwritten minute of a FO official: "Pretty good cheek? What do you think?" For Churchill's reply see below, entry for April 28.

16 Parker T. Hart (1910-1997). US diplomat. Director, US State Department (USSD) Office of Near East Affairs (1952-1955); Counselor and Chef de Mission, US Embassy, Cairo (1955-1958). Later Deputy Assistant Secretary of State for Near Eastern and South Asian Affairs and Ambassador to Saudi Arabia, Kuwait, Turkey and North Yemen, among others.

[in Jerusalem], but he will be so kind as to meet Ministry officials at the King David [Hotel]. Walter asked whether I was willing to receive him for tea at home, and I replied in the negative. He said, "But they may already consider themselves invited." I answered that I would give it further consideration, but even if I should receive them, I would talk to them about the weather, and archaeological discoveries, and would not touch upon any political matter. They must understand that a private visit at home is no substitute for official contact, and we must not make the embargo any easier for them.

[- - -]

Friday, April 9

Raphael Bash, the Party Secretary, came in all insulted and wrought up. Why was the Political Committee postponed? The members were angry and he had no explanation. I had no alternative but to tell him the truth: I had asked for an internal discussion first, but all in vain because of a lack of cooperation by a few key *haverim.* If such a discussion is not held, then nothing doing – I shall not participate in the deliberations of the "political" unless it convenes with full participation by all members, including Ziama. I explained to him the reasons for my behavior, to which seemingly the party is not accustomed. It became apparent that there are *haverim* who presume that they can ignore their responsibilities on the assumption that I shall in any case carry on and see that matters are attended to. I have no alternative but to make them aware of their responsibilities by shattering this assumption. I have taken on my office not in order to be a single decision maker. I had explicitly said that I looked forward to teamwork. No team – no office. It is only by this behavior that I see any chance of making some *haverim* realize the seriousness of the situation when they abstain from cooperation.

Gideon telephoned from Jerusalem. The situation along the Gaza Strip border has seriously deteriorated. Last night the Egyptians launched some military ambushes, and five of our soldiers were wounded. I saw these actions as a response to our ambush, the object of which had been the abduction of a single Egyptian soldier and which had led, in addition to the abduction, to the killing of an Egyptian officer and two soldiers. Some time ago Gideon had spoken to me about renewing his proposal of a direct appeal to the Egyptian government for a meeting designated to settle border security arrangements. He and the DG have prepared a draft, and are sending it to me for confirmation. Perhaps I would like to pick Lavon's brain?

Meanwhile, he told me about the conversation held with Hart yesterday. It turns out that some time ago three American Ambassadors in Arab capitals reported to the State Department that, according to verified information, the Israeli government had prepared a detailed plan of retaliations according to timetable: such-and-such an operation on such-and-such a date against such-and-such a target, and so forth. Russell also admitted that he himself had also reported to the State Department a few days ago that, according to reports circulating among the diplomatic corps in Tel Aviv, a decision on a certain retaliation had been adopted at the Cabinet meeting. Our people had vigorously denied it, and made a mockery of these fictions. Hart had voiced a stern warning against additional retaliations. The US was trying to relax the tension, and may have succeeded in arranging a secret meeting between me and [Jordanian Prime Minister Fawzi al-]Mulki. Retaliations only upset their various efforts. (Whenever we take action, it always turns out, post facto – they by no means let us in on the secret beforehand – that the US had been on the threshold of bringing about our salvation, but we had dealt it a deadly blow by our own hand!) If we continue our course, we will eventually force them to intervene vigorously and no good would come of it. He had asked that we return to the IJMAC and issue a statement against retaliations. He was answered in the negative.[17]

At 12:30, met with Lavon together with Eshkol in the Defense Ministry in the *Kirya*, Tel Aviv. We went over the budget for special arrangements for the security of the roads of the southern Negev and its main points. I brought up last night's events. It was learnt that six ambushes had been set, but we had been caught in only four of them. I told Lavon that this was a response to a response, and that I saw no point in another response on our part. The question whether retaliations prevent new incidents has not been answered in the light of experience. At any rate, in this case our response did cause counter-incidents, and it was best we restrain ourselves.

Lavon's face puckered. He said that he had in mind not an ordinary retaliation but something which would not involve bloodshed, but nonetheless make an impression, let us say, the demolition of a bridge. I asked how could he be sure that everything would go according to plan, and that we would not encounter armed resistance, as in the case of the abduction, and be forced to open fire and cause casualties? I noted incidentally that the abduction had been implemented without any prior coordination with me.

Eshkol posed another question: "How can we be sure that the demolition of a bridge will not open another round of sabotage operations on the part of the Egyptians?" Lavon's answer was: "We don't have any such targets in the area." I said: "Must the Egyptians seek exact mutuality? How can we be sure that they will not attack a settlement?"

I said that I would not countenance any action without a consultation of the *haverim*, and proposed that the five of us meet: he [Lavon], myself, Eshkol, Golda and Ziama. He wondered when such a consultation could take place. I said: "On Sunday." "It would be too late," slipped out of his lips. It was hard to escape the impression that the matter of the bridge wasn't just a vague idea, but an operation

17 For Russell's brief account of this meeting, see *FRUS 1952-1954*, doc.787.

which had already been decided upon. That meant that again a retaliatory action by the IDF was decided upon without obtaining authorization from me. I expressed astonishment at his certainty that a retaliation, even if it were necessary, must come immediately. Has the Army truly become so accustomed to pull the trigger immediately, or otherwise its morale would be broken? I would not agree that such a consideration should be the determining one.

He said: "Perish the thought, it is by no means a question of the Army's morale but a question of policy of action: retaliations or no retaliations."

I said: "Quite so. Let us clarify the policy once and for all."

He said: "But if so, then not just by means of the opinion of 'the five' [i.e., five senior Mapai Cabinet ministers] alone, but in the Party Political Committee."

I laughed and said: "Am I not the one who is asking for a debate in the Political Committee? But it is best that this be preceded by an internal one."

With that I left the room.

A few minutes later a consultation on German reparations matters began in the adjacent meeting hall. I had just opened the meeting when Lavon entered: "When can we convene that consultation?" I said on Sunday afternoon. I understood what had happened in the meantime; he had contacted the General Staff and had ordered them to postpone the operation. This entire exchange perturbed me not a little.

[- - -]

In the evening we dined at Shmuel Bendor's. It was proper a *Shabbat* meal with candles and *kiddush*[18] as was his custom. Michael Simon, who accompanied Baron Rothschild's remains from France on board an Israel Navy ship, recounted the highlights of the journey, including the ceremonies in Paris and Marseille and the machinations of the [French branch of the] Rothschilds who did their best to play down the whole event in the French press. Bendor told us about Hart's visit to the border area by the Gaza Strip, and his seeing the aftermath of the Egyptian attacks of last night. Shalev had asked him there: "What would you do in such a situation?" Hart replied that he had come to see, not to solve problems.

Saturday, April 10

For lunch at home with James McDonald[19] and his wife, Fletcher-Cooke[20] and

18 Sanctification ceremony.

19 James Grover McDonald (1886-1964). First US Ambassador to Israel (1948-1951). Chairman, Advisory Council, Development Corporation for Israel (1951-1961). Former League of Nations High Commissioner for Refugees Coming from Germany (1933-1935), and a member of the Anglo-American Committee of Inquiry (1945-1946).

20 John Fletcher-Cooke (1911-1989). Colonial service in Malta and British Mandatory Palestine. Chief Secretary of the British administration in Cyprus. Later Governor of Tanganyika, and Conservative Party MP.

his new American wife, as well as nine others. The conversation with Fletcher was interesting. He came over for a holiday and to learn of Israel's achievements in the spheres of housing and professional training, and was much impressed. I asked him about Cyprus and he discussed the problems created by the strong penchant for unification with Greece. While the Cypriots are by far above the natives of African colonies, the regime in the island is harsher than anything experienced in mandatory Palestine, since the population opposes the suggested new constitution and is not cooperating with the government. The only grains of democracy are to be found at the municipal level, but the trouble is that three of the island's five cities are in the hands of the Communists. Politically, the population is divided between supporters of reactionary Archbishop Makarios and identification with communism. There is no middle-of-the-road force, and no labor movement with roots in the tradition of democratic socialism.

I said Israel's extraordinary fortune and achievement was because, thanks to mass immigration of working people, a democratic labor movement had established itself before communism had even appeared in the historical arena as a serious competitor of democratic socialism. This is why this country had succeeded in fending off attempts of expansion by the Cominform[21] forces. In neighboring countries such as Cyprus, Lebanon or Egypt, labor organization is a late phenomenon; the masses of workers there were completely submerged in ignorance and lethargy, and upon awakening they saw before their eyes only communism as a counter-weight to capitalism and reaction. My interlocutor fully agreed with my analysis.

[- - -]

After the guests departed I sat with Walter, who was one of them, over current Foreign Ministry matters. Then I napped for a quarter of an hour, then wrote my diary – endlessly.

Gideon telephoned to ask what he was to say to Hart at the final meeting tonight with him in Ramat Gan. I said two things: (a) He rejects retaliations? Fine. What solution does he propose? The State Department can content itself with negative counsel: objection to retaliations. The Israeli government requires affirmative counsel. What might that be? (b) In such a situation, are they truly ready to justify the lack of direct contact between themselves and the Government of Israel here [in Jerusalem]? What is their Embassy doing in Ramat Gan? Moreover, they should not tell us such fairy tales, such as that we upset a plan of theirs to solve the problem of Jerusalem by moving our Ministry of Foreign Affairs there. They have a bad habit of revealing their plans for our salvation *post facto*. We did notify them in advance that we would move the Ministry and they did not notify us in advance that they had a miraculous plan.

---

21 Cominform (Communist Information Bureau, 1947-1956), successor to the Comintern, official coordination body for Communist and workers' parties under Soviet direction.

In an earlier conversation with Reuven I had told him to contend with the State Department people that there was no point in relying on the situation which existed last year concerning Jerusalem, for right now it is clear that the transfer of the Foreign Ministry at the time was a god-send. What would I have done today if the Ministry had stayed on in Tel Aviv? Would I have refused to become Prime Minister? Or agreed to be cut into pieces? Or let somebody else be Foreign Minister? Aren't they ready to reach a decision in view of this new situation?

Sunday, April 11

The press is raging over a speech made by my "friend" Henry Byroade somewhere in Ohio. He taught the Arabs a lesson, but for the sake of balance went one better in giving Israel a sound smacking. He set out to censure Zionism as though he had come upon a hitherto unknown truth. He constructed a flimsy edifice on the basis of shallow knowledge. He made a silly but malignant remark learning about the Jews being of various nationalities but belonging to one religion, and admonished Israel to identify itself with the Middle East and avoid any attachment to the diaspora.[22]

Gideon telephoned the PMO about his talk last night with Hart. He had spoken to him about Jerusalem according to my instructions. When he asked him for the reason the State Department had not informed us beforehand about the plan they were preparing for a solution to the problem of the Holy City, Hart pretended to be puzzled while Russell and his companions blushed. This was an undisputed proof that a miraculous plan never existed but was invented as a means to censure us. Hart said that in the wake of his talk with Shiloah, he had an idea how to begin untying the tangle of Jerusalem. As to the matter of border security, he wondered whether the solution may not lie in putting up a security fence. He once again said that they were seriously looking into the possibility of a high-level meeting between us and Jordan.

[- - -]

In the afternoon there convened the meeting of "the five." It was a strained, two-hour-long discussion. Are we to respond to the Egyptian ambushes, or desist, and what method of response should we choose in general? We were four against one, the differences of shades and choice of words notwithstanding. For lack of choice, Lavon accepted the verdict – for the time being. We examined the manner of presenting the problem in its entirety to the Political Committee. We were of one mind that the complete picture could not be unfolded, since we could not rely on secrecy being

22 Henry Byroade, "The Middle East in New Perspective," address to Dayton World Affairs Council, April 9, 1954, US State Department Press Release 185, *Department of State Bulletin*, April 26, 1954, pp.628-33.

kept. Pinhas, who in our previous conversation contended that he could not accept the decision of "the five" on the question of retaliation policy and that the matter had to be resolved by the Political Committee, did not raise this concern at all.

At the PMO I received Golda and Bernstein for a consultation on the ship "Agamemnon," which is due to dock at Haifa on next Saturday morning, the eve of the first day of Passover. Several hundred tourist-pilgrims will embark from it and, according to their agency's itinerary, are to arrive in the Old City of Jerusalem the following day. That means that the port of Haifa must work on *Shabbat*, Israeli buses must transport the travellers to Israeli Jerusalem on *Shabbat* for the night's lodging and transport them again the next morning, at the height of the holiday, from the King David to the border gate leading to Eastern, Jordanian Jerusalem. The Rabbinate has raised a loud complaint and the transportation networks are at a loss for a solution. To work on *Shabbat* – a new scandal. Not to work on *Shabbat* – a mortal blow. As it is, tourism is limping because of the border incidents.

Here, before us, is a flow of pilgrims which we are interested in attracting and cultivating with every allurement and amenity. Shall we lock our gates in the face of these travellers? And at such a time? I said that it was inconceivable to turn the ship away. A "little bit" of work is done at the port of Haifa on *Shabbat* anyway. Buses run in Haifa on *Shabbat* anyway. They will be able to drive on the road from Haifa to Jerusalem without giving affront. Upon entering Jerusalem, let them be driven to the hotel along Ruppin Street. The sting is the drive to the border gate along a route which passes by the ultra-orthodox Meah She'arim quarter. But the Jerusalem District Officer, Biran,[23] is contemplating a detour for them. And God will come to our rescue. The problem of what to say to the Rabbinate remains. I said that I would consult with its "fifth column" inside the Foreign Ministry, meaning Yaacov Herzog.[24]

[- - -]

Reuven came for dinner, a farewell conversation and summing-up. We went over the whole list of issues and studied each one from every angle: the insoluble situation in the border areas, a constant nerve-wracking and compelling need for restraint and holding back, on the one hand, and for relaxing the reins occasionally, on the other; the troubles still awaiting us regarding the Jordan channel; free passage to Eilat; the delusion in assuming that by parliamentary maneuvers at the UN or by establishing personal contacts [with Arab personalities] in Europe, it is possible to win hearts and impregnate them with a desire for peace when this does not arise of its own. The only two areas in which we do have the power to establish new

23 Avraham (Bergman) Biran (1909-2008). Born in Palestine. Archeologist. Israel Delegate to IJMAC (1951-1955); Israel Consul-General to Los Angeles (1955-1958); later Director, MFA Division for Armistice Affairs and Director, Israel Department of Antiquities and Museums.

24 Herzog, himself religious, was son of Chief Rabbi Isaac Halevi Herzog.

facts and thereby perhaps generate new processes in Israeli-Arab relations are the conditions of the Arab minority in Israel (with the enlistment of a new "motor" for this arena in the person of Shmuel Divon), and the matter of compensation payments for abandoned Arab lands (accepting the plan to set aside a sum from the German reparations for that purpose).[25]

All of these were issues I raised. Reuven added the matter of Eric Johnston's mission and not only in connection with irrigation plans, but as aimed at considering possibilities of general economic development.

Reuven managed to undo the snag of the "invitation to tea." He explained to Russell that I cannot invite him to my home in Jerusalem without setting a precedent for other members of the diplomatic corps and must therefore insist upon his visiting me at the PMO as a precondition for the renewal of relations. There were signs of a planned "thaw" in the conversation with Hart: a "green light" to visits by the heads of delegations to me at the PMO, and visits by others to the heads of divisions at the Foreign Ministry.

[- - -]

A letter from Ben-Gurion arrived in reply to my last letter. Ben-Gurion contends that he would not have dreamt of demanding of anyone in the government to consult with him after his resignation. He meant these should be a "coalition" of the two streams in the party. What still remains completely unexplained is how he justifies his refusal to participate in the preparation of the party council. This letter is appended.

Sde Boker, 8.4.54

Moshe, Shalom,

When I am free I may address a few remarks in reply to your letter. But I feel an urgent need to forestall one mistake, which I fear may have arisen due to what I said to you. I never entertained the notion that members of the Cabinet and the Prime Minister would be obliged in any way to consult with me from time to time, or ask my opinion or take it into consideration. When I decided to leave the government I considered the matter very, very well in my heart, and when I came to a conclusion I knew its significance well. I had no need and I did not think I had any right, and I had no hint of any desire, to be unofficially or in any way a partner or adviser or counselor

25 While appreciating important differences between the two cases of refugee compensation, Sharett was an early advocate of cautiously considering links between German-Jewish and Israel-Arab reparations. During the Cabinet meeting of February 8, 1951, Sharett said: "The two matters are dissimilar – what Germany perpetrated against us is unlike what happened between us and the Arabs, but the fact remains that Arab people were uprooted from their homes, and we agree, within a certain framework, to pay compensation [to Arab refugees. [- - -] I take this opportunity of presenting the question of whether we should link this with the matter of our compensation to the Arabs and say, 'If we obtain compensation from Germany it will enable us to pay generous compensation to the Arabs'" (Y. Sharett, *The Reparations Controversy*, 46-47).

on government matters. My decision to leave meant not only to withdraw from any official post and residence in Jerusalem or Tel Aviv, but to withdraw from all government matters in every possible sense.

I did not for one moment entertain the notion that anyone would be required to consult with me. To continue giving advice is possible in the most proper and responsible way – by serving in the government. The reasons for my leaving the government are also applicable to my withdrawal from interference in any manner. This is the conclusion with regard to myself. I certainly understood that every member of the Cabinet, and every Prime Minister especially, must bear his full responsibility, and he has no right, no option – and no need, I believe – to whatever extent to transfer his responsibility or part of it to someone else.

What I said in regard to a "coalition" is not a personal but a party matter. The two different approaches are not merely personal. I more or less know our public, and I know that both approaches are prevalent there, and for this reason I at first thought that the coalition would continue to exist, but after examining the matter from a distance I saw that it had been a naive conjecture on my part. At any rate, my first assumption (which I abandoned after scrutiny) about the "continuing coalition" should also not be construed as a wish or expectation on my part to be consulted or taken into consideration. This would stand in complete contradiction to my decision to withdraw.

Finally I wish to thank you for sending a passage from [Sharett's daughter] Yael [Medini]'s letter. Greetings to Zipporah and to you.

D. Ben-Gurion

To complete the day's events, it must be noted that there was a hitch in our communication to the Egyptian government. We sent it to Paris and Washington at one and the same time, for delivery in both places, just to make sure. The directive stated explicitly that it was to be delivered to the Egyptian representation directly. But the devil played a trick. Ambassador Jacob Tsur apparently didn't understand the directive properly; he upped and gave the communication to the French Foreign Ministry to relay it to its destination. Alexandre Parodi, DG of the French Foreign Ministry, refused. He found the communication too scathing. Meanwhile, however, Parodi got wind of the matter and is sure to have divulged the matter already, or to do so soon, to the British and the Americans. This entirely upsets our plans. We specifically meant to conceal this step from the Western powers for a few days, until we should have ascertained whether the communication had any direct effect in Cairo.[26]

Monday, April 12

[- - -]

Received Fontaine of *Le Monde*'s editorial board, who is touring Israel, and spoke with him for an hour or so at the Foreign Ministry.

26 The text of message to be communicated to the Egyptian Embassy, Paris, is in *DFPI* 9, doc.164. See also *DFPI* 9, docs.166-167.

Afterwards, from 12:00 until 2:30, there was a broad consultation, both in composition and scope, on the foreign-policy situation and the courses to be determined. The DG, Gideon, Arthur, Bendor, Herzog, Emile, Shabtai [Rosenne] and Tekoah participated. Everyone had their say. My summation lasted more than an hour. Among other things, I argued sharply against those who oppose retaliation. It was strange that a sceptic of the positive value of retaliations such as myself should have been forced to exact redress from those who oppose retaliation totally, in all circumstances. This decisive rejection stems from a view of the problem from only the aspect of foreign relations and with total disregard for the facts of security and their psychological effect on the settlers in the border areas and the entire public. Among other things, I proposed that we now submit to Great Britain a detailed dispatch in regard to its responsibility for Jordan in view of the defense pact between the two countries. I concluded that, in my view, constructive progress on our initiative is possible in only two fields: compensation for Arab abandoned lands, and the treatment of the Arab minority in Israel.[27]

[- - -]

Yesterday I decided to give up an evening for James de Rothschild so that he wouldn't return to England feeling upset about me not giving him a chance for a serious talk. Around 8:00 pm we met at The Sharon Hotel in Herzliya, and the two of us conversed alone for three quarters of an hour and then dined with his wife and Lord Victor. In private I told him about the exchange of messages with Churchill. In the morning I had cabled Elath to ask whether I should share this secret with him, and waited all day long for an answer. Finally I decided to tell him, since he still maintains contact with the old man. While in the middle of reading the messages aloud, a note was slipped in: Shamai telephoned from Jerusalem to inform me that Elath had answered in the positive. The conversation with Jimmy was cumbersome as usual. He showered me with a lot of good advice, some of it to the point.

Tuesday, April 13

The General Zionist ministers asked for an urgent discussion of security matters yesterday. I received them this morning. Only three of them came – Rokach took sick again (his health is most precarious!). They came to pour out their heavy hearts, that there might not be efficient political control over the IDF, and that the IDF might be set on war, no matter what. They also wanted to know whether the arrangement whereby retaliations were to be carried out only with my authorization was being kept. I replied frankly, admitted to disagreements with Lavon, but precisely delineated their essence and extent. In the final summary I put their fears to rest.

27 For a translated excerpt of Sharett's remarks, see WebDoc #9.

[- - -]

I received a memorandum from Lavon vigorously protesting against the line taken by Elath in his talk with Eden [on April 6]. This document depressed me due to its rancorous language.[28]

[- - -]

Pinhas Rosen came to discuss border defense policy. He contended that the benefit to our security from retaliations is nil, while they abound in political damage. Why do I not stand in the breach, my views being known and correct? I enjoy more support than I think, and I would be warranted to act more resolutely. I told him what he hadn't known until now: how many military actions I had forestalled and against what debacles I had put up barriers. As opposed to this, I explained the need for a military response from time to time, and my effort to space it out and exercise restraint and limitations.

[- - -]

Wednesday, April 14

[- - -]

Gideon Rafael and Yaacov Herzog (the latter now in charge of the US Division, Bendor's pending transfer to the Paris embassy) invaded my office with evident agitation to warn of another imbroglio. A few days ago we sent our Embassies in Washington and Paris a message for delivery to the respective Egyptian Embassies for the government in Cairo, to warn it of the deterioration in the Gaza Strip border area and to propose an urgent high-level meeting to settle matters. The effort has met with hitch. As I already indicated, Jacob Tsur did not understand that direct delivery was intended. Instead he bothered the French with it. Our intention had been not to reveal the operation to the Western powers, so that the Egyptians would not get the impression that we had no practical purpose but merely wished to find favor in the eyes of the world. We

28 In his memo to Sharett, dated April 12, Lavon expressed his "great amazement" over several replies and comments made by Ambassador Elath, including his apparent willingness to abandon the call for a conference with Jordan under Article XII and to examine British suggestions for a "surrogate" to Israel's rights under the Armistice Agreements. Lavon also "protest[ed] vigorously" Elath's mild and apologetic – rather than proud and defiant – response to Eden's criticism of the retaliatory raid on Nahhalin. Lavon ended his memo with three accusations: "Who authorized the Israeli Ambassador to define Israel Government ministers as 'law-breakers'? Who authorized the Israeli Ambassador to say these things? Who authorized the Israeli Ambassador to describe the Nahhalin action as 'inappropriate'?" ISA FM 130.02/2446/11; see also *DFPI* 9, p.237, n.4, and English Companion Volume, p.142. For Sharett's reply to Lavon, see below, entry for April 20.

said we would tell them in due time. The truth of the matter is that we had no hope of any concrete response, and thought that this step would help us actually clear our slate vis-à-vis the powers in the final reckoning.

And now suddenly the American Chargé d'affaires, Russell, contacts us and announces that an affirmative reply to our appeal has been received from Caffery,[29] the US Ambassador in Cairo. The government there is ready for a meeting, and is about to despatch Col. Mahmoud Riyadh,[30] in charge of Palestine affairs in the GS, in order to confer with our representatives. Our people were astounded. How did Russell and Caffery, i.e., Washington, know about our dispatch? Had our embassy been so quick to tell the tale, when it had been specifically instructed to keep silent? By a stroke of a miracle, Herzog did not blurt out anything inappropriate, and it was speedily ascertained that Russell knew absolutely nothing about our written missive. It was only Reuven Shiloah who had suggested, while talking to him, that it would be beneficial to have high-level military representatives of both sides meet for urgent negotiations on the prevention of border incidents and attacks. Russell would not have missed having this charitable deed come his way, and immediately contacted Caffery (by means of the State Department?) and the latter acted as quick as lightning also, and now Cairo's assent has been given.[31]

A scandal erupted in the Foreign Ministry. How could Reuven have dared to take action on such a serious and delicate matter on his own accord? And what could be the meaning of his concealing it from the Ministry both before and after the fact? How long will this anarchy prevail in our midst to make a travesty of areas of responsibility, initiative and authority?

The scandal immediately spread to the Defense Ministry and the GS. There is no dearth of people there ready to celebrate the disgrace of the Foreign Ministry and revel in its ignominy. I was thoroughly dejected by the whole episode. Russell is pressing for a reply. Heaven forbid that we reveal our internal lack of coordination to the outside world. We have no choice other than to pretend that everything is right and proper, legitimate and correct. And essentially, no matter what the weird chain of events may have been, it would be inconceivable to give a negative answer now, which would mean back-tracking and subverting the US after it had acted in our name and on our behalf.

I immediately picked up the telephone and contacted Lavon and told him

---

29 Jefferson Caffery (1886-1974). US Ambassador to Egypt (1949-1955).

30 Mahmoud Riyadh (1917-1992). Member of the Egyptian Delegation to the Armistice negotiations with Israel (1949). Director, Department of Arab Affairs, Egyptian Foreign Ministry; Officer in charge of Palestine Affairs, Egyptian Army; Egyptian Ambassador to Syria (1958-1962). Later Egyptian Ambassador to the UN, Foreign Minister, and SG of the League of Arab States.

31 For further details, see *FRUS 1952-1954*, docs.787, 793; *DFPI* 9, docs.171, 177; Russell-Lourie [*sic.*, probably Herzog] conversation, April 14, reported in Russell to Dulles, April 15, 1954, USNA 684A.85/4-1554.

what had happened in an open and friendly manner, and said that a distinction had to be made between the internal-disciplinary aspect – at any rate we must first ascertain from Reuven himself what happened here – and the external-political aspect. Lavon agreed that we had no choice but to respond positively and requested a consultation prior to our setting out for the meeting.

By the way, Reuven thought that he had extricated me from the difficult business of inviting Russell to tea at my home, but not so. Yaacov Herzog and Russell escorted Hart to Lod Airport upon his departure from Israel. On the way they touched on Byroade's speech [of April 9]. Herzog condemned the perversion of truth expressed in the idea of a division between the State of Israel and the Jews of the diaspora and the rejection of the existence of one Jewish nation all over the world. He said that it was too bad they had no opportunity to hear what the PM had to say on this subject. Russell's reply was that he was willing and ready to come to the PM for tea, but the PM had refused...

It is amazing how a man as wise, perceptive, and experienced and responsible as Reuven unwittingly tramples underfoot the basic principles, rules and standards as ordained in the Civil Service code of behavior. He belongs to the Washington Embassy and that is his sphere of responsibility. He comes back to Israel for debriefing and consultation. Here, others are in charge of contacts with foreign elements. Of course, he deserves to meet with the people of the US Embassy in Israel and it is important that he does, but how is it that he does not distinguish between relaying information, on the one hand, and taking diplomatic initiative to submit proposals and new ideas meant for action, on the other? And, added to this, doing so without the assent of the local authorized people in charge, and even without their knowledge? Is all this anarchy and the dismay stemming from it an unavoidable fatality?

I kept Yaacov with me after the others had gone and asked for his intercession with his father, the Chief Rabbi, not to make fuss for us in the matter of [allowing *Shabbat* transit of Jerusalem-bound pilgrims from the ship] the "Agamemnon." We may be under siege, but we still serve as a gateway to sea-faring travelers who come to Old Jerusalem. Shall we shut this opening too, and by our own hand?

A meeting of *Shabbat* Work Permits Committee was convened again. This time MK Warhaftig[32] represented the religious interests instead Shapira. He struggled with us vehemently over each and every permit, and made me lose my temper several times. I decided against him in regard to all items, and the permits were granted. I said to him that the observance of *Shabbat* was dependent on the State of Israel. However, all those truly concerned for the future of the Jewish *Shabbat* must

32 Zerach Warhaftig (1906-2002). Born in Russia. Settled in Palestine in 1947. Jurist. Among *Hamizrahi* leaders. MK and Deputy Minister of Religious Affairs. Later Minister of Religious Affairs.

take account of the imperatives of a modern state, and adapt to them. Otherwise the whole issue will explode. It is inconceivable that, in a twentieth-century state, Jews should behave as they never behaved in their own state two thousand years ago, but as they behaved in Polish or Lithuanian townlets in accordance with a way of life that is extinct. Again, I said that just as *Shabbat* cannot exist without the State of Israel, so the State of Israel cannot exist without work on *Shabbat*.

Zalman Shragai,[33] head of the JA's *Aliya* [Immigration] Department, came to report on his problems having returned from his trip to Western European countries. The number of immigrants from October 1953 to the end of March 1954 was, all in all, 4,083. Until September 1954 no more than 2,200 will arrive. Meanwhile, about 4,000 have emigrated this year; but on the whole emigration is on the decline. In three countries he sensed a "strong will" to come over: England, Holland and Austria. He was very critical of the state being oblivious to the needs of middle-class immigrants. Prospective immigrants of this kind are under the impression they are not needed in Israel. As to prospects for mass immigration, the source is North Africa. It can be assumed that around a quarter of a million are willing to come over. It is possible to bring over whole villages from Tunisia, but there is a problem of taking in people living on relief. If a whole village is transferred, it is impossible to leave the unfortunate to their plight there. "The Joint" is prepared to help these people in Israel on condition that they don't constitute more than 10-15%, but the whole matter is not resolved. Josephthal contends that as long as we have not economically absorbed those who are already here, we should not start a new immigration wave.

[- - -]

Thursday, April 15

A day consisting entirely of meetings.

Set out at 8:00 am for Tel Aviv with Gideon and Shamai. On the way Gideon updated me on Security Council matters and other problems pending, as a briefing prior to the Knesset Foreign Affairs and Defense Committee. [- - -] The FADC commenced at 10:30 and went on until 1:00. I began by speaking about issues in and around the SC. As usual an extensive, quite interesting, argument developed, which did not lead to a conclusion. Lavon advocated a strike at the Egyptian Army in the Gaza Strip in order to force it to restrain infiltrators – and this after such a strike has already been carried out and had only roused the Egyptian Army to strike at us with retaliations, without having restrained a single infiltrator! The session will resume on Monday.

33 Shlomo Zalman Shragai (1899-1995). Born in Poland. Settled in Palestine in 1924. Among leaders of *Hapo'el Hamizrahi*. Since 1948 member of JAE and head of its *Aliya* Department (1954-1958), often engaged in clandestine trips.

After the meeting Lavon lectured me on his plan for "Judaizing" Nazareth.[34] For years now we have been raising this slogan with nothing being done. Now there is talk of moving the district offices [of several government departments] to this "Judenrein" city, but the settling of families of the officials would not bring about a real change. Now a plan has been prepared which would assure this: the moving there of several military enterprises and workshops and the building of housing there for hundreds of workers. I commended this initiative but made two points requiring attention: It is necessary that, from the very beginning, the Arab inhabitants of Nazareth be made aware that this shall bring them a new source of livelihood (such as work in building and selling supplies to the new Jewish inhabitants), and secondly, serious attention must be devoted to the architecture of the housing projects so that they do not harm the landscape.[35]

In the afternoon I prepared for my lecture before the party's Political Committee tonight.

[- - -]

At 8:00 the Political Committee commenced. I spoke for two hours and explained the background to the undermining of the Armistice Agreements, the aggravation of Arab hostility, the strengthening of Western links to the Arabs, and the change in Soviet policy in support of the Arabs against the West and against us. From this, to the problem of "slipping" into war and an analysis of the retaliation philosophy, including its benefits and severe limitations. There was enough time for only Lavon and Ziama to take part in the debate. The former disputed my line of self-restraint and the caution of my thinking and portrayed retaliation as a principal weapon, the efficacy of which was beyond all doubt. When he finished I said to myself: the argument begins only now. Ziama took a middle line and surprised most of those gathered by forcefully stating at the end of his remarks the need for our active integration in Western defense planning, so that we might not remain completely isolated and come out empty-handed on both sides.[36]

Friday, April 16

[- - -]

An envelope containing two telegrams arrived from Jerusalem. One was from Reuven in Paris in answer to the censure aimed at his unauthorized initiative in proposing the meeting with the Egyptians. He hadn't proposed a thing to Russell.

---

34 I.e., for settling Jews in an area adjacent to the mixed Christian-Muslim city of Nazareth with the aim of checking the growth of the Arab city and enhancing Jewish domination in the Arab-populated Lower Galilee under the slogan *Yihud Hagalil* ("Judaization of the Galilee").

35 An all-Jewish town, named Nazareth-Ilit ("Upper Nazareth"), would be founded in 1957.

36 For extracts of Sharett's important speech, see WebDoc #10.

But in answer to both Russell's and Hart's questions about what they could do in Cairo in view of the aggravation of the situation on the Strip border, he had said that for months now we have been demanding a high-level meeting with Egyptians of authority to settle our relations. It had not entered his mind that Russell would view this statement of fact as a new proposal. He therefore had not bothered to stress this point in the report of the conversation which he had delivered to Lourie and Rafael. The second telegram was from Eliahu Elath. It contained details extracted from the British Foreign Office on what went on between Eden and Dulles concerning us. It was an ugly picture of concessions to the Arabs and a cover-up of their malignant behavior by the advocacy of quack remedies.[37]

At 3:00 returned to the Foreign Ministry at the *Kirya*. I consulted with Gideon and Tekoah on our reply to Cairo's announcement of Col. Riyadh's willingness to meet, pending the meeting with the IDF General Staff on the same matter. In the meantime, Russell has contacted Herzog wishing to know (a) what agenda we propose; (b) who is to come from our side; (c) where the meeting will be held. We concluded that, for lack of better choice, our course must be to propose a discussion of border area security. But we ought to strive for an extension of the framework to include the political problem of putting an end to hostile actions generally, including embargo, blockade and propaganda.[38]

At 3:30 met at the Defense Ministry with Lavon, Dayan, Givly,[39] and Shalev. The CoS had at first posed a sulking mien, but Lavon made him give up this silly mood by decisively stating that we had to attend [the high-level meeting with the Egyptians]. I reported on Reuven's explanation of the source of the misunderstanding which had occurred. I proposed the twofold approach regarding our meeting with the Egyptians. Dayan pointed out what was not to be discussed: (a) an arrangement of local commanders' meetings (which does not ensure an absence of incidents but only ties our hands from responding to them); (b) the blockade of the Canal and the Gulf, unless we are willing to deliver an ultimatum and to act in accordance with it later. I said that there was no need for our using the term "ultimatum." To be sure, we are obliged to bring

---

37 See *DFPI* 9, docs.172,175. For American and British accounts of the Dulles-Eden talks, see: *FRUS 1952-1954*, docs.794, 796; Eden to British Embassy, Washington, April 12, 1954, TNA FO371/111070 VR1072/56.

38 Cf. the earlier talk between "Lourie" [probably Herzog] and Russell, reported in Russell to Dulles, April 15, 1954, USNA 684A.85/4-1554. Cf. *FRUS 1952-1954*, doc.798, n.2.

39 Brigadier-General Binyamin Givly (1919-2008). Born in Petah Tikva. Senior officer of the *Hagana*'s *Shai* during the 1940s. Head of the Intelligence Branch, IDF GS (1954-1955). Was deeply involved in the "Egyptian Mishap" – the failed operation activated by the IDF Intelligence Branch of a secret group of young Egyptian Jews for the purpose of sabotaging Western institutions in Cairo and Alexandria aimed at deteriorating relations between the governments of Egypt and Britain and destroying the Anglo-Egyptian agreement to evacuate British bases from Egypt. See, esp. Teveth, *Ben-Gurion's Spy*.

up the blockade problem – otherwise it would be construed as our conceding the whole issue – and must announce, adopting the statement I had delivered at the Knesset, that we are resolved to exercise our right by all means available to us. Lavon did a good job in defining wisely our line of contention regarding border security: the Egyptians must once and for all declare whether they are responsible for the Gaza Strip or not. If not, let them withdraw. If they are [responsible], it is incumbent upon them and not upon us to find efficient means for maintaining security. Lavon wished to go even further and contend that, if Egypt is responsible for the Strip, it must deal with the refugees under civilian law and settle them throughout Egypt, for as long as they remain locked in the Strip there was no way of preventing their disturbances. This sharpening of our position did not seem realistic to me. I proposed the following addendum: if the Egyptians should contend that they are unable to control the infiltrators, we must confront them with their sin of hostility and aggression in territory under their full control – the embargo, the blockade, the propaganda. Having deliberately transgressed in these, no trust can be placed in their claim to honesty as regards their maintaining security. On the contrary, let them prove themselves by putting an end to hostile political actions; then, if they fail to prevent any disturbance along the border, it would not be for lack of desire but for lack of ability. In the end we formulated the agenda: the prevention of all hostile actions, especially security violations in the border area. After the discussion I determined with Lavon the make-up of our delegation: Harkabi, Tekoah, Shalev. At Gideon's urging, I later added Ziama Divon. As to the place, I accepted Lavon's proposal that we suggest Be'er Sheva or Gaza.

At 7:00 we were about to leave for supper when the telephone rang at the last moment. Gideon and Joe Tekoah had just left Russell's. There was a new complication and they had to report to me verbally at once. I asked them to come immediately. Upon hearing their story I could hardly believe my ears. As though the mix-up in the matter of the proposed initiative concerning a meeting of officers wasn't enough, there has already been another one. Upon seeing the formula for the agenda and hearing the proposed make-up of our delegation, Russell was astonished. According to him, the meeting discussed by Shiloah and himself was meant to be of an entirely different nature. Shiloah had been the one to suggest inviting Riyadh. Caffery himself had approached Riyadh directly. He hadn't at all suggested to him that he provide himself with authority. He hadn't talked to him about wide-ranging, high-level negotiations. The intent had been a friendly conversation "over a cup of coffee" between Riyadh and one of ours – just in order to try to contribute to a relief of the tension, without any commitment. A comprehensive agenda such as ours and such a heavy-weight delegation would only frighten and deter the Egyptians, and the entire initiative would come to nil.[40]

It is easy to imagine Gideon's and Joe's bafflement. They had indeed been briefed by Herzog on Russell's questions concerning the formulating of the agenda, the make-up and the place. They tried to toss the ball back into Russell's lap. But the latter disavowed the questions; he had not asked any. Herzog is ostensibly the one who told him that we are willing to propose these terms of reference.

I was flabbergasted. What is going on around me? What kind of a chaos is this? Since when has the Foreign Ministry become a band of confused men who don't know what they are saying, or don't understand what they are hearing? Or is it Russell who is bedeviling them all? The Ministry's disgrace in the eyes of the military is unimaginable. For what reason did I convene that consultation? For what reason had we surveyed the issue and discussed the meeting with such gravity? All our assumptions as regards its nature and purpose have been proven wrong!

But that wasn't the end of Gideon and Joe's report. Russell had hinted at the news he had received about Dulles' meeting with Eden, and said that an impression had been created in the highest quarters that we are resolved to bring about a political decision in our favor by means of a calculated aggravation of the situation. We should know that the powers will not support such a tactic in any way. They have come to the conclusion that any attempt to coerce the Arabs to make progress towards peace would be in vain. Therefore, "technical" improvements only should suffice. Israel apparently wants "all or nothing," Russell contended. The powers view this line as utterly invalid.

On the basis of all these revelations, in view of the web of suspicions and evasions and with the confusion created, Gideon and Joe had come to the conclusion that I must be persuaded to renounce my position in principle not to meet with Russell as long as he maintains a ban upon me in Jerusalem – "making void my law,"[41] so to speak. In order to clarify our position and prevent a potentially disastrous misunderstanding, I must meet with Russell in Tel Aviv. No explanation can equal the things he would hear directly from me.

I totally rejected this spirit of appeasement. We shall not yield to the ban. I told Gideon to tell Russell that I deeply regret that the State Department has seen fit at a time like this to sever the US Embassy's contacts with Israel's PM, but I am unable to help them because it is not a personal but a national issue, and I am in

---

40 In the days immediately following their initial overture to the Egyptians, American representatives became struck by Egyptian suspicions of Israeli intentions. "I have never seen Egyptians more deeply and universally disturbed," wrote Ambassador Caffery, than they are at present over recent Israeli tactics.... Egyptian officialdom, press and public profess to view [the] plan [for a] general S[ecurity] C[ouncil] review of [the] Palestine case as [a] western plot to force Arabs into [a] peace treaty with Israel...." *FRUS 1952-1954*, doc.795.

41 See *Psalms*, 119:126.

charge of a trust which is not mine but the state's. They must be chastised over and over again, for it was they and not I who strayed from the previous custom as regards the PM.

To the crux of the matter, I instructed them to reply to Russell: first, that we are prepared for a meeting with Riyadh, even without a defined agenda and our representatives would be Tekoah and Shalev. Second, the assumption that we are interested in aggravating the crisis in order to resolve it by causing its explosion is both erroneous and harmful. We would welcome the slightest relief. We are not initiating any aggravation but responding, politically or in the field. But we will denounce any false remedy which merely serves to cover up crimes and absolves the other side of responsibility. We have not heard any counsel on the part of the powers for improving the situation, and so long as there is no real barrier against border incidents, everything remains dependent upon them.

[- - -]

Gideon telephoned late at night with the results of the second conversation with Russell. He had sighed with relief upon hearing of our assent to meeting with Riyadh "just for the sake of talking." He had taken down the statement of our position of principle in order to relay it immediately to the State Department. He had been impressed by the contention against window-dressing measures which do not prevent anything. Nevertheless, he also dug from his briefcase the local commanders' agreement which Roger Allen[42] had presented to Elath as the pinnacle of the inventive capacity of the Western powers' leaders.[43] He blurted out something about our being approached, and hinted that it had to do with the territorial integrity of Israel. Gideon got the impression that we would receive an announcement following the Dulles-Eden talk consisting of three items: (1) we must renew the local commanders' agreement; (2) we must abstain from retaliations; (3) they will guarantee our territorial integrity if we behave well.[44]

As to the ban on [official meetings in] Jerusalem, for the first time he did not repeat the mendacious and hackneyed condemnation but openly agreed that the existing rupture is unbearable; that Hart had taken note of this stumbling block; that he himself was conducting ceaseless exchanges with the State Department on this subject; and that he hopes for an early rectification of this wrong, in any event, with the coming of the new ambassador.

---

42 Roger Allen (1909-1972). Assistant Under-Secretary of State, FO, until June 1954. Subsequently British Minister to Bonn, and later Ambassador to Greece, to Iraq and to Turkey.

43 Allen's report of his talk with Elath is reported in FO to British Embassy, Tel Aviv, April 20, 1954, TNA FO371/111070 VR1072/58(II). See also FO Levant Department minute, "Suggested Practical Measures to Improve Frontier Control on Israel's Borders," April 20, 1954, FO371/111070 VR1072/56.

44 See also *DFPI* 9, doc.177, and *FRUS 1952-1954*, doc.798.

To complete the day's pleasures, I received a letter from BG containing a reply to the main content of my last letter to him. The letter is written with obstinance and implacability. The main point is that he remains firm in his refusal to participate in the political activity of the party. The letter would require a proper answer. But where shall the time be found? I am writing beside the sofa on which Zipporah is asleep and my head is like a whirlwind from the intense stress, extreme exhaustion and the feeling of a growing, oppressive suffocation.

Sde Boker, 13.4.54

Moshe - Shalom and Greetings,

This time I shall attempt to touch upon a few things in your letter which I think need to be answered and clarified.

Having relinquished my original notion that the "coalition" [between us] would endure, I am now exempt from addressing the questions you raise concerning the "continuation of the coalition," even though it seems to me that a uniform course is becoming predominant, and perhaps under the given circumstances there is no escaping it, and I must accept the verdict.

I can't see any blessing resulting from the argument with which you confront me in your letter concerning the response to the Ma'aleh Akrabim incident. I know your reasons and position on these questions. These should be expressed at a meeting of the *haverim* or before the Political Committee. And I am a little surprised that you should address this argumentation to me privately, and that you do not know me well enough to realize that this reasoning is alien and unacceptable to me. I did not act in accordance with it during the past six years, and there is no reason why it should convince me now. Our entire history in the recent past would have been completely different if everything had been done according to this reasoning. In a few cases, this reasoning tilted the decisions of the government, and I view them as a cause for weeping for generations to come.[45]

I told you in my next to last letter that we have different **positions**. I do not suppose that you will change your approach, and there is no reason for you to suppose that you will change mine with reasoning of this nature.

And since I am certain that you will act according to your assumptions in keeping with your approach, I have relinquished my naive original belief that the coalition would continue to exist.

And I certainly accept – and as self-evident – your remarks about the responsibility under which you act as Prime Minister, and insofar as the decision is in your hands you must act according to your understanding. And this conclusion I have not abandoned: not to disagree with the government's political actions, after resigning from the Cabinet; not to disagree in public and not to disagree in party debates, for nothing will remain secret. But no one can ask me to say "amen" to things with which I do not agree. Even an individual citizen has a certain amount of responsibility, and he has a conscience which is no different in its validity from the conscience of the Prime Minister.

You speak about the issue of rehabilitating the party as of some abstract concept on Mars which has no relevance to political matters. If I do not wish to – indeed, it seems to me that I am not allowed to – disagree with the government's actions and your views and leadership in political matters, I must desist from any **political** activity. I have defined my boundaries

45 On Ben-Gurion's use of this ominous expression, see below, p.1512 n.15 and p.1862 n.45.

and shall not transgress them. I shall deal with settlement problems and issues pertaining to education and the young generation and wish that I could do all I would want to see done in this field. Your question – whether it is possible for a party member to withhold his help and cooperation in cases when his view isn't accepted – is not a question. A member who fights for his view or expresses it is obliged to accept the verdict willingly even though it has been decided against him. But a member who for special reasons does not want – or is not allowed, which is one and the same – to express his views on political questions, is also obliged to accept the verdict, but does not have to say amen. No one can ask me to say amen. No one can ask me to say amen to things which I repudiate most fundamentally. And if someone should ask me to, I will not be able to comply with his wishes.

I will not discuss the matter of the elections this time. They are far off and our political controversy has nothing to do with the elections. Your political line is not only shared by the large majority of the *haverim* in the government, but by the GZ, *Hapo'el Hamizrahi* and the Progressives.

In the coming days I shall concentrate, to the extent that I deal with public affairs, on matters pertaining to the youth of the country and stimulating the pioneering spirit. [- - -]

I do not know whether all the hopes I invest in these young will be fulfilled, but if a major part of them is, I shall be gratified.

I consider the core of our foreign policy to be internal – in moral, military and economic fortitude. And if I shall be able to do something towards the first, I shall do so willingly, and no harm will come to the party because of it.

With comradely greetings,
D.B.G.

[- - -]

Saturday-Sunday, April 17-18

[- - -]

Monday, April 19

[- - -] On 15:00 I received James McDonald at my *Kirya* office for a conversation regarding our relations with the US and for guidance regarding his mission in Holland and Sweden on behalf of the State of Israel Bonds.

At 4:00 I went over to the Defense Ministry for a meeting of the Knesset FADC. The debate lasted some two hours. At its termination I answered questions for over an hour. It seems to me that this time I succeeded in explaining well and in appropriate scope the complexity of our situation and why a policy of retaliation devoid of restraint and devoid of proper consideration is inconceivable; that a sterile delusion is inherent in this course; that it involves serious dangers that might cause us to slide into disaster as if blindfolded. Binyamin Mintz of the *Po'alei Agudat-Israel* Party came to me after the meeting and said that I had been most persuasive. I had indeed spoken like a teacher to his students this time. Sometimes this style is necessary.

[- - -]

Tuesday, April 20

[- - -]

At the Foreign Ministry I received [Christopher] Mallalo, a Labour Party MP [- - -], who on his own initiative has been calling for the establishing of a British military base in the Negev resulting from a mutual pact between Britain and Israel. Naturally, our conversation touched upon this subject and I asked him for the Foreign Office's reaction to his views. He said: "They are fearful lest this arrangement would prove a new provocation in the eyes of the Arab world." I explained to him that there was no point in us starting to talk along these lines; we would only cause a useless argument at home and in the end we would be embarrassingly defeated on the foreign front. It would be a different situation if HMG proposed the matter to us, in which case we would consider it.

[- - -]

A letter from Bennike was delivered to my home describing the untenable situation created by our leaving the IJMAC and imploring us to return.[46] Not so that simple, I said to myself. Clearly it is inconceivable that we should return "just like that," without any compensation. Two forms of compensation can be considered: a demand upon Jordan to confer with us[47] and the removal of Hutchison from the IJMAC chairmanship. Bennike's letter prompted me to draft, by myself, a letter to him regarding Hutchison. I had asked the Ministry for that letter to be written for days and days, and had not received it because of the slow pace of internal discussions. I composed a draft, the likes of a bombshell. I pilloried, as the epitome of stupidity and perversion of truth, Hutchison's contention during IJMAC deliberations that it hadn't been proven that all of the Ma'aleh Akrabim murderers were Arabs. We have, in our hands, Hutchison's report to Bennike where he explicitly states the possibility of the perpetrators having been terrorists whose aim was to increase the tension and cause trouble for the present government. He was careful to refrain from saying "Jewish terrorists," but the allusion to the *Irgun* and Stern Gang was clear. I therefore went on to add in my letter that I had heard a rumor that Hutchison had expressed such an original idea, and that this further aggravates what he had said in committee. I suggested that Bennike himself draw conclusions, and announced that I would be expressing to the SG my assessment of this chairman's ability to properly consider the facts brought before him for adjudication.[48]

I wrote to Lavon.

---

46 *DFPI* 9, doc.179.

47 Under Article XII.

48 *DFPI* 9, doc.180. The Israelis gathered further evidence to question Hutchison's character and challenge his neutrality (e.g., Rafael to Eban, April 27, 1954, ISA FM 130.02 2425/8b). For Bennike's reply, see *DFPI* 9, doc.186.

Jerusalem, April 20, 1954
279/54

To: Minister of Defense
From: Minister of Foreign Affairs

I am afraid you went too far in your remonstrations about Ambassador Elath in your letter to me dated the 12th of this month,[49] which unfortunately I have had no time to answer till now.

As to the first contention, regarding Elath's qualified assent in his talk with Eden to the proposal that our meeting with the Jordanians should not necessarily be arranged in accordance with Article XII of the Armistice Agreement, let me say first of all that he did have the authority to do so in keeping with the instructions he was given. In my cable to him of April 5, which served as instruction for that meeting, it was said: "You will ascertain the need for a direct meeting between us and Jordan, whether in the framework of Article XII, or under a specific decision taken by the Security Council, as a main aim (of the discussion in the SC)." If there is any cause for complaint, it should be directed towards myself.

Thus, if there is room here for argument, it should be directed to me. Not only did Elath himself make a reservation regarding his assent by saying that it was personal and did not obligate his government; he added that clearly we would not give up our demand based on Article XII.

As to the matter itself, it seems to me there are two sides to the coin. It would indeed have been an important achievement if we had induced the SC to adopt a resolution explicitly requiring Jordan to attend a conference in accordance with Article XII on the basis of our invitation. But under the given circumstances – Britain's pact with Jordan, US avoidance of any strong pressure on an Arab state, and the Soviet veto which has become routine – from the start, and all the more so now, there was no chance of it. On the other hand, if the SC had adopted a resolution requiring Jordan and Israel both to confer in order to make border security arrangements, this would in effect have satisfied our desires. The difference in phrasing would not have made much difference to the essence of the matter. Everyone would have known that this resolution was the result of our initiative, and that its formulation had left Jordan an opening to respond positively out of obedience to the SC's ruling rather than in fulfilment of an Israeli demand.[50]

Factually, the situation as it really is is quite different, but I will not discuss it here.

And, after all, it is possible that a mistake was made in our raising the second possibility. If so, then it was not the only mistake we made during these weeks. I believe, for instance, in view of what has happened since then, that we made a grave mistake by not tabling a complaint to the SC immediately after the Ma'aleh Akrabim outrage. Possibly there were more mistakes steps.

Your second complaint seems to be more serious, but here I believe you are completely wrong. No instructions whatsoever were given to Elath on how to explain or justify the Nahhalin retaliation, and I felt no need for such instruction, assuming that in this matter there is a routine formulation, used by the government and our legations for a long time.

---

49 Above, page 333 n.28.

50 In his April 21 meeting with Roger Allen, Elath raised some of Sharett's reservations regarding the tactics of using a UN subcommittee. See TNA FO371/111070 VR1072/59. Israel's representatives in Washington and New York displayed an even more unwelcoming attitude to this proposal. See, e.g., conversation between Wainhouse, Ludlow, Eban and Eliav, April 30, 1954, USNA Lot File 58D33 box 3; and ISA FM 130.16/2948/6.

In my opinion, Elath clearly spoke in accordance with this formulation, and there is no point in citing a particular word he used. He totally rejected Eden's argument that the government should denounce the operation and punish its perpetrators and this answer was worded, in my opinion, fully honourably. If you compare the former PM's public explanation of the Qibya affair with the explanation given by Elath for the Nahhalin one, you will find a strong resemblance if not a complete one. You are especially angry with the expression "improper means." Do you think that an Israeli Ambassador, when conversing with a Foreign Minister of another country, should define the act of killing ordinary people out of vengeance or for the purpose of instilling fear, as a moral act? I have no idea what word Elath used in this instance, but we always express our sorrow at the shedding of innocent blood, and, in fact, morally detest all violence, while at the same time proving that in the given circumstances these acts were justified and unavoidable. Indeed this was precisely Elath's explanation, and I have no doubt that this and no other was Eden's impression of it.[51]

Wednesday, April 21

[- - -]

I finished editing my letter to Bennike with the DG.

I was handed a detailed and depressing report concerning the internal situation of our mission in Moscow. The principle of "*cherchez la femme*" has taken hold there and it seems the only way out is by uprooting.[52]

[- - -]

Thursday, April 22

[- - -]

51 Sharett to Lavon, April 20, 1954, ISA FM 130.02/2446/11. Sharett was replying to Lavon's memo of April 12; see above, entry for April 13.

52 In a commonly-used ploy, the KGB had succeeded in entrapping a member of the Israeli delegation with a woman operative, then produced a picture of their intimate contact and tried to blackmail him into divulging secret information. He confessed to the Ambassador and was flown immediately back home.

Are We All Against War?

Friday, April 23

A meeting with the CoS, at his request, at the PMO. Relations with him are by no means simple. They are clouded by the problem of trust and complicated by the matter of his subordination to Lavon, the strain in their relations, too. But this time he requested the talk and I willingly responded. He came to summarize the situation along the borders. In his opinion, it hasn't been this satisfactory in a long time. The Lebanese border is all in order. There is one gang, though, roaming the border area, sometimes slipping into Lebanon and sometimes looking for a nest in the Galilee villages. The Lebanese authorities are cooperating in eradicating it. With Syria, there are no complications except for the Jordan channel problem which is dormant for the time being. The situation on the Kinneret has changed profoundly since our initiative and the decision of the ISMAC which went in our favor. There has also been a great improvement along the Jordanian border. The Jordanians are taking vigorous action to prevent incursions. Six Arab Legion battalions are now stationed along the border and their presence is inhibiting [infiltration]. Moshe is not convinced that the Ma'aleh Akrabim massacre was perpetrated by an organized military unit. He was opposed to an immediate response on our part and is always willing in such cases to "miss the first bus" – to wait and see if something like it happens once again and to determine our line according to that.

The main evil was now on the Gaza Strip border. The Egyptians are growing impudent. They have not returned the soldier they abducted. There was a time they crossed the border and prepared ambushes. Shooting from their positions towards our patrols continues. There has been an upsurge in the wave of thefts. Here there is need for a vigorous response. I said that here too we must explore the possibilities of warning to the full and cautiously define the dimensions of the response on our part.

[- - -]

To the upper echelon staff [of the MFA] I reported on my conversation with the CoS and specified the need to prepare the press for the possibility of a flare-up along the Gaza Strip border – to see to it that Egyptian provocations are given enhanced publicity.

Saturday, April 24

[- - -]

The DG came to report on a development on the elevation of the Russian Legation here and our Consulate in Moscow to Embassy status. Abramov suddenly came to announce that, if we should apply to them in this matter, they would give their assent.[1]

[- - -]

[From April 25 until May 15, 1954, Sharett kept only skeleton notes for his diary. The most pressing foreign policy issues at this time were (a) continuing Egyptian-Israeli friction along the border of the Gaza Strip, (b) Israel's protest and abstention from the IJMAC, and (c) Israel's fears regarding US plans for selling arms to the Arab states. See *DFPI* 9, docs.188-212.]

[- - -]

Sunday-Tuesday, April 25-27

[- - -]

Wednesday, April 28

[- - -]

With Lavon on [plans for] sailing an Israeli cargo ship though the Suez Canal.[2]
[- - -] Consultation over the Kasztner case. [- - -]
A message from Churchill.[3]

Thursday, April 29

[- - -] [Mapai] Political Committee.

[The meeting of Mapai's PC, convened on this day, was devoted to a continuation of the debate on the question of reprisals. It started at 9:15 pm. When Sharett's turn came to answer the various participants in the debate it was already midnight. The Chairman suggested that since Sharett would need at least an hour for his rebuttal, the meeting would be adjourned and the Committee would re-convene at a later date, to which Sharett added:]

> I would like to say to the *haverim* that I wouldn't dare ask them to stay on for another hour, not so much because of the late hour, but mainly because I intend to say very serious things indeed. For I am aware that we are very seriously divided. Worse, it is not only that there are two different ways of seeing here, but the real division is between seeing and not seeing. It is not that we all see one thing but each side sees it differently.

1 See *DFPI* 9, doc.194.
2 A plan was executed only later, in September 1954.
3 For Churchill's reply to Sharett's message of April 13, see WebDoc #11.

No, there are things which I see and which in my opinion other *haverim* do not see and do not think about, to the extent that I doubt whether [as PM] I am representing some *haverim* and whether I can continue representing them and whether they can agree that I should represent them. Here matters are extremely serious, and they should be clarified with utmost cool-headedness and comradely peace of mind.

This is why I do not want to speak under pressure of time, and my and *haverim*'s tiredness. I would like to explain matters as thoroughly as possible. I also gathered from the discussion this evening that there are several concrete matters, such as the situation of the Jordan [water diversion] canal, which are not clear and thus require factual explanation – apart from the argument of war or no war, initiated war or not, preventive war or not, or this or that policy of reprisals. Therefore, I deem it unavoidable that we convene for a third time so that I can discuss the issue from its beginning and speak for an hour and a half or two.[4]

Friday, April 30

[- - -]

[As noted above, from April 25 to May 15, 1954, Sharett did not write up his diary in full, but kept only skeleton notes, some of which are reproduced below, supplemented by newly-uncovered archival materials.]

Saturday, May 1

[- - -] In the evening [with MFA Spokesman, Michael] Elizur on Byroade.[5]

I composed a reply.[6]

Sunday, May 2

[- - -]

Cabinet meeting. [- - -] Byroade [speech.]

[Here follow extracts from Sharett's political report to the Cabinet meeting of this date:]

Mr Byroade has honored us with an additional speech. He seems to have given up his idea of separating Israel from the diaspora, but instead raises another issue: immigration. He has done something that was unheard of: he has identified the US administration with one of the most fantastic claims ever advanced by the Arabs. When the Arabs demand [a certain piece of Israeli] territory, we can say that this will never be, even if they insist on their right to get that territory. If they demand the return of [Arab] refugees, then

4 For the conclusion of these debates, see below, entry for May 12.

5 On May 1, Byroade delivered a speech to the conference of the anti-Zionist American Council for Judaism in Dayton, Ohio, in which, among other things, he expressed sympathy for Arab fears and called for a basic change of attitude on the part of Israelis. The complete text, "Facing Realities in the Arab-Israeli Dispute," is reproduced in the *Department of State Bulletin*, May 10, 1954, pp.708-13.

6 No reply was found.

again we can say it is unacceptable, but we cannot deny their own logic in claiming this. When, however, they say that the Government of Israel has declared it will adhere to a policy of unlimited immigration and will absorb millions, and when they say this will drive Israel into expanding territorially by way of a new aggressive act, this becomes one of their arguments for abstaining from making peace with Israel. Byroade has [now] justified this fear. He has publicly stated that Israel must find an appropriate formula on the issue of limiting immigration, and should solemnly declare it. After all [it is argued], there are now only two big Jewish communities in the diaspora from which Jews could come to Israel: the US and Eastern Europe. There is no problem regarding the first, since American Jews would not emigrate; and as for the second, immigration is not feasible in the foreseeable future. Thus [they argue], Israel cannot lose anything by making such a declaration.

It may well be that at the opening of the new Knesset session it will be necessary to say something regarding all these pronouncements, but I think that I should direct our Ambassador to approach the State Department on the highest level possible. That is the Secretary of State, and ask him formally in the name of the Government of Israel if these declarations represent the opinion of the American Administration, if they are conducive to the friendship between the USA and Israel. For if they are not, why are they made, thus misleading public opinion and arousing strife between Israel and the USA?

[- - -]

In the speech I am preparing to deliver on the eve of the coming Independence Day, I mean to emphasize the ideas of immigration and the connection between Israel and the diaspora. Intelligent people will understand my purpose, even though I won't mention Byroade's name.[7]

Arms to Iraq, return [of Israel's delegates] to IJMAC, the incident near Budrus,[8] antisemitism [on the part of] the Chairman of the IJMAC [E.H. Hutchison].[9]

In the afternoon at the Foreign Ministry – Byroade, IJMAC.

In the evening [sat over my] papers, unable to sleep, shootings.

Monday, May 3

[- - -]

[Meeting with] the Frenchmen – [headed by] director of a state plant for the manufacture of aircraft, 30 Mystères (jets), 6 Nords, an assembly plant in Israel.

With Sh. Peres – they have clinched it with the Burmese, sold [them]

---

7 For other official expressions of Israel's official displeasure with Byroade's speech, see below, entries for May 3 and May 10; *FRUS 1952-1954*, docs.815, 823; *DFPI* 9, doc.208.

8 A village in the West Bank, across the Israel-Jordan frontier from Rosh Ha'ayin. There is no mention of the incident in the dailies, nor in Morris' *Israel's Border Wars*.

9 Cf. Rafael to Eban, April 27, 1954, ISA FM 130.02 2425/8-b. During the coming weeks, there was some discussion among Ministry officials about the merits and disadvantages of maintaining Israel's boycott of the IJMAC. See below, entry for May 18, 1954, and *DFPI* 9, docs.203, 205.

30 Spit[fire]s with canons and machine-guns and ammunition [for] a million dollars, 3 sample mortars manufactured by the [Israeli] "Soltam" plant.

[- - -]

At the Foreign Ministry – consultation over the [B'not Yaakov diversion] canal.[10] Cable to Eban to see Dulles.[11]

[- - -]

At the PMO – Bentsur, Bash, Divon, Carlebach; phone call from Walter about Russell.

At home – Michael Elizur – a communiqué on the DG's talk with Russell.[12]

[- - -]

Tuesday, May 4

[- - -]

Yosef Weitz[13] – [reported on matters relating to the resettling of the expelled inhabitants of the Arab Galilee villages of Ikrit and Bir'am in various Arab villages in northern Galilee; compensation to Israeli Arabs ready to emigrate; possibilities of exchange of lands with North African Jews.] He and a colleague would like to go to Tripoli (Libya) and Tunis [for this purpose]; critical importance that one united

---

10 See *DFPI* 9, doc.201.

11 *DFPI* 9, doc.198. Eban ended up meeting with Byroade, rather than Dulles, to convey Israel's concerns about Byroade's speech and other matters. See *FRUS 1952-1954*, doc.815. Following this meeting, Byroade wrote to Secretary of State Dulles, complaining that the Israeli press had "greatly distorted" his Dayton speech and had "ignored everything constructive in [it] and concentrated in a bitter attack on what I said about immigration to Israel. Not a single paper quoted me correctly on this subject." He recommended that Dulles himself consider issuing a statement on the Arab-Israeli situation, since Byroade's "own speeches [had] caused ... a minor sensation in the Middle East out of all proportion to my rank or significance." *FRUS 1952-1954*, doc.816. Byroade would later serve as US Ambassador to Cairo during the countdown to the Suez War.

12 Eytan's report not found. Russell's report of (an earlier?) conversation with Eytan at the King David Hotel (April 28) – in which the two men discussed the impact of the communist threat and the arming of the Arabs on the chances of an Arab-Israeli settlement – is given in *FRUS 1952-1954*, doc.813.

13 Yosef Weitz (1890-1972). Born in Russia. Settled in Palestine in 1908. Director of the JNF Lands and Forestry Departments (1932-1967). In 1948 was appointed by FM Sharett to a small committee (with Ezra Danin and Zalman Lifshitz [Lef]) for the purpose of studying plans for resolving the Arab refugee problem, including "transfer" and resettlement abroad. See Benny Morris, "Yosef Weitz and the Transfer Committees, 1948-1949," in Morris, *1948 and After: Israel and the Palestinians* (Oxford: Clarendon Press, 1990), 89-144.

body be established to deal consistently with this matter.[14]

At the Foreign Ministry – Daniel Lewin on [diplomatic relations with] China, a positive answer from [China's Embassy in] Budapest, a race for time [to establish diplomatic relations with China] with Egypt.

[- - -]

Wednesday, May 5

[- - -]

[Saw] Russell at the PMO.

[- - -]

[Prepared] broadcast of PM's Independence Day Speech. 32 minutes.

[- - -]

Thursday, May 6

[- - -]

Friday, May 7

[- - -]

Phone call from Aran regarding party consultation at BG's [see below, entry for May 17].

Saturday, May 8

[- - -] Aran's telephone call regarding the [*Shabbat* party] consultation.

[Spent] the whole day preparing [speech about foreign affairs for the opening

---

14 Citing Weitz's published diaries, one researcher claims that the "Libyan plan was formally approved on May 13, 1954 in a meeting in which took part PM Sharett, Finance Minister Levi Eshkol, Agriculture Minister Peretz Naftali, DG of the Finance Ministry Pinhas Sapir, Shmuel Divon, the PM's Advisor on Arab Affairs, and Yosef Weitz, of the JNF." However, Sharett's diary entry for May 13 makes no mention of such a meeting. See Nur Masalha, "'Dis/Solving' the Palestinian Refugee Problem: Israeli 'Resettlement' Plans in the First Decade of the State (1948-1959)," in *Across the Wall: Narratives of Israeli-Palestinian History*, eds. Ilan Pappé and Jamil Hilal, (London/New York: I.B. Tauris, 2010), 131. Further details about the Libyan resettlement scheme are given in *ibid.*, 127-42. In his memoir, Ezra Danin writes: "In 1954 I was summoned by FM Moshe Sharett to a joint discussion with Yehoshua Palmon regarding the settlement of Arab refugees. [...] The idea, raised by a Palestinian Arab who ran away to London upon the eruption of the 1948 war and who maintained contact with Palmon, was to settle Palestinian refugees in the Cyrenaica and Tripoli areas in Libya, in villages and farms left by Italian colonists who returned to Italy [...] Nothing came of it." Ezra Danin and Yaakov Sharett, *Tsiyoni Bekhol Tnai* [*A Zionist, Unconditionally*], 2 vols. Ed. Gershon Rivlin (Jerusalem: Kidum, 1987 – in Hebrew), 323.

of the summer session of the] Knesset.

Sunday, May 9

Yael [Vered] on the Kasztner trial.

T[eddy] K[ollek] on [Prof. Robert] Oppenheimer[15] concerning the chances of bringing him to Israel to work at the Weizmann Institute in Rehovot.

[- - -]

Cabinet meeting – [- - -] In the midst of [discussion of income tax, news was brought in on an incident near] Mevo Beitar.[16] [- - -] In the afternoon – Eppy on what really happened [between the Israelis and the Jordanians].[17]

Monday, May 10

[- - -]

At 4:00 pm in the Knesset. [I spoke for] 40 minutes.

[Extracts reproduced below. Sharett opened the summer session of the Knesset with a wide-ranging statement on foreign policy matters. The PM accused senior US State Department official Henry Byroade of "a complete lack of insight" and of distorting Israel's unique characteristics and its ongoing relationship with dispersed world Jewry. Byroade, on the other hand, had "demonstrate[d] full understanding for the feelings of the Arab world, the implacable enemy of the Return to Zion from its very inception."]

> If it is true that the Arab states are in mortal fear of Israel's superior strength – the Arab states which in the aggregate are tens of times larger than Israel in area as well as in population [- - -] – why should they not conclude a peace treaty with Israel which would

---

15 J. Robert Oppenheimer (1904-1967). American Jewish physicist credited with being the "father of the atomic bomb" as Scientific Director of the Manhattan Project. In 1954, he was stripped of his security clearance by the Atomic Energy Commission because of his alleged association with Communists. Actively associated with the Weizmann Institute of Science at Rehovot from its inception; an honorary fellow of the Institute and a member of its board of governors.

16 According to an IDF spokesman on May 10, an Israeli Border Guard patrol in the vicinity of Khirbet 'Illin encountered a stronger Jordanian unit, which had penetrated into Israel and opened fire. Two Israelis were wounded and the Israeli unit was compelled to withdraw. When reinforcements returned to the spot, the two wounded men were missing. Amman later claimed that the clash had taken place inside Jordanian territory, west of the village of Surif in the Hebron hills.

17 Basing himself on Sharett's diaries and an American report, Benny Morris provides the following slightly different account: "On May 9, a chain of events was triggered when a large Israeli Border Police patrol crossed the line at Khirbet 'Illin, near Surif, and was attacked by [Jordanian] National Guardsmen. Two policemen were killed, and a third Israeli died when IDF reinforcements joined the fray. A number of Jordanians died in the exchange. [Defense Minister] Lavon later (privately) admitted that the Israeli patrol had been at fault in crossing into Jordan, guided, he explained, by an inaccurate map." *Israel's Border Wars*, 305.

commit Israel formally and solemnly to preserve its present boundaries permanently? [- - -] Why must the sane and sober State Department be impressed by the fallacy of fear, exposed by so glaring a contradiction?

On the other hand, if concern for one's security is a valid political consideration, do not Israel's fears of renewal of Arab aggression deserve justification sevenfold? On all counts – the historic precedent of aggression actually committed, the constant refusal to make peace, the continued campaign of active hostility, the never-ending oaths of revenge and the actual vast superiority of physical strength – it is the Arab states which should be called upon to reassure Israel and not the other way round.

[- - -]

As against the simple and straightforward objective of a comprehensive peace settlement, the rather vague slogan of a gradual and piecemeal progress towards peace is launched.[18]

For the absence of such progress, too, Israel is once again to blame [in Byroade's eyes]. There is no indication that the Arabs on their part are ready even for such a limited programme, but there is an implied charge that Israel is obstinate on the issue by insisting on "total peace or nothing."

Is this true? [- - -] Israel has offered to various Arab states at different times the conclusion of a non-aggression treaty, as an improvement upon the armistice agreements and a prelude to peace. Has there ever been a response to this proposal? [- - -] In order to remove any possible misconception and preclude a false construction, let me restate again on this occasion that Israel is ready at any time to enter into negotiations with any of the neighbouring Arab states concerning either a final and comprehensive peace settlement or any partial or interim arrangements aiming at paving the way towards peace. [- - -] Any such agreement, whether final or interim, must be based on reciprocity, as otherwise it will be tantamount merely to placing a premium upon intransigence and contribute only to the retardation of peace. Let me also make it clear that any settlement with Israel means a settlement with Israel as it is, that is within the present boundaries and without the introduction [i.e., return] of Arab refugees, just as a settlement with any of the Arab states also, naturally, means a settlement with that Arab state as it is.

This principle, which on the face of it is self-evident, requires emphasis, because the representatives of certain Arab states have at times expressed readiness to negotiate a peace settlement on the basis of conditions which bear no relation to realities and which no right-thinking person can take seriously. As long as the Arab leaders set such terms, it must be clear that they do not mean peace but merely seek to mask their intransigence by assuming an attitude which may appear reasonable to people not familiar with the facts of the situation. The purpose of these declarations is not peace but deceit and confusion.

Against this background, statements repeatedly made by spokesmen of the State Department about the need for mutual concessions must necessarily cause concern. For the Arabs may well try to evade their part by abandoning claims, which are both arbitrary and utterly unrealistic, whereas Israel may be pressed to make concessions of substance by giving up something which is an organic part of its system. This kind of quality of concession Israel will never accept.

18 Indeed, this was a major thrust of Anglo-American approaches to peacemaking in the Arab-Israeli dispute at this time. See: Shimon Shamir, "The Collapse of Project Alpha," in *Suez 1956: The Crisis and its Consequences*, eds. Wm. Roger Louis and Roger Owen (Oxford: Clarendon Press, 1989), 73-100; Neil Caplan, *Futile Diplomacy*, vol.4 – *Operation Alpha and the Failure of Anglo-American Coercive Diplomacy in the Arab-Israeli Conflict, 1954-1956* (London: Frank Cass, 1997; Routledge, 2015), esp. 3-69. CZA, A245/198.

[- - -]

Israel owes much to the US. It is intimately connected with American Jewry whose members of course are loyal citizens of the US. It appreciates deeply the political and financial aid she has been privileged to receive from the US. It values highly the sympathy extended to it by large sections of the American people. It regards itself as an organic part of the democratic world. [- - -] Yet Israel's concern for its own security comes first, and in matters of security it must be left to be its own judge. [- - -]

Based upon considerations of her own security and the defense of the region, Israel is categorically opposed to any grant of arms to any Arab state as long as the policy of that state within the region is one of war and not of peace. Israel will continue to expose any such grant of arms as a premium upon the repudiation of the principles of peace enshrined in the Charter of the United Nations, and as an encouragement to a war of revenge and conquest. [- - -] The fact that Iraq, bent upon revenge and loudly swearing its purpose, is about to receive arms, whereas the request for military aid made by peace-seeking Israel has so far been ignored[,] raises questions as to the character of American policy in the Middle East."[19]

Lavon's speech.[20]

[- - -]

Tuesday, May 11

[- - -]

At the Foreign Ministry – With G[ideon] R[aphael] and Tekoah on the [border] incidents. No news on our response. G.R. on China. With Daniel Lewin on [the] Colombo [Conference] and on India.[21]

Should I write to Nehru? I dictated [a draft].[22]

---

19 A Military Assistance Agreement between the US and Iraq was signed on April 21, 1954. Extract from Sharett's Knesset Statement, translation (9 pp. mimeo) forwarded by British Embassy, Tel Aviv, to Levant Department, FO, May 21, 1954, TNA FO371/111071 VR1072/94. See also Evans to FO, May 11, 1954, TNA FO371/111071 VR1072/83.

20 After Sharett's speech a general debate ensued. The final speaker was Minister of Defense Lavon, who harshly criticized Byroade for his anti-Israeli and anti-Zionist remarks and attacked the USA for its policy of appeasing the Arab world at the expense of Israel and of its arming of Iraq. He ended his speech by saying: "When the Arab states are given arms and we are given guarantees and local commanders' agreements, nobody can accept that as a friendly act. [- - -] Jewish blood shall not serve to oil the wheels of the anti-communist pact in the Middle East. When we are told: no peace, no war, no settlement, no punishment for murderers, then this means only one thing: Jewish blood is free to flow. But Jewish blood shall not flow freely in the State of Israel." *Divrei Haknesset*, XVI: 1611-12.

21 The Colombo Conference was an anti-colonial organization founded in Colombo, Ceylon, at a conference held April 28-May 2, 1954. Members were India, Ceylon, Burma, Pakistan and Indonesia. See *DFPI* 9, docs.204, 212. The partners would reconvene again in Delhi in 1956; see below, entry for November 6, 1956.

22 See below, entry for May 21.

With the DG on India: one-sidedness?

[- - -]

In *Hador* [a Mapai evening paper, an item on] 7 Arabs killed. Telephone call with Lavon – [he said it was the work of] the Border Guard![23]

Wednesday, May 12

[- - -]

Cabinet meeting [- - -] with Joe about response to IJMAC's reprimand [of Israel] for [the Khirbet] 'Illin [incident].

[- - -] Preparing for the [Mapai] Political Committee [extracts of Sharett's speech follow:]

> *Haverim*, I shall try to follow the thread of our last discussion[24] and come to a summing up. Well, I don't think the question "war or no war" is solved by saying: "We don't want war." First of all, I am not sure whether we are all against war. After all that has been said in this vein, I am not sure that all of us do not want war. If I am not mistaken, at least one *haver* suggested the mounting of a preventive war as the only solution, and the sooner the better. Obviously, such a possibility exists. Second, those who say "we don't want war, but it should be acknowledged that, militarily, war now would be better than later" are by these very words spreading an atmosphere of war, thereby nursing a wish for war.
>
> Third, I am afraid that those too who are certainly not vouching for war as an aim of our policy are not taking seriously enough into consideration the possibility of our sliding into war. Either they don't care about sliding into war, in which case they shouldn't say they do not want war – since if they don't care they in fact are hinting that perhaps they accept going to war – or, if they really do not want war, they must see to it that we don't slide into war.
>
> I think many among us are victims of a failing which is only natural to humans: they assess the future on the basis of the past. We all know how generals prepare for war on the basis of a previous war experience, and how they ultimately err. Military thinking is at present seriously endeavoring to free itself from such routine. However, it seems that when people among us are talking about a future war, they see it as an additional phase of completing our War of Independence. It is not. And it is not so on at least three accounts.
>
> First, the former war was not initiated by us. Of course, it can be argued that it occurred by our initiative on account of the [1917] Balfour Declaration, or because of the First *Aliya*.[25] But if we shorten the account a bit, then we could say that politically we were prepared to carry out the November 29 [1947] UN decision fully to the last iota, that is we were prepared to accept our state's territory comprising 55% of Palestine and our state's population being 45% Arab. Moreover, we did not plot nor plan nor wage that war in order to expand territory and minimize its Arab population. The initiative to make war came from the other side, and that is what had characterized all our efforts of

23 Morris (*Israel's Border Wars*, 305) notes several sniping and ambush actions initiated by Israel's Border Police in attempts to avenge their losses of May 9. See below, entries, May 18, May 21 and June 1.

24 See above, entries for April 15 and 29.

25 The first wave of Jewish immigration to Palestine, between 1882 and 1904.

holding on and defending ourselves in that war, as well as what established its character in the eyes of the world at large. The whole world knew then that we were fighting a war which was imposed on us, that our fighting was justified, that for us it was a war of life or death, a war fought for saving our very lives; everyone knew we had no other alternative.

I say that this is what determined our feelings during that war, the feeling that we fighting with our backs a glued to the wall, with no other alternative available. And the same goes for the feelings of the Jewish people abroad, and what prompted it to assist us in resources and manpower. This also determined the attitude of the powers, and in this sense the fact that the UN did not lift a finger, as some say, is of no relevance – although the truth is that the UN did lift its finger, since there were [two] cease-fires [arranged by the UN] which did not only stop us; they saved us. And in this sense the American [arms] embargo too did not decide matters. The sympathy of the world was decisively directed towards us.

When we speak about a future war, it will be different on all these accounts.

We would not be able, however we maneuver and play around, to evade being accused of initiating and instigating this war, and even if it would not be so, it would still be possible to present it as such, since this war would not occur as a result of declaration, nor as a result of sending expeditionary forces; rather some entanglement will occur and, lo and behold, a war will erupt all of a sudden, and thus there will be a full gamut for speculation and [conflicting] versions. And this is what would determine our standing and the attitude of the Jewish people. I wonder whether it would be worthwhile to examine all the hypothetical possibilities, but when people talk so easily about war, such an examination becomes necessary.

The people of Israel would not feel that there was no other way, that there was no alternative. People would not be able to say: "This was a clear-cut case – war was imposed on us." They would say instead that the government played its cards wrongly, that the Army embroiled us and perhaps this war was not at all necessary. And over and above that we must remember that while in the meantime our population has more than doubled, its composition has changed dramatically [i.e., less prepared for fighting]. The attitude of the Jewish people [abroad] would be different, too. I assume they would not shun us; volunteers would probably come, if only they would be allowed to do so. But the people's hearts would not be calm, for they would not be assured that it was all necessary. And this attitude could take 101 forms.

Second, then [in 1948], since there was no alternative, we went into the war without any financial consideration. In fact, at the beginning the State of Israel was not yet in existence. It was all in flames when it was born. But now, in view of the alarming economic and financial complications of the state, in view of the burden which is breaking our back, if we slide into war we would find ourselves in a highly more complicated situation than in the past.

Lastly, as one can guess, the future war would not end like the former did. I am prepared to assume that we shall win militarily. But this victory may be disastrous, as the saying goes: "one more victory and we are lost." In what sense? In the sense of the war's demographic consequences. I do not assume that a future war, by which supposedly we shall occupy the territory of western Palestine up to the Jordan River, will end with a mass exodus of the Arab inhabitants, as happened in the former war. First of all, if we examine that 1948 war not as one whole, but as a series of phases, we would find that the longer it continued, the less was the size of the Arab exodus, and in the war's last phases it almost stopped. For the Arabs learned their lesson.

Let us compare. On the one hand, our present situation, with its seemingly unbearable configuration of the border, the incessant infiltrations and terrorist incidents, and the various complications involved and sometimes the breakdown of the border settlers' morale as well. On the other hand, we reach the River Jordan, thus contributing enormously to the border's security and defense possibility, but at the same time engulfing in our midst one million or so Arabs. I don't know which is preferable: an explosion from without or an explosion from within?

I would really like to suggest to the *haverim* who are talking somewhat loosely about a preventive war, and to those *haverim* who argue that [- - -] militarily it would be better to fight now than later – I would suggest to them that they take into consideration all the complications which may arise from our making war at the present time – before being more buttressed within, before having made more improved successful efforts to build up our economy, before we have educated our new immigrants, before having planned other possible solutions for the problems to be created by the addition of a large Arab population.

I would also like to remind the *haverim* that such a new war would occur after Korea, not before, that is, after it was proven that the UN can intervene militarily. One can argue that in fact the UN did not intervene in Korea, that its intervention was a fiction and that truth was that it was America which had intervened along with a few other states who felt it was their duty, or their international interest, to cooperate with the USA. However, even if we take this line, is it not possible that the US and Britain would intervene in this war under the guise of the UN? On what basis can one assume they would not do so?

Moreover, there is really no need for the powers to intervene by military force. It is difficult to assume that America would send troops over here as it did in the case of Korea. It is not so simple. There is no need at all for sending troops here, nor sending even an air force in order to strangle us. It is enough if the navies of the USA and Britain blockade our ports for that purpose. And such possibilities have been discussed; they are not just a fruit of my imagination.

I think we are very, very far from a situation whereby America starts arming the Arab states so that they could annihilate the State of Israel. It may of course be, that in the process of the arming, if it does reach big dimensions and include heavy weapons, we may find ourselves in a dire situation; but as of now we are far from such a phase. But being far from this phase does not preclude, in my opinion, that a situation may evolve in which both America and Britain would be interested in teaching us a very hard lesson. A concrete lesson, not in words only. Because the State of Israel is gradually assuming a reputation of a state convinced it can do whatever it wants, or, at least a state which can permit itself to do what others cannot – that the State of Israel is some kind of an international "only son." [Just because] it has a long history and international ties with a people dispersed all over the globe; [just because] it performs all kinds of interesting social experiments, has high spiritual presumptions, and succeeds in enlisting support and sympathy – thanks to all these benefits it thinks that, at the same time, it can perform any impermissible act and remain unpunished. Such a nation [so the powers may be thinking] should be taught a lesson once and for all. Once and for all an end must be put to the prevalent assumption among the Arabs that Israel is immune to any strong action taken against it. I think we cannot play with this fire.

We are not deliberating here in order to decide whether we shall or shall not make war. I think even the most extreme of our *haverim* is not going to suggest here today that we declare a preventive war. We are deliberating here over what ways we are to choose in our political thinking. I recommend that the *haverim* add my considerations and my way of thinking to their weighing of the situation both individually within themselves and with discussing of opportunities and dangers with others. I believe they would arrive at the conclusion that war is out.

Of course, if war erupts, if in spite all caution or lack of it, we slide into war, then there is no question that we must fight it out like devils not only in order survive but also to force the whole world to recognize our viability and might. But this is not the subject we are talking about. We are talking about the necessary policy for conducting ourselves, about what we should strive for, about what we should avoid.

I also suggest again, in view of what was said earlier in our discussion, that we should not talk so lightly about abolishing of the Armistice regime. Let us not ease our minds by proving that abolishing it does not mean war, since anyway we are in a no-war-no-peace situation and thus the Armistice regime does not shield us from troubles, and therefore there is no difference between the existence or non-existence of the Armistice regime. There are even those among us who even claim that our abolishing the Armistice regime will be highly beneficial to us, since it can provoke the powers to take notice and do something about the problem.

I am warning ourselves against this mode of thinking. Everything depends on language. One can say: "In such a situation the Armistice regime is out." But one can also say: "Are the neighboring states really interested in the ending of this regime? They have already done much to undermine it; are interested in its final demise?" There is a difference between the two formulations.

In my opinion we should not be interested in appearing as the initiators of the formal abolition of the Armistice regime. For in such a case we would attract the suspicion that this is our interest; and in as much as such a suspicion already exists, we shall be enhancing it. And in our international struggle this is not necessary; neither is it helpful in our military sphere. For if there persists a suspicion that this is our ulterior motive, then this means that we want to pave the way towards war. And then, right from the beginning, we would be seen as potential initiators of war, and then, whatever happens, it would be easier to accuse us, rather than others, of attempting to clear the road to war. [- - -] And since we are not living in a void, then even while relying to the utmost on our own might we must realize that there exists a whole net of international connections, of economic and financial policies, in which our Jewish people too is interwoven. We cannot be oblivious to international reaction to such a declaration by us.

There is also a simple question: suppose we declare that, as far as we are concerned, the Armistice regime doesn't exist. What next? In fact we took this step on a small scale when we left the IJMAC. True, when we left the IJMAC we said we were not revoking the Armistice Agreements; we made it clear that we were not leaving the Syrian, Egyptian and Lebanese MACs. But what next? If by taking this step we could achieve an immediate significant change for the better, or the disabling of the IJMAC, then perhaps it would be worthwhile. But time has passed and what is the situation? Incidents continue to occur, the Commission convenes, makes decisions which anger us, which distorts facts to our detriment. We are not present there. We cannot protect ourselves there, nor attack. The decisions are publicized. As far as the international community is concerned they carry the stamp of the UN. We then react by publishing communiqués, by sending our reports directly to the SC; we condemn the distortions and injustice. But the very first question which cannot but be directed towards us is this: "Either/or. If you are oblivious to the IJMAC, if you don't care, why are you raising hell, why are you accusing and protesting, why are you appealing to the SC? If you do not care, then so be it, pay the price! But if you do care, if you get excited and decide to react, then why aren't you looking after your interests on the spot, that is, why aren't you going back to [participate in] the [Mixed Armistice] Commission?"

This question takes on a more serious character if we are talking about the abolition of the Armistice regime itself. Suppose we took this step. What next? What tomorrow? The armistice demarcation lines [the "Green Line" borders] are in existence or are they not? Are we interested in their existence or not? Are we going to declare them annulled, and start amending them according to our interests? Doesn't this mean war? Or, on the contrary, shall we insist on maintaining them and accuse the Arabs who cross the lines of being transgressors? If so, then we in fact do recognize the Armistice regime, so why did we declared it annulled? Isn't it better if we accuse others of being the transgressors? This is why I asked: What next?

Too often we are executing a calculated stratagem, but only a very short-range one, with no long-range considerations. We are making a move on the chess board without taking into account the other side's possible next move, and then what our next move will be. In other words, we are playing a primitive game of chess. I am aware that one does not always enjoys this luxury while playing this game. I am not a master player; I am not able to plan more than 2-3 moves ahead, and sometimes it turns out that I erred in planning both of my two next moves. But I think we should make an effort to be more calculating and act more wisely on a basis of long-range thinking.

And again, what is the meaning of "we shall declare"? Within the context of the Armistice there are three factors: we, the other party to the agreement, and the UN. Are we totally oblivious to this third party? One of the *haverim* said that we should not cling too much to this body. I would agree that the UN nowadays is not, as far as we are concerned, the same as what it was in 1947. However, I would put forth a second assumption: that this doesn't mean the UN has ceased to exist, and that we can act as if it doesn't exist. Moreover, it is impossible to talk at all about the international arena and about international inter-dependency without taking account of the UN. I fully agree that the public should be taught that it should not blindly love the UN as omnipotent body. However, at the same I think that the public should be taught to develop some international sensitivity. We cannot let our public develop a total insensitivity, an utter rigidity towards international considerations; this is not because we need to be liked by somebody, but because ignoring reality and international complications can clearly be detrimental to us. If we care for ourselves, then we must develop within us an international sensitivity in the same way that we all develop that sensitivity which protects us from putting our hand onto a flame.

Our public is highly capable of isolating itself and losing all awareness of international obligations. But it also can move to the other end of the spectrum and lose its self-assuredness and experience an exaggerated fear of "who knows what the UN can do us?" Our educational efforts should be aimed simultaneously in two directions. Together with enhancing the sense of assuredness and with bolstering the awareness of our might, it is necessary to enhance the awareness that we are not a people that dwells alone, that we are connected to the world, that we are dependent on it, that our dependency may be detrimental or beneficial, and that our task is to see to it that it is beneficial.

And there is another thing I would like to note, and this is the need to differentiate between our vision of our distant future and the vision of the present hour. And by "hour" I don't mean necessarily an exact hour, but perhaps a span of several years. From the long-term perspective, the prospects for Israel are indeed terribly foreboding. The Arab people are clearly able to make war against us with a million soldiers, not necessarily weaklings, who could overcome and annihilate us, which means that we should see to it that the world realizes that the whole Middle East could be thrown into flames and destroyed.

I do not propose that we discuss here what tasks should we give to our military experts. One can assume that these people are busy with all kinds of projects, and it is good that they are busy. And we should be prepared, perhaps, in terminal situations, for [the use of] terminal means.[26]

But generally speaking, if we think in terms of the Arabs' potential ability to enlist against us a million soldiers, then the question arises: Was Zionism really a delusion which has enticed the Jewish people to this corner of the world in order to send it into a death trap?

But the enlisting of a million soldiers cannot be executed in one sudden stroke and the issue is not only between us and the million [Arab] soldiers. There is, after all, a world [community] to which both us and they belong. And for the time being the Arab states are busy not only with arming themselves; they are also busy with constant internal conflicts and tribulations and coups d'état and the overthrow of monarchs. Moreover, our ability to grow and fortify ourselves is by far greater than theirs, so I don't think that our long-term thinking should delineate for us the directions of concrete actions we should take today or tomorrow.

I say we must arm ourselves with forbearance. Forbearance does not mean missing some opportunity in the meantime; neither does it mean insensitivity, closing one's eyes to danger, not taking seriously a problematic situation. Forbearance means avoiding the assumption that the fate of historical struggles is decided for good at every phase. No, there are always several phases in any given battle, in which ups and downs and all kinds of changes occur, so that when we lose one fight it doesn't mean that the [larger] battle is lost, even if the results of a given fight are not exactly those we had wished for and, consequently, if so, all is lost. This is definitely not so.

Let now go back again to the subject of reprisals. *Haverim*, I don't think there is an argument here between a camp that says no reprisals whatsoever and a camp that says reprisals only, constantly and on all occasions. However, it is clear that in our debate quite serious differences of opinion have emerged. When I claim that we should be cautious in this sphere, it is not in order to find favor with anybody, but in order to achieve greater efficacy for our standing as a whole, and first and foremost for our military standing.

Whether or not we are divided on the question of reprisals, whether or not all of us agree on a policy of reprisals, we all hold that we shall not create, out of the blue, so to speak, a new *ETZEL* or Stern Gang[27] and let them go berserk on their own, that we shall not create a *Golem*[28] and let it sow destruction. Naturally, whether we establish [for the purpose of executing reprisal operations] a border guard, or a special unit, or indeed organize settlers whom we would arm and direct – I am not rejecting this variation – this [reprisals] unit will be connected somehow to the center [of state power], which means of necessity taking precautions, since such groups which disobey the central authority are by nature unbridled in their actions.

But I must say – and I say it among us within these four walls – that the very fact that we are using, and must be using, the Army for this purpose creates a situation

26 This seems to be the only reference made by Sharett to Israel's development of a nuclear bomb. See Cohen, *Israel and the Bomb*.

27 Dissident Jewish militias operating independently of the JA against British and Arab targets in Palestine during the 1930s and 1940s. Frequently engaged in "reprisals" and "terrorist" actions. See above, page 48 n.50.

28 Reference to the fabled monster, created by a Kabbalist, who saved the Jewish ghetto of Prague from antisemitic attack, but went out of control.

whereby "sin lieth at the door" [*Genesis*, 4:7], and we must be aware of this. I think that in such actions a much stronger discipline and caution is necessary than is practiced in ordinary military exercises. Here a far greater stricture must be imposed on those in direct command of operations and on their chain of command, indeed, because later, after a military operation is executed, it is much more difficult to ascertain [what happened]. Since, when a unit is sent at night to execute a difficult and dangerous task, to which you cannot add accompanying competent observers as is done during military exercises, you must be able to trust and believe that the information presented later [by the commanders of the operation] is true. Here a most strict education is necessary.

It is incumbent on us that there shall be full trust in IDF reporting, that each word said is the truth and the whole truth. But there are [in IDF operational units] new people [i.e., new immigrants] and young soldiers with natural impulses, and the connection between them and their immediate commander is much tighter than that between him and the line of command above him. Here then an extreme and cruel stricture must be exercised.

Moreover, in this sphere [of IDF operations] we are entangled in a highly complicated problem, for we are compelled to say things which the world at large does not accept as truthful. This is an uncontested fact. I will not challenge here the political logic of the explanation given at the time by Ben-Gurion [regarding the Qibya raid, i.e., that it was mounted by enraged settlers], but at the same time I must state that factually, in utmost clarity, the world did not accept Ben-Gurion's explanation as truthful.

What does this mean? It means that the outside world has learned that a PM is capable of standing behind a microphone and making a solemn declaration which is not truthful. Worse, our people know that it was not truthful – this was the impression outside Israel – and as far as the people of Israel is concerned, this was okay. Here, again. "sin lieth at the door." For if we [the government of Israel] are stating things which are not truthful, then it becomes acceptable for an operational report not to be fully accurate, and for the Foreign Minister not to be informed, or even for the Minister of Defense not to know everything;[29] and it is also possible to then send Abba Eban to make a statement [at the United Nations or to the US administration] which is not always fully true.

I would like to tell the *haverim*: our reputation of being a people who tell the truth is on the decline. Perhaps this impression is not fully justified, but it is an uncontested fact, and this makes it incumbent on us to impose strictness, certainly among ourselves.

Another thing which we should be aware of is that, if we can carry out only large-scale reprisals with a large force, which naturally entails people being killed or the possibility of their being killed – and sometimes, when the operation succeeds, and it also happens that it succeeds too much, which is sometimes unavoidable – we cannot prevent the impression that we are behaving provocatively, that we are capitalizing on incidents carried out against us as a pretext to mount a large-scale operation, and that we do not care if our action brings about a more serious response by the other side, and never mind what happens next. There might arise circumstances where we have no alternative. But if so, then we must be very cautious that a mood of "not caring", of "we have nothing to lose" should not prevail among us. [Rather, we must act on the calculation] that this is the only option, no matter what the results; or, even though [negative] results may be significant, there is no other way; that this is the road to be taken, for otherwise matters would be worse.

We must take into account all kinds of possibilities. For instance, there is a constant

29 See above, page 43 n.39, and below, page 426 n.44.

argument going on among us – not yet in the open but it is simmering – regarding the American grant-in-aid. No one among us accepts the grant with shouts of "Hallelujah", but it is seen as a necessity. I, for my part, see it as a necessity not to be ashamed about, indeed as a honorable necessity, but I would have been happy if we could have done without it. If we do accept it, then it is quite easy to say very convincingly that both the giving and the receiving of the grant are honorable deeds. This is, to my mind, an important point. It is also true: if there is a need, then it is honorable to make a grant. By the way, there is a real question of whether we are utilizing the grant properly, so that we would be prepared to hold on during periods of no grants, and I think that here many sins are committed. However, I don't want, and I don't think any of the *haverim* would want, the grant to be cancelled by way of punishment, or cancelled in such circumstances which as would curtail the ability of American Jewish public opinion to oppose such an annulment. I would not welcome such an annulment.

I would be happy if the American grant would come to its end the same as it was ended in Burma, whereupon one bright day Burma notified the USA that she doesn't need it anymore: "Thank you. We are deeply obliged. We shall never forget that at a dire moment you gave us your hand, but there is no need anymore." And if this cannot be, then there is no alternative but that the grant will die a natural death along a process of its becoming smaller and smaller until the day comes when we receive nothing. What I don't want is that a grant be annulled as step of punishing us while the whole Arab world rejoices.

There is no need for a war for measures to be taken against us. Every day we hear not only warnings but threats as well, and in the past we stood fast and carried out a few actions in spite of warnings and threats. But there is no need to ignore warnings and threats, and if it is possible, while continuing with ongoing reprisals, to curtail the danger of carrying out these threats, so much the better.

I cited [at the previous meeting of the Political Committee] one outcome of the reprisals – that they are fanning the flames of hatred against us. Some *haverim* have said, and rightly so: "And when there are no reprisals? Do the Arabs then sit beside you, ready to negotiate peace?" Still, I cannot ignore this consideration, and I think we all should not ignore it since, after all, the question boils down to what is our purpose here. Is our purpose here peace or not peace? And peace, mind you, with those very same Arab states. If so, are the seeds of hatred being sown meanwhile in the [Arab] hearts of any value, or not?

We are constantly talking with the Arab world via our state radio broadcasts in Arabic. What is the purpose of this activity? Are these broadcasts made only to frighten, to threaten, or also to achieve a positive response in the hearts of the listeners?

If words carry weight, deeds carry weight. If there is no alternative [to reprisals], so be it. If it is a must, so be it. But to completely ignore [the sowing of hatred among Arabs] is just impossible. This attitude of "in any case there will be no peace; whatever we do, it makes no difference" – well, it does make a difference. And there are matters which the Arabs understand more and matters they understand less. There are things which they resist more and things they resist less; matters which they justify more and matters which they justify less. They are people with a very fine understanding and sensitivity. They are not desert savages. True, there is a wall between us, and there is a tragic development created by this wall which grows higher and higher. But, in spite of all this, if it is possible to prevent [this wall from] being made higher, it is incumbent on us to do so as much as possible.

However, we are not talking only about long-range impact on [Arab] feeling and political orientation. There are here, before us, much more direct results, much more immediate consequences. Some *haverim* say: "Not responding [by military reprisals] encourages aggression!" True. But the opposite is also no less true: response provokes aggression. Certainly, there is the question of who is provoked and where. It may well be that the provoked aggression occurs not in the same region, not in the same village [against which an IDF reprisal was mounted], but the [Israeli] provocation spreads around and is encouraging aggression. Possibly a reprisal operation deters the inhabitants of the village which was hit, but it doesn't deter the marauding gang operating in that area; on the contrary, it may encourage it.

I have presented the case for mounting of reprisals, and I did not do that only for the sake of argument; I did that in all seriousness. Among other considerations I mentioned the serious consideration that, if not for reprisals, the government on the other side of the border could sit still and do nothing. There was a time when we said that they were taking it easy – the Jordanian Army was mounting military exercises but at the same time it was abandoning the border area to the marauding gangs. We said: "Let us mount reprisals that will force the Jordanian Army to take up positions and compel it to guard the borders." However reality does not always obey our wishes. In response to our reprisals they established the "National Guard." This body is our child. The "National Guard in the West Bank" evolved not necessarily only to be a preventive instrument, but to be an instrument of aggression as well. Lately we have been witnessing the phenomenon of Jordanian Army posts along the borders participating in aggressive acts. They are shooting at us. No doubt, we must respond – this goes without saying. But as for the question of the efficacy of reprisals, it rather makes it more complicated, not less. And, in addition, the level of alertness in the West Bank villages across the borders has become heightened; their defending themselves [against IDF operations] has become much more serious.

What am I aiming at by saying all this? I am calling for a more calculated behavior, not mechanical, not continuous. There should be lulls in between reprisals. It is necessary to break the chain once in a while, so that it becomes clear who is the instigator. In general, I think it is necessary to investigate anew and thoroughly this whole question of reprisals. I am deeply afraid we have let ourselves come under the sway of a routine whereby it is accepted that we can act only by using the Army – and naturally, the Army can act only by way of mounting reprisals. I think that even on the military level it is possible to look for new ways, and that we should also add other, non-military means.

Let me elaborate what I am aiming at. It may well be that I am not well-read enough; I am so immersed in my day-to-day work that I lack the time to investigate every matter thoroughly and I capitulate to superficiality. [---]

I do most certainly think that, inasmuch as possible, it is preferable to mount small-scale and non-ostentatious reprisals, perhaps even more numerous, than big ones, because this way we would be responding to what is being done by the other side. This would also ease our political battle afterwards. This would also make the occurrences look as natural – it is possible to plan this naturalness just as it is possible to plan improvisation. Moreover, it seems to me that we must devote more attention to hitting directly the people who operate against us [and not just innocent villagers], and this could be achieved as a result of more thorough intelligence activity. I mean investigating, identifying individual culprits, and then hitting our targets. The psychological and moral impact of a direct hit is immeasurable in comparison to a blind attack.

I am not suggesting that we stop mounting reprisals if, in the meantime, owing to certain considerations, they are seen as necessary. But since this is a long-term matter – we don't know how long this is going to last – I suggest the appointment of a special committee, composed by selected members, let's say one of whom would be an IDF man, one an experienced Arabist who is well versed in what's going on among Arab villagers, etc., which would delve into an objective, open-eyed investigation of the situation along the borders during a given period, look into processes which have been evolving, review the methods used and results achieved, positive as well as negative, mistakes made and how to avoid them in the future, successful operations which should be intensified. I am very much afraid of our thinking being pushed along one narrow course while, at the same time, we free ourselves from searching out new and different ways and means.

Let me cite one example – an example taken from the pattern of our recent relationship with the Egyptians in the Gaza Strip. Infiltration in that area is a malignant plague. I have no idea whether Lavon spoke here, or perhaps somewhere else, about transferring the refugees from there to Egypt.

Pinhas Lavon: I did not say that.

Moshe Sharett: You said: "The Egyptians should realize that they must take these people to Egypt and then the problem would be solved."

Pinhas Lavon: I am all for that, but I did not say this.

Moshe Sharett: I am prepared to bring witnesses from the Ministry of Defense. Anyway. There is an infiltration plague, and it should be noted that recently the Egyptian Army went into action against it. There was the case of the abduction of an IDF soldier owing to his foolish behavior. They invited him over, he approached them and was abducted. The assumption is that they are holding him – they did not kill him – for the same reason we are holding somebody who falls in our hands, that is to gather information from him. Well, we wanted to get even and we mounted an abduction operation. The plan was to get somebody alive without casualties being involved. But, bad luck! Since we had not arranged beforehand with the other side that he would not misbehave, he behaved somewhat otherwise and opened fire. We then had to fire back, the result being that we, while operating in their territory, killed three soldiers, an officer an two privates, and then retreated without suffering casualties, with the abducted soldier. Our aim of abducting one man alive was achieved, but at the price of three unplanned deaths. The Egyptians responded to this affair. One can say that our operation was a response, that they should have realized it was a response [to their abduction of our man] and that they should have been deterred by it. As it happened, they were not deterred, but mounted a more serious operation. One night they crossed the border into our area – something, it seems, they had not done, even once – and mounted five or six ambushes, four of which were activated, resulting in several deaths on our side, a burnt-out IDF jeep and damage to one or two of our settlements. It was a "joyful" night along the Strip border.

Now, at this stage a question arose: what should we do, and should we act at all? There were considerations for and against. On the one hand, it was the first time [- - -] the Egyptian Army crossed our borders – not just civilian infiltrators, but Army units which mounted a series of quite daring actions. If we don't teach them a lesson, the situation would only worsen, and therefore we must respond, whatever the results may be, since we cannot allow ourselves to sit still.

On the other hand there was a different consideration: We cannot be oblivious to the process, to the chain of events. Their action came as a response to our action. There is no proof that the Egyptian Army has changed its strategy and decided to mount operations inside Israel from now on. Let us then consciously "miss one bus" - this would not shatter the stature of the IDF in the eyes of the Egyptian Army. Let's see what happens next. If it turns out that they made a probe inside our territory and, upon realizing that this probe remained without response, they continued in this vein, then we should give them a hard lesson. However, if it turns out otherwise, then we have succeeded in breaking the chain.

It was finally decided to opt for the second line of reasoning. And as it happened, the crossing by Egyptian soldiers into our territory did nor recur.

Then, lately, the Egyptians, without crossing the borders, started shooting from their posts at our patrols when they passed near the border. We kept silent once, then twice. On the third shooting we responded rather heavily. At the same time we initiated diplomatic moves. We said we would like to meet together in order to clarify matters: Is all this beneficial to you? Are you really interested in these shooting exchanges and ready to bear their consequences? At long last there was a low level meeting, and an Egyptian member of the EIMAC asked our representative to meet with him in private and then told him: "I was ordered to tell you that we have no interest in border incidents, and in as much as our shooting was concerned it happened because your patrols moved provocatively near the border line and our soldiers lost control and started shooting, even though they were under no orders to do so. Now such an order was issued and the shooting will stop."

I think that these small affairs do not necessarily predetermine future developments, but according to my information and on the basis of my impressions, I would say that they can teach us the positive integration of three principles: forbearance when necessary; response when justified; and the value of diplomatic initiative. I don't know if this will prove effective in the long run, but meanwhile tension along the border has eased dangers of all kinds of [diplomatic] censures [against Israel] have been avoided, and, in my opinion, the Egyptians were taught a lesson.

If I am asked by the *haverim* what is my summing up of all this, I would reply: our position is rather complicated. We have no simple panacea at hand. We must move ahead by trying all possible avenues while both buttressing ourselves and exercising caution.[30]

[- - -]

Thursday-Friday, May 13-14

[- - -]

Saturday, May 15

[- - -]

With Teddy – the [Kasztner] trial. BG – [his initiative to establish] "a people's front."[31]

30 Mapai Archive 26/54; *Sharett: Mivhar Te'udot*, doc.132.

31 Ben-Gurion was toying with the idea of establishing a popular movement which would run in the next general elections under the slogan of reforming the electoral system from country-wide proportional representation by party lists to a combined regional/personal-majority ballot. His assumption was that this principle would increase the chances of one party winning more than 50% of the vote, thus stabilizing Israel's democracy and avoiding the frustrating need to form coalition governments. The proposal would be rejected by Mapai. See Giora Goldberg, *Ben-Gurion against the Knesset*, transl. Chaya Naor (London: Frank Cass, 2003), 9.

Sunday, May 16

I am resuming the diary after a month's interval. Who can tell whether and when it shall be made up?

Sat down with Shabtai Rosenne on the development of our new initiative in the Security Council – to uphold Article 35 of the [UN] Charter and, in accordance with it, to demand a prior commitment on the part of Jordan to accept the principles of the Charter as regards the settling of disputes by peaceful means as a pre-condition for Jordan's participation in Council debates. This matter has put the SC in an uproar. The Arabs are furious; the US and France believe there is no avoiding this commitment. Other countries are also afraid of setting a dangerous precedent if the Council should concede to the Arabs, while only England is attempting some worthless compromise which would extricate its ally from its predicament.[32]

The *Shabbat* Work Permits Committee took up a full hour. Warhaftig [Deputy Minister of Religion] fought desperately again and was defeated on each and every item.

[- - -]

At the Cabinet meeting Lavon gave a detailed review of the arms race in which we were immersed with the Arab states, and on our special efforts to catch up and even overtake them in tanks and guns and bolster our jet air power. Our inferiority in sea power is most disturbing.[33]

[- - -]

Monday, May 17

[- - -]

32 See *DFPI* 9, docs.206, 229; conversation between Wainhouse, Hart, Ludlow, Shiloah and Robinson, May 17, 1954, USNA 684A.85/5-1754; Israel Delegation to the UN, meeting no.38, May 18, 1954, ISA FM 130.03/1962/9.

33 The protocol of the Cabinet meeting reveals that Sharett also reported on Eban's meeting with Dulles and [Jacob] Blaustein's meeting with the President. Regarding Byroade's speech, he said, "Dulles, at most, agreed that a way should be found to correct the impression left by the speech. But the fact is that Byroade pronounced a clear direction, while the President and Dulles spoke only in general and vague terms." There was, he warned his colleagues, "no retreating from what Byroade had said. Byroade has opened our eyes to see some directions and trends. We must monitor these developments with no illusions." Regarding Dulles' announcement of American arms supplies to Iraq, Sharett noted that the Secretary had included some general, but unpromising, words about American friendship with Israel. "We would be mistaken," Sharett said, "if we were to say that we can be at ease after these words." Asked by Minister G. Myerson [Meir] whether it was true that, following his talk with Dulles, Ambassador Eban had told the press that the conversation had been "encouraging," Sharett replied: "It is true, and he received a cable in which I told him this word was puzzling. Even if the conversation had been encouraging, there was no need to describe it as such; one could have said it was 'important,' and remain respectful to Dulles."

Ziama finally told me about the consultation held that Saturday[34] at BG's in Tel Aviv. The main idea [promoted by Ben-Gurion] was to strive with all our might to establish a two-party system in the state. He has evidently despaired of ever winning a 51 percent victory for the party, and has therefore come up with a new invention: the creation of a temporary body for the purpose of the elections to be called the "People's Front," which will be joined by people from various camps whose common denominator is an aspiration to establish stability in the state. This "People's Front" would participate in the general election under the slogan of amending the election law, which will put an end to small political parties and make it possible only for two parties to survive. When the Knesset convenes after these elections it would enact such a law after which it and the "People's Front" would disband themselves. Then new elections would be held on the basis of the new regime, and from that moment internal political life would be stable forever.

Ziama said he strongly dissented: is a two-party system really desirable for us in this period of our history? This has not yet been proven. It also means a gigantic growth of the GZ. And can one assure that the "People's Front" would disband itself? Aren't its Knesset members bound to stay put? Will they shorten their days in the Knesset out of their own free will? In addition and above all these questions I asked Ziama who was going to head the "Front." He said he did not know. When I told him that as far as I have gathered from Teddy, BG sees himself as heading the election list of this body, he was doubly dumbfounded.

I said that these grave problems concerning our slogans for the upcoming elections and our preparations towards them would not be solved in private conversation and we must quickly put them on the track of authorized party deliberations. Actually we should already have had a working campaign staff, which would orchestrate our preparations and stand on guard for the same consideration as regards every act of government and party appearance. Ziama proposed that we first hold a consultation on this matter among the team of five [senior Mapai] ministers.

Ziama also told me about the planned national gathering of sixth and seventh graders in the Hulda Forest, before whom BG would deliver his ideas on pioneering with the purpose of directing this entire young generation into settling the country via the *Gadna*[35] and *Nahal* [pioneering youth] formations. The vision is exalted and the impetus daring, in the best tradition, but I raised questions: First, what was to follow the meeting? Was this once again fireworks which would shoot up into the sky and blind the viewers, only to be extinguished and drown the landscape in

34 See above, entry for May 7.

35 *Gadna*, acronym for *Gdudei No'ar* (youth battalions), a paramilitary organization founded in the pre-State era by the *Hagana* for preparing Jewish youth for military service. Its activity in the State of Israel was legislated in 1949, being placed under the authority of *Nahal*. On *Nahal*, see above, page 85 n.36.

even blacker gloom? Or were plans being made for the provision of instruments to ensure continuity and follow-up of effort? I mentioned that, at two meetings which BG had initiated within the past year, I had proposed at the start of deliberations that we should discuss the creation of instruments necessary for implementation. But my view had been rejected and the meetings went by having left no sign or trace, and played no role in the life of the party. Second, and this is the main thing, was there any link between the new initiative and the existing framework of youth movements? These movements may well be of diminutive size but at least they are organic growths, whereas the *Gadna* is a mechanical contrivance. Pioneer settlement is a way of life and not a specific one-time effort to do one's duty, like Army service. We can easily weaken the existing [pioneering youth] movements by directing all our vim and vigor into the mass frameworks which are state-run institutions, but it is doubtful whether any gain will accrue by it to the pioneering camp.

[- - -]

Jon Kimche[36] came for a quarter-hour visit and sat for an hour and a half. He reported, with some surprise, what he'd heard from Moshe Dayan, that the situation along the borders is better than it has been in a long time and, to tell the truth, is quite satisfactory – all this in contrast to the picture painted by the reports of the incidents. Moshe Dayan also admitted that in a few cases the UN reports are more accurate than ours. (I heard from another source just this week that Moshe Dayan said to Israeli journalists that the Ma'aleh Akrabim gang hadn't been proven to be Jordanian – it may have been local – and that these remarks made their way to foreign delegations in Israel.)

[- - -]

Tuesday, May 18

[- - -]

I devoted the early part of the morning at the PMO to preparing my presentation on the Jordan [diversion] channel matter and the Johnston plan before the Cabinet Foreign Affairs and Defense Committee.

[- - -]

At long last I made a special effort to write a letter to David Hacohen, to be delivered to him in Rangoon by Reuven Barkat, who is taking off tomorrow for the conference of Asian socialist states. My prolonged silence towards him was a heavy burden on my conscience.

36 Jon Kimche (1909-1994). Swiss-born Anglo-Jewish editor and author of several books on the ME and Palestine. Edited the *Jewish Observer and Middle East Review* (1952-1967) which was published by the British Zionist Federation and often served as a mouthpiece for Israel's defense establishment.

Dear David,

You must certainly have given up hope of receiving a letter from me some time ago. But, lo and behold – a miracle! I'm writing! Truth is that not only that have I been missing you all this time, at times painfully, but writing to you was for me an inner need which could not be satisfied owing to the wrecking, maddening, decisively inhuman circumstances in which I am living and apparently shall have to live in for a long time.

I will now tell tell you and Bracha [Hacohen's wife] a secret – I'm writing a diary. I started it last year in October, and for the time being I have succeed in carrying it on. This is an unbearable undertaking indeed. I am writing, by hand of course, and not in brief but at some length and detail, mostly at very late hours of the night, on the Sabbath eve and on *Shabbat*, at the cost of sleep and rest, and sometimes at the cost of urgent work. I have by now amassed quite a pile of sheets of paper, arranged by weeks, all covered with crowded lines of very tiny letters. This diary serves me as a substitute for writing letters to at least two people: to you and to my son Kovi [then a student in New York]. True, for the time being you are not enjoying this enterprise, but the day will come when you will have your share during a visit or a vacation; then you will have to devote few days to [reading] the sheets [I shall have] amassed by then, and [you can] learn a great deal and be party to many experiences which by then I would have surely forgotten.

Very few people know about the diary's existence, so please don't mention it in your letters to anybody at the FM. Many would be astonished and alarmed if ever they knew about it. For it is really hard to imagine that, in addition to my input, the scope of which you, even from a distance, can imagine, in the PMO, FM, Knesset and the party, and hosting of guests at home, etc., etc., I manage to enlist time and energy for this unceasing and tiring effort, day by day, week by week.

I will not say much about my personal life. You must be aware, even from a distance, that all the serious and negative complications which have accompanied the birth pangs of the new government, within our small group [of Mapai leaders] as well, are still with us and are even, time and again, born anew as the weeks go by, inside the Cabinet and outside. It seems it is a decree from Heaven that we are destined to live with such complications and accept the verdict of problems which only time can solve, if they are soluble at all.

[- - -]

With all my heart,
Moshe

A consultation at the Ministry on the problem of the IJMAC. I had thought I would find most of the colleagues advocating our return at the first opportunity after obtaining a suitable pretext – let's say, the removal of our arch-enemy Hutchison from the chairmanship of the Commission – but not so! Except for Arthur who voiced some pertinent remarks as regards the foreign front but did not take internal public-relations considerations sufficiently into account, all were of the opinion that there was no harm in our continued boycott. In their words, the world is less and less impressed by one-sided condemnations of us, adopted in our absence. The contradiction between our boycott of the Commission and our protests against it does not overly concern public opinion (I am skeptical!). Walter opined that we must return as soon as the SC demands it. I noted that it wasn't so easy. First, it was a moot question whether the SC would demand anything; the debate there is stuck in the sand, and who knows whether and when it will end somehow. Second, if a resolution is adopted, or if, in the case of a veto, we should desire to act according to the formula of the resolution which the western majority voted in favor of, we would not be able to obey the directive addressed to us without Jordan complying with the directive addressed to it – Article VIII and Article XII. As opposed to this, I expressed doubt whether we could continue the boycott if anything serious doing us grievous harm happens along the border. The conclusion was that at any rate we shall go on with the boycott for the time being, until the fate of the debate lagging in the SC should become clear.[37]

At 3:00 pm a series of meetings began which continued almost without a break until midnight. The first meeting: the Cabinet FADC at the Knesset. Also invited were the Ministers of Finance and Agriculture, *Tahal* engineers Blass and Wiener, and Rafael and Tekoah from the Foreign Ministry. I lectured on the resumption of the Jordan channel project in the DMZ, the chances of which have improved with the positive report of the UN experts[38] regarding the possibility of guaranteeing Syrian water rights. But our chances are not guaranteed since the shadow of Bennike's "military advantages" accruing to Israel [from the change in the Jordan River's course] has not yet receded. [I also lectured] on the proposal floated to buy Syria's tolerance of the resumption of [diversion] work at the price of our tolerance of the execution of the Yarmuk project, which will entail work in the corner of the demilitarized [area] of El Hama. [I also spoke] on the problem of cooperation with [US Envoy Eric] Johnston and the idea that we sell him upon the planned linkage between our Jordan [diversion] project and Jordan's Yarmuk project, as a first stage in the implementation of the [proposed] regional plan without committing ourselves to the rest of its principles for the time being. [Finally, I spoke] on the US request to allow an American survey team to carry out certain measurements in Israeli territory, in the triangle formed by the Jordan, the Yarmuk and the Kinneret, and on the request by Johnston himself that we not resume work [on the B'not Yaakov water diversion] during the time of his visit with us.

Concerning the last two questions, it was decided as I had proposed: to reply to the State Department in the negative as regards the survey team, and to Johnston in the affirmative as regards the non-resumption of [the water diversion] work – the first answer with an explanation that we ourselves can provide all the required data, the second emphasizing that we are resolved not to miss this entire summer. The concession to Johnston is actually only for the sake of appearances, for in any case

37 Israel's boycott of the IJMAC would continue until November. See *DFPI* 9, docs.240, 287 On the eventual removal of Commander Hutchison, see report of talk with Col. R. Hommel (chief military advisor to UNTSO CoS), Tel Aviv, June 15, 1954, ISA FM 130.02//2425/8b; Eliav-Taylor conversation, June 17, 1954, USNA Lot File 58D33 box 3.

38 Dixon and Eysvoogel; see above, entry for March 29.

we do not intend to resume work until the publication of the experts' report and the elimination of the threat of a new prohibition on the part of the SC.

As to the linkage of the two plans, serious doubts arose regarding the danger of conceding all of the Yarmuk's waters which this settlement would involve, and although nothing final was decided, the trend that emerged was not to raise this question on our part and to wait until it should be raised by Johnston, who is due to visit us in the middle of June.

This hearing took two whole hours and there was no time left to discuss the question of relations with Communist China, the second item on the agenda.

From 5:00 to 7:00 at the PMO, the Foreign Ministry's discussion with the Defense Ministry and GS. Present were Lavon, the CoS, Givly, Shalev, Eytan, Rafael, Lourie, Tekoah [now director of Armistice Affairs at the Foreign Ministry] and the secretaries. I posed for examination an assessment of the border situation, the problems in reporting and the meaning of the latest incidents. I hinted at the speculations spreading among the journalists that did not always coincide with our official versions. The CoS understood the hint and felt slightly offended, but suppressed his anger. He contended that in personal conversation with me he had also explained his opinion that the situation, in effect, was all right. This time he elaborated and elucidated. Previous incidents had brought the [Jordanian Arab] Legion to the border area. Four battalions were now camped the length of it. They had got control of the situation and stopped disturbances. This rectification had been bought at the price of increased tension. Now one army faces the other, both of them on the alert. If there is any outburst, a military reaction would be immediately forthcoming. Ordinary murders had ceased, but the danger of a serious altercation had grown. As to the latest incidents, after the Khirbet 'Illin action, in which a Border Guard unit had been unlucky, its units have conducted a campaign of revenge the length of the border area. The Army has now entered the thick of the fray, responding to the behavior of the Border Guards in order to put them in their place and has demanded that the latter refrain from any and all initiative, leaving retaliations to the Army alone.

I said that this hearing had opened my eyes. Until now I knew that I was dealing with the Army as an element which must be held in check. Now I find that evil may break forth from yet another source: the Border Guard of the police, over which the state's discipline has not yet been imposed. I have taken note.[39]

All in all, the meeting with the Army people was conducted in good spirit and contributed towards the smoothing of obstacles and clearing of unknowns. It also contributed to a common language, both internally and externally in the sphere of the state's public relations.

---

39 In a further complication, UNTSO observers investigating this incident reported being fired on from the Israeli side. See Pelcovits, *The Long Armistice*, 61-62.

[- - -]

At 8:00 pm the final meeting of the day was opened – a consultation over the financial situation of the party. It continued until close to midnight.

Utterly exhausted I drank my last tea with Zipporah.

Wednesday, May 19

[- - -]

At 9:00, a meeting of the *Shabbat* Work Permits Committee. Warhaftig didn't come and we had a taste of joy for an hour, Golda and Aharonson[40] and myself. We authorized permits right and left, although we did charitably defer a few requests until further review.

[- - -]

Sent a telegram to Washington on what and how to reply to Johnston as regards his request that we not resume work during the time of his visit to Israel.[41]

Also sent a detailed telegram on the pearls which fell from the lips of General [Arthur] Trudeau, [head] of US military intelligence, who visited us one day and spoke at length with Lavon, the CoS and Arthur Lourie. Incidentally, according to news we've had from Washington, he was about to bring a letter of invitation for the CoS to visit the US, but this wasn't so. He didn't bring any invitation, verbally probed and prodded as to why Dayan wanted to come to America, and in the end left the matter of the trip in limbo. It was decided correctly to cancel the planned trip.

During the talks Trudeau voiced some provocative opinions. He doubted whether Israel would fight on the side of the West. In any event, Israel was not to be armed for a world war because it would be impossible to take the IDF to the north of the region, due to the Arabs' opposition, while the defense of Israel was of no value, for if the fighting reached such an inner part of the region the campaign would be lost anyway. In Iraq they would arm two divisions and after Iraq will come the turn of other Arab states. The Arabs were by no means to be denigrated as soldiers; witness Korea, which had also been belittled as a military factor, but equipment and training had turned its people into proper fighters. We were making a mistake in forcing soldiers to occupy themselves with agriculture by means of *Nahal*; he knew through his contacts with Jews that these did not constitute an agricultural element at all. And more such gems of wisdom![42]

---

40 Yedidia Aharonson, Chief Supervisor, Department of Work Inspection, at the Ministry of Labor.

41 *DFPI* 9, doc.214. On this date, the Israel Delegation to the UN heard a report from legal adviser Jacob Robinson on the question of resuming work on the B'not Yaakov diversion canal. Meeting no.39, May 19, 1954, ISA FM130.03/1962/9.

42 See *DFPI* 9, doc.213.

Thursday, May 20

Meyer Weisgal came to the PMO to report on the progress of his efforts to unify the collection of American funds for the three institutions of higher learning and research – the Hebrew University, the Haifa Technion and the Weizmann Institute. He went on to speak at length about the political and moral standing of Israel in the US. Again the same dirge about a crisis of confidence. We hadn't yet recovered from the blow of Qibya – and now Nahhalin. He tossed out criticism of our representation. I explained to him what I did, including the internal emotional demands of the community and the difficulty of withstanding them, despite which successful efforts were invested in checking passions – for example our restraint during the time of turmoil in Syria. He asked why this was not known outside; why didn't we publicize this kind of information? When I confronted him with my explicit speech at the Knesset, in which I lauded our stability and restraint in the face of temptation to intervene in the complications of the neighboring countries – a speech which had been publicized abroad,[43] he didn't know what to say.

[- - -]

43 See above, entry for May 10.

The IDF's Unreliable Reports

Friday, May 21

A long conversation with Gideon in view of his coming tour in Europe. He was deeply impressed with the protocols of the deliberations of the Political Committee of the party – he came to appreciate the serious inner struggle in which I am involved, and enthused over the level of my argumentation.

[- - -]

Met with Ziama Divon to hear his initial conclusions on the problem of the Arab minority after weeks of study, hearings and talks. His two basic assumptions: (a) the Arab minority cannot but be disloyal to the state; (b) the state will by no means be able to get rid of this minority. Both assimilation and emigration – despite their inherent positive effects, which must be handled and cultivated – offer only limited opportunities and will not solve the overall problem. He agreed with me that, notwithstanding the importance of the security consideration, until now in many cases it has been abused. It is enough for a junior officer on an inter-departmental committee to veto some positive and vital plan for security reasons; all are immediately deterred at this explicit mention of the almighty word, and the plan is shelved – it making no difference whether the security consideration relates to something serious or something entirely trivial.

I spent the afternoon in my flat on Hayarkon Street. I had asked Yehezkel Sahar, Chief of Police, to come. I wished to hear from him details about the Khirbet 'Illin action and the retaliation by the Border Guard. The troubling aspect of the Khirbet 'Illin action was the abandonment of two wounded men at the site of battle by the retreating squad. According to Yehezkel, the reason was simple: the officer who was wounded tossed his weapon to his troops and ordered them to retreat on the double, for they had encountered a force much superior which would have annihilated them. This officer was mortally wounded, but the wounded private had only been hit in the leg and it is clear that the Jordanians tore him to death in cold blood. As to the "wild" retaliations, matters had been taken in hand and would assuredly not recur.

[- - -]

[On this date, Sharett wrote the following letter to PM Jawaharlal Nehru of India (cf. entry for May 24, below).]

My dear Prime Minister,

Although it has never been my good fortune to meet you, circumstances have arisen which I believe impel my addressing you this personal message.

I understand from U Nu, the Prime Minister of Burma, through our Minister to Rangoon, that in a conversation with him at Colombo you indicated your readiness to establish diplomatic relations with Israel and to welcome a properly accredited representative of Israel in New Delhi.

For myself, I have always followed, on the subject of Israel's diplomatic relations with India, as on many other issues, the advice of the *Song of Songs*: "Stir not up, nor wake love, till it please." The message which has reached me from U Nu seems to indicate that the moment envisaged in that verse has now arrived. But before I authorize any formal step, I should be happy if I could have confirmation of the fact from you or your Government.[1]

Saturday, May 22

Most of the day spent at Hayarkon working quietly, not even one uninvited guest or pestering phone call interrupting. At 5:00 pm we drove to Jerusalem and in the evening went to a concert by the pianist Rivka Gvili. Mozart's sonata was a *chef d'oeuvre* to my ears.

Sunday, May 23

In the morning Teddy dropped in. A first solution has been found for the problem of Robert Oppenheimer, the brilliant physicist, who is being victimized by Senator [Joe] McCarthy and his people for his leftist views. Weisgal will invite him to be this year's lecturer for the Weizmann memorial day on November 2. Here we shall test his mettle, and see whether it is appropriate to speak about a permanent association. In the meantime, this invitation in itself will serve as a honorable redemption on behalf of the Jewish people and the State of Israel.

Teddy also told me about the planned letter to Foster Dulles' brother[2] in which we shall settle accounts with the Americans in light of General Trudeau's enthralling declarations. Finally, he proposed that I agree to give him and the Finance Ministry people authorization to look into the possibility of obtaining a recommendation from the American Embassy for an increase in the current US grant. I agreed to this procedure which relieves the Foreign Ministry of a very dishonorable task. We excel in typical inconsistency in the matter of the grant. In internal political discussions almost all of us have fallen into routine repugnance at this dependence of ours on the US and are willing to arrive at far-reaching conclusions to snap this link which

---

1 *DFPI* 9, doc.218. For Nehru's reply, dated June 5, see WebDoc #12.

2 Allen W. Dulles (1893-1969), Director, CIA (1953-1961). Brother of US Secretary of State John Foster Dulles. Code-named "*Ha'akh*" (the Brother) in Israeli documents.

has verily begun to be like a thorn in our side from every moral and political angle. On the practical side, though, we scheme and plot all sorts of stratagems on how to increase the aid which has become anathema to us.

[- - -]

Ehud came by. We discussed the situation at the [Kasztner] trial. He is going to appear as the main witness when the trial resumes. He reminded me of my talks with the British High Commissioner in Jerusalem and with the Foreign Office people in London about Joel Brand's mission. He was astonished at my remembering details of those talks.[3]

We asked Ehud to stay for dinner and the conversation turned to the subject of BG. At long last I heard a detailed report on his plan for the new political party and the "People's Front." It appeared that these two aren't the same but two stages. Apparent too was the confusion reigning in BG's head regarding the conclusions resulting from his plans. Are these bodies designed to serve as additions to Mapai or as its alternative? Where is their membership to come from? How shall Mapai members be prevented from joining them? How would the loyalty of these bodies to Mapai be guaranteed? Is BG going to head them? On all these aspects BG's ideas are just one big confusion, unless he isn't divulging all his planning.

I said that these expressions, when added to his plan of establishing a state-run youth movement and the correspondence between him and myself show, as far as I see it, that psychologically he has become fed up with the party and that in fact his activity is clearly sabotaging it. Ehud confirmed that BG evidently sees a possibility of returning to political activity only within new national, non-partisan formations. He is building castles in the air for himself and destroying existing ones. Indeed, in today's *Yediot Ahronot* there was an item about his meeting with university students who were summoned to Sde Boker and to whom he expressed harsh criticism about all the existing political parties. Another man in my place would have alarmed the party in face of this danger.

We spoke on and on, and I gathered for the first time that Ehud is strongly opposed to the whole policy of retaliations.

Ehud also related, as having heard it from his brother Haggai, who is a member of Kibbutz Sde Boker, that BG had returned irritable and depressed from his visit to Tel Aviv on Independence Day. In Tel Aviv he spoke with Ehud about the danger of assimilation and surrender threatening both American and Soviet Jewries, and the danger of destruction looming over Israel.

This morning at the Cabinet meeting, Pinhas [Lavon] passed me a note he had received from the CoS. An Arab sniper had shot over the wall of Old Jerusalem and wounded a Jewish woman. Dayan was asking: should one of our snipers be placed

3 See below, page 398 n.32.

opposite the wall in the same place? I replied in the negative. A severe warning must be sent to the Jordanians that if they do not curb their people they will bear the responsibility, but in the words of Moshe himself in conversation with me, it is best "to miss the first bus" [i.e., skip instantaneous retaliation]. Initiating sniping on either side along the entire wall and cease-fire line inside Jerusalem is just the thing we need like the air to breathe at this time! And in the evening news, *Kol-Israel* reports further Jordanian provocations and a bold attack by Arabs from the Gaza Strip on an Israeli Bedouin tent encampment, with blows and injuries, and again in broad daylight. It is clear that the tide of retaliations will swell again!

[- - -]

On the midnight news – a statement by our acquaintance[4] the Egyptian Abd al-Mun'im Mustafa, now SG of the Arab League, that the Arab-Israeli war [of 1948] was a colossal mistake and that the refugees should be resettled in the neighboring countries and that, if enough resources were found, the Sinai Peninsula was the right place for them.

Barney Joseph phoned with good news: the Greek cement ship arrived safely at the Port of Eilat. She had sailed from Haifa and the Egyptians, who knew her destination, let her pass through the Suez Canal after delaying her for three days.

At this moment, the distant and faint strains of the midnight chimes above one of the church towers in the Old City are carried to my ears through the open window. The day has come to an end.

Monday, May 24

[- - -]

I wrote a personal letter to Nehru regarding the problem of the diplomatic relations between us and India, following up on [Burmese PM, U] Nu's conversation with him in Columbo and the okay for this approach that I received from David [Hacohen] in Rangoon.[5]

[- - -]

A meeting of the Government-Jewish Agency [joint] committee for the coordination of immigration from North Africa, on the eve of Shragai's departure for that part of the world. He cited illuminating figures. In 1953 immigration was 10,347, and emigration 7,095. In 1954, 2,200 and 1,940. To the figure of immigration are to be added the tourists and temporary immigrants who stay on in permanent residence; to that of emigration, those who leave without stating their decision not to return. Shragai posed the problem concerning the immigration of

4 From the 1949 Egypt-Israel armistice negotiations and the Lausanne Conference.
5 Apparently mis-dated. See above, entry for May 21.

whole villages, especially from southern Tunisia; there were some thirty thousand Jews there. Clearly, in regard to them, it would be necessary to circumvent the prohibitions currently in force against the immigration of the aged, the infirm and the incurable. The JDC is willing to help such welfare cases as long as they do not exceed 15 percent. There was a lively and constructive discussion on the problem of absorbing village Jews of this type. Eshkol posited as an aim their transfer to large state farms where they would work as hired laborers at first, until sufficiently trained for settlement. Avraham Granot[6] of the JNF was appalled by this heresy. I supported Eshkol, having been impressed by the ideas of Sam Hamburg[7] from California, an agricultural expert who came over to advise us. At the end of the discussion I concluded that towards 1955 we would set ourselves the goal of bringing in ten thousand immigrants, and even this in two stages of 5,000 each, for everything depended upon our means. Eshkol noted that we might have to prod the UJA for an additional and special effort for this purpose. We also determined that the chief representative of the JA in North Africa would set out with Shragai to examine the human element in terms of its suitability for settlement; that detailed planning would be performed here on the basis of the data which the delegation would bring; and that the survey in Tunisia would be carried out covertly and with the cooperation of "the Joint" and the *Alliance*.

[- - -]

At 8:00 pm a meeting of the party's Political Committee. In the middle of the meeting, Barney called me out into the adjoining room to tell me what had happened in Sdom. A few days ago the Jordanian authorities disclosed that an Israeli attack had taken place on el-Saffi near Sdom, and the IJMAC had issued a condemnation of us in this matter. The IDF responded with a vigorous denial of the entire story: nothing of the sort happened, and *finis*. But it wasn't true. All the hundreds of workers at Sdom Potasium Works knew the truth, and are jeering at *Kol-Israel* and the Israeli government. The truth is that two Arabs were sent on a mission of revenge to el-Saffi for actions perpetrated by one of its residents. They threw a grenade into a house, killing a woman and wounding a man.8 The affair generated excitement in el-Saffi and its Jordanian surroundings, and a retaliation is to be feared. This situation threatens both life and work in Sdom which occupies an key economic position situated along the border facing Jordanian forces. Is the Army indeed authorized to act as it sees fit and endanger such a vital enterprise?

---

6 Avraham Granot (1890-1969). Born in Moravia. Settled in Palestine in 1924. DG JNF (1945-1960). Author of books on the land question. MK Progressive Party (1949-1951).

7 Sam Hamburg (1899-1976). American cotton farmer and Zionist enthusiast. Helped to pioneer the development of cotton growing in both California and Israel.

8 See below, entry for May 31, 1954.

Tuesday, May 25

I wrote a personal letter to Pinhas Lavon in which I asked him to see to it that a swift and accurate report is delivered to me on every incident, whether disclosed or not, and regardless of the official version released by us for the public:

> The matter of reporting to me personally on security matters is not being carried out properly. Things are happening which do not come to my knowledge. I hear announcements on *Kol-Israel* and later read them in the press without knowing their true background. The correct procedure would have required that I know the facts, if it had been practically possible, before the official version is announced publicly. At the very least I must know the facts. It seems to me that it is possible to ensure such a procedure, but the initiative of [implementing] this arrangement is in your hands.[9]

[- - -]

Ziama Divon, who has already entered into the thick of Arab affairs and displays an extensive familiarity with details like an old hand, came to share his ideas as a prelude to the party consultation scheduled for this evening.

A comprehensive consultation [at the MFA] on the whole of the water issue. I presented my conclusions. As a sequel I composed an extensive briefing to the Washington Embassy for the talks with the UN SG on the Jordan channel and with Johnston on the regional [water-sharing] plan.[10]

At 3:00 a meeting of the Cabinet FADC. One item on the agenda: our relations with China. I described the chain of events. In November the Chinese representative in Helsinki asked our Consul whether we were prepared for diplomatic relations. We haven't replied to this day. The Chinese representative in Rangoon approached our Minister and said that they were interested in commercial relations. We replied with a proposal to send a commercial delegation to Beijing to be headed by our Minister to Rangoon. No reply has arrived to this day. It appears that they are not replying to the proposal of a commercial delegation because we haven't replied to the proposal of diplomatic relations. In the meantime China is already ensconced in a seat at Geneva for negotiations about Vietnam conducted by French Premier

---

9 Sharett's original letter was not found; it is quoted here, possibly not in its entirety, from Ben-Gurion, *Devarim Kahavayatam*, 23. Ben-Gurion also quotes from an earlier letter sent by Sharett, then acting PM and Foreign Minister, to Lavon, then acting Minister of Defense, on August 14, 1953: "Between myself and the PM and Minister of Defense [i.e., Ben-Gurion] a procedure had been agreed upon whereby I must be notified in advance regarding any serious retaliation operation against a neighboring country, as well as any serious step to be taken against the Israeli Arab population. This procedure was not maintained in the case of the curfew and search carried out in [the Israeli-Arab village of] at-Tira as well as regarding operations held on the night of the 12th of this month. Therefore I must ask you to notify me from now on – in advance and in time – regarding any serious action of the kinds mentioned above to be carried out by your order or with your approval."

10 *DFPI* 9, doc.223; see also *DFPI* 9, doc.222.

Mendès-France,[11] and there are growing signs of a rapprochement between it and the Arab countries. We shall lose the day in Beijing if the Arabs precede us there.

I tried to obtain the assent of the *haverim* to notifying China now of our readiness in principle to establish relations, without carrying this out immediately, and for the time being propose again a commercial delegation. They were opposed. Lavon proposed that we wait and see how things unfold at Geneva. Aran contended that it would be bad for Israel to constitute the first open gate for Communist China into the Middle East. The GZ joined those demanding a postponement of the decision.[12] Golda, who might have supported me, was absent from the meeting because of the anniversary of her husband's death.

[- - -]

At 7:30 a limited consultation of *haverim* on BG's plans about which the press is abuzz: a "People's Front," the two-party system, a supra-party national youth movement, and more. All of these are perceived by the public either as overstepping any party framework, in effect placing BG beyond the bounds of Mapai, or they serve as a pretext for troublemakers to find secret conspiracies culled from the imagination. It is not clear what the rally of pupils of the seventh and eighth grades will achieve, and what kind of follow-up it would have, if any. On the other hand, the ferment BG has stirred has seemingly borne first fruit among the youth of the moshavim: Especially among the older people of the second generation, in Nahalal, a movement has sprung up to leave their parents' farms and to settle for two years with their wives and children in the immigrant moshavim, in order to share completely in their difficult life and provide constant teaching and instruction. We concluded that the secretariat should apply to BG officially and propose a meeting with him to clarify the whole of this issue.

At 8:30 a well-attended consultation on policy towards the Arab minority. Ziama Divon's opening lecture during the first part made a deep impression with its penetration to the root of the problem, comprehensive analysis and articulateness. During the second part, the discussion flagged and suffered from vagueness and verbosity. [- - -] The general assumption was that, by its very nature, the Arab minority is a hostile element to the state and it is impossible to create in it a change of heart. We ought to contain the evil so far as is possible by eradicating some of the sources of bitterness, and yet strictly apply security considerations. I did not argue with this assumption. In fact, I had affirmed it in advance in our morning discussion.

However, deep in my heart I do not hold with this despair. I believe that a change of heart in many among this minority towards genuine loyalty to Israel

11 Pierre Mendès-France (1907-1982). French politician, leader of the Radical Party. Descended from a Portuguese-Jewish family. Served as President of the Council of Ministers (June 1954 – February 1955).

12 See *DFPI* 9, doc.231; Brecher, *Israel, the Korean War and China*, 58-63, and *Decisions in Israel's Foreign Policy*, 138-42.

is feasible by means of constant effort. It is better to establish a mode of action and afterwards rely on the results achieved than to sink into a bout of guesses and speculation beforehand. In my conclusion I focused on the importance of coordinated and guided action. I further determined two guiding principles: (a) the different Ministries, foremost those run by Mapai, should abide by the counsel of the Adviser for Arab Affairs; (b) the PM should have the prerogative to intervene and decide in every case where the Adviser's opinion is unacceptable to a Ministry.

Lavon made some harsh remarks during this discussion. Among other things, he launched into a diatribe against the Education Ministry's promotion of Arabic as the language of study in the Arab schools. In his opinion, from the very start we should have established Hebrew as the language of study, and this had to be done now at any price. I said that I entirely disagreed with this conclusion, and proposed devoting a consultation to two special problems: education and military government [over the Arab sector].

[- - -]

Wednesday, May 26

[- - -]

After 8:00 pm we drove to the Edison Hall for the second part of the [Israel] Philharmonic concert and heard Brahms' first symphony – a brilliant and stormy execution. Later, at a reception for the conductor Paul Kaletzky at the Krongolds, he told us enthusiastically about the recording of our Philharmonic music by a team of the Columbia Records Company. Now, for the first time, the Philharmonic will become known internationally. Any big broadcasting service, such as the BBC, would be able to broadcast classical music played by Israeli musicians. He also recounted how the CBS people were enthusiastic about everything they saw in Israel. They were convinced that nowhere in the world is there such a country, and that nobody in the world really knows what is being achieved here. There are still naive *goyim* [gentiles]! One of the recordings is that of the "*Hatikva*" national anthem as orchestrated by Molinari.[13] Kaletzky asked me for an audience and I invited him over for tomorrow morning.

Thursday, May 27

[- - -]

At the Foreign Ministry a consultation over the trials and arrests [of several Zionist leaders] in Romania. What should we do? I said we had to hand a note to

---

13 The Italian opera conductor Francesco Molinari-Pradelli (1911-1996). Sharett was particularly fond of his orchestration of "*Hatikva*."

the Romanian Government, even though it may not be answered. It cannot be that the State of Israel would remain silent on this issue. At the end of it all I took it upon myself to compose a draft, so that we could have something concrete to discuss.[14]

[- - -]

Dictated a letter to Lavon regarding the argumentation we should use with the USA on the subject of our participation in regional defense schemes.

[- - -]

The whole evening was devoted to paperwork. I wrote to Pinhas Lavon that I had spoken to him ten days ago about the appointment of a committee which would carry out an in-depth examination of the *modus operandi* against infiltration and other Arab lawlessness in the border areas, including the effectiveness of military responses, preventive means by intelligence, etc., and that I had proposed Shmuel Divon, Lt.-Colonel Givly and Ezra Danin as members of the committee. It wasn't clear to me whether he agreed at all with the need for such a committee. At any rate he objected to one or two of the proposed members. In the end, we had agreed that he would look into the matter and inform me of his considered opinion.

Now I was again asking for his response. If for some reason the appointment of such a committee was not to his liking, or if we could not come to an agreement as to its make-up, the I would resolve to appoint such a committee on my own accord, so that I might make use of its conclusions or recommendations for my own personal instruction. Of course, in this case I would not be able to appoint an Army man to such a committee unless he agreed that the appointment be made in accordance with my wishes. But if the committee should be established without IDF participation, then I want to ask that the CoS be instructed to respond to the committee's questions and bring to its attention his and his colleagues' considerations regarding the methods of handling the problem of curbing infiltration on the basis of their long-standing experience.

[- - -]

Friday, May 28

[- - -]

At my party office [110 Hayarkon Street, Tel Aviv] a conversation with Shaftesley,[15] editor of the *Jewish Chronicle*. He bitterly complained about the pressure put on him, a Zionist, by Jewish leaders in England who harbor reservations

14 *DFPI* 9, doc.227.

15 John Maurice Shaftesley OBE (1901–1981). English journalist and writer; editor of the *Jewish Chronicle* (1946-1958).

towards Israel, including former Zionist Leonard Stein.[16]
[- - -]

Saturday, May 29

All day long I sat over my papers. I composed a draft note to the Romanian Government and detailed instructions on the water issue for our people in Washington.

From copies of despatched cables I learned of another ugly incident that occurred. A patrol that crossed the line encountered the Jordanian National Guard and inflicted four casualties.[17]

Sunday, May 30

In the morning an urgent consultation at the Foreign Ministry on water issues: Johnston's regional plan. It was initiated by me. We are submitting the Cotton Plan, which includes the Litani [River in Lebanon], as a counterbalance to the [January 1954] Arab League plan.[18] We discussed the preparation of a summary for publication and the coordination of our activity in this matter with the Embassy in Washington.[19]
[- - -]

At 1:30 drove with Zipporah to Haifa for the opening of the International Modern Music Festival. [- - -] We attended the opening concert. Modern music lovers came from all over the country – composers, music teachers, musicians and music enthusiasts. A symphony by a Brazilian dedicated to Israel, a piano concerto by [French composer] Darius Milhaud and two symphonic pieces by an Italian and a Frenchman were played. I was mostly impressed by the two French pieces. A new and strange world of sounds, but interesting and even enchanting. [- - -] All in all I was satisfied with the effort involved. A window was opened

---

16 Leonard J. Stein (1887-1973). Barrister. Stationed in Palestine during WWI. Political Secretary of the London ZE (1920-1929). Legal Adviser to JA (1929-1939). Opposed partition and also the Biltmore Program. Member of the Board of the London *Jewish Chronicle*. Author of the much-cited *The Balfour Declaration*, London: Jewish Chronicle / New York: Simon & Schuster, 1961.

17 Reference is to the May 26 attack by a small group of Israeli paratroopers under the command of Lieutenant-Colonel Ariel Sharon near Khirbet Jinba, ostensibly in retaliation for missing sheep from Kibbutz Ein Gedi. The raiders "ambushed and killed two National Guardsmen and murdered two Jordanian farmers (and killed two camels) before returning (without any sheep) to Israel." Morris, *Israel's Border Wars*, 305.

18 At Israel's request, American water expert Joseph Cotton had prepared a plan in February. For summaries of the two plans and their differences, see Lowi, *Water and Power*, 88-91; Lonergan and Brooks, *Watershed*, 167-69.

19 *DFPI* 9, doc.230.

for me to a hall inside the edifice of music which had been previously closed before me. I also realized how justified were we in organizing this international congress in our country. First, so many of Israel's modern music lovers were deeply satisfied. How easy it is for such people to feel inferior and cut off – there, in the big world, wonders are taking place while they are fated to being shut off in a faraway corner. Naturally they dream of Paris, Vienna, New York. But here a possibility was opened to bring home "the big world." Instead of flying over to Paris they can take a bus to Haifa. Local citizenship and permanent living in Israel do not impose seclusion and narrowness of horizon. Second, the cream of foreign musicians are able to appreciate Israel's musical qualities. They are also deeply impressed by the amalgam of our musical life with our economic and social attainments. Third, the whole world, learning that this festival, which until now was hosted by Salzburg, Edinburgh, Paris and New York, now takes place in Haifa, has ceased seeing Israel as a place immersed in fire and blood, thus looking similar, owing to our sins, to any of our neighboring countries. Now it is learning to appreciate Israel as a unique country in the whole region, for it is only she that can serve a background to such an international demonstration of one of the most exalted arts of present-day human civilization. Should I elaborate on all this at the Cabinet meeting? They would look upon me as being carried away, talking nonsense...

Monday, May 31

[- - -]

Lavon reported on progress on plans to prevent infiltration. Within a month, experiments with new devices invented by the Science Corps will be completed. These constitute fences with electric detectors. It will then be possible to begin the use of these new methods in vulnerable locations.

[- - -]

At 4:00 pm the first visit of the Turkish Minister to Jerusalem. This is one of the signs of the thaw which has been gradually taking place. On Independence Day I was visited by the British Ambassador. A few days ago one of the Frenchmen showed up at the West European Division at the MFA, and according to our information the American Chargé d'affaires will pay me a visit at the PMO. And once this floodgate is opened, all the rest shall come to Jerusalem one by one.

The Turk asked me for a few explanations and came out satisfied. I explained to him our stand on the water problem as well as our thinking about curbing Arab infiltration by preventive means. He was very pleased and said it is only from me that he hears serious explanations which go down to the root of the matter. He then congratulated me on my political wisdom and said everyone is nursing the hope that I will expedite peace and that all those who had met me in Israel are full of admiration for me, and so on and so forth. I said all these are just expectations, since I have not yet achieved anything. He disagreed, saying that already many improvements are obvious. I said let all this be.

As if to contradict all this, Yosef Tekoah came into my office with answers to my questions on what I found incomprehensible in the latest incidents. I finally came to learn the secret official version of the el-Saffi incident. Two Arabs who were sent by us attacked the village chief, who had been ostensibly involved in thieving, and killed his wife. In another incident, an IDF squad had crossed the line "by mistake." In a third incident, three of our soldiers patrolling deep inside Jordanian territory had encountered the National Guard, which opened fire on them (who's going to check?), returned fire and killed four men. This incident earned us severe condemnation and a noisy press campaign on the part of Jordan. *Ha'aretz* came out this morning with an article hostile to the government, demanding clarifications, while our lips remain sealed.

I suppressed the helpless wrath devouring me and went to the Knesset to listen to Golda's speech on unemployment.

[- - -]

Teddy drove me home. I poured into his ears my darkest thoughts at the conduct of Lavon and the IDF. It seems that Lavon himself had not known in advance about some of the Army's operations. This further exacerbates the situation. It means, in the first place, that he exercises no control, and second, that he has not the courage to admit the truth to me.

Nahum Goldmann visited. He declared that he would not stand at the head of the Jewish Agency again. He would resign at the next Zionist Congress. He wishes to discuss the future of the Zionist movement with Mapai. He will pursue the negotiations on the unification of the GZ and Progressive Zionists; however, should it turn out that not all of the Progressives are willing to unite, he will drop the matter. In no way does he wish to have a hand in splitting his camp. He would then attempt to unite GZ supporters in the diaspora so that the united organization might sever ties with the parties in Israel, and constitute an over-all body for Zionists of all shades, devoid of partisan affiliation.

I rebuked him sharply for his declarations concerning Israel's obligation to "become integrated" within the Arab Middle East. He denied there had been any criticism in his statements. He contended that he had expressed nothing but a positive aspiration, in keeping with official and proclaimed policy.

I inquired into the question of his appealing to the Russians in Geneva on the matter of opening the Soviet Union's gates for Jews wishing to emigrate to Israel. He agreed to try his hand at it, as well as to include in his talks there the matter of the "Prisoners of Zion" in Romania.[20] I asked him whether he wasn't apprehensive, as an American citizen, to approach the Soviets without receiving permission from the State Department. He replied that the thought hadn't entered his mind.

[- - -]

I asked the CoS to confer with me tomorrow for a basic clarification on the question of the latest incidents. My purpose is once and for all to put an end to this reckless behavior of crossing the line every other day without a thought for the harmful consequences.

In my file of the day's papers, a cable from Eban on his talk with [Senator] Herbert Lehman[21], who complained bitterly about the drop of Israel's prestige in the eyes of its friends owing to their loss of confidence in the truth of its statements.

I sat up until 1:30 over my papers and diary. I am at my wits' end whether to persevere with the diary. It is truncated and partial almost beyond repair. It is missing an entire continuous month. From the following two weeks there are barely "skeletons" of some days. My strength and time are by no means enough to maintain a daily writing-up. Woe unto me for not writing. That burdens me with disappointment and frustration. And woe unto me for writing. That fills up all my scraps of free time, distracts me from my work and thought, and strikes me with stupor and suffocation.

I do not get more than six to six-and-a-half hours of sleep a night. During the day I yawn incessantly. What a disgrace! Abba Hushi[22] told me that he sleeps

---

20 Cf. above, entries for May 27 and 29. On May 23, Sharett had written to Goldmann in Paris, suggesting that Goldmann should take the bold step of meeting with Soviet FM Molotov in Geneva for direct talks about letting Soviet Jews emigrate to Israel. This move, according to Sharett, was justified by two considerations: (a) Byroade's anti-Zionist speech in which he opposed Soviet Jewish immigration to Israel; the Soviets might be interested to allow Jewish emigration for the sake of "angering" the USA; (b) recent efforts by the Soviet Union to improve relations with western Europe, to which such immigration would be conducive. As to the chances that the Soviets would respond in the negative, Sharett was not deterred. He believed that one should not abstain from prodding the Soviets on this subject, demonstrating that it would never be taken off the Jewish people's agenda. In concluding his letter Sharett said: "I don't think you should quote numbers, but between you and me I will tell you that if we reached one thousand immigrants a year, this would be a major thing for the state, for Russian Jewry and for the Jewish people as a whole. If we reached ten thousands it would be great. I may well be just dreaming, but indeed this has been the way of Zionists from time memorial. Our heavily burdened serious life as a state has not cured us from this childhood illness." *DFPI* 9, doc.221.

21 *DFPI* 9, doc.228. Herbert Henry Lehman (1878-1963) was an American Jewish banker, politician, and statesman. Former NY State Governor, Senator and financial advisor to FDR. A founder of the JDC. While opposed to Jewish statehood before 1948, was active in the cause of free Jewish immigration into Palestine. Influential Democratic Party figure in American politics.

22 Abba Hushi (1898-1969). Born in Poland. Settled in Palestine in 1920. Mapai MK (1949-1951); Mayor of Haifa (1951-1969).

four-and-a-half to five hours a night. Every morning he leaves for work by 5:45. He says that one can form the habit.

Tuesday, June 1

[- - -]

Lavon appeared suddenly. It seems that my having summoned the CoS to come and answer for the latest incidents brought him up to Jerusalem. This time he spoke frankly and openly, without giving up any shrewdness. He explained the incidents in the vicinity of Tulkarm as a perfectly proper matter. By contrast, he was severely censorious of the IDF operation at Khirbet Jinba.[23]

Indeed, some entirely false details had found their way into the description given of this incident in the MAC decision, but even the true facts are most serious. After the retaliatory actions of the Border Guard, which we had discussed at the last joint meeting, an order had been given to refrain from any retaliatory action and stop preparations which had already begun. An order had also been given that, in the case of patrols encountering Arabs, they were on no account to kill. If a patrol sent out could not avoid engagement, then it would have to withdraw. In this incident the patrolling squad had clearly acted contrary to orders. It had not avoided engagement, and it had killed four men. He had conducted a rigorous inquiry. He showed me a letter he later received from the CoS. Moshe Dayan admitted the failure and its gravity, termed it "disgraceful," said that it was clear he had no knowledge of the action, but, of course, accepted full responsibility. Lavon added that this time the blame lay with Yosef Avidar,[24] Head of the Operations Branch. The young men surrounding him have him under their thumb, and he either lets himself be dragged along by them or gives them free rein. The inquiry will continue and judgement will be meted out. Meanwhile, the orders have been made more severe and a prohibition against patrolling beyond the line has finally been issued.

I said that this was all well and good but not enough. There have been some shocking announcements from the other side while we remain silent. That is tantamount to admission. Admission by silence is not to our credit. Furthermore, by our silence we also confirm the malignant falsehoods which have found their way into the Jordanian story: the killing of a youth and more. Pinhas replied that he too acknowledged the need for our disseminating information (*hasbara*) and had given the CoS an order to gather our reporters and report the truth of the matter to them but not for publication. I again said that this wasn't enough. We must deliver

23 Cf. above, entry for May 29.

24 Yosef Avidar (1906-1995). Soldier, diplomat, author. Born in Russia. Settled in Palestine in 1925. Senior *Hagana* leader in charge of supply. GOC Central Command (1952-1954); Head of Operation Branch, GS, IDF (1954-1955); Israel Ambassador to Moscow (1955-1958). Later DG of the Ministry of Labour; Israel Ambassador to Buenos Aires.

a version for publication. It must be true, though carefully worded. Admitting the truth would only enhance our prestige and strengthen our moral stature. It would help to re-establish trust in our statements, which has drastically plummeted in recent weeks, if not been utterly destroyed. Pinhas responded that he was willing to consider a press release. I again said that a press release was a must, and demanded that he consult with his people tomorrow on a draft and deliver it to the press for publication on Thursday morning. He agreed.

I continued to pester him on the matter of military exercises in the border area, which lead to shooting from the other side. Was it really an absolute necessity to train in the vicinity of the lines? Pinhas replied that he too had become aware of this problem and had demanded a report on the training areas. I said that the most vigorous orders were required to heighten all units' awareness of the border line, not to be crossed by any means except by special order, neither to come near it for no reason. Sensitivity to this issue must be created within the Army, otherwise lawlessness will continue and there will be no end to incidents casually ignited, causing us complications and disgrace for no reason.

It has been a while since I felt such a degree of mutual understanding between the Defense Minister and myself as in this conversation. When we parted I had a feeling that my struggles with him and my explanatory efforts in the party's Political Committee and on other occasions, including my public speeches, which helped to fan a certain atmosphere, had not been in vain.[25]

[- - -]

Wednesday, June 2

[- - -]

In my office at the Knesset I received Minister [of Transport] Yosef Sapir who came to report on his trip to the US. His remarks expressed a great appreciation for Eban, Shiloah and Elath. And as for Abe Harman, whom he had met for the first time, he couldn't praise him enough. He also defended, as far as was possible, the Republican administration in the US and blunted the sharp edge of criticism usually accorded it. Most of the Jewish activists there denied that there had been a change for the worse in US policy. Byroade and his ilk at the State Department did not necessarily hold sway. All the same, Thomas Dewey,[26] who had defined Byroade's speeches as foolishness, in effect said: "But as regards the crux of the matter, he is

25 Allusions to his recent speeches in the Mapai Political Committee (above, entry for May 12), in the Knesset (above, entry for May 10), and on *Kol-Israel* radio, on the occasion of Independence Day (May 5). In all these speeches he emphasized Israel's need to rely on itself, while at the same time behaving wisely and keep its moral standing in the eyes of the world at large.

26 Thomas E. Dewey (1902-1971). Republican Governor of New York State (1943-1954).

right" – that is to say, Byroade had spoken the truth, but it had been silly to express it publicly. All are agreed that Dulles is not hostile to us. Dewey also told Rabbi Silver that he hadn't seen Byroade's speeches before they were delivered, and implied that he deplored the undue severity on the part of the State Department towards us. He also noted that he wished to replace Byroade and was searching for a suitable candidate.

Sapir was very impressed by [pro-]Zionist Senator Jacob Javits (Republican!) who believes that we have to devote more attention and educational effort to the Pentagon. He's under the impression that Javits knows the figure for next year's grant, but is not at liberty to reveal it. It seems that it is lower than this year's. Sapir had questioned his Jewish interlocutors on what would be the consequences if our policy would be to adopt *Herut*'s line which calls "for not missing any opportunities" [for territorial gains]. All unanimously replied that this would be the kiss of death to any identification by American Jewry with Israel. The Jews would be obliged to justify any step that Washington might take against Israel to protect crucial US interests. He concluded: "They will march with Washington."

The practical conclusion is that it is not enough for us to criticize US policy, but that it behooves us to initiate proposals for an affirmative US policy. In Sapir's opinion, it would benefit the PM of Israel to invite the leading Jewish activists in the US to a political consultation in Jerusalem. He hasn't suggested it to Eban, for fear that it might be construed as an insult to him.

[- - -]

In the evening, a party consultation at my house on the question of Goldmann's negotiations on the unification of the GZ and Progressives. In keeping with the renowned precedent of US President Calvin Coolidge – who, in answer to his wife's question upon his return from church on Sunday as to what the pastor had preached about, said: "About sin." And when she went on to ask: "What did he say about sin?" he replied: "He was against it." – I too will no more than note the fact that the entire group was against the unification, and won't go into the details of their reasons. We determined that, as regards the future of the Zionist Organization, we would hold a consultation with BG and afterwards accede to Goldmann's request to confer with him.

[- - -]

From a telephone conversation with Lavon it transpired that, after consulting with the CoS, he had realized that an official admission on the action at Khirbet Jinba is out of the question. Therefore, an unofficial version would be drafted, to be published in one of the newspapers as though from its own sources.

Thursday, June 3

[- - -]

At the Foreign Ministry I conferred with Herzog and Elizur on the problem concerning the publication in the media of the Cotton Plan [for utilizing the Jordan waters] that we are submitting to Johnston.

[- - -]

In the afternoon I set out to Tel Hashomer Hospital for a visit to BG who is confined to his sick-bed, a victim of an attack of lumbago. I found him in good spirits after the relief he was accorded, so he contended, following the bouncing in the ambulance from Sde Boker. The conversation went smoothly, both because it constituted a fulfillment of the age-old injunction to visit the sick and because we did not touch upon any stinging issue. When he asked me what was new, I expressed my concern for the economic situation. He was surprised to hear that in my opinion the situation is deteriorating. He asked whether this was true of agriculture too. I said no, agriculture is the only sector wherein there is much that is pleasing. His mind was immediately set at rest. I said that the progress of agriculture doesn't solve the problem, for the greater part of employment and production is dependent upon industry, and the development of the latter does not keep pace with the need because of our high standard of living and the lack of capital investment – two interlocked impediments.

When I mentioned the instability of currency as an obstacle to the flow of investments, he said: "The currency must be stabilized no matter what!" I said that the currency couldn't be stabilized *per se*, but that this was a matter of putting our economy on healthy ground in general and it involved all the other problems – balancing the budget, efficient use of foreign aid, etc. I could see that these connecting links were not entirely clear to him.

[- - -]

I was late for the opening of the Party Central Committee meeting which again discussed the government's subsidies for imported oil, raw materials and foodstuffs, or rather their abolition. There would be a battle raging on the front between the Finance Ministry and the [*Histadrut*'s] trades-unions. Instead I drove straight to my place on Hayarkon Street. I sent Shamai to the Central Committee to report to me. I wanted to sit down and work, but a wave of exhaustion overwhelmed me. I suddenly rebelled against the curse of my papers and broke the yoke of discipline. I felt like Willie Loman of "Death of a Salesman" – no comparison, of course, with his piteous tragedy, but I was simply too fed up to go on with the day-in, day-out, endless bother of work, even if I am beyond despair at keeping pace with it. I found in the apartment a collection of Chesterton's stories and essays and became immersed in the heroic, clever exploits of the worthy Father Brown until very late.

Friday, June 4

In the press were reports about the Cotton Plan, on the one hand, and the action at Khirbet Jinba on the other.

All morning at a consultation at Tel Hashomer Hospital on the future of the ZO. Present were BG, Eshkol, Golda, [Dov] Yosef, and six others. It was a good and constructive meeting. Successfully avoiding the snare of BG's argumentation against the very existence of the Zionist Organization, we did arrive at several conclusions accepted by all. However, we did not leave the room confident of having embarked upon the high road of dynamic, spirited activity in the diaspora. It is one thing to formulate logical principles, quite another to activate the forces of concrete action and creativity.

[- - -]

Saturday, June 5

[- - -]

Sunday, June 6

Awoke this morning after a nightmarish and horrifying night. I dreamt that Zipporah and I had been sentenced to be shot to death for high treason. The last scene that remained vivid in my memory was our farewell from each other before execution. This dream cast a bleak pall over the entire day, which was actually a sort of secular holiday, being sandwiched between *Shabbat* and the Feast of *Shavu'ot.*

[- - -]

According to a telegram from Washington, Johnston is about to raise with us questions of the country's development beyond the water issue: exploitation of the Dead Sea, transportation projects, the Mediterranean-[Dead] Sea canal, atomic installations. We must prepare for this most seriously.

In the meantime, I ascertained with Walter the state of atomic research in Israel, which he is constantly following. I learned that in this matter there is a very serious disagreement between Professor Shmuel Sambursky[27] and Professor Ernest David Bergmann.[28] The latter is certain that we can achieve the actual production of [atomic] energy through the extraction of uranium from phosphate and the manufacture of heavy water by a special process. The former views all these plans

27 Shmuel Sambursky (1900-1990). Israeli scientist and historian. Born in Germany. Settled in Palestine in 1924. Joined the faculty at the Hebrew University, Jerusalem, in 1928. Executive Secretary of the Board of Scientific and Industrial Research set up by the Mandatory government in 1945. Architect and first director of the Research Council of Israel (1949). In 1957 returned to full-time academic life as Dean of the Hebrew University's Faculty of Science. Opposed the trend of research aimed at production of the atomic bomb in Israel.

28 For the rift between Sambursky and Bergmann, see Cohen, *Israel and the Bomb*, 32-34.

as vain dreams, and contends that we should only train people and leave the work of production to the Western powers. Indeed, there is a hint of a promise contained in Johnston's announcement that we might be assisted by the US in the financial aspect of establishing production facilities. This could alter Sambursky's pessimistic assumptions.

[- - -]

In the evening [my sister] Ada came over. The policeman on guard took her announcement that she was my sister with some philosophical scepticism and called us up to make sure, leaving her in the meantime standing outside the gates, suitcase in hand. When told to let her in, he let her carry the suitcase by herself, apparently not much impressed by her attire and the suitcase tied around by a rope. I went downstairs and found three policemen by the gate and gave them a lesson. They were ashamed and begged forgiveness. A few days ago the policeman on guard came running in a panic, announcing: "There are some people there – they say they were invited for lunch!" – leaving them all standing on the sidewalk. We do not always remember to tell the guard in advance of our guests, but he himself could do with a little more common sense.

Monday, June 7

The festival of *Shavu'ot* – what a pity it's only one day!

The day's event: a dinner in honor of Herbert Morrison,[29] who is visiting the country as a guest of the government. He came by an hour earlier for a talk. I have never respected nor liked him. He is most talented, even brilliant, but one cannot compare him to Attlee as far as graciousness is concerned, nor to Bevin in terms of political stature. Our conversation never reached any climax and went on almost tiresomely. There was nothing special in it, only general and accepted formulas regarding Middle Eastern issues and problems of Anglo-Israel relations. Except perhaps for his complaining against Jewish MP's not understanding that it's better to arm Germany within the framework of the European Defense Community [EDC] than allowing her to become armed on her own with no limits. He also maintained that there were not in present-day England any serious issues dividing Conservatives and Labour which could grab the attention of the voting public.

[- - -]

29 Herbert S. Morrison (1888-1965). British Labour leader. Deputy PM and Leader of the House of Commons (1945-1951); briefly served as Secretary of State for Foreign Affairs (1951). In July 1946, together with US Ambassador Henry F. Grady, proposed the "Morrison-Grady Plan" for the solution of the Palestine problem, calling for provincial autonomy under overall British trusteeship. By February 1947 the plan was dropped after its rejection by both Arabs and Zionists.

Tuesday, June 8

[- - -]

In the morning papers again shattering news about Israel's plans to attack Syrian and Jordan this summer. United Press from New York and Sulzberger in the *New York Times* are prophesying, in fact, in the same vein. I called up Walter and suggested that the Foreign Ministry spokesman release a sarcastic statement which, after calling these prophesies wildest nonsense, would go on to ask whether the American circles who are issuing them are doing this so as to appear afterwards as the saviors of peace.

[- - -]

A consultation on the development plans which we shall submit to Johnston. Present were Eshkol and Sapir, Yosef, Lavon, Naftali, Aran. I had meant to discuss principally the development plans beyond the water issue which we should be able to submit to the US President's emissary, but the conversation immediately turned to irrigation matters. The general opinion was that there was a plot inherent in Johnston's willingness to discuss other development plans with us. Since the main intent was to shortchange us in the division of regional waters in favor of the Arab states, the promise concerning development in general was being offered only to assuage us, to tempt and compensate us with trifling matters for the rout awaiting us on the main front. For this reason, we have, first and foremost, to stand our ground on water issues and insist – come what may – on a regional plan that includes the Litani. We should not budge, even if it meant undermining the entire regional settlement dreamed of in Washington. Against a background of such insistence on our part, we could allow ourselves to weigh other plans, so that it should be clear that we are willing to discuss them in their own right and not as compensation for the loss of water for irrigation.

The following items were indicated to be included in the list submitted to Johnston: an oil pipeline from Eilat to the Mediterranean; a railroad from Sdom to Eilat; the extraction of magnesium from the Dead Sea; a canal from the Mediterranean to the Dead Sea, for the production of electric power; a canal from the Mediterranean to Eilat as a substitute for the Suez Canal (this last item remains with a question mark for the time being.) Since Johnston mentioned transportation projects, I will also consult on this matter with Yosef Sapir. IDF plans in this area should also be reassessed.

In the discussion I did not subscribe to the "diabolic" interpretation of Johnston's proposal as the only explanation for his attitude. I assumed the possibility of a US desire to enter into development projects in general in the Middle East, including Israel. Furthermore, I did not ignore the chance that we might make use of this new attitude to transfer the dwindling US grant to other areas, more stable and long-range.

Likewise, I did not accept the line of sticking obstinately to the inclusion of the Litani, which was in effect a continuation of the position we have taken until now. And what's more, I did not see the Litani as the overall solution, for it is not within our power to make the Litani flow into the Jordan Valley. Even supposing our rigidity bears fruit and Johnston's regional plan falls apart, there still remains the problem of the Jordan as a river in which more than one country has rights. Likewise the Yarmuk. Barney Josef tried to argue that we can sit and wait until Jordan deigns to enter into negotiations with us, and meanwhile continue our work on the upper Jordan [diversion] channel. Lavon has altogether changed his tune about the urgency of work in the DMZ. In his view, we can exercise patience for years, work meanwhile on the canal to Beit Netofa outside the Beitar, and postpone the end of the dredging there until the storm abates. I noted that these proposals ignored one serious consideration: our interest in speeding up resettlement of the refugees. True, we must oppose strongly any resettlement plan in the lower Jordan Valley; no factor there is suitable – neither the land, nor the water, nor the climate, nor the people. The Palestinian refugees are not the pioneers of Kibbutz Beit Ha'arava.[30] Even this valiant experiment remained shaky to its last day because they were unable at the time to raise productivity to the extent of financing air-conditioning in the houses during the hot season. To say nothing of a resettlement plan for tens of thousands of bitter refugees, corrupted by being supported by UNRWA and themselves lacking any impetus for prolonged pioneering effort. In no uncertain terms we should warn against the waste of millions of dollars on this useless project. By contrast, we should not be able to object to resettlement in the Yarmuk Valley or the upper Jordan Valley. Two hundred meters below sea level is not the same as 400 meters.

We are insisting on no return of refugees, and demanding their resettlement in neighboring countries as the only solution. Could we take a position of indifference and even sabotage towards a practical resettlement plan, even if adjacent to our borders? This means that we are once again being pushed in the direction of an attempt at a *quid pro quo* arrangement: our Jordan River project as against Jordan and Syria's Yarmuk project.

[- - -]

I summoned Ziama Aran to come and tell me about his talk with Nahum Goldmann pending the party leadership's discussion with him this evening. Nahum remains firm: the Progressives must be united with the GZ. There is no hope of resurrecting the Progressives as an independent party. If they should unite, General Zionism will be transformed. Such is his wishful thinking.

30 Kibbutz founded in 1939 by Palestinian born-members of a *halutz* [pioneering] youth movement on the northern shore of the Dead Sea, where the climate is unbearably hot in summer and the land thought to be uncultivatable unless painstakingly drained of its salinity. The kibbutz was abandoned at the beginning of the 1948 war and destroyed by the Jordanian Army.

[- - -]

Urgent news arrived from the Defense Ministry, in accordance with the new procedure which Lavon established in compliance with my demand. There was an incident in Kissufim. A vehicle of ours drove over a land-mine. Immediately when it exploded, it was fired upon from an Egyptian emplacement. We returned vigorous fire and silenced it. One of our soldiers was wounded. I said that we must give this attack wide publicity. This Egyptian provocation is surprising. There are reports that there is an active Palestinian National Guard which provokes and incites the Egyptians to actions without knowledge of their own command.

[- - -]

From 8:00 until midnight a meeting in my house of the party leadership with Nahum Goldmann. Two matters were discussed in tandem: the future of the ZO and the unification of the Progressives with the GZ. A lot of time was devoted to the first subject and little new was added. We held to the lines sketched at the Tel Hashomer discussion, albeit without much inner conviction on my part. Goldmann pretended to be resolved to retire from the Executive of the Jewish Agency, and so to be discussing the problem on its own merit, as if personally disinterested. This may truly be his intention. But anyone who has taken his measure knows that he is willing to consider remaining on the Executive if the post of president should be reinstated in the JA and he should win the title – in plain words: if the state should accord this position a proper stature. This was impossible to examine because the presence of Berl Locker. As to the matter of unification, there was a great argument between Goldmann, affirming it, and ourselves, opposed. At the heart of argument were the true colors of the GZ. In this matter, I offered some restrained remarks and Ziama made some open and biting and most colorful ones.

Goldmann stuck to his own: The Progressives have neither future nor purpose, and if they should unite they would carry much more influence. When the discussion began it was had already known that Goldmnan had visited BG at Tel Hashomer Hospital and had received encouragement from him to continue with the unification effort – everything is appropriate in the name of the hallowed principle of a two-party system. BG sees nothing but this abstract goal whereas we, as practical people, think that no strengthening of the party will result from this process. Only the GZ benefit from it; and with them the fanatical bourgeois element will carry the day rather than those toying with the liberal Zionist philosophy. The entire discussion only scraped the surface, and did not penetrate to the roots of the problems, neither as regards the first item nor the second. This was caused by the attitude and manner of presentation of Goldmann himself. He was quite long-winded when he opened the discussion of which he was its principal discussant.

My head was like a spinning wheel at the end of this day, both compressed and torn apart. And after the house was emptied and quiet reigned, I sat for over an hour on my papers and stacked up quite an impressive pile for tomorrow morning. [- - -]

Wednesday, June 9

Already yesterday I had begun getting ominous echoes concerning BG's speech at to-morrow's scheduled meeting of students of the two upper grades of the country's secondary schools, organized by the Ministry of Education. [- - -] Members of the opposition are vehemently protesting and the issue is bound to raise a storm in the Knesset today. I called up Rokach and asked him: "What's all this noise and excitement over BG's speech to the youth?" He said he was not involved at all in this matter so I said the same thing to [Yosef] Sapir. We decided to discuss the matter at the Knesset.

[- - -]

Later, at the Knesset, I sat down with Sapir for a talk. I tried to put him to shame for the GZ allowing themselves to besmirch BG's appearance before a youth meeting. But he remained adamant and maintained that the organizational aspect of the meeting was wrong. Why wasn't "someone" else invited to speak there, as well? Why wasn't it announced that following the meeting more [activities] would be arranged in which people from other parties would appear? I reminded him of the praise and adoration they heaped on BG upon his retirement as a national figure whose all interests were devoted to the national good. He was not impressed, and said BG was no exception: he's a member of a specific party and the whole affair of the meeting seems like a kick-off to the general elections campaign. [- - -]

Meanwhile members of the opposition parties started speaking during the Knesset session. [- - -] Vilner[31] maintained all this was an American machination. [- - -] In the vote taken our coalition was saved by a single, solitary vote. The whole affair was a blasphemy. A great Prophet is needed here to express his wrath. If Providence has favored our nation in these momentous times by granting it a central figure emanating moral authority, unclean hands from all corners are trying to remove his crown and topple him from the national pedestal into a partisan side-corner. I went home with a heavy heart.

[- - -]

Thursday, June 10

[- - -]

Again a conversation with Teddy about the continuation of the Kasztner trial.

31 Meir Vilner (1918-2003). Born in Lithuania. Settled in Palestine in 1938. MK and leader of the CPI.

I had no idea at all that, on the eve of *Shavu'ot* [June 6] *Ma'ariv* had published my report on the Joel Brand affair from those past days, which I had given to the Zionist Executive in London when I came there immediately after my meeting with Joel in Aleppo.[32] Teddy says the report made a very strong impression. It's totally convincing and makes one marvel at the accuracy and restraint of its contents. Even though it was written in the very midst of those tense and hectic days, it reads like a historian's lecture composed at some distance from the ongoing events so as not to be carried away by their impact. Teddy suggested this report should now be published as a booklet for wide dissemination.[33]

[- - -]

At 10:00 pm *Kol-Israel* started broadcasting BG's speech to the youth meeting. I tried to listen but soon became too tired to follow. His delivery was slow and I felt no need to waste my time. When it is printed I shall read it through much more quickly. And what's more, there were many repetitive parts, some of them including eternal truths. The whole speech took an hour and a half.

Friday, June 11

[- - -]

With Isser on the subject of our relations with the Americans. At his disposal are more proofs of hostile attitudes. Despatches concerning Israel from Baghdad or Damascus are unlike those sent from Tel Aviv. He also favors taking the initiative to develop more direct and intensive ties with Turkey. [- - -] There arose the question of leftist academicians in the USA, a few of whom have started knocking on Israel's gates [under McCarthyist pressures]. Isser suggests that whoever comes in as an immigrant under the Law of Return be accepted, but those who come over for work should be individually scrutinized.

[- - -]

After lunch, another consultation with Blass and Wiener pending Johnston's

---

32 On June 6, 1954, *Ma'ariv* published Sharett's report over two full pages under the headline: "Sharett Reveals Brand's Rescue Mission – Secret report about the meeting in Syria and the negotiations with the British authorities in Jerusalem and London – Unknown facts about conversations with Eden, MacMichael and Lord Moyne." The original, "Preliminary Report to Zionist Executive, Dorchester Hotel, London, June 27, 1944," is available in CZA Z4/14870. See also aide-memoire by Weizmann and Shertok, left with Anthony Eden, Foreign Secretary, following their interview, July 6, 1944, reproduced in *Letters and Papers of Chaim Weizmann*, series A: Letters, vol. XXI, January 1943-May 1945, ed. Michael J. Cohen (Transaction Books, Rutgers University, 1979), 321-22. Cf. above, entry for March 31, 1954. See also Weitz, *The Man Who Was Murdered Twice*, 136-38.

33 No such booklet seems to have been published.

arrival.[34] They accepted the line of argumentation I had proposed but Blass suggested in addition that we threaten all sorts of horrors, such as the pumping of water directly from the Sea of Galilee to Beit Netofa, the digging of a tunnel south from the Hula which would detour around the DMZ (and cost IL.10 million), a canal from the Mediterranean to the Jordan which would flood the Ghor [the Jordan Valley plain] with salt water.

[From June 12, 1954 until January 1, 1955, Sharett did not write up his diary. Notes for the diary (the "skeleton," in the diarist's words) jotted down in his calendar pocket-book with a view towards their subsequent amplification, were found and a few, which are of greatest importance, though not always clear, are given, as well as several letters from this period, found attached to the diary. Where appropriate, the "skeleton" is enhanced by material from archival sources.]

Saturday, June 12

[- - -]

Sunday, June 13

[- - -] Border incidents discussed at Cabinet meeting. Lavon's new approach. The problem of accurate reporting. In the midst of the meeting, news of the al-Baqqara incident. My reaction.[35]

[Extracts from Sharett's remarks during the Cabinet meeting:]

> Any intelligent man will conclude that our setting out to destroy a whole village indicates a joyous willingness on our side to provoke the other party into war. One Qibya has destroyed an information campaign of years. [- - -] The whole argument [regarding retaliatory policy] revolves around proportionality, and here a big educational effort must take place. Recently, during IDF military training in the border area, [our] shooting hit people on the other side. The question is: must military training take place precisely along the borders? My impression is that in our Army there is a lack of sensitivity to the borders from a political point of view. On the one hand, we strongly emphasize the significance of the border, but at the same time – whether because we see it as temporary or because of a certain attitude regarding the Arabs – we do not consider it a serious act for us to cross the border. Other nations are very sensitive in this respect; they cannot imagine that we are conducting patrols on the other side of the border. This is a very serious matter. Such an action must be considered ten times before it is executed. The senior echelon of the IDF should be educated politically. When I pass a military sentry on the road to Jerusalem, I ask myself: who is the Foreign Minister of whom? Am I his Foreign Minister, or is he perhaps my Foreign Minister, because he can do something which would compel me to defend him and tens of others because of the problems he creates? [- - -] It must be clear that there is a crisis of disbelief in the State of Israel's announcements.

34 See also *DFPI* 9, docs.243-244.

35 al-Baqqara is a village situated in the Israeli-Syrian DMZ. All its Arab inhabitants were transferred to the Arab village of Sha'ab in western Galilee in March 1951.

> Our announcement on Qibya was not believed. Our announcement on [the] Nahhalin [reprisal] was not believed. [- - -] We are not believed when we say that it was not the Army but civilians who took revenge. We are seen as a disciplined nation, so we must decide if we are prepared to pay the price of losing credibility in our pronouncements. [- - -] The impression is that our people do not care when Arabs are killed. But if we are not touched by such acts, if we do not care, what then is the point of our discussing our international political situation here for four hours? On the other hand, if we do care how Israel is perceived in the eyes of the world, then we must develop the degree of our sensitivity. We must instill an awareness of the border line and seek opportunities to tell the truth, because the truth convinces. It enhances faith in our announcements – a faith which sometimes is very thin.

[- - -] After the meeting, Lavon [presented me] with his version [and] his criticism of the CoS.

Monday, June 14

[- - -]

The truth about the al-Baqqara incident. Nehru's letter. With Walter on Nehru

[- - -]

Tuesday, June 15

[- - -] Consultation regarding Johnston, attended by many. [- - -]

Wednesday, June 16

[- - -]

Thursday, June 17

News regarding mutual elevating of Israel's and Soviet Ministries into Embassies released. [- - -]

Friday, June 18

[- - -] Atomic [consultation in advance of meeting with Johnston with Weizmann Institute physicists and chemists Bergmann, [Aharon] Katzir-Kachalsky, [Israel] Dostrovsky, [Yigal] Talmi, [Victor] Zalkind.[36]

Bergmann: Uranium – if factory established, we could start in 2-3 years producing 5-8 tons uranium a year. Heavy water is a longer process.

36 Physicist Israel Dostrovsky (1918-2010), later DG of the Israel Atomic Energy Commission; electro-chemist Aharon Katzir-Katchalsky (1914-1972); nuclear physicist Yigal Talmi (1925-); hydrologist Victor Zalkind (1900-1986).

Dostrovsky: [We need] not only uranium and [heavy] water but technical know-how. A matter not for 20 years but for a few. If we could get a nuclear reactor from America it would be very worthwhile.

Kachalsky: The matter is real, not imaginary. The more a country is poor in fossil fuels, the more it needs [atomic energy]. We need a power reactor producing at least 30,000 kw. Building [one] by our own means is a very long road.

Talmi: Unlike in America, here [atomic energy] will be cheaper than electricity. It would be worthwhile to receive gratis [from America] the basic investment since [building an atomic power plant is] 2.5 times more expensive than a regular power plant.

Bergmann: [- - -] [meaning unclear]

My conclusions: 1. We shall not raise [the subject of an atomic reactor]; 2. If he [Johnston] raises it – no yielding [on our part]; 3. If they want to discuss the subject for its own sake – by all means.

[Meeting or phone conversation with US Embassy Counselor Francis H.] Russell [about] Johnston [visit].

Saturday, June 19

[- - -] Biran [reported] on the killing [of three settlers] from Mevo Beitar.[37]

Sunday, June 20

[- - -] [Message from] Russell.[38]

[- - -] P. Lavon [reported on] on Mevo Beitar. Cabinet meeting. I reported on

37 Cf. the May 9 incident described above, page 353 n.16. Benny Morris notes that this incident was started by "seven armed Israeli farmers from the right-wing *Herut*-affiliated settlement of Mevo Beitar," who on June 19 "crossed 1,200 metres into Jordan and fired on Arab shepherds and farmers. National Guardsmen engaged them, killing three of the Israelis." (*Israel's Border Wars*, 306).

38 Russell delivered an important aide-memoire, dated June 19, outlining eleven points for frontier pacification that the US and UK were suggesting in parallel démarches to Jordan and Israel. The eleven suggestions were: 1. Acceptance by the parties of their obligations to attend MAC meetings and to resume operations of the Local Commanders' Agreements; 2. Amending the rules of MAC procedure so as to allow the Chairman the power to propose resolutions; 3. Appointment of UN translators and politico-legal advisers to the MACs; 4. Publicity for MAC decisions; 5. An increase in the number of UN Observers, to be stationed more evenly on both sides of the border; 6. Broad freedom of movement and investigation for UN Observers at all points along the border; 7. Additional equipment for UN Observers; 8. MAC to be informed of any persons convicted of infiltration and similar offenses; 9. Demarcation of borders by UN Observers, erection of physical barriers at important points; 10. A system of passes to enable Arabs to travel from Gaza to the Jordanian West Bank under UN supervision; 11. "Any other preventive measures, whether by the parties or the United Nations Truce Supervisory Organization." *FRUS 1952-1954*, doc.836.

Russell's aide-memoire.[39]

Lavon's deadly sniping.[40]

From 4:00 to 7:00, discussion with Johnston. [- - -]

Monday, June 21

[- - -] Lunch at Russell's. Private talk with Johnston on the President's attitude and the role of Egypt.[41]

[- - -]

Tuesday, June 22

[- - -] Lunch with Johnston, Eshkol, et al. Prepared a speech. [- - -]

Wednesday, June 23

Preparations for the Cabinet meeting and press conference. 8:30 at the *Kirya*. Heard a report on last night's meeting [with Johnston which lasted until] 3:00 am. At 9:00, Cabinet meeting. I put off the press conference. 4:00 pm consultation [on Johnston's proposals] with Eytan, Eshkol, Sapir, Herzog and Teddy. 8:15 pm with Johnston & Co.

Thursday, June 24

[- - -] Condemnation [of Israel in the IJMAC] over Mevo Beitar.[42]

Yaacov Herzog [came to prepare for] the continuation of the talks [with Johnston]

39 In addition to these two items, the agenda of this Cabinet meeting began with the question of CoS Dayan's visit to the USA and also included Sharett's update on the water negotiations with Eric Johnston's team. For a summary of these Cabinet discussions, see WebDoc #13.

40 During the Cabinet meeting, Sharett, while recognizing serious problems with the American aide-memoire, did not wish to open a debate on the subject at the present meeting. In the ensuing discussion among the ministers over whether to ask the press to refrain from public comment on the aide-memoire, Lavon said he saw no harm in it, taking a jab at the PM by noting that Sharett had a "fund" [*keren*, in Hebrew] in one of the Israeli dailies, an allusion to *Ha'aretz* political commentator Moshe Keren, with whom Sharett maintained personal contact.

41 Johnston arrived in Israel from Jordan on June 18 and held talks daily with Sharett and other Israeli officials from June 20 to June 23. See: *DFPI* 9, docs.258, 264, 280; *FRUS 1952-1954*, doc.838; Sara Reguer, "Controversial Waters: Exploitation of the Jordan River, 1950-80," *Middle Eastern Studies* 29:1 (January 1993), 59-61.

42 The IJMAC met on June 23 without the participation of Israel's delegates, who were still boycotting it. Gen. Bennike wrote to Sharett on that date protesting IDF interference with this and one previous (Khirbet 'Illin) investigation, and on June 24 the UN SG echoed these protests in a letter addressed to Sharett, who replied to the UN SG on July 27, 1954. See *DFPI* 9, doc.299.

and a briefing for the press. [- - -] Consultation at the MFA on the 11 [points].[43]

[- - -] Afternoon at home for a major discussion on the water issue. BG's letter on the Gaza-Hebron passage.[44]

Friday, June 25

[- - -]

At the MFA with Joe Tekoah. The issue [of how to deal with] the 11 [points proposed by the US] was cleared up. Four points: (a) no patrols, (b) [our] attitude to [UN] observers, (c) praises, (d) return to [participating in the Israel-Jordan] MAC.[45]

New *Shin-Bet* version about Mevo Beitar incident.[46] [- - -]

Saturday, June 26

[- - -] Eshkol reports on their visit to Sde Boker and BG's response which I interpret as "accepting compromise [on water] with the Arabs, [but] against US intervention."

---

43 I.e., the eleven "suggestions of possible practical measures for reduction of frontier incidents" conveyed by Russell on June 20 (above, entry for that date). According to the summary of the MFA minutes of the consultation, officials debated whether to (a) reject the list for its unacceptable clauses, its omissions (especially on preventive measures), and its origins (especially the British involvement), (b) endorse the document, or (c) use stalling tactics to keep the matter open for continued discussion and clarification. *DFPI* 9, doc.261. See also *DFPI* 9, doc.267.

44 Letter not found.

45 Israel's official reply to this démarche would not be delivered until a full month later, following extensive discussions and consultations among Cabinet ministers, MFA officials and senior IDF officers. See entries for July 1954, passim, and esp. explanatory note for July 27, below.

46 On June 26, the Director of Military Intelligence (*AMAN*), Binyamin Givly, reported on this incident to the CoS and Minister of Defense, noting that five settlers from Mevo Beitar had approached the Arab village of al-Qabu, apparently "for the purpose of reconnaissance and sharp-shooting at 'live targets' as they are in the habit of doing from time to time." The settlers were shooting at targets inside al-Qabu and its vicinity when they were ambushed by soldiers of the Jordanian Legion. A firefight ensued; reinforcements arrived on both sides. Three of the Israeli settlers were killed, and one pregnant Jordanian woman was killed by IDF mortar fire. Defense Minister Lavon accused the Jordanians of setting a deliberate ambush and of murder, and the official Israeli version was that the killings had taken place in Israeli territory, and that the three bodies were dragged across the border. An internal IDF investigation of the incident revealed "contradictory evidence" coming from the Mevo Beitar settlers, and "an intention to cover up several matters from us." In spite of these conclusions, Dayan requested approval for a series of sniper attacks against Jordanians in the area, but his request was apparently blocked at the political level. See Morris, *Israel's Border Wars*, 306-07. Morris offers more detail on this action in the subsequent Hebrew edition of the book, *Milhemet Hagvul shel Israel, 1949-1956*, transl. Yaakov Sharett, ed. Eli Shaltiel (Tel Aviv: Am Oved / Harry S. Truman Institute, 1996), 335-36, 596-97 (notes 113-16).

In the evening a consultation on water.[47]

Sunday, June 27

[- - -] Lavon on the murder of a man by infiltrators near Ra'anana. He suggests retaliation. [- - -] 3:30 pm Cabinet meeting on water till 6:30. Lavon's demand for a vote.

[Herewith extracts from the 90-page protocol of the marathon Cabinet meeting. Sharett began with an assessment of the Anglo-American proposal (11-points) for calming the Israeli-Jordanian frontier.]

> There are two main hitches in this document. First, it recommends arrangements which are not in line with the Armistice Agreement, that is, they suggest changes to it. Second, the tendency is to enhance the authority of the UN machinery, changing it from an observing factor to an executive factor, capable of initiating action by itself. This second trend should concern us. [- - -] I suggest that we answer in a way which would not be final, thus putting an end to the negotiations, because it should be clear to us that a formal clash between us and the three [Western] powers will not contribute to the health of the state and its international relations. [- - -] I suggest that we first show a positive attitude towards the powers' interest in improving the situation along the border, but that we should say that all dealings with border problems should be done on the basis of the Armistice Agreement. [- - -] We must add that as long as Jordan chooses what parts of the Agreement she will execute, the same goes for us. [- - -] As to the tendency to enlarge the authority of the UN machinery, we must make it clear that the UN can operate only within the framework as agreed by the two parties to the Agreement.

[Later, when the Cabinet discussed the regional water-sharing plan under negotiation with Eric Johnston, Sharett argued that Israel should be prepared for a compromise on the division of the Jordan waters between her and Jordan.]

> When Cabinet members say, "We have given up the Litani [River]," I cannot understand their language. They are talking as if the Litani was in our hands and we gave it up. When they say, "We gave up 295 million m3 of water in the lower Jordan Valley," I don't understand what are they talking about. They seem to be saying that these waters were in our hands and we have given them up. What is the [true] situation? It is that we do not have complete rule over any part of the Jordan, to say nothing about the Yarmuk. [- - -] The sources of the two main tributaries of the Jordan lie inside territories which are beyond Israel's borders. If the Arabs are adamant and prepared to invest resources, they would be able to divert these sources before they enter our territory. [- - -] We are relying very much on our ability to to establish facts, but they too are able to establish facts. They can divert the Hasbani [source in Lebanon] into the Litani, and the Banias [source in Syria] into the Yarmuk. It is [technically] possible. If we took the whole of Jordan, then I am not sure whether England and the USA would enter into a real fight with Lebanon and Syria, for our sake, if those two diverted the Hasbani and the Banias. But if we attempt to take the whole of the Jordan for our use, leaving not a drop of water to the Kingdom of Jordan, then we can be sure that England and the USA will engage in

47 Ben-Gurion's diary on this date contains nothing on this subject.

a big fight with us. I have no idea of the result, but a big fight it will be. [- - -]

We should also view this problem from a wider angle. There is a war going on between us and the Arab world. This war is conducted along the borders, in the field of international trade, along waterways, in the arena of oil supply, inside international bodies and in the capitals of the Great Powers. And there is this war over water too. In what way are we bettering our situation, our chances in the light of this [general] war, if we do not exploit an opportunity which is perhaps being given us to achieve something? If we avoid such a move, will the Arab war against us be weaker? Will the powers' support of us be stronger? Is time, from this point of view, on our side? I'm very much afraid that is running against us in this context. [- - -] If, on the basis of all these circumstances taken together, and while we have several cards in our hand – not all the cards, but a few – we can arrive at an arrangement which would guarantee us development for many years to come, then it is very doubtful if historical responsibility can allow the Government of Israel to miss this opportunity. [- - -] If we do accept the proposed work [on the regional water-sharing plan], work which would involve many years, which is fraught with chances of bettering the situation [between Israel and the Arabs], which is a beginning of a project which would be concretely a partnership between us and the Arabs, then this would be a step forward, not backwards from the point of view of relations in the areas, [a step] which could be some beginning of a settlement.

And I would like to say this to the Cabinet members following what I said regarding chances of the continuation of war: you take it that all situations are possible, but [do you consider] the evolution of a situation in which the USA is on the side of the Arabs against us, and we are against the USA and the Arabs? Do you think that such a situation, such a chain of developments, would bring us nearer to peace between us and the Arabs? If you think so, you are clearly mistaken, for here is an aggravation of the vicious circle. For if the Arabs see the American intention as an encouragement for no-peace, an encouragement for war, then what sense is there in our being justified in warning [the USA against Arab threats of war]? We must see the concrete results. We must see where are we going. The dilemma of our policy is not simply to be just, but to act in order to reach a goal, and that we shall be supported, that we shall be helped [in doing so] – not to be strong in our own eyes while being oblivious to what facts are in reality.

[- - -] In the evening meeting of the party's Political Committee till midnight.[48] Then I prepared press communiqué regarding Johnston.[49]

Monday, June 28

[- - -] Lavon telephoned about last night's retaliation in 'Azzun [a village east of Qalqilya] against an Arab Legion encampment. [He said:] "They mistakenly crossed

48 For excerpts of Sharett's remarks to the Mapai Political Committee, see WebDoc #14.

49 "In response to a communiqué published in Cairo about the meetings between Mr Johnston and representatives of the Arab states, the spokesman of Israel's Foreign Ministry said last night that, contrary to what was published in Cairo, as of the present time no final agreement has been reached.' The spokesman said that indeed several possibilities are being discussed, but until now no final conclusions have been reached and the conversations between Israeli with American representatives are continuing." *Ha'aretz*, June 27, 1954.

the border by 13 km." They [the IDF] are again lying brazenly. Uncivilized [behavior].[50]
[- - -]

Tuesday, June 29

[- - -] Ziama [spoke to me] about BG [who criticized] mainly the 11 [points proposed by the US aide-memoire to relieve border tensions]. My response: "[BG is] undermining the government's authority."

[Spoke for] two hours and a quarter about water before the Foreign Affairs and Defense Committee.[51]

Eytan on an anti-Hutchison article in the *Jerusalem Post.* At night [I telephoned chief editor Gershon [Agron who informed me] it was inspired by one source at the highest echelon.[52]

[- - -]

Wednesday, June 30

[- - -]

In the afternoon with Joe on [IDF] patrols across the borders. CoS and Givly contend they are essential, otherwise any action is impossible, [that] Jordanians and Egyptians are doing that too. [Our] training of new cadets sometimes [involves them on the other side of the border], our patrols [there] are rare, conducted only for certain precise purposes, [Tekoah said we have] to see that the patrols stop. The CoS responded positively, agreeing on politeness towards the [UN] observers.

---

50 The 'Azzun operation was an Israeli retaliation for the killing of an Israeli near Ra'anana on June 27. According to Israeli information, the killers came from 'Azzun. Benny Morris (*Israel's Border Wars*, 307) describes this incident as follows: "The IDF struck on the night of 27/8 June, targeting the Arab Legion camp at 'Azzun, 13 km. east of Qalqilya ... killing 3 and wounding 3.... Next morning Israel announced that a patrol had 'mistakenly' strayed into Jordan." Dayan mentions this in his *Avnei Derekh*, 126: "I suggested that we inform the UN that a patrol of ours crossed the border mistakenly." One IDF solider, Itzhak Jibly, whose unit was under the command of Ariel Sharon, was taken prisoner by the Jordanians. See also below, entry for July 29, 1954.

51 Sharett's report to the FADC was similar to the one he gave to the Mapai Political Committee; see WebDoc #14.

52 The reference is to the CoS, Moshe Dayan, who (along with Defense Ministry DG Shimon Peres) periodically fed anti-Sharett material to correspondent Sraya Shapiro. Shapiro's "Marginal Column" of June 29, 1954 (page 1) ends with: "In Israel any attempt to bring a [former British] High Commissioner in through the back door would be resisted. And nobody in his senses would insist that Israel regard all [UN] observers as truly neutral. For the name of Hutchison is known to all ." The allusions are to Sharett's alleged deference to outside rulers, like the pre-1948 British High Commissioner, and to the UNTSO which had its HQ in Jerusalem's former Government House, known in Hebrew as *Armon Hanatsiv*, "the High Commissioner's Palace."

The issue of wording the announcement about Mevo Beitar. [- - -]

Gideon Rafael, Josh[53] reported Azmi[54] has been appointed [to head Egypt's delegation at the UN and has] set conditions for contact with us, [and said to Palmon that] Nasser is not at all stable. [- - -] [Regarding the Palestinian] refugees [Palmon] met for the first time with representatives of their organization, Aziz Shihadeh from Jaffa and Mahmud [*sic.*, for Muhammad] Yahya from Tantura, [who said they were being] trampled down by Jews, deceived by Arabs. [They nurse] unreal dreams of a territorial concentration of the scattered [refugees] lacking any rights.[55]

[- - -]

A shooting [in Jerusalem. The Jordanians are] retaliating for our retaliation in 'Azzun. Bennike['s response]. [A talk with] Ziama about Lavon and his contentions: why [should we retaliate in] Jerusalem, why not [against] a village, for here they are not strong (as if we are able to penetrate the Wall). [Several were] wounded. Panic. I waited for Bennike. Lavon [reported] to Teddy: [shooting escalated] from machine guns to mortars. Cease fire at 00:10, went to sleep at 2:00 am.[56]

[- - -]

Thursday, July 1

[- - -] In the morning a consultation with Aran at the PMO [about the 'Azzun] retaliation and its lessons. Talk with G[ideon] R[afael], Yaacov and Joe. Lavon has agreed to a meeting. Ziama [to arrange] a press conference. I composed a communiqué, Hebrew and English. Problem of Bennike's visit.

12:45, Bennike's visit, an ad hoc meeting. 1:30 journalists. [- - -] Eppy [reported] on the shooting on the Kinneret. We [responded with] cannon fire. [A talk] with Lavon about instructions not to retaliate. [- - -] Investigation [was carried out]. Later renewal of shooting. [- - -] 5 wounded. Weighing visit with

53 Yehoshua ("Josh") Palmon (1913-1995). Born in Tel Aviv. Member of the Arab Department of the *SHAI* and a senior member of the JA Arab Department. After the establishment of the state, an adviser on Arab affairs at the MFA and the PMO.

54 Mahmoud Azmi (1889-1954). Egyptian intellectual, journalist and politician. Married to a Jewess. He had maintained contact with Sharett (then Shertok) during the 1930s and 1940s. Azmi would die suddenly while participating in a UN SC debate on November 3. (See Moshe Sharett, *Yoman Medini* [*Political Diary*] vol. II (1937) (Tel Aviv: Am Oved, 1971 – in Hebrew), 12-13, and *Yoman Medini*, vol. V (1940-1942) (Tel Aviv: Am Oved, 1979 – in Hebrew), 246-47, 349n.

55 See *DFPI* 9, doc.239.

56 Israel reacted strongly to the sniping across the lines in Jerusalem, directing complaints to the United Nations in New York and to representatives of the Western powers. On July 1, US Secretary of State Dulles sent messages to Tel Aviv and Amman "deplor[ing] this serious outbreak of violence in the Holy City" and urging "immediate steps [to] insure observance [of the] cease fire." See *FRUS 1952-1954*, doc.839; *DFPI* 9, docs.269-273, 275-276.

[British Ambassador Francis] Evans [on the spot of the shootings]. Lavon also to see Evans, hinted [at our?] stratagem. Conversation with Evans. [- - -] Contradictions [as to] details of our shootings.

[- --] Herzl telephoned [and said that he was] instructed [by Lavon to write] against "Britain's machinations." I lost my temper [and told] Lavon he had started an open dispute. Shamai to instruct H. Berger to cancel [the article].

Friday, July 2

A soldier was killed on Mount Zion. Several wounded. The sniping continues.

[An extraordinary] Cabinet meeting [with the participation of CoS Dayan, on the sniping in Jerusalem]. Clashes with Lavon.[57]

In the midst of the meeting [we were inforned that] the Jordanians had issued orders [to stop the shootings]. [- - -]

Saturday, July 3

[- - -] With Teddy and Memi[58] on plans for the CoS visit [to the US]. The 11 points [above, entry for June 24.]. Went walking. In the evening Lavon [reported] on an incident involving the Border Police. [- - -]

Sunday, July 4

[- - -]

Cabinet meeting – the usual agenda. I proposed that Lavon make a statement in the Knesset.[59]

With Ziama and Lavon re: meeting with BG. Consultation with Lavon on the CoS's trip [- - -]. Dictated [a memorandum] re: [water negotiations with Eric] Johnston.

Monday, July 5

At the Ministry of Foreign Affairs [worked on] the Romanian Note.[60] With Teddy, who's against [Dayan's] leaving the country. Diplomatic luncheon. Eytan stayed

---

57 There were a few sharp verbal altercations between Lavon and Sharett during this meeting. For extracts of Sharett's remarks, see WebDoc #15. See also *DFPI* 9, doc.272.

58 Meir ("Memi") De Shalit (1921-2007). Born in Lithuania. Settled in Palestine in 1925. After serving as liaison with UN officials during the armistice negotiations, joined the MFA in 1949 and was dispatched to Washington as a *Mossad* representative. Deputy DG of the PMO (1954-1964). Later DG, Ministry of Tourism.

59 See below, entry for July 5.

60 The Romanian government had complained of an Israeli-inspired "defamation campaign" being waged against it over the punishment of "several elements found guilty of espionage against the Romanian State." See *DFPI* 9, doc.286.

behind [to discuss] the CoS's trip.

At the Knesset. Lavon's rage (after I asked him). Hutchison.[61]

[- - -] [Exchange of] messages [with Lavon]. [- - -] Enlargement [of] memorandum [to] Johnston.

Tuesday, July 6

At the MFA. [- - -] With D. Lewin on a delegation to Burma and a delegation to China.[62]

From 3:00 to 7:00 pm with the FADC. [- - -] At the Knesset in the evening. Lavon's reply [in the debate over defense matters.][63] [- - -]

Wednesday, July 7

[- - -] [Conversation with] Teddy and Ehud [regarding a unit of] paratroopers under Command of Ariel Sharon].[64] [- - -] At the MFA – our line on the MACs after the inquiry [into the Jerusalem and Kinneret incidents]. [- - -]

---

61 In a fiery speech to the Knesset, Lavon reported on recent incidents, including the Jordanians' opening fire from the Old City of Jerusalem into the Jewish western sector, and the Syrian shelling of an Israeli police boat on the Kinneret which killed two policemen and wounded five. Lavon declared Israel ready to discuss the Jerusalem incident in the IJMAC on condition that its head, Commander Hutchison, not participate. "With all respect to the UN, we must declare that we cannot be oblivious to the attempts to rob us of our dominance over Lake Kinneret. The IDF will react to the cold-blooded murder by the Syrians with all the means at its disposal." Finally, Lavon denounced rumors regarding IDF provocations being aimed at determining Israel's foreign policy. "The IDF has no policy of its own; it's a loyal and disciplined instrument of the state." *Divrei Haknesset*, XVI: 2104-05.

62 On the ongoing internal MFA debates over upgrading Israel's relations with China, see *DFPI* 9, doc.281.

63 Among other things Lavon said that, in spite of Israel's justified criticism of the IJMAC, it was necessary to avoid total and exaggerated criticism of this body. He ended his speech saying that "Israel's aim is attaining peace, but she is prepared to defend herself, her population, assets, rights and borders." *Divrei Haknesset*, XVI: 2126-28.

64 Ariel ("Arik") Sharon (1928-2014). Born in Palestine. Joined the IDF upon its creation in 1948 and quickly became an officer known for his daring. In August 1953 Sharon was appointed Commander of commando Unit 101 and became known for his penchant for exceeding orders. Later served as IDF General, Minister of Defense, and PM (2001-2006).

Unit 101 was a formation especially created for the purpose of executing unorthodox military reprisals. It was disbanded in January 1954 by CoS Dayan because of its disorderliness, and was merged with paratroop Battalion 890 and placed under Sharon's command. The Qibya raid of October 1953 was carried out jointly by Unit 101 and the paratroops before their official merger. For details, see David Landau, *Arik: The Life of Ariel Sharon* (New York: Knopf, 2013), 24-32.

Let There Be Havoc in the Middle East

Thursday, July 8

[- - -] Drafted an announcement on [negotiations with] Johnston by telephone with Yaacov.[1] [Heard from] the CoS [re: the incident at] Kissufim.[2] Drafted a memo to the CoS.[3] [Drafted] a letter to BG [see below].

Friday, July 9

[- - -] At the Foreign Ministry. [- - -] In the afternoon with Lavon on the CoS's trip. Dictated a brief. [- - -] Walter on Russell's worry and Hammarskjöld's instructions [presumably re: maintaining confidentiality on the Dixon-Eysvoogel report on water-sharing between Israel and Syria].[4]

[- - -]

July 9, 1954

Ben-Gurion, Shalom,

I owe you an answer this long while for your last two letters [neither found]. I experienced great emotional difficulty in replying to them, until finally my distress at not answering them overcame my distress at their contents.

In your next-to-last letter you ventured to justify your withdrawal from party activity due to your inability to be party to the responsibility for the government's political course. I am abandoning the attempt I made to prove to you that this conclusion is defective from every aspect of our party life. I will say only this: I do not know whether you have rendered an accounting to yourself as to the consequences of your stand on the internal

---

1 For a detailed account on Johnson's visit to Israel, see Sharett's report to Eban and Shiloah, July 7, 1954, *DFPI* 9, doc.280.

2 On the night of July 7-8, Egyptian scouts mined an IDF patrol road near Kibbutz Kissufim, exploding an armored car and injuring three Israeli soldiers (one losing his eyesight). See Morris, *Israel's Border Wars*, 314.

3 Likely a briefing for his trip to the US. *DFPI* 9, doc.282.

4 Israel had been hoping to publish the report (dated April 3), whose findings appeared to justify its position that creating a water-diversion canal at B'not Yaacov could be accomplished while meeting conditions that would satisfy Syria's water needs. The UN SG feared that publication of the findings would give Israel a green light to resume work on the diversion project, and thereby cause an upsurge in tensions in the Israel-Syria DMZ. See above, entry for March 29, 1954; *DFPI* 9, docs.138, 183, 241; Hammarskjöld conversation with Wadsworth and Barco, June 24, 1954, USNA Lot File 58D33 box 3.

life of the party and the impact on your open relationship with the unfortunate *haver* who has been compelled to become, despite his reluctance and not due to any initiative on his part, the Prime Minister of Israel.

You will surely understand that I am always ready for any consultation with you in any setting, with no insistence [on my part] on an "official" framework, as long as the cooperation or friendly contact between us has the common background of activity within the party and responsibility towards it. Without this common background, we become two private persons, between whom cooperation is not woven into the framework of political responsibility. But if the basis of authority and party responsibility is swept from under my feet, then I lose all my standing, and consequently there is no value to consulting with me or to my participation in any consultation whatsoever.

In your last letter you write that, with regard to your plans for the youth of the country, you have consulted with haverim who are close to these matters and that, since the growth of the number of agricultural settlements established by the youth would necessitate roads, housing and the like requiring allocations from the state treasury, for this reason only you see fit to notify me too of the matter, since I am now Prime Minister and therefore have some connection to budgetary issues. I did not know what to find more astonishing: your "professional" conception of the functions of the PM, or your idea of who are exactly the haverim close to the matters of youth.

I am sure that you did not mean to insult me and I should be very sorry if the reply I am writing you hurts you. But how else could I reply to such a letter from you to me? Or would it have been best if I hadn't answered it at all?

With best wishes for a quick recovery,
Moshe

Saturday, July 10

Joe Tekoah. 10:00 am with BG [to discuss] the coalition, youth – settlements,[5] the electoral law. Lavon [called] regarding a response to Kissufim.

From 3:00 to 5:00 with BG – the 11 points; he [spoke about the powers infringing on Israel's] sovereignty, the water[-sharing] plan.

[- - -] At Lavon's.

Sunday, July 11

Lavon on the operation [in reprisal for the mining of the road near Kissufim]. The mishap that took place.[6]

---

5 Ben-Gurion had been advancing the idea of calling on Israeli youth, mostly from moshavim, to volunteer for service in new immigrants' settlements, with the aim of boosting their morale and assisting them in their daily work.

6 Operation "Eye-for-an-Eye" was executed on the night of July 10-11. "[A] company-sized force of paratroopers, led by [Arik] Sharon, stormed and captured Position 79, opposite Kissufim, killing nine or ten Palestinian gendarmes, wounding several more, and taking two prisoners. [- - -] The Israelis suffered one dead and five wounded (including Sharon, who was hit in the leg) before the defenders were overpowered." Morris, *Israel's Border Wars*, 314. Cf. *DFPI* 9, p.533 n.5.

Cabinet meeting.[7] After the meeting, [spoke to] Lavon about the need for an announcement [re: the Kissufim reprisal].

Afternoon [with] Joe Tekoah [regarding] Lavon's order to reject 7 of the 11 points. Joe did not say so. Complications over the press conference. [IDF spokesman] Nahman Karni. Phone call to Lavon.

Monday, July 12

[- - -] To the Foreign Ministry [- - -] Consultation with the DG, Gideon and Joe on the MAC. Phone conversation with Lavon. A second call with him. He went out [of his mind]. [Lavon gave] written instructions to Shalev. A letter to Lavon [not found] on a tripartite meeting [possibly Sharett, Lavon and Dayan].

[- - -]

Prepared my lecture [for the Mapai Political Committee]. Lectured for one hour and a half, came back shattered and shocked.[8]

[- - -]

[The MFA and the IDF GS experienced recurrent difficulties in sharing responsibilities for the MACs. Below begins an exchange of letters as disagreements came to the fore.]

The *Kirya*, 12.7.1954

Foreign Minister,

In the wake of [discussions on] the "handling" of IJMAC matters, I have come to the conclusion that there can be no continuing of the present state of affairs which causes disruptions and a flurry of colliding policies.

I am unwilling to bear the responsibility for the activity of the MACs under these conditions and, since you are unwilling to rely on my responsibility, it is best that you accept the entire responsibility and the handling of all the MACs. Whatever the course according to which the Foreign Ministry representatives on the commissions act, at least it will be a uniform delegation which draws its instructions from only one source of authority and is fit to act in accordance with the course determined by it.

It is self-evident that Army representatives will cease to function as chairmen of the Israeli delegations. If you are interested, I shall request the CoS to assign to the delegations suitable officers for technical tasks exclusively.

This arrangement will go into effect as of August 1 this year. To prevent a vacuum,

---

7 During the meeting, Defense Minister Lavon reported on the ill-fated Kissufim reprisal. Several ministers expressed doubts about the efficacy of the operation, whereupon Sharett said: "Dear friends, there is a fundamental matter here: Are we totally rejecting reprisal actions, or not rejecting them totally? If we are rejecting them totally, then this would be a clear-cut policy; if it is followed, then such incidents [in which IDF soldiers are killed or seriously injured] would not happen. If we are not totally rejecting reprisal acts, then, clearly, we shall have to execute them [- - -] inside the territory of the other side."

8 No record of Sharett's talk has been found.

it is desirable that all the new personnel and administrative arrangements be determined by the above date.

P. Lavon
Defense Minister

Jerusalem, July 12, 1954

To: Defense Minister
From: Foreign Minister

In answer to your memorandum of today, I accept your proposal to transfer the handling of the MACs to the Foreign Ministry.

Clearly, this new arrangement will also demand close cooperation between the Foreign Ministry and the Army. Representatives of the Foreign Ministry will serve from now on as the heads of the Israeli delegations to the MACs and act in accordance with my instructions, but the delegations must include military personnel too. Moreover, contact with UN Observers in different locations will in the future also be conducted by IDF officers.

The function of delivering reports for disclosure on the course of deliberations at the MACs and briefing the press on these matters will also pass to the Foreign Ministry. The IDF Spokesman will deliver bulletins concerning incidents, and this too will be done through contact with the person in charge of Armistice Affairs at the Foreign Ministry.

The Foreign Ministry will draft a detailed plan for this matter on which I hope I can reach agreement with you.

The very transfer of authority from the Defense Ministry to the Foreign Ministry in a matter as serious as the responsibility for our delegations and the course taken by them at the MACs demands, in my opinion, the approval of the Cabinet. I therefore intend to bring the matter before next Sunday's Cabinet meeting.

I accept your decisive statement that this arrangement will go into effect as of August 1 this year as your wish, to which I, for my part, agree. But this too requires Cabinet approval.[9]

Tuesday, July 13

[- - -] Conversation with Lavon and Aran. [---] Telephone call from Lavon about a message from Kane.[10]

[- - -]

At the Foreign Ministry – [Discussion about] inviting Russell. [Talk] with the DG on a solution to the question [of liaison with UNTSO] by [seconding Aryeh] Shalev [to the MFA]. Afternoon consultation on the MAC. We must conclude [the matter] and not keep ignoring it. The talk with Russell [about Dayan's trip to the US]. [Back] to the Foreign Ministry – dictated a cable.[11] [- - -]

9 Cf. *DFPI* 9, doc.284.

10 Lt-Col. Michael Kane, Jr., Military Attaché at the US Embassy.

11 The cable (text given as WebDoc #16), expressed Sharett's anger at the apparent American about-face undermining the status of the invitation issued to Dayan. Sharett also gave a detailed report to the Cabinet on this matter; see below, entry for July 18, 1954.

Wednesday, July 14

[- - -]

[Extraordinary] Cabinet meeting.[12] Lavon at the Knesset about Dayan [who left on July 11 for a month's tour of the US].[13] The matter of China.[14]

[- - -]

Thursday, July 15

The *Kirya*, July 15, 1954

Foreign Minister,

Following the exchange of letters and the discussion held between us with the participation of Minister Aran, I hereby bring to your notice that my opinion, as formulated in my letter of 12.7.54, remains valid and that at any time you wish to transfer the handling of the MACs to the Foreign Ministry, I shall be ready for it.

But as long as the status quo is in effect, I shall consider myself fully responsible for determining the course of conduct of our delegates to the above-mentioned MACs, within the framework of the Cabinet's decisions to be sure.

I shall always be ready for consultations with you, but the issuing of instructions will be under my exclusive authority.

P. Lavon
Defense Minister

---

12 Finance Minister Levi Eshkol presented the Cabinet with the proposed State Development Budget of IL.194 million for 1954/55. Dov Yosef, Minister of Development, suggested that the sum of IL.350,000 be allocated to the first phase of building up the port of Eilat. He emphasized the importance of building a port there, arguing that "in case of the eruption of a world war the Mediterranean Sea could be blockaded as it was in World War II" and in such an eventuality the Eilat port would be essential for feeding Israel's citizens.

PM Sharett then said: "I would like to support, as much as is possible, this demand by the Minister for Development for starting the building of the port at Eilat. I am convinced that our diplomatic and military efforts – which we have been constantly making while repelling all attacks in this sphere and while exploiting any opportunity of strengthening Eilat's position as our southern port with a view to our maritime connections to the Indian Ocean, South-East Asia and East Africa – that these efforts must be accompanied by the creation of significant economic facts in Eilat – first and foremost, a port. The main reason is not our becoming prepared for a world war, but the buttressing of our position in the world, making countries near and far used to the fact that we envisage Eilat as a potentially important port in the future, and proving this stand by carrying out concrete deeds."

13 Responding to speeches by two leftist MKs, who accused the government of sending CoS Dayan to the USA in order to involve the IDF in "aggressive American anti-Soviet planning," Lavon replied that Dayan had gone to the USA on a study mission. "His visit has no political aims. Talks on political matters are conducted by representatives of the government, not by IDF officers." *Divrei Haknesset*, XVI: 2163.

14 On July 20, MFA DG Eytan wrote to Sharett requesting that the matter be raised again in the Cabinet's FADC. *DFPI* 9, doc.293.

Friday, July 16

Met with Benyamin Givly [and asked him] who had publicized [the matter]?[15]

[- - -]

[Met] with Evans on [the] water [issue]. [Told] Moshe Keren [that] *Ha'aretz*'s line was going too far. [- - -] Who leaked it to the press? Not Foreign Ministry, but Defense.

Isser on Lavon. Warned [me about him and recommended his] dismissal. Lavon's talks. [- - -]

Walter on staffing the MAC. – Ehud + Tekoah, Navon, Chaim Herzog.[16] In the evening [worked on my] papers. [Wrote a] message to Bennike. [- - -]

Saturday, July 17

Paperwork – Reply to the 11 [points]. Nahum Goldmann. Communiqué [for the press] regarding CoS [visit to the US] – [Prepared] a denunciation of the Pentagon.[17]

[- - -] Completed the draft on the 11 [points].

Sunday, July 18

Prepared my report for the [Cabinet] meeting. At the Cabinet meeting I reported on the CoS's trip [to the US]. Should we bring him back? Lavon and I are against, [but] Serlin is making political capital out of [the fact that Dayan had] not been [formally] invited.

[Extract from the Cabinet protocol:]

> Moshe Sharett: Last year, when Moshe Dayan was Deputy CoS, he was sent on the initiative of the MFA to New York in order to assist our UN mission on military questions

---

15 *Ha'aretz* of July 11 published a report about UN SG Hammarskjöld's message to Bennike regarding his views on the handling of the shooting incidents in Jerusalem by the IJMAC. In his talk with Givly, Sharett stressed the political and security damage caused to Israel by this leak. See Givly's report of this meeting to Lavon, No.585/500, July 20, 1954, Lavon Archive, ISA.

16 Vivian Chaim Herzog (1918-1997). Born in Ireland. Settled in Palestine in 1935. Israeli politician, general, lawyer and author. Served in the *Hagana* from 1936 and in British Army intelligence during WWII. Director of IDF Military Intelligence (1948-1950 and after 1959). Military Attaché at Israel Embassy, Washington (1950-1954). Military Commander of Jerusalem (1954-1957). Israel's sixth president (1983-1993).

17 The next morning, Israeli newspapers carried the following item: "The Foreign Ministry spokesman pointed out last night that the announcement regarding CoS Dayan's visit to the US which was published by the Israeli Embassy in Washington before he had left the country, and in which it was said that he would be the US Army's guest, had been transmitted to the Department of Defense of the US prior to its publication, and had been approved by it. It was also known to the Embassy that, in answer to correspondents' questions, the Pentagon had then announced that, during his stay in the US, Dayan would be the Pentagon's guest." See also entry for July 18.

which then were rather complicated [immediately following the Qibya operation]. While on this visit he got in touch with American military [officials] and became interested in the military training methods of the Americans. After he returned home he broached the possibility of going there again for this purpose. The Defense Minister consulted with me on this idea and I saw the [second] visit as a positive step politically, even though the purpose of the visit was solely study. This was after Qibya. The impression [in the US] was that the IDF was a bunch of bloodthirsty people and I thought Moshe Dayan's appearance in the US would demonstrate a different climate of relationship. I also thought the visit would cause the Arabs some headaches while at the same time bring some solace to American Jewry by showing them that [US-Israel] relations were good. It is also possible that the CoS will succeed in explaining some defense matters to the upper echelons of the US Army.

Our Embassy people were happy with this idea and started negotiations with the State Department and the Pentagon regarding an invitation to the CoS. At the time the response from the two bodies was positive. Meanwhile, a senior American [intelligence] officer, General Trudeau, planned a visit to the Middle East, including a day or two in Israel, and we heard that he was bringing over a letter of invitation with him. General Trudeau came; not only did he not bring a letter of invitation, but he discussed the whole matter very strangely. He asked the CoS what the purpose of his journey was, and spoke disparagingly of the visit. There is evidence, which is well founded, that Trudeau had brought with him a letter of invitation; but when he divulged this to Arab and US representatives in the Arab capitals he visited before coming to Israel, they convinced him that the visit would nullify all their efforts at building US friendship with the Arab countries, and that it would be better if he did not hand over the invitation and [instead] saw to it that the Pentagon reconsider the matter.

A very strange situation evolved. There were talks on the matter in the State Department and in the Pentagon. From the Pentagon they phoned our Military Attaché and said everything was OK regarding the visit. When Russell came to my office with Johnston, I told him that we could not tolerate any confusion and disrespect over the CoS's visit. We were not imposing the visit on them; if it was not desired, that would be the end of the matter. But if he was invited, then we were asking for a written letter, after what happened with Trudeau. He said there was no problem – "when I return to Tel Aviv I'll write you a letter, or, if you prefer, I'll consult with the State Department." I said: "It is not for me to tell you what to do, but it seems to me that it would be better if you inquired at the State Department." A few days later a letter from the Pentagon was received by our Embassy. But at the same time we were informed by our Embassy that they found out that letters of invitation were sent only if the guest represented a state that maintained a military pact with the USA; a different procedure governed invitations to friendly states. Still, the Pentagon announced, in an answer to correspondents, that CoS Dayan would be a guest of the US Army. We decided to be satisfied with this letter and their announcement to correspondents, and on the basis of these assumptions the CoS flew over to the US on Sunday, July 11. On the same day the Pentagon announced that Dayan would be the US Army's guest; the Embassy announced his visit and sent its communiqué to the Pentagon for approval before publication, and received an approval [- - -] Dayan left Israel after our Embassy's announcement, approved by the Pentagon, was published.

On Monday evening the American Military Attaché Kane came to the home of his vis-à-vis, Colonel Ami Perlin, and said he was instructed to inform him by the US Army that (a) all of CoS Dayan's expenses in his journey should be paid by IDF and not by the USA; (b) it should be clear that no department of the Pentagon had sent any invitation to Dayan to come to the US. Kane said he regretted personally that he had to say this, and that the announcement was secret. Perlin understood that the matter was political, and thought it strange that the US announcement should be transmitted to him, and therefore he asked Kane if Russell was in the know. To his surprise, he was answered that Russell did not know; the matter was confidential between Kane and the IDF.

On the next day I was informed [of this] by the Defense Minister and I immediately summoned Russell. Before Russell's arrival *Ma'ariv* was published and printed the Pentagon announcement issued after Dayan's arrival. There were two "lovely" things there: (a) it was explained that Dayan had come to the US because he pronounced a keen interest in coming to the USA; (b) he would be flying in the US only on commercial airplanes.

I cabled Eban and he immediately went to see Byroade.

Now, what happened here? According to all kinds of American sources, the picture is clear: when it became known that the CoS was going to the US, panic arose in American legations in Arab capitals, which was enhanced by recent events in Jerusalem, and the result was that Washington instructed its military attachés in Arab capitals to inform their vis-à-vis that Dayan was traveling at the expense of the IDF and that, as a matter of fact, he had not been sent any invitation. [- - -] This was a shameful and insulting retreat by Washington. [- - -] Meanwhile Dayan was continuing his visit according to plan. He paid a visit to General [Matthew Bunker] Ridgway [CoS of the US Army], and all the American generals participated in a dinner arranged for him. [- - -] As for our response, we should be aware that the situation is highly complicated and serious. Any additional tension, any clash, any strong altercation between us and the US would be very damaging politically and militarily, to say nothing of economically. We have no interest in pushing things to the limit.[18]

[- - -]

Tekoah [reported on] the Syrian MAC. Once again [Israeli representatives have been] instructed by the CoS to leave the meeting. Wrote to Lavon.

Jerusalem, July 18 1954

To: Defense Minister
From: Prime Minister and Foreign Minister

I understand that tomorrow the ISMAC is to be convened and it can be assumed that the Syrians will again try to raise the subject of their [fishing] rights in the Kinneret,

---

18 Dayan gives no background on the origins of this trip in his memoirs. He mentions it only in a letter to Givly, dated July 15: "The Pentagon announced publicly, in order to satisfy the Arabs, that the visit of the Israeli military mission to army bases in the US was a private visit and the Israelis would pay their expenses. When the matter became known to us, we were already here and it was necessary to decide whether we should 'swallow' the insult, or return to Israel and end the visit. I think, and I assume you think so too, that cancellation of the visit at this stage would cause us more harm than good, and I did not recommend this. I don't tend now to dig into this matter and I see it as finished. Of course, I did not hide my opinion about it from the Pentagon people." Moshe Dayan, *Avnei Derekh: Autobiografia [Stepping Stones: An Autobiography].* (Jerusalem: Edanim (with Dvir, Tel Aviv), 1976 – in Hebrew), *128*. For one of Dayan's reports of his meetings, see his cable to Lavon of July 16, *DFPI* 9, doc.290. Dayan's July 16 meeting at the State Department is also recorded in *FRUS 1952-1954*, doc.842.

which has already decided upon.[19]

In case the Chairman votes with the Syrians on the procedural question of whether the Commission is allowed to discuss the subject anew, the question of our response will arise. I want to inform you that, if this happens, then I would strongly object to our leaving the meeting. Our leaving would not prevent acceptance of a decision against us on the subject. On the contrary, it may ensure such acceptance, since, at least theoretically, it is possible that in the voting on the subject the Chairman would abstain from voting and thus the Syrian draft resolution would fail, while if we would not be present, then the abstaining of the Chairman, or even his opposition, would not prevent the adoption of the decision. This consideration is added to the general consideration against creating an impression in the world that we are prepared any time and hour to leave meetings and undermine "normal functioning" of the armistice machinery. I very much hope that my opinion is accepted.[20]

Consulted with Teddy and Tekoah about my letter to Lavon [see below] and corrected it. Instructions are to be given by me. [Discussion about the] IDF Spokesman and his selective [dissemination of] news.

Jerusalem, July 18, 1954

To: Defense Minister
From: Prime Minister and Foreign Minister

1. I have received your letter of the fifteenth of this month.[21] I had meant to write to you again in any event, for my letter to you, which reached you after our meeting with the participation of Z. Aran, was written prior to it.
2. First of all, a comment concerning "the exclusive authority." Although you write to the Foreign Minister, one must be aware that there is also a Prime Minister in existence. If my predecessor was given to making political decisions in between meetings, I do not think he would have done so as Defense Minister. No doubt that, if this matter of principle is ever brought before a Cabinet meeting, the Cabinet would draw up a rule of procedure that when issuing political directives the Prime Minister is the one to do so.
3. This argument may be purely theoretical at the moment, for we have both agreed that the responsibility for issuing directives to our delegations to the MACs must be transferred to the Foreign Minister, and in my opinion the sooner the better. In fact, it is desirable and possible that this be done immediately.
4. I certainly agree with Aran that especially now it is not desirable to emphasize the transfer of authority for external consumption. I therefore propose – and strongly urge you to agree – that Lt.-Colonel [Aryeh] Shalev and the members of his staff who appear in our name at the MACs should remain in place, but receive their directive instructions from me from now on. I am proposing this arrangement for a limited period of time, until experience shows whether it is worth maintaining or whether the military heads of delegations should be replaced by civilians.
5. Should this arrangement not be amenable to you, I will have no choice but to bring the matter to the Cabinet for resolution.
6. At any rate, I believe that the task of briefing the press about the deliberations of the

19 At the ISMAC meeting of March 15 it was decided that the Syrians had no fishing rights in the Kinneret. See *DFPI* 9, doc.110.
20 *DFPI* 9, doc.291.
21 Letter not found.

MACs should be transferred to the Foreign Ministry immediately. The IDF Spokesman will henceforward focus on issuing communiqués of details of incidents.
7. More about the IDF Spokesman. Since explaining or briefing the press on matters that touch upon the state's relations with foreign elements can, in effect, be construed as determining foreign policy, the IDF Spokesman will henceforward refrain from issuing such explanations or briefings, both in public and behind the scenes, unless this should be necessary in some special case, whereupon the explanation will be delivered in full coordination with the Foreign Ministry.
8. A special issue is the "filtering" or "leaking" of secrets to the press. From experience I well know that sometimes there is a need to resort to this stratagem. But here too the action is directed towards a political purpose, and therefore the decision whether to exercise it or not should lie in the hands of the authorized political institution, i.e. the Foreign Ministry. Evidently, one of the decisive considerations, if not the overwhelming one, which must accompany any such decision is whether disclosure may prejudice the security of the source. It is therefore incumbent upon the Foreign Ministry to accept in this matter the authorized opinion of those [in the IDF] responsible for the [secret] sources [of information].[22]
9. The routine procedure of prior consultations between the two of us and between the people responsible at the Foreign Ministry and the General Staff on all political-military matters is to be continued as before.

Monday, July 19

[- - -] Straight to the Foreign Ministry. Ze'ev Sharef on his talk with Eppy. [With] Yosef Tekoah – it was decided that he would not participate in the Syrian MAC. Telephoned Lavon. A cable on the CoS's visit to Washington: "The insult remains."

[Text of Sharett cable to Washington Embassy:]

Personal to Ambassador, Minister and CoS. Found it necessary to report yesterday at Cabinet meeting in detail the whole background and circumstances of the CoS's visit. The general feeling was that although we acted in this matter bona fide and had every reason to rely on the Pentagon's approval of our announcement and its own announcement to corespondents that the CoS would be the Army's guest, we have indeed suffered a failure here. Even if we pass over the incident with Kane, which revealed a shameful picture of an intention to humiliate us, then the Pentagon's announcement after his arrival in which it went out of its way to explain the evolution of the affair, that, God forbid, he was not invited and anyway would not enjoy military transport, is an act of a public lack of courtesy, clear and deliberate, which up to now has not been rectified. Afraid style of Pentagon's official announcement has annulled the visit's value as an encouragement to [American] Jews. In view of present situation see as very desirable a festive departure meeting in New York with participation Jewish and non-Jewish VIPs such as Governor Dewey and others. Let there be a positive public response to the visit in order to blur the marred impression created by the government. Sharett.

22 The allusion here is to the IDF and *Mossad* wiretapping and other intelligence-gathering activities directed at UN personnel in the region.

[- - -] Consultation on [the British evacuation from] Suez. I read a draft reply [probably by Lavon] to the 11 [points proposal]. *Consternation* [English word used here]. Not to allow freedom of observation.[23] [Received] an answer from Lavon [see letter below]. He's not budging; it's either [Foreign Ministry] or [Defense Ministry taking charge of relations with MACs]. I decided to bring the issue before our *haverim* in the Cabinet.

[- - -] Cabinet FADC on the 11 [points]. An astronomical gap [between Sharett's and Lavon's positions]. I succumbed and showed the [Lavon] draft. I spoke about the [British] evacuation of [the] Suez [Canal zone[24]]. There was a serious and in-depth discussion [on Israel's policy vis-à-vis the British departure from Egypt]. Lavon said: "Let's go berserk" – [conquest of the] Gaza [Strip], abrogation of the Armistice Agreement. [He was] rebuffed by Golda and Aran.[25]

[- - -]

A meeting of *haverenu*.[26] [We discussed] Jerusalem, the conflict with Lavon, the conclusion [of the conflict between Foreign and Defense Ministries over the MACs]. [- - -]

The *Kirya*, July 19, 1954

Prime Minister and Foreign Minister
Re your letter of 18.7.54:

To my regret, I cannot accept your proposal, as I have notified you twice in writing and once in person.

I am willing to transfer the entire handling of the MACs to the Foreign Ministry, so that this be handled under your guidance, and by people whom you will choose. The task of briefing the press about the contents of the meetings of the MACs will be in the hands of the Foreign Ministry.

I cannot agree to your proposal of having the officers currently at the MACs remain in responsible positions. As I wrote to you in my letter of 15.7.54, I will be prepared to appoint officers of suitable rank to liaison positions.

---

23 Point 6 of the 11 proposed points called for "Broad freedom of movement and investigation for UN Observers at all points along the border."

24 See above, page 210 n.2.

25 For excerpts of the Cabinet FADC discussions, see WebDoc #17. Here, as elsewhere, Israel was watching with great concern as the British prepared to leave their bases in the Canal zone. Fear grew among Israelis that, with the signature of the agreement with England and the disappearance of a British "buffer" element, Egypt would gain important strategic advantage, add equipment and bases to her arsenal left by the British, and would generally be encouraged to adopt a more belligerent posture towards the Jewish state. Such fears were indeed behind Lavon's adventurism and the decision to activate a sabotage ring in Alexandria and Cairo (see below). For other expressions of official Israeli concern at this time, see *DFPI* 9, docs.295, 305-306; M. Gazit's talk with Tripp at the FO, July 29, 1954, TNA FO371/111073 VR1072/162; G. Avner to C. Davies, July 29, 1954, TNA FO371/111073 VR1072/167.

26 *Haverenu*: the term denoting Mapai's Cabinet members. See above, page 150 n.29.

So long as the job is not transferred into the hands of the Foreign Ministry, I will not be willing to accept interim arrangements of divided responsibility. I too am of the opinion that it is best that a fundamental solution to the problem is found in the next few days. In any event, the matter will not remain secret, for there are no secrets in the State of Israel, and too many people know about the differences of opinion and conflicting wills in this matter. It would therefore be best to act decisively, rather than give rise to doubtful predicaments which can only increase bad feelings, gossip, and the like.

With this fundamental resolution, there will also be no need for numerous prior consultations, except for matters in which basic issues of policy are determined, something that should usually be done within the Cabinet and within the Cabinet Foreign Affairs and Defense Committee.

P. Lavon
Defense Minister

Tuesday, July 20

Report by Shragai. Till the end of 1955 regular immigration from North Africa – 15,000 (excluding emergency immigration), from other parts of the world – 7,000. Problem of "emergency villages" – in Tunisia they are asking to move immediately half of the community – 100,000 people – all the ghettos and all the villages. Among the urban poor much spiritual and material backwardness, while in the southern Atlas Mountains health is excellent (5,000 people). Estimated emergency immigration – 25,000. For immediate approval – 4,500. Opinion regarding economic situation in Israel positive. Returnees from Israel have no influence and many would like to go back, but there is a problem regarding big families, parents of killed soldiers [during the War of Independence], etc.[27]

Teddy Kollek – the results of yesterday evening [meeting of *haverenu*]. An indirect indictment [by Teddy] of the Foreign Ministry. In fact, the Ministry of Defense has been briefing the press while the Foreign Ministry sits idly by. A joint team [of the two ministries should be established for briefing the press].

At the MFA I signed letters to Johnston. Ze'ev Sharef [reported on his talk] with Eppy, who said he had not heard one word of disrespect towards Lavon from my lips, but rather the other way round. I told the DG about the results of yesterday. In the taxi [I heard from] Joe about the Syrian MAC.

[Meeting of the] Coordination Committee [of the government and the JA]. Shragai reported self-defense [was organized] in the ghetto [of Casablanca], panic in the mixed cities.[28] The French High Commissioner and the French Commander: A storm is nearing. We are advocating a strong hand [by the French authorities], Paris not so. When it [i.e., anti-French disturbances] erupts, it will be [aimed] against Jews

27 *DFPI* 9, doc.296.

28 Likely in view of the approaching independence of Morocco; the colony would gain its political independence from France within two years, on March 2, 1956.

[since they are] loyal to France and marketing its products. [- - -]

[On this date Sharett spoke at the meeting of the Mapai Knesset faction. For his reply to those opposing the *Dayyanim* (Rabbinical Courts) law, mainly women MKs, see WebDoc #18.]

Wednesday, July 21

[- - -] Letter from Avner[29] re: the CoS.

[On this date Sharett spoke at the meeting of the Knesset FADC. For his remarks on the Anglo-Egyptian negotiations, the Johnston water plan and Israel's relations with the IJMAC and Col. Hutchison, see WebDoc #19.]

Thursday, July 22

[- - -]

In the afternoon I dictated [letters] to Lavon and Avner. A personal letter to Lavon.[30] [- - -]

Friday, July 23

[Meeting with] Isser in the morning. An argument with him about Lavon, whether there is any remedy or not. He [advised me to get rid of him] immediately, before he does damage to [Mapai's chances in] the elections. [Lavon] was preparing himself with support from outside the party.

[- - -]

Ziama about his talk wih BG. He knows one cannot rely [on Lavon?] but is against [creating a] crisis [by his dismissal?].

With Lavon in the car. The prisoner [Itzhak Jibly being held in Jordan since the IDF 'Azzun raid] will be returned.[31] [He suggested sending] a warship [through the Suez] Canal. My reaction. I wrote to Lavon[32] the [idea of sending a] ship [to be decided by] "the five."[33]

Shaul [came by] in the afternoon. I spoke to him at length.

Eisenhower will invite Israel and [Jordan to] the US for a conference on

29 Brigadier-General Elimelekh Avner (1897-1957). Born in Russia. Settled in Palestine in 1913. Served as an officer in the Ottoman Army in WWI, then deserted and joined the Jewish Legion of the British Army. Active in the *Hagana* and one of its first commanders. After 1948, headed the IDF Branch of the Military Government in the Arab-populated parts of Israel.

30 No letters found.

31 See above, page 406 n.50.

32 Letter not found.

33 See above, page 150 n.29.

non-belligerency. [- - -]

Jerusalem, July 23, 1954

To: Defense Minister
From: Prime Minister and Foreign Minister

I view as follows the summary of the consultation held in my home on Monday evening, the 19th of this month:

A. The representation of Israel at the MACs will remain in the hands of the Defense Ministry until further decision.
B. In each case where a problem arises regarding the position to be taken at the MACs and vis-à-vis UN staff, a consultation will be held, so far as is possible ahead of time, between the Defense Ministry and the Foreign Ministry.
C. In each case where differences of opinion arise and there is a need for a final decision, the PM's position will prevail.

To this summary of the consultation I hereby add two [*sic.*, three] assumptions:

1. The Foreign Ministry can always send its representative to any meeting of a MAC as it sees fit, giving prior notice only to the Defense Ministry.
2. Prior to issuing press communiqués on the contents of the meeting of the MACs and relations with UN staff, the IDF Spokesman will coordinate his statements with the Foreign Ministry.
3. Articles 7 and 8 of my memorandum to you of the 18th of this month remain in effect.

I hope that the lengthy deliberations on questions of representation and coordination in matters of armistice policy will come to an end with this summary.[34]

Saturday-Monday, July 24-26

[- - -]

Tuesday, July 27

[- - -]

[With Joe] Tekoah: [situation in the] Kinneret, Bennike's letters to Syria.[35]

[Knesset] FADC – [evacuation of British bases from] Suez, the IJMAC.

[- - -] 3:30 pm – [A meeting of] the ministerial committee [on the] 11 points.[36] I reviewed [Israel's relations with] the US. [- - -]

Bennike – [proposal that] Lavon invite [him for a talk] about Hutchison –

34 *DFPI* 9, doc.297.
35 *DFPI* 9, doc.300.
36 After nearly a month of internal consultations, the MFA would finally, on July 29, send a formal note replying to the US Embassy in Tel Aviv, expressing appreciation for the powers' concern about border incidents, but insisting that efforts needed to be directed at "removing [the] root of [the] trouble." For more details and a summary of Israel's response to the 11 points, see WebDoc #20.

If he refuses, I will invite him.

[A meeting of] "the five" [on the dispatch of] a warship through the Suez Canal, the sinking of a merchant marine vessel [there], [the kidnapping of] a hostage [to exchange] for an [IDF] prisoner, The ISMAC. Getting caught in Egypt.[37]

[- - -]

Wednesday, July 28

[- - -]

G[eorge] Flash[38] [who had just returned from a visit to the US and the UK] burst in [reporting remarks by Tory MP, member of the dissident "Suez Group"] Julian A[mery]: The evacuation is a *fait accompli*.[39] The House [of Commons] can do nothing about it given Labour's support. He warns about British policy following the evacuation. So long as they [the British] were relying on power it was OK, but when the power is gone one should rely on goodwill. There's room for an initiative on our part as long as the Old Man [i.e., Winston Churchill] is around. He's under the impression that they are not interested in transferring the [Suez] bases to the Negev. In the US, he had seen senators, and Hart and Jernegan[40] at the State Department. Jer[negan] had written him asking him to return. [There would be] a strong attack [by the Democrats] from September through November. The Republicans are afraid of the elections. [Senator Homer] Ferguson [of Michigan] expressed his fear openly. It's clear that the administration's policy is being influenced by the [coming] elections (Flash will be returning to the US). Hart tried to convince him that everything [will work out] in Israel's favor. (He had spoken in 37 cities.) [He suggested] that I travel to the US.

[- - -] Dinner with Teddy. Talked about Cyprus and BG, my editing of the

---

37 This is the first reference by the diarist to "the Mishap" of the sabotage activities by Israeli agents there (also known as the "the Affair" or the "Lavon Affair"). The allusion is to the first arrests of the accused undercover agents in Alexandria on July 23, 1954. First reports were published on July 26. On the background and long-term implications of this affair, see: *DFPI* 9, doc.418; Teveth, *Ben-Gurion's Spy*; Haggai Eshed, *Mi Natan et Hahora'a? [Who Gave the Order? The "Lavon Affair" and the Resignation of Ben-Gurion]*. Jerusalem: Edanim, 1979 – in Hebrew; Isser Harel, *Kam Ish al Ehav [When Man Rose Against Man – The Authoritative Documented Analysis of the "Lavon Affair"]*. Jerusalem: Keter, 1982 – in Hebrew; Kafkafi, *Pinhas Lavon – Anti-Messiah*.

38 George Flash (1909-1990). Born in Austro-Hungary. Settled in Palestine in 1933. MK GZ (1951-1955). Chairman of the Maccabi international Jewish sporting federation.

39 The draft agreement was initialed by Egyptian and British negotiators the day before, July 27. On Amery and other critics, see Keith Kyle, *Suez* (New York: St Martin's Press, 1991), 42-43.

40 John Durnford Jernegan (1911-1981). US Diplomat. Deputy Assistant Secretary of State for Near Eastern and South Asian and African Affairs (1952-1955). Later US Ambassador to Iraq, Algeria.

Jerusalem Post. [- - -] Lavon convened the [IDF] upper echelon; harsh words of censure for the Foreign Ministry and its policy.[41]

Straight to Ohel Shem Hall in Tel Aviv, [where I gave] a speech.

[The newspaper *Zmanim* of July 29, 1954 carried the following front-page story under the headline: "Sharett: State of Israel Shall Continue its Struggle against Suez Blockade"]:

In a gathering of Israel Air Force officers at Ohel Shem Hall, Tel Aviv, Prime Minister and Foreign Minister Moshe Sharett said that the State of Israel shall continue its struggle against the arbitrary blockade carried on by Egypt against Israel by all legitimate means at her disposal and by enlisting international support.

"In these very days a grave change is taking place in the balance of power between us and the world surrounding us. We wish any nation to achieve its justified aims for freedom and full independence, but not for the purpose of instilling strife and enhancing enmity and undermining the security of a neighboring state, but for the sake of peace, stability and cooperation.

"Egypt will be tested by the way in which it utilizes the precious national asset [of independence], which indeed is a world asset, in her new position of strength which she is about to assume after such a long struggle. [But] from the mouths of her leaders we have heard declarations of aggressive threats, which justify our serious concern and oblige us to become highly alert.

"The transferring of the new position of strength to Egypt [through the British evacuation of the Canal zone] without her binding herself to resolving her relationship with Israel by peaceful means can be understood, and concretely functions, as an encouragement to aggression. And what's more, according to our information, the new agreement is not even conditioned on complete cessation of the arbitrary blockade executed by Egypt against Israel in the Suez Canal, which is contrary to Egypt's international obligations, the clear decision of the Security Council and the vital interests of the nations which are making use of passage through the Canal.

"The State of Israel shall continue its struggle against this arbitrary blockade by all legitimate means at her disposal and by enlisting international support in this struggle.

"Our grave concern is enhanced by information regarding the intention of the US Government to accompany the agreement between Egypt and Britain by a plan to supply quantities of arms to Egypt. We are warning against supplying arms to Egypt as long as she declares that a state of war exists between her and Israel, and as long as she maintains this state by boycott and blockade and by incessant outbreaks along the border. As long as such a state continues, and as long as no clear change is evident in the declared position of Egypt, as well as in her concrete behavior, we shall consider any arms supplied to her as intended to be directed at us. The supply of arms to Egypt, following the [American] decision to arm Iraq, adds insult to injury.

"We are from time to time in need of the world's support. Many a time we are ignored. Still, while we must rely on our physical strength, we must at the same time rely on our moral one.

"We shall not be able to overcome the difficulties we are facing if we do not unite and become one, if we do not see to it that the awareness of our destiny and future is possessed by each and every one of us." [- - -]

41 For an account of Lavon's remarks, see WebDoc #21.

Tekoah's report on his talk with Bennike. Flexibility. Good news. [- - -] MAC. Lavon's talk with Bennike about Hutch[ison].

Thursday, July 29

Davar surpassed all the other papers – broad coverage of my statement on Egypt [and American arms sales] and of the replies [to questions] in the Knesset. But, apart from *Zmanim* [reproduced above], not a word from the second half of my speech.[42]

Telephone call to Lavon; his talk with Bennike – to no avail. The captive [Itzhak Jibly].[43]

Golda came to my office. I told her about Lavon's elasticity. I found her tense and grim [because of] the news concerning Egypt [i.e., the arrests in Alexandria]. Shimon Peres had been to see her [and had told her that] it [i.e., Lavon's activities as Minister of Defense] had come to an intolerable pass. [Lavon] gave orders to set off bombs in several Middle Eastern capitals – in Baghdad and Ankara – [saying:] "Let there be havoc in the Middle East." The firing of our cannons [in the Kinneret incident; see above, entry for July 1]. [Lavon's] requisition of a pessimistic report [possibly on Arab intentions, in order to justify radical action on Israel's part.] The counterfeiting of the Qibya operational order [which specified to] kill and destroy.[44] Everyone knows that he was deceiving the Prime Minister, [and that] he was being deceived [as well, presumably by Dayan and Givly]. [Peres] told [all this to] BG [who was shocked and] seized his head in his hands. BG realizes that he made a devastating mistake [in appointing Lavon Minister of Defense]. [Golda noted that BG] can size up people like her granddaughter. She will demand that BG order him to resign. Incidentally, [Lavon] said to Aran that he did not accept my summary [regarding the MACs]. Earlier he had said to Aran: "He [Sharett] will take responsibility for armistice [affairs] and I shall contrive incidents." A completely different story about [Lavon's speech to

42 *Davar*'s front-page story covered Sharett's speech at the Ohel Shem Hall, as well as his replies in the Knesset debate. Ambassador Evans also reported on the important speech in a despatch to the FO dated August 3, 1954, TNA FO371/111073 VR1072/164.

43 Itzhak Jibly served in the parachutist battalion commanded by Ariel Sharon and was known for his courage. He was wounded and captured in the retaliation carried out by this battalion against the Arab Legion camp of 'Azzun on June 27. Subsequently five Legionnaires were captured by parachutist battalion units in a series of four operations, and CoS Dayan suggested (on Sharett's advice) to the new UNTSO Chief, Canadian General E.L.M. Burns, that Israel would release the 5 Legionnaires "unconditionally," to be later reciprocated by Itzhak Jibly's release. The Jordanians agreed and Jibly was finally released on October 29, 1954. See above, entry for June 28, and Morris, *Israel's Border Wars*, 311.

44 For an in-depth study of the Qibya attack and its operational orders, see Shabtai Teveth, *Moshe Dayan: The Soldier, the Man, the Legend*, transl. from Hebrew by Leah and David Zinder, (Boston: Houghton Mifflin, 1973), 210-14, and *"Secrets of Qibya,"* cited above, page 43 n.39. See also Eyal Kafkafi, "The 'Latent Function' of the Qibya Raid: David Ben-Gurion's Weapon Against Pinchas Lavon," *Israel Affairs* 8:3 (Spring 2002), 118-33.

the IDF upper echelon]. He boasted: "I, during one year, [initiated more retaliations than in the past]." Insanity. [His brother] Zelig Lavon has admitted that he drinks. [Golda added that] Dayan should replace him.

I summoned Isser [and remonstrated him:] That intelligence unit [in Egypt] to which he once drew [my attention] was "activated" in the meantime! He admitted that he had overlooked this possibility. [- - -] What Givly related about Egypt. He [Harel] will write a report and then I will bring pressure to bear on Lavon.

I fretted and fussed over my speech [to be delivered] in Kibbutz Ma'agan. [- - -] It was a solemn occasion.[45] A huge crowd gathered. There was a symbolic flight of light planes over our heads. I resented this very much. The accident [one plane crashed right in the midst of the people gathered]. 13 dead. 26 injured.

[- - -]

Friday, July 30

We awoke dazed with shock [at the news of yesterday's accident at Kibbutz Ma'agan].[46] [Planned to go] to the Foreign Ministry at the *Kirya*. While still at home [I telephoned to] Lavon regarding a commission of inquiry [into the accident].

[- - -]

Saturday, July 31

[- - -] In the evening consultation at home over Suez; the problem of tomorrow's Cabinet meeting. My fatigue is unprecedented.

Sunday, August 1

Letter from Lavon – he has turned everything upside down.[47]

[With] Haim Cohn on Kasztner. [- - -]

At the Cabinet meeting. Obituary[48]

[I gave a] report on [the situation in] London.[49]

[Gave] a report on [the situation in] Washington. Much melancholy.

---

45 I.e., the memorial ceremony for Peretz Goldstein, one of the *yishuv* parachutists dropped in cooperation with the British Army in occupied Eastern Europe during WWII.

46 The death toll reached 17 people, among them 4 of the surviving *yishuv* parachutists who had dropped into Nazi Europe during WWII.

47 For the text of Lavon's letter of July 29 regarding responsibility for liaison with UNTSO, see WebDoc #22.

48 For those killed by the plane crash during the memorial ceremony in Kibbutz Ma'agan on July 29 (see entry above).

49 Sharett's report was based on a detailed briefing by Eliahu Elath, Israel's Ambassador in Britain, regarding the Anglo-Egyptian Agreement on the evacuation of British forces from Egypt. See summary of consultation at Sharett's home, July 31, 1954, *DFPI* 9, doc.305.

[Here follows an excerpt from the Cabinet protocol. Sharett describes his meeting with Francis Russell.]

The conversation, which was at his initiative, poured more light on the very grave trend of the American policy towards us. He told me the deterioration of relations between our two countries causes him sleepless nights. He doesn't think it is possible to stop America from supplying arms to the Arab countries in the near future, since it is viewed as an axiom derived from the defense strategy of the West. I got the impression that he had informed the State Department that he was going to see me and was instructed what to say. He held a paper in his hands and read it out, but said it was not a "note verbale." He began with the [dredging] works on the B'not Yaacov canal and said it would be to the benefit of Israel and of the whole region if these works were not carried out inside the demilitarized zone nor outside it. Any step implemented there could be taken only by prior agreement of the UNTSO chief, by a SC resolution, or by Syrian consent. If the works are renewed, then it should be assumed that Israel is aware of its consequences.

I said I was astounded by the State Department's behavior, finding it appropriate to suddenly throw this bombshell [at us], using such language. There can be only one response to such an attitude: we have full rights to renew work inside the DMZ, and we shall decide if and when work is to be renewed – this matter is entirely within our discretion. The State Department is now threatening us by building up three walls: the first is the UNTSO commander, the second is the SC and the third is Syria's consent. And above all that, America is threatening taking sanctions against us.

I had no interest in going any deeper into this subject since I was aware that our talk would touch upon more serious issues. Indeed, he went on to discuss the main question of Israeli-American relations against the background of American regional defense planning. He again stated that he was not reading a formal document and asked that any note-taking by us should be destroyed. I will now read from what I wrote down while listening to him.

I answered him that I must deplore the insult implied by such a presentation of the issue. [- - -] What are they offering Israel? To Israel they offer nothing, because what is the essence of the Tripartite Declaration [of 1950 – for the text, see WebDoc #1]? They promise that if they become aware that Israel is threatened by aggression, they will take steps to prevent such an aggression, which means taking diplomatic steps that might succeed or fail. Such an obligation seems to be directed at both sides of the conflict, but American arms are supplied to one side only. You are talking about the need to defend the free world, but you are not offering anything to Israel in this context, which means that as far as you are concerned Israel is not a part of the free world – even though it is the only country in the region whose democracy is deep-rooted, it is the only country whose existence is being threatened, and it is this country you are not including in the sphere of the free world. You are bringing in Iraq, to which you have already supplied arms; tomorrow you will bring in Egypt; and after tomorrow – Syria. What is left to us in view of this situation? Only protesting, deploring and warning. You are telling us: "Do not do that!" Do you want us to give up the only response possible? Under no circumstances will we oblige. You say that any protesting and warning of ours sounds aggressive, but can we do otherwise when you are forsaking us? An abandoned people can only rally around itself and rely on itself. How can you contend that we are being aggressive? The accusations that we are about to attack the Arab countries are an unbearable insult.

At this point he interrupted me and said: "You are possibly aware that rumors have it that you are planning an attack. I myself deny this time and again, but such talk is being spread and it causes harm."

I said: "It is you who are responsible for that. Your policy cannot but make us talk more harshly. This is the only natural reaction to such a policy." Here I gave him a short historical survey of the Arabs as a political factor; how they behaved during WWI and WWII, and how they would certainly behave during a third World War, Heaven forbid. "If what we know about the Arabs is correct, they have no intrinsic interest in defending democracy. We shall protest, we shall deplore, and we shall warn against such an American policy." Here our conversation came to an end.

In the course of our talk I said to him: "You already promised arms to Egypt some time ago, but you postponed supplying them because of Egypt's conflict with Britain. You are not supplying the Balkan countries with arms because of Yugoslavia's conflict with Italy. But you are supplying arms to Egypt in spite of its declarations that it is in a state of war with us. You are giving it arms with which it can attack us. Apparently this eventuality is not important to you, and if that's the case then how else can we behave towards you?"[50]

[- - -]

Monday, August 2

To the Foreign Ministry [to prepare] a briefing for Eban for his meeting with Dulles.

[Meeting with new Soviet Ambassador, Alexander Nikitich] Abramov. [I asked him] when he was going to present his credentials. [He asked about] Suez: did they [i.e., the British] ask for [Israel to accord them facilities to move their Suez bases to] the Negev? I spoke about the British deployment.

Isser [reported] on the [IDF intelligence] unit [in Egypt].

With Gideon Rafael and Yaacov Herzog on the briefing [for Eban's meeting with Dulles.] I added a lot.[51]

[- - -]

Tuesday, August 3

Bennike has resigned [and will be replaced by] Burns.[52]

---

50 See also *FRUS 1952-1954*, doc.847 and *DFPI* 9, docs.304, 307.

51 *DFPI* 9, doc.308. Sharett instructed Eban to aggressively stress Israel's vulnerability if US ME policy were to proceed, as announced, with arming of the Arab states in ways that would obviously change the balance of forces in the region to Israel's disadvantage. If the US did not clarify its intentions favourably, it should be openly accused in the press of abandoning Israel.

52 Major General (later Lt.-General) E.L.M. Burns (1897-1985). Canadian career soldier and diplomat. CoS of UNTSO (1954-1956); Commander of the United Nations Emergency Force (UNEF) (1956-1959). Israeli representatives regarded his appointment to UNTSO as auguring well for having their situation more sympathetically understood. See, e.g., Eytan to Comay, July 26, 1954, ISA FM 130.02/2425/8-b; MFA telegraphic correspondence between Ottawa and Tel Aviv, August 6-24, 1954, in ISA FM 130.02/2425/9.

[- - -]

The Druze are asking to be organized as a recognized community. [- - -]

The Foreign Affairs and Defense Committee – Lavon and the officers.[53]

An additional cable to Eban [regarding his scheduled talk with Dulles] on a security treaty.[54]

[- - -] [Discussed some negative aspects of proceeding with] the China matter [i.e., diplomatic recognition].[55]

[- - -]

Jerusalem, August 3, 1954

To: Defense Minister
From: Prime Minister and Foreign Minister

Re your memorandum of July 29 [see WebDoc #22, and above, entry for August 1].

For trivial reasons you keep harping over three words which are neither here nor there.

The main question is who decides in the case of differences of opinion. In my opinion, the Prime Minister and Foreign Minister. In your opinion, the Defense Minister. In this matter, my position was supported by all those who participated in the consultation and expressed their opinions – excepting yourself, of course. This is, in fact, the summation of the consultation.

If it is your wish that I bring this factual summation to an explicit formulation within the same framework in which the consultation was held – or even to a vote in the Cabinet – I am prepared to do so. At any rate, you have to know that I cannot in any event concede the right to decide on the matters under discussion.

Wednesday, August 4

[- - -] Evans is leaving.[56]

[Spoke to] Rokach on the need for Lavon to resign. At the Foreign Ministry with Gideon Rafael regarding a consultation with the Army on [the subject] of Suez.[57]

[- - -]

---

53 The FADC meeting was devoted to the Anglo-Egyptian Agreement on the evacuation of British forces from the Canal Zone, which was already initialed and approved by the British Parliament. Lavon and three IDF senior officers lectured on the subject and were followed by a summary by PM Sharett, who mainly raised the points he had emphasized in his conversation with Russell on July 30, reported above, entry for August 1.

54 *DFPI* 9, doc.309. Sharett wanted Eban to insist on the dangers to Israel if American defense of the area against Soviet penetration region were to be anchored in the collective security pact of the Arab League. Dulles and Eban met on August 4; for accounts of their discussions, see *FRUS 1952-1954*, doc.851 and *DFPI* 9, doc.313.

55 See *DFPI* 9, doc.316.

56 British Ambassador Sir Francis Evans would leave on October 1, to be replaced by Sir John ("Jack") Nicholls.

57 See *DFPI* 9, doc.318.

Thursday, August 5

[- - -]

At the Foreign Ministry – Joe on MAC affairs. Gideon Rafael [told me about his meeting yesterday] with [Da'ud] Dajani.[58]

[- - -] The letter to the PCC. I put G. R[afael] in touch with Dolik [of the Bank of Israel, presumably re: arrangements with Barclays Bank for frozen assets of Arab refugees].[59]

[- - -] [Went to] the meeting of the [Mapai] Political Committee.[60]

[Following are extracts from Sharett's speech to the Political Committee:]

> If it were clear that the present coalition would be the last one and the agreement we signed upon establishing it would be the last one, and if we had a chance of winning a clear majority in the general elections and establishing a government composed of a majority of our party's ministers, I would say – even then – that such a government should stand by its word. But who can guarantee us that we shall not be compelled to enter negotiations for establishing a coalition with the religious parties or with another party, and how can we do that if they all know that we are a party which does not abide by its word and [resorts to] all kinds of pretexts to that effect? What will our reply be in public gatherings during the election campaign to those who accuse us of having gone back on our signature? We will be put to shame.
>
> I think we have no alternative but to enact the law we gave our word to submit to the Knesset. [- - -] A party which finds it possible to decide that it is free from its obligations testifies that it does not take its obligations earnestly, which means its obligations are worthless.
>
> Are we a party which honors its word or not? [- - -] It may seem to you that interest dictates this or that action; but long-term consequences will reveal that interests dictate ethical behavior in public affairs, not otherwise. [- - -] Let it be known that there are people – at least here is one man – who will not accept immoral behavior of

---

58 Y. Palmon and Rafael had previously met with Dajani, Aziz Shihadeh and Muhammad Yahya on June 5. See *DFPI* 9, doc.239.

59 See *DFPI* 9, docs.333, 353.

60 The committee was convened to discuss a proposal by several party activists to annul the agreement with the GZ party regarding the percentage of voting below of which no party participating in the general elections is eligible to be represented in the Knesset ("blocking percentage"). Upon the establishment of the Mapai-GZ coalition under Sharett's premiership, Sharett signed an obligation to enact legislation raising the blocking percentage from the current 1 percent to 4 percent before the next elections. Because the Progressive Party opposed such legislation owing to its small share of the vote, and since Mapai was interested in the participation of this party in the coalition, it was agreed with the GZ that enacting the 4% law would be postponed until June 1954. Mapai's earlier obligation was not yet fulfilled, but now several party activists proposed to annul the agreement and go back to the 1% "blocking percentage", while others proposed to raise it to 10%. Still others proposed to immediately break up the coalition with the GZ, a by-product of which would be the annulment of Mapai's commitment to the 4% law. Sharett opposed both the annulment of the commitment signed by him and the break-up of the coalition.

a political party, which is not an improvised group of people born anew every day, but an organization based on continuity, maintaining a certain past and present record which guarantees its future.

Friday, August 6

[- - -] Cable from Abba. – Paragraphs for the [proposed public] statement [to be issued by Dulles to allay Israel's security concerns and fears of isolation in the context of Suez evacuation and of Western arms sales to Arab states in pursuit of a regional defense alliance]. My reply. Gideon Rafael on the choice re: Barclays [Bank]. [- - -] Another letter to Abba [re: his follow-up talk with Dulles].[61]

Saturday, August 7

[Spent] the whole morning on my papers. [Dealt with Eliyahu] Dobkin about Golda['s mission to] the US.

At Eshkol's home [we discussed] the State Bank, Barclays, Pinhas Lavon. [We heard] Aran's take [on Lavon].

Dayan [was awarded] the *Légion d'Honneur* [for his role in fighting the Vichy regime in Syria in 1941]. The *haverim* [Mapai Cabinet members] are [meeting] with Lavon.

Gideon Rafael and Yaacov Herzog on a talk with [Francis] Russell.[62]

Dead tired.

Sunday, August 8

Couldn't get up. Finally [arrived] at the PMO [consulted] with Teddy on Suez; Lavon's problems. 11:00 am consultation on Barclays.

Afternoon, at home. Teddy on the planning.

Atom: (1) We sold the formula for uranium from phosphates [to the French] for $190,000 and will be able to produce and, if we renew or they cease, we will replace. (2) Heavy water: they will set up a facility and sell to us at $40,000 a ton (the market price is $200,000), and if we have the money we will also set up

61 Sharett instructed Eban to stress the absolute impropriety of the US supplying any arms to Egypt prior to its making peace with Israel, and to warn that the Arabs should not be relied upon to fight against the Soviet Union. See *DFPI* 9, docs.313, 317, 320. For Eban's detailed report of his talk with Dulles and his subsequent comments, see *DFPI* 9, docs.321-322. The suggestion for a public statement of US reassurance was soon changed to one for an exchange of Notes.

62 The reference is to Russell's informal talk with Herzog on Friday afternoon regarding (1) American attitudes to Israel's resumption of work on the B'not Yaacov diversion project and (2) secret US pressures on Egypt to show a more positive attitude towards Israel, which would require Israeli restraint in face of possible border provocations. See *DFPI* 9, doc.325; *FRUS 1952-1954*, p.1603 n.5.

[a production facility]. (3) We sold propellant for a million. (4) The British have approached France. France stated that she is connected with us. The head of the [Israel Atomic Energy] Commission has agreed to a triad, requests confirmation. The French suggest that we make the disclosure. I asked: "Who decided?" Problem of reporting to Cabinet.

Traveled to Tel Aviv. Gideon Rafael phoned about the Eban-Dulles talk [of August 7]. During a meeting about Golda I received the report of the Eban-Dulles conversation.[63]

Monday, August 9

[- - -] At 7:00 am left for Jerusalem. At the PMO with Yaacov Herzog and Ze'ev Shek went over cables in preparation for reporting to the Cabinet meeting [- - -] I studied again Aubrey's cable on his talk with Dulles.[64]

[- - -]

Cabinet meeting. I reported on Mendès-France; Eban-Dulles [meetings]; Herzog-Russell [talk].[65]

[Following are extracts from Sharett's remarks during discussion on Israel-US contacts and relations:]

As you know, there has been some quite intensive activity there, including two meetings of Ambassador Eban with Dulles. Let me say in parenthesis, that from time to time we witness *clumsiness* [this word in English] in the working of the great USA. We too are sending directives to our ambassador, but it is not our intention that he read them out [verbatim] before Dulles, rather that he should express them in appropriate diplomatic language. But Russell, who was afraid that he might not say exactly what he was directed to say to us, read out the directives he received. I think that in doing so he served us well, for he divulged the very truth [of American policy]. Now we could not refrain from reacting to what he said, and our ambassador has made a protest, and it seems that Russell was then reprimanded for what he did.

In his [August 4] meeting with Dulles, Eban felt he was in dire straits to find some solution and asked for a second meeting [which took place on August 7]. I then directed him to keep to his previous line and to totally refute the conception of our military preponderance. As far as heavy armament is concerned – tanks, guns, planes and maritime power – Egypt alone is perhaps twice as strong as we are, and all Arab countries taken

63 For reports of the meeting, see *DFPI* 9, doc.321; *FRUS 1952-1954*, doc.854.

64 See *DFPI* 9, doc.322.

65 The Cabinet meeting on this day dealt, among other items, with Moshe Dayan's current visit to France as guest of the French Army. In discussing PM Pierre Mendès-France's suggestion to bestow a medal on him, Sharett said that, although in principle Israelis should not accept medals from foreign states, an exception should be made here in view of the warmth of hosts' attitude towards Dayan, the good friendship between the two countries, the fact that the French Premier was a Jew, and the bad feelings caused during Dayan's US visit. He thus accepted the Minister of Defense's recommendation to allow Dayan to receive the medal.

together – three times stronger. I cabled Eban to vehemently demand the abrogation of the Suez blockade. Recently we reached an agreement with the Persians on purchasing oil. We have so far not bought oil from Persia, not only because it was impossible to ship it through the Suez Canal, but also because we did not want to interfere with the British coming to terms with Persia. Now it is only the impossibility of passage through the Suez which is preventing us from purchasing Persian oil, and this creates not a small economic burden for us.

[- - -]

The Americans experience two kinds of fear: the fear of the impact of the elections there, but in addition they fear the harmful results of the Israeli isolation complex. And both these fears are healthy from our point of view. Recently a good Jew visited me. I don't know whether he is formally a Zionist. His name is Schiff and he is quite close to Pentagon circles and well involved with the politics of the Republican Party. At the end of my conversations he said: "I am American, I don't have to tell you where I stand as far as the East-West conflict is concerned. But it is crucial that they [i.e., the US Administration] will not be under the impression that you are tucked in their pocket. Thus said a Jew who is an American patriot.

It is now necessary to draw the line for the coming meetings of our people [in Washington], and I propose five points: a) we oppose any change in the present balance of power; b) if they are clearly decided on arming Egypt, they can find a way of arming us too immediately – let them sell us arms for payment, but on credit. If they decide later to grant us these arms, they can waive the payment; c) they should inform Egypt that economic aid would be granted them on condition that they do away with the blockade in the Canal; d) if any Arab country enters into a defense pact with them, there must be also a defense pact with us. I would not make it a condition that we enter into the same defense pact, for our interest is to have a separate arrangement, but if any Arab state enters a defense pact, an arrangement must be made with us; e) if within a certain period the Arabs are not moving towards peace [with us], then the whole situation must be re-considered.

[- - -]

6:30 pm – Saw Russell with Herzog.[66]

Gideon Rafael phoned and gave me some good ideas [possibly regarding meeting with Russell]. The meeting of *haverenu* did not take place; I was outraged. Eshkol came late and we talked.

Tuesday, August 10

[- - -]

10:00 am FADC. – [Ambassador Eliahu] Elath [on home visit from London], endless questions. I gave a summary of [the] Eban-Dulles [talks]. Decided not to speak in the Knesset next week. [- - -]

4:30 pm – Pinhas [Lavon told] me and Golda [about the sending of] a ship

66 For reports of this meeting, see *DFPI* 9, doc.326, and *FRUS 1952-1954*, doc.858.

("Bat Galim") [from the Eritrean port of Massawa to Israel through the Suez Canal], 3 possibilities [of Egyptian reaction]. [- - -]

9:00 pm – Walter and Ze'ev Shek – the ship to Suez.

[- - -]

[No notes were found for Wednesday, August 11.]

Thursday, August 12

[Visit to] Sde Boker [and discussed local and Negev matters]

[- - -]

Friday, August 13

[- - -] Lavon on [retaliatory operation against] Gaza water pump installation.[67]

Saturday, August 14

[- - -]

Yaacov Herzog came to the house to prepare for Eban['s arrival]. Eppy telephoned – The retaliation [for the sabotage of the water pipeline near Nir Am] will be carried out tonight. At 3:00 am [he called to say] it was done.[68]

Sunday, August 15

[- - -]

My conversation with Ziama [Divon]. [I explained what would have happened] had I insisted on preventing [yesterday's retaliation], and why I did not.

[- - -]

At 5:00 departure of the Burmese [delegation of high-ranking military and civilian officials, after an 8-week visit to Israel]; Shimon Peres raised the question of compensation [presumably for military materiel]. Eliahu and Zehava [Elath] to dinner. I spoke with Eliahu, [heard his] impressions of the country, his analysis and his criticism of me, the appreciation and criticism [in the Israeli public] of me, the Lavon problem. His dedication [to me].

Aubrey arrived [from the US].

---

67 A response to the blowing up by Egyptian saboteurs of the national water pipeline near Kibbutz Nir-Am in the north-western Negev on the night of August 11-12. See Morris, *Israel's Border Wars*, 314-15.

68 During the night of August 12-13 an Egyptian intelligence unit blew up the main water pipe near Nir Am. The IDF retaliated on this night by blowing up a water pump in the northern Gaza strip. See Morris, *Israel's Border Wars*, 314-15.

Monday, August 16

[- - -]

Consultation at the Foreign Ministry [on political and security questions, involving Ambassadors Elath and Eban].[69]

Walter on Emile's and Gideon's ultimatums. Eliahu drove us crazy.

At the Knesset, the calm before the storm. With Ziama – [he said] I must think about the party [presumably, its unity facing the crisis caused by Lavon's Egyptian operations, losing its popularity in view of Sharett's restrained defense policy]. With Golda [on] the evolution of Lavon [from a moderate to an "activist"], the elections.

[- - -] Briefing with Aubrey.

[- - -]

Tuesday, August 17

10:00 to 2:30 FADC.[70]

Lunch with Aubrey. [- - -] 4:30 to 6:30 pm Foreign Ministry consultation at home. [- - -] [Returned] home at 11:00 pm, [stayed up] until 1:00 am [writing] a letter to [Burmese PM] U Nu [on the return of the delegation to Rangoon].[71]

Wednesday, August 18

Zipporah [gave her views] on BG. Press coverage of the EIMAC decisions [regarding the blowing up of the water pipeline].[72]

Short conversation with Ze'ev Sharef before his trip to BG.

[- - -]

Yaacov Herzog phoned about a briefing to Shiloah [in Washington]. Gideon Rafael on a letter about the blocked [Arab accounts]; Barclays has confirmed and sent a draft.[73]

[- - -]

Thursday, August 19

[- - -]

---

69 See summaries in *DFPI* 9, doc.332, 334.

70 The entire FADC session was devoted to an extensive and thorough report by Ambassador Eban on Israel-American relations. Sharett was present but did not speak.

71 *DFPI* 9, doc.331.

72 Cf. above, entries for August 13 and 14.

73 The following day, August 19, DG Walter Eytan wrote to the Chairman of the PCC. *DFPI* 9, doc.333.

Meeting of the Political Committee of Mapai.[74]

[Following are extracts from Sharett's speech to the Political Committee:]

As I see it, the state will be dealt a severe blow if the present coalition does not hold till the end of the Knesset term. It will cause grave harm in view of the situation on our foreign front as well as various internal difficulties. Second, I do not know what would be the results of a general election. I wish that our party, myself and all of us, will win over 50 percent of the votes; however I cannot promise myself that we will not be confronted with the necessity of finding partners. It is one thing if the GZ behave like scoundrels, and compel us to throw them out; it is another if we have to negotiate with them for establishing a coalition after the elections.

As to the "blocking percentage" issue: if, as some *haverim* argue, changing circumstances justify our going back on our promises, then this cuts both ways and others too can do the same. And this means that agreements are not agreements. Perhaps the party can take this road, but I would like it to be clear that it cannot demand from people whose signature was abrogated to sign agreements anew. [- - -] It is impossible to demand from a man who signed, and whose signature was demonstrated in public to be void, to again be a signatory. I hold this as an elementary political principle. During the three meetings we have devoted to this issue I have not heard an answer to this contention of mine. The party entrusted me with directing the negotiations. It gave me instructions. It clearly authorized me to agree to the "blocking percentage" of 4%, and only in this capacity did I put down my signature. How can the party now tell me that I should go back on that signing and, after that, that I should start negotiating again?

[- - -]

Lavon reported on the three [IDF] corpses in Jordanian hands; the land-mine was ours [see below, entry for August 21]. Before that [I received] a letter from Lavon castigating the Foreign Ministry spokesman's response to the verdict of UN Observer Bertoldi [of the EIMAC, regarding sabotage of the national water pipeline on August 11-12 and the IDF retaliation in Gaza on August 14].[75]

[- - -]

Friday, August 20

[- - -]

[Spoke to] Isser – [- - -] He was pleased with the consultation.[76]

---

74 This meeting, in which the Mapai Knesset caucus participated, was a continuation of the meeting of August 5. It began at 3:10 pm and ended at 1:15 am. The various speakers dealt with both issues of annulling or changing the "blocking percentage" and the break-up of the coalition with the GZ. Sharett spoke at length.

75 Cf. above, entry for August 12. Lavon's letter not found.

76 I.e., the MFA and inter-office consultations of August 16, 17 and 18 on a political action plan in response to American policy in the ME and the Anglo-Egyptian agreement on evacuating the Suez Canal Zone. See *DFPI* 9, docs.332, 334.

[- - -] Yaakov Krauss[77] will coordinate matters [i.e., *aliya* organization] in North Africa in our Paris Embassy, organizing self-defense in North Africa.

At the Foreign Ministry – press conference.

[- - -]

Saturday, August 21

Prepared my speech to the Mapai Council [- - -] and spoke for an hour. Eshkol replied.

[After three hours of discussion and debate, Sharett's reply included the following remarks:]

> *Haverim*, what has happened recently in the sphere of our political position? What is perturbing and worrying us? It is, in fact, a change in degree, not one of essence. What has happened is that the fundamental reality of our existence has become sharply evident, a reality which will stay forever with us – the reality of the uniqueness of the State of Israel in its confined area as well as in the wider world, which is its smallness and aloneness, its being the only one of its kind.
>
> True, there is an element which compensates for this uniqueness and smallness of territory: it is the Jewish people of ten million, perhaps a little more, residing outside the State of Israel all around the world. There is in this a significant compensation to the physical weakness of the State of Israel at the present time. It is not only a moral compensation; it is a concrete one in many ways. But let us not minimize the serious limitations which govern this compensation. Let us not forget that, when we talk of ten million – not a big number even for a small people like ours, for only yesterday we were 18 million – let us not forget that close to a fourth of the Jewish people [i.e., those residing in the Soviet Union] is completely cut off from any contact with the life of our people. [- - -]
>
> Our state, both in terms of space and time, is dominated by difficulties unheard of in the experiences of any other people or nation. And in spite of these limitations it has shouldered tasks and undertakings while being highly prepared to fulfill its vision which has no equivalent in any other people or country, in view of its small and relatively poor territory and being surrounded by hostile countries, bigger and richer than it.
>
> We are facing here facts dictated by nature. We are nowadays experiencing a serious confrontation with international Great Powers who are clearly enhancing and enlarging this inequality [with the Arab countries]. Let us remember: this inequality exists anyway in spheres of territory, population, geopolitical position and natural resources. [- - -] And from the point of view of time, fate dictated that we would raise the flag of our national redemption in the mid 20th century, in a divided world, pregnant with conflicts, experiencing ups and downs of tension in its political life.
>
> In addition, we are witnessing the phenomenon of [the big powers'] contest over friendship, sympathy, support, and identification, which is conducted wholly on the basis of size considerations – size and depth of territory, size of population, size of natural resources – and consequently this contest operates against us and worsens our isolation.
>
> The factual isolation of the State of Israel does not mean that it has no deep roots

77 Yaakov Krauss (Karoz) (1920-1993). Born in Transylvania. Settled in Palestine in 1938. From 1946 a member of *Hagana* Intelligence. In 1948 headed its operations in North Africa, organizing illegal emigration to Israel. Joined the *Mossad* in the early 1950s and later was its Deputy Head.

in the hearts of numerous people outside the pale of the Jewish people, too. We witness expressions of sympathy, deep understanding and anxiety regarding our future and fate time and again wherever we travel all around the globe, in every meeting with an open-mined guest or tourist who arrives in our country. But let us not mistakenly think that this sympathy and support are powerful enough to extricate us from our failures and to attain what we are unable to achieve by our own efforts. This very sympathy, understanding and faith in us and our future are always [- - -] derived not so much from a recognition of our righteousness but from an enormous appreciation of our own efforts, our fighting ability, and our acumen in getting things done. It is first and foremost born out of our own faith in ourselves which is no longer manifested in prayers or in demands of others, but in the concrete doing of things, in an unceasing series of decisive acts.

In view of this situation, the decisive political direction of our state lies in the harnessing of the fullest energies possible at our disposal. [- - -] This cannot be achieved without planning from above and without maximum equality in the efforts demanded from the people. We have witnessed in recent times how nations, by far bigger and richer than ours, in times of crisis and existential dangers, manage to get organized unaware of socialist principles: how they manage to cut incomes, to narrow the gap between utter need and luxury, to enhance equality in economic and social life and to harness an entire nation to a regime of equality and general stepping up of the national effort. All the more so in our life, for it is an hour of emergency for our generation, and who knows if not for generation to come.

[Here Sharett explains the unavoidable necessity of maintaining a free economy in the country, making it possible for private wealth and initiative to participate in the development of the country side by side with state enterprise and economic structures and organizations bearing a socialist character.]

In the sphere of foreign relations we can note the failure of the illusion, nursed by our neighbors, of our destruction. After this first illusion of defeating us in war was completely shattered, they started nursing new illusions, according to which our state had achieved a quick victory by all kinds of subterfuges and deceit, by violating truce agreements, by getting help from mysterious sources, by exploiting the lack of unity within the Arab camp, etc. But this [according to these illusions] is only a temporary victory. This state must collapse; it is a suicidal entity. It has shouldered unachievable tasks. It is an artificial creature; it will survive one year, two, or three, and then it will fall apart. The entire world will have nothing to do with it for it will realize it is dealing here with a bunch of madmen who took upon themselves to carry out something logically unacceptable. It cannot but end in a shameful disaster.

Lo and behold, [several] years have passed. Sources of outside support have not dried up and, by and large, the well from which the people of Israel draws its energies and ability to build has not dried up. Our production is growing. The standard of living has generally gone up, especially in housing and availability of food. Employment is satisfactory. Contacts with the outside world were not cut off; on the contrary, they are being developed with the West and the East both in the geographical and political sense. At the same time we are witnessing contests between historic processes around us. In the political sphere there should have been a process of getting nearer to peace and stable relations with our neighbors. But there is another process organizing the world for the defense of certain values, preparing for the eventuality of [West-East] war or for its prevention. These two processes are not easy and simple. It took years for the first one to move a bit, but [- - -] the second one moved much more quickly. The Arab world is sliding much more quickly into a certain organization in order to receive arms. We are convinced that these arms are wanted for use against us, and not for the purpose for which they are supplied [by the Western powers]. [- - -]

We are witnessing also another pair of colliding processes. On the one hand there is the process of the enhancing of our economy, which cannot go on without outside aid, first of all Jewish, but also large scale non-Jewish aid. However, I am afraid that the process of diminishing non-Jewish outside aid is moving more quickly than that leading us to economic independence.

During the last three years in which we received constantly increasing Jewish aid, we also received grants from America and reparations from Germany. These two channels have a time limit. They are not eternal or even long-term. As far as aid by Jews is concerned, it is secure insofar as there will be no economic crisis and as long as they maintain their right to devote part of their wealth towards their preferred purposes. Here everything depends on our initiatives.

The situation regarding non-Jewish arena is different.

Perhaps you would be interested to listen to the following numbers: in the American fiscal year 1951/52, the entire sum of American foreign aid, economic and military, was $7.6 billion; in 1952/53, $6.6 billion; in 1953/54, $5.3 billion; in 1954/55, $3 billion. If we take only economic aid – and we are among the nations receiving economic aid only, it was $1.8 billion in 1952/53; only $800 million in 1953/54; and $450 million in 1954/55.

What did we receive? Although our grant went down from $70 million in 1952/53 to $52 million in 1953/54, an enormous decrease of $18 million, our percentage of the sum total of American economic aid went up from 3.9% to 6.5%. You must be aware of this fact in order to rightly judge the situation. We are witnessing an unceasing, cruel pressure towards decreasing the overall sum of American aid, but at the same time – in such dire conditions – our share is growing. [- - -] True, our percentage may go up but at the same time the total grant may diminish down to a negligible point, not in the current year, of course, but in the distant future.

As for the reparations, it may be worthwhile to quote what the opponents of this initiative said at the time: "What are we going to receive? A few thousand lipsticks, nylon stockings?" Two weeks ago I went aboard one of our ships in Haifa port that imports cargo financed by the reparations. I did not see there any stockings nor any cosmetics. What I did see was iron, fertilizers, building materials, machines.

However, the reparations payments are bound to end one day, and the American grants may cease coming too. What then? [How] will we overcome the gap between our needs and the dwindling outside aid? [- - -] We must plan our economic policy even though it may be highly painful. And planning cannot be based on expectation of miracles, although miracles are part and parcel of our life. We must rely on certainties, at least on preparing ourselves for future eventualities, and this makes it incumbent on us to plant this anxiety regarding our economic future in the hearts of our people.

The policy pursued at present by certain international elements is not promising us a reduction of our military budget. Most certainly not. But the question of how much arms are supplied to the Arabs, how much they had had before and how much is to be added, is not the only problem. Inasmuch as high quality arms or large quantities of it are supplied, one should consider, in addition to the military aspect, the political and psychological impact of this on the distancing of peace and on the promotion of war. We must prepare ourselves accordingly.

The Minister of Finance has said here that our balance of payments has improved.

This is true. We are not living now from hand to mouth as we did only recently, when we were forced to employ all our ambassadors in raising money instead of tending to urgent political matters, or when we were forced to hastily send ministers abroad for the same short-term tasks instead of tending to the carrying out of their duties. However, I would like to remind our Minister of Finance about one item which, agreed, is not included in the accounting of our national debt but should be included in our account of commitments.

I have in mind the compensation we owe for the land of Arabs [occupied in the 1948-1949 war]. We have committed ourselves in this respect, and we have not yet gone back on our commitments. Let me put it this way: no commitment of this kind stays on indefinitely. It was made in a certain period, against a certain background. We did not promise that it would stay on forever. But, for the time being, it has not expired. We still own up to this commitment. If it is demanded, it will be fulfilled; if not – it will expire. We are well aware that the Arabs have several times missed opportunities, such as in the case of the 1947 partition plan and all kinds of proposals regarding [the return of] refugees. They must seriously take care to not miss this commitment of ours. It should be clear that it is inconceivable that they would be free to demand our fulfilment of this commitment while they openly cause us deficits daily by blockade, by all kinds of sabotage and machinations.

This must be clear, and it also must be clear that these lands changed hands not as a result of open market transactions, but as a result of a bloody war of aggression and invasion, a war which cost us enormous sums and precious blood. We will take all this into account when we deal with the other side, but among ourselves we should see to it that we remember this still-standing commitment and that it is possible that the hour of its fulfillment will come.

At the same time, and this is the main task, I am confident that a new surge of immigration is about to happen. I do not know what peak it will reach and whether it will happen tomorrow or the day after. I do not want to make prophecies about potential changes which may happen inside Morocco or Tunisia, or about the reactions of their Jewish inhabitants to this or that change that might effect their psychological preparedness to immigrate to Israel. I know only one thing. Historically and objectively, these Jews are bound to immigrate to Israel in their masses, for it stands to reason that the processes which have taken place in other countries [of the Muslim world] will not skip over these two. It is difficult to assume that history will not repeat itself there. We must correctly read the writing on the wall and prepare ourselves accordingly.

Clearly, we should forward a new appeal to Jews abroad and make them partners in shouldering this burden, but the effectiveness of our appeal to them depends first and foremost on our deeds, which must be highly impressive in order to kindle a big fire of devotion to the task of immigrant absorption. If we are appealing nowadays to American Jewry to unite in extending support for our position [against the supply of arms to Arab states] in spite of the serious difficulties involved [in their opposing their own government], we must ask ourselves whether our demonstrations of disunity among ourselves will be conducive to this appeal.

At 6:00 [meeting of the] Political Committee.[78] [- - -].

78 From 6:10 until 9:55 pm, Mapai's Knesset members participated in another Political Committee meeting devoted to the issue of the whether to change the "blocking percentage" in the coming general elections.

[Following are excerpts of Sharett's speech to the Mapai Political Committee in reply to the preceding debates:]

We are now prodding American Jewry to shoulder two efforts: (a) We want them to be deeply aware of the seriousness of our situation and understand that the problem [of arming Arab states by the US] is crucial for us, and that they should now act accordingly and, if they cannot, at least let them be aware of this and find other ways of reacting such as increasing contributions to the [United Jewish] Appeal. I don't think they would dare wage an open fight, and we should explain to our people the dilemma they are confronting. (b) We are demanding from them to carry out, in as much as possible, a united wall-to-wall effort by the entire community with the exception of the American Council for Judaism – how can we, in these very days, break up the coalition, or let it break up, with the result being the GZ are left out? [- - -]

The break-up of the coalition would also act as an encouragement to the Arabs. They immediately wrote [that the whole dispute regarding the "blocking percentage"] was just a camouflage [to cover] the truth that there is anxiety and panic here because of the British evacuation of the Canal Zone. The Israelis [they claim] are at a loss; Sharett has suffered a defeat. He maintains that it is all about the "blocking percentage" issue, but it is really a deep crisis caused by the utter defeat of the government of Israel in view of the Suez evacuation. This argument is debatable, but it should not be ignored.

Lavon said that the matter of the three [corpses; see above, entry for August 19] never happened. [- - -] Edited my speech and [gave] the [press] conference [which was covered by] the *Jerusalem Post*.

[Following is the text of the *Jerusalem Post*'s report of Sharett's monthly meeting with the editors of the Israeli press:]

The government has no knowledge of a rumored agreement between Egypt and Israel following the Anglo-Egyptian Agreement on the evacuation of the Suez Canal Zone, said the Prime Minister in answer to a question. "It will not be assumed," continued Mr Sharett, "that we shall regard mere verbal assurances as capable of compensating for the fundamental change likely to adversely affect our position in the balance of forces in the Middle East – with all appreciation of the goodwill expressed in statements we hear from time to time."

As for US policy as it emerged in the recent talks of Ambassador Abba Eban with Mr Dulles, Mr Sharett, answering another question, gave a somewhat similar reply. Mr Dulles was clearly disposed to reassure Israel, in light of the grave concern Israel had shown at the developing situation, Mr Sharett said. But he did not consider that these assurances met the issue.

"We take the same utterly negative view we have always held of the American Middle East policy as expressed in the arming of the Arab states," he proceeded. "We are convinced that these arms will not serve their intended purpose, and are sure to disappoint the hopes reposed in them. We say this on the basis of clear experience of two World Wars."

"On the other hand, we have no doubt that, on the Arab part, these arms are designed to be used against Israel. The very grant of these arms can only be regarded by them as a reward for their refusal to make peace with Israel. In no sense is this action calculated to restrain them in their negative line; and both in its political impression and effect, we consider arms grants to Arabs as making peace in the Middle East more remote. Nor do we think that, internally, the rulers can be consolidated by these grants."

The Prime Minister said Israel's opposition to these arms grants was "derived not only from Israel's concern for her own security. We believe that this one-sided grant is liable to undermine peace and stability within the area."

"Israel would look after its security under any circumstances." Mr Sharett said he could not say anything in the moment on details of Mr Dulles reassurances to Israel. Mr Eban will report to the Government on Sunday, and will continue his contacts with Mr Dulles when he returns to the US.

Asked how Israel could think to bridge the gap between the arming of Israel (if arms were given her) and the arming of seven Arab states, Mr Sharett said that we were not faced now with the first step in the arming of the Arabs. The gap already exists, but is now being aggravated. The disparity in strength between Israel and the Arabs was a part of history. But Israel is now to join issue with the US for deliberately making that disparity even greater. The problem should engage international attention. We are a people of one and a half million against tens of millions around us.

Israel has presented no further request to the US for arms, as we have never withdrawn our previous requests, Mr Sharett said.

Asked if Britain had ever hinted at the possibility of bases on Israel territory, Mr Sharett said emphatically: "Never!"

Mr Sharett welcomed Major General Burns, the new [UN]TSO Chief, saying that Israel was eager to co-operate with him, seeks his understanding for Israel's viewpoint regarding the nature and operation of the Armistice Agreements. The first meeting with him would probably be devoted to a general explanation of our attitude on the subjects. "I presume that in view of the continual incidents, we shall have to discuss with him new matters also."

Mr Eric Johnston, President Eisenhower's personal representative on Middle East water problems, intends revisiting the area again in the autumn. Since his return to the US there had been further contacts with him for purpose of clarification.

Mr Sharett revealed that a group of Burmese military personnel had already arrived in Israel for training here. We have been favorably impressed by the official military and government mission which had visited this country and they have been favorably impressed by what they had seen here, the Prime Minister said, pointing out that in his letter to the Prime Minister of Burma he had said that we were happy to have been able to give the delegates a chance to see something of our work here, and we are pleased that they found them worthy of study. But we would also welcome their criticism and their suggestions, as we were interested in an exchange of ideas and cooperation between two people whose historic purpose was one: the rehabilitation of a country from neglect of centuries.

The Prime Minister recalled that two items had been published in Burma on the same day: the intention of the government to bring in a Compulsory Service Law, and the official announcement of the despatch of the military mission to Israel, to study manpower questions here.[79]

79 Extract of the PM's speech in *DFPI* 9, doc.336. The above *Jerusalem Post* report was summarized for the State Department by Russell. See *FRUS 1952-1954*, doc.868. *Davar*'s report on the press conference is identical with the *Post*'s, but concludes with an additional paragraph: "To a question regarding possibilities of military talks between France and Israel, the PM replied: 'I had not yet the opportunity to hear the CoS's report and I can say nothing. It is well known that at various stages we have found possibilities of arms purchases in France and it is possible that the intention is to continue in this vein. France has also significantly aided us in training IDF senior officers. We highly appreciate this attitude and will be deeply grateful if it continues.'"

Sunday, August 22

Teddy Kollek and Memi De Shalit on the consultations.[80] Gideon Rafael and Yaacov Herzog at the office. [- - -] My briefing to Abba. Namir visited BG. Hasty conversation with Dayan [on his recent trip and his impressions about] nuclear war, [feelings of] depression in the US. [- - -]

Monday, August 23

To the Foreign Ministry – My letter to U Nu (re: Nehru).[81] Joe Tekoah on Burns.[82]

[Arye] Levavi [Deputy DG of the MFA] and Lavon have their doubts about [our military] dealings with Burma. Memos to Lavon (reply re: publicity and Burma). [- - -]

Tuesday, August 24

Davar's interview with me was well reported.[83]

[- - -]

Meeting of the Knesset FADC, lively debate. My summing up speech.[84]

[Excerpts of Sharett's speech to the FADC:]

> If the committee members think that I spent the time between the end of the morning session and the beginning of the evening one weighing my response, they are mistaken, for I had not one free moment to do that. Thus my response will not be well organized, but haphazard by way of my stream of thought. I will use a language of general assumptions rather than that of final conclusions.
>
> I am prepared to agree with those members who said that a decision was taken [by the US administration], albeit I do not go for either term, "decision" or "taken." I would prefer saying that a certain tendency has been consolidated, according to which American policy is implemented at present. It is of course permissible – not only permissible but incumbent, inasmuch as it is possible – to foretell things in advance, to see them evolve, and then one is allowed to guess that this tendency continues. It might also be that it will be enhanced and consequently its results would worsen. However, I do not go for the definition of "a decision was taken," that is, that something final has happened, something fateful which is unchangeable. No, this is not my reading of the situation. Members should not conclude, however, that I am prepared to reach optimistic conclusions. My opinion is that we are now going through a certain stage of our political

80 Of August 20, see entry above.

81 Cf. above, entry for August 17.

82 Cf. Sharett's consultation (August 25) with Tekoah, Eytan and Rafael regarding Burns' introductory meeting scheduled for August 26. ISA FM 130.02/2425/9.

83 Reference to the lead story on the front-page, "The PM on the 'Blocking Percentage.'"

84 The FADC discussions took place in two consecutive sessions. Sharett did not take part in the morning session (10:00-1:30) but summed up the debate in the evening session (9:05-11:45).

battle. Who knows what kind of future stages are awaiting us? Who knows what changes, disappointments, retreats, recoilings, but perhaps also jumping-forward and possible worsening, will be experienced due to American policy [towards us]?

At the same time, I am not prepared to come to the far-reaching conclusions reached, or seemed to be reached, by members who made an extremely negative appraisal of the situation. And this, again, not out of optimism on my part, but, while not out of pessimism, out of some endeavor not to lose a sense of proportion in the appraisal of the seriousness of our situation.

What do I have in mind? I would like to say that our situation should not be viewed only through the prism of the change that has occurred in the American policy or in the trend it has chosen. Inasmuch as it is fraught with serious dangers, they are not built-in, but in the objective historical background on which this trend is being implemented. And the objective historical background is the gravity of the matter, a gravity that can be enhanced and that can be eased, but the gravity is obviously there, and it derives from the fact that we are stuck here, in this corner, at the heart of the Arab world; that we are small in number, located within a limited space as a wedge which was thrust into the flesh of the Arab world and caused it to bleed. It is irrelevant whether this [Arab] world chose to invade and make war [against us]. The wedge that was thrust was the stimulus. What was decisive was the spilling of much blood and the inflammation of hatred, a fierce and unmitigated hatred which shall be burning in the hearts of a multitude of people for who knows how long.

And we went straight into this. We went not only when we promulgated the Declaration of Independence. We went when our parents came here in the eighties of the 19th century, whether consciously or not, but we went on towards this situation which is fraught with the terrible danger constantly hovering over our heads. And we must be cognizant of this.

If such is the situation and if it is our fate to live a life fraught with danger for generations to come as dictated by decisive, perpetual geopolitical circumstances which it is beyond us to change, then we must come to terms with this situation and should not daily, hourly, sound the alarm against this danger. We must accept this danger as a constant. One can compare this situation to that of people living by the mouth of a volcano. I would say that we live here as if our heads are thrust inside a lion's mouth, that we are destined to lead such a life, that we are fated to build [our nation] in such circumstances.

Any oscillation this way or that in American policy can of course worsen or ease our situation. But let as assume for a moment that no change had taken place in American policy. Let us as assume for a moment that America did not, after all, embark on the path of arming other countries for the purpose of containing Communism. Let us assume for a moment that there is no East-West conflict in the world, that the world is not torn into two rival, clashing camps. Would that have made the danger facing us evaporate? Assuming that America is not going to supply arms to Iraq tomorrow, and to Syria sometime later – wouldn't these countries be arming themselves? Do they not have money for purchasing arms? They have more arms than we do. It may well be that twenty million Egyptian fellahin are starving to death, but the situation of the Egyptian Minister of Finance is by far better than that of the laborer from [Kibbutz] Degania Bet who became the Finance Minister of Israel. There is no comparison between the two. And we have not found oil. There is a continuous stream of gold flowing to Iraq for its oil sales. Syria too has all kinds of resources and they purchase arms the world over. Their populations are growing and they are generally developing. Their pace of development is not as quick as ours, but it is constantly advancing. And in all these countries, precisely because they lack democratic foundations and democratic organizations on which a somewhat stable regime could be built, precisely because of that there is in all these countries, or in most of them, a process of gravitation towards military regimes since the Army there is the only strong and stable factor. And if military juntas seize power there, then, naturally, because they are military and because they have no other stable foundation within the people, they must first of all amass arms, both for the purpose of buttressing their rule and also in order to be able to carry out external military adventures with which they can distract the attention of the masses from the troubles which they did not succeed in solving, and also in order to put down revolts.

The prevailing circumstances are conducive to rearming, and there are factors here which may not only preserve the power advantage of the Arab states but also, in the course of time, enlarge it. This is the situation we find ourselves in.

In view of all this I do not think that it would be wise on our part to react to the further worsening of the inequality [in armaments] caused by the present American policy or to its worsening in the future by creating panic inside our country and in the diaspora, on the one hand, or by crying out "SOS!", on the other, in the ears of other factors. For it would be quite easy for others to tell us: "This indeed is your situation!" Shall we always cry out: "SOS!"? Shall we always cry out: "Our life is in danger!"? These SOS cries may mar our clear thinking, and may sabotage what we are trying to achieve.

Of course, we, as always, are situated between two extremes, but if we aim at strengthening our position, we must not only cause panic among Jews regarding our future but also inculcate in them a belief in our ability to buttress ourselves and overcome the danger. If we are talking about strengthening ourselves economically, then I would join in this matter the member of the committee who demanded an increase in capital investment in our country now. However, it is not easy to encourage investment while at the same time creating a big panic. And this is why I am not talking about what should be said to many responsible diaspora Jews, who are immune to disappointment and despair. I am talking about slogans created for the general public.

Generally, when we embark on such a campaign in America, we must always consider all its aspects and take care not to become entangled in internal contradictions. What are, generally, the means we must resort to in order to overcome the dangers threatening us? The slogan, the main theme of our open public political battle vis-à-vis the Great Powers, should be the imposition of responsibility. They should realize their responsibility for endangering our security. They should be made aware of their responsibility for creating negative processes inside the Arab countries; that they are not stabilizing their regimes; that they may cause internal conflicts in the region; that they are not bringing about stability and peace – that their policy will not achieve their professed declarations.

We must never turn our gaze away from the power equilibrium which we can build. In what ways do we think we can ease this constant tension, this continuous danger which can have its ups and downs, but is nevertheless always there? First and foremost, by strengthening our own power, which means immigration, settlement building, industrial growth, building up the Army. All these necessitate resources. We cannot, while striving for these aims, take steps that disconnect us from resources; I now have in mind the American grant-in-aid. We must weigh the demonstrative gain, which in my opinion is doubtful – I am not saying it does not exist, but it is doubtful – we must weigh the results of this demonstrative step vis-à-vis the grant. We must juxtapose this doubtful demonstrative step against the concrete, certain damage, clearly undoubted, which would be caused to our economic position.

For what do we have here? There are those who say: the grant should be given up, we must throw it back in their faces. This is at least $40-45 million annually. I will not bother you now with the fact that, this very day, a colleague of mine is making a special effort talking with people with the aim of convincing them to grant us perhaps $5 million more next year. Perhaps at least $5 million more. I am talking about $40 million, which means more arms. Do you want the Minister of Finance to give up $40 million which are secure in our hands, and simultaneously find additional $40 million for arms, which means that he must find $80 million? Where is he going to find $80 million? Well, there are opposition MKs who say that a tax should be imposed on the country and on the diaspora. I admit I still do not know how a tax of millions can be imposed on our country. If it is said that more tourism and more exports should be developed, then this is a plan for many years. But how such magic tricks are to be performed within a year or two – that is unclear to me.

What is the meaning of imposing additional taxes on the people? One conclusion is that we must increase our manpower. Well, let's assume we are soon going to have surge of immigration from North Africa. [- - -] This means that we shall have to appeal to the diaspora for an additional effort. It can accept such a demand. However, can we say to American Jews that they should contribute more not because the State Department cancelled the grant, but because we ourselves decided to give up the grant? They will ask: "What reason did you have to give it up? Why didn't you ask us?" I am quite an expert on American Jewry, and I know that raising money is among them is not done by hitting a rock by a stick. We must appeal to people who consider themselves to be quite wise and knowledgeable. We will not be able to explain our behavior to them. We will not be able to explain this behavior to British Jews, South African Jews, and even more so to American Jews. We are worsening the conflict between us and America, and are asking the [American] Jews to pay the price for it? We shall not succeed in this.

Our people in Washington, first and foremost our ambassador, are stressing time and again that the grant-in-aid, more than being an assistance or aid by the government, is money given by the American people. The people's representatives have decided to give this money, and we well remember how it all started. In the beginning the State Department proposed giving us $23 million and the Congress decided to give us $65 million – about three times more. Then, the next time, after the State Department realized what happened, it proposed more. And you all know that while the total sum of American grants-in-aid is diminishing under Congressional pressure, our share has been growing from 3% two years ago to 6% this year and to perhaps 9% in the next year. It is not a simple thing – neither financially, nor politically, nor in view of our connections with the diaspora – to give up the grant.

This consideration holds true in other aspects of our political battle as well. It is very easy to say: "This [the giving up of the grant] is not a step taken out of enmity to America. It is in opposition to its policy." But this policy has deep roots in the ethos of the American people, and if there is something deep-rooted in that ethos, then our Jewish brethren in America are very sensitive to it, because they are sensitive not only to the Israel's future and to the dangers it faces; they are also sensitive to their position as American citizens, and you will not succeed to uproot that sensitivity from their hearts. Moreover, they will prove to us, black on white, that their ability to aid the State of Israel is a direct result of their being good American citizens. We are demanding much from them and they are capable of giving much, but we must always be on guard and not lose the sense of proportion. Then, when certain steps are proposed which they would not be able to justify, not only will we not advance our position on our political front in America, but we may well suffer setback and failure.

Generally speaking, it is either/or. Either we all say at one moment that we are an isolated state, an entity numbering one and a half million Jews and nothing more; or we say that we are the vanguard of the Jewish people, that we are the state of the Jewish people, and consequently we see the entire Jewish people in the world as one entity. And if we say so seriously and in good faith, then some conclusions must be drawn accordingly. If we take the second view then we cannot forget it the next moment and propose that we behave like any other small nation which has no connections over the world and which does not expect at all to receive outside aid in times of trouble. For if we do expect such aid and if we demand it, then we should weigh every step we are taking and foresee whether it is conducive to attaining it or, God forbid, liable to curtail it.

I am not proposing here any simple medical formula that is always usable. We are facing here highly complicated considerations. As an example I'll take one proposal advanced by the committee chairman. There is talk of sending a vessel carrying Israel's flag through the Suez Canal. This is a plan we are now working on, but we do not think the time is ripe for sending a tanker, for, first of all, such an operation costs tens of thousand of dollars and a tanker will probably cost more. But there are several stages in such an operation. I will not promise that we will do it tomorrow or the day after. [- - -] What if the Egyptians seize the vessel? This is not going to be a simple matter. We can of course bomb [them]. Technically we are able to do this. But then the Egyptians can bomb [us] too. Or we can seize an Egyptian vessel in the Mediterranean, but the Egyptians can seize an Israeli vessel. The Egyptians have more sea power than we have, and if this happens then, first of all, there will be publicity over the world, and then the question will be how the whole affair is perceived by the press – who was first to seize a vessel on the high seas? Egypt can claim she has a legal base for seizing the vessel; she can also claim that she was about to free that seized vessel after conducting a search on board. There are here very precise considerations to be taken. And if they seize a vessel in the Suez, will we seize a vessel in the Mediterranean on the very next day? We will not. We will have to resort to political action [first]. How much time will we earmark for this stage? I have no idea. It depends on the response of world public opinion and also on that of the powers. This is no simple matter, to move from a policy of retaliation on land to a policy of retaliation on the seas. Let us not push ourselves into these narrow straits with our tactics at sea as well.[85]

One more thing, perhaps more serious, is the emphasizing of our independence by contacts with one world camp. I would like to express myself clearly on this matter. It may well be that America was far from pleased with the fact that we renewed our diplomatic relations with the Soviet Union. I am aware that there are circles, places, where it is thought that we have not been stubborn enough in shunning this renewal and that something suspicious was going on here. We have never taken this into consideration. Possibly, certain American circles did not approve of our expanding trade with the Soviet Union. Not only am I not prepared to take this into consideration, but in these very days we are preparing serious plans for the expansion of trade with the Soviet Union, an expansion which may perhaps carry a political aspect as well. And this because, first, it suits us financially. We can save millions this way and open up new markets both

85 See also above, entry for August 10. A month later, Israel would dispatch the "Bat Galim" to test freedom of passage for Israeli ships through the Suez Canal. See below, entries for September 2 and after.

immediately and in the future. Second, because every such activity enhances in numerous indirect ways the contact between Israel and Soviet Jews. Whenever an Israeli orange, banana or olive finds its way into Jewish hands, it carries a promise with it, and if somewhere in the Soviet Union there are still dying Jewish embers, these symbols are kindling them anew. Third, we do not know how things will evolve in the international arena, and we are a state that must forge chains of contact with all world factors inasmuch it does not harm our vital interests but only serves them.

During diplomatic talks and while presenting our policy I do not refrain from hinting a warning that a certain American political line may cause serious opposition and consternation inside the State of Israel, that such a line will not enhance America's position, first of all in Israel and then in the Middle East. I am certainly prepared to play this card. But what I think will not succeed and can only cause us harm is making believe that we are searching for, or weighing the possibilities of, some other attachment [other than to the West]. This will either not be taken seriously altogether and will only lower our standing and present us as charlatans in the international arena; or, if taken seriously, it will case us much, and decisive, harm. I do not wish to mince words and analyze anew where is the center of gravity of our international ties, where our main interest lies in this context. I take this as an established constant. Let me say, though, that there are here very grave dangers of becoming entangled with big international factors. [- - -]

This whole situation obliges us to strengthen the pace of our ties with Asian countries, that is trade ties as well as other ties behind the Iron Curtain, but up to a certain line. I mean various cultural ties with the Soviet Union, not on their conditions, of course. There was an initiative taken by the Soviet Embassy here to buttress the "League of Friendship with the Soviet Union." We told them plainly: There can be leagues. Ours is a free country and people can organize, but as long as the party dealing with cultural ties on the other side is the Soviet government, then the opposite-number here is also the government, and they must come to terms with it. And to come to terms with the government is possible only on a reciprocal basis. They want to send people over here? We shall decide who is acceptable and who is not. And we shall send our people over there. If we come to terms, then there will be an exchange.

Of course, we should develop ties with any element who can, to some extent, aid us instead of America, inasmuch as America is not aiding us. And even if it does aid us, other ties will add to our strength. But even here there are serious limits. There is talk about France. I would like to say something regarding the enormous benefit of our ties with France, but also regarding the limits of this factor. There is no question, France has given us invaluable aid throughout all these years, and it is aiding us in these very days in numerous areas, known and unknown. But if any among you thinks that France is prepared to do everything without having regard for America, he is most seriously mistaken - because France is dependent on America and is interested in America's friendship, and does not want to be isolated in Europe, devoid of any attachment to America.

If, for instance, we have purchased very modern planes in France, that was discussed [by the three Western powers under the terms of the Tripartite Agreement] and America did not voice any opposition. Another party [i.e., Britain] was very much reserved, but not America. This we have learned from French sources. And this justifies the appraisal that America will not oppose our getting arms on every occasion. America is now wooing the Arabs, and consequently has no interest at present to arm us, but it is not opposing that we receive arms.

French sources had a big laugh at the *Herut* article which claimed a formal alliance between us and France was possible. We did not enjoy hearing that for, after all, it was an Israeli newspaper reporting it. But we heard very decisive comments on this subject and they were fully unreserved and unmitigated: How stupid it is to assume that France is capable of taking such a step, and what a senseless political idea it is to write articles which burden the Israel-France relationship with such a superfluous weight; that there is among us a lack of understanding of the value of what is possible and can be preserved, and no refraining from provoking responses which can only cause reservations and negative reactions.

This battle will not be a short one, and during it we must seek props of support within the American public as well, and we must refrain from acts and stratagems which may alienate these props from supporting us.

What are the slogans that we should use in this battle? I fully accept the notion that these slogans must be, first of all, negative: a negation of this [American] policy, a negation of its very foundations, although this does not mean a negation of its aims. Let me explain my intention: No arms to the Arab states, no arms because they are endangering Israel; no arms because these weapons will not serve their aim [of containing the Soviet Union]. We should not, however, reject the purpose for which these arms are to be supplied, that is, we should not do battle against the conception that the Middle East is endangered by Soviet penetration or invasion. It is not, by any means whatsoever, in our interest to say that we have no information regarding active Soviet machinations toward war in the Middle East. For tactically it would be tantamount to cutting the branch on which we are sitting, to declare that we are sitting here and there is no danger whatsoever, and hence there is no need to supply us with arms. If we take this line, we will thereby clash with opinions and feelings that are deeply rooted in the psyche of the American people, and it is not within our power to heal this people of this, if you will, psychosis. We must conduct this battle among the American people as they are, while they are governed by this madness [fear of the onslaught of Communism], assuming it is a madness. But even given this madness, it is possible to come out and say to the American people: "What you are aiming at [by rearming the Arabs] will never be achieved. These people have no interest in defending democracy, they have no democracy in their countries. If a war erupts tomorrow and the Soviets invade [the Middle East], there will be no [Arab] force to oppose them. It [the rearming of the Arabs] is a waste. It is an illusion."

Well, then, we must fight against the breach of equilibrium [in the supply of arms] and at the same time denounce the absurdity of the Tripartite Declaration of 1950. First of all, it is not binding. Inasmuch as it calls for some principle of arms balance, we are now witnessing its open breaching. We must fight against Israel being so obviously abandoned, abandoned even from a formal point of view in the Anglo-Egyptian Agreement. [- - -] However, it should not be said in our public campaign: [- - -] "However, if you are giving – give arms to Israel," because this destroys the ideological basis of our entire position.

Certainly, this campaign is being waged with the aim of achieving something. Certainly, if it is possible to bring about the total annulment of arms supply and the disappearance of the agreement with Iraq and the promise to Egypt, that would be well and good. [But] it is not so simple to hope for such results. Inasmuch as we may achieve a slowing down of the process or its reduction, so much the better. But it may well be that this campaign achieves nothing. There are here no guarantees for positive results.

Still, a positive achievement may result from the negative situation. If it is said: "No arms to the Arabs because it endangers Israel," a possible response may be: "We shall give arms to Israel too," or "We shall give Israel a guarantee." If it is said: "Do not breach the equilibrium," it is possible to respond with "We shall maintain the equilibrium." If it is said: "Israel should not be exempted from the defended countries," this can be responded to by: "We shall include Israel together with the defended countries."

If the other side, that is America, starts putting up such suggestions, we cannot allow ourselves to reject them outright or in principle. I mean, if it does propose [to provide] us [with] arms, then we should weigh whether or not it is worthwhile to accept it on such or other conditions. If it proposes a guarantee, it should be asked whether its purpose is that we declare that this will satisfy us. There can be a guarantee which perhaps satisfies us; [but] there can [also] be one which we will find unsatisfactory. If the US proposes a[n unsatisfactory] guarantee, we should not reject it out of hand. Take the 1950 [Tripartite] Declaration: it is now serving us as a weapon. We are now proving to them that they have gone back on their promise. Did we ask them to come out with this Declaration? No. But we are now using it to our advantage. Thus, if they start giving out guarantees which cannot satisfy us, we will declare that these are no more than guarantees on paper, and continue on with our campaign. At the same time, though, it is possible that on a rainy day this guarantee will serve us in some way. This is the thrust of our campaign. There can be no other.

Wednesday, August 25

Consultation at the MFA to wrap up [our policy considerations re:] the US and England: the DG, our two ambassadors [Elath, Eban], Gideon Rafael. At noon, a meeting of "the five" on the same subject.

In the afternoon, the Cabinet FADC. I opened with a summing up. An important and moderate meeting. They were surprised about Lavon [presumably his restrained tone in the discussion following Sharett's analysis].[86]

[- - -]

Jerusalem, August 25, 1954

To: Defense Minister
From: Foreign Minister

I hereby reply to your memorandum of the 19th of this month. I did not see eye-to-eye with all that is contained in it, either in substance or in formulation.

The Foreign Ministry is authorized to respond publicly to any occurrence on the Israeli foreign affairs front. It is self-evident that if the matter under discussion lies not in the realm of "pure policy," but has a practical side pertaining to another ministry's field of activity – whether defense, finance, commerce, and the like – it is obligatory to coordinate the response with the ministry concerned. On the other hand, the other ministry similarly has a duty to see to it that its position in regard to the matter, which in any event becomes public knowledge and subject for discussion, be known to the Foreign Ministry ahead of time.

86 An extract of Sharett's remarks in the Cabinet FADC is reproduced in WebDoc #23.

In the case under discussion, it was wrong of the Foreign Ministry to issue a statement without first contacting the Defense Ministry or the General Staff, but the Army would also have done well had it, immediately upon consolidating its position, notified the Foreign Ministry of the course it saw fit to take.

More to the point, in this case the Foreign Ministry was faced with an urgent need to take a step which might correct in some small measure the negative balance of international public opinion against us created by our one-sided condemnation in the matter of our blowing up of the water pumping installation of Gaza [on August 14th], with no condemnation of Egypt for the blowing up of the Negev pipeline at Nir-Am [on August 11th]. A sensitivity to the widespread impressions that international public opinion gets of events happening between Israel and her neighbors is not one of the traits with which the IDF is generously blessed. Perhaps possession of this quality should not even be demanded of it. By contrast, the Foreign Ministry is the state's organ enjoined to cultivate and manage this sensitivity and act accordingly. For example, immediately after the blowing-up at Nir-Am, I do not know what steps were taken to denounce this barbaric attack on a large project of agricultural development, and on the functioning of many settlements, in international public opinion – apart from the severe damage it caused to general state security and its being a willful violation of the Armistice Agreement. At that time I was in the Negev, word of the explosion was late reaching me, and even then there was no possibility of my directly influencing the course of events. But when the results of the discussion at the EIMAC were disclosed, I expressed an urgent need to publicize our refusal to accept the verdict in this case. This had to be done lest our silence reinforce the impression, bound to arise in the world immediately upon the disclosure of the EIMAC Chairman's conclusion, that in this case Israel rather than Egypt had violated the agreement. Had we kept silent, it would clearly have meant that we too confess our guilt. Concern for our relations with the Chairman must not in any way distract our attention from concern for our stature in international public opinion. By no means did the Foreign Ministry disregard concern for the former. Its statement was formulated in general and moderate language, and even commended the Commission's activity in general.

In the matter of sanitation in no-man's land in Jerusalem, I understand that in this Yosef Tekoah is in contact with the CoS or Lt.-Colonel Givly. I was entirely ignorant of the matter until I received your memorandum, but I do know that:

(a) Avraham Biran has since long past maintained direct contact with the Old City authorities on matters outside the framework of the Armistice Agreement, and he does so in constant liaison with the Foreign Ministry and with our delegation to the IJMAC.

(b) Upon our withdrawal from the IJMAC, all military contact between ourselves and Jordan through this channel was severed.

(c)This rupture can by no means justify a lack of response on our part to the other side's proposal concerning a meeting of medical personnel to consult on questions of sanitation that pertain mutually to both parts of the city. The question is one of a practical resolution. At this juncture I leave its handling to Yosef Tekoah.

Thursday, August 26

Straight to the Foreign Ministry. Arye Levavi [Deputy DG] on his colleagues. Aubrey again: Gideon Rafael is urging him to come over in order to be appointed

Foreign Minister and then he, Gideon, shall become DG. [- - -]

Full consultation on the [upcoming UN General] Assembly. 12:30 – Burns-Bennike visit.[87]

[- - -]

Afternoon [discussion with] Yaacov Herzog on [his visit to BG in] Sde Boker. He [BG] swallowed the briefing. He was inquisitive about what was being done. Yaacov did not mention my name. Perhaps BG didn't mention it, or perhaps Yaacov had pity on BG. BG praised Eshkol. What was his advice? He spoke about [the problem of low public] morale, a mood of frustration. He's fed up with the Knesset and the Government. Everything is rotten, the press, etc. A different road should be taken – [educating] the youth, moving [settlers] to the Negev, etc. "But what is to be done right now" [asked Yaacov]. He [heaped] fire and brimstone upon [US water negotiator, Eric] Johnston: "Who made thee a prince and a judge over us?"[88]

He's against [launching a] war; only over [a blockade of] Eilat should we respond with force. From all the compositions [i.e., BG's various articles in *Davar* in recent weeks] nothing will come. Paula was hysterical [about her unhappy life in Sde Boker].

I spoke with Yaacov about Aubrey – perplexed and complicated. He [Eban] has been telling everyone about his relations with Reuven: he needs an adviser, not a minister.

I wrote my speech[89] until 4:00 am.

---

87 Following earlier meetings at the Ministry of Defense, the departing Vagn Bennike introduced his replacement as UNTSO CoS, Major General E.L.M. Burns, to senior officials at the Foreign Ministry. Present, along with PM / FM Sharett, were Rafael, Tekoah and Ze'ev Shek. Shek's record of the meeting is in ISA FM 130.02/2425/9. Later that day, Burns was also introduced to members of Israel's delegation to the IJMAC (who were still boycotting the body in protest against statements by Cmdr. Hutchison in the March 1954 Ma'aleh Akrabim terrorist attack on an Israeli bus). Shalev's record, loc.cit.

Burns' diary account of these meetings includes the following passage: "Saw PM Moshe Sharett in FO. He made quite a speech about Israel's history and circumstances - and said the GAAs must be maintained until something better can take their place. [...] Mr Sharett also referred to desire to return to [the IJ]MAC. Their loss of confidence in Hutchison. I said the Chairman of the MAC had to have a secure position, like a judge. He later said he had to be agreeable to both sides. No doubt the negotiations about this will be difficult." Burns diary, August 26, 1954, Library and Archives Canada (LAC), MG31G6 v.7. (See photo below, p.914.)

88 *Exodus,* 2:14.

89 Over the coming days Sharett worked hard on the speech he was to deliver to the Knesset, excerpts reproduced below, entry for August 30.

Friday, August 27

[- - -]

Saturday, August 28

Yitzhak Navon: [- - -] BG will certainly come back. [- - -]

In the evening, Gideon – the speech [- - -], Syria-Iraq unification.

Teddy: BG won't come back. [He spoke about] Aubrey-versus-Reuven and himself and about a public-relations program. In the evening, Walter stayed till midnight – [going over Foreign Ministry] staffing, etc. [Worked on] the speech from midnight to 5:00 am.

Sunday, August 29

[- - -]

At 6:00 pm. Harry Levin, organizing our *hasbara* [in the US]. New people. His future. [Worked with] Lilian on the English translation [of tomorrow's Knesset speech] until 2:00 am. Completely drained – collapsed.

Monday, August 30

[- - -] Edited the speech in both languages. To the PMO [for a meeting with] Russell and Herzog. Herzog's assumption that the talk comes as a sequel to [Russell's talk with] Gideon Rafael [on US facilitating direct secret Israeli-Egyptian contacts].[90]

[- - -] In the afternoon, the speech to the Knesset.

> The Government of Israel is not aware of any concrete guarantee given by or even demanded of Egypt to ensure her compliance with the [September 1951] Security Council resolution [on freedom of passage], in a treaty that gives her such tremendous gains. Yet Britain and the US were among the foremost sponsors of the SC [resolution] with regard to the canal. Only a few days ago the government of the US reiterated its support of this resolution, and proclaimed its desire to see it implemented. But the powers have not yet taken any effective step to ensure implementation.
>
> The question is: Are they not putting these efforts to open the canal [to Israeli shipping] to naught, by fulfilling most of Egypt's desires, by failing to call that country to account, while there is still time, for her violations of international law? Are they not in effect approving these violations?
>
> The transfer of the Canal Zone to the military control of Egypt increases, at one stroke, and to a very substantial extent, her effective military strength and her capacity for aggression against Israel. Suffice to mention the airfields with which the Zone is well supplied to make clear what is here involved. Large-scale material reinforcements are

90 On Sharett's talk with Russell, see *DFPI* 9, doc.343, and *FRUS 1952-1954*, doc.879. Rafael had invited Russell to lunch on August 24. See *FRUS 1952-1954*, doc.871, and *DFPI* 9, doc.338.

falling into the hands of a state which invaded the Land of Israel in defiance of the United Nations [partition resolution of November 1947, and] which, as a result of that invasion, still occupies an area [i.e., Gaza] to which she has no sovereign title; which constantly reiterates the existence of a state of war with Israel, and its intention of carrying out the plans at which it failed on first attempt.

In recent days, it is true, we have heard from the rulers of Cairo words that seem to hint at readiness for a peaceful settlement with Israel. In spite of all our yearning for true signs of peace, we must, in the light of our experience, beware of being led astray by deceptive tactics. Only time will tell whether Cairo's words were sincerely meant, or whether it was merely an attempt to lull and mislead the authorities in Washington, and to frustrate our efforts to win American public opinion to our side.

We are far from falling into panic, but we shall avoid illusions. We have been in grave situations before, when our entire future hung by a hair, and came out unscathed. We should be able to endure new trials if such are in store for us. But we shall not exempt from responsibility those who by their policies may bring nearer or aggravate these orders. Today we are isolated in our region, but we are not alone in the world. Millions of our fellow Jews will stand by us in this struggle and will continue to support us with a brotherly hand. The more we here in Israel do with our own strength what is incumbent upon us, the more will we enjoy loyal and united support by diaspora Jewry. The more firm and united we stand on the political and military fronts, while at the same time strengthening our moral structure and the spiritual quality of our undertaking, the more will the best elements of humanity show sympathy for Israel, faith in its future, and willingness to help. [91]

[- - -]

Lavon received permission for a reprisal for [a terrorist attack against Ramat] Raziel.[92]

[- - -]

Tuesday, August 31

[- - -]

---

91 *Divrei Haknesset,* XVI:2547-51; translation above is from David Ben-Gurion, *Israel: A Personal History*, trs. Nechemia Meyers and Uzy Nystar (New York: Funk & Wagnalls, 1971), 438-39. In his speech, Sharett also spoke on the recently initialed Anglo-Egyptian Treaty for the evacuation of British bases in the Suez Canal Zone. Cf. *DFPI* 9, doc.357, n4. The complete English and Hebrew texts are in CZA A245/35/III.

92 On August 28, infiltrators from Jordan shot and killed one guard and wounded another in Moshav Ramat Raziel in the Judaean Hills. Morris, *Israel's Border Wars*, 309.

"Bat Galim" Sailing Delayed

Wednesday, September 1

[- - -] Went to the Knesset. [- - -] Spoke for 40 minutes. My jabs hit the mark. Praises (Ziama was happy; [received] notes from [visiting Ambassador Eliahu] Elath and Gideon Rafael). I edited the protocol immediately.

[Following are excerpts from PM Sharett's reply in the Knesset debate begun on August 30 (see entry for that date).]

In this debate quite a wide measure of unity was expressed regarding our response to the policy against which we must be fighting. At the same time, voices of controversy were heard as well, and all kinds of panaceas were advanced which can only lead us to the very opposite aim towards which are striving.

Some [Knesset] Members spoke as if the danger we are facing threatens us with a fundamental change of our situation, and as if, from the standpoint of our international policy, we find ourselves before a clean slate from which everything has been erased and it is in our power to write on it whatever we want. I will not be disclosing anything new if I say that, just as new technological innovations do not change an iota of the permanent laws of matter, energy and movement, so too do political changes, conflicts and struggles take place against the permanent background of fundamental facts of reality.

When MK [Moshe] Sneh [of the "Leftist Faction," later CPI] attempted from this podium to make a sham of the concept of "the open [free] world" [of the western democracies], he only reiterated his illogical contention, for his very speaking here was a clear proof of the crucial existence of the "open world." If an MK can come up and make a speech which is an anathema to 95 percent of the House; if his words are spoken, heard, taken down and published and all are allowed to listen to them – then such a phenomenon is possible only in the "open world." And if one is allowed to publicly attempt to expose the criminality and stupidity, so to speak, of Israel's state policy, then this, too, is possible only in the "open world." Moreover, if we, who are conducting the state policy which is totally rejected by MK Sneh, can expose the criminality and stupidity of a policy of a great and formidable power, as we see it, [- - -] then this too is possible only in the "open world." On the other hand, if a policy which decides the future of peoples and countries, and at times that of the entire world, is determined in closed rooms and then forced upon the people in the name of which, as it were, it is determined – and nobody is allowed to speak up against it or criticize it – then this is possible only in the "closed world" [of the Soviet bloc].

We are very much interested in the friendship of every people and nation, first and foremost, that of the big powers – which means the friendship of the Soviet Union too. But what are the prospects of this friendship which must be based on mutual foundations? Can we develop a full friendship with a power which maintains an abyss between us and its Jewish citizens? This power is holding in its hands an asset which, if it uses it, it will enormously enhance the mutual friendship between the two of us. But it chooses to not use it, and is thus directly and severely limiting such a friendship.

Suppose the Soviet Union opens up its consumer markets for our exports – how then would we be able to produce more without building new factories? And from where will we be able to get the necessary resources to build them? Whoever tells us: "Reject American grants and open up trade with the Soviet Union" is simply entangled in a contradiction.

We must conduct a well-considered policy, free of internal contradictions. One cannot ask American Jews to support us staunchly and, in the same breath, throw out slogans which can only demolish any possibility of acting hand in hand with them. One cannot speak loudly of immigration and settlement building and, in the same breath, oppose being "enslaved by the American grant."

The grant is given to us by the American Congress, by the elected representatives of the American people. It represents a response by a prosperous nation to the needs of a nation which is very limited in its resources while building its future. And we are deeply interested in relying on that nation in the present struggle facing us. Rejecting this grant of our own will and, at the same time, appealing to the American people to stand up against the policy of its government is, again, an obvious contradiction in which we are apparently being advised to become entangled by certain MKs [of the left].

What reason have we, as a state whose vital interests are now being endangered by American policy, to enter into a total rejection of America's global policy? Are we going to strengthen the power of our *hasbara* efforts aimed at the American people?

It's about time that each of us decides for himself what, in his opinion, the State of Israel should wish for at the present moment. True, there is always the question of what this state should be prepared to do in response to one calamity or another. But inasmuch as it is completely free in initiating action, what is its interest these very days? Is it peace or no peace? Is it stability or pandemonium? Is it building quietly, even if this is disturbed by border incidents or general turmoil?

We are once again faced with the deterioration and deformation of the Armistice Agreements. Much has been said already on this subject and I will not repeat myself now. But the basic problem is clear: What do we want? What is our own policy? Is our aim to stick to the Armistice Agreements, such as they are, so that we can get on with our building up of our state and buttressing ourselves? Or are we consciously interested in doing away with these agreements and in widening the bloody strife, letting the other side embark on adventurous moves? [Are we interested] in becoming entangled in more serious international conflict which nobody knows how it will end?

Our quarrel with the powers is acute and serious, for in practice they are encouraging the aggressor to take the road of war while, as far as peace is concerned, they are content with words alone. If that is not so – let them prove it in deeds, that is, by taking certain steps and by avoiding others. Let them not ignore warnings by a small but ancient people; let them not disregard the stamina of this small nation, deep-rooted in its land, a nation without which no peace and security can exist in the Middle East, nor [can they exist] at its expense.

Continuing our campaign vis-à-vis the powers and doing so wisely and efficiently, enhancing our assault on public opinion in the free world, strengthening our existing friendly ties and seeking new ones, unceasing efforts to buttress our position and power by harnessing the energies of the people of Israel and the support of the Jewish people all over the world – these are the guidelines of our policy.[1]

1 *Divrei Haknesset*, XVI:2571-2604.

[- - -] In the evening a meeting on a plan for *hasbara* in the US.

Thursday, September 2

[- - -] The incident [at Beit Liqya].[2] [- - -] Lavon phoned – the freeing of [Israeli] prisoners. Dayan at lunch with the generals.

Gideon Rafael – the ship ["Bat Galim" setting out from Massawa to Haifa via Suez, to test freedom of passage]: should we warn the Americans? The Arabic service of *Kol-Israel*. [- - -]

Friday, September 3

[- - -]

Tekoah about his troubles with Dayan. He was not invited to [the farewell] lunch [arranged by Dayan for Bennike on September 2]. Dayan's interventions in "the crisis" [between the Defense and Foreign Ministries over dealing with UNTSO]. What business is it of his? Dayan's attitude of vengeance, his threats: "If you make any arrangements, they will not work. I shall sabotage [them]." The DG [declared: Dayan is] a "MacArthur."[3] I: We must make an effort to be on speaking terms.

[- - -]

5:30 pm – meeting with Aubrey. He would like to be appointed minister without portfolio towards the end of 1955. [- - -]

Saturday, September 4

10:00 am – With Aubrey, Gideon and Yaacov to finish off the guidelines [see below, entry for September 5].

---

2 On the night of September 1/2, in an operation in retaliation for the murder of a guard at Ramat Raziel on August 28, IDF troops under Arik Sharon attacked the village of Beit Liqya in the Latrun area, killing 4 or 5 Jordanians and capturing 3 Legionnaires. Three Israeli soldiers were killed in the attack. See Morris, *Israel's Border Wars*, 309-10.

The incident, the first he was called upon to mediate, caused serious concern to General Burns, as he felt morally uncomfortable with Israel's thinly-disguised motive of kidnapping Jordanian Legionnaires in order to set up a prisoner exchange. In Amman, King Hussein summoned both British and US ambassadors, and spoke in the most forceful language yet heard by these envoys. The US State Department was also severely critical of the IDF action, as it came just as a new initiative for reducing tensions was being launched. See: Burns diary, September 2 and 3, 1954, LAC MG31G6 v.7; *FRUS 1952-1954*, docs.883, 890; Duke-Hussein talk, reported in Duke to FO, September 2, 1954, TNA FO371/111105 VR1091/189; Duke to Falla, September 4, 1954, TNA FO371/111074 VR1072/189; *DFPI* 9, doc.349 n.1.

3 Douglas MacArthur (1880-1964). CoS, US Army, during the 1930s. Commander of US Army in the Far East (1941-1945). Effective ruler of Japan (1945-1951). Led the UN Command forces in the Korean War (1950-1951). A controversial general, noted for his colorful personality.

1:30 pm – Meeting with [Tennessee Democratic Senator Estes] Kefauver, Russell, [Lincoln B.] Hale, Whiteman [*sic.*, probably Ivan B. White, the latter two of the US Embassy staff in Israel], Eshkol, Agron, Eytan. Had a short conversation with Kefauver. He is pressing for action. Will contact Eban. [Said] if they [the Democrats] win [in the Congressional interim elections of November], they will exert influence and the President will have to consult with them. They will enter the State Department and rejuvenate financial grants. [- - -]

Saturday night spent entirely on paperwork. Wrote to Lavon about the gossip over the prisoners. Wrote to Dayan on his failure to invite [Tekoah to the September 2 luncheon for Bennike].

Sunday, September 5

Cabinet meeting.[4]

[In his remarks before the Cabinet, Sharett linked the discussion on retaliations with the larger issues of Israel's campaign to block US arms sales to the Arabs:]

> It was only very recently that a Democratic leader made an impressive speech in our favor by which he, so to speak, launched our campaign. In addition, Democratic Senator Kefauver just came over here. The American Embassy was instructed to not let him out of its control and their people accompanied him wherever he toured the country. I first wanted to invite him over alone for lunch at my home, but when I became aware of that instruction and that he would be accompanied by several people from the Embassy, I invited, at the last moment, whomever I could reach in order that they would engage the people around him so that I could manage to talk with him privately for at least 10-15 minutes. And now, suddenly, in the midst of our campaign [in the US], we are creating a counterproductive fact! We are thus prompting the Americans to ask themselves if they can give us arms. I think that, after all, some thought should be devoted to the possibility of planning small-scale operations [instead of big ones]. I am aware that the mounting of reprisals, among other things, serves as a means of training our soldiers in real action; that it is much more than just an exercise. It also keeps the Army on the alert. But meanwhile a routine is being created. Reprisal operations are thus seen as justified in their own right, because they are playing an important part in training the Army. It is crucial that some effort must be made to break out of this routine and, perhaps, move along different rails.

In the afternoon I dictated the briefing to [the Israel Embassy in] Washington.

[Briefing and guidelines are reproduced below:]

> 1. In our public briefing and propaganda we should use negative slogans. Opposition to any arming of the Arab countries – first, because they cannot be relied upon to be

4 In addition to Sharett's remarks reproduced here, topics included Israel's participation in an international conference to be held in Germany and the raid on Beit Liqya. See WebDoc #24.

fighting along with the western democracies against a Soviet invasion and second, because these arms would serve them for attacking Israel. Strongly protesting against destroying the arms balance in the Middle East since it must undermine stability, endanger security and postpone peace. Warning against abandoning Israel as a result of making its enemies militarily preponderant and encouraging them politically and militarily to wage a war of revenge against Israel. Stressing the discrimination characterizing the State Department's attitudes towards the Arab countries and Israel: the Arab countries are given clear and public promises and formal ties are made with them, while negotiations with Israel are held in the back rooms without anybody being aware of their contents and binding character. Protesting the granting of economic aid to Egypt without stipulating the condition of the cessation of its economic boycott and maritime blockade against Israel, which means, politically, the recognition of the boycott and the blockade and, financially, the support of a state which is inflicting damage on Israel which the USA then covers by making a grant-in-aid to Israel.

In this campaign of briefing and propaganda, in as much as it is conducted and directed by us, no positive demands should be advanced for the time being, such as arms to Israel, guarantees against aggression, a defense pact and the like, so as not to become entangled in contradictions and weaken the impact of our attack by hastily suggesting an offer of compensation which will imply acceptance of official American policy.

2. A special effort should be made with the aim of influencing the Democratic Party to oppose a policy whose main aim is supplying arms instead of, first of all, concentrating on the stabilizing of the economic and social foundations of the Arabs and inculcating in them the principles of democracy. If people and circles are found that are unwilling to oppose the plans of arming in principle, but are prepared to castigate the discrimination against Israel, they should not be prevented from voicing their criticism in their own way.

3. The campaign of definitely opposing the State Department-Pentagon policy should go on even if it seems fruitless, for even if the aim of the current campaign is not immediately achieved, it will serve as warning for days to come by preparing the background and harnessing energies for future struggles. However, there is no room for giving up hope now that our propaganda campaign will not achieve at least partial results – by postponing the shipment of arms, limiting their scope, the addition of conditions, putting pressure on the Arab states to change their attitude towards Israel, and the like.

4. Following are guidelines for the continuation of talks with the Secretary of State:

(a) An appreciation of his goodwill, sincere sympathy and serious concern about Israel, which were obvious in his previous announcements, should be expressed.

(b) It should be explained patiently, but with utmost clarity, why the government of Israel cannot accept his soothing expressions and suggestions as resolving the problem. We are being faced with the creation of concrete and immediate facts in favor of Egypt, against which we are offered only vague promises for the future. The very evacuation of the British bases grants Egypt an enormous military advantage which seriously disrupts the balance in our disfavor. The supply of arms, gratis by the USA and by sale from Britain, will increase the gap. "Light arms" means, certainly, also mortars, machine guns and perhaps light guns – all of which cannot be ignored as tilting the balance against us. We have no idea of the quantity of these arms in the next two-three years. The very granting of them, even if we ignore their military value, is politically a prize to Egypt and a penalty for us. In the meantime, arms will be supplied to Iraq, Britain will continue arming Jordan, and tomorrow or the day after tomorrow Syria will become involved. Our security must be based on a total equilibrium with all our Arab neighbors. In view of the present situation, the promise to consider the possibility of granting us arms – how much or in what proportion is not clear – if the continuing of arms supply to Egypt would seriously disrupt the equilibrium between us and Egypt [- - -] – can by no means satisfy us.

(c) The principle of an arms balance in the region, as long as there is peace here, should be stressed by every means. This principle is one of the three bases of the [May 1950] Tripartite Declaration [WebDoc #1] and the clearest among them. It is now being violated. The beginning of this violation is perhaps frustrating, but the end of this process is foreboding. If the tendency now is to arm the Arab countries while they maintain a state of war against us, then, in spite of all goodwill towards us, it would be impossible to prevent a constant worsening of the balance and the widening of the gap which already exists, for the Arab countries are by far better able to absorb quantities of arms and military equipment than we are. Would we be promised arms in quantities equal to those supplied to all the Arab countries taken together, by far greater than our ability to absorb? If there is a serious and sincere intention to maintain a military balance, then the end result should be seen at present and consequently the dangerous process should be stopped at its beginning. Military support to Israel could perhaps act as a political compensation to us as against the political advantage to the Arabs resulting from the supply of arms to them; but Israel's security concerns can be allayed only by a clear obligation that no disruption of the balance will take place.

(d) Stress should be put on the absence of any concrete and binding guarantee for our security in face of the danger of Arab aggression. It should be pointed out that they are not suggesting a clear-cut defense pact. It would be very interesting to watch the response to this contention (a defense pact is, of course, an agreement that any injury to Israel's security is tantamount to an injury to the security of the US).

(e) In addition to the contention regarding the arms balance, it should be made clear that the incorporation of the Arab countries into a regional defense organization without, at the same time, some kind of a parallel commitment to Israel is by itself a very serious disruption of the balance of power.

(f) Our demand for military aid should not be raised at this stage. If they offer it, we shall ask them to clarify its dimensions and conditions so that we can evaluate it per se.

(g) As to [American] economic aid [to Egypt], we should denounce the discrimination between its stipulation on an arrangement with Britain and the absence of its stipulation on stopping the blockade on Israel. How can the Administration justify financial support to Egypt when, while determining its grant to Israel, it is compelled to take into consideration the financial loss caused by Egypt to Israel? Suppose this was just a mistake and the promise given by the Administration [to Egypt] cannot be taken back, but that promise did not include a specific sum. Is the US prepared to inform Egypt that, following the first symbolic instalment, it is awaiting the cessation of the blockade (i.e., among other things, letting Israeli ships and oil tankers [sailing to Israel] pass through the Canal without interference, and that otherwise further instalments would not be executed? Is the US prepared to inform us that it has served such a notice to Egypt and that it will staunchly execute this stipulation?

(h) With all due respect to the importance of the problem of free passage through the Canal, the Secretary of State should not be allowed to concentrate on this issue, thereby evading the main issue of the arming of the Arab countries. It is also necessary to prevent them from evading this issue by an attempt to impress us with promises regarding future gains from US prodding for peace in Cairo. Such attempts made by the US in Cairo should be commended, but at the same time it should be stressed that there is no certainty whatsoever that they will bear positive fruit. Consequently, the Americans can by no means present the chances of bringing about peace in the future, which may well be only wishful thinking, as justifying an American demand from Israel to ignore military facts being created against her, as well as tilting the political equilibrium to her detriment.

(i) The difference between American negotiating methods with Egypt (and Iraq) and with Israel should be denounced. The facts being created, or about to be created, in favour of Egypt are clearly seen by all, while the promises to Israel are given in back rooms. When the government of Israel wishes to publicly report its situation to the people it is responsible for, it is prevented from giving even a hint of the existence of secret promises, for if it does, it would be accused of sowing illusions or even cheating. Thus it faces a choice between revealing those promises in full and consequently being guilty of not keeping its word [to the US Administration], or not disclosing these secret promises altogether, and [being guilty of] not reporting the true situation [to its worried population]. In fact, as was already said above, the government is not convinced that, despite all the goodwill involved in the American promises which have been given so far, they can balance out the military facts established for all to see [in the Arab countries].

(j) The negative aspects of the Anglo-Egyptian Agreement from our point of view – the exclusion of Israel from the group of countries on which a new basis for defense is being established, and the recognition of the collective security pact of the Arab League as bona fide – should be denounced time and again. The approval of such serious blows to our security position resulting from US approval of that pact, and following which came the US expression of its readiness to recognize this pact as the appropriate instrument for the organizing of regional defense, should be denounced as well, and the same goes for the State Department's disavowal of its clear past promises [to us].

5. By no means should we aspire to conclude this phase of our negotiations with the US by an exchange of Notes. Such a conclusion would represent an intention to extricate from us an expression of satisfaction with American policy, or at least our acquiescence in it. We have no interest whatsoever in granting such a justification to the State Department's behaviour. Any justification by us would totally destroy the momentum of our public campaign, which has only started, and would kill off our chances of reaping any political harvest in the forthcoming [American] elections. If it were the case of a Note sent to us by the American government, to which we would give this or that answer, that should not be rejected. However, if the intention is to draft in advance an agreed wording of the two Notes, then we must frustrate this plan. Inasmuch as a final decision has not been taken within the State Department itself – whether to take the road of an exchange of Notes or that of a public announcement, it's better to push our interlocutors to the second option; then we shall respond to the pubic announcement according to its contents and wording. Be that what it may, we must beware of any step that may tie our hands and shut our mouths in our ongoing campaign.

M.S.[5]

Monday, September 6

[- - -] At the Foreign Ministry – We need someone in Turkey for high-level economic talks (including tourism) for the long-term; I'll write to Fischer [- - -]. With [Deputy DG] Levavi on Jerusalem: Emile will check into the matter and

5 Sharett, Guidelines for Continuing Political Activity in the US, September 5, 1954, *DFPI* 9, doc.350.

report back on two issues: France and the joint commission.[6]

Aliya from the Soviet Union. With Herzog on a reply to Russell regarding the [Beit Liqya reprisal] incident. [- - -] With Daniel Lewin on David Hacohen's trips. [- - -] With Abba Eban on the UJA and the [Beit Liqya] incident. [- - -]

9:30 pm [meeting of the Mapai] Political Committee [lasting] until 1:30 am [- - -][7]

Tuesday, September 7

[- - -]

Jerusalem, September 7, 1954

To: Minister of Defense
From: Minister of Foreign Affairs

In view of the rumors or reports concerning Jordan's intention to carry out retaliations for the latest incident, and the possibility that the target may once again be Israeli Jerusalem, it seems it would be worthwhile to issue an order calling for high degree of restraint in the event of sniping from the Old City Wall, should it be resumed.

In general, having come to the realization that the issue of Jerusalem has again entered a stage of high sensitivity from an international viewpoint, it is best we make sure not to ask for trouble by any imprudent action in this area. It might also be of benefit to propose again to the UN Chief of Staff to arrange for direct contact between the commanders in the Jerusalem area.

In the matter of the demilitarization proposal, I sent you the report of my conversation with the French ambassador. We are trying to ascertain the boundaries of the proposed demilitarization more precisely before conducting the mutual consultation.[8]

Wednesday, September 8

[- - -]

The *Kirya*, September 8, 1954

Foreign Minister,

To my regret, I must once again write about the behavior of your Ministry.

A few days ago, Mr Y. Tekoah assembled Israeli and foreign reporters in order to explain the border incidents, their nature and consequences. As a result of this meeting,

---

6 France and Britain had submitted a joint proposal for the demilitarization of the Holy Places in Jerusalem. See *DFPI* 9, doc.344 and below, entry for September 7.

7 Sharett opened the meeting by saying he had not much new to say after his last two speeches in the Knesset (August 30 and September 1). He then proceeded to deal with the subjects of arms from the US; free maritime passage in the Suez Canal; immigration of North African Jews; diminishing contributions to the UJA and the US government grants-in-aid. He then argued that Israel's military behavior could not help but be reflected in the US attitude towards her and have an impact on American readiness to provide her with arms. For extracts, see WebDoc #25.

8 *DFPI* 9, doc.351.

an article was published in *Davar*, and there were also reactions in other local newspapers. It is not clear to me what was published abroad.

Without going into the question whether wise statements were made at this meeting or not, I cannot accept the procedure whereby a representative of the Foreign Ministry, with neither my consent nor the CoS's, would handle matters that by general consent are under the authority of the Defense Ministry and the Army.

If it is a matter of "snatching," for the sake of keeping an even balance, I shall have to enjoin one of the Defense Ministry officials to gather the press and deliver explanations to them on matters of foreign policy. Of course, this "nice" procedure will only "enhance" the welfare of the state and its dignity.

P. Lavon
Defense Minister

Thursday, September 9

At the Foreign Ministry with Joe Tekoah, on the IDF spokesman, the CoS' talk with Burns,[9] and the CoS's letter to Burns. "I did not see the letter" [Tekoah complained.] With the DG on our reply to the *sharp rebuke* [orig. in English].[10]

Russell's invitation [to discuss US good offices re: sabotage from across the Egyptian frontier on an Israeli] pipeline [near Gaza.] Lavon came up to the apartment [in Tel Aviv; we agreed on] no retaliation in the south [for the pipeline sabotage]. [Discussed the activity of the] IDF spokesman. His reply to Burns in writing and orally.[11]

The ship ["Bat Galim" was given the order to leave Massawa for Haifa via Suez].[12]

Friday, September 10

[- - -] Talk with Russell at the office. They will approach Cairo [regarding recent border incursions] and publicize [the fact of this approach].

[Here follows Herzog's account of the conversation as reported to the Israel Embassy, Washington:]

9 The two men met on September 8, along with Vigier, Hommel and Ladas (UNSTO), Givly, Tekoah and Shalev, and dealt with the following items: 1. Protection for Kinneret patrols; 2. New appointments to chair MACs; 3. Sabotage from across the Egyptian lines; 4. Burns' suggestion to restrict IDF military exercises near the DL; 5. Meeting between Jerusalem Area Commanders. Shalev's minutes of the meeting are in ISA FM 130.16/2948/17.

10 The reference is to a Reuters report after a September 7 State Department press conference divulging the confidential information that the US government had issued "a severe reprimand" to Israel over IDF retaliations. Israel regarded herself as being the victim of a double-standard, since only quiet diplomacy was being used in Cairo. See: *DFPI* 9, docs.349, 357 and below, entry for September 10, 1954.

11 For Lavon's letter to Burns, September 8, see WebDoc #26.

12 The ship was scheduled reach the Canal around September 16. The MFA was hoping that Eban could hold his next meeting with Secretary of State Dulles before that happened. See *DFPI* 9, doc.354.

Jerusalem, 12 September 1954

PM ["Roham" in orig. English transliteration] invited Russell Friday, Tel Aviv, Herzog present.

PM detailed latest chain Egyptian violence, murder tractor driver [on Kibbutz Ruhama, on September 4/5], blowing up bridge opposite outpost protecting western flank Elath [*sic.*, for Eilat, on September 2], renewed breach pipeline Nir Am [on September 7]. Stressing extreme gravity two acts sabotage, PM said absence civilians on Egyptian side opposite Eilat and nature both operations led to conclusion Egyptian mil[itary] involved inspiration, planning, and very possibly execution. Conclusion supported by fact we lately apprehended Egyptian infiltrees who admitted [being] sent as spies by Gaza mil[itary] authorities. Eilat incident act naked provocation, demonstrative sabotage, without particular harm apart from offence our army's amour proper, but pipeline outrage much graver affecting existence settlements all around who dependent on water lifeline. Very serious matter if Israel had to acquiesce in recurrence such acts. In view US's ["Ahav's" in orig. English transliteration] increasing links with Egypt, PM wished query whether US would agree call Egypt's attention to most disturbing state affairs and publish this had been done. This was not request but question and PM wished add that so far as it lay within power organized authority, special care been taken prevent any imm[ediate] and direct reaction. "What Cairo does or fails to do indirectly involves you." PM mentioned theory this chain part carefully prepared plan provoke Israel into sharp and far-reaching action so she could be represented as aggressive party and her protests against arming Egypt thus nullified. Egypt might be told her game known and seen through.

Russell promising communicate to Washington, continued, since last meeting with PM he had been instructed raise two points with him and as didn't do so wished utilize present opport[unity] (1) Week before [Beit] Liqiya incident[13] Department of State cabled him report from US missions Amman, Damascus, Israel in course maneuvers intended attack to east, and asked whether suggestion of another gov[ernmen]t (ref[erring] clearly Britain) approach Isr[ael] ask for guarantee this would not be done, should be made. He replied negatively basing his assessment on fact Israel special efforts in US during past two months. Liqiya thus adversely affected his reputation. (2) Department of State requested he convey general feeling which Jernegan mentioned to Shiloah.[14] He had not done so as knew PM would hear from Shiloah on effect Liqiya might have on efforts US been making. "Fair and expedient say that Dep[artmen]t's extraordinary efforts put through what Dulles said to Eban and work out practical details for discussion on Eban's return had not been reciprocated". Mentioned Sharett's statement Knesset[15] and Eban's public statements here.[16] Could not say what would happen consequence Liqiya. Department of State felt she not in good position influence Egyptians towards peace with Israel or psychologically deal with question assuring Israel's security if no cooperation forthcoming in mutual effort.

After expressing regrets both for Russell's and for US-Isr[ael] relations sake Russell should feel his personal standing affected, PM continued Russell was perfectly right in saying manoeuvres not intended as incentive to launch attack against Jordan. Liqiya in no way connected with manoeuvres. Odds were it was direct result of killing at

13 See above, entry for September 2.
14 On September 1; see above, entry for September 2.
15 See above, entry for August 30.
16 Reference to Eban's news conference broadcast over *Kol-Israel*, September 2.

Ramat Raziel. While did not have details could say that in no way was anything as spectacular as suggested planned. Described cumulative tension on frontier from Mevo'ot Betar [*sic.*] to Raziel incidents.

On charge of lack reciproc[ity] replied US's line placed Isr[ael] Gov[ernmen]t in peculiar position. Approaches and undertaking to Arab countries publicly and above-board while assurances to Isr[ael] in camera. Isr[ael] gov[ernmen]t quandary still greater since assurances although prompted by sincere approach were by no means adequate offset effects of policy vis-à-vis Arabs which involved inter alia putting back clock of peace. In Knesset [debate] bound speak out true feelings but had done so with all reservations, localising and qualifying issue between Isr[ael] and US and setting it against background basic friendship, also acknowledging aid we had received from US. Confident Eban would explain situation fully to Dulles [during their scheduled talk on September 15].

Returning to main subject convers[ation] PM reiterated query whether US would talk to Egypt on acts of violence. Press interpreted Department of State's approach Israel on Liqya as "sharp rebuke."[17] Such language never quoted by press as having been used vis-à-vis Arabs although plain incontrovertible fact contemporary history initiative always came from Arab side. If US would not now react toward Egypt she would lay herself open to charge of discrimination.

Russell promised convey.[18]

Saturday, September 11

[- - -] With the DG and Tekoah on a reply to Burns: either us [the Foreign Ministry] or them [the Defense Ministry], but we are to decide the [final?] text. The [enlargement of our] UN delegation. [- - -]

Sunday, September 12

[- - -] Cabinet meeting. [- - -] Approval of the delegation [to the UN GA].[19]

I was asked [by Minister Dov Yosef] about the killing of two soldiers[20] – was it [a proof of the] failure of [our] reprisals? [We] also [discussed] the pipeline [sabotage].

[Following quotations are taken from Sharett's reply during the Cabinet meeting:]

It is clearly assumed that this was an action avenging our [Beit Liqya] reprisal operation for the killing of a guardsman at Ramat Raziel. The Jordanians had threatened

17 Cf. above, entry for September 9.

18 *DFPI* 9, doc.357 (orig. in English). For Russell's telegraphic report of this conversation, see WebDoc #27.

19 The delegation consisted of Aubrey Eban (head of delegation), Michael Comay (deputy head), David Hacohen (Israel's Minster in Rangoon), Dr Jacob Robinson (legal adviser, Israel Mission to the UN), Maurice Fischer (Israel's Minister in Ankara), Moshe Tov (Director, Latin America Division), Mordechai Kidron (deputy permanent representative to the UN), Zena Harman (assistant, Israel Mission to the UN), and Avraham Livran (assistant, Israel Mission to the UN).

20 *Davar*, September 12, 1954, reported two soldiers were killed in broad daylight by Jordanians who crossed into Israeli territory not far from the Latrun road.

us with a reprisal, but I assumed it would take place in Jerusalem, since they are aware that politically our situation there is more vulnerable than theirs. And indeed there was some shooting there one evening. Even before that I had contacted the Minister of Defense and asked him to see to it that a special order be issued to the Jerusalem garrison to keep cool. There was some firing from the walls and one Israeli was lightly wounded, but that was all. It was also assumed that by doing that the Jordanians had got satisfaction, since (a) in our reprisal a few of our men were killed and (b) we returned all three captives and two more captured in past IDF operations. But our fears came true. They intentionally attacked one of the IDF posts. During the same week two incidents occurred which put into question the efficacy of our reprisal operations. After our water pipeline [in the vicinity of the Gaza Strip] was bombed, we responded by a very effective action: the detonating of the Gaza water pump installation. If a reprisal operation should bring about positive results, this one surely had to. Two weeks passed and there was again a very successful blowing up of our water pipeline. After that I had a very severe conversation with General Burns. Last Friday I summoned Russell and I did not ask him for something or demand anything, but put a question to him: Egypt is about to receive economic and military aid from the US. The US thereby becomes morally responsible for actions Egypt takes or does not take. I am asking now: Is the State Department prepared to direct its Ambassador in Cairo to bring to the attention of the Egyptian authorities this act of sabotage, and to the sabotaging of a bridge near Eilat, and to clarify that the US government cannot accept such an act? Furthermore, is the US government prepared to announce publicly that it has approached the Egyptian authorities regarding this matter, parallel to what it announced regarding us?

I then added that these two acts of sabotage testified to an Egyptian tendency to provoke us into carrying out very severe reprisals, which will serve them in undermining our propaganda activity. We contend that they are an aggressive factor and that we are on the defensive, and they have an interest in provoking us to carry out reprisals in order to change this picture. One can still explain the sabotaging of the water pipeline by a wish to cause us damage, and indeed that action has caused us severe damage. But sabotaging an unimportant bridge near Eilat was carried out for the sake of sabotage. It was simply an act of provocation. I also said that if this sabotaging of the water pipeline continued, we would not be able to compromise on that, for it is one of our biggest national development projects. It's a lifeline for our people.

As to our own accounting of our reprisal operations, we must take notice that our reprisal operation after the Ramat Raziel incident brought about the killing of two soldiers of ours. This was caused by our reprisal action. It was carried out by the Arab Legion. The Legion took revenge for its killed soldiers.

It is true, as was publicized, that the number of murderous infiltrations has declined. It is reported that they went down to 15% of such acts committed last year. This is a result of several factors. One of them is the stationing of the Legion along the border. This has a preventive effect against infiltration, but it did not prevent the Ramat Raziel incident. We must take into account the fact that in carrying out reprisal operations we are engaging the Legion even we have no such intention. When we are operating against a village, when we are blowing up a building, when we are attacking the Jordanian Home Guard, the Legion immediately rushes in its troops to the spot and they immediately engage us in battle. So the fighting is against the Legion, and the Legion does its arithmetic. It does not want to let its casualties go on without responding. These are only thoughts to be considered. I am not suggesting any conclusion.

Monday, September 13

[- - -] Tekoah on Lavon; he postponed the sailing of the "Bat Galim" [from Massawa, Eritrea, to Haifa, via Suez] by one day only. Consultation with DG, Rafael, Tekoah – the crisis with the Army again reaching a peak. Who is going to maintain contact with General Burns? [- - -]

Dictated a letter to Lavon to postpone [the sailing of the "Bat Galim"] for a week. [- - -]

Jerusalem, September 13, 1954

To: Defense Minister
From: Prime Minister and Foreign Minister

I must request you to order most urgently that the sailing of the "Bat Galim" be postponed for a week, i.e., until Tuesday, September 21. I view this postponement as a necessity of the highest order pending Ambassador Eban's planned talk [on September 15] with Secretary of State Dulles. That talk should be carried out without the appearance of our ship at the entrance to the Suez Canal casting its shadow over it.

That we are merely exercising our incontestable right to send the ship through the Suez Canal is a consideration that does not escape me. But we know from experience that whenever we take such an initiative, the Americans contend that we have sabotaged their efforts on behalf of a settlement and peace, and have brought down the entire edifice they have built. I am willing to face the argument with them this time as I have withstood previous conflicts of this kind (the transfer of the Foreign Ministry to Jerusalem, the beginning of work on B'not Yaakov [water diversion project] and the like). However, I see no point in undermining the main argument we are conducting with them at present. Eban's talk with Dulles should be devoted principally to the arming of the Arab states and the disruption of the balance of power between us and them. We are by no means interested in dealing Dulles cards [to use] against us pending this meeting. He already has one card in hand and that is the Beit Liqya incident.[21] I do not wish to concede another card.

Since I am aware in advance that you may disagree with me, I must add for the sake of clarity that I view the passage of the ship through the Suez Canal as distinctly an operation of foreign policy and not a security measure. The Ministry of Defense is here serving as an executive agent, but it does not determine policy.

If after this explanation you are still unwilling to accept my opinion, I will have no choice but to convene a meeting of the Cabinet Foreign Affairs and Defense Committee tomorrow morning in order to decide the issue. I shall be very sorry if you should have to interrupt your short vacation in order to take part in this meeting, but under the circumstances I can see no alternative. Therefore, in case you should not see your way to acquiesce to my request immediately, I ask you to view this letter as an invitation to a meeting tomorrow morning at 9:00.[22]

Tuesday, September 14

Phoned Joe – Lavon has "cancelled" the sailing. Dayan's rationale.[23]

---

21 See above, entry for September 2.
22 *DFPI* 9, doc.358. Cf. Dayan, *Avnei Derekh*, 133.
23 Cf. Dayan to Lavon, September [14], 1954, IDF Archive (IDFA), file 636/56/33.

My additions. The press is full of [my interview in] the *US News & World Report (USNWR)*.[24]

A conversation with Teddy about Lavon's [militant] development; his reply to Burns, the publicity, the ship ["Bat Galim"]. In his opinion, he must go. [- - -] Ehud is filled with wrath at the [IDF] retaliations, etc. I said: "By all means, stir up peoples' thinking!"

Phone call from the CoS on the DG's letter to Burns regarding the concluding paragraph of Lavon's letter. [- - -]

At the Foreign Ministry – A cable from Abba, congratulating me [for the interview with the *USNWR*.] Met with Eliahu and Arthur on our line to adopt in London; how to speak with [Labour Party leader, Clement] Attlee and his colleagues, to attack Eden on exploiting public opinion for defending their policy. I resolved the complications over the delegation: Comay will be its deputy. With the DG on the ship ["Bat Galim"] and our reply to Burns. With Yaacov on an invitation [to send] lecturers [to the US] and news from Johnston.

In the afternoon with Joe Tekoah. He has spoken with Burns [and found him in a] peaceful state of mind. Dayan's elasticity. His dispute with Lavon regarding Lavon's letters to Burns. I said: "It's impossible to give up Dayan in our contacts with Burns." The article in *Ha'aretz*.[25] I said: "[It is written by] Gideon Rafael." I called *Ha'aretz*. Gross [admitted]: "Rafael!" [I put] *Shin-Bet* censorship [into action to prevent its publishing]. [- - -]

Worked all evening, until midnight, on my speech to the [Mapai Party] Central Committee. Eliahu ate at the President's home and came over to spend the night. I told [him] about Lavon [and he said Lavon] is unbalanced.

Wednesday, September 15

Ha'aretz did not publish [the article submitted by Gideon Rafael].

A consultation at the Foreign Ministry on North Africa.[26]

[- - -] Joe Tekoah [reported that] *Ha'aretz* [had issued] a "correction" – "political sources in Jerusalem"! No way! [- - -]

Thursday, September 16

[- - -]

24 E.g., *Davar*'s headline: "M. Sharett – Arming of Arabs Political Failure for US." The September 17, 1954, issue of the popular American magazine contained a feature interview (which took place on July 27) with Sharett by J. Fromm under the title: "Warning to the West: Don't Arm the Arabs." For excerpts of this article, see WebDoc #28.

25 Sharett was somehow informed of the contents an article criticizing the IDF's attitude towards Burns submitted to the newspaper. See below, Sharett's letter to Lavon dated September 23.

26 See *DFPI* 9, doc.356.

[Mapai Central Committee meeting] in Rehovot from 4:00 to 9:00 pm. I spoke after BG. His speech [main points]: no need to exaggerate, sovereignty, and reprisals.[27]

[Following is the concluding portion of Sharett's speech:]

In view of all this it is incumbent on us to devote much thought to our economic planning geared to a timetable [- - -]. Are we going to bide time till an economic crisis erupts, or begin planning now for how we shall deal with possible future gaps between expenditure and income?

I must remind you in this context about our state's obligation to pay compensation for a large number of Arab landowners [whose property was confiscated by the State of Israel following 1948 War]. True, no such obligation stands forever; it was given in a certain period against a certain background. If steps are taken to see that it is carried out, it will be implemented; if the landowners refrain from demanding it, if there is a refusal to create circumstances conducive to our carrying out our obligation, it will evaporate in due time. For the time being we admit this obligation, but we are not prepared to acknowledge it forever. The Arabs of Palestine and our neighboring countries have already missed opportunities more than once – all of us remember their opposition to President Truman's proposal of allowing 100,000 displaced Jews in post-war Europe to immigrate to Palestine,[28] their opposition to the partition plan of the UN GA in 1947 and to various proposals we advanced regarding the solution of the Arab refugee problem. They should now seriously take care not to miss the carrying out of our obligation in this matter. They also should be aware that we shall by no means consider payment at a time when they are daily causing us financial losses by blockade, boycott and all sorts of actions undermining our economy. It should also be clear that these Arab lands came into our disposal not as a result of purchasing them in the free market, but as a result of bloody war, of aggression and invasion, of a war for which we paid an enormous cost in blood and resources. All this will be taken into account, but we ourselves should be cognizant of the fact that for the time being our obligation [to offer compensation] is valid.

However, above all, we should be aware that our population is not going to stand still. Apparently, we are now facing a new wave of immigration. I have no idea what internal changes are going to take place in Morocco and Tunisia and how Jews there will react to

27 For extracts of Ben-Gurion's remarks at the meeting, see WebDoc #29.
Sharett's speech was similar to the one he delivered to the Mapai Council on August 21 (see above, entry for that date). Among other things, Sharett repeated his appraisal of Israel's isolation and vulnerability, and urged realism in his listeners' expectations of the extent of diaspora Jewish support. He also presented the hard facts of Israel's difficult struggle for economic self-sufficiency, and reminded his audience that, on top of everything else, they must also factor in compensation for Arab property losses during the 1948 war.

28 The recommendation was first made in August 1945 by President Truman's envoy, Earl G. Harrison, following his visit to European Displaced Persons (DP) camps. The proposal became part of post-war discussions on US and British postwar policy, and was included among the recommendations of the Anglo-American Committee of Inquiry. For details, see: M. J. Cohen, *Palestine and the Great Powers, 1945-1948* (Princeton: Princeton University Press, 1982), 55-60, 113-14, 119-22; Allis Radosh and Ronald Radosh, *A Safe Haven: Harry S. Truman and the Founding of Israel* (New York: HarperCollins, 2009), 92-111, 188-96.

them as far as *aliya* is concerned. But I do know one thing: the *aliya* of the multitudes of these Jews is a matter of a historic necessity. It is only logical to think that the processes which took place in other countries will not skip over these two countries. We must read the writing on the wall, and be prepared.

Clearly, we shall have to advance a new demand for support to Jews abroad. But the efficacy of our appeal to them depends, first and foremost, on our own efforts. [- - -] If we are now asking Jews abroad to unite in supporting us politically [against American supply of arms to the Arab countries] despite the difficulties involved, and to ignore all kinds of divisions among themselves for our sake, surely we must ask ourselves if we can allow ourselves to undermine all that by demonstrating at this very time a new disunity in our country.

Let me sum up with four slogans: More planning, more productiveness, more economizing, and more volunteering for aiding the new immigrants' settlements!

[- - -] Returned to Tel Aviv dead tired and dying of hunger.

Received a cable from Abba on his talk with Dulles – extremely worrying.[29]

[- - -]

Friday, September 17

8:30 - 10:30 am – A tense meeting at the Foreign Ministry with Lavon, Golda, Ziama. My summation: [UNTSO is the only political instrument available for Israel's contact with the other side]. I told Golda about Dayan's treatment of General Burns. She was shocked.

[- - -]

The Elaths took their leave. Eliahu [spoke] about [Shimon] Peres [probably on his direct contacts with the French Ministry of Defense]. He said: "For God's sake, [responsibility for dealing with] UNTSO [should lie with] the Foreign Ministry." I explained why not. Eliahu [complimented me for] my patience and my dedication.

At the apartment – Palmon, Maklef, Eppy, Isser (on Dayan), failure in Germany. [- - -]

Saturday, September 18

[- - -]

In the evening the DG, Arthur and Gideon on the letter.[30] Sat over my papers until 1:00 am (the ship).[31]

---

29 *DFPI* 9, doc.359; cf. *FRUS 1952-1954*, doc.893. For Israeli reactions to Eban's report, see *ibid.*, docs.363-365.

30 Possibly the much-delayed letter that would be sent, over Eytan's signature, on September 23, in reply to Burns' letter of September 7; see below, entries for September 20, 21, 22.

31 On September 16, Eban had cabled from Washington asking that the "Bat Galim" not sail for a further two weeks. *DFPI* 9, doc.362.

Sunday, September 19

[- - -]

During the Cabinet meeting still more questions. Extensive debate [regarding Sharett's attack on press leaks by ministers of their questions to the PM during Cabinet meetings]. [Visiting Ambassador from Paris Jacob] Tsur's report was interesting and detailed, preparing our minds for the question of *aliya* [from North Africa.]

[At the end of Ambassador Tsur's report, Cabinet minutes record PM Sharett as making the following remarks:]

> I would like to add a few words. It was decided in the Coordinating Body to differentiate between regular *aliya* from North Africa, which would go on naturally according to selection criteria, and rescuing *aliya* (aimed at extricating Jews under threat). The second *aliya* applies mainly to southern villages in both Morocco and Tunisia. These are not Jewish villages; these are villages in which there are Jewish communities which are like islands in the middle of an Arab sea. The French say that they cannot quickly send help to such remote villages – it can take 24 hours before news about a persecution arrives. It is estimated that, by the end of 1954, 15,000 people from these two countries would emigrate under regular *aliya*, and 25,000 under rescuing *aliya*, which, although under more lenient selection rules, still prevents tuberculosis victims, the insane, etc., from emigrating. Possibly, by the end of 1954, we shall have to absorb 40,000 people within a year and a half or less.

[- - -] In the afternoon Tekoah discussed Dayan – I told him of the arrangement [with the IDF concerning relations with UNTSO].

Monday, September 20

G. R. on [PM] N[uri] S[a'id][32] in London.[33]

I cabled Elath about a proposal for *non-aggression* [orig. in English] as the seed of an initiative to counteract a renewed flurry of activity by the Arabs.

I drafted a letter to Burns.[34]

[- - -] Tons of paperwork. A conciliatory cable to Aubrey, a cable on the final decision about [the sailing in the coming days of] the ship ["Bat Galim" towards the Suez Canal].[35]

Tuesday, September 21

[- - -] At 10:00 am with the Knesset FADC. Tsur spoke on *aliya* [from North

32 Nuri al-Sa'id (1888-1958). Iraqi politician, held various key cabinet positions and served eight terms as PM under the British Mandate and later in independent Iraq.

33 Cf. record of talk between Selwyn Lloyd and Nuri Sa'id, September 20, 1954, TNA FO371/111074 VR1072/203. See also below, entry for September 26 (Sharett's report to Cabinet).

34 Possibly a delayed response to Burns' letter of September 7 – See *DFPI* 9, doc.352.

35 *DFPI* 9, doc.368. Cf. *ibid.*, doc.369.

Africa].[36] Questions [were raised].

[Following are extracts from Sharett's concluding remarks:]

We should be prepared for catastrophe, but we must take a constructive approach. We must take care and refrain from a deterministic approach. There are indeed historical processes, but there are also facts which slow them down. The process of independence there can take four, five, six years. Meanwhile, factually, Tunisian and Moroccan Jews are not taking flight. True, the number of those registering for *aliya* is higher, but possibly not all of those registered are prepared to leave now. There is also the problem of preventing immigrants from returning, but one should not become alarmed by this phenomenon. It is evident in all countries absorbing immigration. It is called "back-wash." I do not consider this as a major problem.

The problem is preventing "un-immigration." When speakers here said: "Let us bring the tens of thousand of North African Jews and put them in camps and, come what may, American Jews will arise and contribute more money," I am afraid these Jews will not come over. For the same as *aliya* should encourage contributions, so *aliya* must encourage *aliya*. Immigration will enhance immigration if it becomes evident that the immigrants can make a living. But if they experience all kinds of complaints, there will be no *aliya*.

When will the push of *aliya* become stronger than the hardships of making a living? When Jews in North Africa face massacres. If there are no massacres there will be no *aliya*, and the mood prevailing now among North African Jews is not a fear of slaughter tomorrow. Therefore there is logic in saying that we still have time on our hands for some planning – planning both here and there. For instance, I am a staunch supporter of what is called "selection," especially when there is, in any case, a big reservoir. For years now we have been "breaking our heads" over how to bring over eight Jewish families from Albania, for how can we abandon the elderly there? But when we are talking of hundreds of thousands – and nobody suggests absorbing hundreds of thousands within one year – it would be a crime and sin to fill up the country with the sick [with tuberculosis], crippled, lepers, madmen and deranged old people. It seems cruel – shall we let them die there? It is not. We have always existed on pennies, and those pennies should be invested in creating work, in educating the young. They should not be thrown out for nothing.

Therefore we must, every hour every time, have in mind a definite operative number of immigrants. At present the number is 40,000. For bringing over this number we turn on several wheels, here and in America. If these wheels forge ahead and we can bring over 60,000 – let us do that; if 70,000 – let us do that. The number of 40,000 is not scientifically based, but it was reached by people like the Minister of Finance, the treasurer, the chairman of the Absorption Department of the JA, and the Minister of Labor.

I have never visited North African communities, but I know something about the situation there. The vast majority of Jews, both in Tunisia and Morocco, are concentrated in towns and townlets; a minority lives in villages. I understand that when talking about villages, the entire community must be taken out, even though when you are taking out 200 families at once this cannot be done quietly, as the French ask us to do. A commotion takes place: "The Jews are leaving!" This drives the Arabs to voice

36 The FADC dealt uniquely with the subject of *aliya* from North Africa. Tsur, the first and main speaker, gave a very long, detailed report. Some members of the committee contended that because the North African countries would soon reach independence, a special effort had to be carried out to encourage *aliya*. Sharett summed up the discussion.

opposition and undermines our control of the situation. But what about our activity in Casablanca or Marrakesh? Would we take out an entire block or perhaps the entire city? Clearly, one must be careful to take out a certain composition of people, to see to it that there will be among them as many people of means and professions as possible, to see to it that the composition is well balanced. One must then act on the basis of a plan outlined so that it fits the entire Jewish community there.

We have no interest in doing all this while constantly quarreling with the French. Anyway, if the French see our activity as causing them harm, then our entire project will be lost. They will undermine our actions, and they will under no circumstances agree that the *aliya* process be accompanied by public announcements, intensive publicity and the like.

How can you raise money without publicity? How can you otherwise approach American Jewry? It is a question of "hot ice." Quite recently I met with [Pierre] Mendès-France. When I tried to explain this problem to him, he said: "Yes, but without publicity. It must be dome with caution – carefully and quietly." Somehow we will have to act accordingly.

In closing I would like to inform committee members that this meeting has taken place behind closed doors. It must not happen that there will again be all kinds of bombshells in the press resulting from this meeting.

[Spoke to] Givly about the ship ["Bat Galim"] and the orders that were issued.

In the afternoon Walter and Joe [worked on] the letter to Burns [see below, entry for September 22]. Again things are murky. [UN] Observers will be patrolling; a fear of clashes. Dayan [is convening] a conference of [newspaper] editors. [Sent] briefing cables to London and Washington [embassies] about the ship. [- - -] Michael [Elizur] phoned about Selwyn Lloyd's statement [offering British] mediation. My reply: direct negotiations.[37]

[- - -] At night Walter [came by and] we both worked on the aide-memoire [to the British Government re: the Anglo-Egyptian agreement on evacuating the Suez bases].[38]

I approved [Foreign Ministry] appointments to the US.

Wednesday, September 22

The press [carried reports of] Selwyn Lloyd['s offer of good offices] and my response.[39]

I accompanied Golda to Lod [Airport] with a briefing for [her visit to] the US.

[- - -]

37 For a discussion of Lloyd's statement in his meeting with Arab Ambassadors on September 17, and his offer of "good offices" for resolving Arab-Israeli differences, see Caplan, *Futile Diplomacy* IV: 73-75; TNA FO371/111074 VR1072/202; *DFPI* 9, doc.374.

38 See *DFPI* 9, doc.376.

39 "Britain Offers its Mediation for Attaining Peace Between Israel and the Arab Countries" (*Davar*); "Britain Proposes to Mediate Between Israel and the Arabs" (*Ha'aretz*); "Britain Offers to Mediate Israel-Arab Differences" (*Jerusalem Post*). Cf. "British Reply to Arabs – Seeking Peace on Israel's Borders," *The Times* (London).

At the Foreign Ministry for a [phone] conversation with Elath. Completed drafting a reply to Burns.[40]

At home, a phone call with Elath regarding [his meeting with] Eden.[41]

Tekoah [reported] on Burns' letter to Dayan – a very clever formulation.[42]

In the evening Herzog, the DG and G.R. – I told them about the arrangement [with the Ministry of Defense]. Eppy phoned with "Lavon's position on a reply." I said: "I'll read it. Tomorrow Tekoah will join in."

September 22, 1954

Major-General E.L.M. Burns,
Chief of Staff, UNTSO
Jerusalem

Dear General Burns,

1. This is to confirm receipt of your letter of September 20, 1954, which requires study.

2. I must, however, inform you immediately that our opposition to the carrying out of patrols in Jerusalem or to any other action by United Nations Observers not in accordance with the General Armistice Agreement, as expressed to you by me in writing and in conversation[,] has been confirmed again, after further consideration.

Yours sincerely,
Moshe Dayan, Rav-Aloof
Chief of General Staff, IDF[43]

Thursday, September 23

In the morning with Tekoah. I was about to give instructions, but there was no point in view of a copy of Lavon's letter and Givly's apology. All of a sudden we have a crisis, more acute than ever [over contact with UNTSO]. [- - -] I wrote to Lavon.

Jerusalem, September 23, 1954

To: Defense Minister
From: Prime Minister

1) I have seen a copy of the Chief of Staff's letter yesterday to the UNTSO Chief of Staff. Contrary to our understanding this letter was drawn up without the participation of Yosef Tekoah. Furthermore, this was done in full disregard of what I said to your personal secretary over the telephone last evening – when he notified me what you had in mind to reply – that I hadn't yet read General Burns' letter, that I would read the letter by

40 See *DFPI* 9, doc.381.

41 See *DFPI* 9, doc.375; Eden to Evans, September 22, 1954, TNA FO371/111074 VR1072/209.

42 Burns complained to Dayan about Israeli police obstruction of the movements of a UN Observer investigating stone-throwing on September 20, contrasting the incident with one the following day when the same Observer was able, with cooperation on all sides and to everyone's delight, to rescue two turkeys that had strayed into the "no man's land." Burns to Dayan, September 22, 1954, ISA FM 130.02/2425/9.

43 ISA FM 130.02/2425/9.

morning, and that Yosef Tekoah would participate in drawing up the reply this morning after receiving instructions from me.

2) I would like to note especially that the reply to the UNTSO Chief of Staff was signed and sealed evidently under the assumption that it was written in English.

3) Since it has become clear that the understanding reached between us is insubstantial in its results – and this not only in light of the above-mentioned letter – I have decided to bring the settlement I have in mind concerning the spheres of authority in this whole matter of contact with the UN Observers' staff before the Cabinet for approval. I would have been ready to do so this coming Sunday, but I understand that you will not be able to participate at this meeting due to your vacation. On the following Sunday I myself will be on vacation, but due to the importance and urgency of the matter I will come to the meeting and submit my proposals.

4) Until the matter is cleared up at the Cabinet meeting and a decision is made in regard to it, I hereby determine that no letter be sent to the UNTSO Chief of Staff before I have seen its draft and confirmed it. I also hereby determine that until the Cabinet's decision no political briefing shall be given by the IDF Spokesman or by anyone else from the General Staff to the press on armistice affairs and our relations with the UN staff, whether publicly or behind the scenes. I reiterate: every suggestion that you or the General Staff may have in this area will be transferred to the Foreign Ministry.

[- - -]

[Received] a cable from Elath on his talk with Eden.[44]

[- - -] Phone call to Elath: What is the meaning of N[uri] S[a'id's latest moves] – [Was Nuri maneuvering towards] Iraqi-Syrian unification?[45]

[- - -]

Friday, September 24

[- - -]

The CoS's statement [against UNTSO border patrolling] in the press. – He claimed they violated our sovereignty. No news on the ship ["Bat Galim"]. [- - -]

Press conference [summoned by] the Chief of Staff? [No] coordination! Later [I discussed it] with Isser [who said]: "Fire him!" [Discussed] relations with Dayan with Joe [who claimed] the CoS himself was relenting. [- - -] In the afternoon I decided that the UN Observers [problem be discussed and decided] in Cabinet,

---

44 *DFPI* 9, doc.382. This cable commented on his original report of September 22, and focused on the active role played by Nuri Sa'id in London. See also below, entry for September 26 (Sharett's report to Cabinet).

45 See Colin Reid, "Irak Move for Arab Peace with Israel – Observance of UN Terms for Jerusalem a Condition," *Daily Telegraph*, September 17, 1954. In his discussions at the FO, Nuri hinted that the Arabs might accept a final settlement with Israel based upon the 1947 UN partition boundaries, and British officials sent feelers in Israel's direction. See Lloyd to Troutbeck, September 24, 1954, TNA FO371/111074 VR1072/203; Shuckburgh-Elath conversation, October 1, 1954, reported in *DFPI* 9, docs.392-393, and in TNA FO371/111075 VR1072/216.

to which the CoS would be invited. [- - -]

[Spoke] to Shamai about my assumptions regarding N[uri] S[a'id], which were subsequently confirmed in a cable from Gazit.[46] [Held a] press conference [on Nuri Sa'id's London overtures].[47]

7:30 – Return to Jerusalem. I thought about Iraq-Syria unification as solution of the peace problem. [- - -] With the DG [I discussed] the idea [of Syria-Iraq union]. He wanted to broaden [the discussion to include] the partition of Jordan, but I rejected that.

Saturday, September 25

[- - -]

With G.R. on the idea [of using Iraq-Syria unification as a move towards peace.] N[uri] S[a'id] is prepared to settle [Palestinian] refugees [in Iraq]. The unfreezing of blocked [accounts] will be added to the equation.

Joe Tekoah on the CoS. He had consulted with him personally on the formulation of the IDF spokesman's [statement] on Friday morning, as well as the text of the IDF spokesman's [statement] on the prevention [of free movement] of UN Observers. Three incidents had taken place. Admiration among the General Staff at my reply [to Lavon on September 23, see above]. I told Joe to carry on contact with him pending reaching a decision. Eppy told Joe that Lavon "regrets" his letter [to Burns which was sent] contrary to the arrangement between us. Invited the CoS to a meeting.

Again with G.R. regarding Barclays Bank. We reviewed N[uri] S[aid's initiative]. He spoke of resettling refugees. The Arab countries are in a state of turmoil. I said: "It's the first time [that the Arabs have] an interest [in making peace with Israel]."[48]

G.R. again in the evening. [- - -]

[Worked on my] papers – cables about N[uri] S[a'id], our statement on China [at the UN],[49] response to Selwyn Lloyd.

---

46 Mordechai Gazit (1922-2016). Born in Istanbul. Brought to Palestine in 1932. Joined MFA in 1949. First Secretary, Israel Embassy, London (1952-1956). Chef de bureau under FM Meir (1956-1959). Later DG MFA and PMO; Israel Ambassador to Paris.

47 For the British Ambassador's report on Sharett's press conference, see WebDoc #30.

48 Sharett truly felt that the current juncture represented an unprecedented window for Arab leaders to seek a peace settlement with Israel. See also *DFPI* 9, doc.388.

49 On September 21, Eban had voted in favor of a US resolution to not consider the question of China's representation during the current (ninth) session of the UN GA. Eban took this decision (which was not consistent with Israel's previous votes on this question) on his own responsibility, in fact disobeying his instructions from Jerusalem. See *DFPI* 9, doc.378; Brecher, *Israel, the Korean War and China*, 66-68, and *Decisions in Israel's Foreign Policy*, 143-45.

At midnight with Teddy. I poured out my bitterness over the situation. [He told me] Lavon was "sorry" and that it was Lavon who ordered Givly to apologise. He [Lavon] had asked Teddy to convince me not to bring the matter before the Cabinet. I said: "All trust [between us] is gone, perhaps I should resign in order to demonstrate the seriousness of situation[?]" Why do I get so entangled? Perhaps I am the one to blame[?]

The N[uri] S[a'id] matter: Should I go to Sde Boker [to consult with BG]? I pored over all this till 3:30 am.

Sunday, September 26

Got up at 7:30. Eppy reported that two Israelis were murdered and two wounded [near Beit Shikma in western Negev]. [- - -] [Sat] with David Hacohen on his report [to the Cabinet] on [entering into diplomatic relations with Communist] China. At the Cabinet meeting [- - -] he made quite an impression.[50]

I reported on the CoS and Tekoah, Burns' press conference, CoS's threat of resignation. [- - -] I suggested a solution. Dayan accepted it, and will invite Burns. I protected Lavon.[51]

[In the following excerpt from the Cabinet meeting Sharett deals with Nuri Sa'id's London overtures:]

> We will try to find out Nuri Sai'd's intentions, for it appears that he has come to the conclusion that any attempt to unite Syria with Iraq without making peace with Israel will spark a war with Israel, resulting with Israel's further expansion. If this assumption is right – and indeed in a cable I received [from London] it was said that in a conversation with an Englishman Nuri told him that it [peace with Israel] will facilitate unification of Syria and Iraq – then this is the first time we are witnessing a clear Arab interest in peace with Israel. Up till now we have not seen any Arab leader – except the King of Jordan who wants an outlet in Haifa – who shows a geopolitical interest in making peace with Israel. It seems Nuri does not see our threats as empty ones. Nuri is certainly an Arab patriot, at least an Iraqi patriot. His patriotism is interwoven with his personal ambition. Incorporating Syria into Iraq is his life's dream; he was already politically active during WWI. He is now approaching seventy and with age he becomes more desperate to achieve results, and thus he is able to pay a higher price. I am familiar with this phenomenon, because I found it characterizing people much closer to us, such as King Abdullah and our late President. Nuri is burning

---

50 Immediately following the meeting, Sharett cabled Eban regarding Israel's stance on the China question at the UN. *DFPI* 9, doc.385. Hacohen's memoir expressed bitter disappointment with Sharett, the Foreign Ministry and the Cabinet for not sharing his enthusiasm for moving quickly towards establishing full diplomatic relations with China during 1954 and 1955. *Time To Tell*, 230-45.

51 At the Cabinet meeting Dayan gave a detailed report in which he explained that Burns wanted his observers to enjoy free movement around the country without any IDF permission. Dayan said this was not included in the UN decision creating UNTSO. Sharett generally agreed with him, but clearly wished to prevent a deterioration of relations with Burns. He suggested that Dayan invite him for a talk with the participation of a MFA representative, and Dayan agreed.

with his urge to see Iraq bridging the Persian Gulf with the Mediterranean. He does not need the territory of Jordan for that purpose. If he can add Tripoli [on the Mediterranean in northern Lebanon, close to the Syrian frontier] to Basra [in southern Iraq, near the Arabian/Persian Gulf], his dream [of Fertile Crescent unity] comes true.

After the meeting Dayan discussed retaliation [for the Beit Shikma incident] with me. [He suggested] an attack on Gaza. I said not immediately, and that [the decision would] not be [taken] by myself alone. He said: "In this case, the whole thing is cancelled." I thought to myself: [Do we need such a retaliation now, on the eve of convening the] UN GA, Burns [just appointed UNTSO CoS], sailing of the "Bat Galim", [our] peace offensive, [our relations with] the USA? We agreed that the MFA would reply to Burns.

At 4:00 [I met] with UN and USOM [US Operations Mission] personnel. 250 [people attended], atmosphere was excellent. [- - -] Gideon telephoned [to say] they had closed the deal and signed with Barclays Bank [for unblocking frozen Arab assets].[52]

I told him there would not be a retaliatory operation. He said, "Maybe [we should contact Mahmoud] Azmi?" [We] also [talked about] the ship ["Bat Galim"].[53]

[- - -] Tekoah and Michael [Elizur came by with] a draft [press communiqué] that I cancelled and rewrote from scratch. When they returned I dictated the English [version].[54]

Drafted cables to Abba – no retaliation, but ... – and to Eliahu [regarding] Nuri [Sa'id]. [Perhaps we can contact him through Richard] (Cross[man?])[55]

Monday, September 27, *Erev* Rosh Hashana

Straight to the Foreign Ministry Finished off some business. News received from the ship; [the "Bat Galim"] is expected [to reach Suez] tonight. [- - -]

Tuesday, September 28, Rosh Hashana

In the morning Shamai called to say that the ship ["Bat Galim"] has arrived at Suez. Canal officials boarded it routinely. Then, Tekoah [reported], radio communication went dead. We are awaiting word from Cairo.

Moshe Dayan [informed me] of the flock [of Kibbutz Ein Hashofet stolen by infiltrators].

---

52 See *DFPI* 9, doc.386.

53 See *DFPI* 9, doc.387.

54 Possibly the official government statement on the unblocking of frozen Arab assets. See Editorial Note, *DFPI* 9, doc.386.

55 Richard Crossman (1907–1974). British Labour leader and MP. Pro-Zionist. Member of the Anglo-American Committee of Inquiry for Palestine, 1946.
See *DFPI* 9, docs.387-388. Elath had recommended the use of Crossman as a go-between for contacts with Nuri (*DFPI* 9, doc.382).

Shall we issue a press release about the ship? After consultation with the DG and G.R. we decided to wait one day. At 3:00 pm Rafael reported the [Egyptians' claim that the "Bat Galim" crew had] "fired" [on an Egyptian fishing boat], etc. [- - -] We composed a press release, cabled our embassies and legations. I edited the English version, gave it teeth, as well as the Hebrew one. Broadcast at 6:00 pm. In the evening [came] an Egyptian statement that was more moderate.[56]

Wednesday, September 29

[At the Weizmann Guest House, Rehovot] At 10:00, a discussion for two and a half hours [with Moshe Dayan] – the Bedouin of Be'er Sheva, [- - -] the [Ein Hashofet] flock has been returned![57]

The whole world is taken [with the "Bat Galim" affair]. Reuters is reporting from Cairo. The ship's captain's denials; only revolvers. We: "Only one revolver." [*Ha'aretz* correspondent Moshe] Medzini [reports] from the UN: "Nobody believes it." Arabic broadcast at 2:15, quite bitter, ended with a threat.

Thursday, September 30

The flock was not returned. No news from the ship. Waves in the world. [- - -] *Ma'ariv* [published] an attack on the release of the frozen [refugee] assets. The DG may see Burns about the flock – they had already seen him and Shalev will see him tomorrow.

Friday, October 1

At the Foreign Ministry. We must demand a discussion [on the "Bat Galim" seizure] in the Security Council.[58]

[- - -]

With Joe on new troubles: Shots [by IDF soldiers were fired at UN Observer Colonel Charles] Brewster's car. A strong letter by Burns.[59]

Problems in the EIMAC [We discussed] the idea of not participating if [the untenable accusation against] the ship ["Bat Galim" firing on an Egyptian fishing

56 For the Egyptian Foreign Minister's brief account of the "little [shooting] incident" on the arrival of the "Bat Galim", as given to the US Ambassador, see *FRUS 1952-1954*, doc.899. On this date, Ambassador Eban issued a protest over the seizure of the ship to the President of the UN SC. See *DFPI* 9, doc.389.

57 This meeting, and the episode of the flock, is described in greater detail below, entry for October 26. This report of the early return of the flock turned out to be incorrect.

58 See Eban to MFA, October 2, 1954, *DFPI* 9, doc.394; Eban to President of the SC, October 4, 1954, *DFPI* 9, doc.395.

59 Burns to Dayan, September 30, 1954, ISA FM 130.02/2425/9. On October 20, Brewster would replace Hutchison as head of IJMAC.

boat is maintained.][60]

With Arthur about an appeal to the British. Afterwards [I met with] Yosef Avidar [to discuss] an operation [against] the village [of Paku'a, on the other side of the border, in the area of Kibbutz Ein Hashofet] and the Legion [in retaliation for the flock stolen from Ein Hashofet] – [the idea is to take] people [hostage] against the sheep. I felt I shouldn't decide alone and called for a consultation.

Walter reported on his talk with Russell [in accordance with] my instructions.[61]

Burns is sullen and displeased. He's evading dinner with Dayan [because of the shooting against UN Observers in] the Old City [of Jerusalem]. [- - -] Arthur [commented] on disasters [orig. English] following the cancellation of the trip to Mount Scopus. Dinner at Meyer Weisgal's.

Saturday, October 2

With Ziama on Lavon's problem – moral and political. I have no trust in him. How can I allow this to continue? And, if I actively intervene, what would be the repercussions in the party? Ziama will go to BG [to see whether BG would agree to replace Lavon as Defense Minister]. "Meanwhile [BG advised] don't bring this up in Cabinet." I said: "Look, Nehru [has recently announced that he] is tired. So am I. I cannot start up all over again with BG."

---

60 "The Egyptians claimed that the 'Bat Galim' had opened fire and killed several people. The UNTSO found no substantiating evidence: the ship was armed with one unserviceable pistol. Despite the seriousness of the charge, the Egyptians were most reluctant to discuss it in the MAC or anywhere else." Earl Berger, *The Covenant and the Sword: Arab-Israeli Relations, 1948-1956* (London: Routledge, 1965), 162 n.2. In a clever diversionary tactic, the Egyptians pursued a complaint against the alleged shooting with the EIMAC, resulting in lengthy proceedings and legalistic arguments before Egypt eventually withdrew the complaint. See Burns, *Between Arab and Israeli*, 73. See also below, entry for October 3.

61 The two men had met that morning at Lydda (Lod) Airport during the British Ambassador's leave-taking. According to Russell's telegraphic report of the conversation, Sharett had asked Eytan to deliver the following message: "Prime Minister is upset and anxious as result border episodes, especially along Gaza Strip. He had hoped, following his last meeting with me [September 10], that US would take energetic action against Egypt and publicize it. US has in past been expeditious in making public its condemnation of Israel for similar acts and it looks as though US applying double standard. Israel's restraint, instead of having tranquilizing effect, has been rewarded by two extremely serious incidents including killing of two men at Beit Hashikma. As result, atmosphere in that part Israel extremely grim. Sharett says he has taken pains to see that as far as lies within power of Israel Government nothing will be done but doesn't know how long he can maintain restraint in light of new incidents. Would like to feel US would take energetic action and publicize it. That of itself would have tranquilizing effect. Also, situation on Jordan frontier getting serious again. Three days ago one of most valuable flocks of blooded sheep in country, worth IL.75,000, was stolen from Kibbutz. ..." *FRUS 1952-1954*, doc.900.

Meeting of the six [Mapai members of the Cabinet to discuss the retaliation for Ein Hashofet suggested by IDF GS]. I gave my analysis, opinions were divided. I managed to call off the operation, at least to postpone it. Later Ziama telephoned: "Dayan is depressed." Better [to bring the matter] to the Cabinet.

Phoned Joe – the plan to return the ship ["Bat Galim"] southward [to its port of departure]. Phoned Walter [- - -] Possibility of an announcement in the *New York Times* [perhaps denouncing Egypt for its blockading the Suez Canal]. His talk with Burns. Our *démarche* [orig. French] towards the British.[62]

[UN SG] Dag [Hammarskjöld] will warn the Egyptians.[63]

Sunday, October 3

The press carried the EIMAC decision – strongly urging [the Egyptian authorities] to immediately put an end [to raiding across the Gaza frontier with Israel].[64]

[- - -] Spoke to Eshkol about bringing the issue of "authorities" [of the Foreign Ministry or the IDF vis-à-vis UNTSO] to the [Cabinet] meeting. He implored me not to; took it upon himself [to find a way out].

At the Cabinet meeting, an extensive examination of retaliations, in principle and in practice. The decision arrived at was against certain acts at a certain time. Lavon was *visibly* [orig. English] put out of countenance.

---

62 In high-level talks in London on October 2, John Foster Dulles and Anthony Eden agreed on the desirability of a joint Anglo-American effort "to persuade the Egyptian Government to abandon their interference with Israeli shipping in the Suez Canal – "at the right moment." On October 5, the Foreign Office cabled Anthony Nutting, then in Cairo to finalize the Anglo-Egyptian Agreement: "[- - -] if the atmosphere after, repeat after, signature of your Agreement is propitious, you might suggest to Nasser and Salah Salem that they release the Israeli ship 'Bat Galim' and if possible even allow it to pursue its course through the Canal. Nothing would be better calculated to ease tension and to get the Anglo-Egyptian Agreement off to a good start with world opinion generally." On October 8, Nutting replied that such a move "would only invite a rebuff" from the Egyptians. See: Eden-Dulles talk, October 2, 1954, TNA FO371/111075 VR1072/223; FO to Cairo, October 5, 1954, loc. cit., VR1072/222; Nutting to FO, October 8, 1954, loc. cit., VR1072/229.

63 Cf. Kidron to Eytan, September 30, 1954, *DFPI* 9, doc.390.

64 Under the headline, "Egypt Severely Reprimanded and Asked to Put an End to its Aggressiveness against Israel," *Davar* of this date reported as follows: "At its emergency meeting convened yesterday following Israel's demand, the EIMAC strongly called upon Egypt to immediately and decisively put an end to any hostile aggressiveness against Israel. The meeting ascertained that on 25 September an armed and well-trained five-man group, coming from Egyptian-controlled territory, entered Israel's territory and attacked at close range four Israeli citizens who were on the road between Migdal and Beit Shikma, and then retreated to Egyptian territory. Two Israeli citizens were killed by shots in the back and two were wounded. No money or personal belongings were taken from the murdered and the wounded."

[Here follow some excerpts from Sharett's speech during the Cabinet discussions:]

The first subject is that of our sailing a ship ["Bat Galim"] through the Suez Canal. Initially we faced the question of what to do first: we should sail a ship carrying an Israeli flag through the Canal, or send such a ship to Eilat. On the face of it, we have an uncontested right to send a ship under the Israeli flag to Eilat, since in this case no international covenant of regimen is involved. On the other hand, there were considerations to the contrary: (A) First of all, if the Egyptians stop our ship in the Suez Canal, it will have a strong international echo, for everybody is cognizant of this waterway and its purpose to serve as a free maritime passage for all nations at all times, while the number of people who know what Eilat is and where it is situated is meager. In the case of Eilat, Egyptian contentions can cause confusion. (B) If they hinder the sailing to Eilat, it can be considered a breach of the Armistice Agreement. We would then have to place a formal complaint with the EIMAC and this can drag on, the Egyptians can appeal against the MAC's decision, and this can drag on and on, and who knows what the end of it will be. There is also the possibility that the Egyptians would use force, in which case we may have grounds to respond with force, and this can lead to serious complications. In view of these considerations it was decided that it would be better to postpone the Eilat operation to a later stage. There is no question of the use of force in the Suez Canal.

The ship we purchased was carrying a Greek flag. It went through the Suez Canal and reached the port of Massawa [in Eritrea], where its flag was replaced by an Israeli one. The crew was sent by air to Massawa and the ship was loaded there with purely non-military goods, such as were allowed to pass through the Canal [in non-Israeli ships]. The ship was not armed at all, besides the Captain's revolver, which is the accepted routine. We maintained constant radio contact with it.

Politically, we considered the time was now appropriate, for it was after the initialing of the British evacuation [agreement] from the Canal Zone and [before] the final signing. From the Egyptians' point of view, if they seriously accept the obligation [included in the Canal Covenant], they would have an incentive to demonstrate it now; on the other hand, if they are decided to ignore their international obligation before the final signing, all the more so after it, when they are completely free to interfere with our ships.

The ship's voyage took longer than planned, for its motor broke down. At long last it reached the Canal and went through the formal registration procedure, but some time later a police boat approached it and since then our radio communication with it has been cut off. Meanwhile a meeting of the EIMAC took place and our man exchanged some words with the Egyptian representative. From what the Egyptian said he gathered that they are going to release the cargo and the crew and let the ship go back. For they will not let it sail through the Canal; they would not mind if the cargo is brought to Haifa by another ship.

I directed our UN mission to table a complaint in the SC on this matter. We have already contacted the UN SG. He said he would summon the Egyptian representative and prod him to see to it that his government puts an end to the policy it is has maintained so far. I do not know whether he has done so and what are the chances of his approach.

Meanwhile, during the last four weeks there occurred several serious incidents on both the Egyptian and the Jordanian fronts, in which several Israelis were killed. In this period we did nothing – the last reprisal operation was the one in Beit Likya, a month ago. The Army captured one infiltrator who told his interrogators that the two last acts in the south were carried out by a gang which is directed by the Egyptian Intelligence in the Gaza Strip.

A serious incident on the Jordanian front was the robbery of Kibbutz Ein Hashofet's flock of high-breed sheep. We approached the UNTSO people two and three times. They promised to take action, but so far to no avail. The subject of a reprisal for this incident was discussed. Usually, we inform the government after a reprisal is carried out – what was done, why and how, but in this instance I would like to inform you of our considerations before any action is taken.

I am going to meet with Burns today and write a very serious Note to the British government, then wait for a few days and see what happens. I think we must restrain ourselves for the next several days. We will give the press a detailed list of all incidents which occurred during the last four weeks and see to it that it is publicized abroad. Indeed, it can add a blow to tourism, but by such publicity we shall make the public aware of the concrete situation. It will also prepare the background for our [reprisal] actions, if there will be any.

Recently, after the murder near Ra'anana, the perpertrator, as we have learned, was caught in Jordan and sentenced to three years in prison. The judge who punished him said: "It is not my intention to avenge Jewish blood, but this man is a criminal from the national point of view, because the Jews mounted an operation against 'Azzun after the Ra'anana murder and killed many Arabs there. The criminals who steal property inside Israel in order to enrich themselves do not take into consideration the possible result of their deeds, and therefore they must be punished severely." Such is the logic operating there.

Another consideration which I saw as a very serious one was the fact of our being now in the midst of a campaign against arming the Arab countries. We are investing great efforts in this campaign and we are seeing some results. It seems that the State Department tends to be more cautious and more considerate in view of public opinion, though its policy of arming the Arab countries remains the same. Let us not delude ourselves in this matter. What is our contention? We argue that we are defending ourselves while the Arabs are the aggressors. However, the stark facts created by us demonstrate to opposite, because our [reprisal] operations are widely publicized, and this undermines our entire plan; it distorts our image in world public opinion.

It is in view of this consideration, and of the present convening of the UN GA, that I decided to not approve the proposed reprisals, and I wanted the government members to be aware of this matter.

[Several Ministers expressed their opinions on the issue and spoke for or against mounting reprisal operations. Minister of Defense Lavon was adamant in opposing Sharett's position. PM Sharett wound up the discussion:]

I am afraid we shall never reach a consensus regarding the reprisal policy, since it is a matter beyond proof. Not only here, but elsewhere too, there are people who are convinced that had there been no reprisals, our situation would be worse by far. We are surrounded by a huge accumulation of hatred, frustration and lawlessness which can quite easily be expressed in actions against us and, therefore, it is only the reprisals which are curbing attacks and make it possible for us to lead our lives. I am taking into account the fact that a man like the CoS born in this country, a man of highly developed sensitiveness to security matters, is of this opinion. Still, I am not entirely convinced of the wisdom of this position. I cannot, by any means, be confident that the recent growing number of incidents against us was a result of our restraint. I did not intend to put down an absolute policy regarding reprisals. I pronounced my opinion in face of certain two reprisal proposals which were put before me, and I expressed my negative opinion regarding them at this moment.

It seems to me that here, just as in other matters, we have assimilated a certain routine, to what is meant by the English word "pattern" – of what is the only thing to be done, as if there is no other way possible. We do not take into account the overall impact [of our reprisal operations] on the Arab world. Every such operation, when publicized, is like a fireball thrown into an explosive powder keg. It arouses, it inflames anew, the entire fire of hatred. It immediately becomes an item on the Arab League agenda. It serves as a slogan for money-raising campaigns in the Arab countries. It does not matter that it only rarely led to [Arabs] taking action [against us]. But it immediately creates dangerous clouds. It enhances anew Arab unity. Each and every such reprisal operation shuts the mouth of any Arab who dares express a moderate opinion. It may well be that the situation is a tragic one, from which no escape is possible; but we cannot ignore this aspect of the dilemma. I say, and I have already said this in one of our previous meetings, that we must think of other means. We must have at some point an overall discussion devoted to this issue. I have already suggested that a number of people should be assigned to probe and investigate what has been carried out in the last year or two in this sphere of reprisal operations, to ascertain how they evolved and what they have achieved, and try to reach conclusions.

The decision taken yesterday at the EIMAC was a strong one. It is possible that it will remains only on paper. But it is impossible that we, only one or two days later, should do something which is a negation of the contents of the decision which we ourselves demanded at the EIMAC meeting. We must allow time for the possibility of the implementation of the EIMAC decision. Meanwhile there is the problem of the ship ["Bat Galim"] outstanding. I am certainly against a compromise on the robbery of the [Ein Hashofet] flock.

I would now like to inform you something regarding Burns. Here both negative and positive developments occurred. There is clearly much tension in our relationship with him in view of the clashes we've had with him. I am not prepared to release him from any guilt, because he started by overacting and exaggerated in using a tone of a ruler. It is possible that it was good that he was repulsed a few times so that he should be restrained in the future. But this will be achieved only if he's not poisoned to an unmitigated degree. There is no doubt, inasmuch as it is possible to see, that he is an honest man, an able and a very wise one, and that he will insist on his powers or rights.

Clearly there is not only a question of personality here, but this question is present as well, and should not be ignored. There is the problem of the political background. The international political background which has evolved before his coming here and which he has inherited. I mean the mode which has crystalized among the powers to intervene more than in the past, to the point of granting authority to the UN machinery. Burns represents this attitude. Recently we were warned by the US – we were told that they viewed our relationship with Burns with deep concern; they wanted to be assured that we understood that if we got entangled with him, it would have serious repercussions on world public opinion. A second warning came from the UN SG [Dag Hammarskjöld] precisely when we came to discuss the issue of the ship with him. He first said that Egypt's position in this matter was weak; he would see the Egyptian Ambassador and emphasize the UN interest in the Suez Canal. But then he proceeded to discuss what he called "the argument" we were having with Burns, and told us that he unconditionally supported Burns both juridically and historically. He said he and Burns would pursue this position. The last piece of information regarding this issue is that Burns has informed us that he received an advice, or a directive, from the SG to the effect that he, Burns, should execute the arrangement he has initiated only when he becomes convinced that any of the MACs is not operating correctly. Clearly, Burns does not agree with our basic position that he has no authority in this respect.

In the afternoon, a talk with Burns on the flock; his promises. His anger at the shots [fired at] Brewster [and Lombet]. [We talked about] the next [meeting of] EIMAC [Special Committee, and the proposal to reduce the backlog by each side withdrawing many of its] appeals.

[Consulted with] Walter on various matters and with Gideon Rafael on the frozen [refugee] accounts and on an appeal to the [Red] Cross [regarding] the ship. [- - -] I asked Joe if I could be sure of the truth of the version that there were no arms [aboard the "Bat Galim"] and no shooting.

Monday, October 4

[- - -]

At 9:00 [went] to Rehovot [for a vacation, at the Weizmann Institute Guest House]. G. R. [reported] on Abba's talk with [Mahmoud] Azmi. I said: "No threats." News of peace feelers in Egypt – support for Nuri [Sa'id's peace feelers].[65]

Walter [reported] on the meeting of the Special Committee of the EIMAC, which went off well. [He also informed me that] Hutchison has reported to Burns

65 Several days earlier, at a farewell dinner for the departing British Ambassador, Sharett was critical of Anthony Eden's reported assessment of Nuri Sa'id as the only Arab leader "who had any conception of the major strategic considerations involved in the ME, and of the importance, in relation to this problem, of peace between Israel and the Arabs." Sharett's remarks were as follows: "Mr Sharett, who claimed to know Nuri well and to understand his psychology, feared that Nuri's interest in peace with Israel, if it existed at all, sprung less from a desire to serve the strategic interests of the West than from his ambition to establish a union of Syria and Iraq. This aspiration, which envisaged a Greater Iraq, stretching from the Mediterranean to the Persia Gulf, and controlling the land bridge between Europe, Asia and Africa, could only be fulfilled after peace had been restored to the Middle East. [- --]. If [- - -] normal peaceful relations existed between Israel and Iraq, Nuri would, no doubt, expect there to be less opposition from Israel to his [unification] plans. This, Mr Sharett felt, was the sole motive underlying Iraqi efforts to move towards peace with Israel, since at the moment there was no other incentive for her to do so. He clearly thought the possibility that this was the case should be borne in mind by HMG in case Nuri should pursue the question." Tel Aviv Chancery to Levant Department, September 29, 1954, TNA FO371/111075 VR1072/220.

In a note to Eliahu Elath in London, Arthur Lourie of the MFA noted skeptically that Nuri's "efforts to create an impression of moderation and sweet reasonableness" were "flatly contradicted by the violence" of the statement made to the UN GA by Fadhil al-Jamali, Iraq's Permanent Representative to the UN. Lourie to Elath, October 4, 1954, ISA FM 130.16/2593/23.

[on efforts in Amman to retrieve the sheep taken from Ein Hashofet]; a letter was sent to Nusseibeh,[66] and a reply is expected tomorrow. If it's negative, [Burns] will go [to Amman] the day after tomorrow.[67]

[- - -]

Tuesday, October 5

I phoned Tekoah [and heard] details on the EIMAC Special Committee [meeting]; contact with [Egypt's chief delegate Lieut.-Col. Salah] Gohar[68] did not help at all. Burns had declined Dayan's invitation for Sunday [dinner] before the shooting [at Colonel Brewster's car]. Afterwards he called to say that the dinner was OK [for Sunday October 10] after all. Burns has corrected the formulation regarding [freedom of movement of UN] Observers, but it's obvious he is looking for a compromise way out.

[- - -]

[Drafted] my comments on Abba's speech for the GA.[69]

[- - -]

Wednesday, October 6 [*Erev* Yom Kippur]

[- - -] [Consulted] with the DG about the [stolen] flock, discussing how and when. [- - -] With G.R. - I reported on Isser's adventure; calculations vis-à-vis Nasser, in spite of everything.

Kol Nidre evening prayers – we read from Chaim Weizmann's *mahzor*.[70]

[- - -]

Thursday, October 7 [Yom Kippur]

[- - -]

In the evening the DG [reported that] Burns had gone to Amman, and had conducted tiring negotiations. The flock is to be returned by Sunday. [- - -]

At night [we heard] Eban's speech on the radio.[71] G.R. is against our discussing

66 Anwar Nusseibeh (1913-1986). Palestinian politician born in Jerusalem. Since 1951 member of the Jordanian Parliament. Minister of Defense (1954-1955).

67 Cf. Burns diary for this date. Eytan and Burns had dinner together. LAC MG31G6 v.7.

68 Lt.-Colonel Salah Gohar. Egypt's chief delegate to the EIMAC. Head of the Palestine Department, Ministry of War. Later Deputy Foreign Minister.

69 In his speech to the Seventh GA on October 6, Eban raised the proposal that Israel and the Arab states sign non-belligerency agreements. See Editorial Note, *DFPI* 9, doc.399.

70 High Holiday prayer-book. Sharett's family spent Yom Kippur at the Weizmann residence in Rehovot.

71 See above, note 69.

the ship [issue] in the MAC. A lawyer [would have to be added] to our delegation. I reported these suggestions to the DG. [We are considering exchanging] the sheep [for] the Chevrolet [that crossed the demarcation line from Jordan into Israel]. I warned against publicity for the Foreign Ministry following the return [of the sheep], but for us it was clear [that the sheep would be returning as a result of MFA negotiations rather than an IDF retaliation as proposed by the CoS].

Friday, October 8

In the morning [I worked with] Yaacov Herzog on a final briefing for Eban's talk with Dulles. With the DG regarding the MAC and the ship ["Bat Galim" still being held by the Egyptians]. Burns insists he will be dealing only with the [specific] incident, not the [principle of freedom of] passage. [Spoke to] Tekoah about Burns – the atmosphere has improved thanks to [- - -] [ellipsis orig.] Consulted with the DG about not giving visas to the Russians.

Saturday, October 9

[- - -] The flock has been returned. I breathed more easily.

Eban's report of his talk [with Dulles] was brought to me.[72]

[- - -]

Sunday, October 10

7:15 went to Jerusalem, with Teddy [and talked about] about Lavon, the [return of the Ein Hashofet] flock, and what the Army is capable of. He: "That's not the trouble, but that the Defense Minister authorizes [such operations]". The IDF espionage operation in Egypt (Moshe Dayan: "An order was given!"). I told this to Ze'ev Sharef too.

During the Cabinet meeting [I reported on] the flock, the Eban-Dulles talk,[73] visas for the Russians, German ships [as part of the reparations payments – excerpts follow:].

> The Ministers have already read in the press that the [Ein Hashofet] flock was returned, in fact only 90% of it. We are still negotiating the return of the remaining 10%. This affair demanded quite an intensive effort which lasted a whole week. It started with my talk with the UNTSO Commander. I told him it was indeed strange that

---

72 Eban and Shiloah met with Dulles, Bedell Smith, Byroade and Bergus on October 8 and discussed possible US measures to allay Israel's apprehensions. See *DFPI* 9, doc.402 and *FRUS 1952-1954*, doc.905. Eban wrote at length afterwards to Dulles to express his "disappointment" with their meeting. *DFPI* 9, doc.403 and *FRUS 1952-1954*, doc.906. Dulles replied on October 18, 1954, *ibid.* doc.909.

73 See above, note 72.

a Prime Minister and the chief representative of the UN should meet to discuss a flock; however, since they were meeting, it stands to reason that the matter is important. I presented him with a choice: either he sees to it that the flock is returned, or, if this proves to be impossible, a period of flock rustling along the border would be initiated. Burns took some intensive steps. He wrote a personal letter to the Jordanian Defense Minister and then traveled himself to Amman. We also contacted the British Embassy regarding this matter, and they too sent a man to Amman. In order to be on the safe side, they recalled that some time ago a Jordanian car mistakenly crossed the border near Eilat and demanded its return, and this was done.

Now to more serious matters, even though the solution of the flock problem prevented quite serious ones [i.e., IDF reprisals].

An additional meeting was held between Ambassador Eban and Dulles during which it was hinted that the problem is not that the cow stopped wanting to give milk, but that the calf stopped wanting to suck. Nasser is having a very difficult fight with the "Muslim Brethren" who are accusing him of being a servile slave of the Americans; he seems to be getting rid of the British while, at the same time, he becomes enslaved to the US. This is why it is not comfortable for him now to become stained by American military aid.

I will not say the approaching [US Congressional] elections have not played a part here, but surely Egyptian neutrality did.

Meanwhile, in London, Ambassador Elath met with one of the FO people. In the midst of their talk, Eden rang and directed the FO man to ask what can we offer, or can the Arabs offer, in order to break the ice. This question by Eden should be seen as a continuation of Selwyn Lloyd's offer to mediate between the two sides. I told Elath to say: Let the Arabs cease all their misdeeds and then we shall refrain from mounting reprisals and thus peace and quiet would reign along the borders for some time and this will create a more comfortable climate for discussing further steps. All this is impossible as long as blood is being spilled, or could be spilled at any time. I made no specific offer, for this would have implied our consent to British mediation.

On the matter of the ship ["Bat Galim"], the Egyptians pulled a clever trick by accusing our crew of firing on an Egyptian fishing boat. They tabled a complaint before the EIMAC and we did too. However, it was clear that the MAC said it is not authorized to deal with this matter. At the time, General [William] Riley gave his opinion that our passage through the Canal was a matter for the SC to decide. Our impression of Burns' position in this matter is that it is clear to him that the Egyptian accusation holds no water, but he would not be surprised if the Egyptian produced a boat with bullet holes and even some corpses.

Two additional matters I have to report on have to do with Russia and Germany. After diplomatic relations with Russia were renewed, a new Minister arrived here – later he was named Ambassador – and he immediately started talking about developing cultural ties. I told him I was all for it, but on a reciprocal basis. We tried to open negotiations with this purpose in mind, but nothing came of this. Meanwhile they invited us to an agricultural exhibition. A mission of three went there and was very well treated as state guests. Sometime later we appealed for a few entry visas to the Soviet Union for our agricultural experts. While still awaiting a response, we were asked to issue visas for six Soviet guests who were invited to a celebration organized by the CPI. The Foreign Ministry is against fulfilling this request. The Soviets should be told that we are certainly in favor of contacts, but these must be maintained on a reciprocal principle. When our people go to the Soviet Union, they are treated as state guests; their people too should be state guests, not guests of an organization opposed by the vast majority of Israelis. Such a visit cannot contribute towards advancing mutual friendly relations. I bring up this position for the approval of the government, since our refusal nay cause quite a tension, but I think there is no other alternative in this case. Once and for all a line must be drawn.

Another item I must bring before you is an old issue which has now become actual. It is the use of German ships for importing German products purchased with reparations money. During the Reparations negotiations it was agreed that the treaty would include a clause against such use, and indeed the Reparations Agreement signed by me included such a clause. However, when the agreement was about to be ratified by the Bundestag, an uproar arose there. The elements favoring the ratification contended that this item was an insult to the German people. Long negotiations ensued and at the end of it we agreed to give up this clause. However, in practice, shipping German products by German ships was postponed for half a year, then again for half a year. Recently the president of the German shipping association demanded our consent to the arrival of the first German cargo ship in Haifa poet in November. He suggested that this first ship would not fly the German flag and that its crew would be confined to the ship while it was being unloaded, but from then onwards their ships would fly the German flag. When we argued against that, they contended that this was a political issue which should be decided by their Foreign Ministry. They will accept whatever this Ministry decides.

Our Mission in Germany recommends that we do not appeal to the German Foreign Ministry, for this would mean asking a favor. In fact, we are asking them for all kinds of favors, above and beyond the Reparations Agreement which they are fulfilling meticulously; we were advised not to ask for a favor the fulfilment of which means our breaching of the agreement.

There is also the question of the arrival of German experts in connection with the installation of certain German-made machinery coming in as a result of the Reparations Agreement, and these experts hold German passports. The government must define its position on these issues and consequently the public should be briefed and guided on these matters.

Following [some Ministers'] feelings in these matters, which are quite justified in themselves, while abstaining from political considerations cannot but put our political thinking to sleep. In this matter we are dealing with a Great Power – it is today the strongest in Europe, it is fifty million working people. We can, by no means whatsoever, even if the Reparations Agreement would not have come to pass, abandon our relations with it to the domination of feelings. On the contrary, the Reparations Agreement is enabling us to evolve honorable relations. There was a clear admission by the German government of its debt to us. It is now expressed daily, hourly, by an incessant stream of products which are made thanks to the taxes paid by every German. Every German taxpayer is aware of this. There is Arab and Nazi propaganda against this in Germany; our interest is to check it. Are acts of boycotting Germany going to isolate it? We shall only isolate ourselves. Soon an international congress of social workers will convene in our country. It will include Germans. The same goes for an important scientific symposium which will take place next year in Rehovot. Are we to decide that such events will not take palace in our country? Are we going to withdraw from these and similar international organizations, or are we to participate in conferences abroad but shut our country's gates before such events? We should better prepare our public for all this in time. I think our public is ready for this more than we assume. This does not mean that there are no lunatics in our midst. A lunatic tried to break Jasha's Heifetz's hand, but there are phenomena

Moshe Sharett accompanied by Defense Minister Lavon and CoS Dayan inspecting parade at end of IDF officers' training course, Jerusalem

Moshe Sharett conducting party members' singing at end of Mapai conference

testing to the public readiness to accept such steps.

[- - -] As to the issue of the German ships carrying German goods, I gather that there is majority here for its solution by allowing the ships to start coming to Haifa without flying the German flag.

[- - -]

In the afternoon [participated in] a graduation ceremony of [400 IDF] officers [in Jerusalem]. My speech – [stressed importance of loyalty to] moral [standards; danger of the Army developing] sectarianism.

[Worked] with Herzog on briefing Eban following his talk [with Dulles].[74]

Monday, October 11

[- - -] With Tekoah on the [UN] Observers' investigation at the "Dolphin". [- - -] A way opened for a compromise during Burns' talk with Dayan [at dinner on Sunday]. [- - -] In the evening, at the Weisgals, met with Shalom Asch[75] and Gershon [Agron, who stated:] " Burns [is] double faced" [orig. English], following a talk [*Jerusalem Post* journalist] T[ed] L[urie] had with Dayan.[76]

[- - -]

Tuesday, October 12

I am sixty. Depression. In the evening a family gathering [celebrating my birthday] at [my sister] Ada's. [There was much] singing.

Wednesday, October 13

[- - -]

Thursday, October 14

At the office in the *Kiyra*. Isser on Lavon and [the mishap in] Egypt.

At home in the afternoon. Tekoah [reported on] the Burns affair, the [possible

74 Sharett to Eban, October 11, 1954, *DFPI* 9, doc.406; US Division to Israel Embassy, Washington, October 11, 1954, *DFPI* 9, doc.407.

75 Sholem (Shalom) Asch (1880-1957). Polish-Jewish novelist, dramatist, and essayist in the Yiddish language. Emigrated to the US in 1938 and in 1954 settled in Bat Yam, Israel. His house in Bat Yam is now the Sholem Asch Museum. The bulk of his library, containing rare Yiddish books and manuscripts, including the manuscripts of some of his own works, is held at Yale University.

76 This negative view of General Burns stands out as the exception among many praiseworthy private reports received from various informants. For examples of the latter, see correspondence in ISA FM 130.02/2425/9. See also Burns to Lourie, November 2, 1954, loc.cit.

return of Israel's representatives to] IJMAC, and the "Bat Galim" [case] in the EIMAC. [- - -]

Friday, October 15

Morning meeting at the office in Tel Aviv with Denis Healey [Labour MP]. [I spoke about] the myth of Arab[-British] friendship and the roots of [Arab] neutralism, practical and philosophical. He: "The trouble is that you are so logical and straightforward; the Arabs are irrational." I: "In any case, [I asked him for] two [things]: 1. Don't abandon [us]; 2. If we are right – say so." [- - -]

To Jerusalem. [- - -] A glitch blocking the signing [of the Israel-Jordan Local Commanders' Agreement]. Went home. Got a report from Walter – Woe is me! Phoned Moshe Dayan; his version was that "they requested an extension" (meanwhile the UN has issued a communiqué).

In the afternoon with G.R.:

1) "Bat Galim"; the Egyptian communiqué, with photos, sweet faces, "criminals", etc., *feda'yin* [orig. Arabic].[77] A ship is traveling from the north with journalists. Reassure the families and pay the salaries. A lawyer.

2) "Nasser's [regime] is shaky". Institutional crumbling.

3) The Alexandria debacle, [fixing] our line. Consultation. Should we cry "blood libel"? I toyed with the idea of a personal approach to Nasser.[78]

4) The triangle between us, the [Arab refugee] depositors and the PCC, which presents the affair as being in the hands of the banks alone. The depositors are ready to sign with us.

5) The representatives of the depositors on the Johnston [development] plan: they are opposed to resettlement in the Jordan Valley. The earth is salty, the climate deadly [- - -].

6) Haifa – [its proposed use] for trade with Jordan (Eden's note).[79]

Afternoon [meeting] with Walter – Burns' version is completely different. He placated him.[80]

---

77 *Feda'yin, feda'yun.* "Self-sacrificing" saboteurs. Commonly rendered "fedayeen" in English.

78 The charge-sheet against those implicated in the July sabotage attempts in Alexandria and Cairo was announced by Radio Cairo on October 12. See *DFPI* 9, docs.418, 434, 435.

79 The idea of creating a free port at Haifa for use by Arab countries was a suggested ingredient of post-1948 peace plans devised first by Count Bernadotte and taken up subsequently in the USSD, the British FO and elsewhere. See, e.g., Caplan, *Futile Diplomacy* III and IV, *passim*. The proposal was again under active consideration for several months following Sharett's September interview in the *USNWR* (WebDoc #28).

80 According to Burns' diary of this date, the signing of the Local Commanders' Agreement was delayed because of the objections of the Israeli delegates to having him sign the agreement as a witness. Eytan offered to sort the matter out and to overrule Dayan, if necessary. LAC MG31G6 v.7. See also Dayan to Burns, October 17, 1954, *DFPI* 9, doc.414.

Saturday, October 16

[- - -]

After midnight [- - -] with Walter correcting [the final draft of] the letter to Burns. He told me of his visit to BG at his home in Tel Aviv. Strange company [was there]. He argued with Dayan who was convinced that the Foreign Ministry sided with the UN. Burns [had told him] about the report of the observers [sent to visit the crew aboard] the "Bat Galim." [The report] proved nothing one way or the other. The result: a draw in the EIMAC [i.e., no decision; our initiative to attain an EIMAC] decision [condemning Egypt] was defeated.

Sunday, October 17

[- - -]

I dictated the letter to the three [Elath, Eban, Shiloah] on the [stolen] flock [see below, entry for October 26]. I finished [working] with the DG on a reply to Eliahu regarding [Israel's offer to Jordan to use] Haifa as a trade outlet.

[- - -]

Walter [added impressions] of his conversation with Dayan, who claimed the Foreign Ministry was interested in the existence of UNTSO forever; "we [the Army] are concerned with the interests of the state, while they [the Foreign Ministry] are concerned with what the *goyim* say."

[- - -]

Monday, October 18

[- - -]

Tuesday, October 19 [Simhat Torah]

With Giora who has returned from a visit to the US. [- - -] One has the impression abroad that there are two governments in Israel. He spoke sharply giving his opinion of Pinhas Lavon: Giora [would have told him:] "Go!"

[- - -]

An announcement on the [forthcoming] signing of the [Local Commanders] Agreement.

[- - -]

Wednesday, October 20

Prepared for the meeting of the FADC at the Foreign Ministry in the *Kirya*. I lectured for two hours on the "Bat Galim", the blocked [accounts], Dulles, and the visas for the Russians.[81]

[Excerpts of Sharett's remarks during the FADC discussions follow:]

Let me say first something about the logic behind the "Bat Galim" operation. Political logic is a two-edged sword – one can always prove it sound or the other way around. The same goes for timing – one can always prove it was wrong, especially after the act in question was already carried out and not too successful at that.

Factually. Until the "Bat Galim" affair, Egypt has never sent back any ship carrying cargo to Israel or from it. There were cases of interference, but they all ended up by letting the ship sail through the Canal. However, Egypt has not allowed two things: passage of an oil tanker, no matter under what flag, and passage of a ship under Israeli flag. Indeed, there is also a third test: passage of an Israeli warship or a ship carrying Israeli arms, for instance, to Burma. We have left this third test to the future, and so far we have not put Egypt to the first two tests.

The implementation [of a plan] to sail a ship under Israeli flag through the Canal is not so simple. We would not risk a big, good ship; we need to purchase a ship for this special purpose. There is the problem of where the flag would be changed to an Israeli one. There is the problem of organizing the crew. These steps take time, usually longer than planned, and meanwhile the operation must be coordinated with the political calendar. Our reasoning was that it would be better if we sailed the ship at a time when Egypt's international sensitivity was high, and we assumed that as long as the Anglo-Egyptian treaty had not yet been signed, this would be the right time. Morever, if Egypt won't let the ship pass at this stage, it would certainly not do so later. We also reasoned that we could fail, but our test would make it clear that the Suez Canal was serving ships of all nations except Israel, and this would give us a good attacking position.

It is difficult to foresee what will happen in the SC when it discusses our complaint. We will strive for a clear decision stating that the seizure of the ship was illegal and that Egypt must allow it to continue its voyage to its destination. But even if the SC makes a decision, there is still the question of what Egypt would do.

Clearly, there arises the possibility of us detaining an Egyptian ship. Here, too, there is a gamut of considerations. Detaining for what purpose? If it's against their detaining of the "Bat Galim," then we would have to release it when the "Bat Galim" is released, even if it is not allowed to continue sailing northwards. If we detain an Egyptian ship in the open seas, the Egyptians could do the same to an Israeli ship – and their navy is stronger, and we have more cargo ships. Such a step must be seriously weighed before undertaking it. I suggest that we advance step by step and examine the various possibilities in each. The fact that the Egyptians falsely accused the "Bat Galim" crew of shooting at Egyptian fishermen testifies to their awareness of the weakness of their position. This raises the possibility of us sending another ship, this time with journalists aboard. We must realized we are dealing here with a prolonged campaign.

I will now move on to the issue of the IJMAC. On this issue here can be two opposing positions. I will elaborate the two and then state the government's one.

It is possible to contend that the tragedy of Ma'aleh Akrabim offered us an excellent excuse to fully justify our leaving the MAC in order to never return to it, or pose such

81 On the issue of Israel's refusal to grant visas to members of the Soviet delegation to the Israel-Soviet Union Friendship League Congress organized by the CPI, see *DFPI* 9, docs.416, 438.

conditions to our return which will make it impossible, and [some would] see this as a blessing. Similarly, we would wait for opportunities enabling us to extricate ourselves from all the other MACs, and then the Armistice regime would disappear and a situation of catch-as-catch-can would evolve. Perhaps this is what we are striving for.

There is another position which says that, as long as there is no peace, we have no alternative but to be living within the Armistice conditions. Indeed, this regime embroils us in all kinds of complications and struggles, which at times compel us to take sharp demonstrative steps, sometimes even walking out of the MAC. However, it must be clear that it is not our intention to destroy this regime. We have no intention of leaving the IJMAC for good. If we left it was only a demonstrative act and consequently we must find a way of returning to it honorably, because in the long run we would be losing if we stayed out. If, by our staying out, the entire Armistice regime was dismantled and UN supervision was gone, and if the disappearance of these elements was in our favor, then it would be incumbent on us to take this road. But if the result is different, what have we gained? In fact, we have not done away with the Armistice Agreements, we have not done away with the Armistice regime – we are only not participating in it, and this behavior is causing us very grave damage. If we stipulate our return [as being conditional] on the replacement of the MAC chairman [Hutchison], such a change is possible. But if we only demand such a replacement, why should the UN do us this favor? Accordingly, in view of this consideration, we informed the IJMAC at quite an early stage after our first act of walking out, that we would certainly return if the chairman is replaced. The UNTSO command could easily have extended the chairmanship of Commander Hutchison, but it did not do so, which is significant. Of course, the UN command could have panicked, or demonstrated unexpected good will and replaced him immediately, but it did not. At the same time, it could have ignored our announcement and gone on with the situation as it was, and we know such opinions were advanced in the State Department. The decision they arrived at was not to replace him while his term was still on, but since his term was about to end, not to renew his appointment.

By the way, it is difficult to say that the removal of General Bennike – obviously against his will – can be seen as a clear and friendly step towards the Arab states. But meanwhile a replacement took place in the UNTSO command, and inasmuch as there was a better chance of [us] getting along with the Canadian commander [Burns], there was also a possibility that clashing with him could be much more serious than clashing with Bennike – and this not only because he is a Canadian, but also because a very serious effort was made by the British, Americans and UN Secretary-General to find a person of high quality to man this post. Consequently, clashing with him, especially at the beginning of his term, could be much more serious. The present situation – in which the UNTSO commander was replaced, and meanwhile we are not participating in the most important of the MACs, which is constantly holding meetings and dealing with most important issues – creates a very uneasy background to our relationship with Burns, albeit we did not go back on our announced position that we shall return [to the IJMAC] only upon Hutchison's replacement.

I was asked by one of the committee's members point blank whether it is true that the government had decided on a total avoidance of military retaliations against Arab aggression and that, consequently, the Army was ordered to abstain from any military response to Arab action along the borders. Well, nothing of the sort has happened. No decision in principle has ever been taken to never retaliate to any action. The same as it is impossible to instruct the Army to respond freely to any anti-Israel action, so it is

> impossible to instruct it to abstain from response, no matter what happens along the borders. If a group of soldiers is fired on, it immediately fires back. It would be absurd if in such a situation the Army should [have to] ask the Prime Minister what to do. However, no serious military response can be executed without an approval. The fact that no military retaliation was carried out against Jordan during the last three weeks was a result of the fact that during this time there was nothing to retaliate against.

The question we must ask ourselves is: what is the purpose of retaliation? I do not exclude the element of revenge from the gamut of considerations. But do we retaliate just for the sake of taking revenge, or is our purpose to stop acts of terror? It can well be that in a given situation we could say: let us abstain from retaliation this time and see whether the wave of terror rises or declines? Let us take a risk, let us miss one bus, so to speak, and thereby prolong peace along the border.

[- - -]

At home [in the evening]. Joe telephoned: the IJMAC.[82]

The Army is burning with desire for new clashes. Tomorrow the EIMAC.

[- - -]

Thursday, October 21

The British letter [of reassurance to Israel, upon the signing of the Anglo-Egyptian Agreement on withdrawal from Suez] was published.[83]

[- - -]

Joe Tekoah – things are not well with the EIMAC. Burns' plan (demilitarization). Failures on the Eastern [i.e., on the Soviet] front – Argaman's letter [from the Israel Embassy in Bucharest, Romania].

I'm heavily depressed.

Teddy came by and reported on the Jerusalem Convention [of UJA leaders]. I said: "Perhaps BG should return and I should leave?" He: "The day will come when this year will be counted as a great one." He himself would like to leave government service now. [He claims] BG is against retaliations.

---

82 On this date, Israeli representatives returned to attending the IJMAC.

83 In his letter to Ambassador Eliahu Elath, British Foreign Secretary Anthony Eden wrote that he was "convinced" that the Anglo-Egyptian Agreement would "result in a general lessening of tension in the ME. By increasing confidence between the Arab States and the West it should facilitate the solution of major problems in the area." Letter dated October 19, 1954, *DFPI* 9, doc.424. For the text of the Agreement (Cmd.9298), see *Documents on International Affairs, 1954*, ed. Denise Folliot (London / New York / Toronto: Oxford University Press [under the auspices of the Royal Institute of International Affairs], 1957), 248-54. See also *DFPI* 9, docs.422-23, 425-36.

Friday, October 22

Conversation with Isser – the problem of Tunisia is not resolved.

Meeting of our Cabinet *haverim* on [the] Alexandria [mishap; protocol not found] – [aspects of] practice and principle. The MACs and Burns. My relationship with the CoS. Patents and the atom.[84]

With Isser. He is against denying [our part in the mishap]. To Jerusalem, straight into a meeting on Alexandria [mishap]. Dinner with Shalom Asch. His confession. [- - -]

Saturday, October 23

With Eliezer Livneh – [his] warning against BG. [- - -] Lunch with [retired US] General [George H.] Olmstead [formerly Pentagon's head of Military Assistance operations]. Joe [reported] on five hours in the EIMAC.[85]

[- - -] With Yaacov on Eban.[86]

[- - -]

Sunday, October 24

Prepared my report [to Cabinet] with Yaacov Herzog and Ze'ev Sharef. [- - -] At the Cabinet meeting [- - -] the CoS and DG took part in [the] security [discussion]. Lavon reported on arms purchases in France and connections developed there.

[Excerpts from Sharett's remarks to Cabinet follow:]

> During the last two weeks intensive activity has been taking place in the US, and as a result about 50 Republican and 100 Democrat candidates signed an obligation to oppose arming the Arab countries. Although the Democratic Party did not take a formal decision regarding this issue, the general impression in the American public is that it will make it an election issue. This led Nixon to publicly deny that the Republican administration has abandoned Israel. A special effort was made to convince [Adlai]

---

84 Israel sold the patent for a chemical process for creating heavy water to the French. See Cohen, *Israel and the Bomb*, 60.

85 Following the marathon meeting of October 22, General Burns noted in his diary that Egypt's chief delegate, Salah Gohar, was "obviously stalling" and that he planned to "say privately to Gohar that further procedural delay will be taken to mean Egypt has no confidence in her case." LAC MG31G6 v.7. Another observer refers to this meeting as "the longest session of filibustering any MAC had suffered." Berger, *The Covenant and the Sword*, 162 n.2.

86 Following major Israeli disappointment in not obtaining from the State Department a firm declaration of American support on October 8, the Washington Embassy (esp. Reuven Shiloah) continued to lobby for a favorable statement. See *DFPI* 9, docs.427, 429-30. Some of the frenetic diplomatic activity of the previous weeks is captured in *DFPI* 9, docs.406-07, 410-11, 413, 419-20.

Stevenson[87] to issue a statement regarding this matter, and he indeed said something. According to our information, his statement made the appropriate impression in the Republican camp. [Averell] Harriman[88], too, made a quite strong speech on the issue. One of the State Department's senior officials told somebody that forty Republican candidates who depend on Jewish voters told the Administration that they must do something in order to strengthen them, otherwise they would be defeated.

There is very secret information about what is going on inside the Republican machine. I must point out the courageous position taken by American Jews who are active in the very heart of this party. [Eric] Johnston approached our people in Washington and said he was prepared to help us regarding the arms issue. While he did not say so, it was clear he wanted us to reciprocate regarding the water issue. We were informed that Bernard Baruch, too, has been active regarding the arms issue.

According to cables we received from our Washington embassy, the State Department people contend that the US cannot treat the Middle East as a vacuum in its overall security system. They see a clear possibility of strengthening Nasser in Egypt, for if he falls who knows what would happen in Egypt and in the entire Middle East. Therefore they must continue with their policy, but they are confident that Israel is not threatened by any danger, for it enjoys "a position of strength" and, secondly, the arms they are starting to give to Iraq and Egypt are in small quantities. In fact, an agreement with Egypt has not yet been signed.

The facts that we refrained in recent weeks from military operations in spite of the surge of Egyptian aggressiveness and several actions on the Jordanian border; the broadcast by our Arabic radio in which it was said that Israel is prepared to negotiate peace; our releasing of Arabs' frozen deposits; and our return to the IJMAC – all these have created a much better climate which we have not experienced for quite a long time, perhaps not since the Qibya reprisal.

In the meantime there is the problem of the "Bat Galim." We are constantly demanding that American aid to Egypt be granted on condition that it ends its blockade in the Suez Canal.

We recently received a Note from the British government in which it wants to pacify us in view of the coming parliamentary debate regarding the Anglo-Egyptian Agreement. There are some positive points in this Note and at the same time there some missing points. The Note calls for peace between Israel and the Arabs, and inasmuch as this is our policy it gives us moral support and criticizes the Arab negative policy. Missing from the Note are answers to our previous Note, which we concluded by a few questions. We asked – in view of their announcing that they would intervene if there is an attack [against Jordan] – on what basis would they intervene and what kind of an intervention would it be. We also asked what are they going to leave in the Canal Zone, and were answered that they are not going to leave large quantities of arms there. A third subject we raised was their announcement that they would continue to maintain a balance in arms supply.

---

87 Adlai Stevenson (1900-1965). American Democratic politician and diplomat. Promoter of progressive causes. Governor of Illinois (1949-1953). Unsuccessful Presidential candidate 1952, 1956. Later US Ambassador to the UN.

88 Averell Harriman (1891-1986). American businessman, Democratic politician and diplomat. Served under FDR and Truman. Former US Ambassador to the UK and the Soviet Union. Governor of New York (1955-1959). Lost the Democratic Party nomination for President to Stevenson in 1952, 1956.

We shall have to answer this Note, appreciate its courteous tone and note what is missing in it, mainly the lack of any expression regarding the repair of the balance in view of its being strategically undermined by the transfer of the Canal Zone to Egyptian hands.

At the same time we should avoid panicking our public by stressing the dangers involved. It is enough to note that the evacuation of the British greatly enhances the power of the Arabs, but to call upon our public to be self-confident.

[- - -]

According to the weekend papers [- - -] BG told [British journalist] Ritchie Calder that war [with Egypt] was inevitable. [- - -] Letter from U Nu. I drafted another letter for Abba [to send] to Dulles.[89]

Monday, October 25

Bartur on Turkey. Yosef Weitz on resettling [Palestinian] refugees [in North Africa], his group.[90]

[- - -]

To the Foreign Ministry – Daniel Lewin on problems in Burma. G.R. says we have] a victory on [the] Cyprus [issue]. The problem of Egypt (death sentence [for the captured spies] and the "Bat Galim"). Walter reported on BG's talk with Ritchie [Calder] on [chances of a] war [with Egypt].

[- - -] Returned to Jerusalem. Paperwork, horribly tired. [Finalized the] letter on the [return of the stolen] flock [see below, entry for October 26]. Joe [reported] on the results of the EIMAC; he had made an error. Burns had already reported.

Tuesday, October 26

[Press report] in *Ha'aretz* that Egypt proposes exchanging the [Gaza] Strip for the Southern Negev. [- - -]

Meeting of Knesset FADC. A hot debate. In the middle came news about the blowing up of the water pipeline [last night, near Mefalsim, opposite the city of Gaza.]

[This was quite a long meeting during which leftist committee members demanded Israel's leaving the MACs, and criticized Israel's lenient policy on the subject of American policy in the Middle East. Sharett concluded the meeting with a long reply. Some excerpts follow:]

I was asked whether our political situation has improved or worsened. My answer is

---

89 Eban's response to Dulles's note of October 18 (page 488 n.72) would be sent on October 29, 1954, *DFPI* 9, doc.443.

90 The group included Ezra Danin, Yehoshua (Josh) Palmon and Yoav Zukerman. Weitz's published diary account of this meeting is translated by Masalha, "'Dis/Solving' the Palestinian Refugee Problem," 131-32.

both. America's and Britain's position on the main subjects has not changed. However, our standing in the sphere of public opinion there has improved by steps we have taken as well as by steps not taken. A more comfortable background for continuing our campaign has been created. The fact that precisely during the recent period we have not mounted military reprisals has contributed enormously to American Jews' and generally to Israel's friends' ability to come out and support us, because they did not have, while attacking the Administration, to advance all kinds of excuses for our retaliation operations, no matter whether they were justified or not. It would have been a pinnacle of stupidity on our part if, while castigating the Arab states for their aggressive stance and presenting Israel as a stable, constructive state, counterproductive facts would have shown us to be an aggressive force, or one intent on provoking a war in the Middle East.

Britain is clearly endeavoring to strengthen its position in the Arab countries. It sees the Anglo-Egyptian Treaty as a most important step within this context. But it is not ignoring the problem of Israel's survival. It is prepared to sell us weapons to a certain degree and demonstrate its attitude of favoring Israel's existence while taking care that it would not jeopardize its relations with the Arab countries. On the issue of peace or no peace it openly sides with us.

Now to America. The State Department's policy is to create a background for a serious contact between the US and the Arab states in order to fill the void in the Middle East, contain the tendency toward neutralism and bring the Middle East into an evolving anti-communist front. The State Department contends time and again that not only is this policy not to Israel's detriment, but, in the long run, it favors Israel, because only after the Arab countries pass through a stage of being unilaterally armed and involved in pacts with the US would the US be able to bring to bear its influence for making peace with Israel. Otherwise the US has no chance to attain that.

When Israel's friends contend that meanwhile the US is abandoning Israel, the Americans say: "We are prepared to issue a pro-Israeli declaration, however, a declaration which satisfies Israel will undermine our Arab policy. Are you interested in an empty declaration? Since you are not interested in this kind of declaration, we decided to not issue any declaration before the coming elections."

I must point out that while in the clash between the interests of the Republican Party and those of the American state, the latter has had the upper hand, the problem of the danger threatening Israel has become an important issue, and that is a positive result of the election campaigning.

One should also note the preparedness of all American Jewish circles and personalities, including Jews high up in the Republican Administration as well as those who have so far never spoke up in our favor, to attack the State Department. Moreover, one cannot say that our campaign has had no result whatsoever. There is no doubt that it had an effect on slowing the pace of arming the Arabs and limiting its dimensions, even if the fundamental policy has not changed.

In our propaganda campaign in the US we cannot evade the fact that the Middle East is becoming an arena of defense pacts. While an Israeli-American defense treaty is not realistic, demanding it demonstrates that we are being discriminated against. Here we have a very sharp weapon: we are not against defending our region, but we argue that all the money invested by the US in the Arab states for the defense of the region is totally wasted. What a pity that dollars earned by the sweat of American people are criminally, stupidly, thrown into the treasuries of the Arab governments so that they defend democracy – they will never defend democracy. This idea is foreign to them.

In an interview I gave to the *USNWR* [WebDoc #28], which had interviewed Nasser two or three weeks before [me], I made it clear in all sharpness that this was just a waste of money, to no avail; for the Arabs will never defend democracy. And I analyzed the political psychology of the Arab world in this context. I asked: is it not a natural conclusion that the only state in the Middle East capable of defending democracy is Israel, for its very being a democracy makes it interested in defending it.

One member of the FADC, [Mapam] MK [Yaakov] Riftin, contended that our very demand for a defense treaty with the US, although unrealistic for the time being, will create an abyss between us and Asia. It seems to me that I have had no small part in inculcating in the Israeli public an awareness of our being part of Asia. But let me say plainly that seeing ourselves as only being a part of Asia is absolutely senseless. We are situated in a specific geographical corner which from more than one aspect makes us by far closer to Europe than to China or India. We are clearly part of Europe, as we are of Asia. We are part of the Western world, and first and foremost we are connected with those parts of the Jewish people who are free to support us.

Another Committee member, [*Ahdut Ha'avoda*] MK [Yitzhak] Ben-Aharon, cried out from the bottom of his heart against the fact that UNTSO observers are freely roaming our country. I share with him some of his criticism in this respect. However, what is he proposing? He does not want us to announce that we are abrogating the Armistice Agreements. He proposes that we announce that as long as the UNTSO commander does not agree with us on every point we shall boycott him. Can that be? Is he not allowed to interpret these agreements as he understands them? There is an entire literature of the agreements' interpretation. Each Arab state has its own interpretation, and so do we. If our withdrawing from the IJMAC was a positive act, logic dictates that we withdraw from the other three. Is our policy to breach the agreements? To boycott the UN? Would our position get two-thirds of the GA's vote? Is this campaign going to bring us positive results? The UN is first and foremost the US and Britain, and the Soviet Union has a say there too. Do you think that we can gain anything by clashing with the US and Britain on the issue of the UN's position in Israel?

There is a four-legged table – I mean four armistice agreements. One leg has broken down and the table began shaking. If it is possible to throw it out, to dismantle it to pieces, fine. But if this is impossible then, first of all, it is necessary to repair the broken leg and see to it that he table leans on four legs. True, this UNTSO command has all kinds of appetites, initiated perhaps by Britain and the US. We have never taken upon ourselves to satisfy them and we are conducting a struggle on this background. It is one thing to cooperate with the UN while, at the same time, guarding our sovereignty. But it is another thing altogether to boycott and clash with this body based on a rejection of its authority in the area of the Armistice Agreements.

The situation would be different had we enjoyed peace. But there is no peace on the armistice front. Yesterday the water pipeline was blown up near the Gaza Strip. Whose interest was it to summon UNTSO observers to the spot? Do you think that if we announced that the pipeline was blown up the world would believe us? It was crucial that UNTSO observers be brought down there to ascertain that three men had carried out that action. It is by far more important that UNTSO announces that rather then we.

We are going to have a political debate in the Knesset. It is my wish that this debate not become an electioneering debate, that the very grave issue of our foreign policy and the foreign relations of the State of Israel not become an election issue.

One last remark. Committee members spoke here about the need to enhance our political standing physically. Let me point to an additional improvement in our relations with France. It is not a formal, declarative one, but a concrete one, especially in the military area, and not only in the sphere of purchasing arms but also in the planning of production and in the accompanying research [possibly a veiled allusion to nuclear research]. All in all it intensifies our military industry.

[- - -]

The DG [reported] the telegram [from Washington] about Blau[stein's[91] proposed visit] to Egypt.[92]

Isser regarding the proposal for contacts in France.[93]

News about blowing up the pipeline [near Nir Am by infiltrators from the Gaza strip]. [- - -] [Later that day] Lavon suggested retaliation [for the blowing up of the pipeline.] Telephone from [Shmuel] Bentsur: Shimon Orenstein was released. I issued a communiqué and phoned Mizra [Mordechai Oren's kibbutz].

A cable from the UN SG to Burns on the rights of [free movement of UN] Observers.[94]

[- - -] Finished my letter to the three with "one can never know what the next day – or night – may bring."

26.10.54

To: Eliahu Elath [London]
Abba Eban [Washington - N.Y.]
Reuven Shiloah [Washington]
From: M.S.

I feel a need to write to you personally, and describe one chapter in the internal struggle I am engrossed in these days and in which you share as my partners from afar. The subject of this chapter is the struggle over the question of retaliations against Egypt and Jordan in recent weeks.

91 Jacob Blaustein (1892-1970). American-Jewish businessman. President of the AJC (1950?-1954; subsequently its Honorary President). Member of US Delegation to the UN (1955). Frequently served as a trusted link between senior Israeli and American officials.

The AJC was founded in 1909 to advance civil liberties and social equality for Jews in the US. Later its focus moved to global advocacy on Jewish issues, and shifted from ambivalent "non-Zionism" to support for Israel. In September 1950 Blaustein reached an agreement with PM Ben-Gurion respecting the political allegiance of American Jews as being solely to their country of residence.

92 Blaustein had met with Mahmoud Riyadh, with Nasser's knowledge, at the initiative of Henry Byroade of the State Department. The generally positive outcome of the meeting included efforts to arrange for his visit to Cairo. For details, see *DFPI* 9, doc.433; Zvi Ganin, *An Uneasy Relationship: American Jewish Leadership and Israel, 1948-1957* (Syracuse University Press, 2005), 195-99. Cf. below, entry for November 17, 1954.

93 Cf. *DFPI* 9, docs.436-437.

94 Reference perhaps to Hammarskjöld to Burns, September 29, 1954. The SG gave a copy to Israeli delegate, Reggie Kidron, at the beginning of October. See ISA FM 130.02/2428/1-b.

I shall begin with Egypt. The series of sabotage activities and murders committed by Egyptian gangs in the Gaza Strip border area and the vicinity of Eilat during the period between September 2nd and 25th is well-known to you from our cables. At the start of this new wave of incidents on the part of Egypt, the Minister of Defense himself proposed not to respond with retaliations but to address a special demand to Burns and give him a chance to show his mettle. To this course I contributed an appeal of my own to [Francis H.] Russell, [Chargé d'affaires at the US Embassy,] which was formulated not as a request, but as a query put to the State Department, asking whether they were ready willing to express severe condemnation to the government in Cairo and publicize that they had done so. The intention was to demand of them an even-handed attitude towards Israel and for Egypt, and to denounce in advance the double-standard of judgement that they have adhered to in practice. These appeals bore no fruit, and the murder at Beit Hashikma, which followed them, was enough to wear our patience thin. This action was most impudent and also seemed especially dangerous due to its destructive effect on the morale of the settlers and its encouragement of more bloody assaults of this kind. This was on the night of Saturday, September 25.

The day after, on Sunday, I invited the CoS to the Cabinet meeting (the Defense Minister was then on vacation) to report on the dispute with Burns over the question of observers' patrols. In the wake of the debate held on this matter, it was decided, in accordance with my proposal, to seek a compromise along certain lines. After the meeting, the Chief of Staff asked to see me privately, and proposed my authorization of a retaliation against the Egyptian in the Gaza Strip. He contended that matters had come to an intolerable pass, and that we had to cease our "self-restraint."[95]

If we did not act vigorously, the [terrorist] wave would constantly swell in magnitude and result in the utter collapse of the settlements. On the other hand, vigorous action on our part would put an end to Cairo's indifference to what was happening along the borders of the Strip and rouse it to take preventive measures. Until then the Egyptian government had acquitted itself by only imposing a curfew on Gaza for several nights: more a demonstration of activity for the sake of appearances than an efficient operation to root out the evil. I would like to cite an incident that sheds a special light on the situation. Once, one of our patrols aborted the plans of a gang of infiltrators it clashed with. One of the members of the gang was wounded and captured. In his interrogation he frankly confessed that the gang was organized and dispatched by Egyptian intelligence and attributed instructions for least two of the previous operations to guidance from this source. The CoS contended, again and again, that there was no point in "retail" retaliations that would strike at some military outpost or simply at groups of civilians or refugees. Cairo would not be impressed by this, or be roused from its lassitude. Only an action of great impact would force Cairo to act energetically and without delay. If such an action was unacceptable to me, it was best in his opinion to desist from any action at all. I asked what action he was proposing. The answer was: a nighttime sortie into the city of Gaza in order to blow up a central government building or at least one of its wings: the

95 A reference to the *havlaga* (self-restraint) doctrine adopted by the JAE and the *Va'ad Hale'umi*, and maintained by the *Hagana* organization – the clandestine military arm of the organized *yishuv*, controlled by the JAE – during the 1936-1939 Arab Revolt against the British Mandate and Zionism. While the concept normally suggests ethical behavior towards non-combatant Arabs, it was denigrated at the time by the Revisionist Party led by Ze'ev Jabotinsky and ignored by the *Irgun* (*ETZEL*). Dayan was no doubt using the term in the present context as one of derision, to mock Sharett's and the MFA's approach.

district offices, or police headquarters, or the municipal water installation. The operation would require the use of two companies: one to create a sort of corridor from the border to Gaza and one to pass through this corridor in order to carry out the mission. Obviously, it would involve a clash with Egyptian military forces. The CoS thought that the number of casualties killed by us would not necessarily exceed ten. Evidently, we ourselves must be prepared for a number of casualties, but if we are successful we would perhaps lose no more than two or three.

I said to myself that there was no guarantee the proposed operation would end with this total of casualties from both sides; the numbers could be much higher. I was also sure that, in practice, three or four companies would be activated in such a case, and the size of the operation be augmented per force. Breaking into the city of Gaza with a large force would in itself have a resounding effect, beside which all prior Egyptian raids would pale in comparison. As regards the [UN General] Assembly which had just begun its deliberations, the action would ill serve us as a helpful "overture" in just the same way as the Qibya action last year. Furthermore, at the very time of our being engrossed in a public campaign in the US to prove that arms given to Egypt were intended for aggression against us and that first of all we must be strengthened as a peace-seeking and beleaguered party, the attack on Gaza would prove to the whole world that we are bent on aggression and conquest. Thus, by our own efforts, we would assist Egyptian counter-propaganda and undermine our own efforts at persuasion. Finally, any day now we are expecting the appearance of "Bat Galim" at the mouth of the Suez Canal, and it is best that we focused on this campaign rather than open a "second front."

I told the CoS that my own inclinations were negative, but I would not want to decide the matter without consulting with several haverim. This consultation could take place only on Thursday. the day after Rosh Hashana.

The CoS said that he had meant to take action at the close of Rosh Hashana, on Wednesday night. I repeated that there would be no authorization before the consultation and the consultation which, as noted before, could not take place before Thursday. The CoS's response was that, in that case, he proposed to abstain from any action this time. Retaliation for a certain action could only have purpose if executed soon after that action; there was no point in taking action after a prolonged interval. In this state of affairs it was best we pursued our restraint and reap benefit from it.

I accepted this summation and while I was at it invited the CoS to visit me at the Weizmann Guest House in Rehovot on one of the two days of Rosh Hashana for a general discussion of relevant topics.

This discussion took place on Wednesday, the second day of Rosh Hashana, and shifted the center of gravity to the Jordanian front. The CoS told me what I hadn't known – for lack of newspapers and not listening to *Kol-Israel* – that on Monday morning, the day of Rosh Hashana [which began later, at sunset], [Kibbutz] Ein Hashofet's flock of sheep had been carried off forcefully by three hooligans from the Arab village of Fakua across the border: 480 head of pedigree sheep, perhaps the finest in the country. Even though this had happened on the Jordanian border, and we were still not cooperating with UN Observers in this field,[96] the theft of the flock was reported to Colonel Hommel,[97] who promised to take prompt action to obtain its return. I asked

96 Israel had been boycotting the IJMAC since late March, in protest against Cmdr. Hutchison's handling of the Ma'aleh Akrabim terrorist attack.

97 Col. Richard Hommel. US Marine, Assistant CoS of UNTSO and one of General Burns' trusted advisers.

whether Burns personally had been spoken to regarding the matter. The answer was that, following the appeal to Hommel, there was no doubt the matter had come to the notice of the [UNTSO] CoS. Better still, the next day, when Burns would tour the border accompanied by Aryeh Shalev, he would be approached directly on the subject. The CoS was very severe in his assessment of the malignant consequences arising from the flock not being returned in the absence of retaliation on our part. It would mean the abandonment of the border areas to acts of lawlessness, murder and pillage, without any retribution (by sheer miracle the Ein Hashofet's shepherd wasn't killed; the bullet only grazed his neck). The border area in question consisted entirely of agricultural settlements. A situation could easily be created in which it would be impossible to take flocks out to pasture, to plow and sow the fields, to install and operate irrigation pipes, etc. Hopefully, the flock would be returned. If it wasn't, there was no escaping taking action. The trouble was that it wasn't at all easy to seize an Arab flock as a pawn against ours. We did know that much tumult and anxiety pervaded the village from which the robbers had set out. The sober-minded folk there contended that the theft of the flock threatened their entire village and demanded it be returned. The hotheads objected. Meanwhile, the village watch had been reinforced. As a result, there was no point in choosing it as a target for a raid. In general, due to the disposition of armed forces in the Jordanian border area, the situation was such that any penetration by daylight, even for such a "modest" objective as the capture of a flock, would necessarily lead to a bloody engagement. What was called for was a surprise, a well-planned night operation. Several plans could be taken into consideration, the lightest of which was the encircling of another village, at some distance, taking control of it for several hours and removing from it all cattle and sheep. Of course, such an operation would involve bloodshed, but every effort would be made not to overdo it. The operation was planned for Friday night if the flock was not returned by then. And again, it was the CoS's firm hope that it would be returned.

I said that I well understood the severity of the matter, and that it was clear to me that if the flock was not returned, we would have to do everything possible to seize a large-sized Jordanian flock. Nevertheless, I would want to hear a more detailed description of the proposed operation before authorizing it. I suggested that meanwhile h-hour be postponed to Saturday night – also in order to give the UN people another day to act – so that on Friday I could get the detailed plan from the CoS.

The postponement from Friday night to Saturday night was not well taken by the CoS, but he accepted the verdict.

While we were talking, the telephone rang. Mrs Dayan had something to relay to the CoS. A minute later he returned to the room with beaming face: word had arrived that the flock had been returned. I sighed in relief, and I am sure that was the CoS's reaction too.

But next morning, on Thursday, I received a short note from Yosef Tekoah: a "slight" mistake had befallen the message relayed by Ruth Dayan: the negative had been dropped, and the message was that the flock had not been returned.

At that stage, I sent you a telegram to alert you to the possibility of a retaliation for the plunder of the flock.

On Friday afternoon, Lt.-General Avidar, appeared at the Weizmann Guest House to explain the details of the plan. I listened, and I was staggered. The intention was to capture a village with a force of two companies (again, practically speaking, three or four). Since a Jordanian Legion company was stationed in that area, each platoon separately, and one of them encamped right next to the designated village, it would be necessary to direct a platoon or two against it in advance. There was no doubt that, in the village itself, we would also encounter resistance from the National Guard, and perhaps from the Legion too. In this situation, despite the strict orders not to strike at civilians unnecessarily and especially to refrain from harming women and children, there was no guarantee that peaceful inhabitants wouldn't be killed or that there would be no women and children among the casualties.

The picture became clear: an inevitable frontal collision with the Legion; (despite our authentic desire to make do with little) the killing of villagers in numbers which could not by any means be anticipated; the certainty of casualties in our ranks. The attempt to remove flocks from courtyards and corrals might or might not succeed, but blood would be shed, and probably much blood. Furthermore, it would be most easy for the other side to portray the entire operation in the nature of a premeditated provocation, the intention of which was to prod Jordan into a large-scale battle which might well lead to the renewal of war – a devilish scheme of aggression on the part of Israel, for which the matter of the stealing of the flock served merely as pretext. Even un-poisoned public opinion would not understand an act involving the taking of human lives for of a flock of sheep. And while this were likely to be the political consequences, from a practical point of view the attack on the Legion might lead to military retaliations on its part, as already proven by experience, and there would be no end to the matter.

I said to Avidar that the proposed plan threatened graver consequences than I had imagined beforehand, and therefore there could be no way of its execution on Saturday night. Over *Shabbat,* I would hold a consultation at my home, and its results would decide the matter. I added that I doubted, even after Shalev's talk with Burns which had taken place in the meantime, whether we could put enough pressure on the UN apparatus, and whether we had exhausted other possibilities of putting pressure on Jordan; the same morning I had asked Arthur Lourie to speak most emphatically to the British Chargé d'affaires, [Anthony R.] Moore.

On Saturday morning a consultation was held at Weizmann Guest House, to which several ministers and the CoS were invited. The Defense Minister, who participated for the first time in this affair upon his return from vacation, insisted upon the need for an urgent retaliation for the stealing of the flock, and he renewed the proposal concerning the Gaza operation, which in all innocence I had thought was eliminated for good. I completely objected to both proposals. About Gaza, in addition to the above-mentioned reasons, I said that now that we were at the thick of the campaign over the "Bat Galim," we had no reason to upset our appeal to the SC and turn instantly from the prosecutors to the prosecuted. I also relied on the fact that only the day before (Friday), a decision of the EIMAC had been publicized, insistently demanding that Egypt once and for all put an end to the raids directed against Israel. It would be total idiocy on our part to welcome such a resolution with an act of aggression, rather than holding back to see how the resolution might influence the Egyptian behavior. As to the matter of the flock, I expressed my absolute conviction that we had not exhausted the possibilities open to us by using peaceful means to prevail upon Jordan, including threats, to return it. I announced that I was willing to personally summon Burns to a meeting with me the next day in order to put the fear of God into him.

A variety of observations were voiced during the discussion, but I was content with its common denominator. Eshkol viewed the theft of the flock as a very grave matter, and was ready to endorse any vigorous action in response to it, even if it should involve serious bloodshed, but he was impressed by my contention that not all the peaceful remedies had been tried. He whole-heartedly agreed that if something could be accomplished by political pressure, it was best to postpone the retaliation for a few days. Aran subscribed to retaliations against both Egypt and Jordan, but not sizable and high-powered actions, only limited and dispersed ones. He argued that it would have been permissible to respond to the murder at Bar-Giora, which had taken place a few days earlier, with the killing of an Arab or two, but objected to the operation being proposed by the GS. Another colleague who took part in the consultation was opposed to any retaliation against Jordan for fear of complications at the UN GA, but all the same he agreed that retaliation against Egypt was called for, though not wholesale retaliation.

Thus, no one aligned himself with the proposed high-voltage retaliation for the robbery of the flock – with its immediate execution, at any rate -- neither with the plan of breaking into Gaza. This indeed was the common denominator with which I was content enough.

While this consultation was going on, an argument developed over the efficacy of the method of retaliations in general. The CoS vigorously contended, and quite persuasively too, that if not for the retaliations the situation would have been several times worse, resulting in utter chaos. We are surrounded by Arab populations so suffused with bitter hatred towards us, and the refugee camps harbored such explosive forces, that only vigorous retaliations executed from time to time held back the gales of raidings which could flood the border areas and reduce the security of the state to shambles. It was only our sharp reactions and the pressure generated in their wake which had forced the Jordanian government to station Legion units along the border, and these latter had curtailed infiltration to some extent. True, the containment could not be absolute and, on the other hand, retaliations for damage inflicted while Legion patrols were still posted along the border necessarily brought us into confrontation with regular forces. However, there was no evading this. At any rate, there was less risk in such confrontations than in refraining from any retaliation altogether.

I said that this analysis possessed great deal of logic, but it was impossible to prove its correctness. Likewise, it was beyond me to prove the opposite.

The next day I reviewed the entire issue before the Cabinet meeting. I related what the Army's proposals had been, and why I could not accept them. In summation, my position was supported.

That same Sunday afternoon, I invited Burns to my home and saw him in the presence of the DG, without our military. I began by saying that any bystander would be astonished to learn that the PM of a state could confer with the highest representative of the UN in the region just to discuss the fate of a flock of sheep, but the fact that I'd invited him for that exclusive purpose should prove to him of itself how serious the matter was, and what importance we attributed to it. The honor of the UN representation was at stake. Not returning the flock meant the abandonment of the entire border area to the mutual brigandage of flocks which could only lead to grave bloodshed. The UN apparatus had to stand in the breach, and I demanded that he exert himself personally. According to our information, the flock was in the hands of the Legion, and its non-return meant the official justification of the robbery by the Jordanian authorities. If that was their position, they had to be notified that they would be responsible for the consequences. At any rate, it must be clear that we would not tolerate a situation that meant our flocks were available for theft.

Burns immediately acquiesced, and said that the UN staff had already addressed the Jordanian representative to the IJMAC, who had promised to handle the return of the flock. (We found out, in black-and-white, that this person notified Legion HQ that if their intention was to confiscate the flock, it was best to do so before the middle of the month – the date set for Israel's return to the MAC -- in order to confront the Israelis with a *fait accompli* when they try to raise the flock issue with the Commission.) He himself would now write urgently to the Jordanian Defense Minister. He would have been ready and willing to drive immediately to Amman but for the special session of the EIMAC, which had been scheduled for the next day and which he had to chair. If his letter should prove fruitless, he would indeed drive to Amman two days hence.

On Monday morning, the British Chargé d'affaires was invited to the Foreign Ministry. Walter and Arthur heaped coals on his head. Immediately after the conversation, he crossed into the Old City, and contacted his opposite number in Amman by telephone.

Burns' letter to [Anwar] Nusseibeh was sent to Amman with one of the officers from the UN staff. Burns himself kept his word. After returning from the special session of the EIMAC, he drove to Amman himself. I didn't follow all details of the course of negotiations between Burns and the Jordanians; that was done by the DG and Tekoah from Jerusalem, while I myself stayed in Rehovot. By the eve of Yom Kippur we had reached a stage at which the discussion was no longer whether the flock would be returned, but when and how. The Jordanians sought to save face by pressing a counter-claim for the return of some old vehicle which had strayed and crossed the border near Eilat and had been confiscated by us. They also presented us with a demand for the payment of 240 dinars for the feeding of the flock. This was a brazen demand, for the flock had been plundered inside our territory and hadn't strayed into Jordanian territory while grazing. The Army itself agreed to the return of the vehicle. (At first, they weren't sure whether it still existed or had been dismantled for spare parts). From Rehovot I gave instructions not to be stubborn in the matter of the payment. After all, the Legion could have claimed that in order to save the flock from extinction, it had taken it out of the hands of its robbers and kept it until its return could be arranged. It certainly did not have to bear the costs of its upkeep. On the other hand, since we knew that several dozen sheep had already been slaughtered and suspected that the Jordanians would replace these high-pedigreed ones with ordinary local ones, I suggested that we submit a financial claim for the missing sheep and present one sum to offset the other.

In conclusion, on Saturday, October 9th – 12 days after the plunder – I was notified that the flock had returned to Israel. A few days later I received a letter of thanks from Ein Hashofet, accompanied with an invitation to a celebration of the event to be held at the close of Simhat Torah.

The lesson from the entire affair is very instructive, a real eye-opener. True, "only" 90% of the flock was returned (I heard that someone in Army circles tried to make much of this matter), but the return was accomplished without a single shot fired and without a drop of blood shed. By contrast, if the Army's impatience had determined the course of events, who knows what political complications or even disaster we would have been facing now. Moreover, from a practical aspect, it was doubtful whether Ein Hashofet would have found several dozen scrawny Arab ewes, even with the addition of a few goats, an appropriate compensation for its fine flock.[98]

As for the Gaza Strip, since the murder at Beit Hashikma, a full month ago, nothing

98 For General Burns' interesting account of what UN Observers jokingly called "Operation Bo-Peep," see his *Between Arab and Israeli*, 41-44. Extract in WebDoc #31.

serious has happened there. Of course, one can never know what the next day – or night – may bring.

Notes: (A) The writing of this letter was completed on Monday, the 25th of this month, in the evening. When I wrote that "one can never know what the next day – or night – may bring," I could not have imagined that the very same evening the central irrigation pipeline of the Negev would be blown up once again, this time near Mefalsim. A retaliation for this action will certainly follow.

(B) This letter is meant for your eyes only and is by no means to be shown to anybody at the Embassy. I must ask you to return the letter to me in a sealed envelope addressed to me personally.

Wednesday, October 27

[- - -] With Yosef Tekoah on Burns' report to [the UN SC in] New York. [We also discussed] the CoS's reply to Burns on procedural matters and on the IJMAC; signing of the Jerusalem [Local Commanders] Agreement;[99] and arrangements for [Foreign Ministry] cooperation with the Army. Consultation about Johnston's team of experts. In the afternoon at home. At 4:00 pm [discussion regarding] the scandal of the fighter planes to Burma. 9:30 pm – *haverenu.*[100]

[- - -] Afterwards regarding retaliation [for the pipeline blowing up], I decided in favor. Why.

Thursday, October 28

Felt quite depressed all day long; what if there are casualties? Navot;[101] [what would be] the impression in the world[?]

[- - -]

In the afternoon a meeting of our Knesset faction. I wrote a note to Lavon: "No hitting!" He replied he had postponed [the retaliation, and added] orally [that] the circumstances had changed. [- - -]

10:00 pm [at home] on Hayarkon Street [a consultation] with the DG, Joe, Lavon, Dayan, [Binyamin] Givly, Shalev and Eppy. [We discussed] replies to Burns [about free movement of UN Observers]. Later, a consultation on retaliation. We were divided 50:50. He [Lavon] was for, I was against, and that was that; it was as if a stone was lifted off my heart. In the car [afterwards,] Eppy told me the history of the Alex[andria] disaster.

---

99 Cf. Shalev-Burns meeting, October 28, 1954, ISA FM 130.16/2948/17.

100 Protocols of meeting of Mapai Cabinet members not found.

101 Navot Sharett (1934-). Sharett's nephew, his brother Yehuda's son. As member of special commando Unit 101 under Ariel Sharon, participated in its retaliation operations. Member of Kibbutz Degania Bet.

Friday, October 29

[- - -]

Saturday, October 30

[- - -]

11:30 – Gershon Agron [came by. Told me] the IDF spokesman [Nahman Karni] is still "dictating" [to the *Jerusalem Post.*]

[- - -] On the evening news, three [infiltrators] killed [after crossing] the Egyptian [Gaza] border. [- - -]

Sunday, October 31

[- - -]

[Here follow excerpts from Sharett's report to the Cabinet meeting of this date:]

As you know, some time ago an agricultural mission of ours was invited to the Soviet Union on the occasion of an all-Soviet agricultural exhibition. Three people went there and were very well received. According to the principle of reciprocity, we will invite three Soviet agricultural experts for a visit to our country and thus start a series of mutual visits which would have nothing to do with proposed visits connected with the CPI. True, we have no agricultural exhibition now, but while one can spend two or three years surveying agriculture in the vast Soviet Union, two or three days will suffice for surveying agriculture in our small country.

However, there is another aspect to this subject. As is well known, Jews are not allowed to emigrate from the Soviet Union, but recently there was some amelioration of this rigid principle when six visas were granted not only to people older than 65 [as in the past] but to young people as well. I am not building castles here, but precisely because they are not letting Jews leave, we are very much interested in getting in there. Every visit of an Israeli makes a sensation within Soviet Jewry and brings them some hope – be it a soccer team, a visit by a journalist, or an agricultural mission, or for instance the recent visit of Mrs Vera Weizmann. News about such visits spreads quickly. The Israelis are seen, most of them show up in local synagogues and their very appearance there raises the Jews' spirits. There is no greater duty [*mitzva*] we can perform for the sake of Russian Jewry than to keep up such visits. And the more Soviet visitors we invite over to Israel, we can expect that more Israeli visitors will be invited by the Soviets. We should see this as an integral part of our efforts to penetrate that area

The Noose Tightens in Cairo

Monday, November 1

Went straight to the Foreign Ministry. Lourie [reported on] his talk with Moore. [Local] Commanders Agreement [will serve as a] test. Joe on his problems with Dayan.[1]

Wrote Dayan and Lavon [see below]. Edited my speech on Weizmann [on the second anniversary of his death] in English.

Jerusalem, November 1, 1954

To: Defense Minister
From: Prime Minister and Foreign Minister

I understand that the meeting between the CoS and the CoS of UNTSO has been scheduled for tomorrow.

Of the three questions under consideration, at our last meeting we determined the course of one of them, i.e., the procedural amendments in the IJMAC. I would like to comment on the other two questions.

In the matter of the [UN] observers' patrols, there is a standing Cabinet decision concerning the compromise to be sought. Obviously, if there is a possibility of settling the matter with Burns on more favorable terms, so much the better. But if this hope is in vain, we must go back to the Cabinet decision.

As for the matter of the Local Commanders Agreement in Jerusalem, we should keep in mind that we have complicated the matter by our refusal to sign the agreement which was formulated exactly according to our own wishes, just because the UN representative was going to sign it as a witness. Far be it for us to create a situation in which we should be responsible for the failure of the entire matter, all the more so after we took the initiative for this agreement. I do not know whether this agreement will have any practical value, but it is clear that our not signing it gives the powers and other elements an opportunity to saddle us with the blame for any deterioration of the situation. Therefore I believe that we should not insist on the issue of the presence of UN personnel at the meetings of the [local] commanders. I am sure that the operative element here, more than being a conspiracy on the part of the UN staff to stick its nose into every matter, is a morbid fear on the part of Jordan to enter into a routine of meetings with us without a third party, a fear that we have exacerbated by denying the right of the UN staff to sign as a witness. Our refusal to sign will disrupt our relations with the UN without improving our relations with Jordan. From every practical and international aspect, this road we are embarking upon will not add to our glory.

On the other hand, it seems that we cannot agree to the exclusion of the Mount Scopus area from the scope of the agreement. If the Jordanians should insist on this point,

---

1 See Dayan to Sharett, October 29, 1954, and Dayan to Tekoah, November 19, 1954, both in IDFA 636/56/33.

the blame will lie with them.[2]

Tuesday, November 2

[- - -] Joe was not invited to [Dayan's] talk with Burns. An announcement on the agreement with the Refugee Congress [regarding blocked bank accounts' release].[3]

[- - -] In the afternoon [I heard from] Dayan about his talk with Burns.[4]

[- - -]

Wednesday, November 3

[- - -]

Nicholls[5] visited, [we discussed] Eden, Egypt.[6]

[- - -]

Thursday, November 4

The whole morning at the MFA I sweated over my lecture to the UJA conference. In the afternoon – 3 hours UJA, then a party for the conference [participants]. Later, a consultation on [Eric] Johnston's dam [i.e., proposal to use the the Kinneret as a catchment basin in his regional water development scheme].[7]

Friday, November 5

[- - -]

In the afternoon, Moshe Dayan at [my home on] Hayarkon.

[- - -]

---

2 *DFPI* 9, doc.445.

3 See *DFPI* 9, docs.446-447.

4 On this meeting, see *DFPI* 9, doc.445, n.3; Tekoah to Israel Embassy, Washington, November 3, 1954, ISA, FM 130.16/2948/17.

5 Sir John ("Jack") Walter Nicholls (1909-1970). British Ambassador to Israel (1954-1957). Later Ambassador to Belgrade, Brussels, Johannesburg.

6 Sharett's report on this meeting is in *DFPI* 9, doc.454; for Nicholls' reports, see WebDoc #32. In response to parliamentary questions at the end of the ME debate on November 2, Eden had stressed the importance of the Tripartite Declaration of 1950 [WebDoc #1] in terms of both maintaining the balance of arms between Israel and the Arab states and the powers' commitment to come to Israel's aid if it was attacked by an Arab state (and vice versa). For extracts of Eden's remarks and Israeli press coverage, see WebDoc #33. Israel continued to be concerned about the possible negative impact of the signature of the Anglo-Egyptian Agreement, despite official assurances given in Eden's letter of October 19 (see above, entry for October 21).

7 An earlier consultation was held on October 27. See *DFPI* 9, doc.441. See also below, entry for November 12.

Saturday, November 6

[Gershon] Agron [told me that] Sraya Shapiro was adding his own embellishments [to the anti-Sharett material being fed to him by the Defense Ministry]. [- - -]

My conversation with Burns. At home with Tekoah. Told him about my talk with Burns, my outpourings about [Mahmoud] Azmi, my talk with Dayan. [- - -] Let Elath go to [meet formally with] Eden.[8]

Nothing public [was done in Britain to honor] Churchill on his 80th birthday. [- - -]

I sweated blood over my speech about Enzo Sereni[9] [for the memorial meeting on his tenth anniversary of his murder by the Nazis].

Sunday, November 7

Cabinet meeting.

[Here follow excerpts of Sharett remarks at the Cabinet meeting:]

> At a previous meeting[10] I said mistakenly that recently younger Soviet Jews were permitted to immigrate to Israel. While there was an increase in the permissions' number – in past years no more than five permissions were issued and in this year the number rose to thirty-nine – the minimum age of the immigrants was fifty two, maximum seventy nine.
>
> I move now to the British parliament's political debate in which, for the first time, we heard a statement [by PM Anthony Eden] which attempted to put teeth into the Tripartite Declaration of May 1950. Eden said: If Israel is attacked, Britain would intervene by force of arms on her side. This has now been announced in the open; you will recall it was said privately by Selwyn Lloyd to Counselor Gershon Avner,[11] but afterwards Shuckburgh,[12] who deals with our matters in the FO, retreated from that position in his conversation with Elath.

---

8 The day before Elath had reported a casual conversation with Eden at a reception. See *DFPI* 9, doc.455.

9 Enzo Sereni (1905-1944). Born in Italy. Settled in Palestine in 1927. Organized youth *aliya* from Europe (1931-1934) and from Iraq (1942). During WWII he served in the Special Operations Executive (SOE), Cairo, recruiting Italian war prisoners to the Allied war effort and broadcasting propaganda in Italian to Italy. In 1944 he joined a group of 37 younger Palestinian Jews who volunteered to be parachuted into Nazi Europe – a clandestine operation organized by the JA Political Department under Sharett (then Shertok) in cooperation with SOE HQ in Cairo. On May 15, 1944 Sereni was parachuted into Northern Italy; he was soon captured and sent to Dachau concentration camp where he was shot on November 18, 1944.

10 See above, entry for October 31, 1954.

11 Gershon Avner (1919-1991). Born in Germany. Settled in Palestine in 1933. Joined JA Political Department in 1946. In MFA since 1948.

12 Sir C.A. Evelyn Shuckburgh (1909-1994). Private Secretary to Secretary of State for Foreign Affairs (August 1951-May 1954); Assistant Undersecretary of State for Middle East Affairs at the FO (May 1954-June 1956). Undertook a tour of ME capitals from late October until early December 1954, laying the groundwork for what was to become the Anglo-American secret peace initiative code-named "Operation Alpha." See also, below, page 525 n.43.

Now Eden has stated it explicitly and publicly, not behind closed doors. In the mean time I met the new British Ambassador [Nicholls]. He confirmed Eden's position. I asked: Suppose we do not ask for Britain's help – will it intervene on its own, for this would mean an invasion? He said: The assumption is that you will ask and we will respond. He asked if a defense pact between our two states was necessary. I said that we have not asked for a pact, but we would not reject such an eventuality. Ambassador Elath, who is going to meet with Eden probably this week, suggested that he would raise this matter with him and I gave him my approval.

Elections in the US. Debate in the British House of Commons.
[- - -] I asked Lavon about the incursion from the [Gaza] Strip.

Monday, November 8

Cabinet meeting [dealing with internal problems of maintaining the coalition with the General Zionists].

[- - -] At 12:30 went to receive [Edward B.] Lawson[13] [the new American Ambassador to Israel]. [- - -]

Tuesday, November 9

[- - -] At the Foreign Ministry consultation with Daniel Lewin on [Israel's recent vote in the UN on] China.[14]

[- - -] Later [a consultation] on [the passage of Israeli ships through] the Suez Canal.[15]

Got home at 2:00 pm and had a phone call from London: Eliahu [will meet with] Eden [and will request] a written undertaking [of Britain's protection in the event of an attack on Israel].[16]

At 3:00 the Cabinet [Foreign Affairs and Defense] Committee: the [Suez] Canal, China, Eden['s statement].[17]

---

13 Edward B. Lawson (1895-1962). US Ambassador to Israel (1954-1959).

14 See *DFPI* 9, doc.458.

15 During this period American officials were attempting to formulate a successful draft resolution in the UN SC. See, e.g., *FRUS 1952-1954*, docs.913, 919; *DFPI* 9, docs.448, 456, 463, 464, 466.

16 See *DFPI* 9, doc.461.

17 During the discussions various participants made proposals for follow-up actions after the arrest of the crew of the "Bat Galim", such as sending another ship through the Suez Canal or through the Gulf of Aqaba straits. Sharett concluded by saying Israel should wait and see how things evolved in the SC regarding the "Bat Galim" issue. On the subject of relations with China, Sharett said: "At a certain stage, both in Helsinki and Rangoon, Chinese representatives asked their Israeli colleagues if Israel desired to enter into diplomatic relations with China. The FM considered this matter and concluded that it was not comfortable to say No, but it was not desirable to say Yes [in view of the American position]. Upon our instructions, our Minister in Rangoon answered his Chinese colleague: The Chinese offer is being considered, but meanwhile we are prepared to consider sending an economic mission for a visit. The mission would take place in December or January."

Lavon: No incident took place [as reported November 7]. [- - -]

[Text of note received from Ben-Gurion:]

Tiberias, 9.11.54

To Moshe, Shalom and Greetings,

I read with great satisfaction what you said in your talk with Shuck[burgh]. But Shuck[burgh]'s and Nich[olls]'s words are deeply worrying. The mentality of the London Conference of 1938 [*sic.* for "1939" – the "Round-Table" Conference at Saint James Palace] still exists – with no change al all. Thus spoke [Malcolm] MacDonald and [Lord] Halifax. They undoubtedly represent the position of Anthony [Eden], and that is even worse than Dulles' position, and it is without doubt influencing the S.D. [orig. in English; i.e., the State Department] position.

And again I see no other conclusion but strengthening ourselves internally. But this is known and clear to all, and yet no one seems to be doing anything about it.

Yours,
D. Ben-Gurion[18]

Wednesday, November 10

Kesse [came by] with Shlomo Hillel [to discuss Jewish] bank accounts [abandoned] in Iraq. A committee has been appointed.

Meeting with our party members of the Knesset FADC. My speech. A useful clarification of [the subjects of] - Germany, China, immigration from the Soviet Union, US, Britain, Arabs, Jerusalem, France, Burma.

Presentation of Nicholls' credentials. [- - -] Nicholls [delivered] a nice speech, and so did the President [Yitzhak Ben-Zvi] But he [found it appropriate to say on this occasion that he] thinks that Soviet Jews are discriminated against in view of their being prevented from emigrating to Israel.

[- - -]

In the afternoon at Eshkol's house: (1) Financing a refugee survey [by appealing to the] Rockefeller [Foundation]? [Yosef] Weitz and his colleagues should look into this.[19]

---

18 The date of Ben-Gurion's note might be incorrect. Sharett met with Shuckburgh almost three weeks later (see below, entry for November 26), suggesting that November 29 or December 9 might be the correct date of this note.

19 Citing Weitz's diaries, Nur Masalha describes a meeting convened at Sharett's home on November 1 attended by Danin, Divon, Kollek and Rafael. Weitz and Danin were to follow up by preparing an outline of the proposed work and its costs, on the basis of which Sharett promised to consult his Cabinet colleagues. Nur Masalha, "'Dis/Solving' the Palestinian Refugee Problem," 132-33. See also above, entry for May 4, 1954. Weitz was a member of a "transfer committee" established by Sharett in 1949-1950 to investigate possibilities of settling Arab refugees abroad, in places such as Libya and South America. Nothing came of these discussions. See Morris, "Yosef Weitz and the Transfer Committees, 1948-49."

Thursday, November 11

[- - -]

At the Foreign Ministry. [- - -] Consultation on the problem with the refugee congress (not to hold up implementation [of the unfreezing of bank accounts]).[20]

Talk with Nicholls.

[- - -]

Friday, November 12

9:00 am – at the PMO. Consultation (Eshkol, *Tahal* [representative]) on the American [Kinneret] catchment [proposal]. I composed a cable to Elath [transmitting] a summary of the Cabinet committee meeting and my talk with Nicholls.[21]

11:00 am – presentation of the letters of accreditation by [incoming US Ambassador Edward] Lawson; his address.

12:00 – at the Foreign Ministry. Consultation about Mount Scopus. The DG reported on Khirbet [Sulam] (yesterday he had heard about the expulsion from Lavon).[22]

I immediately phoned Ziama [Divon]. Leo [offered] comments on my [Knesset] speech [scheduled for November 15. He emphasized there were] no guarantees [by Egypt to refrain from aggression against Israel included in the recently signed Anglo-Egyptian Agreement].[23]

[- - -]

[Text of note received from Ben-Gurion:]

Sde Boker, 12.11.54

To Moshe, Shalom and Greetings,

Even though I assume my saying this is superfluous, and while you yourself correctly interpreted the meaning of Eden's statement [of November 2], I consider it my duty to inform you of my opinion. Eden cleverly answered the question put to him [in Parliament]. However, he did not add any strength to the Tripartite Declaration, nor did he take upon himself any additional obligation. The reservation "pending consultation with the two other Powers" annuls the promise to come to Israel aid if it is attacked.

There is no need to ignore nice talk, but at the same time one cannot take nice talk

20 *DFPI* 9, doc.469.

21 *DFPI* 9, doc.470.

22 The editors were unable to find details regarding the Khirbet Sulam incident.

23 Sharett often labored hard and long in advance over his Knesset speeches. See, e.g., Tekoah's November 2 comments on an earlier draft, in CZA A245/76.

as an obligation which is unreal.

With a strong Shalom to you and to Zipporah,

Yours,
D. Ben-Gurion

Saturday, November 13

All day long pangs of composing my speech [for the November 15 Knesset session, in response to Eden's statement on November 2 on the Tripartite Declaration]. I read the Hansard in the morning and struggled [over the speech]. [- - -] In the evening Joe Tekoah [reported] success against Jordan regarding irrigation from the Jordan River and Burns' promises to step up [efforts to release] the "Bat Galim." Wrote up my speech till 4:00 am.

Sunday, November 14

[- - -]

Cabinet meeting. I announced I wouldn't touch on Germany [in my Knesset speech]. [Discussed] the *hasbara* budget. A losing battle [for the GZ critics]. I replied to Rokach.[24]

Serlin wanted an outline of my [Knesset] speech [tomorrow] and I refused. An exchange of notes with Lavon about retaliation over Khirbet [Sulam?] and a continuation of [IDF's retaliation against] Nebi Samuel.[25]

[- - -]

I wrote up the speech, throwing out [references to the] Jerusalem [incidents]. In the evening [I dictated the text] to Lillian until 1:00 am. Went over the speech with Walter.

Monday, November 15

At the Foreign Ministry.

[- - -]

[Worked] all morning on the speech; everything is ready.

[- - -]

In the afternoon [went] to the Knesset. [Spoke for] 40 minutes, everything

24 During the Cabinet discussion on the *hasbara* budget, the GZ ministers questioned the necessity of hasbara, seeing it a tool in the hands of Mapai for partisan manipulation of public opinion. (The Minister responsible for *hasbara* was Z. Aran.) The budget was approved by a majority vote in the Cabinet.

25 Exchange of notes with Lavon not found.

got compressed.[26]

[- - -]

Tuesday, November 16

The papers were full [of coverage] of the speech. [- - -]

At the Foreign Ministry. [- - -] I was busy preparing material for my reply [in the Knesset debate]. Ze'ev [Sharef] went to great lengths [to assist me]. [- - -] Afterwards I had a talk with Leo Kohn. I developed an idea: It is doubly disrespectful for us to be both cajoling and being repulsed, and for becoming a mistress [of the Western powers]. It is not respectful to behave like the Arabs and beg the US and Britain. With this idea in mind I composed the end of the speech and sent it for translation into English – meanwhile, there is something to cable [to the Israeli legations] abroad.

2:00 pm at home. Immediately after lunch sat down till 4:00, writing paragraph after paragraph [of my reply to the Knesset debate].

[- - -] Got to the Knesset at 8:00 pm and was immediately given the floor. [I spoke] for 50 minutes.[27]

[In his reply, Sharett said, inter alia:]

In general, the doctrine that the assertion of an international right has prospects only

---

26 Sharett opened with remarks on the Anglo-Egyptian Agreement, signed on October 19, and its potential negative impact on Israel's security because of the geopolitical and strategic advantages reaped by Egypt. He expressed appreciation for Eden's letter to Elath of the same date (see above, entry for October 21) and also for his Parliamentary remarks on November 2 (above, entry for November 3), which constituted a welcome public statement of Britain's undertakings under the Tripartite Declaration (1950) to come to Israel's assistance if it were attacked and to preserve the balance between Israel and all the Arab states in terms of arms supplies.

In the section of his speech dealing with "Arab Threats," Sharett drew quotations from a recent flurry of particularly intransigent and hostile declarations by Jordanian, Egyptian, Syrian, Lebanese and Saudi rulers. "Far be it for me to exaggerate ... the possible influence of this poisonous verbiage. It may be that these are only the frenzied cries of members of a declining generation petrified in their conceptions and blinded by their own hatreds. Yet these things are being said in public and reach the ears of multitudes." Then, in a thinly-disguised rebuke to the Western powers' wooing of the Arab states to join in a regional anti-Soviet defense alliance, Sharett added: "Those who are taking pains to consolidate and encourage the regimes which now hold sway in the Arab countries ought to realize what it is they are consolidating and to whom they are giving encouragement. The striving for peace and the strengthening of the hands of rulers of this type is ... a contradiction in terms." The full English text (9 pp. mimeo) of the speech is in CZA A245/76. Cf. *Divrei Haknesset*, XVII: 64-67; *DFPI* 9, doc.476.

27 Part of Sharett's reply dealt with criticism of his government's handling of the freedom of navigation (Suez, Eilat) issue, the recovery of assets of Jews who left Iraq, and the release of blocked Arab refugee accounts.

if it is backed at every stage by a capacity to demonstrate and forthwith deploy physical force does not to my mind betray a particularly wide understanding. By embracing this theory [- - -] it can lead you to abandon every form of purely political or legal struggle in the international arena. This would mean never to apply to the SC, never to burden the big powers. Is it really the case that when we turn to these powers [- - -] and when we condemn this international scandal which Egypt is perpetrating [by not allowing unhampered Israeli passage through the Suez Canal, as enjoined by the UN SC resolution of September 1951], do we really thereby invite [outsiders] to wage the struggle on our behalf while we sit back with folded arms? Our enlisting of international support is only one of the forms of our own struggle – it is one of the weapons we use in this campaign. [- - -]

[- - -]

The release of Arab blocked accounts in Israel [- - -] was a timely step. It has been of moral value to Israel on the international front. Financially, also, we have lost nothing. Notwithstanding the outcry of one of our newspapers whose acquaintance with the facts often stands in inverse ration to the categorical character of its judgments, we have not thereby surrendered any card that was in our hands. On all counts this was the right thing to do. In connection with this release, direct contact was established between us and the representative body of Arab refugees. There is no alliance between us, nor any joint conspiracy against anyone, as some Arab newspapers are alleging. On the contrary, they and we are two litigants. Yet we see virtue in this direct contact between us both for their sake and for our own. [- - -]

MK Yitzhak Raphael has condemned partial agreements as prejudicing the prospects of complete peace. I could not follow exactly to what he was referring. What kind of partial agreement have we concluded? In replying to a query in the course of an interview given to a certain American journal[28] I did say – and I think I have said it more than once before, so that if I have sinned I must have sinned many a time – that if the Jordanians stopped the boycott and agreed to enter into mutual trade relations with us we should be prepared to give them free port facilities at Haifa. What kind of unrequited benefit is there here? Is such a partial arrangement really harmful to Israel?

[- - -]

And now, Mr Speaker, a few observations of a general character in reference to some of the more sweeping criticism that has been voiced here. An attack was launched in this debate on the entire foreign policy of the Government from certain sides, mostly voiced very loudly and with rage unbridled. On this occasion, Mr [Yitzhak] Ben-Aharon outreached everybody else, so that the cup is undoubtedly his. He is definitely the victor in this contest. And yet not a single piece of concrete advice was offered by any of the critics nor did they trace an alternative road. [- - -][29]

[- - -]

[Afterwards in the Knesset cafeteria, MK Baruch Azaniah [Mapai]: "Our party's MKs were highly satisfied," MK Yaakov [Shimshon] Shapira: "a wonderful speech."

28 *USNWR* – cf. above, entry for September 14, 1954 and WebDoc #28.

29 Sharett's reply is in *Divrei Haknesset*, XVII: 102-07. For fuller excerpts see WebDoc #34.

Hannah Lamdan:[30] "a great speech." In the Knesset [received] a note from Tekoah: "Some progress on [attempts to release] the 'Bat Galim'."[31]

[- - -]

Wednesday, November 17

[- - -] [Met] with Yael Vered [of the MFA Research Division] about her [planned] book and Arab affairs – Khirbet Sulam.[32] Yael told me of the impression made by my first speech on the radio. [- - -]

Ha'olam Hazeh [maverick weekly owned and edited by journalist and later MK, Uri Avnery].[33]

At the Foreign Ministry with G.R.: The PCC has maneuvered itself to leave. British subversion. Deathly fear [among the British] of the rise of Palestinian power [in Jordan] (Glubb). The incentive [which is driving the] refugees [serves their] political goal – it enhances their position in [the West Bank of] Palestine [and creates] an opening for [our] negotiations [with them] on [their] lands [now situated inside Israel territory]. G.R.'s steadfastness against doubts or retreats on our part [vis-à-vis the PCC].

Blaustein's mission [to Cairo] has been shamefully cancelled.[34]

For lunch at [Ambassador] Nicholls' home with the Moores and others. Nicholls complimented me [on the Knesset speech]: "*dexterously*" [orig. English].

[- - -]

A long conversation with Shaul [regarding Jews in the Soviet bloc] – method of our activity, mishaps, new ways, people to man [*Nativ*'s cadres in Israel's Soviet bloc embassies], [preparation of] literature [to be disseminated among Soviet Jews].

---

30 Hannah Lamdan (1905-1995). Born in Serbia. Settled in Palestine in 1926. Mapai MK (1949-1955). Deputy Speaker of the Knesset. Later MK for *Ahdut Ha'avoda* and Mapam.

31 Ironically, General Burns' diary of this date notes how "very tiresome" he found the continuing delays caused by Egyptian-Israeli wrangling. LAC MG31G6 v.7. The "Bat Galim" affair was scheduled to be discussed at the EIMAC meeting of November 18.

32 See above, entry for November 12,

33 On this day *Ha'olam Hazeh* published a sensational report under the headline: "The Secret Plan of Ben-Gurion," in which it was stated that "Mapai is again on the verge of decision which will determine the future political development of the country for the coming months. Ben-Gurion and Sharett are ready to do battle. Their secret plans, in broad outline, have become known." The weekly purported to outline the composition of BG's cabinet upon his return to premiership, for instance: PM and FM – Ben-Gurion; Defense – Lavon; *hasbara* – Sharett. Sharett's plan, according to *Ha'olam Hazeh*, was to purge BG's people from key government posts. An effort would be made to get rid of Defense Minister Lavon, MK Argov (head of the Knesset FADC), Teddy Kollek (DG of the PMO), and Ze'ev Sharef (Cabinet Secretary).

34 For details, see *DFPI* 9, docs.459, 489 (n.4); Ganin, *An Uneasy Relationship*, 196-99; above, entry for October 26, 1954.

The DG [discussed] atomic research. Authority [for dealing with the nuclear issue as between the Defense Minister and the PM] is not clear. A[n Atomic Energy] committee was appointed by [Defense Minister] BG, Lavon inherited it. [Members are] experts + Peres + CoS. They want the Foreign Ministry DG, but who is authorized to appoint him? There are two schools: Sambursky and Bergmann[35] – [the first is for] research and [the second is for] production. The DG of the Ministry of Development ignores atomic [energy for purposes of] irrigation etc., [his opposition] based on out-dated assumptions. A French expert [has arrived?]. [The activity aimed at production of atomic energy is, in Eytan's words,] "like the crossing of the Atlantic [Ocean] by air in 1925/26 – it is clear that we will succeed, but it is not clear how much the ticket will cost." Oil-rich countries might afford [this enterprise], but [can] we? And [on the other hand] do we want others to precede us? I: "[This issue] must be brought before the Cabinet, but not before the elections, because the GZ will undermine it by leaking to the press. I will talk with Sambursky [in order] to change his mind [on account of his opposition to Bergman's ideas, [presumably for developing a nuclear weapon. Will also talk] with Eshkol, Lavon. I will ask BG who appointed [the Atomic Energy] Committee."

I dictated the reply letter [to BG] to Lillian.

Thursday, November 18

Straight to the Foreign Ministry. Completed the translation of the [Knesset] speech. [Learned] from GR about his mission to Paris, and the cancellation of Blaustein's trip to Cairo.[36] [- - -]

Lunch with the American [Ambassador, Edward Lawson]. Mrs Lawson [spoke of] Jews' domination, and [reportedly told] Hermona [Simon] that "the State Department is against [you], but we shall be your friends." I gave a farewell speech for [Francis] Russell. Went to tea at Yaacov Herzog's.

Eytan exploded against Lavon. He [Lavon] had let loose in front of Russell and his people over Eban's exaggerations regarding the atom. Joe [reported] from the [MAC] meeting, almost everything was going well, and he retreated again. Conversation with Burns during the party, "territorial waters."[37]

With T[eddy] K[ollek] on [- - -] the atom, the possibility of getting a reactor from the US. – A compromise between Sambursky and Bergmann.

[- - -]

35 See above, entries for June 6 and November 17, 1954.

36 See above, entry for November 17.

37 Burns recorded in his diary on this date that the Arabs and the Israelis appeared to be coming closer to accepting Johnston's water-sharing scheme. LAC MG31G6 v.7. MFA officials continued to fear undesirable complications and consequences to Johnston's latest suggestions. See *DFPI* 9, doc.487.

[Text of note received from Ben-Gurion:]

Dear Moshe,

From your letter[38] I gather that the press version regarding Eden's reply was not accurate. The authoritative Hansard protocol is not classified.

When [Labour leader] Arthur Greenwood paid me a visit I discussed with him Eden's declaration (at the time I had not yet seen the press version on the basis of which I wrote you my previous letter) and I told him: if Eden really thinks that England must come to our aid if we are attacked – why does he not deal with us the same as he is dealing with all of Britain's allies, in NATO, the European pact and the Jordanian one? Why is he not prepared to sign a written pact [with us]? Consequently, there is a difference and therefore we cannot rely just on his declaration (I was not aware then of the accurate wording). Greenwood thanked me [for clarifying this].

Now that I have read his authentic words, I see that his declaration was more positive than I had thought, both in its first part (regarding help in case of an attack) and in the second part too – regarding keeping a balance in giving arms. And perhaps the second part is more important, because it determines an immediate obligation, and in peaceful times, not in a hypothetical case which should be prevented. However, the naked fact remain: if this is the intention, why not a bilateral pact, written and signed? [- - -]

Yours,
D. Ben-Gurion

Friday, November 19

Attacks on Burns by military correspondents in the newspapers.

Went to Tel Aviv in the morning. At the Foreign Ministry in the *Kirya* I phoned Walter, then to Elath, [asking him] to postpone [his meeting] with Eden [- - -]. [Phoned] Eban [asking] why he overdid it.[39]

[Met] with Isser – recorded separately.[40]

[- - -] Phoned Yosef Tekoah [and learned of] a victory in the EIMAC.[41]

According to Tekoah, the CoS had arranged the [anti-Burns] briefing for the correspondents.

Saturday, November 20

[- - -]

38 Letter not found.

39 Possibly a reference to Eban's note to Secretary of State Dulles, November 18, 1954, *DFPI* 9, doc.484.

40 Record not found. Presumably they discussed the "mishap" in Egypt.

41 I.e., the passage of an Israeli motion on the groundlessness of Egyptian complaints regarding the "Bat Galim" incident. See *DFPI* 9, doc.486. Burns' diary records an unhappy undercurrent to the EIMAC meeting of November 18. Lt.-Colonel Shaul Ramati of the Israeli delegation "made a statement ridiculing the Egyptian story of the ["Bat Galim"'s] attack on the fishermen, and referring to Major Salah Salem, which was offensive to the Egyptians." LAC MG31G6 v.7.

Eppy phoned about the IJMAC – our representative walked out of the meeting.

[- - -]

Walter phoned [to say that] Egypt is appealing [the EIMAC ruling on the "Bat Galim"].[42]

Burns isn't supporting [Egypt's appeal of the EIMAC ruling].

Sunday, November 21

[- - -]

Monday, November 22

[- - -] At the Foreign Ministry [a consultation] on the continuing [dispute over the] "Bat Galim" – [consideration of] an appeal to the SC.

[- - -]

Tuesday, November 23

Meeting of the Knesset FADC: We pointed to the victory [in the EIMAC] on the "Bat Galim." [I explained] the need for exploiting what was achieved without carrying out an additional operation. As always, confrontation with Argov [FADC chairman].

[- - -]

[The minutes of the FADC record the following remarks by Sharett:]

> I would first like to make is clear that when the government decided on this operation it took into account two possibilities: that it would succeed and that it would not. Our reasoning was that even if the operation was fated to not succeed in one of its stages or at its end, it was better to execute it than not, and this for two reasons: first of all it is impossible to be sure in advance that it would not succeed. If we do nothing there would certainly not be any success and then the situation as it is, i.e. the blockade, remains; if you do act, then there is a chance of breaking the blockade. The second reason was that in case the operation failed, it would be better that the failure be a result of action taken than of doing nothing. If you do something, you can expect results; if you do nothing, no results can be expected. The situation as it is unbearable, and thus it is better, if we are preparing ourselves for the future, that this physical protest be executed than not executed. This is how we reasoned.
>
> It also should be clear to us that what we have embarked on is a long battle. We must realize it will involve a time scale if not of years, then certainly of months. If you want today to mount an operation against Gaza, it can be done on the next day. If you

42 See also *DFPI* 9, doc.490.

decide to send a ship, preparation alone takes two-three months. The government has decided to go on with this battle on both fronts, Suez and Eilat, with the intention of constantly staying active.

Wednesday, November 24

[- - -] Went to the Foreign Ministry. [Discussed] arrangements for Shuckburgh with the DG. G.R. is anxious [to meet Shuckburgh]. Consultation.[43]

[- - -] [Received] an annoying letter from G.R.

[No "skeleton" was found for the period from November 25, 1954 to January 2, 1955, when the diarist resumed writing (even though he then mentioned that he had written a "skeleton" for this whole period). In place of the diary we have reconstructed some of Sharett's political activity of this five-week period from archival documents.]

Thursday, November 25

[On this date the Cabinet FADC met and devoted its attention to relations between Israel and the US and Britain in view of the evacuation from the Suez Canal Zone, and the one-sided policy of arming the Middle East countries. It was opened by a presentation by PM Sharett. Excerpts follow:]

The impulse for discussing our relations with the US is the initiative of Secretary of State Dulles' in his two last talks with our Ambassador, proposing to us some coming to terms by way of an exchange of Notes. The impulse for our discussing our relations with the Britain is a series of talks, especially the last talks between Mr Selwyn Lloyd and our plenipotentiary Gershon Avner.

I have no intention of making a lengthy analysis. Let me say in short: we are not finding ourselves in a completely new situation as a result of American and British policies. It is not these which created the extreme and foreboding quantitative disproportion

---

43 Rafael went to meet with Shuckburgh and Nicholls the following day. During the meeting with Shuckburgh, Rafael outlined his country's ideas for the first steps towards a settlement. For details, see WebDoc #35.

Shuckburgh's fact-finding mission would indeed become the basis of top-secret Anglo-American plans for an Arab-Israeli settlement that would be undertaken during 1955 under the code name "Alpha." Upon his return to London, Shuckburgh reported that there was a certain "weariness" and a "desire for a relaxation of tension" in the Arab countries, but without "much disposition to compromise." Most leaders in the region said "privately" that they would like a settlement, although publicly they were "committed to oppose it except on terms known to be unobtainable." Shuckburgh singled out the attitude of Egypt as different from that of the other Arab states: the Egyptian government, he felt, was "less emotional on the subject and less subject to public opinion." Egypt would "probably like a settlement if [it] could play a part in obtaining it and if it led to increased Egyptian influence in the Arab world." Nasser was described as "a man of courage[,] capable of leading rather than following public opinion." Shuckburgh, Notes on Arab-Israel Dispute, December 15, 1954, TNA FO371/111095 VR1079/10G; extracts in Caplan, *Futile Diplomacy* IV, doc.4. See also above, page 514 n.12; *DFPI* 9, docs.549, 565; Caplan, *Futile Diplomacy* IV: 84-89.

between us and the Arab countries. This disproportion is a constant, basic phenomenon, dictated by fate, and we have taken upon ourselves to wrestle with it inasmuch as it is in our power, being aware that there is no guarantee that we shall succeed. What has happened now is that the disproportion has become aggravated by the policy of the two Powers, and our response must be more putting the onus of responsibility on them instead of us pointing out to our weakness, to the danger of our being destroyed and annihilated.

I say this in view of the Knesset debate next week, in which we should not evoke too much panic, for panic may seriously damage the spirits of the people as well as those of the diaspora, and it would serve the Arab world as a powerful encouragement. Indeed, in our struggle with the Arabs we should only be strong; we must instill an impression that we are powerful, for otherwise we can be lost.

Clearly, our very warnings against the American policy mean that we are worried, that the security of Israel has been undermined and could be further undermined. However, what we should emphasize is the danger threatening the entire Middle East, the danger of undermining its stability, of moving it further away from peace – rather than pointing to the direct danger threatening Israel. I'm not suggesting covering up the truth in talks with responsible Jews abroad. I'm not suggesting blurring reality in direct talks with American and British leaders. But we are going to have a Knesset debate, which serves as a public expression of our state of mind, and such debates are echoed all over the world, including the Arab world. [- - -]

Our aim should be exerting maximum pressure on the Western powers, especially on the US, with the aim of deterring them from their policy of arms sales [to Arab countries]. If we do not achieve our aim, and it may assumed that we shall not, then our pressure should aim at limiting or deferring the pace of arms sales.

In earlier stages we succeeded in deferring some changes and perhaps in limiting them too. We put the [American] Administration in a defensive position and self-justification, and this bore fruit. We must continue in the same vein. We must not limit ourselves to slowing and limiting, but strive at receiving concrete compensation for the additional power granted to the other side.

Ambassador Eban explained to us that we cannot entertain much hope that the Democratic Party would pursue a partisan policy fully opposing that of the [Eisenhower Republican] Administration, but there is ground for our hope that within both parties our demands would be listened to with empathy and support. Our activity should be directed at those congressmen and senators whose elections are not assured or are dependent on Jewish votes. At the same time our demands should not be limited to the elections; they are aimed at winning public opinion, first and foremost Jewish.

Here we should use a series of negative principles. First, "no" to arms to the Arab countries as long as there is no peace; no arms to the Arab countries as a means against Soviet penetration or invasion. We shall not succeed in uprooting the American general fear of Communist expansionism. We should attempt to convince Americans that there is no danger of the Soviets invading the Middle East, just as they are trying to convince us that the Arabs are not plotting to attack us. What we should say is that the Arabs can by no means whatsoever be trusted in the defense of democracy; they don't have any democracy to defend. Their position would depend on the result of the struggle between the two world camps; they will finally, at the last moment, join the winner. Hence all arms given to them is just illusionary and a waste of money, while at the same time these arms may be used for other purposes, mainly that of endangering Israel's security.

Second, "no" to undermining stability in the Middle East. If there is some kind of stability now, it should be preserved. While we think that the British evacuation of the Canal Zone is justified by itself, it must be emphasized that it will greatly enhance Egyptian military power, all the more so since Egypt is daily announcing that it is in a state of war with us. Consequently, it must be clear that we should be compensated. The fact that Egypt is going to be unilaterally armed clearly undermines the balance of power.

Third, "no" to abandoning Israel, for in practice it is abandoned not by commission but by omission. In the Anglo-Egyptian Agreement, initialed and enthusiastically hailed by President Eisenhower, it is said that the [military] base [in the Canal Zone] would be activated if one of the Arab countries or Turkey is attacked. Israel is not mentioned. It is the only exception. The bases would not be activated if it is attacked. Our security is not dependant on the activation of the bases, but insofar as the powers' policy is expressed in the agreement, it demonstrates abandoning us – all Middle Eastern countries are entitled to be defended by the Canal bases, except Israel.

Fourth, "no" to discrimination. In addition to what I said so far, we are witnessing British ties with Jordan; Britain is now working on an agreement with Iraq; the US is connected with Turkey via NATO and the Turkey-Pakistan ["Baghdad"] Pact. Britain has an agreement with Egypt and an agreement between the US and Egypt is in the making. True, a regional defense pact in the Middle East is far away; the Arabs are not yet ready for it, but there is a whole gamut of connections between the two [Western] Powers and countries in our region, with the exception of us. There are talks with us, we are being pacified behind closed doors, but we are not proposed anything concrete.

Fifth, "no" to economic aid to Egypt as long as it does not put an end to the blockade [of Israeli shipping] in the Canal.

In view of our demands of the Administration, it should be noted that Dulles, in his recent talks with Eban, said that if the supply of American arms to Egypt goes on to reach a point of undermining the military balance with us, the US would consider supplying arms to us as well. Here we must take care to not sell ourselves cheaply, or half-gratis. We should take care to not enter into some superficial negotiations which will prevent us from continuing with our campaign aimed at the American public, especially now before the elections.

According to very reliable sources on the American side, Dulles was prompted to start talking with us by two considerations following his conversations with Ambassador Eban, whom he deeply respects:

a) He realized we are experiencing feelings of fear and loneliness, that this state of mind is foreboding for the stability of the Middle East, and consequently we should be extricated from this complex at the earliest possible time by strengthening our trust in their good intentions.
b) The coming election in the US.

I think that, in future talks with Dulles, we can advance two ideas:

a) You are not proposing a defense pact to us; had you done this, matters would have been totally different.
b) You must be aware that as long as there is no peace between us and the Arab countries – and one should take into account that peace does not always mean love and real friendship – and as long as they continue announcing their enmity towards us, we must weigh our military strength against their combined strength, and thus no policy of arms supply which does not contribute towards a military balance would not satisfy us.

As to Dulles' suggestion that he write us a Note, we certainly should not oppose the idea. However, if it turns out that the Note is to contain only niceties with no concrete promises, we can tell him that while we appreciate his positive attitude towards us, it may well be that the Note would only do us more harm than good.

Now to our future relations with Britain.

Here sending of a Note is necessary, for we have already sent four or five Notes to the British during the campaign around the evacuation of the Suez Canal and they sent us two. We have heard some announcements by Selwyn Lloyd who emphasized that he was instructed to make them by the Cabinet, which means that Churchill himself stood behind them. I think that in our Note we must again stress three points:

a) We have noted that you are announcing that in case of an Arab attack against us, you would be willing to act and intervene.
b) Supplying arms – for they are not granting but selling – you will cling to the principle of balance in the future too. Indeed, they are interpreting "balance" in a certain way – they claim that one airplane in our hands is tantamount to three in the hands of the Arabs. They contend that the Arabs would reach our standards in use of airplanes in perhaps fifty years from now.
c) They have informed us that they are concluding the agreement with Egypt on the basis of evacuation all arms from the Canal Zone. Their arms would not be transferred to the Egyptians.

It is suggested that, in addition, we should say that we are prepared to enter into negotiations with them for the purpose of reaching agreed conclusions in the sphere of defense. If we reach an agreement, we would be able to discuss the form of their intervention and later to discuss common interests in the region.

I doubt whether they would respond positively to our proposal, for their policy at present is to reach a new agreement with the Arab world, and thus they fear that any contact with us may undermine this process. Thus, they are talking with the Arabs in the open and with us behind closed doors. We are making an attempt which possibly might succeed. If it does not, we would know exactly our position.

I think our Note should include two questions and two complaints. The questions are:

a) We want to receive a written answer to their idea of free passage through the Canal.
b) What exactly are the supplies they will leave in Egypt? What is the guarantee that they will not pass into Egyptian hands? And also, are they prepared to sell us cheaply anything from these supplies?

The two serious complaints are:

a) That they are about to sign a treaty with Egypt without making it conditional on the cessation of acts of violence against us.
b) That article 4 of the treaty is flawed in view of the fact that we are not mentioned together with the countries for whose defense the usage of the bases would be allowed. This article mentions only Turkey and the members of the common defense pact of the Arab League.

Another matter is American military aid to us. This coin has two sides: the military and the political. In our case the first is not so simple, for it is not clear that it not all positive from our point of view. Generally, we have no chance of receiving much armaments or heavy arms. If we receive something it will be incremental. Possibilities of purchasing weapons are open for us, sometimes with the full agreement of the US. We purchased Mystère planes in France. A reliable French source later informed us that they consulted their two partners – the British were against, the Americans agreed. This means that France is not always prepared to act on its own in spite of our friendship, and also that America is not entirely opposed to us getting all kinds of weapons. Purchasing is thus possible. We are limited here only by our ability to absorb new weapons. Had America been prepared to grant us what is prepared to grant all the Arab countries, we would have a serious problem how to absorb it all. Our manpower is limited. Our army is not growing. By purchasing certain weapons without growing in numbers we might become choked.

On the other hand, any American military aid is tied to conditions that are not always quite comfortable. It involves the presence of a military mission. A military mission endeavors to penetrate behind the scenes, to find out all the Army's secrets, and this leads to problematic relations. Thus, as long as it is not crucial, there is a question whether we should expedite the creation of such complications. But, at the same time, Ambassador Eban has made it clear that the very fact of receiving American weapons and military aid elevates our relations with America to a different plane. It greatly enhances relationship. It leads to solidarity. It obliges America far more than economic aid does.

We are living in a world which is all organized in patterns of defense pacts. In the Middle East we are almost the only exception. A question arises then whether such a situation adds to our health and whether we should not strive to attain some engagement. There is the issue of the Balkan Pact, in which Greece, Turkey and Yugoslavia participate. Interestingly, on two occasions we were asked by two of these three – once by the Yugoslavs in Belgrade and once by the Turks in Jerusalem – what we thought about the pact and whether we had any aspirations in this respect. It is thus important that we establish some position regarding this matter.

Friday, November 26

[On this date Foreign Minister Sharett met with Sir Evelyn Shuckburgh. Here follows Arthur Lourie's account on the meeting:]

The Minister saw Shuck[burgh] and Nicholls for an hour and a half.

1) Shuck[burgh] described his impressions of the Arab countries and his consternation regarding the mounting danger of communist penetration, especially in Syria. The Western powers were powerless in view of Arabs' hatred towards them on account of Israel.

The Minister doubted the reliability of his analysis. [He said:]

(a) The Soviets will not act directly, since this will involve a danger of a World War.

(b) The Arabs themselves are not able to carry out a social revolution of their own.

(c) Their non-neutralism during WWII [when they sided with the Germans], despite the White Paper [of 1939], is still deeply rooted, except as regards the issue of Israel.

2) Arab-Israeli peace. Shuck[burgh] said the Arabs feared Israel, on the one hand, and on the other they were prisoners of their own public opinion. He suggested we give a push to the situation by:

(a) Our agreeing with the principle of the refugees' return, on the assumption that only few will do so.

(b) Compensation.

The Minister staunchly opposed item (a) and gave his reasons. Answering a further question he said that we could see, within the framework of a peace agreement, the granting of broader rights regarding families' unification.

As to item (b), assuming that we would receive foreign financial aid, we would be prepared to pay compensation on condition that the Arabs ceased their policy of harming our economy [through blockade and boycott]. The Arabs cannot have it both ways.

Answering Shuck[burgh]'s question with what Arab country we feel that we could attain peace first, the Minister said: Egypt. It was obvious that Shuck[burgh], fearing the answer would be Jordan, felt comfortable with the Minister's answer.

(It should be noted that Shuck[burgh] did not even hint at territorial concessions.)

3) The Minister stressed that by no means would Israel agree with Egypt's interfering with the sailing of our ships, and especially pointed to oil tankers. Shuck[burgh] contended that the "Bat Galim" operation was not carried out at an appropriate time. The Minister rejected this contention.

4) Regarding Anglo-Israeli relations, the Minister positively appreciated Eden's speech, which by itself was a step towards peace, but noted that there had been no response to our proposal for holding meetings on security matters. The Tripartite Declaration, which was based on the idea of a[n arms] balance, was, on the face of it, valuable. An undermining of the balance was caused as a result of the fact that Jordan, which is opposing us, enjoys assured guarantees arising from its [mutual defense] pact with Britain. We are not demanding an [equivalent] agreement precisely, but some form of solution must be found. Shuck[burgh] did not react.

In his conclusions the Minister emphasized that peace with Israel meant with Israel as it is.[44]

Sunday, November 28

[At the Cabinet meeting of this date Defense Minister Lavon reported that a serious lull had been achieved in the "Book of War" with General Burns, with almost all bones of contention with him – e.g., the local commanders agreement with the Jordanians in Jerusalem and the UNTSO patrols – resolved. There were, however, several issues still unresolved, including two important ones: Burns' proposals regarding the Gaza Strip, and the problem of Majdal. Burns was promised that these matters would not be reported in the press. Prime Minister Sharett added the following remarks:]

I highly commend the way that the defense people, and mainly the CoS, took in seeking to avoid clashes with Burns while insisting on maintaining our principled positions and demonstrating elasticity and inventiveness in reaching a compromise.

I would like to note that we don't always avoid publicizing agreements reached with Burns behind close doors. It is not always right to enlist the press to attack him. Of course, any correspondent is free to report that he has heard something, but when four or five newspapers simultaneously publish a report "by our military correspondent" which are very much alike, it is clear that it is not an individual reporting but the result of guidance [by the Army]. This antagonizes him. This time he restrained himself, but

44 *DFPI* 9, doc.498. This report also includes a brief summary of a subsequent talk involving Lourie, Rafael, Shuckburgh and Nicholls. For other accounts of this meeting, see below, entries for November 30 (Cabinet FADC meeting) and December 21, 1954 (Knesset FADC meeting). The following day, the MFA DG dined with Nicholls and Shuckburgh. See Eytan to Elath, November 29, 1954, ISA FM 130.02/2410/10.

this will not always be so and it is plainly unnecessary. Anyway, what has been achieved is immensely valuable.

Tuesday, November 30

[On this date, Sharett met with the British, French and American Ambassadors. The following is US Ambassador Lawson's telegraphic report to the State Department of their meeting:]

Prime Minister called British, French [Ambassadors] and myself independently to Jerusalem today to request three governments support of IG [Israel Government] position in *Bat Galim* case before SC. He emphasized strongly very great importance [of the] SC decision to Israel Government. After reviewing conditions of [the] case, and particularly [the] decision and final report of [EI]MAC to SC[,] the Prime Minister described the proposed IG procedure as follows:

IG will endeavor to have SC pass resolution strongly and clearly defining rights of freedom of Suez passage for ships of all flags and basing resolution specifically on *Bat Galim* case. This to be [a] new resolution and not merely refer to September 1, 1951 resolution [WebDoc #2] which Egypt has completely ignored in [the] past. He felt that [a] resolution reiterating [the] terms ignored [in the] 1951 resolution would be completely ineffective as Egyptians would grant it little respect in view of past experience. He is convinced that only [a] clear, precise and strong resolution based on *Bat Galim* case and on principles clearly involved will settle [the] basic issue and permit Israeli flagships [to] pass unhindered through Suez in [the] conduct [of] Israeli foreign trade – an international right which should not be denied Israel alone among all nations.

He claimed that [a] decision on ths important principle [is] clearly a responsibility of [the] SC and was so recognized by its resolution [of] September 1, 1951.

He said US Government had specific responsibilities as (a) permanent member [of the] SC, (b) as supporter [of the] September 1951 resolution, and (c) because of special relations with Egypt, especially economic aid commitments which [were] made despite Egyptian attitude towards SC 1951 resolution.[- - -]

In describing [the] seriousness of [the] matter he pointed to [the] greatly weakened position MAC would occupy due to failure of SC to back up recent MAC decisions on [the] *Bat Galim* case; that SC itself would lose great prestige in [the] eyes of [the] world should it fail to face up to [its] manifest responsibilities; Israel public would lose confidence in both MAC and SC; and that there would be widespread disappointment in US in that "it had deserted Israel". However, he was emphatic and expeditious in his statement that these opinions did not mean there was any "threat" on his part or that there would be any diminution in the IG's loyalty to the UN or to [the mixed] armistice commissions, with which it would continue to work "provided Egypt did not go completely mad."

However, he thought he should tell me that if the Security Council failed to meet its responsibility in the case and if, under instructions from my government I should at some future date complain to him about the failure of the IG to abide by Security Council resolutions or MAC decisions, I should not be surprised if he recalled this discussion to me. Apparently alluding to the logic and consistency of US action in supporting IG position, he mentioned what he termed "the very strong position your government took with regard to Banat Yaacov" and the attitude the US took at that time regarding strict adherence to Security Council resolutions by Israel.

He said that the IG based its case largely on terms of the September 1, 1951 Security Council resolution, and he read the complete text to me. He emphasized articles 5 to 8 inclusive.[45]

I inquired as to what he considered the likely decision of the Security Council. He said he was hopeful but had no tangible basis for opinion other than generally encouraging discussions with the US, British, and French delegates at [the] UN of principles involved. He did not mention the probability of the Security Council referring the matter to I[nternational] C[ourt of] J[ustice] but I feel he would consider that an unsatisfactory and unnecessary delaying procedure.

He said he had presented the Israel Government case to [the] Soviet Ambassador[46] much as he had to the British Ambassador and me. He had done so because the Soviets are permanent members of the Security Council. He said, in confidence, he had talked as strongly and emphatically as he could in an effort to prevent a repetition of the Soviet veto to the New Zealand resolution on Suez transit earlier this year. He pointed out to the Ambassador the similarity in Soviet interest in principle involved in Suez and through Dardanelles. He received no impression or indication of Soviet reaction to his present request.

He expressed the very great hope that the US would support the IG. I replied that I would report to my government this conversation, the several points he had emphasized and the very great importance he attached to the matter and to the benefits of effective support on our part.[47]

[On this date, Sharett also appeared before the Cabinet FADC and reported on two issues: (a) the "Bat Galim" affair, and (b) his talk with visiting British FO official Evelyn Shuckburgh. After summarizing his discussions on the former with the Ambassadors of the US, Britain, France and the Soviet Union, Sharett went on to the second item, as follows:]

Shuckburgh, who is about 40, has been in service at the FO from a young age. He later became Eden's private secretary and was recently appointed one of the FO aides responsible for Middle Eastern affairs. He came here on a study mission and first visited Persia, Iraq, Syria and Jordan. From Israel he will continue to Lebanon, Egypt, Cyprus and Turkey. Our London embassy advised us that his report would certainly have effect on Eden, with whom he is warmly connected.

When he came to see me I asked him first what the Arabs had told him about us. He then touched upon a subject which clearly has been dominating his thinking – the communist danger in the Arab countries. He was impressed by a communist surge in Persia, Iraq, and especially in Syria. There are strong governments in Persia and Iraq, but Syria is a divided country and communism there is very active. Generally, the situation is dangerous because of the difficulty to achieve concrete, unified cooperation with the Arabs against communism. The reason for this is the [Arabs'] lack of trust in the Western powers because of their support of Israel. Israel is thus an obstacle to friendly cooperation between the West and the Arab countries at a time when it is incumbent to save the Arab states from communism.

---

45 For the text of UN SC Resolution 95, see WebDoc #2.

46 See *DFPI* 9, doc.506.

47 *FRUS 1952-1954*, doc.923. In the coming week, Israel's representatives would continue to lobby at the UN and in world capitals for a strong resolution at the SC on the "Bat Galim." See, e.g., *DFPI* 9, docs.516, 517, 519, 523.

I said I saw the situation differently. I did not see a serious communist threat to the Middle East. This is not to say that there are no problems posited by communism – we too have problems with [communists], but I do not believe Russia is plotting a serious adventure in the Middle East because this could ignite a big fire which I don't think [Russia] is interest in, and there is no seriou s human element capable of carrying out a communist revolution from within.

Second, I rejected the idea that, if not for Israel, the ruling elites in these countries would be prepared for an efficient and concrete alliance with the Western powers against the communist danger. They are fundamentally neutralistic because they worry only about themselves and they only use Israel as a fig leaf.

Third, it seems the Western powers had not learned from experience, if they think that by sacrificing Israel or by betraying her they would be able to achieve something in the Arab countries. I said: "You entered WWII armed with a very efficient weapon – the 1939 White Paper in which you fully accepted the Arab claims against us and decided that we would remain an eternal minority of 33% in Palestine. In what measure did that help you? Did it help you against the Rashid Ali al-Kaylani revolt [in Iraq in 1941], or against King Farouk [who flirted with the Axis powers and declared war on Hitler only in 1945, under British pressure].

Shuckburgh had no answer but, as his conversation the next day with the Minister of Defense proved, he kept to his view.

Another subject at our meeting was the problem of peace. Here he posed several ridiculous questions. He asked what did we prefer: a complete peace, or peace step by step? I said: are you offering us a choice between these two? In this case, of course we would prefer a complete peace, but this is not to say that if it is possible to advance towards peace step by step, we shall reject this alternative. He then asked if we prefer negotiating with them all, or with every Arab state separately. I said again: if such a choice exists, then negotiating separately would be preferable. This is what Ralph Bunche had wisely done [at Rhodes and elsewhere in 1949]. Then he asked: if separate negotiations, with whom first? I said: if you ask with whom it is desirable, then it is with Egypt, because it is the major Arab state, and because objectively there are fewer conflicts of interest between us and her than with any other. I told him that at one time a lethal criticism was directed against me in the Knesset FADC on account of my preferring to make peace with Jordan than with Egypt. They said I had a weakness for King Abdullah. My answer to my critics was that we were facing a wall. We want to start extricating bricks from this wall. I am feeling my way around this wall with my hands. If I find a loose brick – it would be easier to extricate it than another. When King Abdullah was alive [- - -] – he died a political death before his physical one – he had understood the matter and wanted to do something with us. We worked in that direction.

Shuckburgh said it would be possible to bring Egypt around to a moderate and acceptable position. I said by all means. I then expected that he would say that the main thing for Egypt was territorial continuity with Jordan, for only a short time ago Nasser said that we must give up the Negev. At that time [Sir] John Strachey was here and I discussed this subject with him.[48]

Then he went to Egypt and on his way back to England he stopped in Cyprus and met our man there. He told him in a vulgar language: "When you are going through Israel and then move to Egypt it is as if you're leaving some clean house and starting to

48 John Strachey (1901-1963), Labour MP and Minister of War (1950-1951).

tread in shit." I told Strachey before he left: "You are going to meet with Naguib. Would you not agree that he is more moderate than Nasser? Do ask him what Nasser had meant. Had he really assumed that Israel would give up the Negev? It is an absurdity." Naguib answered that they would insist on a land link outside Israeli territory. That meant either giving up Eilat or granting them a strip in the middle of the Negev, that is cutting the country to two. Both obviously an impossibility.

But contrary to my expectation, Shuckburgh did not raise this matter. He said the main thing for the Egyptians was the refugee problem. While they are presenting the slogan of the right of return, they would be satisfied with a symbolic return. I said we could agree to the return of a family and then some more, but we will reject any return which would mean resettlement. It is absurd to assume that the Government of Israel would shoulder the reintegration of these people into the economy of the country, and what's more, among Jews who emigrated from the Arab countries. As long as you are talking about the return of even a very small number, you are preventing an accommodation to the situation as is. This assumption must be totally erased.

[No "skeleton" was found for the period from November 25, 1954 to January 2, 1955, when the diarist resumed writing (even though he then mentioned that he did write a "skeleton" for this whole period). In its place we have reconstructed some of Sharett's political activity of this five-week period from archival documents.]

Tuesday, December 7

[On this date, after a dinner party at the home of the US Ambassador, PM Sharett spoke with George V. Allen,[49] on an important mission to Egypt. Ivan White described the "friendly atmosphere after dinner" and the "very frank discussion and exchange of ideas, which at times bordered on the blunt." Prime Minister Sharett, he noted, was "aided, and on occasion, interrupted by Minister of Defense Lavon." See WebDoc #36. Also on this date, Sharett sent the following cable to the Israel Embassy in London, clarifying the real meaning of the campaign to free the "Bat Galim" and allow her to continue her voyage northwards through the Canal:]

I cannot avoid the impression that you too are seeing the release [of the "Bat Galim"] back southward as some achievement. Let it be clear that this will clearly be defeat. Even if the crew and the cargo are allowed to proceed northwards, but the ship southwards, it will still be a defeat. The campaign of the "Bat Galim" is not about the passage of cargo, an act carried out dozens of times in the past, not about the release of the crew which was accused of a false charge, but about the free movement of the Israeli flag in the Suez Canal and this is what we must stress and accentuate incessantly.[50]

Wednesday, December 8

[On this date Sharett wrote to Jacob Tsur, Israel's Ambassador to France, with instructions for his talk with Pierre Mendès-France:]

---

49 George V. Allen (1903-1970). American diplomat. Assistant Secretary for Near East, South Asia and African Affairs (January 1955 – July 1956).

50 *DFPI* 9, doc.524.

Urgent

It is desirable to continue the conversation with Mendes [France] from the point we reached in his meeting with Eban [on November 24 in Washington].

(a) Mendes promised France's and his personal support to the strengthening of Israel. He should be told that these words were a source of encouragement of unique value to your government.

(b) Mendes expressed his opinion that our concrete security situation is not so serious, while our concern regarding US policy of arming and organizing Arabs, which continues unchanged and regarding Britain's positive attitude towards the idea of a common Arab organization, is justified. Mendes expressed his positive evaluation of the Turkey-Pakistan Pact and its enlargement by including Iraq and Persia. You should thoroughly explain that we see no justification in differentiating between the aim of the pact and that of a common Arab [defense] organization. As we see it, Iraq is being used as a means to attract all other Arab states in its wake. The result will be more cohesion and more reliance on the Arab League, which is incapable of assuring the region's security but only of spreading hate against Israel and France. The identified interests of France and Israel in the Middle East call for practical cooperation and we are prepared to discuss practical plans with all appropriate agencies.

(c) In the meantime, the Arabs' war against Israel goes on incessantly. We are relying on France to assure us the necessary arms supplied under acceptable financial conditions. We are also looking forward to their political support and help towards breaking the economic boycott and all other aspects of Arab enmity. In this regard, the problem of the blockade in the Suez Canal is of major importance. Here you can point to the examples of "Bat Galim" and Alexandria trial.

(d) [- - -]

(e) It is not desirable to demonstrate any doubts regarding France's goodwill. [- - -]

(f) You should bring up the problem of North Africa. Stress the need for direct and close contact between government of Israel and government of France in this matter. On our part we shall act with a view to coordinating Jewish activity with French interests. On their part we expect assurances for the security of North African Jews and their free movement, including their property.[51]

Thursday, December 9

[On this date Sharett wrote to Ambassador Abba Eban in Washington, giving instructions for mobilizing US representatives in Cairo to prevent death sentences in the Cairo trials against accused Jewish saboteurs:]

Following the hanging of the six [Muslim Brotherhood members accused of conspiring to bring down the revolutionary regime] in Cairo, the danger looming over ours in Alexandria has increased. It is necessary to prompt US to take a most strong stand and propose that they announce in Cairo that, whatever the accusation against the people, their execution means: (a) A serious setback to US government developing its friendly attitude towards Egypt, this not because of Jews but because of surge of general public opinion. (b) Undermining prospects of peace in the Middle East by arousing impulses for revenge and renewed bloody strife.

51 *DFPI* 9, doc.529.

In connection with "Brothers" we do not mind if they [the Americans] either contend that the hanging of the "Brothers" is an internal Egyptian matter while the same verdict in Alexandria creates an additional and serious complication vis-à-vis Israel, or that they point out that tension has already been created between Egypt and the Arab countries [*sic.* should read: the US] and warn against an additional complication which would put additional burden of the position of Egypt's rulers. Any one of these arguments would help.

Generally, they should emphasize that the line of restraint we have adopted could break down completely under the accumulating of pressure of constant unilateral provocations, the intensifying fear of the West evading the matter of "Bat Galim" and bringing matters to a crisis by death[-penalty] verdict[s] of Alexandria. You can also point to the emotional reaction of the American public following the espionage trial in China [of 11 American pilots and 2 citizens captured in the Korean War and sentenced to imprisonment on November 22], and note that the existence of an Egyptian espionage ring in Israel which we exposed several times did not lead us to organize show trials and certainly not to death sentences. The last argument should be advanced without hinting any admission to the truth of the Alexandria accusations. I briefly and vehemently talked with [George] Allen accordingly and it seems that he was very much impressed.[52]

Friday, December 10

[On this date Sharett met with US Ambassador Lawson. The following is Ambassador Lawson's report to the US State Department of this meeting:]

Prime Minister separately saw British Ambassador and myself today at his request in Tel Aviv. He said purpose of conversation was that there would be no misunderstanding Israel Government point of view re developments [in the] "Bat Galim" case.

Sharett said Israel Government sees rather abrupt interruption [of the] SC proceedings as [an] interim stage but is anxious US and G[reat] B[ritain] know Israel Government aim. Israel representative told by British, and he believes by US representative [at the] UN, best course was to have time to consider matter and take soundings Cairo and possibly influence Egypt [to] release [the] vessel.[53]

He termed release proposals by Government of Egypt vague and he emphasized Israel's aim and main point of issue is to establish not a special privilege, but Israel's undisputed right to have its ships pass through [the Suez] canal under its own flag.

52 *DFPI* 9, doc.530. Neither the memorandum of the conversation between Allen and Sharett (WebDoc #36) nor the cover letter penned by the American Chargé d'affaires, Ivan White, mentions the trial of the accused Jews in Egypt.

53 The US Embassy in Cairo reported to the State Department on December 3 that Egyptian Foreign Ministry "officials have [- - -] stated categorically that, all other considerations aside, it is politically impossible for GOE (Government of Egypt) to allow an Israeli flagship to transit Canal at this juncture. To do so would be catastrophic they say for [the] R[evolutionary] C[ommand] C[ouncil] not only internally, but also in respect [to] relations [with] other Arab states whose foreign Ministers [are] presently gathered here in A[rab] L[eague] session are already aroused over [the] Jerusalem credentials matter." *FRUS 1952-1954*, doc.923, n.2. See also *DFPI* 9, docs.528, 531, 532.

He expressed the hope that US diplomatic efforts in Cairo were pointed [in] this direction.

Israel, he said, would be patient and was not protesting reasonable delay for purposes mentioned but could not wait indefinitely; Israel Government would not drop [the] issue and did not want to let its case go by default. He hoped US Government could let him know in a few days how Cairo démarche was progressing. There should be no misunderstanding, he repeated, as to Israel's aim, release of ship, crew and cargo as a unit to proceed to its destination. He was grateful for Cairo effort but will welcome information as to how matters stand. Israel Government will be guided by this information as to its next move.

In answer to my query that Israel Government had then no objection to the postponement, if for a reasonable time, Sharett agreed but said again that Israel would not stay quiet indefinitely. If too many days went by, Israel would have to ask for another meeting of SC. [- - -] [H]e indicated that about [the] middle of next week should produce reply from British and US and Israel Government would be guided by report on Cairo thinking. Eban, he said, would also be in touch [with] US representative at [the] UN.

In [a] brief exchange of views following above, he said Israel Government felt Government of Egypt could explain giving in on this case to their public on [the] basis of being up against a combined and solid international front and [that the] acknowledgement [of] freedom of passage was part of [the] bargain for British evacuation. I made no comment. Regarding my reference to [the] Arab League meeting in Cairo and possible relation to desire delay by Government of Egypt, Sharett said Israel Government not completely blind to tactical considerations but could not accept a dragging out of [the] case to better Egypt's position if that was to remain intransigent.[54]

Sunday, December 12

[On this date Sharett addressed the Cabinet meeting as follows:]

I am prepared to report very briefly on the tragic trial [in Egypt]. It is clear that the situation has worsened since last week, after the Muslim Brotherhood leaders were issued death sentences and since these sentences were executed in spite of the very harsh protests pronounced in all Arab capitals. If they acted like that towards the Muslim Brotherhood, it is impossible to assume that they would not act the same towards the Jews. We have been active in this matter for weeks now. Attempts were made to enlist the US, Britain, France, the Vatican and other bodies commanding influence. An attempt was also made to find a direct path to the Egyptian and tell them that if the trial ends with executions, it would be a very serious matter. I met with [George] Allen, who went from here directly to Egypt. He took it upon himself to act in this direction. We are trying to send people to Cairo, to talk with Nasser. I know that a defense for the accused was organized in spite of great difficulties.

This all I can report. The people are in the hands of an enemy state. Confessions were extorted by torture and threats. We do not know what these confessions were.

As to the question of appealing to the UN in this matter like the Americans did in the case of the eleven American pilots imprisoned in China, the difference is that the

54 *FRUS 1952-1954*, doc.930. Sharett's report of the meeting to the Israel Embassy in Washington, dated December 12, 1954, is in ISA FM 130.09/2312/8.

people are not Israeli citizens. The US is contending that the Chinese violated the Korean armistice agreement – we have nothing similar to contend. And when the US appeals to the UN, immediately dozens of states support it, seeing this as a part of the war against communism. If we appeal to the UN there is no certainty that we would be supported at all, to say nothing of our appeal immediately creating in the UN a front of the six Arab countries together with the Muslim countries against us. I also wonder whether countries like the US, or Britain or France are convinced that the trial is only a show trial, that the accusations are false; they may also be assuming that the accusations are justified.

I touched upon this matter in the Knesset, and my statement was twice broadcast in Hebrew, English, French and Arabic. Had we kept silent, it might have been concluded that our conscience was unclean. Some people said that if we cared about the people, it would be better to refrain from any statement, but my opinion was that keeping silent on this matter would be more dangerous than making that statement.

Monday, December 13

[On this date, Sharett briefed the Knesset Foreign Affairs and Defense Committee on the trial in Egypt. Excerpts of his remarks:]

First, I'd like to determine one principle: our intensive action in this matter we have now only one aim: saving the men. Any other consideration is shadowed by this one. It is possible to use this trial for castigating Egypt, and possibly we can use it as an example of Egypt's and in fact all Arab countries' treatment of the Jewish minority and make it our main aim. We are abstaining from doing that. We think that, first of all, everything should be done in order to save the men's lives, if it is impossible to save them from conviction. Our intensive activity in this matter is executed mostly behind closed doors. The governments of France, USA and Britain have been approached, as well as the Vatican. We have also activated local Jews in those countries for this purpose.

I must say that I'm not convinced that all these bodies and people are convinced that the accusations are baseless. Our impression is that these governments would not like to see death sentences because they fear the bloody consequences of such verdicts. We are, time and again, making them aware of the serious situation in the event of hangings.

At the same time I must say that our chances are not encouraging, especially after the death sentences [meted out to six members] of the Muslim Brotherhood were carried out in spite of the wave of protests in all the Arab and Muslim countries.

Still, we do not think our efforts are without purpose, but we think that they should not be carried out in the open. For instance, if the Americans do something, it would be counterproductive if the Egyptians are under the impression that we are behind it. Publicized activity can also lead to extreme antagonism within the Egyptian public.

However, we are not favoring complete silence in this matter. By all means no. This has led to my statement in the Knesset, which was indeed short but explicit.

In view of all this I don't think we should have a Knesset debate on this subject because speakers will castigate the Egyptian regime and this will only harden its position.

At one of the first stages of the affair an attempt was made to present it within the context of anti-Jewish persecution in Egypt. People who went to Egypt to deal with this matter on our behalf told us it was impossible to advance such a contention. The opposite is true. All in all, one hundred Jews were interrogated and thirteen were indicted. What happened had no connection whatsoever with the situation of Egyptian Jews.

At 8:15 pm Sharett opened the evening Knesset sitting with the following statement:

Mr Speaker, members of the Knesset. The trial which began two days ago in Egypt against thirteen Jews is stirring up and causing deep bitterness in our country and across the entire Jewish world. It cannot but arouse anxiety and fear in the hearts of seekers of justice and peace around the world. The Knesset FADC devoted, and will devote, its attention to this grave subject, but at this hour I find it necessary to make a brief statement:

In my speech of November 15 in the Knesset I said: "Egypt's unrestrained activity does not testify that a spirit of moderation and peace-seeking is dominating its rulers. The plot which is now being woven in Alexandria testifies to the distance separating Egypt from this spirit, in view of the show trial which is now being organized there against a group of Jews who have fallen victims to a false accusation of espionage and on whom, so it seems, pressure is being mounted in order to extract form them confessions to imaginary crimes by threats and torture."

This foreboding assumption has now been verified and exposed as a factual truth in the light of the statement made by the defendant Marcelle Ninio before the military tribunal in Cairo, published this morning, that she had been tortured during the pre-trial interrogation, and that under torture a false confession of crimes not committed was extracted from her.

The government of Israel voices its strong protest against this procedure which is prepared to implement methods of the Inquisition of the Middle Ages in the Middle East. The Government of Israel strongly rejects the false accusations included in the charge sheet presented by Egypt's Prosecutor-General, which attributes to the Israeli authorities horrific deeds and dark designs against Egypt's security and international relations.

From this podium we have time and again warned against persecution and libels which have been taking place against innocent Jews in certain countries. We see the Jews accused by the Egyptian authorities of such grave crimes as innocent victims of wild enmity towards the State of Israel and the Jewish people. If their crime is their Zionism and devotion to the State of Israel, then multitudes of Jews the world over are partners to that crime. We do not think that Egypt's rulers have any interest in smearing Jewish blood over their heads by their own hands. We are calling all those standing for of peace, stability and human relations between nations to prevent a distortion of justice harboring calamity.[55]

Tuesday, December 14

[On this date, the Knesset FADC continued its deliberations over the trial in Egypt and the "Bat Galim" incident. Excerpts of Sharett's remarks:]

[- - -] The matter as whole is a disaster and, while we are discussing means to forestall the climax of the disaster, we are right to doubt whether this is possible in view of circumstances.

I would like to remind you that it is not the first instance in the Middle East. There were hangings of Jews in Iraq. Years have passed since then and the affair has been

55 *Divrei Haknesset*, XVII:306.

somewhat forgotten. We are facing a problem; anyone suggesting a solution must prove its efficacy, or at least prove it will cause no harm. There are instances in which no solutions are to be found beyond what has already been done.

First of all I would like it to be very clear: we cannot hold the stick at both ends – to conduct ourselves as a state and at the same time not as a state. We cannot contend that Egypt is not behaving like a state. It is possible that the accusations are exaggerated, it is possible that the Egyptians have some sinister purpose, but as far as the outside world is concerned, the facts are that the men were caught inside Egypt, that something started to burn in a cinema hall, that it led to an investigation, that a trial is being conducted in the open with a prosecutor, with a counsel for defense, and with outside observers.

We said what we had to say in the Knesset. This announcement was an act of state. We approached friendly states and asked for their help. This step was an act of state. But kidnaping Egyptian officers, as was just suggested here by MK Haim Landau of Herut – that is not what a state does. To say nothing of the practical question of how are you going to kidnap: by going into battle? Can you foresee its results, how would it end? Would it not be seen as us invading a foreign territory, a step which could lead to a possible disaster?[56]

Moreover, suppose we did kidnap people – are we sure the Egyptians will mind? Are we sure they would be deterred, that they would be panicked, that they would not be confident that we would not hang the kidnapped? After all, the State of Israel is not the *Irgun*, is not the Stern Gang, it is not even the *Hagana*.[57]

It is the State of Israel, which is a totally different entity. There are people in our midst, perhaps they are present even in this very room, who are still living in a state of past cognition, not in a cognition of statehood. Statehood is something granting enormous benefits, but it also involves far-reaching limitations, and one cannot live in two worlds at the same time. And can we be sure the Jewish people would support such an act? American Jewry is composed also of different Jews than MK Landau. Perhaps it's a pity, but it's the reality, and when we deal with political issues we must stick to reality. It seems to me that we are witnessing here an intellectual process of attempting to climb up a slippery wall just because something impressive must be done.

---

56 Benny Morris writes: "*AMAN* chief Binyamin Givly proposed to *Mossad* head Isser Harel that Israel should kidnap Egyptian hostages from the Gaza Strip or 'from Cyprus or in Europe' and that it should attack the Egyptian Embassy in Amman if death sentences were pronounced. On December 10 and 11 [CoS] Dayan and the operations branch issued orders to kidnap Egyptian military personnel and civilians (and also Syrians) as hostages against the execution of the accused in Cairo, but the carrying out [of the orders] was not approved by the civilian authority" [i.e., Sharett]. *Milhemet Hagvul shel Israel*, Hebrew ed., 348. Cf. the brief reference in the English version, *Israel's Border Wars*, 318. See also below, entry for January 14, 1955.

57 Reference to the three major pre-state Jewish underground militias. The *Hagana* was under the political command of the JAE, while the others did not accept the authority of the Agency or other elected *yishuv* bodies. In 1947, *Irgun* and *LEHI* ("Stern Gang") responded to arrests and death-sentences of their comrades by abducting British personnel and threatening to kill them in reprisal. In late July, two captive British NCOs were murdered after three *Irgun* memberswent to the gallows for their part in a daring attack on the Acre Prison. The booby-trapped bodies of Clifford Martin and Mervyn Paice were hung near Netanya. See also below, entries for December 28, 1954 and January 14, 1955.

In a way, similar considerations apply to the suggestion advanced here by MK Zissman [GZ] and supported by MK Argov [Mapai] of sending an IDF brigade down to the Negev. Can we be sure the Egyptians or the Powers would be impressed by such an act? Don't we realize it would entail a financial cost? We are dealing here with very serious matters. I must admit I woke up this morning with quite an unrequited conscience because of my statement yesterday, for I'm not sure I that it was truly beneficial. Still, I'm not opposing the establishment of a public committee whose activity would be directed towards the outside world, but I'm against organizing mass meetings and demonstrations.

As to organizing activity abroad, it should timed between the pronouncement of the verdict and its date of execution, in spite all the danger involved. It is possible that after the verdict is given, action taken to prevent hanging would be justified and perhaps beneficial, although it is doubtful. We know of similar cases during the Mandate period when the British were not impressed by our appeals. It happened in Britain too, in most similar cases. However, it is not human to refrain from trying even if chances are naught. Sometimes this kind of activity should be taken in order that the accused become aware of it.

[The FADC decided to establish a public committee for enlisting public opinion abroad, without resorting to public meetings and demonstrations. Sharett then presented his report on the "Bat Galim" affair:]

Let me say that we see this chapter of the "Bat Galim" as a link in the chain of a long struggle which will not necessarily end swiftly. We must arm ourselves with a measure of patience and at the same time see to it that, at each stage of this struggle, matters don't stand still but develop at some pace. We are now situated at the stage of a renewed dealing with the issue at the SC. As you are aware, after hearing statements by the two sides, the British representative proposed to stop the discussion and renew it at an appropriate time. Immediately afterwards the American and British representatives informed us that they had discussed the matter and had concluded that it would be better if they were given time to act diplomatically in Cairo with the aim of influencing the Egyptian government to take a desirable course.

In response to this step I summoned the American and the British ambassadors and told them that we were prepared to patiently wait for a limited time in order to let the two Powers deal with the issue. However, there should be no misunderstanding regarding the holy trinity of the ship, the crew and the cargo. We oppose the dismantling of this trinity. This trinity must continue sailing northwards and reach its destination. The ship entered the Suez Canal not in order to be turned around. It entered one end of the Canal in order to get out of it at the other. Consequently, we would like to know within a few days what the US and Britain have done in Cairo and what the Egyptians were intending to do. If we are not satisfied, we shall raise the issue again at the SC and forcefully demand a discussion on the subject of free passage through the Canal. The blockade is against the UN Charter; it is a threat which we shall not let the Powers ignore.

This is the situation of as now. We shall wait till the end of this week. If by then nothing new happens, we shall demand a meeting of the SC. From the Americans we have not yet heard a clear response. The British are advising us not to take an extreme line. They say it is impossible to have it all and that they cannot risk their relations with Egypt just because of the "Bat Galim" affair – they also have other problems with Egypt to tend to. Generally speaking, they think Nasser's regime should be strengthened, for if it falls down, who knows who will come in its place. As they see it, this regime is prepared to get closer to the West and, in the course of time, to reach a settlement with the State of Israel. Therefore the Egyptians must be dealt with smoothly, not harshly.

The Egyptians have announced that they are releasing the crew and the cargo. Juridically they are conducting themselves according to their doctrine of being in a state of belligerency with us, and thus article 10 of the Constantinople Charter allows them to take defensive precautions against us in the Canal.

[Later this day Sharett sent the following two cables to the Israel Embassy in Washington, setting out guidelines for action regarding the Cairo trials:]

Following two intelligent and penetrating discussions in the Knesset FADC, one of which took place before my statement [in the Knesset on December 13] and the other after it, I am summing up:

(a) The one and only aim at this stage is saving lives.
(b) A most intensive action on our part to activate the [US] administration.
(c) Jewish activity in all directions, including (b).
(d) Items (b) and (c) without bombastic publicity, but it may be desirable that there will be signs pointing to sensitivity and awareness.
(e) Articles in major press organs appealing to Cairo rulers' wisdom, rather than castigating them.
(f) Emphasizing in appeals and in the press that even according to the accusation, which must be denied, there is a difference between [the] Alexandria [accused] and the [Muslim] Brothers, who attempted to assassinate the head of state and conspired to overthrow the regime.
(g) It must be taken into account that, if there are death sentences, it is possible that they would be executed within a day or two, and therefore action must be taken in time.
(h) We shall consider this at an appropriate stage, but in all probability we would go for extensive public action immediately following pronouncement of death sentences in spite of an obvious danger.
(i) The committee rejected demonstrations and public meetings in Israel and abroad at this stage.
(j) A public committee for mounting of pressure, but not for organizing mass activity, would be formed in Israel.
(k) Tension in Israel is mounting daily and giving vent to it is necessary at least in order to prevent unbridled initiatives, therefore (j).[58]

Apparently US government has so far not taken any serious step, and perhaps has not taken any step towards saving the accused in Cairo. Allen was impressed by what I said. He said: It is very good that you told me this now, thus promising by implication that he would act in Cairo, but in the last 48 hours he has not answered my message to him [transmitted on Dec.12 through Ambassador Lawson in Tel Aviv] in which I asked him for results. The transmitting of Blaustein's message [to Mahmoud Riyadh on December 12] by state [department] channels was indeed valuable, but it emphasized the lack of a direct formal appeal. It must be clear to them that lack of action on their part, or action which would only be taken as doing one's duty, will demonstrate US indifference to the possibility of hangings. I think we are entitled to a clear answer: would Washington appeal to Cairo or not? Cable your opinion immediately. Every day counts.[59]

58 *DFPI* 9, doc.540.
59 *DFPI* 9, doc.541.

Wednesday, December 15

[Sharett sought to enlist the help of British MP and Anglo-Zionist leader, Maurice Orbach,[60] in creating a back-channel to Nasser's circle in Cairo:]

Jerusalem, December 15, 1954
Most immediate

Dear Mr Orbach,

I have read with great interest the report [forwarded by Easterman and Barou on November 30] of your conversation with the PM of Egypt. As you know, many of us admire his integrity, idealism and tenacity of purpose.

We feel sure that his aims are peace and progress and that he fully realises the interdependence of the two. It is for this reason that we regret the absence of practical evidence that he is preparing the ground for peace by educating his public opinion accordingly. What we would like to see is some positive steps in that direction, such as the recognition of Israel's elementary right to free passage through the Suez Canal, which would come not as a concession to her, but in fulfillment of Egypt's unquestionable international obligation and in deference to an overwhelming consensus of international opinion.

But there is also the question of the avoidance of certain acts which are liable to set back the clock of peace indefinitely. What I have primarily in mind is the outcome of the Cairo trial against a group of hapless and helpless Jews. I fervently hope that it will not result in death sentences, for their execution would inevitably cause a fatal breakdown of moral restraints and frustrate those who are making superhuman efforts to curb passions and lead their people into ways of peace. We look forward to counsels of farsighted statesmanship prevailing over considerations of the moment and preventing the erection of a scaffold as an insuperable barrier between Egypt and Israel.

Yours sincerely,
Sharett[61]

Friday, December 17

[On this date Sharett met with Ivan B. White, Chargé d'affaires at the US Embassy. Here follows Sharett's account of their talk:]

Tel Aviv, 17 December 1954

Mr White brought me the following message from Acting Secretary of State Hoover

60 Maurice Orbach (1902-1979). Anglo-Jewish Labour MP. Had previously visited Cairo and would become involved as an emissary between Sharett and Nasser. See: *DFPI* 9, docs.510, 553, 562 and *Documents on the Foreign Policy of Israel*, volume 10 (1955), ed. Yemima Rosenthal; Executive Ed., Yehoshua Freundlich (Jerusalem: Israel State Archives, 2016), docs.2-3 – hereafter *DFPI* 10; below, entries for January 2, 4, 11, 27, and February 8, 22, 1955 and Orbach's articles: "The Orbach File: First Visit to Cairo," *New Outlook* (October 1974), 8-23; "The Orbach File (part two): Second Visit to Cairo," *New Outlook* (November-December 1974), 8-21; "The Orbach File (part three): Third Visit to Cairo," *New Outlook* (January 1975), 12-20.

61 *DFPI* 9, doc.542.

[in response to Sharett's conversation with Ambassador Lawson on December 10.]. I have recorded it almost, but not quite, verbatim:

There is no change in the basic position of the US regarding the right of Israel shipping to use the Suez Canal.

With regard to the "Bat Galim", strong demarches have been made vis-à-vis Egypt, both in Cairo and in Washington. The Department is not sanguine about the possibility to effect a complete reversal of the Egyptian attitude in this context.

In the United States' judgment the "Bat Galim" incident has demonstrated the correctness of US belief that progress in a quiet atmosphere can be conducive to effective negotiations, whereas dramatic test cases can only hamper a progressive relaxation of the Egyptian attitude in the matter.

It may well be that such cases will also contribute to arouse emotions in Israel.

The US Government has some reasons to hope for the release of the vessel as well as the cargo and crew, and they look forward to an increasingly effective response to their efforts for the total easing of the restrictions – a process which has been interrupted by the "Bat Galim" incident.

I asked Mr White whether he could throw any light on the meaning of the word "release" in the last sentence – release of the ship to proceed whither? Mr White smiled understandingly and said that he himself had no additional information to what was stated in the message, but it stood to reason that if the meaning had been that the boat would be free to proceed to its destination this would have been plainly stated.

I then said that I had only one comment to make. The assumption of the State Department that Egypt was likely to change her attitude as a result of peaceful persuasion alone, without the pressure of facts which focused international attention on her behavior, was not borne out by experience. At the beginning Egypt intended to obstruct the traffic of any goods shipped through the Canal to or from Israel. It was only because we started sending cargoes through the Canal – at first under foreign flags – that Egypt, after repeated attempts to prevent the passage of such ships, take the cargo off, etc., had had eventually to give in, with the result that the practice of a more or less free passage of ordinary goods in non-Israel ships had been established. It was therefore clear that as far as the passage of Israel ships proper was concerned, Egypt would again give in only if her hands were forced. Without the creation of such facts as "Bat Galim" it was idle to expect any relaxation.

Mr White said in reply that the next step might profitably be the sending of an oil shipment from Persia through the Canal.

I asked him point blank whether he could tell me that the US Government saw an early prospect of securing passage for an oil tanker bound for Israel, but he evaded a direct reply and merely indicated that they were aware of our negotiations with the Anglo-Iranian [Oil Company] in this regard.[62]

In conclusion I said that with regard to "Bat Galim" we shall probably have to press for a SC meeting next week, so as to wind up the affair. Mr White expressed doubts as to whether a winding up that way was practicable, to which I remarked that what I had in mind was at least a formal winding up, such as would clarify the situation, so that we might know where we stood in the whole business.[63]

---

62 On negotiations regarding the supply of Iranian oil to Israel, see *DFPI* 9, doc.537; Uri Bialer, *Oil and the Arab-Israeli Conflict* (London: St. Antony's College/Macmillan Series, 1999), 171-83.

63 *DFPI* 9, doc.547. For White's telegraphic report of this meeting, see WebDoc #37.

Saturday, December 18

[On this date Sharett cabled Ambassador Eban in Washington as follows:]

White brought me yesterday afternoon T[el] A[viv] foll[owing] message from Allen replying mine:[64]

"Have discussed matter with Caffery. We both agreed best chance success is for Caffery to take it up with Egypt authorities stating he was doing it on his own."

White added orally, Caffery already acted, this he gleaned from copy Cairo Embassy cable to [Washington] DC. He unaware reaction.

Inferences obvious:

Till Allen's visit Cairo no steps taken by US.

Instead Allen doing it himself which would [have] indicated extraordinary important [of the] matter, he relegated it to routine level.

Even then care was taken not lend it to full weight special approach. In circumstances doubt very much veracity statement made [by Byroade] to Engel [of the AJC on December 14 to the effect that Americans had put pressure on Nasser regarding the trial].

Believe we should return to [the] charge by mobilizing all available forces [with a] view [to] securing, in [the] event of [a] death sentence, direct personal message from President to Nasser advocating clemency. Cable prospects.[65]

Sunday, December 19

[On this date Sharett reported to the Cabinet as follows:]

First to the "Bat Galim" operation. I conducted talks with the British and American Ambassadors ten days ago. I told them: the last meeting of the SC was stopped at the suggestion of the Britain representative in order to enable Britain and the US to take steps in Cairo towards settling the matter. We were prepared to give them some time, but not an unlimited one. We want it to be clear what a resolution entails – it means the release of the ship, its crew and cargo so that it can continue sailing on to Haifa. It does not mean allowing it to sail back southwards. We are expecting urgent replies. If they do not come, we shall again knock at the doors of the SC. Last Friday I was informed by the American Embassy that the State Department had grounds to hope that the ship, the crew and the cargo would be released. To my question whether they would be allowed to sail to Haifa, the answer was that it did not seem that the ship would be allowed to do so and that the basic Egyptian position regarding free passage for Israeli ships in the Canal has not changed. The State Department is of the opinion that it is possible to ameliorate the Egyptians' position gradually until they put and end to all limitations "not by a drastic test case" but through the American influence in Cairo, and that such a process had been going on until it was cut off by the "Bat Galim" operation.

I said I could not accept the State Department's reasoning in this matter. It is not

---

64 On December 12, Sharett had transmitted to Allen in Cairo, via the US Ambassador to Israel, a message expressing his deep concern regarding developments in the trial of those accused on spying for Israel. See ISA FM 130.02/2453/20.

65 Sharett to Eban, December 18, 1954, *DFPI* 9, doc.554.

supported by the facts. At the beginning Egypt was determined to maintain a complete blockade in regard to all cargos going to and from Israel. Had we relied on changing this position by peaceful means, nothing would have changed. What has changed the situation was our direct action in sending cargo by foreign ships. The Egyptians tried to stop us by detaining and delaying the cargoes, but we went on sending them and the Egyptians gave in in view of international public opinion which was aroused by our initiative. Thus, at the end, a procedure whereby cargo sailing freely to and from Israel by non-Israeli ships was established. The same goes for ships flying the Israel flag. If several attempts are not made by us to sail Israeli ships through the Canal, the situation will remain as it is. If a second and third attempt is made, the Egyptians would have to give in.

We shall demand a ruling by the SC and see what happens. Both the British and the Americans discern signs of Nasser's willingness to come to terms with the West. They must take into consideration all parts of the front and cannot concentrate only on the "Bat Galim" issue. They are of the opinion that if the ship, the crew ad the cargo are released it would constitute an achievement – we cannot have it all at once.

Regarding the Cairo trial, action is being taken in several directions, including quite effective attempts to reach direct contact with Abdul Nasser and explain t him the serious results in case of death sentences. At the same time we are intensifying our pressure on other governments. Clearly, if there can be an effective pressure at all, it must be exerted by the US.

I have no factual evidence, but my feeling is that America is not willing to put its full weight here, perhaps because it does not wish to appear too pro-Israel vis-à-vis the Egyptians, perhaps because it fears a negative answer which would be awkward, perhaps somebody was offended because the people are accused of sabotaging American institutions. Still the Americans are doing something. This issue is the main topic in all our meetings in Washington. I raised it in my meeting with Allen and said to him point-bank that if they do not want a new wave of bloodshed, they must prevent any hangings. He said: "It is very important that you told me so, because tomorrow I am going to Cairo." However, later he sent me a personal message in which he said he had discussed the matter with the American Ambassador in Cairo, Caffery, and they decided that Caffery would tell the Egyptians that he was approaching them on this matter on his own initiative, that is, not formally in the name of his Government.

I must inform you that yesterday I received a secret message from Washington in which it was said that inside the State Department it is assumed that here will be hangings. I am being careful not to say anything which would be interpreted as sowing illusions among the public, but I cannot evade informing the Cabinet of facts written black on white.

Now to the matter of the Syrian plane. First, the Minister of Defense will report the facts and then I'll add something.[66]

[At this point in the meeting Minister of Defense Lavon informed the Cabinet of the background to this episode. On the night of December 8-9, while on an action "the details of which, with the permission of the PM,

66 On December 12, a Syrian civilian airliner travelling between Damascus and Cairo with 5 passengers and 5 crew on board was intercepted by Israeli aircraft and forced to land at Lod (Lydda) Airport. The IDF's idea was to exchange the Syrian airliner for the five IDF POWs held in Damascus. The airliner was released two days later. For details of this episode, see *DFPI* 9, doc.563 and Morris, *Israel's Border Wars*, 366 n.35. See also below, entries for January 10, 13, 17, 25 and 30, 1955.

I will not divulge," five IDF soldiers were captured inside Syrian territory. In order to prevent their being murdered or mishandled, Lavon explained, it was decided to bring down a Syrian military plane if it entered Israel's airspace. Regrettably, a civilian plane was compelled to land. Meanwhile the Syrians reported that the captured Israelis were alive and well, so Israel's main fears were over. The Syrian plane was released on December 14 following an investigation.]

PM Sharett: Let me say this: a version was spread among Israeli public, and it was expressed in the press – strangely enough first and foremost in the *Jerusalem Post*, and most sharply at that – that the government made a serious mistake by releasing a plane which it had rightfully caught, because it flew over Israeli territory, and that this act of indulgence bordered on a crime. In one paper it was reported that, when the Army was asked why was the plane being released, it replied that "we are the executing organization; it was the Government that decided."[67]

The *Jerusalem Post* was indeed scandalous. In fact, the plane was by no means flying over Israeli territory. There is no doubt that its flight could not be rightfully curtailed. [- - -][68]

I must say I breathed freely when the plane was released. I thought that once and for all we should decide whether we are a state or not – we cannot, being a state, employ methods which non-state organizations can use.

[On this date, Sharett sent the following draft text to Gideon Rafael in Paris, for transmission to Gamal Abd al-Nasser in Cairo through his personal emissary, Abdel-Rahman Sadeq, who had been in secret contact with Ziama Divon of Israel's Paris Embassy:]

I am addressing myself to you despite the present state of tension and animosity[,] feeling confident that, while determined to serve the best interests of our respective nations, and because this is our aim, we are both eager to achieve an honorable understanding between them.

Many of us admire your integrity, idealism and tenacity of purpose and wish you the fullest success in attaining the emancipation of the land of the Nile from the last vestiges of foreign domination and the initiation for the masses of Egyptian people of an era of social regeneration and economic welfare.

We feel sure that your aims are peace and progress and that you fully realize the interdependence of the two.

It is for this reason that we are keenly looking forward to more tangible evidence that you and your friends are preparing the ground for an eventual settlement with Israel by educating your public opinion to appreciate the vital importance of peace within the Middle East.

The recognition of Israel's elementary right to free passage through the Suez Canal – not as a concession to her, but in discharge of Egypt's international obligations and in deference to an overwhelming consensus of world opinion – would indeed be a positive step in that direction.

But there is also the question of avoiding certain acts which are liable to set back the clock of peace indefinitely. What I here have in mind is the outcome of the trial now proceeding in Cairo. I cannot emphasize too strongly the gravity of the issue which hangs there in the balance for our future relations. I fervently hope that, whatever the

67 *Lamerhav* of December 15 reported that the order was issued by the PM.

68 Here the ISA censor struck out a long passage.

guilt established, no death sentences will be passed, for their execution would lead to dire results: it would inevitably produce a most violent crisis, kindle afresh the flames of bitterness and strife, and defeat our efforts to curb passions and lead our people into ways of peace.

We look forward to your farsighted and constructive statesmanship to prevent the erection of a scaffold as an insuperable barrier between Egypt and Israel. We probably hold different views of the culpability of the accused, and I will not attempt to persuade you to accept mine. But I would appeal to you to exercise forbearance for the sake of the goal which I assume we pursue in common – a settlement between Egypt and Israel and a state of peace and contentment inside the region as a whole.[69]

Tuesday, December 21

[In the FADC, Sharett was first asked for details about the forced landing of the Syrian plane in Israel and the five IDF soldiers captured by the Syrians.]

As to the five soldiers, they were not kidnapped. They went [into Syrian territory] on a certain mission, not a fighting one nor for demolishing anything, but for a certain reconnaissance. There were two alternatives: announcing that they were kidnapped, or that they crossed the line by mistake. On account of a certain consideration it was announced that they were kidnapped.

In circumstances of this sort of complication, the public's impression is that what happened was a result of some Syrian act of aggression. It is a stark fact that in a similar instance we killed five [Jordanian] Legionnaires. They too did not cross our border for carrying out an act of terror; they simply chose to take a short-cut. Juridically we were justified. Our five soldiers [sent to Syria] were armed and were inside their territory, but they [the Syrians] did not kill them. One was lightly wounded. UN Observers saw them and said they are all right physically. It is not yet clear what will happen to them. The Syrians can stall their release. They can first get a censure decision against Israel in the ISMAC. They may possibly attempt to prove our version is not true and theirs is. Or they may put them on trial.

Now, as to the Syrian plane it must be clear that it was not flying over Israeli territory. It did not violate our sovereignty nor the armistice agreement. It did pass, while flying over the Mediterranean, through the airspace controlled by Lod Airport air traffic control, and according to international regulations it should have announced this fact to our controller. But it did not violate our sovereignty. There is no precedent of any state finding itself in a similar situation and requiring a plane to land. In this matter a totally

---

69 Message quoted in *DFPI* 9, doc.555. Under instructions from Sharett, Ziama Divon had opened informal "back-channel" contact in Paris with Abdel-Rahman Sadeq, who reported directly to Gamal Abd al-Nasser. From Israel's point of view, the above message was one of several last-ditch appeals, added to ongoing international diplomatic efforts, to resolve the "Bat Galim" deadlock and to influence the outcome of the trials of Israel's spies in Cairo. For details of these back-channel negotiations, see: Michael Oren, "Secret Egypt-Israel Peace Initiatives Prior to the Suez Campaign," *Middle Eastern Studies* 26:3 (July 1990), 354-56; Avi Shlaim, *The Iron Wall: Israel and the Arab World* (London: Allen Lane / Penguin Press, 2000), 78-80, 118-20. For an interesting British assessment of the chances of a Sharett-Nasser rapprochement at this time, see WebDoc #38.

mistaken impression was created in our public.

The situation is much more complicated because while they [the Arab countries] are not flying their planes over our territory, we fly [over theirs]. We fly over their territory when our planes fly to South Africa. We do not inform them and they do not inform us. However, if we insist that the state controlling the area under air traffic control is entitled to require a plane which flies through it to land, then they too can insist on that as well. And then we would lose more than they because we, not they, are under blockade and each air route is of crucial importance for us.

In this case it was an error and the sooner we put an end to it, the healthier for us.

The *Jerusalem Post* published an article on this matter, which in my opinion was scandalous. The article entirely distorted the facts and castigated the government for not knowing how to deal with the Arabs – as if we were living outside the international community; [as if] there were only us and the Arabs [on earth] and inside this jungle a duel was going on between Israel and the Arabs. All the world exists outside this jungle, and there are no British or Americans or plain human beings flying around. It was twice said in this article that the Syrian plane flew over an Israeli territory, which was absolutely untrue. There was a demagogic treatment of this matter in both the *Jerusalem Post* and *Lamerhav*, where it was said that the Army was only carrying out directives [from the government], which was a clear distortion and a harmful brainwashing of the public. For the public should be taught that it exists in a state, and that this state exists not in a jungle but on earth, and there are on this earth international laws which must be observed while at the same time protecting our interests.

Let me add that there have been no arrests of Jews as Jews in Egypt. There have been arrests of communists, some of whom are Jews. There were arrests among the Muslim Brothers. But since the establishment of Israel, when there was a wave of arresting Jews, there have been no arrests or persecutions of Jews in Egypt. I am saying this behind these closed doors: there is now no persecution of Jews in Egypt.

It so happens that the "Bat Galim" operation and the trial occurred simultaneously, which is not beneficial, neither to the first nor to the second. For inasmuch as Nasser faces an internal front against which he is fighting forcefully, including mass arrests, hangings and the dismantling of a subversive organization, it makes it politically difficult for him to demonstrate leniency towards Israel at the same time.

As to the direction of the trial, there are conflicting views. On the one hand, there are some quite foreboding reports. But on the other, we were informed that the Egyptian authorities are not keen on hangings, even though they are convinced that the accusations are true. Inasmuch as their conscience is concerned, it is clean. Inasmuch as they are approached by outside elements – and there is an extensive activity in this sphere up to the intervention of the Italian Prime Minister which I appeal to you not to publicize, and the Americans are intervening too – the Egyptians vehemently deny that the accusations are trumped up for the sake of their internal struggle with their opponents. At the same time all foreign observers present at the trial, including the French Consul and Americans, say there is no doubt the trial is being conducted decently; it is open, and the defense is doing a good job. The prosecutor demanded the trial be conducted behind closed doors, but the chief justice accepted the defense request that it would be held in the open. There is there no anti-Jewish atmosphere, not a hint of anti-Jewish incitement. The linen take by the defense is not to absolutely deny the accusations. Possibly, it was convinced this would be to no avail. I assume the aim of the defense is to save the accused from execution. The defense line is to show that the accused are not too sophisticated or fully mature developed people;

that they were enticed to act by some clever and sinister man who managed to escape. The accused did not know exactly what was his purpose; they did not realize the seriousness of what they did; they assumed they were doing something for a good purpose.

Why did the only woman [Marcelle Ninio] among the accused announce courageously that she was tortured while the others did not? One assumption is that she has a stronger character. Another is that she is a solitary person with no family or relatives, and thus she was not afraid of revenge taken against anybody.

I would now like to report on my meetings with Evelyn Shuckburgh and George Allen. Let it be clear that each man came here on a fact-finding tour, and it was only by coincidence that they arrived together.

Shuckburgh had already visited Syria, Iraq, Jordan and Persia. He is the son of Sir John Shuckburgh, who during the British Mandate years was for a long time a [Colonial Office] official and an opponent of Weizmann, Ben-Gurion and myself. He is also quite close to Eden – he was his private secretary and now his is one of the aides to the Minister of State and heads the Western Asia and North Africa desk at the Foreign Office. He was nominated to this post a month or two ago. The strongest impression he has brought from the countries he visited is of the strength that communism is gaining there. In some places it is forcefully contained, in others, like Syria it is unrestrained. There is no strong rule in Syria; there is a total anarchy there. It is a result of internal strife and Soviet machinations. The situation is highly dangerous. In normal circumstances it would be possible to settle things with the authorities with the aim of containing communism with the help of the West. At present [however] it is impossible to speak with the Syrian authorities who have no trust in the West, and this distrust is because of Israel.

An important part of our conversation was devoted to the refugee issue. He tried to convince me that we should at least agree to the return of a symbolic number of them. I contended that the very talk about a symbolic return undermines the entire solution of the problem, since it strengthens the Arab refusal to accept a different solution for any refugee hopes to be included within the symbolic returnees. We discussed whether Israel could or should absorb refugees while there is no peace. He said: "Suppose peace is possible, but at the price of a return of a certain number of refugees. Will you say then: let there be no peace, but at least no refugees would return?" I said: "No! No return whatsoever is possible [except] as a part of an overall solution of their problem by their resettlement. What is possible in case of peace is that we shall be more lenient in the sphere of family-reunions; we shall be more liberal in humanitarian cases. We are now enabling the return of wives and small children, but we may consider the return of a brother, a sister or an old uncle. But there will be on no account a partial return as a contribution to the solution of the refugee problem by resettling them in Israel. No Israeli government would shoulder the resettling of refugees. It is economically an absurdity. Israel is the most densely populated country in the region, and the cost of settlement in it is the highest in the region. Israel is also a country in which the internal security problem is the most serious on account of the Arabs, and this danger will be heightened if Arab refugees are settled in the neighborhood of immigrants who have fled from Arab countries. It is a totally different situation if a returnee is absorbed by members of his family who have remained within Israel. If there is peace, we would be able to be more liberal.

To this he responded by saying there would be peace. I asked him if he was able to promise me that there would be peace, but got no answer to that. Instead he advanced the customary contentions – while on the face of it not saying they are his – of the Arabs living in fear of our future inevitable expansion. I said that on this subject the Arabs are entangling themselves with two contradictions: a) They are constantly contending that we will attack them and occupy their territories, while at the same time they are refusing to make peace. This is senseless. True, no peace treaty is eternal, but if they are afraid, then peace would serve as a guarantee. Why are they refusing such a guarantee? b) They say that we shall expand because the territory at our disposal will not suffice for settling our immigrants and because of our dynamism, but at the same time they demand that we give up parts of this territory.

I also made some stinging remarks regarding the defense pact. I asked: As staunch supporters of democracy, what price haven't you paid to the Arabs? In fact, we were your payment – you have abandoned us. What have you done for the sake of the Arabs and what have you received in return? Why are you not learning a lesson from your experience?

The most important thing about the meetings with Allen was the man himself. He impressed us as being a man of caliber, serious, honest, conscientious. He is clearly not a State Department type person, as Shuckburgh is a Foreign Office type. I think he understood our position on the refugees. It seems so me that he absorbed our understanding of Arab mentality in general and our outlook regarding the world's problems. When I told him that we are confronted not just with the problem of Arab mentality; we are confronted with something by far deeper in that the Arabs view the serious conflict which is tearing the world into two camps, West and East, as a kind of an internal family conflict. They do not realize that, in the final resort, the world is one, and that one must at long last take a clear position in view of the conflict which is taking place between two civilizations, one of which will win. To this he replied that he was well aware of this attitude, since he had been serving in India.

Our conversation was conducted on a higher intellectual level than the former, but it turned out that the man does not know much [about the Middle East] and thus I had to explain matters to him from the very beginning.

Also on this date Sharett authorized the following draft of a message for transmission to Gamal Abd al-Nasser "on plain paper no form address no signature, but state orally this is from Roham [*rosh hamemshala*] to Roham", i.e., from Prime Minister to Prime Minister:

I have received a report of your message transmitted through a special emissary now in Paris.

I have noted with deep satisfaction that it is your desire to bring about a peaceful solution of the problems outstanding between Egypt and Israel. I welcome particularly your readiness to consider measures for improving the present situation and reducing the prevailing tensions. We for our part are eager to cooperate in efforts directed towards this end.

Many of us admire your brave idealism and tenacity of purpose and wish you the fullest success in attaining the emancipation of the Land of the Nile from the last vestiges of foreign domination and the initiation for the masses of the Egyptian people of an era of social regeneration and economic welfare.

We feel sure that your aims are peace and progress and that you fully realise the interdependence of the two.

It is for this reason that we are keenly looking forward to more tangible evidence that you and your friends are preparing the ground for an eventual settlement with Israel by educating your public opinion to appreciate the vital importance of peace within the Middle East.

There are two matters in particular the handling of which may well have a decisive effect on the development of relations between our countries.

In the first place, freedom of all shipping to and from Israel to pass through the Suez Canal would be in keeping with Egypt's international obligations and would be widely acclaimed by the international community.

Secondly, there is the urgent question of the trial now proceeding in Cairo. I cannot emphasize too strongly the gravity of the issue which is there in the balance. I fervently hope that no death sentences will be passed, as demanded by the prosecution. They would inevitably produce a violent crisis, kindle afresh the flames of bitterness and strife and defeat our efforts to curb passions and lead our people into ways of peace.

We look forward to counsels of farsighted statesmanship prevailing over considerations of the moment, for the sake of the goal which I assume we pursue in common – a settlement between Egypt and Israel and a state of peace and contentment inside the region as a whole.

This message which I am addressing to you above the din of daily conflict in a spirit of sincere quest for peace and friendship will, I hope, evoke a corresponding response.[70]

Wednesday, December 22

Jerusalem, December 22, 1954

To: Defense Minister
From: Prime Minister and Foreign Minister

Although we have conducted inquiries into the matter of the [civilian] Syrian airplane that was forced to land at Lod [Airport on December 12th, and released two days later], the gravity of the matter does not leave me satisfied with the explanations given to me.

It must be clear to you now that not only did we have no justification for detaining the airplane, but having transgressed in forcing it down, it was incumbent upon us to release it immediately rather than continue to detain it and conduct interrogations of its passengers for 48 hours.

I have no reason to doubt the statement of the State Department of the US that the step we took has no precedent in international conduct.

Beyond the severe violation of military discipline, in this case by an action which completely negates an explicit standing order, the narrow-mindedness and short-sightedness shown here by the top echelon of our Army shock and trouble me most deeply. They apparently believe that the State of Israel can – even must – act in the field of international relations according to the laws of the jungle. But even in the thick of the jungle, man's foremost considerations is his own security. Yet it turns out that even this primal wisdom is lacking in the minds of our military leadership.

I must ask you to inform me of the conclusions you have drawn from this serious mishap. Such actions, performed with no authority and out of spurious considerations, create malignant political realities, whose consequences may be disastrous for the state. The government must be absolutely insured against scandals of this kind. It must be clear to all concerned that the government has no intention of tolerating such manifestations of "independent action" within the ranks of the security and military forces.

---

70 *DFPI* 9, doc.559. The above message evoked the following response, also "on plain paper with no address or signature," transmitted by Abdel-Rahman Sadeq to Ziama Divon in Paris: "I have received your letter of the 21/12/54. I have instructed my special emissary to transmit a verbal answer to the questions you have mentioned in your letters. I am very glad that you realise the efforts spent from our side to bring our relations to a peaceful solution. I hope that they will be met by similar efforts from your side thus permitting us to achieve the results we are seeking for the benefit of both countries." *DFPI* 9, doc.576. The oral explanations offered by Sadeq are reported in *DFPI* 9, doc.577.

For the sake of preventing any misunderstanding or imbroglio, and in order to stop inciting adventurous spirits, my opinion is that it is not enough to prohibit any harassment of civilian airplanes, but necessary to entirely discontinue patrol and espionage flights of Air Force airplanes outside the territory of Israel, including the territorial waters. We must root out the erroneous and injurious notion that the area under the supervision of the flight-control of Lod Airport can serve as an arena for any direct action on the part of our authorities against airplanes that stray into it. The problems concerning our flight-control area are those of flight safety, and not of national security or sovereignty. This area does not constitute any zone of action for the activity of our Air Force.

An especially sorry chapter in this whole sad affair, adding disgrace and shame, is the matter of publicity. To this day, most readers of the Israeli press are sure that the Syrian airplane was forced down and apprehended because it violated Israel's sovereignty and perhaps also threatened its security. For this reason, the public does not understand why such an airplane was released, and concludes that an unjustified concession was made on the part of the government. Such an assumption gives renewed currency to the spurious whispers of slander concerning the discord between the Foreign Ministry's policy and the IDF's way of thinking. You must have seen the article that appeared in *Lamerhav* on this subject. You will also find it beneficial to examine the editorial in The *Jerusalem Post*, which is based entirely on distorted facts, presents readers with a political analysis of the problem that in my eyes is the height of provincial inanity, and which, according to my information, was inspired by military sources. This bad habit too must be stopped.[71]

Sunday, December 26

[On this date the Cabinet met and heard the following report from Prime Minister Sharett:]

Let me report first on the Cairo trial. What I'm going to say is unverified and absolutely secret. According to information we have received from three independent channels, two of them Egyptian, one American, it is clear that the Egyptian authorities do not incline towards hangings, perhaps apart from the two defendants in absentia. While sharp threats and provocations against the Egyptians may only harden their attitude, it is clear that pressure by world public opinion is highly valuable, and hence it should not stop.

As to the "Bat Galim" matter, the American government has informed us that it is continuing its efforts to make the Egyptians agree to the passage of the vessel northwards with the crew and cargo, but this is not assured. Convening of the SC at this juncture would not be conducive to these efforts, and the US asked us to agree to the postponement of the SC meeting till early January. I considered this appeal and decided to give them some more time. Moreover, on December 31 Lebanon ceases to be a member of the SC. At the same time the Egyptian government informed the SC that they are going to release the "Bat Galim" crew on January 1 through the auspices of the EIMAC, and to release the vessel and its cargo too. Accordingly, we shall face the question of accepting the crew [sent] across the armistice lines or not. I suggest that this issue be transferred to the Ministerial FADC.

71 *DFPI* 9, doc.564; *Sharett: Mivhar Te'udot*, doc.134.

Monday, December 27

[Herewith a note from Moshe Sharett, evidently passed to one of his Mapai ministers, perhaps during a Cabinet or Cabinet committee meeting:]

27.12.54

I had two questions to pose to Lavon. I did not pose them yesterday out of pity. The questions are:

1) Why did he never tell me about the existence of this network in Egypt?

2) Why, when the disaster occurred, did he not turn to me immediately for counsel and assistance?

One point remains obscure and that is:

3) What exactly did he say to [Head of *AMAN* Binyamin] Givly when the latter turned to him, let us suppose not on the 17th but on the 31st [of July].

The answer to 2 is contained in 1 and 3. His guilty conscience kept him from turning to me. Point 1 means that he deliberately concealed the matter from me. Point 3 means that he authorized the course line of action, after the fact to be sure; but when the news of the arrests became known, he did not know that they had been carried out before his conversation with Givly.

The deeds were done and the arrests carried out after he had authorized the course of action.

This is no more, of course, than a conjecture, albeit a substantiated one.

Tuesday, December 28

[On this date Sharett made the following remarks in the Knesset FADC in response to Menachem Begin's proposal to kidnap several Egyptian soldiers as hostages to be held in exchange for the Jews arrested in Egypt:]

As to the proposals for capturing [some Egyptian] men, the committee chairman already said that this is an adventure, and above all an extremely doubtful adventure as far as its political results. But first of all it is adventurous from the operational point of view. Those several officers are not waiting to be kidnapped while sitting *unguarded* in some coffee house *which we know how to reach*. Certainly a whole operation could be mounted for such kidnaping, *well prepared in order to maximize its chances of success, but this means a very serious operation*. The first results would be major headlines in the world press about Israeli aggressive action against Egypt. This will *immediately tip the scales, for instead of various elements being impressed by Israel's restraint, such a step by Israel would* direct all the rage against us, and those powers in whom we see a chance of their helping us would be released from any moral obligation towards us and from backing our demands. Moreover, and perhaps this is the main point, I take it for granted that if after this operation our people in Egypt shall be hanged, the State of Israel would not treat the [Egyptians] kidnapped as did a certain well-known organization in a similar case [referring to the *Irgun* in 1947], that is, she shall not hang them. *I believe these concise considerations should put an end to this proposal.*[72]

---

72 Sharett's penchant for editing other people's writing was well known at the time (see, e.g., WebDoc #41). Always a stickler for accuracy, and evidently unhappy at the way the stenographer recorded his remarks at this meeting, Sharett added by hand the italicized words and phrases to his copy of the official protocol of the meeting.

Wednesday, December 29

[On this date Sharett sent the following cable to Eban at the Israel Embassy in Washington:]

The appeal to the President should be made immediately upon the announcement of the verdict and he should be asked to intervene within one hour or two. It must be taken into account that if the verdict calls for hanging it would be executed within hours.[73]

[Also on this date Sharett wrote to Defense Minister Lavon:]

Following my conversation with the CoS a few weeks ago I composed the attached guidelines for cooperation between the Foreign Ministry and the GS, as well between myself and you, regarding everything pertaining to the carrying out of the armistice agreements.

Guidelines for Cooperation in Armistice Affairs

Preamble

The whole issue of the armistice agreements – including the discussions held regarding them, the clashes which are taking place between us and the neighboring countries and the controversies which take place in this context between us and UNTSO Command – is constantly creating political facts which are mirrored in the state's position on our foreign front that the MFA is in charge of and responsible for. These facts influence directly and indirectly the relations of the state with the Powers, which are constant and ongoing, and which are naturally conducted through the channels of the MFA. In the sphere of direct relations with the UN – which again means direct and indirect relations with the Powers – our dealings and representation in armistice affairs, in any case, devolve at a certain stage to the MFA. All these considerations point to the necessity of intensively tightening relations and close cooperation between the [IDF] GS and the MFA in all matters pertaining to the armistice at all stages of activity. Cooperation with the MFA is especially necessary not only in defending positions, decisions and actions already taken, but in the discussions preceding any decision and action. In the following articles guidelines are set for the forms of this cooperation. They do not purport to exhaust the entire problem, and it is doubtful whether it can be exhausted at all in writing, since everything depends on goodwill to maintain real cooperation, and one cannot foretell all possible future circumstances which would arise in view of events and actions and call for forms of cooperation necessitated accordingly.

Guidelines

1) The state's representation in the MACs is handled by the Army. The head of the delegation and its spokesman is an IDF officer. At the same time, the MFA will send, when it sees fit, its representative to any meeting of any of the MACs and to all important meetings and formal ceremonies connected with the armistice. Whenever the CoS, for some special reason, opposes the participation of the MFA's presence at a given meeting, he must discuss this in [due] time and reach agreement on the matter.

2) The authorized state representative for maintaining constant contact with the UNTSO Command and conduct negotiations orally or in writing with the aim of reaching solutions to problems as they arise from time to time, or to define the government's position vis-à-vis the UNTSO Command, is the CoS.

---

73 *DFPI* 9, doc.573.

3) A MFA representative would generally participate in formal meetings between the CoS and the UNTSO commander except in instances in which the CoS would find a special specific reason to conduct the meeting in private. In such instances a report of the meeting's contents must be immediately be transmitted to the MFA.

4) In order to clarify items 1 and 3 above, it is ascertained that Mr Yosef Tekoah is not only the legal adviser of the CoS for armistice affairs, but also the MFA's representative and the liaison between it and the GS. Mr Tekoah has no veto rights regarding positions determined by the CoS unless he is clearly instructed by the PM and the Foreign Minister to oppose a given position or action.

5) MFA officials are free to meet with the UNTSO commander for the purpose of general clarifications but they are not to initiate meetings for the purpose of clarifying concrete issues as they appear on the [MAC] agenda. But they will respond positively to the UNTSO commander's or to his representatives' request for discussion of concrete issues; in such instances they either do not respond to his contentions or else coordinate their response with the CoS according to an agreed line. In any possible event, it should be assured that a GS representative will participate in such meetings and, in any event, they must be immediately be reported to the CoS.

6) The PM and the Foreign Minister will invite the UNTSO commander for discussions on any issue, or for any purpose which he deems appropriate.

7) A MFA representative will participate in the drafting of letters to the UNTSO commander, as well as in the drafting of important letters written to other members of the UN staff, on both levels of the letters' content and style.

8) In instances of special importance a draft of the letter shall be submitted for the PM and the Foreign Minister's approval, if he so requests.

9) In any matter of principal importance, or a matter the results of which may cause complications and difficulties in the realm of foreign relations, a consultation between the PM and the Foreign Minister and the Defense Minister will take place, at the conclusion of which a course of action would be determined. It is assumed that the CoS will participate in all such consultations. The determining of the course of action can be agreed upon also in consultations between the Defense Minister and the CoS and the DG of the MFA. In such instances the DG would be recognized as representing the PM and the Foreign Minister.

10) In day-to-day activity, Mr Tekoah, the MFA's representative who maintains constant contact with the PM and the Foreign Minister, would be recognized as representing his opinion. After the principal course of action is determined, Mr Tekoah will participate in the consultations held between the Defense Minister and the CoS, as well as in discussion held at the GS, in which the position of any of the stages of development of the matter is to be determined.

11) In any matter which allows for no delay, and for which there is no time for consultation, the opinion of the PM and the Foreign Minister will be decisive regarding any step to be taken or not.

12) The IDF spokesman will issue facts, clarifications and military evaluations to the press regarding border incidents, discussions in MAC meetings and their results, as well as negotiations with the UNTSO command. He will not, directly or incognito, issue for publication any political guidance and will not direct the press to take on political positions. The only source for political clarifications and political guidance by the government in the realm of foreign relations is the MFA.

13) The CoS may conduct press conferences, as in the past, with newspaper editors for the purpose of clarifying matters of the IDF's organization and needs. It is desirable

that a MFA representative be present on such occasions and, in any case, the MFA should be cognizant of the guidance given by the CoS to newspaper editors, even when it is not intended for publication, in all matters pertaining to the state's foreign relations.[74]

Thursday, December 30

[On this date Sharett sent the following cable to Eban:]

Most Urgent

A last effort is necessary to prevent the Egyptians from returning the ["Bat Galim"] crew by land. Their last communique to the UN regarding bringing the men to km.95 [on the main sea-shore road, near Gaza] was not publicized and therefore they are able to retreat free of shame, on the face of it fulfilling the verdict of the maritime court in Suez.

You must immediately see Hoover, even if late in the evening and prod him to take staunch and urgent steps in Cairo with the aim of letting the ship sail north with its crew, in which case:

a) The discussion in the Security Council will not be renewed.

b) We will not renew for a certain period our attempts to sail a ship under Israeli flag through the Canal and they will have a respite.

However, if they stubbornly insist, then, first, a discussion will be held and they will be strongly reprimanded; second, we shall continue pestering by sending ships and denouncing them in the international arena causing them much trouble. You could also hint that the Egyptians can themselves sail the ship to Port Said, let the crew join it there so that it can sail on freely, thus extricating themselves from the problem.

For your information only, we are attempting to exert direct pressure [on the Egyptians through the Divon-Sadeq back-channel in Israel's Paris Embassy], which must be kept secret, and thus American help may tilt the balance. This directive is based on the assumption that it is clearly desirable for the US to put an end to the Security Council discussion and get rid of additional complications in the Canal for the time being. An urgent action is necessary since tomorrow, Friday, is the decisive day.

Cable immediately.[75]

[Undated note, evidently written during a Cabinet meeting:]

Moshe,

I am nearing the end of my inquiry into the matter of Egypt. I presume that next week I will be able to submit to you all of the documentary material that presents an entirely clear picture.

I would prefer that this conversation be between the two of us, because the issue in question is explosive.

P[inhas] L[avon]

74 *DFPI* 9, doc.574.

75 *DFPI* 9, doc.575.

www.ingramcontent.com/pod-product-compliance
Lightning Source LLC
LaVergne TN
LVHW010347080826
844660LV00003B/211
* 9 7 8 0 2 5 3 0 3 7 3 5 0 *